SPECIAL EDUCATIONAL NEEDS AND INCLUSIVE EDUCATION

SPECIAL EDUCATIONAL NEEDS AND INCLUSIVE EDUCATION

Major Themes in Education

Edited by David Mitchell

Volume I
Systems and Contexts

RoutledgeFalmer
Taylor & Francis Group

LONDON AND NEW YORK

First published 2004
by RoutledgeFalmer
2 Park Square, Milton Park, Abingdon, Oxon, OX14 4RN

Simultaneously published in the USA and Canada
by RoutledgeFalmer
29 West 35th Street, New York, NY 10001

RoutledgeFalmer is an imprint of the Taylor & Francis Group

Editorial Matter and Selection © 2004 David Mitchell; individual
owners retain copyright in their own material

Typeset in Times by Graphicraft Limited, Hong Kong
Printed and bound in Great Britain by MPG Books Ltd, Bodmin, Cornwall

British Library Cataloguing in Publication Data
A catalogue record for this book is available from the British Library

Library of Congress Cataloging in Publication Data
A catalog record for this book has been requested

ISBN 0-415-28452-X (Set)
ISBN 0-415-28453-8 (Volume I)

Publisher's Note
References within each chapter are as they appear in the original complete work.

CONTENTS

VOLUME I SYSTEMS AND CONTEXTS

CONTENTS

CONTENTS

CONTENTS

CONTENTS

CONTENTS

VOLUME III ASSESSMENT AND TEACHING STRATEGIES

CONTENTS

CONTENTS

VOLUME IV   EFFECTIVE PRACTICES

CONTENTS

ACKNOWLEDGEMENTS

The publishers would like to thank the following for permission to reprint their material:

McGraw-Hill Publishing Company and Open University Press for kind permission to reprint Carol Christensen, 'Disabled, Handicapped or Disordered: "What's in a Name?"', in C. Christensen and F. Rizvi (eds), *Disability and the Dilemmas of Education and Justice* (Buckingham: Open University Press, 1996), pp. 63–78. Copyright © 1996.

Taylor & Francis Ltd for permission to reprint Burt Perrin and Bengt Nirje, 'Setting the Record Straight: A Critique of Some Frequent Misconceptions of the Normalization Principle', *Australia And New Zealand Journal of Developmental Disabilities* 11(2) (1985): 69–74. http://www.tandf.co.uk/journals/titles/13668250.html

American Association on Mental Retardation for permission to reprint Wolf Wolfensberger, 'Social Role Valorization: A Proposed New Term for the Principle of Normalization', *Mental Retardation* 21(6) (1983): 234–9.

Taylor & Francis Ltd for permission to reprint Evangeline R. Danseco, 'Parental Beliefs on Childhood Disability: Insights on Culture, Child Development and Intervention', *International Journal of Disability, Development and Education* 44(1) (1997): 41–52. http://www.tandf.co.uk

From 'Can Disability Culture and Full Educational Inclusion be Reconciled?' by Jean P. Hall, 2002, *Journal of Disability Policy Studies* 13(3): 144–52. Copyright © 2002 by PRO-ED, Inc. Reprinted with permission.

Michael J. Oliver, 'Capitalism, Disability, and Ideology: A Materialist Critique of the Normalization Principle', in R. J. Flynn And R. A. Lemay (eds), *A Quarter-Century of Normalization and Social Role Valorization: Evolution and Impact* (Ottawa: University of Ottawa Press, 1999), pp. 163–73. Copyright © 1999, University of Ottawa Press. Reprinted by permission of the publisher.

Alfredo J. Artiles, 'Special Education's Changing Identity: Paradoxes and Dilemmas in Views of Culture and Space', *Harvard Educational Review* 73(2) (Summer 2003): 164–202. Copyright © 2003 by the President and Fellows of Harvard College. All rights reserved.

From 'Overrepresentation of Minority Students: The Case for Greater Specificity or Reconsideration of the Variables Examined', Donald L. MacMillan and Daniel J. Reschly, *The Journal of Special Education* 32(1) (1998): 15–24. Copyright © 1998 by PRO-ED, Inc. Reprinted with permission.

TASH Connections for permission to reprint Jill Bevan-Brown, 'Evaluating Special Education Services for Learners from Ethnically Diverse Groups: Getting it Right', *The Journal of the Association for Persons with Severe Handicaps* 26(3) (2001): 138–47.

Education and Treatment of Children for permission to reprint Michael L. Wehmeyer and Michelle Schwartz, 'Disproportionate Representation of Males in Special Education Services: Biology, Behavior, or Bias?', *Education and Treatment of Children* 24(1) (2001): 28–45.

Blackwell Publishing for permission to reprint Harry Daniels, Valerie Hey, Diana Leonard and Marjorie Smith, 'Issues of Equity in Special Needs Education from a Gender Perspective', *British Journal of Special Education* 26(4) (1999): 189–95.

Taylor & Francis Ltd for permission to reprint Michael Miles, 'Disability on a Different Model: Glimpses of an Asian Heritage', *Disability & Society* 15(4) (2000): 603–18. http://www.tandf.co.uk

David Fulton Publishers for permission to reprint Alice Bradley, 'Community Based Rehabilitation in Developing Countries', in P. Lacey and C. Ouvrey (eds), *People with Profound and Multiple Learning Disabilities: A Collaborative Approach to Meeting Complex Needs* (London: David Fulton Publishers, 1998), pp. 215–25.

Republic of South Africa: Department of Education for permission to reprint 'Executive Summary', in *Education White Paper 6. Special Needs Education: Building an Inclusive Education and Training System* (Pretoria, Republic of South Africa: Department of Education, 2001), pp. 5–8.

Taylor & Francis Ltd for permission to reprint Mary Warnock, 'Equality Fifteen Years on', *Oxford Review of Education* 17(2) (1991): 145–53. http://www.tandf.co.uk

From 'Special Education for the Mildly Retarded – Is Much of it Justifiable?', by Lloyd M. Dunn, *Exceptional Children* 35 (1968): 5–22. Copyright © 1968 by The Council for Exceptional Children. Reprinted with permission.

McGraw-Hill Publishing Company and Open University Press for kind permission to reprint Garry Thomas and Andrew Loxley, 'Special Education – Theory and Theory Talk', in *Deconstructing Special Education and Constructing Inclusion* (Buckingham: Open University Press, 2001), pp. 1–20. © Copyright 1996, McGraw-Hill Publishing Company and Open University Press.

From 'Commentary: Today's Special Education and its Messages for Tomorrow', James M. Kauffman, *The Journal of Special Education* 32(4) (1999): 244–54. Copyright © 1999 by PRO-ED, Inc. Reprinted with permission.

Taylor & Francis Ltd for permission to reprint Martyn Rouse and Lani Florian, 'Inclusive Education in the Market-place', *International Journal of Inclusive Education* 1(4) (1997): 323–36. http://www.tandf.co.uk

Routledge Kogan Page for permission to reprint Len Barton, 'Market Ideologies, Education and the Challenge for Inclusion', in H. Daniels and P. Garner (eds), *World Yearbook of Education 1999: Inclusive Education* (London: Kogan Page, 1999), pp. 54–62.

Love Publishing Company for permission to reprint Martha L. Thurlow, 'Standards-based Reform and Students with Disabilities: Reflections on a Decade of Change', *Focus on Exceptional Children* 33(3) (2000): 1–16.

UNESCO for permission to reprint UNESCO, *The Salamanca Statement and Framework for Action on Special Needs Education. Adopted by the World Conference on Special Educational Needs: Access and Quality. Salamanca, Spain, 7–10 June 1994* (Paris: UNESCO, 1994), pp. vii–xii.

Lawrence Erlbaum Associates, Inc. for permission to reprint David Mitchell, 'Transfer of Beliefs, Knowledge, and Experiences between Countries', in P. Retish and S. Reiter (eds), *Adults with Disabilities: International Perspectives in the Community* (Mahwah, NJ: Lawrence Erlbaum Associates, 1999), pp. 259–85. Copyright © 1999, Lawrence Erlbaum Associates, Inc.

Taylor & Francis Ltd for permission to reprint Peter Mittler, 'Educating Pupils with Intellectual Disabilities in England and Wales: Thirty Years on', *International Journal of Disability, Development and Education* 49(2) (2002): 145–60. http://www.tandf.co.uk

Taylor & Francis Ltd for permission to reprint Sally Tomlinson, 'The Expansion of Special Education', *Oxford Review of Education* 11(2) (1985): 157–65. http://www.tandf.co.uk/journals/carfax/03054985.html

Peter Evans, 'Equity Indicators Based on the Provision of Supplemental Resources for Disabled and Disadvantaged Students', in W. Hutmacher, D. Cochrane and N. Bottani (eds), *In Pursuit of Equity in Education: Using*

International Indicators to Compare Equity Policies (Dordrecht: Kluwer Academic Publishers, 2000), pp. 253–66. Copyright © 2000, with kind permission from Kluwer Academic Publishers.

Elsevier for permission to reprint Thomas B. Parrish, 'Restructuring Special Education Funding in New York to Promote the Objective of High Learning Standards for All Students', *Economics of Education Review* 19 (2000): 431–45.

Disclaimer

Chronological Table of reprinted articles and chapters

Chronological Table continued

Date	Author	Article/chapter	References	Vol.	Chap.
1995	Catherine Clark, Alan Dyson, Alan Millward and David Skidmore	Dialectical analysis, special needs and schools as organisations	C. Clark, A. Dyson and A. Millward (eds), *Towards Inclusive Schools?*, London: David Fulton, pp. 78–95	II	43
1995	Robert B. Rutherford, Jr. and C. Michael Nelson	Management of aggressive and violent behavior in the schools	*Focus on Exceptional Children* 27(6): 1–15	III	72
1996	Carol Christensen	Disabled, handicapped or disordered: 'What's in a name?'	C. Christensen and F. Rizvi (eds), *Disability and the Dilemmas of Education and Justice*, Buckingham: Open University Press, pp. 63–78	I	1
1996	Dorothy Kerzner Lipsky and Alan Gartner	Equity requires inclusion: the future for all students with disabilities	C. Christensen and F. Rizvi (eds), *Disability and the Dilemmas of Education and Justice*, Buckingham: Open University Press, pp. 145–55	II	32
1996	Michael Oliver	Education for all? A perspective on an inclusive society	M. Oliver, *Understanding Disability: From Theory to Practice*, Basingstoke: Macmillan, pp. 78–94	II	35
1996	Jeanne B. Repetto and Vivian I. Correa	Expanding views on transition	*Exceptional Children* 62(6): 551–63	III	76
1996	C. Beth Schaffner and Barbara E. Buswell	Ten critical elements for creating inclusive and effective school communities	S. Stainback and W. Stainback (eds), *Inclusion: A Guide for Educators*, Baltimore: Paul H. Brooks, pp. 49–65	II	46
1996	Thomas E. Scruggs and Margo A. Mastropieri	Teacher perceptions of mainstreaming/inclusion, 1958–1995: a research synthesis	*Exceptional Children* 63(1): 59–74	II	51
1996	Thomas M. Skrtic, Wayne Sailor and Kathleen Gee	Voice, collaboration, and inclusion: democratic themes in educational and social reform initiatives	*Remedial and Special Education* 17(3): 142–57	II	42

Year	Author	Title	Publication	Part	Page
1997	Evangeline R. Danseco	Parental beliefs on childhood disability: insights on culture, child development and intervention	*International Journal of Disability, Development and Education* 44(1): 41–52	I	4
1997	George J. DuPaul and Tanya L. Eckert	The effects of school-based interventions for attention deficit hyperactivity disorder: a meta-analysis	*School Psychology Review* 26(1): 5–27	IV	87
1997	Monique R. Frazier and Kenneth W. Merrell	Issues in behavioral treatment of Attention-Deficit/Hyperactivity Disorder	*Education & Treatment of Children* 20(4): 441–61	III	73
1997	Garry Hornby, Mary Atkinson and Jean Howard	Peer/parenting tutoring – is it effective?	G. Hornby, M. Atkinson and J. Howard. *Controversial Issues in Special Education*, London: David Fulton, pp. 132–48	III	64
1997	Pam Hunt and Lori Goetz	Research on inclusive educational programs, practices, and outcomes for students with severe disabilities	*The Journal of Special Education* 31(1): 3–29	IV	94
1997	Margaret E. King-Sears	Best academic practices for inclusive classrooms	*Focus on Exceptional Children* 29(7): 1–21	IV	82
1997	Martyn Rouse and Lani Florian	Inclusive education in the marketplace	*International Journal of Inclusive Education* 1(4): 323–36	I	19
1997	Mark Wolery and John W. Schuster	Instructional methods with students who have significant disabilities	*The Journal of Special Education* 31(1): 61–79	IV	92
1997	John Woodward and Herbert Rieth	A historical review of technology research in special education	*Review of Educational Research* 67(4): 503–36	III	63
1998	Alice Bradley	Community based rehabilitation in developing countries	P. Lacey and C. Ouvrey (eds), *People with Profound and Multiple Learning Disabilities: A Collaborative Approach to Meeting Complex Needs*, London: David Fulton, pp. 215–25	I	13
1998	John McDonnell	Instruction for students with severe disabilities in general education settings	*Education and Training in Mental Retardation and Developmental Disabilities* 33(3): 199–215	II	53

Chronological Table continued

Date	Author	Article/chapter	References	Vol.	Chap.
1998	Donald L. MacMillan and Daniel J. Reschly	Overrepresentation of minority students: the case for greater specificity or reconsideration of the variables examined	*Journal of Special Education* 32(1): 15–24	I	8
1998	Barbara J. Scott, Michael R. Vitale and William G. Masten	Implementing instructional adaptations for students with disabilities in inclusive classrooms: a literature review	*Remedial and Special Education* 19(2): 106–19	IV	84
1998	Paula J. Stanovich and Anne Jordan	Canadian teachers' and principals' beliefs about inclusive education as predictors of effective teaching in heterogeneous classrooms	*Elementary School Journal* 98(3): 221–38	IV	85
1998	Paula J. Stanovich, Anne Jordan and Josette Perot	Relative differences in academic self-concept and peer acceptance among students in inclusive classrooms	*Remedial and Special Education* 19(2): 120–6	IV	98
1999	Len Barton	Market ideologies, education and the challenge for inclusion	H. Daniels and P. Garner (eds), *World Yearbook of Education 1999: Inclusive Education*, London: Kogan Page, pp. 54–62	I	20
1999	Roy I. Brown and Jo Shearer	Challenges for inclusion within a quality of life model for the 21st century	*Australasian Journal of Special Education* 22(3): 180–94	II	38
1999	Harry Daniels, Valerie Hey, Diana Leonard and Marjorie Smith	Issues of equity in special needs education from a gender perspective	*British Journal of Special Education* 26(4): 189–95	I	11
1999	James M. Kauffman	Commentary: today's special education and its messages for tomorrow	*The Journal of Special Education* 32(4): 244–54	I	18
1999	Dorothy Kerzner Lipsky and Alan Gartner	Inclusive education: a requirement of a democratic society	H. Daniels and P. Garner (eds), *World Yearbook of Education 1999: Inclusive Education*, London: Kogan Page, pp. 12–23	II	31

Chronological Table continued

Date	Author	Article/chapter	References	Vol.	Chap.
2000	Michael Miles	Disability on a different model: glimpses of an Asian heritage	*Disability & Society* 15(4): 603–18	I	12
2000	Thomas B. Parrish	Restructuring special education funding in New York to promote the objective of high learning standards for all students	*Economics of Education Review* 19: 431–45	I	29
2000	Sheila Riddell	Inclusion and choice: mutually exclusive principles in special educational needs?	F. Armstrong, D. Armstrong and L. Barton (eds), *Inclusive Education: Policy Contexts and Comparative Perspectives*, London: David Fulton, pp. 99–116	II	37
2000	Kevin S. Sutherland, Joseph H. Wehby and Philip L. Gunter	The effectiveness of cooperative learning with students with emotional and behavioral disorders: a literature review	*Behavioral Disorders* 25(3): 225–38	III	61
2000	Martha L. Thurlow	Standards-based reform and students with disabilities: reflections on a decade of change	*Focus on Exceptional Children* 33(3): 1–16	I	21
2000	Sharon Vaughn, Russell Gersten and David J. Chard	The underlying message in LD intervention research: findings from research syntheses	*Exceptional Children* 67(1): 99–114	IV	91
2001	Jill Bevan-Brown	Evaluating special education services for learners from ethnically diverse groups: getting it right	*Journal of the Association for Persons with Severe Handicaps* 26(3): 138–47	I	9
2001	Andy Bondy and Lori Frost	The Picture Exchange Communication System	*Behavior Modification* 25(5): 725–44	III	75
2001	Michael Bullis, Hill M. Walker and Jeffrey R. Sprague	A promise unfulfilled: social skills training with at-risk and antisocial children and youth	*Exceptionality* 9(1–2): 67–90	III	62
2001	Ian Dempsey and Phil Foreman	A review of educational approaches for individuals with autism	*International Journal of Disability, Development and Education* 48(1): 103–16	III	74

Year	Author(s)	Title	Source	Vol.	Page
2001	Department of Education	Executive summary	Education White Paper 6. Special Needs Education: Building an Inclusive Education and Training System, Pretoria: Republic of South Africa, Department of Education, pp. 5–8	I	14
2001	Charles R. Greenwood and Mary Abbott	The research to practice gap in special education	Teacher Education and Special Education 24(4): 276–89	IV	78
2001	Frank M. Gresham, T. Steuart Watson and Christopher H. Skinner	Functional behavioral assessment: principles, procedures, and future directions	School Psychology Review 30(2): 156–72	III	57
2001	Joshua K. Harrower and Glen Dunlap	Including children with autism in general education classrooms: a review of effective strategies	Behavior Modification 25(5): 762–84	II	52
2001	Seamus Hegarty	Inclusive education – a case to answer	Journal of Moral Education 30(3): 243–9	II	40
2001	Mark P. Mostert and Kenneth Kavale	Evaluation of research for usable knowledge in behavioral disorders: ignoring the irrelevant, considering the germane	Behavioral Disorders 27(1): 53–68	IV	79
2001	Thea Peetsma, Margaretha Vergeer, Jaap Roeleveld and Sjoerd Karsten	Inclusion in education: comparing pupils' development in special and regular education	Educational Review 53(2): 125–35	IV	96
2001	Mary J. Pitoniak and James M. Royer	Testing accommodations for examinees with disabilities: a review of psychometric, legal, and social policy issues	Review of Educational Research 71(1): 53–104	III	58
2001	Gary M. Sasso	The retreat from inquiry and knowledge in special education	The Journal of Special Education 34(4): 178–93	IV	80
2001	Roger Slee	Social justice and the changing directions in educational research: the case of inclusive education	International Journal of Inclusive Education 5(2/3): 167–77	II	34
2001	H. Lee Swanson	Searching for the best model for instructing students with learning disabilities	Focus on Exceptional Children 34(2): 1–15	IV	90

Chronological Table continued

Date	Author	Article/chapter	References	Vol.	Chap.
2001	Garry Thomas and Andrew Loxley	Special education – theory and theory talk	G. Thomas and A. Loxley, *Deconstructing Special Education and Constructing Inclusion*, Buckingham: Open University Press, pp. 1–20	I	17
2001	Michael L. Wehmeyer and Michelle Schwartz	Disproportionate representation of males in special education services: biology, behavior, or bias?	*Education and Treatment of Children* 24(1): 28–45	I	10
2001	Wendy Weichel Murawski and H. Lee Swanson	A meta-analysis of co-teaching research: where are the data?	*Remedial and Special Education* 22(5): 258–67	III	66
2002	Shirin D. Antia, Michael S. Stinson and Martha Gonter Gaustad	Developing membership in the education of deaf and hard-of-hearing students in inclusive settings	*Journal of Deaf Studies and Deaf Education* 7: 214–29	II	55
2002	Pauline Davis and Vicky Hopwood	Including children with a visual impairment in the mainstream primary school classroom	*Journal of Research in Special Educational Needs* 2(3): 1–11	II	54
2002	Carl J. Dunst	Family-centered practices: birth through high school	*Journal of Special Education* 36(3): 139–47	III	69
2002	C. Jonah Eleweke and Michael Rodda	The challenge of enhancing inclusive education in developing countries	*International Journal of Inclusive Education* 6(2): 113–26	II	49
2002	Mary Fisher and Luanna H. Meyer	Development and social competence after two years for students enrolled in inclusive and self-contained educational programs	*Research & Practice for Persons with Severe Disabilities* 27(3): 165–74	IV	93
2002	Michael F. Giangreco and Mary Beth Doyle	Students with disabilities and paraprofessional supports: benefits, balance, and band-aids	*Focus on Exceptional Children* 34(7): 1–12	III	67
2002	Jean P. Hall	Narrowing the breach: can disability culture and full educational inclusion be reconciled?	*Journal of Disability Policy Studies* 13(3): 144–52	I	5

Chronological Table continued

Date	Author	Article/chapter	References	Vol.	Chap.
2002	Michael L. Wehmeyer, G. Denise Lance and Susan Bashinski	Promoting access to the general curriculum for students with mental retardation: a multi-level model	*Education and Training in Mental Retardation and Developmental Disabilities* 37(3): 223–34	II	47
2003	Alfredo J. Artiles	Special education's changing identity: paradoxes and dilemmas in views of culture and space	*Harvard Educational Review* 73(2): 164–202	I	7
2003	Alan Dyson, Andy Howes and Barbara Roberts	What do we really know about inclusive schools? A systematic review of the research evidence	Paper presented at the AERA Annual Meeting, Chicago, April	II	45
2003	William L. Heward	Ten faulty notions about teaching and learning that hinder the effectiveness of special education	*The Journal of Special Education* 36(4): 186–205	IV	88
2003	Kenneth A. Kavale and Mark P. Mostert	River of ideology, islands of evidence	*Exceptionality* 11(4): 191–208	II	41
2003	Geoff Lindsay	Inclusive education: a critical perspective	*British Journal of Special Education* 30(1): 3–12	II	30
2003	Cor Meijer, Victoria Soriano and Amanda Watkins	Special needs education in Europe: inclusive policies and practices	C. Meijer, V. Soriano and A. Watkins (eds), *Special Needs Education in Europe, Thematic Publication*, Middelfart, Denmark: European Agency for Development in Special Needs Education, pp. 7–18	II	48
2003	Brahm Norwich	Is there a distinctive pedagogy for learning difficulties?	*ACCP Occasional Papers* 20: 25–37	IV	89

GENERAL INTRODUCTION

Few sectors in education have been as frequently debated and subjected to such wide-ranging policy changes as has provisions for students with special educational needs. In many countries, provisions for students with special educational needs are being transformed or are facing major critical reviews. It would be no exaggeration to claim that, at the beginning of the twenty-first century, special education is facing a crisis of identity, with no issue more acute than its relationship to inclusive education. In responding to this crisis, consideration must be given to broad philosophical principles such as human rights and equity, as well as to technical matters such as assessment and pedagogy.

Aim of the collection

The aim of this collection is to assemble published works that show, first, how the two fields of special education and inclusive education have evolved philosophically and technically over the past 25–30 years and, second, the contemporary state of the art in approaches to educating students with special educational needs. The overarching concern is to assemble a set of material that could assist policy-makers, practitioners and researchers in special and general education to make informed decisions regarding how best to educate students with special educational needs.

In determining what constitutes the most appropriate education for such students, several questions must be addressed. Chief among these are the following:

- What are the goals of their education?
- How should they be categorized; should they be categorized at all?
- What is the intersection of disability, ethnicity, gender and class?
- Where should they be educated – in specialized facilities or regular schools?
- What constitutes knowledge in special and inclusive education?
- What is the impact of wider educational reforms on their education?
- How should their education be funded and how should such decisions be made with regard to such principles as equality and equity?
- What is the most appropriate curriculum?

- How should they be assessed?
- What are the most effective teaching strategies?
- What is the role of parents, for example in making choices as to the placement of their children with special educational needs?
- How should their teachers and associated professionals be trained?
- What is the role of empirical research in making decisions?

Paradigm shifts and clashes

As will become apparent in this collection, the changes that have occurred, and are continuing to occur, can best be understood as reflecting the coalescence of a series of paradigm shifts. Some of these are specific to the field of special education; others reflect shifts in the broader education system. In some cases, one paradigm has clearly usurped another one, at least in some countries, while in other cases opposing paradigms remain contestable. In this collection, attention will be paid to five paradigm 'shifts' or 'clashes'.

First, the conceptualization of special needs is undergoing change. Slee (1998) provides a useful framework of five different paradigms, or perspectives. The first of these comes under the umbrella of an 'essentialist perspective', and is variously referred to as the 'medical model' or the 'psycho-medical model'. Here, students' differences are unproblematically located in their individual pathology, failure at school typically being blamed on some defect or inadequacy located within the student. This approach is usually characterized by a focus on disabilities or impairments, with the assumption that students with particular disabilities have more in common with each other than with differently disabled students or with those who do not have disabilities. The second approach is a 'social constructionist perspective', sometimes referred to as a 'socio-political paradigm' or the 'social theory of disability'. Writers from this perspective portray disability as a socially contrived construct. Slee's third category is a 'materialist perspective' in which disability is seen as a form of exclusion created by the economic system. The fourth category is a 'postmodern perspective' which portrays the experiences of persons with disabilities as discontinuous and ungroupable. And, fifth, there is a 'disability movement perspective' in which the concern is with bringing about social change and empowering persons with disabilities.

The second paradigm clash has to do with the role of assessment. Traditionally (and contemporaneously in many developing countries), assessment has been seen as a tool for sorting or selecting which learners should have opportunities to continue their education or which occupations should be open to them. When assessment is used for such purposes it is inevitable that students with special educational needs will fare the worst. Assessment procedures have had the effect of stigmatizing such students as failures and demotivating them. Increasingly, however, assessment is being seen as serving educational purposes by promoting learning and guiding teaching through providing the best possible account of what a learner knows, can do or has experienced.

The third paradigm clash centres on the extent to which students with special educational needs should and can be educated in regular school settings. The inclusive schools movement argues that regular schools should accept the rights of all students to enrol and receive their education in them; reduce barriers to learning; accommodate to students' different styles and rates of learning; and ensure equality of education opportunity through appropriate curriculum, school organization, use of resources and partnerships with their communities. The contrary view is that not all students with special educational needs can be accommodated in regular schools and that human rights arguments should not obscure the necessity to obtain sound empirical evidence for inclusion. Underlying this debate is the issue of whether there should be a unitary or a dual system of education and, if it is to be the former, how it can be transformed to accommodate to diversity.

The fourth clash arises from the impact on special and inclusive education of the broader education reforms that have recently taken place, or are under way in many countries. As noted by Mitchell (2001), these reforms include such shifts as the following: separating policy and delivery functions; reducing public monopolies and maximizing contestability; moving the balance of responsibility for governance, management and accountability from the centre to local authorities, even individual schools; moving from the use of input controls to quantifiable output measures (and the concomitant issue of 'high stakes testing'); and accepting greater parental choice.

The fifth paradigm clash concerns pedagogical issues. Briefly, these revolve around the relative emphases placed upon approaches involving highly structured, direct instruction strategies drawn from a behaviour analysis tradition, compared with those drawing upon cognitive and metacognitive theories. In turn, these lead to differences in assessment and planning methods.

In all of these paradigm clashes, there are accompanying tensions. Further, it must be noted that different countries are at different stages in reaching settlements. These differences reflect a range of factors, including intellectual traditions, cultural values, economic circumstances and demography.

Definitions and nomenclature

For the purposes of this collection, students with special needs include those with disabilities and associated learning and/or behavioural difficulties that are not attributed primarily to cultural or linguistic factors (although these will be considered as secondary factors, where appropriate). Giftedness *per se*

3

is not systematically covered, except where it co-occurs with disabilities. Special education is interpreted to cover the provisions ranging from institutions to special schools, special classes and resource rooms/teachers. Inclusive education covers provisions ranging from part-time integration of students with special educational needs in regular classes to their full-time inclusion in age-appropriate classes. The focus of the collection is on the compulsory school period, although consideration is given to the transition from school to post-school experiences. For most purposes in the introductions to each volume, the term, 'students with special educational needs' will be used, except where the writers clearly wish to use 'disability' as the referent.

Structure of the collection

In selecting material for inclusion in the collection, several criteria were taken into account. Chief among these were the following: coverage of the main issues in special and inclusive education; significance for the field at the time of publication; potential enduring significance for the field, in the case of recent publications; relevance to an international audience; the quality of the evidence or argument; the quality of the writing (works in English only were selected – a major restriction); an attempt to do justice to the diverse views characterizing particular issues; and the achievement of an international balance. With regard to the last point, 54 of the 98 items selected originate in the USA, the remaining 44 coming from non-US sources. In arriving at the final selection, approximately 1,000 items were surveyed over a two-year period while the editor was located in four different countries: New Zealand, the USA, England and Singapore.

Because of space limitations, preference was given to critiques, meta-analyses, reviews and theoretical perspectives. With a few exceptions, it was not possible to include papers devoted to specific research projects or to country descriptions. Nor was it possible to include more than a few disability-specific papers. Thus, a large number of items of potential significance had to be omitted. The editor recognizes that the final selection is inevitably based on his subjective judgements and that another editor could well have made very different judgements.

The collection is arranged in four volumes, with some overlapping content:

- *Volume I* presents material on systems and contexts, with items to do with issues such as the identity of students with special educational needs, normalization, the over-representation of different groups in special education and the impact of educational reforms on provisions.
- *Volume II* focuses on inclusive education – the concept, its origins and rationale, its implementation, research evidence and critiques.
- *Volume III* is concerned with assessment and teaching strategies and includes material on staff utilization and family involvement.

- *Volume IV* presents research into the effectiveness of various interventions (including inclusive education), issues concerning research and
  the research–practice gap.

Acknowledgements

Preparation of this manuscript was supported, in part, by the following
institutions: the Department of Human Development and Counselling,
University of Waikato, Hamilton New Zealand; the Special Needs Research
Centre, School of Education, Communication and Language Sciences,
University of Newcastle, UK; and the David and Minnie Meyerson Foundation's 'Project on Research, Advocacy, and Policy Studies on Disability'
at the University of Arizona, Tucson, Arizona, USA.

Dr Jill Mitchell provided invaluable assistance in selecting material for
inclusion in the collection and Rebekah Taylor, Senior Development Editor
– Major Works at Routledge, skilfully guided the project.

References

Mitchell, D. (2001) 'Paradigm shifts in and around special education in New
Zealand', *Cambridge Journal of Education* 31(3): 319–35.
Slee, R. (1998) 'The politics of theorizing special education', in C. Clark, A. Dyson
and A. Millward (eds), *Theorising Special Education*, London: Routledge.

INTRODUCTION

The fields of special and inclusive education are replete with controversy and competing ideologies. Some of these are common to general education, but some are specific to the education of students with special educational needs. This volume presents material relating to five issues at the systems and contexts level to do with such students: perspectives on their identity, normalization and social role valorization; the over-representation of different groups in special education; the financing of provisions; and the impact of education reforms. As well, there are papers presenting international and national perspectives on these and other issues. Other volumes also contain material of relevance to these issues and will be referred to in this introduction.

Perspectives on the identity of students with special educational needs

For much of its history, special education has been dominated by what Clark, Dyson, Millward and Skidmore (1995, II: 43)[1] describe as a psycho-medical model, which focuses on the assumption that deficits are located within individual students. In contrast, several writers in this series (Christensen 1996, I: 1; Skidmore 2002, II: 33; Skrtic, Sailor and Gee 1996, II: 42) regard disability as a socio-political construct, defined by Clark *et al.* (1995, II: 43) as focusing on structural inequalities at the macro-social level being reproduced at the institutional level. Christensen, for example, argues that the portrayal of people with disabilities in terms of personal tragedies arising from their diseases, pathologies or deficits is tantamount to oppression. The dualistic segmentation of society into two groups, a majority who are 'whole' and a minority who are 'less than whole', is derived from the medical model. Christensen considers that this model is problematic for several reasons. First, it leads to the attribution of student failure to a defect or inadequacy within the individual, thus masking the role that highly constraining educational systems play in creating failure. Second, it wrongly suggests homogeneity within various diagnostic categories. Third, many students enrolled in special education do not manifest demonstrable pathologies. Fourth, studies show that instruction based on categories is generally not effective. Rather than seeing such students as disabled or defective,

Christensen asserts that all students should be seen as different, complex and whole. Some writers are critical of this socio-political perspective, however, blaming it and its derivatives for what they consider to be an unscientific approach to special education (see Heward 2003, IV: 88; Kauffman 1999, I: 18; Kavale and Mostert 2003, II: 41; and Sasso 2001, IV: 80). Their views are outlined in more detail in the introduction to Volume IV.

A variant of the socio-political model is a socio-cultural view presented by Danesco (1997, I: 4) on the basis of her examination of international studies of parental beliefs about the nature and causation of childhood disabilities and about treatment and intervention. These studies reveal a commonly held duality of beliefs, with many parents in some cultures simultaneously holding both biomedical and socio-cultural views, the latter derived from magical, religious, supernatural or metaphysical beliefs. Among the socio-cultural views is the belief espoused by cultural groups that adhere to the idea of reincarnation, where a disability is perceived as a condition affecting a present life but not necessarily the preceding or following lives. This duality of beliefs leads parents to pursue both formal biomedical help and support from informal networks, including eliciting the help of folk healers, performing religious rituals and changing their own behaviours to atone for past transgressions. Danesco argues that professionals need to identify where their and parents' beliefs are convergent, divergent or in conflict, and to develop strategies to deal with these circumstances. Danesco's argument is echoed by Kalyanpur, Harry and Skrtic (2000, III: 70) who contend that the equity and advocacy expectations embedded in mandates for parent participation in special education decision-making processes may well be in conflict with the values held by many families from culturally diverse backgrounds. This is particularly so in the case of those who do not share beliefs in the primacy of participatory democracy, individual rights and freedom of choice. Instead of equity, some cultures may believe that inequality is a right and proper principle; instead of asserting individual rights, some cultures emphasize social obligations; instead of valuing choice, some cultures accept the primacy of ascribed roles. It is therefore incumbent on professionals that they develop an awareness of their own cultural and ethical values and understand that these may not be universally shared. A similar perspective is taken by Miles (2000, I: 12) in his discussion of historical meanings of disability in Asia. He suggests that these meanings should not be forced into modern Western categories, but rather that they should be used to challenge and refresh them.

Yet another way of looking at disability is argued by Oliver (1999, I: 6). Drawing from a Marxist political economy theory, he presents a materialist view of society, claiming that the category 'disability' and the oppression that disabled people (his term) face is produced by the economic and social forces inherent in capitalism. Even the move from institutions to community can be seen as but an extension of the processes of control within the capitalist state, the balance of power between disabled people and pro-fessionals remaining unchanged: 'it is still professionals doing it, whatever "it" is called, to disabled people' (p. 166). Oliver concludes by reiterating that the demands of disabled people all over the world are not so much for improvements in existing services, but for control over them.

While not presenting an alternative model, the view expressed by Thomas and Loxley (2001, I: 17) should be considered in juxtaposition with the foregoing. They challenge the validity of much of the 'knowledge' in special education, bringing into question the legitimacy of the enterprise. They argue that many notions of learning difficulty that underpin special education rely on theories that purport to be something more than they really are and often distract attention from simpler explanations for children's failure to thrive. They reject the view that special educators should adopt particular 'formulaic schema for collecting data, some analytical sieve for sifting it or some theoretical frame for synthesis' (p. 12). Instead, they mount a case for renewing confidence in practitioners' knowledge in understanding the failure of children in school. This, they feel, would go some way to redressing the power imbalance between practitioners and the possessors of 'privileged knowledge' who have persuaded teachers that they may not be suffici-ently knowledgeable or expert to help children who experience difficulties.

A final perspective on the identity of students with special educational needs is offered by Hall (2002, I: 5) who puts the case for recognizing the existence of a disability culture in which persons with disabilities have opportunities to associate with and learn alongside others who share similar identities and life experiences. Moreover, she points out, the history of the disability rights movement illustrates that major changes do not occur unless people with disabilities band together to address shared injustices. This feature is accentuated by the fact that, unlike other cultural groups, people with disabilities do not usually share that cultural affiliation with their families. The school therefore presents a unique opportunity for students with disabilities to obtain both knowledge and support from others with disabilities.

Normalization and social role valorization

The term 'normalization' was promulgated first in Scandinavia in the late 1960s and had at its core the principle of 'making available to all mentally retarded persons patterns of life and conditions of everyday living which are as close as possible to the regular circumstance and ways of life of society' (Nirje 1976, p. 231, cited by Perrin and Nirje 1985, I: 2). According to these writers, the term came to be misunderstood, with misconceptions such as 'normalization means making people normal', 'special services are incon-sistent with the normalization principle', 'normalization is an all or nothing concept' and 'normalization is appropriate only for the mildly retarded'.

Although Wolfensberger (1983, I: 2) was an early user of the term 'normalization', he eventually decided that it was too ambiguous a concept and should be replaced by a new term, 'social role valorization'. He argues that this concept reflects the highest goal of the original concept of normalization, i.e. the creation, support and defence of valued social roles for people who are at risk of social devaluation. Perrin & Nirje (1985, I: 2) criticize Wolfensberger's 'deviation' from the original concept of normalization, claiming that he interpreted it as specifying various standards of behaviour to which a mentally handicapped person must conform. Oliver (1999, I: 6) presents an even more severe critique, arguing that normalization is based on an outdated interactionalist and functionalist sociology and that, whatever the caveats of its proponents, it is essentially predicated on a normal/abnormal distinction.

Over-representation of different groups in special education

Two groups are widely considered to be over-represented in special education: those from ethnic minorities and males.

First, some writers express concern at what they perceive to be an over-representation of racial minority students in special education, referred to by Dunn (1968, I: 16) as 'socioculturally deprived children'. (An opposite situation pertained in South Africa where, under apartheid, whites were over-represented in special education (Department of Education 2001, I: 14).) The issue of ethnic minority over-representation is explored in some detail by Artiles (2003, I: 7). He notes that in the USA, African Americans and Native Americans are disproportionately represented in special education, especially in the high incidence categories of learning disabilities, mental retardation and emotionally disturbed. Explanations include the lack of congruence between minority cultures and the school culture, the legacy of deficit thinking about racial minorities, bias towards racial minorities and the links between race, poverty and disability. A way of addressing the over-representation of ethnic minority groups in special education can perhaps be found in the work of Bevan-Brown (2001, I: 9). Writing from a New Zealand perspective, she presents a series of guidelines for evaluating special education services for Maori students. She summarizes these requirements in terms of the right person asking the right questions of the right people at the right place and time. While these guidelines have wide applicability, Bevan-Brown cautions against stereotyping members of cultural groups. In the case of Maori, for example, they differ in many areas including their level of education, lifestyle, values, socio-economic status, tribal affiliation and their knowledge and practice of Maori culture.

That the over-representation of ethnic minorities in special education issue is not a straightforward matter, however, is demonstrated by MacMillan and Rechsly (1998, I: 8). In their critique of the US literature, they argue that data suffer from five major problems. First, quite different results are obtained when percentages of groups in categories or programmes are used, compared with the more commonly cited data on percentage of categories or programmes by groups. Second, they urge caution in relying on aggregated data on race/ethnicity from sources that use different approaches to recording these features (in a related point, they note that most data collection fails to account for biracial students). Third, in noting the considerable variability in rates of disability across states, particularly in categories requiring subjective judgements, they question the validity of these designations. Fourth, they note the failure to consider that social class, rather than race/ethnicity, may be the more significant variable to focus on when considering over-representation. And, fifth, they point to the irony of considering over-representation to be a problem if students are purportedly gaining the advantages of special education.

Further, there is the question of gender imbalance in special education. Evans (2000, I: 28), for example, notes that in every one of the OECD countries he studied, boys were in a clear majority by a ratio of around 3 : 2, suggesting to him that they thus received more resources than girls to help them gain access to the curriculum. In addressing the question of the over-representation of males, Wehmeyer and Schwartz (2001, I: 10) put forward three possible reasons: boys exhibit behaviour patterns that are more likely to lead to referrals; there may be biological differences between boys and girls; and there may be a gender bias in referrals and admissions. On the basis of a comprehensive study in some US school districts, they concluded that it is not so much that males are over-represented but that females are under-represented. Writing from an English perspective, Daniels, Hey, Leonard and Smith (1999, I: 11) also report on significant gender differences in the numbers of students receiving special education support, irrespective of the identification procedures employed. Of interest, however, is their finding that this overall pattern obscures considerable inter-school variability, with ratios of girls to boys varying from 1 : 1 to 1 : 8. There is thus a need to investigate what aspects of schools give rise to such disparities. Further, a finding that gender differences were much greater among whites than among blacks suggests to Daniels *et al.* that both gender and race should be considered simultaneously.

Financing of provisions

Two papers bearing on the financing of special education are presented in this volume. First, arguing from John Rawls's 'difference principle', which asserts that institutions should be structured with a built-in bias in favour of the disadvantaged, Evans (2000, I: 28) examines how equity in education occurs in the way resources are distributed to disadvantaged groups, including those with disabilities. He notes that this supply-side model has the advantage of being quantifiable and can be used to determine the extent to which additional resources are being used efficiently and effectively. It also enables comparisons to be made between and within countries. These are often hampered, however, by different definitions of special education and categories of students. Parrish (2000, I: 29) provides a US perspective on special education finance, reviewing funding mechanisms across the states and presenting a detailed examination of current and proposed funding models in one state, New York. He notes that, on average, expenditures for students receiving special education services were 2.3 times greater than for general education students. He also notes that growing concerns about the quantum of special education funding and methods used to allocate it have led to reform initiatives. Although funding has historically been based on each state's count of students with disabilities who were receiving special education services, it is planned that the number of students be capped at 12 per cent of the school-age population. Further, federal special education funding will eventually be census-based, meaning that it will be based on total school enrolments rather than on special education counts. Such an approach would permit students with special needs to be served outside special education and would reduce the incentives to over-identify. On the other hand, according to Parrish, this model would raise issues of equity in states and districts with higher prevalence rates, jeopardize procedural safeguards if students are not identified as having special needs, and may threaten current levels of funding.

The impact of education reforms on provisions

Since special and inclusive education normally exists within the context of education systems, it is important to consider the impact of education reforms on students with special educational needs. In this volume, two aspects of such reforms are considered: market-oriented ideologies and standards-based reforms. (The introduction to Volume II outlines the impact of education reforms on inclusive education.) According to Barton (1999, I: 20), the 'New Right' ideologies introduced by conservative governments in the UK articulate a new vision of the 'good society', one characterized by individualism, competition and the decentralization of planning and decision-making. Underpinning this vision is the belief that market forces are more efficient at allocating resources and more responsive to the needs of individuals. He further writes that the impact of these ideologies on education has been to establish a more hierarchical, status-ridden, selective and exclusionary system, thus exacerbating the deep structural socio-economic conditions and relations in society that serve to maintain inequalities, discrimination and exclusionary practices.

One of the educational battle cries in the USA in the 1990s was for 'standards-based reform', with its goal of higher and more rigorous achievement standards for all students. According to Thurlow (2000, I: 21), students with disabilities do not fare well under these reforms. She cites research showing that such students are frequently excluded from national and state assessments at various points – the setting of standards, participation in assessments, accommodations to enable their abilities, rather than their disabilities, to be assessed, and the reporting of assessment results. Students with disabilities are disadvantaged, too, by the narrowing of the curriculum that emerges as an unintended consequence of the standards-based reforms as teachers focus on the range of knowledge and skills included in assessments. While this latter point could be considered undesirable for all students, Thurlow argues it is particularly relevant when considering the need for students with disabilities to have access to a broader curriculum. Also writing from a US perspective, Artiles (2003, I: 7) predicts that the introduction of such education reforms as standards, high-stakes testing and zero tolerance for anti-social behaviours may well exacerbate the current trend towards over-representation of ethnic minority groups in special education.

International perspectives

Mitchell (1999, I: 24) analyses the ways in which beliefs, principles, knowledge and practices relating to special education are transferred between countries, resulting in what he considers to be a remarkable degree of convergence, both in ideology and in practices, across all types of nations. These transfers arise from such sources as international governmental organizations such as the UN bodies, international and regional nongovernmental organizations, bilateral arrangements between countries, the dissemination of influential legislation and, most recently, the Internet. The transfer of knowledge, beliefs and experiences raises both technical and moral issues, including problems in coordinating international assistance, the need for universal design for such matters as assistive devices, and the cultural propriety of making such transfers. With respect to the last point, Mitchell notes that the challenge to both exporters and importers of philosophies and practices is to determine how far indigenous philosophies, ideologies and practices should be encouraged, respected, challenged, overthrown or blended with those from 'outside'.

The Declaration on the Rights of Disabled Persons, adopted by the UN General Assembly in 1975, stands out as a landmark in the international context (United Nations 1975, I: 22). Its 13-point proclamation has influenced many countries, especially developing countries, in their formulation of policies for persons with disabilities, including special education policies. *Inter alia*, the Declaration asserts that disabled persons have the right to respect for their human dignity, to measures designed to enable them to become as self-reliant as possible and to a range of services,

13

including education, which will enable them to develop their skills. With regard to the education of students with special educational needs, the 1994 Salamanca Declaration was even more specific. At a 1994 conference held in Salamanca, Spain, and sponsored by UNESCO (UNESCO 1994, I: 23), representatives of 92 governments and 25 international organizations proclaimed that every child has a fundamental right to education and has unique characteristics, interests, abilities and learning needs which should be taken into account by child-centred education systems.

Community-based rehabilitation (CBR) is a term used since the 1970s to describe an approach to working with people with disabilities, especially in rural areas in developing countries. Bradley (1998, I: 13) outlines how the World Health Organization instigated it and presents several examples of how it works in practice. She describes CBR's main features as including the goal of working towards social justice and equity for people with disabilities and their families, the dissemination of rehabilitation knowledge to families and communities with no access to conventional rehabilitation services, partnerships between governments and communities, multidisciplinary teamwork and flexibility to take on the shape required to meet the needs of those it serves.

National perspectives

Given that the USA and the UK have played, and are playing, dominant roles in influencing worldwide provisions for students with special educational needs, it is relevant to outline some of the important issues in these jurisdictions. South Africa, because of its radical post-apartheid restructuring of special education into an inclusive system, also deserves separate attention.

'A better education than special class placement is needed for socioculturally deprived children with mild learning problems who have been labeled educable mentally retarded.' So begins Dunn's classic denouement (1968, I: 16, p. 5) of many features of special education that had hitherto been taken for granted in the USA and which he considered to be obsolete and unjustifiable. Among the many arguments he mounts for taking this position, three stand out. First, special classes are based on the premise of homogeneous grouping, which tends to work to the disadvantage of slow learners and underprivileged students. Second, efficacy studies suggest that retarded students make as much or more progress in regular grades as they do in special education. Third, the labelling processes are flawed: they are based on inadequate diagnostic procedures, lead to lowered expectancies of teachers and contribute significantly to students' feelings of inferiority. Instead of special classes for such children, Dunn argues for consideration of 'a comprehensive ecological push' to achieve quality education for 'children from inadequate homes and backgrounds'.

14

A more recent representation of US developments is reflected in President Bush's 2001 ordering of the creation of the President's Commission on Excellence in Special Education. In the preamble to its report (President's Commission 2002, I: 27), the Commission notes that young people with disabilities drop out of high school at twice the rate of their peers; that most public school educators do not feel well prepared to work with students with disabilities; that of the 6 million students in special education, half are identified as having a 'specific learning problem', mostly because they have not learned how to read; and students of minority status are over-represented in some categories of special education. The Commission brought down nine major findings, including the following: (1) the imple-mentation of the Individuals with Disabilities Education Act (IDEA) is overly bureaucratized; (2) too little emphasis is placed on prevention, early identification and aggressive intervention using research-based approaches; (3) general and special education are seen as separate systems; (4) many of the current methods of identifying students with disabilities lack validity; and (5) research in special education needs to be more rigorous, the current system not always implementing evidence-based practice. These major findings led to a wide range of recommendations, with three underlying themes: focus on results, not on process; embrace a model of prevention not a model of failure; consider children with disabilities as general education children first.

From the UK, Warnock (1991, I: 15), chair of the landmark UK Commit-tee of Enquiry into the Education of Handicapped Children and Young People that reported in 1978, recounts some of the features of that commit-tee's recommendations and the background to them. She notes, for example, the significance of the early 1970s transfer of responsibility for the hitherto designated 'ineducable' severely handicapped from the Department of Health to the Department of Education and Science. This led directly to the setting up of the committee of enquiry. Among the committee's central tenets were the beliefs that every person had the right to education; that the goals of education should be independence, the ability to do useful work and the ability to enjoy life; that the concept of 'special needs' should replace diagnostic categories; and that while 2 per cent of children had ongoing significant special needs, as many as 20 per cent had less significant special needs which still required special help. The committee saw equality as equality of entitlement, not identity of provision. Writing some 13 years after presenting the report, Warnock paints a bleak picture of progress in the achievement of this notion of equality, blaming the financial crisis and the new ideal in education, that of cost-effectiveness. Mittler (2002, I: 25) reviews some of the significant developments in the education of students with intellectual disabilities that have taken place since responsibility for their education passed from health to education authorities. These include the shift from a categorical to a non-categorical, needs-based approach to teaching; a greater emphasis on changing the environment rather than the child; a shift from exclusion to inclusion (although the majority of children with intellectual disabilities remain in some form of segregated provisions, with considerable variations between local education authorities); and developments in making the National Curriculum and its assessment more accessible to students with special needs. Tomlinson (1985, I: 26) presents a sociological perspective on the reasons for the expansion of special education in the UK that took place in the early 1980s, attributing it, first, to changes in education as it attempted to fit the perceived needs of a technologically-based society in which a large social group will be partially or permanently unemployed. Second, professional vested interests played a role, with ordinary teachers being pressured to raise standards (which can be accomplished in part by removing 'defective and troublesome children') and teachers in special schools seeking to obtain clients for their schools. Third, comprehensive schools were driven to solve the dilemma of how to accommodate less able or troublesome children by a form of internal segregation.

When it emerged from the apartheid era, South Africa was determined to create special needs education as a non-racial and integrated component of its education system. In a 2001 White Paper (Department of Education 2001, I: 14), several findings of commissions on special needs education are reported, including the following: special education and support have predominantly been provided for a small proportion of learners with disabilities within special schools or classes; most learners with disabilities have either fallen outside the system or have been mainstreamed by default; and the curriculum and education system as a whole have generally failed to respond to the diverse needs of the learner population. Accordingly, South African policies are aimed, *inter alia*, at bringing about qualitative improvements in special schools and their phased conversion to resource centres, the overhauling of the processes of identifying and assessing learners with special needs, and the establishment of district-based support teams.

Note

1 Throughout this introduction, items included in the volumes will be indicated in this manner: author(s), date of initial publication, the volume number in the present series, and the chapter number allocated to the item (e.g. Christensen 1996, I: 1). Other sources will be acknowledged in the conventional manner. When page numbers are referred to, these are as they appear in the original source.

Reference

Nirje, B. (1976) 'The right to self-determination', in W. R. Kugel and A. Shearer (eds), *Changing Patterns in Residential Services for the Mentally Retarded*, rev. edn, Washington, DC: President's Committee on Mental Retardation.

1

DISABLED, HANDICAPPED OR DISORDERED

'What's in a name?'

Carol Christensen

Source: C. Christensen and F. Rizvi (eds), *Disability and the Dilemmas of Education and Justice*, Buckingham: Open University Press, 1996, pp. 63–78.

> 'tis but thy name that is my enemy
> . . . O be some other name!
> What's in a name? That which we call a rose
> By any other name would smell as sweet.
> (Juliet in *Romeo and Juliet* II. ii)

Although this sentiment is intuitively appealing, as Juliet was subsequently to discover, she may have understated the significance of names. In fact quite a lot can be in a name. Language reflects our perceptions, beliefs and understandings of our world. It also helps shape those perceptions. Thus language can exert a powerful influence on social processes which help shape human lives.

The role of language in political and social processes has been often stressed by groups concerned with social justice. Many socially oppressed groups have deliberately formulated an identity around a specific nomenclature. This nomenclature becomes one mechanism with which to challenge the dominant cultural expressions which serve to maintain social injustices. A notable example of this process is found in the fight for racial equality in the United States. Fraser (1995) argues that because of the dominant European culture, forms of expression have developed which valued and esteemed whiteness and disparaged and devalued blackness. Thus, the language of skin colour was a cultural mechanism by which specific racial groups were socially and politically marginalized. The battle for social justice required that aspects of cultural oppression be addressed. 'Black' was redefined in a way to valorize and recognize oppressed racial groups. Nomenclature of

17

'blackness' became a mechanism for anti-racist groups to combat the Eurocentric cultural hegemony.

Disability as cultural oppression

Disability is one of the most frequently forgotten forms of social, political and cultural oppression. As with other groups fighting for social justice, disabled groups have grasped the significance of language and sought to develop a nomenclature in which they control the definition of their own identity. The central issue, around which issues of social justice and the language of disability revolve, relates to notions of personal disease, pathology, disorder or deficit as mechanisms of social and cultural oppression. For much of this century the lives of people with disabilities have been dominated by the medical profession. As a group their identity was defined for them in terms of sickness, involving pathology or disorder. They were labelled as deaf, dumb, blind, mentally deficient, spastic. However, medical terminology inevitably intersected with social values and cultural norms of the time. In societies which valued youth, beauty, physical prowess and intellectual excellence, the medical language of disability soon became the social language of insult and disparagement. For example, medical terms used initially to classify people with intellectual disabilities included imbecile, moron and idiot. Similarly terms associated with physical disability such as cripple and spastic have lost their original medical connotations and become cultural tools to devalue and marginalize specific groups of people.

This process is of course not unique to disability. It has been repeated in relation to other socially oppressed groups, particularly minority racial groups. However, the intertwined nature of linkage between personal medical conditions and social functioning for people with disabilities has meant the nexus between language and social oppression has been particularly pernicious and intransigent in the face of pressure for social reform. During the 1960s and 70s those labelled 'disabled' sought to redefine their identity – and in the process, redefine the popular perceptions of the sources of their 'problems'. People with disabilities contested their identity as medical problems and challenged the personal tragedy view of disability which had underpinned much social policy to that point (Oliver 1986).

Personal tragedy, disability and educational reform

The personal tragedy concept of disability in education is problematic for a number of reasons. It is embedded in the notion that there are those in society who are able (or normal) and those who are not. This dualism segments society into two groups: those, the majority, who are whole; and those who are less than whole, who are imperfect and to be kept apart from the 'able'. As a result the 'disabled' are often portrayed in popular culture as either the 'courageous battler' or the 'pathetic cripple', but are rarely viewed or treated as 'normal people' (Gartner and Lipsky 1987).

Second, after being labelled as disabled or a category of disabled (e.g. blind, developmentally delayed or mentally deficient, emotionally disturbed, or physically impaired) the label tends to become the defining feature of the person. The person becomes 'the disabled' or 'blind' or 'cripple' rather than being viewed as a complex multifaceted, fully human person.

A third area of concern with the personal tragedy view of disability relates more specifically to educational systems and the manner in which they deal with difficulties, problems or failure. A disability or disorder is an inherent characteristic of the individual and consequently attributes student failure to a defect or inadequacy within the individual (Carrier 1983; Christensen *et al.* 1986). However, it can be argued that student disability results from organizational pathology rather than student pathology. Because disability locates the cause of failure within the individual student it masks the role educational systems play in creating and reproducing failure.

A disability implies a non-problematic pathological condition intrinsic to the individual; it fails to recognize that the concept of disability is socially constructed. Rather than being a real and non-problematic feature of the individual, it occurs as a consequence of diverse student characteristics interacting with the highly constraining demands of the classroom. This is particularly the case with 'mild' disabilities such as behaviour disorder, learning disability and intellectual disability. Many students are identified as disabled, stigmatized or excluded, not because their personal characteristics necessitate this but because schooling is structured in such a way that student diversity beyond very narrow prescribed limits cannot be accommodated. The lock-step, grade-based system of schooling requires a homogeneous school population to function efficiently (Skrtic 1991).

Thus, it can be argued that schooling is itself disabling, that its lack of flexibility in accommodating a diverse range of student attributes creates disabled students. However, because the manner in which schools function is taken for granted and seen as unproblematic, the source of students' difficulties is seen to reside in their disabilities or defects rather than the limitations and defects of schooling.

The central issue here concerns the ethics of school practices related to disability as a personal tragedy. It is suggested that ethical practice cannot occur unless there is a clear recognition of the role of both schooling practices and student characteristics in the identification of school failure. The use of concepts such as disability locates the cause of problems and failure in student deficit and thus serves to legitimate and mask the role of schooling in creating the problem. However, by doing so it also serves to obscure productive solutions to enduring and persistent problems.

Although this analysis seeks to reveal the role of previously covert institutional factors in the creation of disability, it is not sufficient as it fails to address the question of how these conditions arise. School practice is largely a result of the values of the people who engage in the practice (Skrtic 1991). Suggesting that school practice contributes to the construction of disabilities ignores the beliefs and values of practitioners which promote equity, justice and student success rather than failure. How is it then that school can simultaneously promote practices which disadvantage and stigmatize students while at the same time seeking to enhance their life opportunities. The answer to this question partially lies in the history and origins of special education. Initial special education programs were established at the conclusion of the last century and were based on a humanitarian ethic. They were designed to care for and educate people with sensory, intellectual or physical impairment who were likely to remain institutionalized without intervention. These programs were closely allied to medical interventions. For this reason and because of the clear physiological basis for many of the students' difficulties, special education practices were based on the personal tragedy view of disability and firmly embedded within the medical model.

Medical diagnosis and educational provision

This medical model assumes that the basic cause of an individual's symptoms is an underlying pathology or disease. The pathology requires appropriate diagnosis which determines the prescription of a treatment. The treatment should result in cure of the disease and the disappearance of the symptoms. In an educational context symptoms are generally based on the failure of an individual to function appropriately in a classroom. A broad range of categorial labels have been developed and used to describe various pathologies. These include sensory disabilities, physical disabilities, intellectual disabilities, emotional, attentional or behaviour disorders and learning difficulties or disabilities. According to the medical model, the diagnosis of the appropriate category of disability results in prescription of a treatment. In traditional special education, diagnosis occurred through an assessment, and treatment comprised placement in a categorially based segregated setting.

While special education was initially developed to assist a small group who had clear physiologically based conditions it grew rapidly during the first half of the twentieth century and increasingly has included students where no physical pathology, disorder, disability or impairment could be shown to exist (Gartner and Lipsky 1987). The rapid expansion and shift in the focus of special education commenced with and paralleled the introduction of compulsory education (Sarason and Doris 1979). Sarason and Doris provide a convincing argument that special education grew to meet the needs of a general education system required to accommodate a diverse range of sometimes recalcitrant and difficult students.

As a system, special education retained the assumptions of the medical model as a set of guiding principles. It also retained the humanitarian ideals which characterized its origins. However, in effect special education often functioned to provide a separate segregated system to contain those who because of their physical, emotional and intellectual characteristics did not fit the regular system. Thus, it served to relieve general education of the pressure to respond to diverse and sometimes resistant students.

While a quiet symbiosis seems to have existed between special and general education for some time, strident criticism of special education during the 1960s and 70s culminated in widespread reforms during the 1970s and 80s. One source of impetus for these reforms was the work of a number of researchers and scholars who demonstrated through empirical investigation that the assumptions of the medical model could not be sustained when applied to the practice of special education. Also, a large literature based on notions of social justice and fundamental human rights questioned the treatment of those labelled disabled. The objectives of the civil rights movement and women's movement articulated with those of the disability rights movement.

The medical model is founded on a logical link between pathology, diagnosis and treatment. In special education practice, this translated into a presumed pathology based on the assignment of a categorial label followed by placement in a categorially defined setting. The question of the role of a pathology in special education placement is a vexed one. First, definition and identification of a disability, disorder or impairment is often a matter of quantitative rather than qualitative deviation from the norm. For example, there is no clear distinction between when a person is a bit long- or short-sighted, or partially-sighted or seriously visually impaired or blind. This problem is even more pronounced with categories such as intellectual disability, behaviour or emotional disorder and learning disabilities, where the line between acceptable and unacceptable classroom behaviour and performance is extremely blurred.

Second, empirical investigation of various special education populations has shown that a number of labelled students demonstrate no detectable evidence of impairment, disorder or disability (Mercer 1973; Algozzine and Ysseldyke 1983). Rather than deviating from the norm on sensory, intellectual, physical or emotional dimensions, many special education students deviated on social, cultural, ethnic and economic dimensions. Special education, particularly for the 'mildly disabled' was shown to comprise disproportionately large numbers of students from poor or minority backgrounds.

Along with findings that many special education students failed to show a demonstrable pathology, assessment procedures designed to identify the pathology and therefore prescribe treatment have been found to be grossly inadequate (Coles 1978; Walker 1987). For example, Gartner and Lipsky (1987: 372) write that 'except for the case of physical disabilities assessment procedures are barely more accurate than a flip of the coin'. Thus, the link between assessment/diagnosis and instructional treatment assumed under the medical model did not hold when applied to assessment processes for special education. Rather assessment frequently served merely to locate the student within a disability category and consequently legitimate placement in special education (Wang *et al.* 1986; White and Calhoun 1987). In such cases assessment information did not provide useful information to guide instruction.

In addition to problems with definition and diagnosis, studies demonstrated that instruction based on categorial labels was not effective (Hallahan and Kauffman 1977) and that generally instruction which was effective for 'special education' students was fundamentally based on the same instructional techniques which have been shown to be effective for all students. Particularly disturbing were a series of studies which found that placement in segregated special education settings diminished rather than enhanced students' education success (Gartner and Lipsky 1987).

Taken together, these studies not only exposed the myth of the medical model which sustained and legitimated traditional special education practices based on student disability, they also raised serious questions about the humanitarian ethos which accompanied these practices. How could it be claimed that special education classes served to enhance and promote the interests of 'disabled' students if it could be shown that many students are better served by avoiding placement in special education?

Disability and the rights of students

During the period that these studies appeared in the literature a number of writers were raising a different set of concerns about special education based on issues of equity and social justice. They argued that exclusion of some children from any form of education based on an identifiable physical condition and the segregation of others in separate schools and classrooms violated their fundamental human rights (Wolfensberger 1972). They argued that these practices were stigmatizing and deleterious to students, and given the demonstrable lack of efficacy of segregated setting, indefensible in terms of serving students' interests.

These criticisms culminated in widespread reforms implemented during the 1970s and 80s. These reforms were international in scope, occurring in the US, Britain, Europe and Australia. Most significant of these reforms has been the trend towards mainstreaming or placement in 'less restrictive' environments. Unfortunately reports suggest that after approximately two decades of turmoil not only have the reforms failed to achieve their stated objectives but in some cases they have exacerbated the situation they were intended to remedy (Gartner and Lipsky 1987).

The reforms have failed because they failed to recognize and address the critical social function of special education and the personal tragedy theory of student disability in maintaining a relatively homogeneous and controllable population within general education. On a surface level there is an obviously incoherent logic in the removal of students from general education classrooms for certification as 'disabled' only to restore them to the classroom with the additional stigma of the 'defective' label. At a more fundamental level,

> the objectification of school failure as student disability through the institutional practice of special education . . . prevents the field of general education from confronting the failures of its practices and thus acts to reproduce and extend these practices in the profession [of teaching] and institution of education.
>
> (Skrtic 1991: 44)

In other words social justice as it relates to disability and special education is embedded within the social institution of schooling and as such reflects broader social structures.

Society, justice and disability

Fraser (1995) argues that struggles for social justice can be theorized along two conceptually distinct dimensions. First is an economic-political dimension which is central to Rawls's (1971) distributive theory of social justice. Social injustice is viewed as primarily a result of the inequitable distribution of economic, social and political resources. According to this view, social justice is primarily an issue of socio-economic allocation, therefore the remedy to social injustice is to restructure the distributive system or develop *redistributive* solutions.

The second dimension of social justice is cultural in nature. According to Fraser:

> The second kind of injustice is cultural or symbolic. It is rooted in social patterns of representation, interpretation and communication. Examples include cultural domination (being subjected to patterns of interpretation and communication that are associated with another culture and are alien and/or hostile to one's own); nonrecognition (being rendered invisible via the authoritative representational, communicative and interpretative practices of one's culture); and disrespect (being routinely maligned or disparaged in stereotypic public cultural representations and/or in everyday life interactions).
>
> (Fraser 1995: 71)

Fraser suggests that socio-economic redistribution does not resolve issues of cultural injustice. Rather, cultural oppression is appropriately addressed through recognition and valorization of the oppressed group. Cultural injustice results from the devaluing, derision and degrading of particular groups because of their cultural practices. The solution is to respect and value these practices, which Fraser refers to as *recognition* remedies.

Fraser argues that while the two dimensions of social justice are obviously intertwined in practice, the solutions to these two forms of social injustice are to some extent contradictory. Redistributive solutions tend to blur social distinctions. As resources are allocated more equitably, differentiation according to economic-political affiliation becomes muted. Redistributive solutions to social injustice aim to undermine group differentiation. For example, redistributive solutions to economic inequity faced by some socio-economic groups aim at the abolition of the class structure. 'The task of the proletariat is not simply to cut itself a better deal, but to abolish itself as a class' (Fraser 1995: 76). In contrast to redistributive solutions, recognition solutions to social injustice emphasize the distinctiveness of social groups, thus increasing social differentiation.

Fraser suggests that most socially oppressed groups are *bivalent* in that they are both socio-economically disadvantaged and culturally marginalized. Thus, they require both socio-economic redistributive solutions and cultural recognition and validation. However, simultaneous pursuit of these contradictory solutions often results in the perpetuation of the inequities they were designed to resolve. Disability is an example of bivalent social injustice. People with disabilities suffer both socio-economic and cultural oppression. Both redistributive and recognition dimensions can be identified in recent policy reforms in disability and special education.

Redistribution, recognition and special education reform

In his distributive theory of social justice Rawls (1971: 6) suggests that socially just practices require 'equal distribution of primary social goods . . . unless unequal distribution is to the advantage of the less favoured'. Initial demands for reform of special education, particularly calls to integrate students with disabilities into regular classrooms (Wolfensberger 1972) reflected a Rawlsian redistributive approach to social justice. Thus, the issue of access to regular schools and classrooms for students with disabilities was interpreted as one of fairness of distribution of educational resources. For example, early arguments for mainstreaming referred to the process of 'normalization' (Wolfensberger 1972). This concept emphasized the intrinsic sameness of individuals and therefore the requirement for consistency and similarity of treatment of individuals. In other words, all students regardless of disability should be treated as 'normal' students.

The Rawlsian fairness view of social justice clearly appears in some aspects of the initial US legislation, PL 94–142, and subsequently the Individuals with Disabilities Education Act (IDEA), which prohibited the exclusion of children with disabilities from the provision of free, public education. PL 94–142 mandated that all children, regardless of disability, have access to a state-provided and publicly funded education in the same way that non-disabled students have access to public education. Also in keeping with the Rawlsian view, PL 94–142 mandated that all children should be educated in the least restrictive environment (LRE). This required that all students have access to the same (i.e. regular classroom) educational environments unless the magnitude of their disability indicated that they would be better served in a separate special education setting.

Despite the dramatic reforms mandated in PL 94–142 recent critiques have argued that pressures for change have not been successful in dramatically altering educational practice (Gartner 1986; Reynolds *et al.* 1987; Lipsky and Gartner 1989). After approximately two decades of turmoil, critics (such as Gartner and Lipsky 1987) charge that not only have the reforms failed to achieve their stated objectives, in some cases they have exacerbated the situation that they were intended to remedy. For example, Gartner and Lipsky argue that following PL 94–142 the identification of students with disabilities and segregated placement of children increased rather than diminished.

The reforms failed in part because they did not recognize the critical social function of special education. PL 94–142 did not address the prevailing place of disability labels in maintaining the legitimacy of school practices which result in an inequitable distribution of school failure. Schools in the United States have been able to comply with federal regulations without either changing the practices which make more students disabled in a school context than in broader society or without recognizing their own role in the academic and social difficulties of many students. Thus attempts at distributive solutions to social injustice which fail to address the personal tragedy construction of disability have led to contradictory outcomes for students in schools.

Oliver (1986) argued that the personal tragedy theory of disability is the root cause of much of the social injustice experienced by people with disabilities. He argues that the personal tragedy theory of disability is one variant of social theories centred on victim-blaming (Ryan 1971). Like other victim-blaming theories it has tended to *individualize* problems of disability and ignore the social and economic structures which serve to disadvantage people with disabilities. In terms of recent educational reforms as articulated in PL 94–142, the process of individualizing the problem was embedded in the individualized education plan (IEP). The IEP process was intended to ensure that decisions related to the curriculum content presented to students and the setting in which their education was delivered should be derived from each student's specific needs as documented by the IEP. The IEP was embedded in a notion of individual need focused on individual deficit or pathology. Thus distribution of educational resources was tied to individual 'needs' contingent upon the identification of a disability.

As with provision of education in the LRE, the IEP frequently failed to function in the way that it was intended. Ysseldyke *et al.* (1982) reported that IEP team decisions often did little more than verify the problems identified by the teacher. In a national US study, Algozzine *et al.* (1982) reported that 92 per cent of students who were referred for assessment for special education were tested and that 73 per cent of these students were subsequently declared eligible for special education services. Ysseldyke *et al.* (1982) suggested that the most potent influence in IEP decision-making was 'teacher squeak'. This was an index of the degree to which the teacher wanted the removal of the student from the classroom. Thus Reynolds (1984) referred to the IEP team decision meeting as a 'capitulation conference'. In his review of the literature Smith (1990: 6) suggested that the IEP was intended as

> an essential component of instructional design and delivery that enhances and accounts for students' learning and teachers' teaching. Yet, data support the contention that IEPs are not functioning as designed, including being inept at structuring specially designed instruction.

Moreover, he contended that 'despite overwhelming evidence that IEPs have failed to accomplish their mission, little has been done to rectify the situation' (p. 6).

Thus it appears that during the implementation process of the reforms posed by PL 94–142, the purpose and nature of the IEP process was transformed. As Smith (1990) argued, the original intent and spirit of PL 94–142 has been met with passive compliance or acquiescence. Rather than constituting a reasoned and compelling response to students' specific educational needs, IEPs tended to function as compliance documents in the process of referring students to special education. As with LRE, the IEP mandate has been transformed through practice to support distribution of resources based on individual pathology, deficit or disability.

Cultural recognition of disability

Oliver (1986) argued that real and enduring reform requires a reconceptualization of the notion of disability from an individual personal tragedy to an aspect of social oppression. Early advocates for 'the disabled' were often parents, members of the medical profession or charity organizations concerned with procuring additional resources for the care and treatment of individuals. These groups perpetuated the dependency relationship which was imposed on many people with disabilities. This is reflected by a commentary on policy by Topliss (1979) on a British policy related to economic provision for people with disabilities which suggested that 'sympathy for the handicapped has been translated into effective legislation' (p. 9). Similar attitudes prevailed in terms of educational provision. Vincent and Troyna (1995) quoted the Chair of the Education Committee's comments regarding an LEA's special needs services: 'In [this policy document] it says people who are vulnerable and in need, we should take care of them . . . the most vulnerable are the special needs' (p. 160).

The emergence of advocacy groups formed by and composed of people with disabilities has provided a forceful challenge to personal tragedy theory. In Britain the Union of the Physically Impaired Against Segregation (UPIAS) has been one strident and effective critic of the unreflective acceptance of disability as personal tragedy. In terms of Fraser's (1995) analysis, the shift from a personal tragedy view of disability to a social oppression theory reflects a shift from a focus on distributive solutions to cultural recognition solutions. The UPIAS set out to address the social marginalization, the perpetuation of dependency relationships and the cultural neglect of people with disabilities. The pervasive nature of cultural oppression of people with disabilities is perhaps best portrayed by Fraser herself. In her otherwise insightful analysis of social injustice she noted that cultural racism has resulted in the depreciation of people of colour which has been expressed through a number of 'demeaning, stereotypical depictions in the media as criminal, bestial, primitive, *stupid*, and so on' (p. 81, my emphasis); demeaning indeed for people with intellectual disabilities.

In 1976 the UPIAS promoted a radical approach to the definition of disability which explicitly located the problem within the social structures which served to marginalize and disempower people with disabilities. The UPIAS definition distinguished between *impairment* (which related to the physical attributes of individuals) and *disability* (which referred to the social structures responsible for cultural oppression).

According to the definitions, 'Impairment' is defined as lacking part of or all of a limb, or having a defective limb, organ or mechanism of the body. 'Disability' is the disadvantage or restriction of activity caused by a contemporary social organization which takes little or no account of people who have physical impairments and thus excludes them from participation in the mainstream of social activities.

While these definitions represented a radical departure from the dominant medical approach to disability, they have received support from a number of sources. For example, in 1981 the British Council of Organizations of Disabled People was formed and adopted the UPIAS definitions.

The acceptability of this redefined notion of disability in relation to nomenclature is reflected in the changed terminology in the US legislation. In 1975 the original legislation was identified as 'The Education for All *Handicapped* Children Act'. In 1990 the bill was reauthorized as 'The Individuals with *Disabilities* Act'. Nevertheless there has not been unanimous support for the revised definitions posed by UPIAS. In 1993 the UN General Assembly accepted new definitions of disability and handicap.

The term 'disability' summarizes a great number of different functional limitations occurring in any population in any country of the world. People may be disabled by physical, intellectual or sensory impairment, medical conditions or mental illness. Such impairments, conditions or illnesses may be permanent or transitory in nature.

The term 'handicap' means the loss or limitation of opportunities to take part in the life of the community on an equal level with others. It describes the encounter between the person with a disability and the environment. The purpose of this term is to emphasize the focus on the short-comings in the environment and in many organized activities in society, for example, information, communication and education, which prevent persons with disabilities from participating on equal terms.

There are a number of examples of dispute around nomenclature in recent special education reform arising from the effort to combat the stigma of pathology, deficit or disorder. For example, Warnock (1978) coined the term 'students with special needs' in an effort to engender similar reforms in England and Wales to those mandated by PL 94–142 in the US. Warnock identified the concept of student disability as a legitimating factor in the inequitable treatment of students in special education. She attempted to transform the systemic conceptualization of special education and disabled students by transferring the locus of the problem from a disability within the child to inflexibility in the system of schooling. By suggesting that some students have 'special needs' she was attempting to encourage the notion that the educational system needed to change and become more responsive to particular student characteristics. Thus, the term 'student with special educational needs' was intended to locate the cause of the problem within the nature of schooling rather than within the nature of the student. This was a clear attempt to address the social and political aspects of the education of students with disabilities and challenged the role of individual deficit in legitimating the failure of diverse students.

However, rather than transforming the system of schooling, the concept of students with special needs was itself transformed by the system (Tomlinson 1982). Thus rather than identifying a child as *disabled* and therefore being inadequate for 'normal' schooling, teachers and administrators identified the child as 'special needs' and therefore inadequate. Dee and Corbett (1994) noted the repetition of this process in more recent attempts to change British nomenclature from 'special education need' to 'learning support'. They suggest that one category simply superseded the other. Rather than identifying specific learning support structures which the school needed to supply to students to ensure equity in educational experiences, schools continued to identify students with disabilities with labels such as 'The students are learning support' (p. 322). Similarly, Fulcher (1983) has documented a process where attempted reform based on educational responsiveness to students' education needs was reconstructed by teachers as resource allocation based on 'needy' students. To some extent these failures of nomenclature can be seen as failures of what Fraser (1995) terms the recognition remedy to social injustice. Rather than recognizing students as valued members of the school community, they were continually redefined as in some way disordered or deficient.

In addition to the distinction between economic-distributive and cultural-recognition approaches to social justice, Fraser distinguishes between *affirmation* and *transformation* strategies to achieve social justice. Affirmative and transformative strategies intersect with redistributive and recognition strategies. Fraser argues that affirmation strategies are aimed at addressing injustices without disturbing the fundamental social structures which generate injustices. Transformative strategies, on the other hand, seek to modify underlying social structures.

Fraser argues that transformative strategies can help the redistributive-recognition dilemma where actions to promote social justice result in contradictory outcomes. Thus for groups which experience bivalent injustice (i.e. both political-economic and cultural discrimination), transformative strategies can help simultaneously promote redistributive and recognition solutions. Students with disabilities clearly represent a bivalent social group. These students frequently fail to benefit from the level of educational resources available to most students. In order successfully to engage in schooling they require additional 'special' educational resources. Yet the provision of these resources has traditionally been tied to a process of social marginalization (segregation from peers) and personal devaluation (labelling as deficit, disordered or disabled).

While the US reform legislation sought to deliver more socially just practices to students, it did so by merely affirming disabled students' rights to educational services. Thus it failed to attack the fundamental perception of the locus of the problem and subsequently modify the outcomes that many students traditionally experience. For example, Nelson and Stevens (1981) argued that one of the major obstacles in developing teacher consultation models to deliver special education services in regular classrooms is the legislation itself. They see two aspects of the legislation as particularly counterproductive. First, provision of funding is based on the identification and labelling of a specific proportion of students. Second, provision of special education services was restricted to those children who were legally defined as 'handicapped'. Thus they suggested that

the law itself provides a highly stigmatizing label which must be affixed to children before they can be served. This label is hardly conducive to mainstreaming, in that regular classroom teachers resist working with 'mental health' problems. The refer-and-remove policy is consequently perpetuated.

(Nelson and Stevens 1981: 90)

Fraser argues that transformative strategies allow for the deconstruction of existing social categories in a way that transforms the identities of all participants. She notes that 'all axes of injustice intersect one another in ways that affect everyone's interests and identities'. For example, in examining gender equity Fraser argues that deconstruction challenges the hierarchical dichotomies (male vs. female, disabled vs. able) and allows them to be replaced by 'networks of multiple intersecting differences that are demassified and shifting' (Fraser 1995: 90).

Fraser argues – and the analysis of recent special education reforms suggests – that transformation of the social location and identity of one group (the dis-abled) will not occur if the social identity of the other group (the abled) remains intact. Fraser's notion of network of intersecting differences is a useful one. Most existing literature, including the literature which acknowledges and critiques the social construction of disability, has left intact the disabled–abled dichotomy. Yet the community of people with disabilities is not a large, homogeneous entity. People with disabilities reflect a diversity of human conditions, even in relation to the characteristics which have contributed to their identification as disabled. For example, many advocates within the deaf community reject the notion of inclusion in schools and wish to fight for recognition and affirmation as a distinct social and cultural group. Within the blind community there are tensions between people who are congenitally blind and those who are adventitiously blind. There are clear distinctions in the concerns and needs of those who are physically disabled and those who are intellectually disabled. Moreover, disability is only one facet of human functioning. Disability intersects with a vast array of other cultural, linguistic and social characteristics such as gender, race and socio-economic background. Deconstruction of the notion of disability allows for flexible and generative analysis and policy formulation which can be responsive to these multiple, intersecting and constantly shifting interests.

In relation to education and disability, transformative strategies require a fundamental reformulation of the dualisms of special and regular education, of able and dis-able – in other words, transformation of the institution of schooling. The dualism of special and regular education has resulted from a form of traditional schooling which cannot accommodate diversity and so must screen it out. However, just as widespread segregation failed to deliver socially-just educational programs to many students with disabilities, the simple wholesale return of those students to regular classrooms without a basic transformation of those classrooms will similarly fail to provide social justice to all students.

If this dualism is to be transcended it seems inevitable that the nomenclature of disability itself will come under question. Whether it is used to designate an individual as in some way disordered, or is used to signify that social structures must be more responsive to individual needs, disability perpetuates the dualism. Real and enduring reforms need to be accompanied by fundamental restructuring of the culture and practice of schooling. This requires the development of a schooling which engenders an inclusive rather than exclusive form of educational practice. In such a practice students are not seen as disabled, defective or disordered. Rather, all students are seen as different, complex and whole. All students are recognized as reflecting a diversity of cultural, social, racial, physical and intellectual identities.

References

Algozzine, B., Christenson, S. and Ysseldyke, J. E. (1982) Probabilities associated with the referral to placement process, *Teacher Education and Special Education*, 5: 19–23.

Algozzine, B. and Ysseldyke, S. (1983) Learning disabilities as a subset of school failure: the oversophistication of a concept, *Exceptional Children*, 52: 242–6.

Carrier, J. G. (1983) Masking the social in educational knowledge: the case of learning disability theory, *American Journal of Sociology*, 39: 949–73.

Christensen, C. A., Gerber, M. M. and Everhart, R. B. (1986) Toward a sociological perspective on learning disabilities, *Educational Theory*, 36: 317–31.

Coles, G. S. (1978) The learning disabilities test battery: empirical and social issues, *Harvard Educational Review*, 48: 313–40.

Dee, L. and Corbett, J. (1994) Individual rights in further education: Lost, stolen or stayed?, *British Educational Research Journal*, 20: 319–25.

Fraser, N. (1995) From redistribution to recognition? Dilemmas of justice in a 'post-socialist' age, *New Left Review*, 212: 68–93.

Fulcher, G. (1983) *Disabling Policies? A Comparative Approach to Education Policy and Disability*. London: The Falmer Press.

Gartner, A. (1986) Disabling help: Special education at the crossroads, *Exceptional Children*, 53: 72–9.

Gartner, A. and Lipsky, K. (1987) Beyond special education: toward a quality system for all students, *Harvard Educational Review*, 57: 367–95.

Hallahan, D. P. and Kauffman, J. M. (1977) Labels, categories, behaviours: Ed., LD and EMR reconsidered, *Journal of Special Education*, 11: 139–49.

Lipsky, D. K. and Gartner, A. (1989) *Beyond Separate Education: Quality Education for All.* Baltimore: Paul H. Brookes.

Mercer, J. (1973) *Labelling the Mentally Retarded: Clinical and Social System Perspectives on Mental Retardation.* Berkeley, CA: University of California Press.

Nelson, C. M. and Stevens, K. B. (1981) An accountable consultation model for mainstreaming behaviorally disordered children, *Behavioral Disorders*, 6: 82–91.

Oliver, M. (1986) Social policy and disability: some theoretical issues, *Disability, Handicap and Society*, 1: 5–17.

Rawls, J. (1971) *A Theory of Social Justice.* Cambridge, MA: Belknap Press of the Harvard University Press.

Reynolds, M. C. (1984) Classification of students with handicaps, in E. W. Gordon (ed.) *Review of Research in Education* (Vol. 11 pp. 63–92). Washington, DC: American Educational Research Association.

Reynolds, M. C., Wang, M. C. and Walberg, H. J. (1987) The necessary restructuring of special and general education, *Exceptional Children*, 53: 391–8.

Ryan, W. (1971) *Blaming the Victim*. New York: Orbach and Chambers.

Sarason, S. and Doris, J. (1979) *Educational Handicap, Public Policy, and Social History*. New York: Free Press.

Skrtic, T. M. (1991) *Behind Special Education*. Denver, CO: Love.

Smith, S. W. (1990) Individualized education programs (IEPs) in special education – from intent to acquiescence, *Exceptional Children*, 57: 6–14.

Tomlinson, S. (1982) *A Sociology of Special Education*. London: Routledge and Kegan Paul.

Topliss, E. (1979) *Provision for the Disabled*. Oxford: Blackwell and Robertson.

Union of the Physically Impaired Against Segregation (1976) *Fundamental Principles of Disability*. London: Union of the Physically Impaired Against Segregation.

Vincent, C. and Troyna B. (1995) The discourses of social justice in education, *Discourse: Studies in the Cultural Politics of Education*, 16: 149–66.

Walker, L. J. (1987) Procedural rights in the wrong system. Special education is not enough, in A. Gartner and T. Joe (eds) *Images of the Disabled/Disabling Images*. New York: Praeger, pp. 98–102.

Wang, M. C., Reynolds, M. C. and Walberg, H. (1986) Rethinking special education, *Educational Leadership*, 44: 27.

Warnock, M. (1978) *Special Educational Needs*. London: Department of Education and Science.

White, R. and Calhoun, M. (1987) From referral to placement: teachers' perceptions of their responsibilities, *Exceptional Children*, 53: 467.

Wolfensberger, W. (1972) *The Principles of Normalization in Human Services*. Toronto: National Institute on Mental Retardation.

Ysseldyke, J. E., Algozzine, B., Richey, L. and Graden, J. (1982) Declaring students eligibility for learning disability services: Why bother with the data?, *Learning Disability Quarterly*, 5: 37–44.

2

SETTING THE RECORD STRAIGHT

A critique of some frequent misconceptions of the normalization principle

Burt Perrin and Bengt Nirje

Source: *Australia and New Zealand Journal of Developmental Disabilities* 11(2) (1985): 69–74.

While normalization ideas evolved in Scandinavia during the 1960's, the normalization principle as concept was developed and articulated by Bengt Nirje and given its first statement in print by him in 1969 (Nirje, 1969). Since then, normalization very quickly has become one of the most influential and widely quoted concepts internationally in mental retardation and in other human services areas, and has played a major role in the movement, however slow, towards community living. The principle has major implications regarding the ways we view and act towards handicapped people and for the programs we develop for them.

Yet the normalization principle has been widely misunderstood, both by many of its advocates as well as by its critics. In some cases it has been misinterpreted so perversely as to produce implications and programs directly opoposite to what is intended by the principle! The purpose of this paper is to briefly identify and discuss a few of the more common misconceptions. As well, the later statement of normalization by Wolfensberger deviates dramatically from the principle as originally conceived and presented by Nirje. Some of the more significant of these differences, particularly those reflecting different values and views of people, will be discussed.

What is the normalization principle? As defined by Nirje (1976 p. 231):

The normalization principle means making available to all mentally retarded people patterns of life and conditions of everyday living which are as close as possible to the regular circumstances and ways of life of society.

Bank-Mikkelsen (1976, pp. 27–28) describes normalization as meaning the acceptance of the mentally retarded with their handicap, offering them the same conditions as are offered to other citizens, inclusive of treatment, education, and training needed to provide for optimal development. Implicit in the principle of normalization is the concept that mentally handicapped people are entitled to the same rights and opportunities as are available to others in their society, including opportunities to exercise personal preferences and freedom of choice.

Some common misconceptions

Eight of the most common misconceptions of the normalization principle are briefly discussed below.

Misconception 1: "Normalization means making people normal"

Probably the most common misinterpretation of the normalization principle is the mistaken belief that it means mentally handicapped people must be expected to, indeed be forced, to act "normal", to conform in all respects to society's statistical norms for all dimensions of behaviour. Normalization frequently has been confused with normalacy.

No, no, no! Normalization does **not** mean normalcy; it does **not** mean that people should be normalized; it does **not** mean that anyone's behaviour should be forced to conform to any particular standard (e.g. what 51 percent of one's neighbours do or what "experts" feel is best); it does **not** mean that mentally handicapped persons are expected to be made normal or to act like other people. It **does** mean that opportunities and support should be provided to permit a lifestyle similar in nature to that of other members of society, including similar opportunities for individual variation and choice. Normalization means the acceptance of persons **with** their handicap within "normal" society, with the same rights, responsibilities, and opportunities as are available to others.

Misconception 2: "Special services are inconsistent with the normalization principle"

The normalization principle, on the contrary, supports, indeed insists upon the provision of whatever services, training, and support are required to permit living conditions and routines similar to that of others in the community. At a minimum, this would include appropriate housing, opportunities for some form of work (or education for children), and leisure. This will vary from person to person depending upon need and personal preferences.

Most "normal" people as part of "normal" life use specialized services when appropriate. For example, a person with heart trouble may consult a cardiologist; in extreme cases a pacemaker, a decidedly "unnormal" foreign object, may be surgically implanted in the body. The purpose of this abnormal treatment is to permit the continuation of everyday living patterns (i.e. "normal" living).

The normalization principle indicates that mentally handicapped people similarly should have access to those forms of special or added assistance they require in order to take part in normal living in the same way that "special" services are provided to other members of society. Where possible, generic services (e.g. regular dentists) should be used. A word of caution: just as with some medical conditions where the treatment or cure may be worse than the disease, some special services, despite their benefits, may actually **detract** from, rather than enhance normal living (e.g. institutions).

It also has been falsely claimed that special administrative organizations to co-ordinate or facilitate needed services for mentally handicapped people are inconsistent with normalization. Normalization, rather, deals with conditions of life; administrative organization is secondary. Those organizational forms and administrative structures that support the furthering of all facets of integration of handicapped people are consequently more appropriate than other, more restrictive, forms and structures (Nirje, 1980).

Misconception 3: "Normalization supports dumping people into the community without support"

The normalization principle has been interpreted falsely to mean that mentally handicapped people should be placed in the community without any support or assistance, however essential it may be. On the contrary, physical placement in the community does not necessarily represent integration or normalization: the pertinent question is how closely the lives of mentally handicapped persons approach those of other members of the community. Where it does not, in the case for example of someone isolated in a rat-infested boarding house, this represents false integration, **not** community living or normalization.

As Nirje (1980, pp. 47–49) has discussed, normalization involves six different forms of integration (e.g. social integration). Physical placement in itself is insufficient and does **not** represent normalization.

Misconception 4: "Normalization is an all or nothing concept"

A common misconception is that normalization refers only to totally independent living. However, there are degrees of normalization, and the principle implies provision of a **range** of support and structure, depending upon the individual's need and abilities (e.g. a continuum of housing – including highly structured settings and various forms of co-operative living; work alternatives – including work stations, other low-support arrangements, as well as sheltered employment; etc.). Normalization can be applied as well to improve conditions and programs within an institutional setting.

Misconception 5: "Normalization is appropriate only for the mildly retarded"

On the contrary, the normalization principle applies to all, and indeed its implications may be most far-reaching for people with more severe handicaps. As Nirje (1976) has indicated, some of the ideas which led to the development of the principle grew out of analyses of facilities and programs for severely handicapped people, in the attempt to make their living situation and patterns of life more similar to that of others.

Misconception 6: "Mentally handicapped people are best off with their own kind, protected from the rigours of society"

This myth, however well-meaning, has led to the creation of large asylums and institutions where in the name of "protecting" people, they too often have been (and still are) subjected to inhumane treatment and living conditions. But even more significantly, this view is contrary to factual evidence. Dybad (1982a), for example, has pointed out that the abilities of mentally handicapped people have been grossly underestimated. Given appropriate training and opportunity, they can function at levels never considered possible (e.g. see Gold, 1972). Thousands of "hopeless" cases, once freed from restrictive institutions, not only have demonstrated their ability to function more than adequately as people, but have expressed a clear preference for this lifestyle.

Misconception 7: "Normalization is a Scandinavian concept inapplicable elsewhere"

Normalization does not mean the application of Scandinavian services elsewhere, and in fact is neutral regarding cultural values. The specific implication of normalization will be different for every culture, as what constitutes normal living patterns and opportunities varies from society to society. Ironically, the principle may be easier to implement in many developing countries which do not have an entrenched infrastructure of facilities and programs, along with a history of segregating handicapped people from the community.

Misconception 8: "Normalization is a humanistic concept, but idealized and impractical"

On the contrary, one of the major benefits of the principle is that it is practical, providing guidance for how we view and treat handicapped people, along with many specific action implications. These implications are, and have been, subject to scientific test and scrutiny (e.g. Kebbon, Hjarpe & Sonnander 1982); very impressive results in many different contexts have been attained when the principle has been applied.

The Wolfensberger deviation from the original concept of normalization

Up until now, we have spoken of normalization as originally defined by Nirje, with its emphasis on normal living oportunities, patterns, and circumstances of life. However, in recent years Wolfensberger's (1972) definition also has received considerable attention, and as he (Wolfensberger, 1980b) notes, most discussions of the pros and cons of normalization have failed to distinguish between the differing versions of the principles.

We wish to clearly indicate that Wolfensberger's version of "normalization" deviates in many significant ways from the original concept of the principle, and thus contrary to Wolfensberger's (1972, p. 28) claim, cannot be considered as a reformulation, refinement, or operationalization of the principle. Rather his version, with its focus on using normative means and on establishing normative behaviour, is built upon a fundamentally different value base and conception of people, with quite different implications for how we view and treat handicapped people.

The original concept of normalization as articulated by Nirje and discussed earlier in this paper is really quite simple: mentally handicapped (and other handicapped) people should be given the opportunity to live a life as similar in nature as possible to that of others, with similar rights and responsibilities. Just as (within certain limits which vary from society to society) a "normal" individual may engage in unpopular, nonconformist or even "deviant" behaviours, the normalization principle implies that the same right also should apply to mentally handicapped people. Normalization as originally defined is based upon a humanistic, egalitarian value base, emphasizing freedom of choice and the right to self determination. It emphasizes clearly respect for the individual and his or her right to be differenct. As Dybwad (1982) has indicated in his own critique of Wolfensberger, it is normal to be different.

Wolfensberger (1972, 1980a), on the contrary, interprets normalization as specifying various standards of behaviour to which a mentally handicapped person must conform. He speaks openly of "normalizing" people through "eliciting, shaping, and maintaining normative skills and habits" (Wolfensberger, 1972, p. 32; 1980a) p. 17) or even through the use of force: "Normalizing measures can be **offered** in some circumstances, and **imposed** in others." (Wolfensberger, 1982, p. 28, italics in original).

Note that the above statements make no provision for a person's **own** preferences regarding his or her lifestyle. Wolfensberger is not **opposed** to the concept to self-determination, and indeed he does include this as one of the ratings in PASS (Program Analysis of Services Systems, a rating system developed by Wolfensberger's interpretations of normalization). However, he (Wolfensberger, 1980b) indicates that this right to choose may be in conflict with what is defined as appropriate, normalized behaviour and he clearly indicated that the latter should take priority. For example, Wolfensberger and Glenn (1975, vol. 1, p. 31) openly indicate that PASS is concerned with program structures rather than with individual feelings or reactions, labelling the latter as irrelevant.

The values and implications of the above are alien to those of the normalization principle as originally delineated. Wolfensberger requires a mentally handicapped person to act in conformity to values chosen by **others**. To us, this authoritarian approach, however benevolent in its intentions, represents an unwarranted abuse of the powers of the therapeutic state, well documented elsewhere (e.g. Kittrie, 1971). Normalization as originally conceived indicates that individuals should be encouraged and assisted in expressing their **own** preferences and making their **own** choices; normalization implies that opportunities and training should be provided to assist in this process.

Are mentally handicapped people capable of making any choices regarding their lives? As previously discussed under Misconception 6, the capacities of mentally handicapped people to do just this have been well documented elsewhere (e.g. Nirje, 1972; Dybad, 1982a). While in some cases assistance with certain decisions may be required, this is no different in kind from the situation faced by "normal" people when faced with unfamiliar areas (e.g. medicine, the law, economics, plumbing). Normal respect and understanding for the silent wishes as well as expressed self-determination of mentally handicapped people should be provided.

Wolfensberger has recently (1980b) clarified that his specification of "normative" behaviour does not necessarily refer to the statistical mean. However, his conservatism corollary is even more limiting: "With a choice from among a continuum of options around the cultural value mean, the more positive (or conservative) option" should be chosen (Wolfensberger, 1980a, p. 16). This once again fails to consider the preferences of individuals by prescribing standards of behaviours which they must follow. We also note with no further comment the value base which automatically asserts that the more conservative options are by definition more positive!

A key element of normalization as originally proposed is the provision of opportunities for mentally handicapped people so that they can live a life similar to that of others. Wolfensberger's conservatism corollary blatantly contradicts this by **setting** different standards than for "normal" people. For example, he indicates that: a mentally handicapped person should not work with animals although he says it is perfectly acceptable for others; handicapped people should not wear their hair long, even though others in the community may do so; a middle-aged man should wear a necktie even though appearing in public with an open collar may also be normative in his community. If any handicapped persons associated with a program under assessment by PASS refused to conform to the above (and to other similar examples), the program would be downgraded in its assessment, irrespective of the personal preference of values of the clients.

At a PASS workshop held in Toronto in 1974, numerous examples along the above lines were presented. A black woman in attendance finally said: "You aren't talking about normalization; you are talking about making people into upper-middle class whites!" Wolfensberger imposes solution whereas Nirje and the normalization principle indicate proper ways to put questions concerning a situation and the development of solutions, allowing for individual preferences.

Wolfensberger's model of normalization in our view is excessively concerned with the notion of mentally handicapped people "passing" in society. As defined by Goffman (1963), passing refers to the ability of members of deviant groups to minimize their differences or signs of deviancy so that they can "pass" undetected into society. For Wolfensberger, this means that mentally handicapped people must not do anything which will lead to them standing out or attracting attention to themselves and risk being labelled as deviant. Hence the conservatism corollary discussed above.

This applies to Wolfensberger no matter how appropriate the difference may be. To cite two examples, he argues that a mentally handicapped person should not wear a visable hearing aid, even if the hearing otherwise cannot be corrected (Wolfensberger & Glenn, 1975, Vol. 11, p. 31); a washroom in a residence would be downgraded in a PASS assessment if it has special gripbars, even though such modifications may be necessary for the convenience of disabled residents (PASS Workshop referred to above). We note that while likely unintentional, the acronym PASS is the same term used by Goffman (1963) to describe the process whereby minority and deviant groups attempt to hide or deny their differences.

This concern with passing and obsession with minimizing deviancy leads to an emphasis by Wolfensberger on the **appearance** rather than the **reality** of normalization. In this respect, with its priority on appearance rather than on self-determination, it is contrary to the original version of normalization, which as Bank-Mikkelsen (1976, p. 27) indicates, means the "acceptance of the mentally retarded **with** their handicap." It is contrary to the direction taken by most minority groups, at least in the Western world, which now are insisting upon their right to equality of opportunity without having to deny or hide their uniqueness. It is also contrary to the recent direction taken by self-help movements of handicapped people, including the mentally handicapped such as People First, who now are demanding the services they need to enable them to participate on the same basis as do others in society.

In a recent comment on the normalization principle and its demand for normal respect for the individual, Nirje (1980) has defined integration as based on recognition of a person's integrity, meaning to be yourself – to be able and allowed to be yourself – among others.

Wolfensberger also takes a narrow reductionistic approach to normalization, focusing on specific behaviours which can be manipulated by others and easily measured. The original definition of normalization involves the availability of and the freedom to choose among the normal range of options, life circumstances, patterns of life, and opportunities, with the ability to participate on the same basis as do others in society. PASS and other such standardized devices are not suitable for measuring normalization expressed in these terms. While the **appearance** of normalization may be subject to measurement by PASS, this is far less significant than the **reality** of normalization as defined above, including consideration of individual preferences and experience. This also is subject to scientific scrutiny (e.g. Kebbon *et al.*, 1982).

Wolfensberger's narrow focus on observable behaviours has led him (and others) to create a meaningless distinction between means and ends. For example, he (Wolfensberger, 1980b) has labelled Nirje's definition of normalization as means rather than ends oriented (presumably because it speaks of **making available** patterns and conditions of life rather than of **imposing** specific behaviours upon people). Yet he also has labelled Bank-Mikkelsen's statement of normalization, which is essentially the same as Nirje's, as concerned only with outcome and not with means! This may be because Bank-Mikkelsen (as does Nirje) points out that normalization is silent with respect to appropriate treatment modalities. As discussed earlier under Misconception 2, pedagogical methods such as precision teaching, early infant stimulation, and techniques such as behaviour modification, are no more or less inconsistent with normalization than pedagogical methods in general. The criteria is the same: do they work? (provided of course that they are ethical).

Conclusion

The normalization principle has been described by Dybwad (1969) as "elegant in its simplicity and parsimony. It can be readily understood by everyone". While we agree with the first part of Dybwad's statement, it is apparent that in the intervening years, normalization has been subject to numerous misinterpretations which this paper has attempted to address.

The normalization principle has been misunderstood and misinterpreted for too long. It does not necessarily imply conformity, but rather the freedom to live a life based on the same values and on the same terms as others in society. Proper understanding of normalization and its meaning can go a long way towards improving services, life conditions, and the dignity of handicapped people.

References

Bank-Mikkelsen, N. E. (1976). The Principle of normalization. In B. Nielsen (Ed.), *Flash 2 on the Danish National Service for the mentally retarded.* Copenhagen, Personal Training School, Copenhagen. (a)

Bank-Mikkelsen, N. E. (1976). Misconceptions of the principle of normalization. Address to the IASSMD Conference, Washington, D.C. (b)

Dybwad, G. (1969). Action implications, U.S.A. today. In R. Kugel & W. Wolfensberger (Eds). *Changing patterns in residential services for the mentally retarded.* Washington, D.C. President's Committee on Mental Retardation.

Dybwad, G. (1982). The re-discovery of the family. *Mental Retardation,* 32, 18–30. (a)

Dybwad, G. (1982). Normalization and its impact on social and public policy. In *Advancing your citizenship. Normalization re-examined.* Eugene, Oregon. Rehabilitation Research Training Institute. (b)

Goffman, E. (1963). *Stigma: Notes on the management of spoiled identity.* Englewood Cliffs, N.J.: Prentice Hall.

Gold, M. (1972). Stimulus factors in skill training of retarded adolescents on a complex assembly task: Acquisition, transfer and retention. *American Journal of Mental Deficiency,* 76; 517–526.

Kebbon, L., Hjarpe, J., & Sonnander, K. (1982). Report of research findings on the evaluation of the normalization principle. Paper presented to the IASSMD Congress, Toronto.

Kittrie, N. N. (1971). *The Right to be different: Deviance and forced therapy.* Baltimore: Johns Hopkins Press.

Maloney, M. P. and Ward, M. P. (1979). *Mental retardation and society.* New York: Oxford University Press.

Nirje, B. (1969). The normalization principle and its human management implications. In R. Kugel & W. Wolfensberger (Eds), *Changing patterns in residential services for the mentally retarded.* Washington, D.C. President's Committee on Mental Retardation.

Nirje, B. (1972). The right to self-determination. In W. Wolfensberger (Ed.), *The principle of normalization in human services.* Toronto: National Institute on Mental Retardation.

Nirje, B. (1976). The normalization principle. In R. Kugel and A. Shearer (Eds), *Changing patterns in residential services for the mentally retarded.* Rev. Ed., Washington, D.C. President's Committee on Mental Retardation.

Wolfensberger, W. (1972). *The Principle of normalization in human services.* Toronto: National Institute on Mental Retardation.

Wolfensberger, W. (1980a). A brief overview of the principle of normalization. In R. J. Flynn and K. E. Nitsch (Eds). *Normalization, social integration, and human services.* Baltimore: University Park Press. (a)

Wolfensberger, W. (1980b). The definition of normalization: update, problems, disagreements, and misunderstandings. In R. J. Flynn & K. E. Nitsch (Eds). *Normalization, social integration, and human services.* Baltimore: University Park Press. (b)

Wolfensberger, W. and Glenn, L. (1975). *Program analysis of service systems (PASS 3): A method for the quantitative evaluation of human services.* 2nd Ed. Vol. I: Handbook. Vol. II: Field Manual. Toronto: National Institute on Mental Retardation.

3

SOCIAL ROLE VALORIZATION

A proposed new term for the principle of normalization

Wolf Wolfensberger

Source: *Mental Retardation* 21(6) (1983): 234–9.

Abstract

The highest goal of the principle of normalization has recently been clarified to be the establishment, enhancement, or defense of the social role(s) of a person or group, via the enhancement of people's social images and personal competencies. In consequence, it is proposed that normalization be henceforth called "social role valorization."

The earliest known uses of the terms "normalization," "normalization principle," or "principle of normalization" were reviewed by me several years ago (Wolfensberger, 1980a). For all practical purposes, we can say that the term was first given prominence by Nirje (1969). Early examples of attempts to implement the concept, though with little emphasis on the term itself, were provided by Bank-Mikkelsen (1969) and Grunewald (1969). I retained the term in my series of elaboration and systematizations of the concept (e.g., Wolfensberger, 1972, 1980a, b; Wolfensberger & Glenn, 1973a, b; 1975a, b; Wolfensberger & Tullman, 1982; Wolfensberger & Thomas, 1983). However, the choice of the term "normalization" itself has clearly been unfortunate, one major reason being that relatively few people have found it possible to separate the different meanings attached to it by various users of the term (Wolfensberger, 1980a, b). Also, in part because of its name, people have failed to take the principle of normalization seriously as a tightly-built, intellectually demanding, and empirically well-anchored megatheory of human service and, to some degree, relationships. Any review of the literature (Wolfensberger, 1980a) will disclose that once people hear or see the term "normalization," a large proportion (apparently even the vast majority) assume—usually wrongly—that they know "what it means." Even otherwise scholarly persons have published inane critiques of the principle without citing, or apparently having studied or even become aware of, the major expositions thereof in the professional literature. It is because of the danger of these preconceived associations to the term "normalization" that I suggested (Wolfensberger, 1980a) with grim humor that a totally unfamiliar foreign or novel word, such as "orthofactorization," might have been preferable.

Ever since 1969, I have attempted to convert the early formalizations of normalization by Bank-Mikkelsen (1969) and Nirje (1969) into a scientific theory that is universal, parsimonious, and congruent with social and behavioral science. I have never been satisfied with the term "normalization," but have resisted a change in name for two reasons: (a) I was unable to think of a superior choice; alternatives suggested by others seemed to be no improvement, and usually even inferior (Wolfensberger, 1980a); and (b) by the early 1970s, the term "normalization" had acquired so much momentum that only a dramatically superior term seemed to warrant the attempt to change it. This opportunity has now arrived, with the advent of two developments.

One development is the recent insight (Wolfensberger & Tullman, 1982; Wolfensberger & Thomas, 1983) that the most explicit and highest goal of normalization must be the creation, support, and defense of *valued social roles* for people who are at risk of social devaluation. All other elements and objectives of the theory are really subservient to this end, because if a person's social role were a societally valued one, then other desirable things would be accorded to that person almost automatically, at least within the resources and norms of his/her society. Indeed, attributes of the person which might otherwise be viewed negatively by society would come to be viewed positively. For instance, a person who has hallucinations that would render the person devalued in some cultures might be held in awe and respect in another culture (as among certain American Indian tribes, or in the Arab world) where such phenomena may be considered manifestations of the divine or of divine favor. Or, in the Far East until recently, a very wealthy person might have his/her hands rendered useless, so that what would be considered a serious functional impairment in the Western world would there be a sign of the person's high status—indeed, so high that everyone would be made aware that the person had all necessary functions performed for him/herself by servants and others. In fact, being seen as filling a valued social role may be the one thing which prevents a person from becoming devalued because of a characteristic which would automatically cast other people who do not have socially valued roles into a devalued status. Even further, a characteristic which of itself is devalued might become valued if it were displayed by a person in a valued social role.

In contrast, people are considered to be of low value when they are not seen as having valued social roles. In consequence, I perceive devalued identity rather than mere differentness as synonymous with deviancy. We know that among other things, being seen as devalued/deviant brings with it three important consequences:

1   Devalued persons will be badly treated. Devalued people are apt to be rejected, even persecuted, and treated in ways which tend to diminish their dignity, adjustments, growth, competence, health, wealth, lifespan, etc.
2   The (bad) treatment accorded to devalued persons will take on forms that largely express the devalued societal role in which they are perceived. For instance, if handicapped children are (unconsciously) viewed as animals, then they may be segregated into settings that look like cages and animal pens, may be located close to zoos or animal laboratories, and their service may be given an animal name, often even the name of an animal that is seen as expressive of the devalued people's identity. Thus, a class for mentally retarded children may be named "The Turtles." Similarly, people perceived to be social menaces (perhaps for no realistic reason) may be served in settings that look forbidding and fortress-like, have (or appear to have) walls, locks, fences, and barred windows, and that are far removed from the rest of society.
3   How a person is perceived and treated by others will in turn strongly determine how that person subsequently behaves. Therefore, the more consistently a person is perceived and treated as being deviant, the more likely it is that s/he will conform to that expectation and will behave in ways that are socially expected of him/her—or at least that are not valued by society. On the other hand, the more social value that is accorded to a person, the more s/he will usually be encouraged to assume roles and behaviors which are appropriate and desirable, the more will be expected of him/her, and the more s/he is apt to achieve.

In my writings on normalization, I have always stressed that the cultural relativity of who gets devalued points to a two-pronged action strategy: (a) to reduce or prevent the differentness or stigmata (i.e., the overt signs) which may make a person devalued in the eyes of observers; and (b) to change societal perceptions and values in regard to a devalued person or group so that a given characteristic or person is no longer seen as devalued. If a human condition (including what might be considered an affliction) were valued in society, then it would be less likely that people would do bad things to the "incumbent" of such a condition. Instead, the incumbent would be respected and have power; other people would tend to censure anyone who attempted to harm the person; the incumbent would be sought out by others as a valuable associate or friend, or at least as a person one would wish to be perceived as associated with. Indeed, many members of society would try to become more like those people who are highly valued. If the most highly valued people in society were those who had no arms and legs, other people would not only strive to meet their every need, but might even pay dearly to have their own arms and legs removed so as to attain the same identity. If a stuttering person were king, many courtiers would be apt to develop at least a slight stutter, much as for over 300 years, first men and then women across the whole world have worn quite inconvenient and unhealthy high-heeled shoes in imitation of Louis XIV—who introduced them because he was short. Other historical facts which support the above point include the centuries-long custom of women of the upper classes in the Far East having their feet bound so that they become crippled; and in Europe, for hundreds of years, especially during the Renaissance, tens of thousands of males gladly submitted to castration in order to attain the socially valued status of castrato singers. If one were to try to restore the bodies of such voluntarily mutilated people, fit them with prostheses, or teach them various self-help and other functional skills, one might actually come to be seen, condemned, and avoided as being "deviancy-making."

A new conceptualization of normalization goals and strategies

In order to pursue the two strategies mentioned above in attempting to attain the goals of socially valued roles and life conditions for (devalued) people, any number of things can or must be done which, for practical and problem solving purposes, can be divided into two large classes: (a) enhancement of people's "social image" or perceived value in the eyes of others, and (b) enhancement of their "competencies." In our society, image enhancement and competency enhancement can be assumed to be generally reciprocally reinforcing, both positively and negatively. That is, a person who is competency-impaired is highly at risk of becoming seen and interpreted as of low value, thus suffering image-impairment; a person who is impaired in social image is apt to be responded to by others in ways that impair/reduce his/her competency. Both processes work equally in the reverse direction; that is a person whose social image is positively valued is apt to be provided with experiences, expectencies, and other life conditions which generally will also increase his/her competencies, and a person who is highly competent is also more apt to be imaged positively.

In recent publications (Wolfensberger & Tullman, 1982; Wolfensberger & Thomas, 1983), we have interpreted the above two broad strategy clusters as themselves expressing and utilizing seven core "themes" which will not be further elaborated here: (a) the role and importance of (un)consciousness in human services, (b) the relevance of role expectancy and role circularity to deviancy-making and deviancy-unmaking, (c) the conservatism corollary of normalization, with its implications of positive compensation for people's devalued or at-risk status, (d) the development model, and personal competency enhancement, (e) the power of imitation, (f) the dynamics and relevance of social imagery, and (g) the importance of societal integration and valued social participation. The recent development of Program Analysis of Service Systems' Implementation of Normalization Goals (PASSING, a new tool that enables the evaluation of a human service against normalization criteria) contributed much to the insight that normalization can be explained in terms of these seven core themes which capture and express most or all the ultimate as well as intermediate goals and processes of the principle (Wolfensberger and Thomas, 1983). With regard to human services specifically, one can now conceptualize normalization as implying a hierarchical arrangement of implications, which can be summarized as in the Figure.

A new term to reflect the new insights

The insight that the creation of valued social roles for people at risk of social devaluation was the epitome of normalization occurred shortly before I discovered that modern French human service language has been using the term *valorisation* to convey the conferring of value onto people, and that in Canadian French, the term *valorisation sociale* has been used during the teaching of the normalization principle since late 1980. This discovery afforded the further insight that the perfect French term for normalization might be something like *la valorisation du rôle social*. A bit of research disclosed that a French encyclopedic dictionary (Larousse) definition of valorisation is "giving value ('valeur') to an object or mental representation." *Valeur*, and the root in *valorisation*, come from the same Latin root and have various English equivalents. "Valeur" exists in English usage only as an imported French word, and is not found in many smaller dictionaries. However, the word "valor" (sometimes spelled valour, at least in British usage) is a venerable English word that goes back at least to Norman English. Webster's Dictionary gives three meanings to it, the first of which is value or worth. "Valorous" is also defined first as having value or worth, and only secondly as meaning brave.

In combination, the above insights and discoveries suggested that in retrospect, an eminently suitable English term for normalization would be "social role valorization." Valorization itself is found in many dictionaries as meaning "attempting to give a market value or price to a commodity." This arcane meaning is a drawback because it implies the attachment of value to objects instead of people, but this dictionary definition is neither very familiar to most people nor would it appear to constitute a compelling negative image juxtaposition. Further, the word "valorization" has very strong meanings corresponding to what we have been trying to convey, while at the same time it is unfamiliar to most people who, therefore, would

The Ultimate Goal:
Enhancement of the Social Role of Persons or Groups at Risk of Social Devaluation, Via 2 Major Sub-Goals

Enhancement of Their Social Image, Via:

Physical Settings	Relationships & Groupings	Activities, Programs, & Other Uses of Time	Language, & Other Symbols & Images
Neighborhood Harmony	Enhancing Juxtaposition to Other Programs	Enhancing Service Workers	Enhancing Personal Possessions
Internal & External Appearance & Features	Grouping Size that Facilitates Social Integration	Enhancing Separation of Program Functions	Personal Appearance
Enhancing Proximity to Other Sites	Enhancing Grouping Composition	Age- & Culture-Appropriate Activities & Schedules	Personal Labels, & Service Names & Acronyms
Enhancing History	Enhancing Other Social Integration	Promotion of Autonomy & Rights	Enhancing Program Funding

Enhancement of Their Personal Competencies, Via:

Physical Settings	Relationships & Groupings	Activities, Programs & Other Uses of Time
Accessibility to Clients, Families Public	Enhancing Size & Composition of Groupings	Address of Real & Urgent Client Needs
Proximity to Potentially Integrative Resources	Enhancing Other Social Integration	Intense & Efficient Use of Time
Comfortable Environment	Programmatic Individualization	Provision/ Promotion of Enhancing Personal Possessions
Challenging Environment	Life-Enriching Interactions	
Individualization-Facilitating Environment	Promotion of Valued Socio-Sexual Identity	

Figure The Hierarchical Structure of Social Role Valorization (Formerly Known as the Principle of Normalization).

be open to being furnished with definitions and explanations rather than attaching their own preconceived ones to it. Considering what happens to people's minds when they encounter the simplistic-sounding term "normalization," we can see that it is actually an advantage that the term "valorization" either (a) is devoid of meaning to most people, (b) carries the meaning of "value," or (c) evokes an unrelated technical concept that is relatively meaningless to most people, and is recognized by the few people who know it as inapplicable to the context to which it is being applied. If one gets too concerned about the commercial meaning found in the dictionaries, one may contrast its benign nature with the meanings that one might find in dictionaries for the term "normalization," with its allusions either to a mathematical process (normalizing distributions of measurements by means of mathematical transformations), or as reference to the relationship among countries, where it implies objective and correct diplomatic relationships and perhaps the absence of hostile tensions, rather than the presence of positive valuation.

Unfortunately, I did not discover the French usage of *valorisation* in time to incorporate it into the most recent update and elaboration of the normalization principle, namely PASSING (Wolfensberger & Thomas, 1983), which is now the most detailed explication of normalization application to human services. However, I have concluded that if the term "normalization" is ever to be replaced by a better one, then it must be done now, and I cannot conceive of a better alternative than "social role valorization," though it is important to distinguish between the valorization of the role of the person, and the valuing (or valorization) of the person him/herself.

It seems to me that within a scientific-theoretical framework—which social role valorization largely is—we can only speak in terms of the valorization of the role of a person. When we speak of valuing the person, we step at least partially outside a theoretical framework that is profoundly anchored to empiricism, and into the realm of supra-empirical value systems. Furthermore, it is readily apparent that people might very well possess ideologies which motivate them to value a person, but that this valuation of the person may not imply a construction of valued social roles for that person in society. For instance, we often hear it said (especially from a religious perspective) that once one values a person, it then becomes irrelevant whether that person occupies a valued social role in the eyes of others and "the world." Yet even if one values a person or group, one might still engage in actions which contribute greatly to the further extensive devaluation of the roles of that person or group in the eyes of others. One can readily cite examples of this. For instance, a lot of people who say they value mentally retarded persons will do nothing to reduce the negative images commonly attached to these persons, enhance their competencies, help them to overcome infirmities, or to acquire habits of socially valued grooming, and so on. Such things may be dismissed as unimportant by the valuing observer, perhaps even with the argument that these things are unimportant before God. Such an orientation often results in a defiant challenge to "the world" to similarly value the person regardless of the person's identity and characteristics.

That such an appeal has merit and validity I do not question, but I do assert that it is almost totally ineffective in bringing about the desired goal. As any unbiased reading of history will reveal, social devaluation and division is so thoroughly laid into human mentality that obviously, people need all the help they can get to overcome these baser inclinations. Furthermore, genuine personal valuation cannot be merely a verbal abstraction but must manifest itself in behavior vis-à-vis people at risk of devaluation. One of the first steps in getting people to be less devaluing is to get them to approach the negatively charged (or at least ambiguous) stimulus object, i.e., a person with devalued characteristics. Again, it is a well-established empirical phenomenon that positive attitude change is not brought about by social contact alone, but by social contact which the actor experiences as positive and pleasurable. This goal can be promoted very powerfully by the various social role valorization strategies.

In terms of practical word use, one would speak of things being "social role valorizing" rather than normalizing, although the adjective "normative" is still useful in some contexts, especially as the concepts of what is normative and valued in a culture are still of the highest relevance to social role valorization. (However, the caveats as to the concept of "norm" or "normative" discussed by Wolfensberger, 1980a, should be noted.) Thus, I submit the term "social role valorization" to the field as a replacement for "the principle of normalization," and have begun to use it in my teaching and in the workshops which our Training Institute offers. I believe that adopting this new term is not only a more accurate descriptor of what the theory of normalization has been all about, but that just as importantly, the phrase can serve as a very instructive consciousness raiser to those who hear and use it.

References

Bank-Mikkelsen, N. E. (1969). A metropolitan area in Denmark: Copenhagen. In R. Kugel & W. Wolfensberger (Eds.), *Changing patterns in residential services for the mentally retarded* (pp. 227–254). Washington: President's Committee on Mental Retardation.

Grunewald, K. (1969). A rural county in Sweden: Malmöhus County. In R. Kugel & W. Wolfensberger (Eds.), *Changing patterns in residential services for the mentally retarded* (pp. 255–287). Washington: President's Committee on Mental Retardation.

Nirje, B. (1969). The normalization principle and its human management implications. In R. Kugel & W. Wolfensberger (Eds.), *Changing patterns in residential services, for the mentally retarded* (pp. 179–195). Washington, DC: Government Printing Office.

Le Petit Larousse, 20th ed. (1965). Paris: Librairie Larousse.

Webster's New International Dictionary. (1919). Springfield, MA: G. & C. Merriam Company.

Wolfensberger, W. (1972). *The principle of normalization in human services.* Toronto: National Institute on Mental Retardation.

Wolfensberger, W. (1980a). The definition of normalization: Update, problems, disagreements, and misunderstandings. In R. J. Flynn & K. E. Nitsch (Eds.), *Normalization, social integration, and community services* (pp. 71–115). Baltimore: University Park Press.

Wolfensberger, W. (1980b). Research, empiricism, and the principle of normalization. In R. J. Flynn & K. E. Nitsch (Eds.), *Normalization, social integration, and community services* (pp. 117–129). Baltimore, MD: University Park Press.

Wolfensberger, W., & Glenn, L. (1973a). *Program analysis of service systems (PASS): A method for the quantitative evaluation of human services: Field manual.* Toronto: National Institute on Mental Retardation.

Wolfensberger, W., & Glenn, L. (1973b). *Program analysis of service systems (PASS): A method for the quantitative evaluation of human services: Handbook.* Toronto: National Institute on Mental Retardation.

Wolfensberger, W., & Glenn, L. (1975a). *Program analysis of service systems (PASS): A method for the quantitative evaluation of human services: Field manual* (3rd ed.). Toronto: National Institute on Mental Retardation. (Reprinted 1978)

Wolfensberger, W., & Glenn, L. (1975b). *Program analysis of service systems (PASS): A method for the quantitative evaluation of human services: Handbook* (Rev. 3rd ed.). Toronto: National Institute on Mental Retardation. (Reprinted 1978)

Wolfensberger, W., & Thomas, S. (1983). *PASSING (Program Analysis of Service Systems' Implementation of Normalization Goals): Normalization criteria and ratings manual.* (2nd ed.) Toronto: National Institute on Mental Retardation.

Wolfensberger, W., & Tullman, S. (1982). A brief outline of the principle of normalization. *Rehabilitation Psychology, 27*(3), 131–145.

4

PARENTAL BELIEFS ON CHILDHOOD DISABILITY

Insights on culture, child development and intervention

Evangeline R. Danseco

Source: *International Journal of Disability, Development and Education* 44(1) (1997): 41–52.

Abstract

This paper examines studies on the interface of culture, parental beliefs, and childhood disability, within an ecological framework. Through a discussion of studies on parents' beliefs about the nature and causes of childhood disability, and their ideas about treatment among various cultural groups, it is proposed that parental beliefs is a means by which culture affects child development. Parents' beliefs about childhood disability provide the structure and context to the development of a child with a disability. Parents' beliefs about the nature and causes of disability likewise provide the context for parents' beliefs about treatment and intervention. The studies also revealed that parents held both biomedical and sociocultural views, reflecting duality in beliefs. Conceptual and methodological considerations for future research on culture, parental beliefs, and childhood disability are discussed. The linkages between parents' ideas and intervention has implications for clinical practice, particularly for multi-cultural societies.

Introduction

Bronfenbrenner's ecological model of child development (1979) proposed that the role of various contexts in which the child is embedded is crucial in comprehending the complex and dynamic nature of development. Although this ecological model has been heavily cited in the literature, there are few empirical studies that have systematically examined both cultural and familial contexts among families of children with disabilities.

Thus, even if both culture and family ecologies have been recognized as potent factors in the adaptation of families of children with disabilities, research on the family and on culture have been separate strands. Their integration in research efforts continues to be predominantly at the level of discourse.

This paper examines studies on parental beliefs among families of children with disabilities across varied cultural groups. Empirical studies included in this paper specifically examined parents' beliefs about the nature of their children's disability, their beliefs about the causes of disability, and their beliefs about treatment or intervention. Case studies, ethnographic reports, quasi-experimental studies, and experimental studies were included. Literature from various disciplines, such as psychology, special education, social work, medicine, and anthropology were surveyed.

The investigation of parental beliefs as the interface between culture, family, and childhood disability is a potentially productive endeavour as it reflects both parental and cultural influences. The developmental niche framework advanced by Super and Harkness (1986; Harkness & Super, 1994) referred to the "psychology of caretakers", while Serpell (1994) noted parental "ethnotheories" as providing the medium whereby culture influences child development. In both frameworks, parents' ideas about parenting and child development reflect cultural systems of meanings. Similarly, this paper proposes that parental ethnotheories on childhood disability, such as parents' views about the nature or causes of disability and their corresponding prognoses and prescriptions, provide the context to the development of a child with disability. Such cultural and familial factors are thus dynamic, non-static entities rather than "objective" social address variables impacting on child development (Betancourt & Lopez, 1993).

Cultural factors have often been treated as extraneous or independent variables, by detecting similarities or differences in beliefs and attitudes based on membership in a cultural group (Berry, 1985). Such a narrow view of culture limits our understanding of the dynamic processes affecting behaviour. Differences among cultural groups, which may afford shifts in (mainstream) psychological theories and methodologies, can instead be viewed as secondary to the notion of "culture as a setting for human behaviour" (Harkness & Super, 1980, p. 2). Betancourt and Lopez (1993) suggest that a definition of culture should specify the subjective aspects of "the human made part of the environment" (Herkovits, 1948 in Betancourt & Lopez, 1993), for example, "familial roles, communication patterns, affective styles, and values regarding personal control, individualism, collectivism, spirituality, and religiosity" (p. 630). Betancourt and Lopez (1993) also clarified the concept of ethnicity, since this term is often used interchangeably with culture. Ethnicity, as proposed by Betancourt and Lopez, "is used in reference to groups that are characterized in terms of a common nationality, culture or language" and that it refers to "the ethnic quality or affiliation of a group, which is normally characterized in terms of culture" (p. 631). While being a member of an ethnic group is a source of transmitting culture, inter-ethnic interactions are also possible sources of influence on behaviour (Berry, 1985).

The studies included in this paper adopt both broad and narrow views of culture. The perspective adopted in this paper is the broader conception of culture as a medium of human development (Betancourt & Lopez, 1993; Cole, 1992). The following sections present studies examining parental beliefs on the nature and causes of disability and studies examining parents' beliefs about prescriptions for childhood disability.

Parental beliefs about the nature and causes of childhood disability

Parents' beliefs or ideas refer to parents' concepts of child development and parents' ideas about parenting (Goodnow, 1984). Areas of study have included belief-behaviour consistency, the likelihood of change in beliefs, the source of ideas, the relation of beliefs and feelings, the relation of beliefs and developmental outcomes, the accuracy of beliefs as compared with objective indices, and beliefs of parents in various cultures (Goodnow & Collins, 1990; Miller, 1988; Sigel, 1985, 1994).

Research in this area originated with studies on parents' expectations and attitudes toward their disabled child and parents' ability to judge the development of their child (e.g., Ehlers, 1964; Ewart & Green, 1957; Heriot & Schmickel, 1967; Levine, 1966; Rheingold, 1945). More recently, in the field of mental retardation, there has been a focus on parents' estimates of their disabled children's abilities compared with estimates of children without disabilities (e.g., Handen, Feldman, & Honigman, 1987), and correspondence between parents' estimates and that of professionals (e.g., Sexton, Thompson, Perez, & Rheams, 1990).

Parents' beliefs about their child with a disability were initially investigated within a model of pathological family functioning and propagated the idea of the "bad mother". There seemed to be a witch hunt for her negative beliefs and attitudes towards her child and in tracing maternal reactions of denial and guilt toward the child's disability. A parent deficit model, albeit with the intention of identifying factors that influence positive developmental outcomes, has been perpetuated by studies that compared parental beliefs with those of professionals. In this model, parents are assumed to lack certain knowledge and skills compared with the experts. Some parent training programs become directed towards making parents quasi-professionals (Mittler & McConachie, 1983). An orientation towards the relative importance of environmental factors, in contrast with a transaction theory, may have influenced such programs.

Beliefs on the nature of disability

What do parents think about their children's biomedical diagnostic labels? What do parents perceive as the differences between disease and disability? Mardiros (1989) provides an extensive analysis of ethnographic data on such issues among Mexican-American parents. She reported that parents regarded their children as being both disabled and healthy. They recognized that their child had impairments in some aspect of their physical or mental development and that this did not mean their child was ill or diseased. On one hand, parents saw their child's condition as permanent or irreversible; on the other hand, "all parents remained hopeful that a cure could be found 'someday' or that a miracle could happen, the first being in the realm of physics and science, and the second through belief in God" (Mardiros, 1989, p. 58).

Regarding their conceptions of the diagnostic labels, Mardiros (1989) reported that most parents were able to describe their child's disability in biomedical terms and considered these labels to be less important than the child's specific skills and behaviours. The child's disability per se was not considered the problem. Rather, functional problems were cited (e.g., limitations brought about by the child's disability and their effects on the family).

Among Chinese parents in New York City, Ryan and Smith (1989) reported that there was a lack of awareness and understanding about their children's disability. This was attributed to language difficulties because most of the parents had poor English and professionals were not able to communicate in the parents' native tongue. Hence, an effective dialogue between professionals and Chinese parents was not instituted. For instance, a parent shares through a bilingual interviewer:

> Very difficult, because we don't understand English and the doctors don't understand Mandarin. We did not know how to ask questions. The only thing we could do was think about it on our own all the time.
>
> (p. 290)

Parents also viewed the child's condition as temporary, with the hopes that the child would outgrow their problems.

Parents' conceptions of childhood disability as a temporary condition are also reported by Leonard (1985) and Reiter, Mar'i, and Rosenberg (1986), based on beliefs on reincarnation. Reiter *et al.* (1986) surmised that Druse parents in Arab communities in Israel had higher positive ratings on attitudes towards persons with disabilities, because they regarded disability as "a temporary or passing condition" (p. 359), with possibilities of change in life after death.

Similarly, Leonard (1985) related a case study of a family from Sri Lanka who migrated to London. After an initial diagnosis of autism in a British clinic, the family went to an astrologer in India who diagnosed the child as "a reincarnation of a warrior who had been severely injured in a battle and was rendered dumb until he died" (p. 200). According to the astrologer the child would have severe speech difficulties until age seven. Leonard's account is consistent with Edgerton's (1981) review of perceptions of mentally retarded children in some parts of India and Nepal, "as possessing divine qualities or because they serve as mediums through which divine intentions can be expressed" (p. 310). Apparently, among cultural groups that adhere to reincarnation, disability was perceived as a temporary condition when viewed along several possible lives. The cause of the disability was seen as resulting from an event in a previous life.

Beliefs on the causes of disability

A duality in beliefs about the causes of disability appears to be predominant among parents of children with disabilities. A biomedical or physical cause for the disability goes hand in hand with sociocultural beliefs which are often referred to in the literature as supernatural, magical, metaphysical, or religious. This duality can be described as a shifting between professional/scientific and lay or "folk" conceptions. This duality can also refer to the deployment of bicultural repertoires because members of the ethnic group traverse between two sets of cultural beliefs and norms. Such eclectic repertoires of beliefs and practices can be inferred from the accounts of parental beliefs on the causes of disability among Chinese-Americans (Ryan & Smith, 1989), Mexican-Americans (Mardiros, 1989), and Jewish-Oriental mothers (Stahl, 1991) which explored the question: What do parents think are the reasons or causes of the child's disability?

About 15% of the Chinese-American parents interviewed by Ryan and Smith (1989), or 9 out of 59 parents, include physical causes for their child's disability (e.g., effect of oral contraceptives, long labour). Ten of the 59 parents regarded having a child with a disability as due to fate or as punishment for a violation of a religious, ethical, or cultural code. The hot-cold dichotomy based on the yin/yang Chinese cosmology was also mentioned by the parents. That is, the child's disability was believed to have been caused by colds or high fevers, presumably a disharmony between the yin and yang forces. It is not clear whether parents regard these beliefs as incompatible or if these Chinese-American parents adopt both biomedical/physical and sociocultural beliefs.

Stahl (1991) reports that Jewish-Oriental mothers in Israel who are "more modern" tend to have "rational explanations" about the causes of the child's disability (p. 362). The less modern, including those who describe themselves as non-religious, ascribe religious or magical causes to the child's disability. Fate, punishment for a specific sin, the "Evil Eye", peculiar prenatal events such as meeting a retarded person, persistent prayers for a child or a son by a "barren" woman, were the most cited causes for disability.

Moreover, the blame for the child's disability is often placed on the mother, even if there may be a history of disability in the father's family. Since children are within the mother's responsibility, the child's "imperfections" are often considered to be caused by the mother. Stahl comments that such maternal blame is often tacitly assumed by both parents.

Among Mexican-American parents, the biomedical causes for their child's disability include chronic health problems during pregnancy, negative health habits, insufficient rest and exercise, environmental factors (e.g., food preservatives, toxic waste, pollution), accidents, and medical interventions (e.g., anaesthesia, medications) (Mardiros, 1989). Sociocultural views included marital difficulties, divine punishment for parental transgressions, wife abuse, and fate or predestination. Mardiros notes that all parents held both biomedical conceptions and sociocultural beliefs about the causes for the child's disability. Parents could competently describe their child's etiology in medical terms and accept the diagnosis, as well as adhere to sociocultural perspectives on what they themselves regard as the causes of their child's disability. Hence, it appears that the duality in Mexican-American parents' beliefs about the permanence of the disability is likewise apparent in their beliefs on the causes of a disability. This traversing between two views may suggest the adoption of several repertoires of behaviour as a predominant mode of dealing with a child's disability.

Affleck, McGrade, Allen, and McQueeney (1985) examined American mothers' beliefs about the behavioural causes for their infant's disability among infants with perinatal medical problems and genetic syndromes. Unfortunately, the authors did not indicate the cultural background of the respondents. Affleck *et al.* focused on beliefs about "behavioural" causes to determine if mothers who attributed their child's medical condition to their (mothers) own behaviour differed in their adaptation to the child's disability and their caretaking behaviour, compared with mothers who attributed other people's behaviour as the cause for their child's condition, or with mothers who did not attribute any behavioural causes. The responses of 51 mothers to questions in a semi-structured interview were categorized into three mutually exclusive beliefs: maternal behavioural causes (e.g., smoking during pregnancy), behaviour of others (e.g., obstetrician's behaviour), or no behavioural causes.

About 25% of the mothers were classified as attributing their child's disability to their own behaviour, about 22% to the behaviour of others, and about 57% did not ascribe behavioural causes. This suggests that mothers' beliefs about the causes of their child's disability were not always rooted in behaviour. Non-behavioural causes included religious interpretations, fate, and medical causes. Since the non-behavioural causes were not the primary focus of the study, distinctions between mothers who ascribed medical causes versus those who attributed their child's condition to supernatural causes were not further analyzed.

Among mothers who gave behavioural causes, those who perceived their own behaviour to be the cause of their child's disability had more optimal scores on indices of mood, caretaking perceptions, and home environment, as compared to mothers who blamed others or mothers who did not indicate any behavioural causes. Mothers who blamed themselves had less caretaking difficulties and less mood disturbances; they also had more positive scores on scales of emotional and verbal responsiveness, organization of the physical and temporal environment, and maternal involvement with the child. The investigators commented that mothers who blamed themselves for their child's disability seemed to adopt more problem-focused coping, consistent with the predominant cultural orientation on events as within personal control. Apparently, mothers who indicated that they perceived their behaviour as causing their infant's condition were able to cope with the demands of their child's disability, perhaps because such demands may have been seen as within their control.

Parental beliefs about treatment and intervention

In the previous section, the studies on parental beliefs about the nature and causes of childhood disability showed that parents comprehend biomedical views and at the same time, adopt sociocultural views, which are often described in the literature as magical, religious, supernatural, or metaphysical beliefs. The studies likewise suggest that although parents practice professionals' prescriptions for treatment and/or intervention, cultural prescriptions prevail as well.

A Chinese-American parent sought medical treatment for a child with epilepsy and also sought the help of mediums to drive evil spirits away; acupuncture, and wearing of silver bangles were other practices reported by some parents (Ryan & Smith, 1989). Jewish-Oriental parents interviewed by Stahl (1991) also sought to drive evil spirits away by "putting an iron object under the child's mattress" (p. 364) or burning the child with a hot iron, based on the belief that evil spirits are afraid of iron. Some parents sought folk healers or rabbis without official religious status to perform rituals or provide parents with amulets. Parents sometimes changed the name of their child, because names are believed to allude to certain desired states or traits. Another practice reported was performing religious rituals, particularly going on pilgrimages. Stahl notes that the kinds of treatments parents sought, aside from professionals' prescribed interventions, reflected both traditional religious beliefs and magico-religious or superstitious beliefs. The latter are regarded as conflicting with traditional or orthodox belief, seemingly in the parents' hope of seeking any kind of cure for their child's condition.

Mexican-Americans employ two repertoires of beliefs and practices. The formal support network is the basis for biomedical views about the child's disability, while the informal support system is the basis for sociocultural perspectives (Mardiros, 1989). Parents had certain expectations of physicians (e.g., to treat their children, refer them to other professionals or services, and to listen to them). However, as Mardiros quotes one parent:

> Whatever the doctor said, we took with a grain of salt. They may know a lot more about medication, but we know a lot more about [our daughter] but they don't listen to us. And so when they say something, I don't assume they're wrong, or assume they don't know what they're talking about. But like I said, I know my daughter better than they do, I know the patient involved. So I take what they say and interpret it to what I know about her and that's how we make our decisions about what to do for her.
>
> (p. 63)

While seeking professional help, Mexican-American parents also sought support from the informal network. This included lay groups from the parents' church, neighbours, and the extended family. Cultural prescriptions were also practiced, such as the use of home remedies, seeking the help of "curanderos" to remove the hex of a "brujera," prayer, pilgrimages, and the fulfillment of vows were the most common practices to "cure" the child or minimize the severity of symptoms.

Hence, beliefs about the nature and causes of childhood disability provide the context for beliefs about treatment and intervention. Parents who believed that the disability was caused by evil spirits sought ways to drive such demons away or sought the help of folk healers to achieve this end (Mardiros, 1989; Ryan & Smith, 1989; Stahl, 1991). Parents who believed that the disability was caused by their past transgressions or negative habits, changed their behaviour to alleviate their child's condition (Mardiros, 1989). Parents who believed that divine intervention caused their child's disability sought to remove divine displeasure by going on pilgrimages, performing religious rituals, or fulfilling vows. Chinese parents who regarded the child's disability as caused primarily by supernatural causes were more inclined to seek corresponding cultural prescriptions and less inclined to follow professional advice (Ryan & Smith, 1989). On the other hand, parents who accepted biomedical perspectives would follow professional prescriptions, but at the same time they often performed various cultural prescriptions to find a cure for their child's disability.

Specific predominant cultural beliefs may also affect ideas and practices related to treatment and intervention. For instance, the greater emphasis on male education among the Yoruba seemed to be reflected in the higher number of male deaf children enrolled in educational programs (Togonu-Bickersteth & Odebeyi, 1985). Similarly, there was a high number of first-born deaf children, reflecting the Yoruba's value towards the first-born. Studies of the role of beliefs regarding reincarnation in ideas about treatment and intervention are inconclusive. Reiter *et al.* (1986) reported more positive attitudes among the Druse—who believe in reincarnation—than among Christians or Muslims in Arab communities in Israel, but relations to treatment or intervention were not explored.

Discussion

Studies on parental beliefs and childhood disability among various cultural groups were examined within an ecological framework, wherein parental beliefs provide a medium by which culture affects child development. The major points that emerged from the studies were that parents' beliefs about the nature and causes of childhood disability reflected both biomedical and sociocultural views and that parents' beliefs on the nature and causes of disability provide the context for beliefs about treatment and intervention.

Parents' were able to express their biomedical conceptions about their children's disability, as well as describe their children's skills, behaviours, and functional problems. Some parents regard childhood disability as a permanent condition, while others regard it as temporary. The latter is most notably found among cultural groups that adhere to beliefs in reincarnation. A lack of awareness and understanding of childhood disability can be traced to language difficulties between parents and professionals from different ethnic and language groups.

Parents' beliefs about the causes of childhood disability likewise reflected both biomedical and sociocultural views. Parents were able to cite biomedical causes, such as medical conditions, environmental factors, genetic factors, and negative health habits. However, parents also often depicted their children's disability as due to fate, divine punishment, peculiar events, and other religious or socio-cultural beliefs.

Parents' ideas on the nature and causes of their children's disability have an impact on their ideas on prescriptions for treatment and intervention. At the same time that some parents seek professional help, they also often perform cultural prescriptions to "cure" their children's disability, or at the least to minimize the severity of functional problems. For example, parents utilized home remedies, performed religious rituals and pilgrimages, or amended negative behaviours, and fulfilled vows.

The deployment of various beliefs and practices by parents from ethnic minority groups, whether they be conflictual or complementary practices, is consistent with Berry's (1985) and Betancourt and Lopez' (1993) assertions regarding inter-ethnic variables as possible influences on behaviour. Ethnic groups are not isolated communities, but interact at various levels with diverse ethnic groups and with the mainstream culture (Berry, 1985; Betancourt & Lopez, 1993). Parents of children with disabilities who are members of minority ethnic groups in a culturally diverse society negotiate professional services as well as ethnic remedies and cultural practices in seeking what they regard as the best intervention for their child. This entails deploying the mainstream culture's beliefs and practices and at the same time upholding their group's cultural beliefs and practices.

This indicates the need for professionals to learn to "speak the language" of ethnic minority parents and be more knowledgeable of parents' cultural backgrounds and their particular practices and beliefs. Professionals need to tap into minority groups' cultural repertoires and initiate the bridging of differences in values and practices. For instance, Leonard's (1985) case studies of families from Greece, Sri Lanka, and Jamaica who migrated to London highlighted the families' need to address cultural beliefs and pre-scriptions regarding the child's disability. Contacts with fellow migrants or visits to their country of origin facilitated acceptance of the child and encouraged involvement in intervention efforts.

Parents' use of various repertoires is not restricted to the ethnic minority-mainstream distinction, but also involves the professional-lay distinction. The studies included in this paper portrayed the tension between Western-trained, biomedically-oriented professionals and parents who adhere to "folk" beliefs. To what extent are these views in conflict? In what specific areas among specific cultural groups are these beliefs incongruent? How can professionals deal with such conflicts (e.g., educate parents on the "sci-entifically correct" views, "tolerate" folk beliefs and practices, be "culturally sensitive")? These are some questions that professionals are now confronting and which research must begin to address. Research on parental beliefs that inform effective interventions are greatly needed.

The dichotomy itself, between parents' biomedical and sociocultural beliefs, may reflect investigators' Western-based theoretical orientations and biases towards biomedical perspectives. Biomedical orientations are cultural tools, as are parents' sociocultural beliefs, but scientifically-oriented beliefs are tacitly assumed to be valid. Professionals in early intervention may tend to adopt such a posture (i.e., only folk beliefs that have corresponding biomedical explanations or beliefs which have underlying scientific explanations, can be considered valid). This is unfortunate because research that does not go beyond such a dichotomy will very much perpetuate a parent-deficit perspective.

The ethnic validity model proposed by Tyler and his colleagues (Tyler, Brome, & Williams, 1991; Tyler, Sussewell, & Williams-McCoy, 1985), developed in the context of the psychotherapeutic relationship between therapists and clients who come from different cultural groups, offers a useful framework towards differing beliefs between professionals and parents. This model suggests that the congruent, divergent, and conflicting interactions among persons from different cultural groups are due to particular conceptions of the self, self-world relationships, and ideals of psychological well-being, with each cultural group having legitimate or ethnically valid world views. Identifying specific areas where parents' and professionals' beliefs are convergent, divergent, and in conflict, is an initial step towards clarifying parent-professional interactions. Ways to expand areas of convergence, ways to respect areas of divergence, and ways to deal with areas of conflict can then be explored.

Similarly, Serpell (1993, 1994) advocates for a process of negotiation between parents and professionals whereby differences in perspectives are initially identified so that they can gradually work towards a "fusion of horizons". Articulating these differences and identifying the frames of reference of various actors involved (e.g., teachers, parents, the community, children) assumes the legitimacy of each perspective. Hence, simply aiming to "correct" parents' beliefs towards a more biomedically-oriented perspective is not a morally responsible course, nor a pragmatic and realistic objective. However, a mere acceptance of parents' sociocultural views and practices is also untenable (e.g., teachers simply cannot accept a parents' practice of putting a hot iron on a child's hand as legitimate) (cf. Stahl, 1991). Rather, a negotiation of specific practices and beliefs between parents and professionals and the articulation of mutually shared goals for the development of the child with disabilities is a process worth exploring. There will be no one formula to address the diverse beliefs from different cultures. However, dialogues on mutually shared goals can form the basis for a "fusion of horizons" between parents and professionals.

Investigating the interface of culture, parental beliefs, professional beliefs, and childhood disability is necessary to inform what constitutes effective intervention among diverse cultural groups. This is important in developing countries wherein research in psychology has an applied focus (i.e., psychology is linked to issues of national development or social, economic, and political concerns, such as research on street children). Such research is likewise important in responding to the challenges of multiculturally diverse societies such as the United States, particularly in addressing the concerns of parents who are jeopardized by poverty, ethnicity, and disability (Brookins, 1993). In multicultural societies, rhetoric on cultural sensitivity is not enough (Brookins, 1993; Rogler, Malgady, Constantino, & Blumenthal, 1987). Examining these issues is imperative if research and programmatic efforts are to be relevant and responsive to the demands of parents, children, and the broader society.

Author note

The author wishes to acknowledge the comments of Drs Maureen Black, Robert Serpell, and Forrest Tyler on previous versions of this paper.

References

Affleck, G., McGrade, B. J., Allen, D. A. & McQueeney, M. (1985). Mothers' beliefs about behavioral causes for their developmentally disabled infant's condition: What do they signify? *Journal of Pediatric Psychology, 10*, 293–303.

BERRY, J. W. (1985). Cultural psychology and ethnic psychology: A comparative analysis. In I. R. LAGUNES & Y. H. POORTINGA (Eds.), *From a different perspective: Studies of behavior across cultures* (pp. 3–15). Lisse, The Netherlands: Swets & Zeitlinger B. V.

BETANCOURT, H. & LOPEZ, S. R. (1993). The study of culture, ethnicity, and race in American psychology. *American Psychologist, 48*, 629–637.

BRONFENBRENNER, U. (1979). *The ecology of human development: Experiments by nature and design.* Cambridge, MA: Harvard University Press.

BROOKINS, G. K. (1993). Culture, ethnicity, and bicultural competence: Implications for children with chronic illness and disability. *Pediatrics Supplement, 91*, 1056–1062.

COLE, M. (1992). Culture in development. In M. H. BORNSTEIN & M. E. LAMB (Eds.), *Developmental psychology: An advanced textbook* (pp. 731–789). Hillsdale, NJ: Lawrence Erlbaum.

EDGERTON, R. B. (1981). Another look at culture and mental retardation. In M. J. BEGAB, H. C. HAYWOOD & H. L. GARBER (Eds.), *Psychosocial influences in retarded performance: Volume 1. Issues and theories in development* (pp. 309–323). Baltimore: University Park Press.

EHLERS, W. H. (1964). The moderately and severely retarded child: Maternal perceptions of retardation and subsequent seeking and using services rendered by a community agency. *American Journal of Mental Deficiency, 68*, 660–668.

EWART, J. C. & GREEN, M. W. (1957). Conditions associated with the mothers' estimate of the ability of her retarded child. *American Journal of Mental Deficiency, 62*, 521–533.

GOODNOW, J. J. (1984). Parents' ideas about parenting and development: A review of issues and recent work. In M. E. LAMB, A. L. BROWN & B. ROGOFF (Eds.), *Advances in developmental psychology* (Vol. 3, pp. 193–242). Hillsdale, NJ: Lawrence Erlbaum.

GOODNOW, J. J. & COLLINS, W. A. (1990). *Development according to parents: The nature, sources, and consequences of parents' ideas.* Hillsdale, NJ: Lawrence Erlbaum.

HANDEN, B. L., FELDMAN, R. S. & HONIGMAN, A. (1987). Comparison of parent and teacher assessments of developmentally delayed children's behavior. *Exceptional Children, 54*, 137–144.

HARKNESS, S. & SUPER, C. (1980). Child development theory in anthropological perspective. In C. SUPER & S. HARKNESS (Eds.), *New directions for child development: Anthropological perspectives on child development* (pp. 1–5). San Francisco: Jossey-Bass.

HARKNESS, S. & SUPER, C. (1994). The developmental niche: A theoretical framework for analyzing the household production of health. *Social Science and Medicine, 38*, 217–226.

HERIOT, J. T. & SCHMICKEL, C. A. (1967). Maternal estimate of IQ in children evaluated for learning potential. *American Journal of Mental Deficiency, 71*, 920–924.

LEONARD, C. J. (1985). Brief outlines of the parent/family reaction to childhood disability in families from 3 ethnic minority groups. *International Journal for the Advancement of Counseling, 8*, 197–205.

LEVINE, S. (1966). Sex role identification and parental perceptions of social competence. *American Journal of Mental Deficiency, 70*, 822–824.

MARDIROS, M. (1989). Conception of childhood disability among Mexican-American parents. *Medical Anthropology*, *12*, 55–68.

MILLER, S. A. (1988). Parents' beliefs about children's cognitive development. *Child Development*, *59*, 259–285.

MITTLER, P. & McCONACHIE, H. (Eds.) (1983). *Parents, professionals and mentally handicapped people: Approaches to partnership*. London: Croom Helm.

REITER, S., MAR'I, S. & ROSENBERG, Y. (1986). Parental attitudes toward the developmentally disabled among Arab communities in Israel: A cross-cultural study. *International Journal for Rehabilitation Research*, *9*, 355–362.

RHEINGOLD, H. L. (1945). Interpreting mental retardation to parents. *Journal of Consulting Psychology*, *9*, 142–143.

ROGLER, L. H., MALGADY, R. G., CONSTANTINO, G. & BLUMENTHAL, R. (1987). What do culturally sensitive mental health services mean? The case of Hispanics. *American Psychologist*, *42*, 565–570.

RYAN, A. S. & SMITH, M. J. (1989). Parental reactions to developmental disabilities in Chinese American families. *Child and Adolescent Social Work*, *6*, 283–299.

SERPELL, R. (1993). *The significance of schooling: Life-journeys in an African society*. Cambridge: Cambridge University Press.

SERPELL, R. (1994). Negotiating a fusion of horizons: A process view of cultural validation in developmental psychology. *Mind, Culture, and Activity*, *1*, 43–68.

SEXTON, D. THOMPSON, B., PEREZ, J. & RHEAMS, T. (1990). Maternal versus professional estimates of developmental status for young children with handicaps: An ecological approach. *Topics in Early Childhood Special Education*, *10*, 80–95.

SIGEL, I. E. (Ed.) (1985). *Parental beliefs systems: The psychological consequences for children*. Hillsdale, NJ: Lawrence Erlbaum Associates.

SIGEL, I. E. (Ed.) (1994). *Parental beliefs systems: The psychological consequences for children* (2nd ed.). Hillsdale, NJ: Lawrence Erlbaum.

STAHL, A. (1991). Beliefs of Jewish-Oriental mothers regarding children who are mentally retarded. *Education and training in mental retardation*, *26*, 361–369.

SUPER, C. M. & HARKNESS, S. (1986). The developmental niche: A conceptualization at the interface of child and culture. *International Journal of Behavioural Development*, *9*, 545–569.

TOGONU-BICKERSTETH, F. & ODEBEYI, A. I. (1985). Influence of Yoruba beliefs about abnormality on the socialization of deaf children: A research note. *Journal of Child Psychology and Psychiatry and Allied Disciplines*, *26*, 639–652.

TYLER, F. B., BROME, D. R. & WILLIAMS, J. E. (1991). *Ethnic validity, ecology and psychotherapy*. New York: Plenum Press.

TYLER, F. B., SUSSEWELL, D. R. & WILLIAMS-McCOY, J. (1985). Ethnic validity in psychotherapy. *Psychotherapy*, *22*, 311–320.

5

NARROWING THE BREACH

Can disability culture and full educational inclusion be reconciled?

Jean P. Hall

Source: *Journal of Disability Policy Studies* 13(3) (2002): 144–52.

Because of the long history of exclusion of people with disabilities, total inclusion in the educational environment has many outspoken proponents. People and organizations favoring inclusion, however, are overlooking the value of the disability culture that is fostered when children with disabilities have the opportunity to associate with and learn alongside other individuals who share similar identities and life experiences. The history of the disability rights movement clearly illustrates that major changes do not occur unless people with disabilities band together to address shared injustices (e.g., Shapiro, 1993). The phenomenon of a disability culture has been convincingly demonstrated by many researchers and writers, and its importance to the development and self-esteem of students with disabilities is discussed. Although the current special education system has many negative aspects, changes to the existing system rather than a movement to full inclusion will be more effective in supporting disability culture and, ultimately, the needs of children with disabilities.

Josh's story

Cindy is the White mother of a 10-year-old Black child with cerebral palsy (see Note). She took Josh home from the hospital when he was 6 days old and weighed less than 5 pounds. Originally, she was to be his foster parent for 2 weeks, but eventually Cindy's family adopted Josh. From the start, Cindy made efforts to reinforce Josh's racial culture. She took him to Black churches and Black Expos, exposed him to books by Black authors, and had him participate in activities during Black History Month. She never really considered getting him involved with other people who had disabilities, however.

A local Black civil rights activist once told Cindy that Josh had two "whammies" against him: he was Black and he had a disability. Furthermore, he warned Cindy that Josh would experience discrimination on the basis of his disability much earlier than on the basis of his color. He was right. Cindy relates stories of how even medical professionals, noting Josh's obvious physical difficulties, were shocked by young Josh's sense of humor, his advanced vocabulary, and his obvious intelligence.

Josh attends public school in a rural area. One of his best friends in school was a White boy with spina bifida who used crutches like Josh. Recently, the friend died due to surgical complications. When Josh found out, his response was: "Now there's nobody like me." Obviously, to Josh, his disability cultural affiliation was stronger even than his racial cultural affiliation, which had been actively fostered by his family. Furthermore, school was the only setting in which Josh had truly enjoyed the opportunity to experience that affiliation.

For most of U.S. history, schools were allowed to—and often did—exclude certain children, especially children with disabilities. In the 1960s, federal legislation began to address the educational needs of children with disabilities, culminating in the Education for All Handicapped Children Act of 1975. Subsequent amendments to the Act have changed its name to the Individuals with Disabilities Education Act (IDEA), which was last reauthorized in 1997. One tenet of IDEA is that education for children with disabilities be provided in the "least restrictive environment" (LRE), meaning that they receive their education, to the maximum extent appropriate, with nondisabled peers and are not removed from general education classes unless their education cannot be achieved satisfactorily there (20 U.S.C. § 1412(a)(5)(A)). Perhaps partly because of the long history of exclusion of people with disabilities, many outspoken reformers have equated LRE with full inclusion of children with disabilities in the general classroom. I argue, however, that inclusion proponents are overlooking the value of the culture that is fostered when children with disabilities have the opportunity to associate with and learn alongside others who share similar identities and life experiences.

Furthermore, the movement toward full inclusion has the potential to undercut the ability of the disability community to advocate effectively for itself. The history of the disability rights movement has clearly illustrated that major changes do not occur unless people with disabilities band together to address shared injustices (e.g., National Council on Disability [NCD], 1996; Pfeiffer, 1993; Shapiro, 1993). Pfeiffer explained how the independent living movement, although initially spurred by the need for services, matured into an organization that was equally concerned with the civil rights of people with disabilities. He detailed how people with disabilities involved in the independent living/disability rights movement came together to lobby for signing of the Section 504 regulations in the early 1970s and how this cause helped to unite people with disabilities from across the country. Even Scotch (1984), who questioned how influential the disability rights movement was in the passage and implementation of Section 504, acknowledged that "[d]isabled people have begun a long march through the institutions of American life, and it is unlikely that they will be easily turned back" (p. 168). Scotch did, however, emphasize that sustaining a unified and effective political movement can be difficult. Charlton (1998) echoed this belief in his statement that "(t)he failure of people with disabilities to identify with other people with disabilities is . . . the principal contradiction that limits the disability rights movement's potential influence and power" (p. 78).

A weakening of advocacy efforts can have monetary as well as civil rights implications. Braddock, Hemp, Parish, Westrich, and Park (1998), for example, clearly documented a direct correlation between the level of advocacy in a state and the level of funding for services for people with developmental disabilities. Another example of the monetary power of grass roots advocacy is the "Drive for 75" movement by independent living advocates. This effort to change the fiscal allocation under Title VII, Part C, of the Rehabilitation Act has resulted in a 21% increase for federal funding of centers, and efforts to increase these funding levels continue. Kimball Gray, executive director of the Maryland Statewide Independent Living Council, described the advocacy effort as follows:

[I]t's good to see the power of the independent living movement in a proactive position with Congress, as opposed to our accustomed role of defending the civil rights of people with disabilities. I think we demonstrated the ability to have a presence in both arenas.

(Topeka Independent Living Resource Center, 2000)

Understanding disability culture

To appreciate fully the importance of fostering disability culture for children, we must first understand that culture itself. Many researchers have documented the existence of a disability culture, its functions, its "core values," and its similarities to and differences from other cultural groups (e.g., Charlton, 1998; Gill, 1995; Gilson, Tusler, & Gill, 1997; Paradis, 1998; Shapiro, 1993). One distinct feature of disability culture that is not shared with any other cultural minority group is that in the great majority of cases, people with disabilities do *not* share that cultural affiliation with their families. As Gilson *et al.* pointed out,

[the] process of identity formation for persons with disabilities is complicated by a social marginalization so profound that it extends into
the shelter of the family. A pivotal point in the identity development
process is the individual's recognition of corporeal and psychological
distinctness from her/his nurturers, followed by a complementary
recognition of similarity to others outside the family boundaries.

(p. 13)

For this reason, the school environment presents a unique opportunity for
children with disabilities to both experience and, more important, learn
from educational experiences shared with their peers with disabilities. This
is especially true for children whose disabilities preclude them from interacting with peers in other community settings due to medical, transportation,
financial, or other limitations.

Regardless of when or how an individual acquires a disability, he or she
can obtain both knowledge and support from other people with disabilities.
Support groups for people with many different types of disabilities can
be found in most communities. These groups provide an opportunity to
exchange ideas, experiences, and coping strategies. Similarly, many hospitals have programs in place to match (a) patients who have been newly
diagnosed with cancer with peers who have previously been diagnosed and
treated or (b) people with recently acquired spinal cord injuries with veteran
wheelchair users. Clearly, there is a recognized need for and a benefit from
the exchange of insights and common concerns among people with disabilities, and these are recognized even among professionals who do not
themselves have disabilities.

Disability culture extends beyond diagnoses, however. True disability
culture embraces *all persons* who have been marginalized by society simply
because they are viewed as defective, not valid ("invalid"), or somehow in
need of pity. Even people with invisible disabilities such as chronic health
conditions or mental illness experience this marginalization: Children
with severe asthma often have to sit on the sidelines while their classmates
participate in vigorous sports; people with systemic conditions or mental
illness often experience extreme fatigue or somnolence due to their illness or
medications and may feel excluded because their participation in many parts
of life is limited; people with HIV/AIDS are still treated as pariahs by many
individuals if their condition is revealed. Think of a child with a severe
learning disability who is asked to read aloud in front of a class. Although
his or her disability may be invisible to classmates, its manifestations
certainly are not, and the resulting rejection is no less profound.

A 1986 Harris & Associates study found that 74% of people with disabilities reported feeling a sense of common "group" identity with other people
with disabilities that cut across disability, age, and employment status.
As Paradis (1998) noted, "Like other minority groups, we must struggle

to . . . integrate with the 'mainstream' while preserving the meaning of our unique life experiences and our own separate identity" (p. 19).

Definition of disability culture

In reviewing various definitions of the term *culture*, Barnartt (1996) noted that "all emphasize norms, values, symbols, language, ideational systems, . . . and arts such as . . . humor" (p. 3). Gill (1995, 1999) defined *disability culture* as including shared, long-standing social oppression; art; humor; history; evolving language and symbols; a unified worldview; beliefs and values; and strategies for surviving and thriving. Although many people are familiar with deaf culture and its accompanying sign language, few are perhaps aware of a larger, more inclusive, cross-disability culture and its language and symbols. Publications such as *Disability Rag* (now *Ragged Edge*) and *This Brain Has a Mouth* (now *Mouth Magazine*) exemplify the often graphic and powerful language and symbols used by disability rights advocates representing all types of disability groups, including people with cognitive impairments and psychiatric disabilities. A *Mouth* staff member, Tom Olin (cited in Gwin, 2000), noted that the magazine's "essential function is to develop a language, a vocabulary to describe us and the inside-out lives we lead, the tyrannies we endure. . . . Language gives knowing." These and other magazines, such as *Mainstream*, emphasize the injustices experienced by almost all people with disabilities and illustrate how mistreatment of one disability group directly or indirectly results in the mistreatment of all people with disabilities. Stand-up comedians such as Chris Fonseca and Kathy Buckley and cartoonist John Callahan share with fellow people with disabilities and with mainstream society the humorous—and often ironic—aspects of living with a disability. Groch (1994) listed many other such "cultural artifacts."

Centers for Independent Living, which are mandated by the Rehabilitation Act to be "cross-disability," recognize the universality of the disability experience in their core service of peer counseling. Peer counselors are veterans of disability who serve as role models and mentors. They do not necessarily share the same disability as the people with whom they work, but they do encounter the same societal barriers and attitudes that may hinder true independence.

Core values of disability culture

The language and symbols of disability culture seem to reflect a series of core values. Although more research may be needed to confirm the presence of these values across disability groups, many people with disabilities appear to share them, regardless of the individual circumstance. Some of these values have been described by Gill (1995) and Kemp (1999), and they include the following:

1 *An acceptance of human differences.* Because people with disabilities are different from the persons who make up the majority population, they are more accepting of others who are also different.

2 *A matter-of-fact orientation toward helping.* People with disabilities often depend on others for assistance with even the most basic and personal of life's daily activities; thus, they view helping others as a natural and right thing to do. Interdependence is a normal part of their lives.

3 *A tolerance for lack of resolution.* People with disabilities, especially individuals with chronic illnesses or progressive conditions, have learned by necessity to live with a great deal of uncertainty in their lives.

4 *Disability humor.* Often seen as a very dark humor by the nondisabled, disability humor frequently plays on the stereotypes of disability held by the majority culture. Disability humor also gives people permission to laugh about circumstances that some individuals see as pitiable but that the disability community take in stride. For example, Kemp (1999), a quadruple amputee, shared the story of how each year he must reapply for his handicapped parking placard. He related how he goes to the motor vehicle office and, after showing them he hasn't "grown any arms or legs," asks "Could you . . . give me 18 months, maybe two years? I don't feel any growth coming on yet."

5 *A sophisticated future orientation.* Think of the person with paraplegia who uses a wheelchair and has been invited to present at an out-of-town conference in 6 months. He or she will immediately begin inquiring about accessible airlines, accessible transportation to and from the airport, accessible lodging, reimbursement for the use of a personal attendant, and so forth. Similarly, an individual with a chronic mental or physical illness requiring medication will be sure to bring a sufficient supply and will probably also locate a place to obtain this medication in the place being visited. Finally, someone with a brain injury or learning disability who is contemplating which college to attend will likely check into the process of obtaining, and the quality of, note takers, readers, or other similar accommodations before applying. Simply put, many people with disabilities are—and must be—great planners.

Importance of the disability culture for children with disabilities

Although Barnartt (1996) questioned the applicability of the term *disability culture*, he did acknowledge that this concept serves as a frame "around which disability consciousness can be built" (p. 2). Groch (1994) suggested that people who possess a disability consciousness have developed a sense of collective identity and acknowledge their oppressed position. These views are incorporated in some of the functions of disability proposed by Gill (1997):

1 fortification against oppression;
2 unification across disability; age, race, gender, socioeconomic status;
3 communication developed through art, language, symbols, and rituals that help to articulate to the world and to others with disabilities their distinctness; and
4 the offer of a sense of belonging to marginalized individuals.

These functions can obviously be quite valuable to children who may feel isolated. For example, a young woman described how her involvement with the disability community not only helped her resolve her own feelings about her disability but also resulted in better relationships for her with people who did not have disabilities. Unfortunately, she was not able to experience this involvement until she entered graduate school.

> I . . . began to look at my disability in a very different way. This change was catalyzed by experiences I started to have with other disabled students. We began to "hang out" and I enjoyed their company. . . . I had finally found a group of people with whom I did not have to consistently play the role of the "happy overcomer." I no longer regard disability as an inherently negative condition, but rather as one of the unique and positive characteristics that comprise our society as a whole. . . . And as I have come to value my disability as an integral part of who I am, others have too. For once, I began to let people pass through the carefully guarded gate of the wall which I built to separate me from others. After having reached the point of accepting and respecting myself and my differences, it has been much easier for me to form a positive relationship with society.
>
> (Gill, 1997, p. 44)

Charlton (1998) remarked on a similar phenomenon whereby the new consciousness of self derived from interacting with others who have similar experiences "allows individuals to recognize themselves in the context of something bigger than themselves and enables them to appreciate the commonalities they have with others. . . . Isolation and estrangement are replaced by association and connection" (p. 118). If we value these roles that disability culture can offer children, we must find a way to support the culture's involvement in their development. A logical place for this support is school, where children spend much of their formative years. First, however, we must understand how current special education and full inclusion practices have evolved and whether they bolster disability culture or suppress it.

Special education legislative and judicial histories

As Lipsky and Gartner (1996) discussed, the history of education of students with disabilities ran parallel to that of other minority groups in U.S. society and consisted of three distinct stages: exclusion by law or regulation; formal inclusion, based on judicial and/or legislative requirements; and progress toward defining the nature of inclusion (policies and practices). Up until the 1960s, children with severe disabilities either stayed home with their families or were placed in private schools or institutions. Children with less severe disabilities were generally served in special classes, day schools, or residential facilities. With the advent of the civil rights movement, public education for children with disabilities began to be addressed. Generally, the legislative trend from the 1960s through the 1990s has been toward expanding eligibility for special education and increasing opportunity for students with disabilities to participate in classrooms with nondisabled students (National Information Center for Children and Youth with Disabilities, 1996).

In most instances, legal cases have reflected the same trend toward increasing opportunities for students with disabilities to participate in the general education classroom. Most litigation has centered on the concepts of LRE and appropriateness, which are addressed in IDEA. IDEA specifically requires that "to the maximum extent *appropriate* [italics added], children with disabilities are educated with children who are non-disabled" (20 U.S.C. § 1412a(5)).

IDEA also requires local education agencies to ensure the availability of a continuum of alternate placements, from least restrictive to most restrictive, within which a child's program can be delivered. Federal regulations indicate that the continuum may include (but is not limited to) general and special education classes (34 C.F.R. § 300.551(b)(1)).

The U.S. Supreme Court has not addressed the LRE issue directly, but federal circuit courts have generated a range of decisions concerning it. In reviewing circuit court cases addressing LRE, Thomas and Rapport (1998) found that both general education and segregated placements have been upheld in different cases. The courts have appeared to recognize that there is no "one size fits all" standard for the most appropriate placement of a child, and they have reaffirmed the need for a continuum of placements, as required by law. Further, in *Clyde K. v. Puyallup School District No. 3* (1994), the 9th Circuit Court found that not only were the plaintiff's educational needs more effectively met in a segregated setting, but also he had become socially isolated in the general education classroom.

Understanding full inclusion

It should be noted at this point that the legislation and litigation previously cited focused primarily on the concept of LRE. The inclusion movement stemmed from but also broadened the concept of LRE. Although the term *inclusion* has become common in the discussion of the placement of students who are eligible for special education services, it has no legal definition. It does *not* represent a *legal* requirement that every child should be educated in the same way or the same place (Bard, 1995). A broadly accepted definition for inclusion might be the one developed by the National Center on Educational Restructuring and Inclusion (1995), as follows:

> Inclusion is the provision of services to students with disabilities, including those with severe impairments, in the neighborhood school, in age-appropriate general education classes with the necessary support services and supplementary aids (for the child and the teacher) both to assure the child's success—academic, behavioral and social—and to prepare the child to participate as a full and contributing member of the society.
>
> (p. 3)

Full inclusion proponents have generally advocated for the total disbanding of special education and the merging of special and general education programs such that all children are educated in the same environment (e.g., Stainback & Stainback, 1984). The inclusion philosophy is reflected in the following excerpt from Downing (1996): "Although some children, especially those with severe and multiple disabilities, may have unique ways of learning, separating them from others who learn in a different way is unnecessary and could prevent them from achieving their full potential" (p. xii). As Block (1999) suggested, to many people, full inclusion has become a human rights issue and even a moral imperative, but "in their zest to promote inclusion, many inclusionists forgot about the child" (p. 31). Put another way, by blindly pursuing absolute adherence to a concept, inclusionists have neglected the educational and social needs of *individual* children.

Although inclusion is not a mandated public social policy per se, in that it is not codified in IDEA, it is a practice that affects the social relationships of individuals and their relationship to the society of which they are a part. This makes it a social policy. As such, inclusion can be analyzed using frameworks developed for conducting policy analyses.

Policy analysis of inclusion

When the analytical framework developed by Chambers (1993) is applied to inclusion, many notable weaknesses in this policy emerge. Chambers's framework directs us to disaggregate the policies in question into their component parts (operational characteristics) and examine them separately. Each part is then critically evaluated using value-based criteria to judge its effectiveness. This framework is especially useful in examining LRE and inclusion policies, because only by looking at the individual parts of these policies do we find their short-comings. In addition, Chambers's framework consistently prompts the analyst to consider the needs of diverse groups under each of the operational characteristics.

Characteristic 1: Policy goals and objectives

One of the evaluation criteria for policy goals and objectives is whether the goals are concerned with the end or outcome rather than only the means. Inclusion policy would seem to fail this criterion because it focuses on the *means* of providing the education rather than the *outcome*, which according to IDEA is that children with disabilities receive educational services that are "designed to meet their unique needs and prepare them for employment and independent living." The outcomes of full inclusion must therefore be considered as part of a policy analysis. Although perhaps representing an extreme view, an attendee with a disability at a round-table discussion held during a meeting of the Society for Disability Studies asserted the following: "The outcome of inclusion is exclusion. Inclusion is a conscious method to keep us from our identity and group identity formation" (Gilson *et al.*, 1997, p. 12). Even a less extreme analysis of full inclusion, as discussed next, indicates that inclusion by itself does not satisfy the stated legislational purpose of meeting the unique needs of children with disabilities.

Characteristic 2: Entitlement rules

To be effective, a policy must not result in the stigmatization and alienation of the individuals it was designed to help. Full inclusion subjects students to an environment in which they may be rejected consistently by their classmates and in which they are always in the minority group. As Charlton (1998) stated, these "groups exist as collectors of people whom the dominant culture selects for exclusion" (p. 81).

Researchers have suggested that this exclusion can be manifested in groups as early as the preschool age. In a study of inclusive preschool programs, Wolfberg *et al.* (1999, p. 78) noted,

A common thread of experience was that each child [with a disability] encountered either brief or prolonged periods of social isolation. In some cases, children with disabilities experienced isolation collectively, as a separate subculture formed within the dominant peer culture composed largely of typically developing peers.

The children in the Wolfberg *et al.* study had a diverse range of both visible and invisible disabilities (e.g., autism, Down syndrome, attention-deficit disorder [ADD], cerebral palsy, hearing impairment/cochlear implants). Not only did these children experience alienation from their nondisabled peers, but they also naturally congregated (across disability types) and provided support for one another. Unfortunately, the context in which they came together was generally a negative one—as the minority "out" group. When the other children in the class did interact with them, it was often in a "helping" role that reinforced a benefactor/recipient relationship between the nondisabled children and the children with disabilities.

Another recent investigation indicated that the isolation does not improve and may actually worsen as children advance through the upper elementary grades. Hall and McGregor (2000) examined the peer relationships that developed between three children with disabilities and their nondisabled peers in an inclusive setting and compared the former's levels of social isolation in kindergarten and Grade 1 with the same levels in Grades 4 through 6. The authors found that the children experienced fewer reciprocal peer relationships during the upper elementary grades and that "in contrast to typical peers during preadolescence, the focal children in this study spent less time in large-group activities, more time alone, and received fewer nominations as preferred playmate" (p. 125). The children with disabilities met the definition of *neglected social status* (Wentzel & Ascher, 1995). In this study as well, one of the main contexts in which any interaction between nondisabled children and children with disabilities occurred was that of helper/recipient.

Foster (1987) conducted a study of the mainstreaming experiences of a group of deaf high school students. She found that many of these students, like the younger students discussed previously, felt "lonely and left out" (p. 3) in regards to social interactions. Perhaps more important, though, she found that the study participants also encountered a range of obstacles and challenges to their *academic* success. These findings suggest that "while there is a formal dimension to classroom learning, there is also a less clearly defined but equally important informal dimension to learning" (p. 17). According to Foster, this informal dimension includes discussion with class-mates, teamwork, and out-of-class study or information sharing, activities in which students with disabilities were often not included. Foster suggested that classroom supports provided by the school system in inclusive settings are not very successful in facilitating these informal interactions that are so necessary to the learning process.

Finally, a personal account by a person with a disability reinforces the fact that a feeling of loneliness exists *throughout* the various levels of an inclusionary education:

As a survivor of "inclusion" in neighborhood schools for nine years, my most vivid [re] collection of this process was how excluded I felt . . . I was subjected to ridicule from my peers, I was painfully and constantly made aware of my disability. . . . Many of my Deaf colleagues and I still bear many emotional scars and continue to feel socially dysfunctional in many ways from such an experience.

(Carver, 1994)

Ohlson (2001), who is a parent of a child with a disability, wrote, "Mainstreaming isn't so bad if you're part of the mainstream. . . . I take little solace in the possibility that all those other kids got a lesson in compassion by being around Matt" (p. 4). In fact, many students with disabilities who have previously attended inclusionary programs in public schools and then enrolled in private, segregated special education programs related that they did not have any friends until they changed schools (Ohlson, 2001; Pierce, 1994).

Characteristic 3: Service delivery systems

Two criteria for examining the service delivery system are relevant in analyzing inclusion policies. The first of these is *accessibility*. According to Chambers (1993), cultural differences can hamper the access clients have to important benefits and services. One recommendation for addressing this problem is the use of *indigenous workers*, which in the context of education means teachers, paraprofessionals, and allied health providers with disabilities.

The literature on inclusion has not made any reference to the importance of teachers and other role models with disabilities for the positive educational experiences of children with disabilities. Part D of the 1997 amendments to IDEA does address the marked shortage of teachers representing racial minorities (specifying African American and Hispanic individuals) and the need to increase their numbers to more effectively meet the needs of the growing numbers of African American and Hispanic students in special education programs. IDEA even funds initiatives to train and recruit minority teachers. Although some, even many, students in special education are members of racial minorities, *all* of them have disabilities. Does it not seem obvious that recruiting teachers with disabilities is even more essential? Neither inclusion policy nor IDEA addresses this critical and fundamental need, however. In fact, Charlton (1998) noted that he has several colleagues and friends who were told they could not become teachers simply because they used wheelchairs. A cultural view of disability clearly indicates that teachers with disabilities are uniquely qualified to meet the needs of their students in a culturally sensitive manner. Charlton illustrated this point when he wrote that other colleagues and friends who are deaf went through 12 years of school without ever once having had a teacher proficient in sign language. According to Charlton, "They were told that it was good for them because they should learn to read lips" (p. 32).

Perhaps an even more compelling reason to recruit and retain teachers with disabilities was provided by Groch (1994). She found that although students with disabilities who attended school in segregated settings had stronger interpersonal links with other children who had disabilities, they were less likely to develop a strong oppositional consciousness, which Groch believes to be a prerequisite for taking social action. Groch contended that part of the reason this consciousness did not form is that the segregated programs were administered and operated by nondisabled professionals. Students who have teachers with disabilities will be much more likely to associate a positive status with having a disability. Recently, the Office of Special Education and Rehabilitative Services [OSERS] perhaps became aware of this issue and began awarding bonus points to research and personnel-preparation grant applicants who demonstrated that they would recruit and advance staff members with disabilities (OSERS, 1999).

The second of Chambers's criteria for evaluating the effectiveness of service delivery systems is the *ability to relate to diversity in client populations.* Chambers suggested that access to appropriate services for certain groups can be increased by developing separate systems to serve their needs exclusively. Clearly, the establishment of a special education system with a full continuum or array of services follows this strategy.

Some people, including Judy Heumann, the former assistant secretary of the federal Office of Special Education and Rehabilitative Services, have compared special education to racially segregated programs (cited in Pierce, 1994). Using this analogy, they have argued that special education, like racially segregated education, is not "separate but equal." This argument is spurious because unlike racially segregated education, special education was created to help the many children with disabilities who have *unique educational needs* related to those disabilities. Arguably, even education for children whose disabilities do not affect their learning style could be "unequal" because the opportunity to develop a disability identity remains a unique need for these children. As one professional put it, "We live in a diverse culture, and the ordinary classroom should reflect our diversity, but it should not trivialize it" (Schroeder, 1993).

Negative aspects of special education, such as lower academic standards and expectations for children with disabilities or the use of special education classrooms as a "dumping ground" for problem students, do exist, of course (e.g., Shapiro, 1993). Full inclusion proponents have repeatedly focused on these shortcomings as a reason to disband the entire system. Conversely, full inclusion opponents have used related arguments about the shortcomings of full inclusion to justify the complete abandonment of this effort. The more logical choice, however, seems to be to find a middle ground that is sensitive to the needs of children with disabilities and provides a quality educational experience for them.

Additional considerations

A final pair of analytical frameworks that can be applied to the evaluation of inclusion as a policy were discussed by Skrtic, Sailor, and Gee (1996). These authors cited Boulding's (1967) work in which it was claimed that social policy should be concerned with building an inclusive system, one that "includes those aspects of social life that are . . . justified by [an] appeal to . . . identity or community . . . to build the identity of a person around some community with which he [*sic*] is associated" (p. 7). Skrtic went on to cite Moroney's (1981) analytical framework to explain that identity and inclusion must be central to social policy because their opposite— alienation—threatens community itself. Although Skrtic *et al.* used these analytical frameworks in support of inclusion as a policy, the frameworks actually seem to support the policy of fostering a disability culture even more strongly. For example, I have suggested in this article that children with disabilities need the opportunity to develop an integrated identity that incorporates their disability and that such integration is facilitated by interaction with other children who have disabilities. I have also documented that full inclusion can lead—and has led—to feelings of alienation for many children with disabilities.

What, then, are the best strategies for supporting disability culture, increasing the effectiveness of educational experiences for children with disabilities, and recognizing the importance of integration as a civil right? It is not necessary to take an "all or nothing" stance, refuting the value of any level of inclusion. I do, however, dispute the practice of *full* educational inclusion at the expense of any opportunity for segregated educational experiences. The great majority of children with disabilities have the opportunity to interact with the nondisabled population not only at school but also in their homes and communities. On the other hand, they may have no opportunity other than school to interact with their peers with disabilities.

Some individuals might suggest that school-sponsored segregated clubs or extracurricular activities would suffice for this interactional opportunity. Such clubs and extracurricular activities are not typically offered at the elementary school level, however. At the secondary level, clubs represent one way to foster disability identity, but they should not necessarily replace other opportunities for school-related interactions. Clubs by themselves do not address Foster's (1987) finding that "informal" learning is an important aspect of the educational process that may be missed by students with disabilities in an inclusive classroom. Segregated programs are not only about identity, they are about learning.

In the following section I identify some recommendations for improved practices that might provide a foundation for future policies that incorporate the positive aspects of both inclusive and segregated settings. These suggestions demonstrate that special education as defined in IDEA can work and that the breach between full inclusion and segregation can be narrowed peacefully and productively.

Suggested improved practices

1   Parents, teachers, and administrators must begin to recognize and learn about disability culture and its importance in the emotional and social development of children with disabilities. They should work to provide opportunities for children with disabilities to interact in meaningful ways.
2   Special education teachers and other service providers with disabilities must be aggressively recruited because they are the most qualified to understand disability culture and to serve as appropriate role models for their students.
3   Schools must establish high educational expectations for all students and be held accountable for the results. The National Council on Disability (1996) has endorsed this practice.
4   School systems must provide a full range (or continuum) of placement options that are consistent with IDEA. Many groups, including the National Education Association (1999), the Council for Exceptional Children (1993), and the Learning Disabilities Association (1993), have endorsed this recommendation. A further suggestion in this area is that the term *continuum* be changed to *array*. The former word connotes an ordered sequence of placements from most segregated to least segregated, suggesting a hierarchy of classes in which students graduate or get promoted to higher and higher (more segregated) levels. An array, on the other hand, implies a *range* of services, none inherently better than any other, from which a person can choose the service that best meets his or her needs.
5   As suggested by students at the National Summit on Disability Policy (NCD, 1996), if students with disabilities decide to form peer groups or clubs, school administrators should support them. In addition, all students should participate in a curriculum that covers the Americans with Disabilities Act, the history of disability culture, positive attitudes, listening skills, patience, and appropriate terminology (NCD, 1996). I would add self-advocacy to this list.

Perhaps the parent of a child with a disability said it best (personal communication, February 13, 2001):

I have observed that Jessica [her daughter, who has cerebral palsy] enjoys being in situations that she is not the only one with a disability. She actually WANTS to attend programs that are only for children with disabilities. I'm sure part of this is because for once everyone isn't in a hurry and things may be more in her time frame. I think there needs to be opportunity for kids with disabilities to interact with other children and adults with disabilities, but that those opportunities need to be with a positive approach toward disability. So often when we have found groups of kids with disabilities they tend to be "special groups" (Special Olympics, special camps) and the volunteers assisting with those groups want to *help* those special children. . . . So I guess I have mixed feelings. . . . I do agree [that children with disabilities should have the opportunity to interact in their own time and space in school]; I also do know that inclusion is important and has great benefits. So, what is the answer . . . some of each I suppose.

Author's note

The author would like to thank Rosemary Chapin, Daryl Mellard, Kathy Parker, Belinda Schuman, Julie Tollefson, Rud Turnbull, and three anonymous reviewers for their comments on various drafts of this article and especially Gary Clark for his comments and support. She would also like to thank the two parents who provided personal accounts of their children's experiences in school.

Note

All names have been changed.

References

Bard, J. F. (1995). *Pennsylvania inclusion policy* (State Basic Education Circular BEC-2-95). Retrieved October 4, 1999, from www.kidstogether.org/ed_policy.html

Barnartt, S. N. (1996). Disability culture or disability consciousness? *Journal of Disability Policy Studies, 79*(2), 1–19.

Block, M. E. (1999). Did we jump on the wrong bandwagon? Problems with inclusion in physical education. *Palaestra, 15*(3), 30–36.

Boulding, K. (1967). The boundaries of social policy. *Social Work, 12,* 3–11.

Braddock, D., Hemp, R., Parish, S., Westrich, J., & Park, H. (1998). The state of the states in developmental disabilities: Summary of the study. In D. Braddock (Ed.), *The state of the states in developmental disabilities* (pp. 22–53). Washington, DC: American Association on Mental Retardation.

Carver, R. (1994, December). Inclusion or illusion? *DCS Newsletter,* November/December 1994. Retrieved October 6, 1999, from http://dww.deafworldweb.org/pub/c/rjc/inclusion.html

Chambers, D. E. (1993). *Social policy and social programs: A method for the practical public policy analyst* (2nd ed.). New York: Macmillan.

Charlton, J. I. (1998). *Nothing about us without us: Disability oppression and empowerment.* Berkeley: University of California Press.

Council for Exceptional Children. (1993, April). *Statement on inclusive schools and communities.* Reston, VA: Author.

Clyde K. v. Puyallup School District No. 3, 35 F.3d 1396 (9th Cir. 1994).

Downing, J. E. (1996). *Including students with severe and multiple disabilities in typical classrooms.* Baltimore: Brookes

Education for All Handicapped Children Act of 1975, 20 U.S.C. § 1400 *et seq.*

Foster, S. (1987). *Life in the mainstream: Reflections of deaf college freshmen on their experiences in the mainstreamed high school.* Rochester, NY: National Technical Institute for the Deaf.

Gill, C. (1995). A psychological view of disability culture. *Disability Studies Quarterly, 15*(4), 16–19.

Gill, C. (1997). Four types of integration in disability identity development. *Journal of Vocational Rehabilitation, 9,* 39–46.

Gill, C. (1999). Disability culture: A framework for understanding disability, family and community. *The Disability Messenger, 11.*

Gilson, S. F., Tusler, A., & Gill, C. (1997). Ethnographic research in disability identity: Self-determination and community. *Journal of Vocational Rehabilitation, 9,* 7–17.

Groch, S. A. (1994). Oppositional consciousness: Its manifestations and development. The case of people with disabilities. *Sociological Inquiry, 64,* 369–395.

Gwin, L. (2000). *Incoming! Watch out!* Retrieved March 19, 2001, from http://www.mouthmag.com/number60/number60.htm

Hall, L. J., & McGregor, J. A. (2000). A follow-up study of the peer relationships of children with disabilities in an inclusive school. *The Journal of Special Education, 34,* 114–126, 153.

Harris & Associates. (1986). *The ICD survey of disabled Americans: Bringing disabled Americans into the mainstream.* New York: Author.

Individuals with Disabilities Education Act Amendments of 1997, 20 U.S.C. § 1401.

Kemp, J. (1999, May). *Keynote address.* Presentation at the ADA Symposium, Kansas City, MO.

Learning Disabilities Association. (1993, January). *Position paper on full inclusion of all students with learning disabilities in the regular education classroom.* Pittsburgh, PA: Author.

Lipsky, D. K., & Gartner, A. (1996). Inclusion, school restructuring, and the remaking of American society. *Harvard Educational Review, 66,* 762–796.

Moroney, R. M. (1981). Policy analysis within a value theoretical framework. In R. Haskins & J. J. Gallagher (Eds.), *Models for analysis of social policy: An introduction* (pp. 78–101). Norwood, NJ: Ablex.

National Center on Educational Restructuring and Inclusion. (1995). *National study of inclusive education.* New York: City University of New York.

National Council on Disability. (1996). *Achieving independence: The challenge for the 21st century.* Washington, DC: Author.

National Education Association. (1999). *Policy statement on appropriate inclusion.* Retrieved October 4, 1999, from http://helpfrom.nea.org/publiced/idea/ideaplcy.html

National Information Center for Children and Youth with Disabilities. (1996, October). The education of children and youth with special needs: What do the laws say? [Electronic version]. *NICHY News Digest, 15.*

Office of Special Education and Rehabilitative Services. (1999). Notice Inviting Applications for Fiscal Year (FY) 2000. 64 Fed. Reg. 167, 47310–47330.

Ohlson, K. (2001, April 5). *Faith in the baby*. Retrieved April 6, 2001, from http://www.salon.com/mwt/feature/2001/04/05/faith/index.html

Paradis, L. (1998, December). Beyond fear and pity. *Mainstream*, 15–19.

Pierce, B. (1994). Are specialized educational settings for children with disabilities immoral? *The Braille Monitor*, February 1994. Retrieved November 1, 1999, from http://www.nfb.org/brlm9411.htm

Pfeiffer, D. (1993). Overview of the disability movement: History, legislative record, and policy implications. *Policy Studies Journal, 21*, 724–734.

Schroeder, F. (1993, July). *Mainstreaming, schools for the blind, and full inclusion: What shall the future of education for blind children be?* Presentation at the 1993 National Federation for the Blind National Convention, Dallas, TX.

Scotch, R. K. (1984) *From good will to civil rights: Transforming federal disability policy*. Philadelphia: Temple University Press.

Shapiro, J. (1993). *No pity*. New York. Random House.

Skrtic, T. M., Sailor, W., & Gee, K. (1996). Voice, collaboration, and inclusion: Democratic themes in educational and social reform initiatives. *Remedial and Special Education, 17*, 142–157.

Stainback, S., & Stainback, W. (1984). A rationale for the merger of special and regular education. *Exceptional Children, 51*, 102–111.

Thomas, S. B., & Rapport, M. J. K. (1998). Least restrictive environment: Understanding the direction of the courts. *The Journal of Special Education, 32*, 66–78.

Topeka Independent Living Resource Center. (2000). *TILRC news*. Retrieved July 12, 2001, from http://www.tilrc.org/docs/national2.html

Wentzel, K. R., & Ascher, S. R. (1995). The academic lives of neglected, rejected, popular, and controversial children. *Child Development, 66*, 754–763.

Wolfberg, P. J., Zercher, C., Lieber, J., Capell, K., Matias, S., et al. (1999). "Can I play with you?" Peer culture in inclusive preschool programs. *Journal of the Association for Persons with Severe Handicaps, 24*(2), 69–84.

6

CAPITALISM, DISABILITY, AND IDEOLOGY

A materialist critique of the Normalization principle

Michael J. Oliver

Source: R. J. Flynn and R. A. Lemay (eds), *A Quarter-Century of Normalization and Social Role Valorization: Evolution and Impact*, Ottawa: University of Ottawa Press, 1999, pp. 163–73.

1 Introduction

At the outset, I should say two things. I have no particular interest in the history of Normalization and, therefore, I am not attempting to provide a revisionist history of it. Neither do I think that Normalization, nor Social Role Valorization as it has become in its reincarnation, has much to offer in developing a social theory of disability. I am interested, however, in the oppression of disabled people in capitalist societies and what Normalization does, or rather does not, say about it.

This interest has led me to begin to sketch out what a social theory of disability might look like (Oliver, 1990). For me, all social theory must be judged on three interrelated elements: its adequacy in describing experience; its ability to explain experience; and, finally, its potential to transform experience. My own theorizing on disability is located in Marxist political economy, which, I would argue, offers a much more adequate basis for describing and explaining experience than does Normalization theory, which is based upon interactionist and functionalist sociology.

In fact I would go further and argue that the social theory that underpins Marxist political economy has far greater transformative potential in eradicating the oppression that disabled people face throughout the world than the interactionist and functionalist theories that underpin Normalization ever can have. And I will go even further than that and argue that already this theory has had a far greater influence on the struggles that disabled people are themselves currently engaged in to remove the chains of that oppression than Normalization, which is, at best, a bystander in these struggles and, at worst, part of the process of oppression itself.

In presenting this argument, I will begin by articulating my own theoretical position based upon Marxist political economy and hereinafter referred to as materialist theory. I will then demonstrate the inadequacies of Normalization theory's explanation of the rise of the institution before going on to provide a critique of the ideology that underpins it. Next, I will take issue with the argument that Normalization has been successful because it is based upon "experience." Finally, I will look at what both Normalization and materialist theories say about change, having briefly described the appalling material conditions under which disabled people live throughout the world.

Before proceeding further, it is perhaps necessary to explain the use of terminology in this chapter. Underpinning it is a materialist view of society; to say that the category "disability" is produced by capitalist society in a particular form implies a particular worldview. Within this worldview, the production of the category "disability" is no different from the production of motor cars or hamburgers. Each has an industry, whether it be the car, fast food, or human service. Each industry has a workforce that has a vested interest in producing their product in particular ways and in exerting as much control over the process of production as possible.

2 Producing a materialist theory of disability

The production of disability, therefore, is nothing more or less than a set of activities specifically geared toward producing a good—the category "disability"—supported by a range of political actions that create the conditions to allow these productive activities to take place and underpinned by a discourse that gives legitimacy to the whole enterprise. As to the specifics of the terminology used in this discourse, I use the term "disabled people" generically and refuse to divide the group in terms of medical conditions, functional limitation, or severity of impairment. For me, disabled people are defined in terms of three criteria: (a) they have an impairment; (b) they experience oppression as a consequence; and (c) they identify themselves as disabled persons.

Using the generic term does not mean that I do not recognize differences in experience within the group, but that in exploring this we should start from the ways oppression differentially impacts on different groups of people rather than the differences in experience among individuals with different impairments. I agree that my own initial outlining of a materialist theory of disability (Oliver, 1990) did not specifically include an examination of the oppression that people with learning difficulties face (and I use this particular term throughout my paper because it is the one that democratic and accountable organizations of people with learning difficulties insist on).

Nevertheless, I agree that "For a rigorous theory of disability to emerge which begins to examine all disability in a materialist account, an analysis of Normalization must be included" (Chappell, 1992, p. 38).

Attempting to incorporate Normalization in a materialist account, however, does not mean that I believe that beyond the descriptive it is of much use. Based as it is upon functionalist and interactionist sociology, whose defects are well known (Gouldner, 1971), it offers no satisfactory explanation of why disabled people are oppressed in capitalist societies and no strategy for liberating us from the chains of that oppression.

Political economy, on the other hand, suggests that all phenomena (including social categories) are produced by the economic and social forces of capitalism itself. The forms in which they are produced are ultimately dependent upon their relationship to the economy (Marx, 1913). Hence, the category "disability" is produced in the particular form it appears by these very economic and social forces. Further, it is produced as an economic problem because of changes in the nature of work and the needs of the labor market within capitalism.

> The speed of factory work, the enforced discipline, the time-keeping and production norms—all these were a highly unfavorable change from the slower, more self-determined methods of work into which many handicapped people had been integrated.
>
> (Ryan & Thomas, 1980, p. 101)

The economy, through both the operation of the labor market and the social organization of work, plays a key role in producing the category "disability" and in determining societal responses to disabled people. In order to explain this further, it is necessary to return to the crucial question of what is meant by political economy. The following is a generally agreed definition of political economy:

> The study of the interrelationships between the polity, economy and society, or more specifically, the reciprocal influences among government . . . the economy, social classes, state, and status groups. The central problem of the political economy perspective is the manner in which the economy and polity interact in a relationship of reciprocal causation affecting the distribution of social goods.
>
> (Estes, Swan, & Gerard, 1982)

The central problem with such an agreed definition is that it is an explanation that can be incorporated into pluralist visions of society as a consensus emerging out of the interests of various groups and social forces and, indeed, this explanation has been encapsulated in a recent book on disability:

> A person's position in society affects the type and severity of physical disability one is likely to experience and more importantly the likelihood that he or she is likely to receive rehabilitation services. Indeed, the political economy of a community dictates what debilitating health conditions will be produced, how and under what circumstances they will be defined, and ultimately who will receive the services.
>
> (Albrecht, 1992, p. 14)

This quote lays out the way in which Albrecht pursues his argument in three parts. The first part shows how the kind of society people live in influences the kinds of disability that are produced, notably how the mode of production creates particular kinds of impairments. Further, he traces the ways in which the mode of production influences social interpretation and the meanings of disability and he also demonstrates how, in industrial societies, rehabilitation, like all other goods and services, is transformed into a commodity.

The second part of the argument shows how intermediate social institutions in America, such as the legal, political, and welfare systems, contribute to the specific way in which disability is produced, and their role in the transformation of rehabilitation into a commodity.

The final part considers what this may mean in terms of future developments in social policy and what effects it may have on the lives of disabled people.

It is difficult to disagree with this formulation at the descriptive level, but the problem with this pluralist version of political economy is that the structure of capitalist America itself goes unexamined as does the crucial role that the capitalist economy plays in shaping the experience of groups and individuals. Exactly the same criticism can be leveled at Normalization theory. Devaluation according to Normalization theory is a universal cognitive process, and economic and social conditions are only relevant to who gets devalued.

Political economy, as it is used here, takes a particular theoretical view of society, one that sees the economy as the crucial, and ultimately determining, factor in structuring the lives of groups and individuals. Further, while the relationship between various groups and the economy may differ in qualitative ways, the underlying structural relationship remains.

> The convergence and interaction of liberating forces at work in society against racism, sexism, ageism and economic imperialism are all oppressive "isms" and built-in responses of a society that considers certain groups inferior. All are rooted in the social-economic structures

of society. All deprive certain groups of status, the right to control their own lives and destinies with the end result of powerlessness. All have resulted in economic and social discrimination. All rob (American) society of the energies and involvement of creative persons who are needed to make our society just and humane. All have brought on individual alienation, despair, hostility, and anomie.

(Walton, 1979, p. 9)

Hence, the oppression that disabled people face is rooted in the economic and social structures of capitalism. And this oppression is structured by racism, sexism, homophobia, ageism, and disablism, which is endemic to all capitalist societies and cannot be explained away as a universal cognitive process. To explain this further it is necessary to go back to the roots of capitalism itself.

3 Disabled people and the rise of capitalism

Whatever the fate of disabled people before the advent of capitalist society and whatever their fate will be in the brave new world of the 21st century, with its coming we suffered economic and social exclusion. As a consequence of this exclusion, disability was produced in a particular form: as an individual problem requiring medical treatment.

At the heart of this exclusion was the institution—something on which we would all agree. In the 19th and 20th centuries, institutions prolifer-ated in all industrial societies (Rothman, 1971) but to describe this, as Wolfensberger does, as "momentum without rationale" (Wolfensberger, chapter 3, p. 48) is patently absurd. The French Marxist Louis Althusser (1971) suggested that all capitalist societies are faced with the problem of social control, and they resolve this by a combination of repressive and ideological mechanisms.

The reason for the success of the institution is simple: It combines these mechanisms almost perfectly. It is repressive in that all those who either cannot or will not conform to the norms and discipline of capitalist soci-ety can be removed from it. It is ideological in that it stands as a visible monument for all those who currently conform but may not continue to do so—if you do not behave, the institution awaits you.

It is for this reason that the institution has been successful. Its presence perfectly meets capitalism's needs for discipline and control (Foucault, 1972). It is also the reason that, despite the fact that the defects of institutions have been known for the 200 years that they have existed, they have remained unaddressed. Indeed, the principle of "less eligibility" was central to the rise of the institution. It is simply not true to say that we have only known of their defects in recent years because, if this were the case, they would then not have been performing their ideological control function. Day trips to institutions, which originated in the 1850s, not the 1950s, were precisely for this purpose; to demonstrate how awful they were for the purposes of social control, not to educate the public about their reform (Wolfensberger, chapter 3, p. 50).

What is also not in dispute between us is that in the second half of the 20th century, the physical and ideological dominance of the institution began to decline (Scull, 1977). What is in dispute, however, is why this should be so. While not claiming that the Normalization principle was the only causal factor in what has become known as deinstitutionalization or decarceration, Wolfensberger (chapter 3) nonetheless claims that it "broke the back of the institutional movement" (p. 72) and without it "there would have been massive investments in building new, smaller, regionalized institutions" (p. 53). I would not wish to dismiss the role of ideas or, more appropriately, ideologies in this process, but there were other more important factors.

Most importantly, the rising costs of institutional care were becoming a major factor in the shift to community-based care. Ideology was turned into political action when this, along with other factors such as rising oil prices, spiraling arms expenditure, and so on, brought about fiscal crises in many capitalist states (O'Connor, 1973; Gough, 1979). This fiscal crisis explanation stands in stark contrast to Wolfensberger's (chapter 3) assertion that while deinstitutionalization may have started in the 1950s, it was a "drift that occurred without much planning, intent or consciousness" (p. 89).

The transition to late capitalism (the postindustrial society, as some writers have called it, or its more recent fashionable manifestation as postmodernity) has seen this process continue apace. The question it raises is what does this process mean. Cohen suggests that it "is thought by some to represent a questioning, even a radical reversal of that earlier transformation, by others merely to signify a continuation and intensification of its patterns" (1985, p. 13).

Those who have promoted the idea of Normalization would, I suspect, place themselves in the first camp. That is to say, the move from the institution to the community is part of a process of removing some of the apparatus of social control by the state. I would place myself in the latter camp, seeing this move as an extension of the processes of control within the capitalist state.

After all, the balance of power between disabled people and professionals has not changed at all. The situation described by Cohen (1985) remains unchanged:

> much the same groups of experts are doing much the same business as usual. The basic rituals incorporated into the move to the mind—taking case histories, writing social enquiry reports, constructing files, organizing case conferences—are still being enacted.
>
> (p. 152)

In the world of late capitalism, the same people, albeit with different job titles and perhaps in plusher buildings, are doing the same things to disabled people, although they may now be calling them "doing a needs-led assessment" or "producing a care plan" in Britain. Elsewhere it may be called individual program planning, social brokerage, change agentry, and the like. But the material fact remains, it is still professionals doing it, whatever "it" is called, to disabled people.

4 The ideology of normalization

All social changes require an ideology to support the economic rationality underpinning them. So the ideology underpinning the rise of the institution was ultimately a medical and a therapeutic one; accordingly, placing people in institutions was not only good for the health of individuals, it was also good for the health of society. Normalization, it could be argued, is the ideology (or one of the ideologies) that allowed people to be returned to the community in that they can be "normalized" or, in its later variant, be allocated normal (valued) social roles. After all, we do not want the different, the deviant, or even the dangerous returned to our communities.

I fully realize that here I am stepping on dangerous ground and that both Wolfensberger (chapter 3) and Nirje (1993) would probably argue that I am confusing normal with Normalization. There is not the space to demonstrate that I realize that this is not the case nor to draw attention to their own published ambiguities on this issue. Instead, I wish to point out that Normalization is part of a discourse that is predicated on the normal/abnormal distinction, and it is certainly clear that Wolfensberger (chapter 3) thinks this distinction is real rather than socially constructed (p. 88).

A materialist approach to this would suggest, as does the French philosopher Foucault (1973), that the way we talk about the world and the way we experience it are inextricably linked—the names we give to things shape our experience of them and our experience of things in the world influences the names we give to them. Hence, our practices of normalizing people and normalizing services both construct and maintain the normal/abnormal dichotomy.

It is becoming clear that the social structures of late capitalist societies cannot be discussed in a discourse of normality/abnormality because what characterizes them is difference: differences based on gender, ethnic background, sexual orientation, abilities, religious beliefs, wealth, age, access or nonaccess to work, and so on. And in societies founded on oppression, these differences crosscut and intersect each other in ways they have not even begun to properly understand, let alone try to resolve (Zarb & Oliver, 1993).

The concept of simultaneous oppression (Stuart, 1993) may offer a more adequate way of understanding differences within the generic category of disability. Certainly, people are beginning to talk about their experience in this way.

> As a black disabled woman, I cannot compartmentalise or separate aspects of my identity in this way. The collective experience of my race, disability and gender are what shape and inform my life.
>
> (Hill, 1994, p. 7)

Kirsten Hearn provides a poignant account of how disabled lesbians and gay men are excluded from all their potential communities. First, "the severely able-bodied community and straight disabled community virtually ignored our campaign" (1991, p. 30) and, "issues of equality are not fashionable for the majority of the severely able-bodied, white, middle-class lesbian and gay communities" (1991, p. 33).

The point that I am making is that the discourse of Normalization (whatever the intent of its major proponents and however badly they feel it has been misused by its disciples) can never adequately describe or explain societies characterized by difference because of its reductionist views of both humanity and society. Individual and group differences cannot be described solely in terms of the normality/abnormality dichotomy, and inegalitarian social structures cannot be explained by reference only to valued and devalued social roles. Normalization can also never serve to transform peoples' lives, a point to which I shall return.

5 The role of experience

In explaining why the idea of Normalization was so powerful for many people, Wolfensberger (chapter 3) claims that it connected with their common sense, it gave them a language or discourse in which to talk about the issues, and it gave them a "unified mental scheme" (social theory) connecting a range of issues (p. 72). Of course, in talking about this he is talking about the connection of these ideas to the experience of academics, professionals, and policy makers, not to the experience of people with learning difficulties.

He also claims that "a single theory or principle could be applied to all; not only to all retarded people and not only to all handicapped people but to all deviant ones" (p. 71). I remember attending the first conference on Normalization in Britain in the mid-1970s when such claims were made. A colleague and I vociferously denied the claim that the half-digested mishmash of functionalist and interactionist sociology we were being presented with had anything to do with our experiences as disabled people.

Our claims were, of course, denied, as they often have been in the past, on the grounds that as isolated, elite disabled individuals, our experiences did not accord with those of the majority of disabled people (a basis on which you may wish to deny my claims in this paper). And, of course, the Normalization bandwagon rolled on in Britain, into social service departments, health authorities, and undemocratic voluntary organizations. But not into the newly emerging democratic and accountable organizations that disabled people were setting up at the time. To this day, not a single one of these organizations of disabled people has adopted the Normalization principle as the basis for its operations or as a rationale for its existence.

Our experiences at that conference mirrored our experience in terms of disability politics more generally. We were already being told by groups of able-bodied experts that not only did they know best what our problems were, they also knew best how to solve them. And disabled people were developing our own views both on those experts who wished to define or colonize our experience and to identify what our problems really were. These views were encapsulated in "a little red book" called *Fundamental Principles of Disability* (UPIAS, 1976), which, I would argue, is far more important for disabled people than all the publications on Normalization put together.

This slim volume is not widely available, but the debt that disabled people owe to it is enormous. I, and many other disabled people, openly acknowledge our debt to the document in the way it shaped our own understanding of disability (Oliver, 1995). Because the document has never been widely available, and with the demise of the Union in 1991, it will become increasingly difficult to obtain. I reproduce two passages here, the first of which exposes the role of "experts" in our lives and the second which defines our own problems for us.

> The Union maintains that, far from being too concerned with the cause of disability, the "experts" in the field have never concerned themselves with the real cause at all. The fact that they had delusions that they were looking at the cause, when they were typically concentrating on its effects, on confusing disability with physical impairment, underlines the imperative need for disabled people to become their own experts. It is only when we begin to grasp this expertise that disabled people will be able to see through the "experts'" attempt to disguise as something "entirely different" the traditional, clearly failed, "spontaneous" struggle against aspects of disability, such as poverty.
>
> Disability is something imposed on top of our impairments by the way we are unnecessarily isolated and excluded from full participation in society. Disabled people are therefore an oppressed group in society. To understand this it is necessary to grasp the distinction between the physical impairment and the social situation, called "disability," of people with such impairment. Thus we define impairment as lacking part of or all of a limb, or having a defective limb, organ or mechanism of the body; and disability as the disadvantage or restriction of activity

caused by a contemporary social organization which takes no or little account of people who have physical impairments and thus excludes them from participation in the mainstream of social activities. Physical disability is therefore a particular form of social oppression.

It was from this work that I and a number of other disabled people began to write and talk about the social model of disability. For my own part, I originally conceptualized models of disability as the binary distinction between what I chose to call the individual and social models of disability (Oliver, 1983). This was no amazing new insight on my part dreamed up in some ivory tower, but was really an attempt to enable me to make sense of the world for the social work students and other professionals I was teaching at the time. The idea of the individual and the social model was taken quite simply and explicitly from the distinction originally made between impairment and disability by the Union of the Physically Impaired Against Segregation in the *Fundamental Principles* document (1976).

The articulation of this new view of disability did not receive universal acceptance. Originally, it was professionals, policy makers, and staff from organizations for disabled people who, because they had vested interests in maintaining the status quo underpinned by the individual model, questioned the experiential validity and explanatory reliability of the social model. However, we have seen a paradigm shift, and many professional bodies and groups have now come to espouse the social model, in theory at least (DHSS, 1988; Gillespie-Sells & Campbell, 1991). Whether it has had much impact on professional practice is another question altogether and beyond the scope of this paper.

The articulation of the social model was received much more enthusiastically by disabled people because it made an immediate connection to their own experiences. It quickly became the basis for disability awareness and later disability equality training.

It was adopted by democratic disability organizations all over the world, including Disabled Peoples International (DPI) and the British Council of Organizations of Disabled People (BCODP), and remains central to their rationale.

In reading Wolfensberger's (chapter 3) comments about how *Changing Patterns* came to be written, I am struck by just how much in the way of economic resources (plane tickets, hotel bookings, secretarial support, etc.) went in to producing it. Similarly the World Health Organization has spent millions of pounds, dollars, and yen on trying to describe and classify us (Wood, 1980) and has lamentably failed.

Disabled people, whose intellectual labors have produced the social model, have done this without access to the kinds of resources available to international academic superstars, professionals, and policy makers, as well as the usual coterie of hangers-on and freeloaders. Imagine how much farther down the road we might be if disabled people had been given these resources to develop our own social theory, our own quality measures for human services, and our own classification schemes.

6 The material conditions of disabled people throughout the world

Developing materialist theory with respect to disability requires us to understand the material conditions under which disabled people live through-out the world. A recent UN report (Despouy, 1991) has confirmed earlier estimates that there are more than 500 million impaired persons in the world; that is 1 in 10 of the world's population. The report goes on to suggest that at least "25 per cent of the entire population are adversely affected by the presence of disabilities."

There have been very few international studies of the lives of disabled people although the UN report did come to the following conclusion:

these persons frequently live in deplorable conditions, owing to the presence of physical and social barriers which prevent their integration and full participation in the community. As a result, millions of disabled people throughout the world are segregated and deprived of virtually all their rights, and lead a wretched, marginal life.

(Despouy, 1991, p. 1)

It is possible to put some descriptive flesh on the bones of these figures, and what follows relies heavily on figures present in a recent special edition of the *New Internationalist* called "Disabled Lives" (1992).

Of the 500 million disabled people in the world, 300 million live in developing countries, and of these 140 million are children and 160 million are women. One in 5, that is 100 million of the total population of disabled people, are disabled by malnutrition. In the developing countries, only 1 in 100 disabled people have access to any form of rehabilitation and 80% of all disabled people live in Asia and the Pacific, but they receive just 2% of the total resources allocated to disabled people. In the Third World, the death rate of people with a spinal injury within 2 years of the injury is as high today as it was in the developed world before the Second World War.

While not being able to put an accurate figure onto it, there is no doubt that all over the world, there is a close link between disability and poverty.

malnutrition, mothers weakened by frequent childbirth, inadequate immunisation programmes, accidents in overcrowded homes, all con-tribute to an incidence of disability among poor people that is higher than among people living in easier circumstances. Furthermore, disability creates and exacerbates poverty by increasing isolation and economic strain, not just for the individual but for the family: there is little doubt that disabled people are amongst the poorest in poor countries.

(Coleridge, 1993, p. 64)

While in an absolute sense, the material conditions of disabled people in the developed world are vastly superior to their Third World counterparts, they still experience conditions of life far inferior to the rest of the population. Thus, for example, more than 60% of disabled people in both Britain and America currently live below the poverty line.

Labor markets in the developed world continue to discriminate to the point where disabled people are three times more likely to be unemployed than their able-bodied counterparts. In education, the majority of disabled children are still educated in segregated special schools and less than 3 in 1,000 disabled students end up in higher education, when, according to prevalence figures, it should be 100. On any indicator, disabled women and black disabled people fare worse than their white, male counterparts.

While the accuracy of some of these figures might be called into question with respect to both the developed and developing world, no one would deny that they paint an authentic picture of the lives of disabled people throughout the world. The point at issue is what can be done about producing the necessary changes. In the next section, I shall discuss the different positions of Normalization and materialist theories with respect to producing changes in the lives of disabled peuple.

7 Economic, political, and social change— how will it be delivered?

In comparing what Normalization and materialist theory have to offer with respect to these changes, I want to concentrate on three interrelated areas: change in individuals, change in social policy and welfare programs, and change through the political process.

Partly, I suspect, because of the unacknowledged impact that the social model has had, both Nirje and Wolfensberger are anxious to claim that Normalization does not mean making individuals normal. They go further and suggest that it can be applied even more fruitfully to environments. Wolfensberger, however, honestly admits that

as long as one grants that abnormalization abnormalizes a person, and not just the person's environment, . . . one cannot say that Normalization only normalizes life conditions . . . In short, I cannot see how Nirje's formulation allows an exclusion of actions on a person.

(chapter 3, p. 88)

93

It is the final sentence which raises issues of grave concern. The history of oppression is underpinned by allowing "actions on persons," and the crucial questions this raises are who decides, what actions, and which persons? To answer, as Normalization does, that prevailing life conditions, environments, and values are the ones into which to normalize individuals, begs huge questions and may take us down the road to death making, sterilization, physical torture, incarceration, and mind control. This list is part of our collective history as disabled people, as we are discovering as we begin to write this history, and not some emotive or exaggerated imagining to make a political point (Morris, 1991; Coleridge, 1993).

Materialist theory does not have the same problem with changing individuals, although it is their consciousness that it wants to change, not their bodies, their behavior, or their social roles. Transforming consciousness is a matter of changing personal experiences into political issues. This materialist theory does, and it also links the two: At the collective level, disabled people may "false consciously" believe that the difficulties they face are because of their individual impairments. Hence they "internalize oppression" (Sutherland, 1981; Morris, 1991) by believing that it is their fault that they cannot get a job, use public transport, and so on.

Social and individual transformations are inextricably linked. However, in materialist theory individuals must transform themselves through collective action, not be transformed by others who know what's best for them or what's best for society. Empowerment is a collective process of transformation on which the powerless embark as part of the struggle to resist the oppression of others, as part of their demands to be included, and/or to articulate their own views of the world. Central to this struggle is the recognition by the powerless that they are oppressed—first articulated with respect to disability by the Union of the Physically Impaired Against Segregation in the 1970s and more recently been given a theoretical reformulation within "oppression theory" more generally (Abberley, 1987).

Normalization theory sees improving human services as a major platform for improving the quality of life for disabled people, and, indeed, much time and energy is devoted to precisely this. Wolfensberger's position on this is unequivocal; he is vehemently opposed to services provided by institutions but has spent much of his working life developing and improving community-based services. As I suggested earlier, this is because he views community-based services as radically different from institutional ones in that they are not part of the social control apparatus of the state.

While his position on community-based human services may be unequivocal, it is certainly contradictory. In the paper he gave at the International Disability Conference in Bristol, in 1987, he came very close to taking a materialist position on all human services, not simply institutional ones, when he argued that their real purpose (latent function) was to provide employment for the middle classes, and in order to continue to do that, merely enlarging the human service empire is not sufficient to meet all the requirements that a post-primary production economy poses. In addition, one has to make all the services that do exist as unproductive as possible—indeed one has to make them counterproductive if at all possible, so that they create dependency, and so that they create impaired people rather than habilitate them.

(Wolfensberger, 1989, p. 34)

The problem with this formulation is that it mistakes the symptom for the problem. If human services under capitalism are part of the state apparatus of social control, as materialist theory would argue, the reason they employ the middle classes is simple: They are not the groups who pose a threat to capitalism and, therefore, they do not need to be controlled, but instead can become agents for the control of others.

It is precisely for this reason that the demands of disabled people all over the world are not, any longer, for improvements in existing services but for control over them. And, further, their struggles around welfare issues are about producing and controlling their own services through centers for independent living, direct payments to enable them to purchase these services for themselves, and peer counseling to enable them to develop the necessary skills and support to meet their own self-defined individual and collective needs. This is not an antiwelfare or antihuman-services position, but one that raises fundamental issues of who is in control and in whose interest.

In looking at the issue of political change, within Normalization theory it is difficult to find anything beyond descriptions of the kinds of things devalued people should be entitled to. How to achieve these entitlements at the political level is not really discussed although Wolfensberger (chapter 3) confidently asserts that if we want to valorize someone's social roles "we know from social science what the overarching strategies are through which this can be accomplished *if* that is what one wants to pursue" (p. 88).

I don't know what social science he is referring to, but I have to say that I know very few social scientists who are, any longer, convinced that the concept of social roles has very much value to the development of social theory let alone for the promotion of political action. Not only are Talcott Parsons and Erving Goffman dead in a material sense but so are their products, the macro and micro versions of role theory. One can only assume from Normalization writings that political change will be a gift from the powerful to powerless once they have come to a true understanding of disability through exposure to the teachings of Normalization and Social Role Valorization. Nowhere does Normalization acknowledge that

the conviction that one's group is worth fighting for has to come at least partly from within. The alternative is to wait passively for the

95

advantaged group to confer limited equality which does not essentially alter the status quo, and which it may be motivated to avoid.

(Dalley, 1992, p. 128)

Again, materialist theory is much more upfront about political change. It will only be achieved through struggle, and that struggle will be by oppressed groups themselves against the forces that oppress them. In order to do this, it is necessary for oppressed groups to organize collectively to confront this oppression. That inevitably means confrontation and conflict with powerful groups, interests, and structures, for there are few examples in human history of people willingly giving up power to others.

As far as disabled people are concerned, we have seen over the past 15 years disabled people coming together to organize themselves as a movement at local, national, and international levels. In Britain, for example, in order to harness this growing consciousness of disabled people, to provide a platform to articulate the redefinition of the problem of disability, and to give a focus to the campaigns for independent living and against discrimination, the British Council of Organizations of Disabled People (BCODP) was formed in 1981, and its success in the subsequent decade is entirely an achievement of disabled people themselves (Hasler, 1993). Its conception and subsequent development have been achieved without extensive financial support from government or from traditional organizations for disabled people. On the contrary, the BCODP was criticized from the start as being elitist, isolationist, unrepresentative, and Marxist by a collection of unrepresentative people with abilities, right- and left-wing academics, isolated and elitist staff and management of traditional organizations, and many professionals whose very careers were bound up with keeping disabled people dependent.

Yet despite these attacks, BCODP has gone from strength to strength, now representing over 90 organizations of disabled people and 300,000 disabled individuals. These initiatives not only established BCODP as the only representative voice of disabled people in Britain, but by its very success it stimulated an ever growing number of disabled people to adopt a disabled identity. Similar stories of the rise of the disability movement could be told from other parts of both the developing and the developed worlds.

With this growing sense of a collective, political identity has developed the self-confidence not simply to ask for the necessary changes, but to demand them and to use a whole range of tactics, including direct action and civil disobedience. What's more, this movement is democratic and accountable to disabled people themselves (Dreidger, 1988; Oliver, 1990; Davis, 1993) and its collective voice is demanding that we be included in our societies everywhere by ending the oppression that confronts us, not by offering us and our oppressors Normalization or Social Role Valorization programs.

8 Conclusion

In this paper I have argued that Normalization as a social theory is inadequate in that it does not describe experience satisfactorily, that its explanation of why disabled people have the kinds of experiences they do is wholly inadequate, and that its potential for transforming those experiences to something better is limited. It is not only those unsympathetic to Normalization who question its future, however.

> What does Normalisation now have to do in order to be a positive force for change in the 1990s? The answer may lie in going back to its roots and realigning itself in relation to other sociological theories.
>
> (Brown & Smith, 1992, p. 176)

Whether such a realignment, even with materialist theory, is likely to resuscitate Normalization is itself doubtful, because what is at stake is a vision of the kind of society we would like to live in. Normalization theory offers disabled people the opportunity to be given valued social roles in an unequal society that values some roles more than others. Materialist social theory offers disabled people the opportunity to transform their own lives and in so doing to transform the society in which they live into one in which all roles are valued. As a disabled person, I know which of those choices I prefer, and I also know which most of the disabled people I meet prefer.

References

ABBERLEY, P. (1987). The concept of oppression and the development of a social theory of disability. *Disability, Handicap And Society*, 2(1), pp. 5–19.

ALBRECHT, G. (1992). *The disability business*. London: Sage.

ALTHUSSER, L. (1971). *Lenin and philosophy and other essays*. London: New Left Books.

BROWN, H., & SMITH, H. (Eds.). (1992). *Normalization: A reader for the nineties*. London: Routledge.

CHAPPELL, A. (1992). Towards a sociological critique of the Normalisation principle. *Disability, Handicap and Society*, 7(1).

COHEN, S. (1985). *Visions of social control*. Oxford: Polity Press.

COLERIDGE, P. (1993). *Disability, liberation and development*. Oxford: Oxfam Publications.

DALLEY, G. (1992). Social welfare ideologies and Normalization: Links and conflicts. In H. BROWN & H. SMITH, (Eds.), *Normalisation: A reader for the nineties*. London: Routledge.

DAVIS, K. (1993). On the movement. In J. SWAIN, V. FINKELSTEIN, S. FRENCH, & M. OLIVER, *Disabling barriers—Enabling environments*. London: Sage.

DESPOUY, L. (1991). *Human rights and disability*. New York: United Nations Economic and Social Council.

DHSS. (1988). A *wider vision*. London: HMSO.

DISABLED LIVES. (1992, July). *New Internationalist, 233.*

DREIDGER, D. (1988). *The last civil rights movement.* London: Hurst and Co.

ESTES, C., SWAN, J. & GERARD, L. (1982). Dominant and competing paradigms in gerontology: Towards a political economy of ageing. *Ageing and Society, 2*(2).

FOUCAULT, M. (1972). *The archaeology of knowledge.* New York: Pantheon.

FOUCAULT, M. (1973). *The birth of the clinic.* London: Tavistock.

GILLESPIE-SELLS, C., & CAMPBELL, J. (1991). *Disability equality training: Trainers guide.* London: CCETSW.

GOUGH, I. (1979). *The political economy of the welfare state.* Basingstoke: Macmillan.

GOULDNER, A. (1971). *The coming crisis in western sociology.* London: Heinemann.

HASLER, F. (1993). Developments in the Disabled People's Movement. In J. SWAIN, V. FINKELSTEIN, S. FRENCH, & M. OLIVER, *Disabling barriers—enabling environments.* London: Sage.

HEARN, K. (1991). Disabled lesbians and gays are here to stay. In T. KAUFMAN, & P. LINCOLN, (Eds.), *High risk lives: Lesbian and gay politics after the clause.* Bridgeport: Prism Press.

HILL, M. (1994, March). Getting things right. *Community Care Inside, 31.*

MARX, K. (1913). *A contribution to the critique of political economy.* Chicago: Chicago Press.

MORRIS, J. (1991). *Pride against prejudice.* London: Women's Press.

NIRJE, B. (1993). *The Normalization Principle—25 years later.* Finland: The Institute for Educational Research.

O'CONNOR, J. (1973). *The fiscal crisis of the state.* New York: St. Martin's Press.

OLIVER, M. (1983). *Social work with disabled people.* Basingstoke: Macmillan.

OLIVER, M. (1990). *The politics of disablement.* Basingstoke: Macmillan and St. Martin's Press.

OLIVER, M. (1995). *Understanding disability: From theory to practice.* Basingstoke: Macmillan.

RYAN, J. & THOMAS, F. (1980). *The politics of mental handicap.* Harmondsworth: Penguin.

ROTHMAN, D. (1971). *The discovery of the asylum.* Boston: Little Brown.

SCULL, A. (1977). *De-carceration, community treatment and the deviant—A radical view.* New York: Prentice-Hall.

STUART, O. (1993). Double oppression: An appropriate starting-point? In J. SWAIN, V. FINKELSTEIN, S. FRENCH, & M. OLIVER, *Disabling barriers—Enabling environments.* London: Sage.

SUTHERLAND, A. (1981). *Disabled we stand.* London: Souvenir Press.

SWAIN, J., FINKELSTEIN, V., FRENCH, S. & OLIVER, M. (1993). *Disabling barriers—Enabling environments.* London: Sage.

UNION OF THE PHYSICALLY IMPAIRED AGAINST SEGREGATION (UPIAS). (1976). *Fundamental principles of disability.* London: Author.

WALTON, J. (1979). Urban political economy. *Comparative Urban Research.*

WOLFENSBERGER, W. (1989). Human service policies: The rhetoric versus the reality. In L. Barton, (Ed.), *Disability and dependency.* Sussex: Falmer Press.

WOOD, P. (1980). *International classification of impairments, disabilities and handicaps.* Geneva: World Health Organization.

ZARB, G., & OLIVER, M. (1993). *Ageing with a disability: What do they expect after all these years?* London: University of Greenwich.

7

SPECIAL EDUCATION'S CHANGING IDENTITY

Paradoxes and dilemmas in views of culture and space

Alfredo J. Artiles

Source: *Harvard Educational Review* 73(2) (2003): 164–202.

U.S. classrooms today look dramatically different than they did thirty years ago, before the federal government passed its first comprehensive special education legislation — the Education for All Handicapped Children Act — in 1975. This law was reauthorized as the Individuals with Disabilities Education Act (IDEA) in 1990. Although educators now have theoretically more sophisticated and effective interventions at their disposal for serving students with disabilities, their work also is far more complex and challenging. For instance, as the population of students with disabilities and the proportion of minority students grow rapidly, we are witnessing the inexorable convergence of two of the most important developments in special education's contemporary history, namely, the inclusive education movement[1] and the overrepresentation of racial minority students in special education.[2] The increasing complexity of diversity in terms of racial background and ability level poses significant challenges to the refinement of special education services, the improvement of policies, and the development of a knowledge base, particularly when we acknowledge that the research literature on racial and linguistic minority students is rather thin (Donovan & Cross, 2002; Gersten, Baker, & Pugach, 2001). Moreover, minority overrepresentation and inclusion pose important challenges to special educators' understandings of culture, the role of culture in visions of disability, and the creation of a research ethos that is mindful of cultural differences.

Inclusion and overrepresentation will undoubtedly influence the transformation of special education's identity. Let us remember that a cornerstone of special education's original identity was grounded in a civil rights discourse for people with disabilities. As a result, IDEA was passed to ensure free and appropriate public education, parents' rights to be informed of evaluation and placement decisions (including the right to due process hearings), individualized and nondiscriminatory assessment, individualized educational and related services, education in the least restrictive environment, and federal assistance to support states' and school districts' efforts to educate students with disabilities (Smith, 2001).

The passage and refinement of IDEA was a major accomplishment in the history of special education that has made a difference in the lives of millions of people with disabilities. However, given ongoing societal and professional transformations, the special education field must still address the following questions:

- How will special education's identity change as this system serves more racially diverse students with disabilities in general education contexts?
- How will understandings of culture be infused in special education's identity?
- How will this field acknowledge race and language background in research practices and how will researchers place these constructs in dynamic grids of cultural influence?
- As understandings of inclusion shift from a spatial location (the general education classroom) to the alignment of educational philosophies with visions of organizational arrangements, how will the new identity of the field account for racial differences, culture, and space?

It is imperative that the discourse communities working on inclusion and overrepresentation begin to craft a dialogue across their respective discourse boundaries to reflect on the implications of their labor for a new, emerging systemic identity.[3] Unfortunately, these discourse communities rarely reflect on their growing overlapping foci or on the implications of such convergence. Hence, in this article I discuss the intersection of inclusion and overrepresentation as it affects school-age individuals with high-incidence disabilities (particularly learning disabilities). I focus on this group because it comprises the United States' largest segment of the school population with disabilities.[4]

I build my analysis of the literatures on inclusion and overrepresentation on two ideas. First, current special education developments ought to be examined in the context of larger cultural and political processes located in educational reforms and society at large. This examination must include an analysis of the power differentials and struggles that shape the educational outcomes of racial minorities and students with disabilities. Second, the convergence of the inclusion movement and the overrepresentation of minorities in special education create paradoxes and dilemmas that can interfere with the development of socially just educational systems in a democratic society.

In this article, I present the preliminary findings of an analysis of the inclusion and overrepresentation literatures, namely 1) silence about racial diversity in the implementation of inclusive models, 2) lack of vision for a culturally responsive educational system, 3) inadequate attention to sociohistorical context and the complexity of culture, 4) limited definitions of space, and 5) problematic views of difference. I conclude with a discussion of the implications of this analysis for a new generation of inclusion and overrepresentation research. Before developing these ideas, I situate overrepresentation and inclusion in the current cultural politics of educational reform.

The cultural politics of current educational reforms

As I witness the ongoing debates about inclusive education and minority representation in special education, I cannot ignore the contexts in which these conversations are taking place. The most immediate is the sociopolitical context of general education reform. For example, the recent neoconservative tide of reforms largely assumes that schools should produce human capital (Apple, 1996). Neoconservative reformers reason that, in an era of increasing global competition and unprecedented economic progress, schools must produce a skilled and competitive labor force. Apple argues that this premise is ingrained in a larger and more complex cultural agenda that values individualism and competition. Implied in this premise is the idea that the educational system will have winners and losers (see also Varenne & McDermott, 1999).

Policymakers and the general public have generally concluded that in order for the United States to be competitive in this era of globalization, schools must produce the human capital necessary to meet the demands of the new economy. This commitment has generated a number of popular reform ideas, including the incorporation of national standards, curricula, and testing and privatized choice plans (see Apple, 1996, and McLaughlin & Tilstone, 1999, for analytic overviews of these reforms). Due in part to concerns over poor outcomes and low expectations for students with disabilities, the most recent reauthorization of IDEA has incorporated several accountability provisions that align with general education reforms. Examples of such provisions include performance goals and indicators, school-based improvement plans, participation in large-scale assessments, access to the general education curriculum, and greater collaboration between general and special education personnel (McLaughlin & Tilstone, 1999). It is feasible that general and special educators' potentially divergent views of effective instruction might create contradictions in the implementation of these policies (McDonnell, McLaughlin, & Morison, 1997). For example, it is not clear whether the new emphasis on standards-based reform for all students will shortchange students with disabilities as teachers feel compelled to cover content and promote more sophisticated forms of learning, thus leaving less time for teachers to support students who lag behind. Confused about when to modify curriculum versus when to provide instructional accommodations in order to access the curriculum, teachers often feel unprepared to apply this new accountability framework to special education populations (McLaughlin, Henderson, & Rhim, 1998; McLaughlin & Tilstone, 1999).

Apple (1996) argues that neoconservative reforms help to maintain economic and political security for the dominant group, preserve the dominant group's traditional values, and legitimize dominant definitions of knowledge and competence. These reforms ratify a politics of difference that favors neoconservatives because such reforms afford them the privilege to construct and impose exclusionary insider and outsider identities (i.e., "we" and "them"). "We" are homogeneous, hard working, and English speaking, and "we" do better in all labor, educational, and health outcome measures. In contrast, "they" are lazy, dirty, heterogeneous, misuse English, and take advantage of the government and the "we" (Apple, 1996). The consolidation of deficit views about "them" has drawn attention to issues of difference in education and beyond at a time when the nation is experiencing unprecedented cultural diversification.

Areas in which we observe the interplay between conservative educational reforms and their implicit pursuit of a cultural agenda that privileges dominant groups are language and literacy reform, particularly in the debates over bilingual education and the English-only movement. As these debates polarized, we witnessed the abolition of bilingual education programs in states including California, Arizona, and Massachusetts. These policies have had dreadful consequences as they became embodied in what some call "backlash pedagogies" (Gutierrez, Asato, Santos, & Gotanda, 2002), which aim to maintain the status quo that assumes inequality is a natural state of affairs in educational practice and reform. Backlash pedagogies disregard the history of oppression and marginalization suffered by minority populations (Gutierrez et al., 2002) and are ultimately grounded in colonialist views of literacy and learning.

As we witness the initial implementation of standards, accountability reforms, and English-only initiatives, we must consider the consequences for historically marginalized racial and linguistically diverse groups. For instance, will referrals of English language learners (ELLs) to special education increase? (Artiles, Rueda, Salazar, & Higareda, 2002). How will special education placement for ELLs influence access to the general education curriculum and affect dropout, graduation, or special education exit rates? How will the principles of the inclusive education movement be operationalized when placing ELLs in special education, considering that

(a) ELLs are likely to be taught by teachers without credentials (Gándara *et al.*, 2000), (b) there is a dramatic shortage of special education and bilingual teachers (García 1996; Reynolds & York, 1996), (c) most teachers receive poor training on the influence of language and culture in children's learning (Zeichner & Hoeft, 1996), and (d) teachers have limited experience with collaborative and/or team-teaching arrangements (Smith, 2001)?

These are the cultural politics enclosing the special education field in which an emphasis on individualism and competition, views of competence and literacy that privilege certain groups, and a troubling politics of difference intermingle. We must not lose sight of these cultural politics as we move toward a more inclusive special educational system and grapple with the overrepresentation of minority students in disability programs. An exhaustive analysis of inclusion and overrepresentation is beyond the scope of this manuscript. Therefore, in the next section, my goal is to sketch their boundaries and highlight key issues as a means to identify paradoxes and dilemmas that exist within and between these literatures.

Outline of the inclusive education movement

Special education legislation requires that students with disabilities be educated in the least restrictive environment (LRE). Although this notion is a fundamental and identifying principle of contemporary special education, it is also one of the most controversial constructs in the field (Smith, 2001). In its early years, special education was provided in self-contained classrooms and separate schools. During the 1970s and 1980s, the LRE requirement allowed schools to mainstream students with disabilities in general education classrooms for a portion of the day, though this practice was done on a voluntary basis (Brantlinger, 1997). In the mid 1980s, Madeline Will, then director of the federal Office of Special Education Programs, challenged the field to transform traditional practices so that more students with disabilities would be integrated into general education classrooms (Will, 1984). These efforts were called the Regular Education Initiative. Although the law requires that LRE be individually determined and that services be available across a continuum of options from most to least integrated, debates ensued between parents, practitioners, policymakers, and researchers about best practices for implementation (Smith, 2001). These debates evolved from discussions about integration (as embodied in the REI) to the development of proposals based on the concept of inclusive education.

The inclusive education movement aims to change a school's ethos and practices to promote truly inclusive models and ultimately to promote student academic learning, social competence, social skills, attitude change, and positive peer relations. In its early years, the movement stressed full inclusion and focused primarily on students with severe disabilities; however, it has steadily expanded to include students with high-incidence disabilities (Fuchs & Fuchs, 1994). The inclusive education movement embodies several important characteristics and beliefs focusing on the student, the teacher, and the system. For example, the movement argues that all children can learn, that learning is supported by a strong sense of community, and that services are based on need rather than limited by location. Also, the movement promotes schoolwide approaches, such as teacher collaboration, enhanced instructional strategies, curriculum accommodations and modifications, and additional supports in general education settings. Finally, the movement focuses on the system, asserting that neighborhood schools enroll natural proportions of students with disabilities and demonstrate a concern for standards and outcomes for all students (Lipsky & Gartner, 1999).

Despite these common characteristics and beliefs, unclear goals and multiple definitions of inclusion seem to permeate the movement's discourse and research practices (Dyson, 1999; Fuchs & Fuchs, 1994). For instance, definitions can range from students' with disabilities part- or full-time placement in a general education classroom to the transformation of a school ethos or the construction of entire educational systems based on an inclusive education philosophy (Dyson, 1999). The diversity of definitions and goals of the movement contribute to the creation of multiple discourses. Dyson argues that discourses about inclusion can be organized along two dimensions: (a) the *rationale* for inclusion and (b) the *realization* of inclusion.

Rationale for inclusion

With regard to the rationale dimension, Dyson (1999) identifies two discourses: 1) the rights-and-ethics discourse and 2) the efficacy discourse. The rights-and-ethics discourse uses a civil rights discourse to argue that individuals with disabilities have the fundamental human right to be educated, ideally alongside nondisabled peers (Brantlinger, 1997). This basic right is grounded in ethical principles of fairness and social justice (Lipsky & Gartner, 1999; Skrtic, 1991). According to Dyson (1999), the rights-and-ethics discourse derives from structuralist analyses that suggest that societal inequalities are reproduced in educational systems. Individuals and groups who possess cultural capital have advantages over marginalized or oppressed people with educational and labor opportunities, since educational systems are built on the knowledge and values of dominant groups. When applied to people with disabilities, this critique asserts that special education, a historically segregated system parallel to general education, further privileges certain groups by separating and marginalizing students deemed problematic or difficult. The existence of this system in turn establishes general education as the norm and special education as deviant, and conceals the underlying need to restructure societal conditions. Therefore, the argument follows, special education placement decisions are inextricably linked to issues of equity and social justice. According to the rights-and-ethics discourse, the maintenance of a segregated special education system is incongruous with socially just educational systems, and ultimately with democratic ideals.

Despite the clear logic of this critique, particularly with regard to equity issues, we must acknowledge that competing definitions of social justice that permeate this discourse and the special education field add confusion to an already complex process (Christensen & Rizvi, 1996). For instance, current reforms based on notions of free market and choice, which in turn are grounded in individualistic meritocratic principles, define social justice as fairness of opportunity for individuals. As such, "social justice is no longer 'seen as linked to past group oppression and disadvantage' judged historically, but represented simply as a matter of guaranteeing individual choice under the conditions of a 'free market'" (Rizvi & Lingard, 1996, p. 15).

Conversely, within the rights-and-ethics discourse, social justice is defined as the access to and the redistribution of general education resources for students with disabilities. Unfortunately, as Rizvi and Lingard (1996) argue, even this distributive view is limited, for it does not "account adequately for either contemporary politics of difference, or the various complex ways in which exclusion and discrimination are now practiced, in both their individual and institutional forms" (p. 21). This is indeed a major shortcoming of this discourse in light of the growing overrepresentation of minorities in special education, which I take up in more detail in the following section.

The rationale based on the efficacy discourse is closely aligned with the rights-and-ethics thesis. This rationale cites evidence that suggests that students with disabilities who are placed in segregated programs do not exhibit greater educational gains than comparable peers educated in integrated contexts. Evidence is also cited about the lack of differentiation between the instructional practices observed in programs for various disabilities and general education classrooms (Lipsky & Gartner, 1996). This discourse's underlying view of social justice is also based on the aforementioned arguments of access and equity. Unfortunately, access does not guarantee meaningful participation, full membership, or more comparable outcomes (Rizvi & Lingard, 1996).

Realization of inclusion

In addition to the discourses advanced to justify the creation of an inclusive educational system, visions of how such a system ought to be realized have been proposed. Dyson (1999) labels these discourses political and pragmatic. The political discourse is concerned with developing forms of resistance against the interest groups that uphold the traditional special education system. For example, the inclusion movement has faced strong resistance from segments of the special education professional community and it has spurred heated debates in professional journals and conferences. Some of these discussions revolve around technical issues, such as empirical bases of arguments or lack of specificity in proposed models (Fuchs & Fuchs, 1994; Kauffman & Hallahan, 1995; Wang & Walberg, 1988). Others are ideological or rhetorical, focusing on values and beliefs about learning, teaching, disability, research, and meanings of expressions such as "all children" (Brantlinger, 1997; Gartner & Lipsky, 1987; Pugach & Lilly, 1984; Stainback & Stainback, 1991).[5]

The pragmatic discourse has received by far the most attention from researchers. This discourse addresses what inclusive education programs and schools do and should look like. Some scholars have developed profiles of inclusive schools related to the ethos, structures, and processes in such contexts, while others have offered conceptual analyses of the fundamental differences between inclusive and non-inclusive schools (Skrtic, 1991; Villa & Thousand, 1995). It is common to find within this discourse practical materials and guides for teachers and administrators interested in developing inclusive programs and schools (Dyson, 1999). A potentially damaging consequence of the pragmatic discourse is that educators might become overly concerned with how to allocate human and material resources, carry out procedures, or create regulatory stipulations aimed at compensating for or avoiding discriminatory practices (Slee, 1996).

A review of research based on the pragmatic discourse reflects the following findings about the inclusion of students with disabilities in general education contexts (U.S. Department of Education, 1999): (a) higher frequency of interactions with nondisabled peers; (b) larger and more enduring nondisabled peer networks; (c) improved social and communication skills (e.g., initiation, self-regulation, choice, contact termination); (d) variations in relationships and status similar to friendships observed among nondisabled students; (e) contingent upon the types of assistance provided, adults as positive mediators of friendships between students with and without disabilities; (f) gains in some academic areas; and (g) success with cooperative learning and peer tutoring, although the impact of mixed-ability grouping on disabled student learning is inconclusive. Some studies that focus on students with learning disabilities find that these students do not always participate meaningfully in general education classrooms. They also show that instruction for this group is undifferentiated. Overall, the results of research "to improve the quality of instruction provided to students with disabilities in general education classrooms . . . have been mixed" (Gersten et al., 2001, p. 699). A few studies suggest that the presence of students with disabilities in inclusive contexts does not have a negative effect on nondisabled students' developmental or academic outcomes (e.g., Staub, 2000). Some argue that gains for nondisabled students is the most consistent finding in this line of inquiry (Manset & Semmel, 1997).

Overview of minority representation in special education

The special education population is increasingly segregated along racial lines, as reflected in the disproportionate representation of these minorities in such programs (Donovan & Cross, 2002; Dunn, 1968). While both over- and underrepresentation patterns are associated with disproportionality (Artiles & Trent, 2000), overrepresentation has by far received the most attention in the literature. African Americans and American Indians are most affected by overrepresentation, mostly in the high-incidence disability categories such as LD, MMR, and ED (see note 4).

Considerable efforts and resources have been spent to understand and address this problem, perhaps with more intensity in recent years. Over the last three decades, insights and alternative solutions to this problem have come about through litigation, new legal requirements, active lobbying and advocacy from professional, state, and civil rights groups, two National Research Council (NRC) reports (Donovan & Cross, 2002; Heller, Holtzman, & Messick, 1982), and increasing attention and support from the federal government (e.g., funding of research, technical assistance, and training projects,[6] coverage in recent annual reports to Congress, and attention from high-level administrators in official speeches, reports, and statements) (Hehir, 2002). Unfortunately, the problem is still reflected in current enrollment statistics (Losen & Orfield, 2002).

Although few question whether overrepresentation exists, there is some disagreement about the causes and magnitude of the problem, and some have even asked why overrepresentation is a problem (see Artiles, Trent, & Palmer, in press). Proposed causes cover a wide range; at opposite extremes of this range we find institutional racism and child poverty. The institutional racism thesis is based on social reproduction theory and argues that minority groups' overrepresentation in special education reflects their oppressed and marginalized status in society. Child poverty has also been offered as the cause of this predicament. The latest NRC report (Donovan & Cross, 2002) devoted a great deal of attention to this issue and sum- marized an extensive literature on the association between poverty and risk for disability. Unfortunately, to our dismay, "we know precious little about the intervening dynamics that connect socioeconomic status to disability" (Fujiura & Yamaki, 2000, p. 196). Sociological and cultural analyses about the connection between child poverty and disability are rarely conducted in the special education field, and thus we rarely consider the historical, cultural, and structural antecedents of the systematic link between poverty, race, and disability (Slee, 1996). A result of this is the implementation of deficit-based studies that overlook the forces that can protect children's development even when they live in dreadful conditions (McLoyd, 1998). Research that aims to document children's deficits also ignores the structural correlates of poverty — for example, schools that serve poor minority students have significantly fewer material and financial resources, lower teacher and instructional quality, and bleak school climates. The existing literature in this field generally falls into two categories: research on placement patterns and research on the precursors to placement, both of which I discuss next.

Racial minority overrepresentation: placement patterns

The bulk of the overrepresentation literature focuses on special education placement patterns in various disability categories. Findings suggest that overrepresentation patterns vary, depending on whether the data are disaggregated by geographic location, ethnicity, or disability program. Overrepresentation trends can also vary according to ethnic representation in the school population, year, and indicator used (Artiles *et al.*, 2002; Donovan & Cross, 2002; Finn, 1982; Reschly, 1997).

Based on 1998 data, the latest NRC report (Donovan & Cross, 2002) indicates that at the national level 12 percent of all students are served in special education, whereas the risk indices by ethnic group are as follows: 13.1 percent for American Indians, 14.3 percent for African Americans, 11.3 percent for Latinos/as, 5.3 percent for Asian Americans, and 12.1 percent for Whites. When racial minorities' placement rates are compared with White students (using odds ratios)[7] across all disabilities, only African Americans (1.18) and American Indians (1.08) are overrepresented (Donovan & Cross, 2002). There is some variability when the data are disaggregated by disability category. African Americans are overrepresented in mental retardation (MR) (2.35), LD (1.08), ED (1.59), and developmental delay (2.06). These patterns reiterate a consistent finding over the history of this problem regarding African Americans. American Indians are also overrepresented in MR (1.07) and LD (1.2) programs. Latinos are slightly overrepresented in LD (1.12), and Asian Americans are underrepresented in all high-incidence categories.[8]

Several caveats relate to the analysis of placement patterns such as problems with the procedures used to collect data for national datasets, variability in the definition and eligibility criteria for disability across states, and lack of data on factors that could deepen understanding of the contexts of overrepresentation (e.g., teachers' and administrators' beliefs, school climate, quality of instruction, and quality of prereferral interventions). For example, based on data gathered in New York's urban schools, Gottlieb, Alter, Gottlieb, and Wishner (1994) concluded that the fact that "1 in 6 students with LD have IQ scores that could render them eligible for classification as mentally retarded calls into question the definition of learning disabilities that is being applied" (p. 455). Thus, it seems that the LD category, which used to be reserved mostly for White middle-class students, may be becoming a repository for poor ethnic minorities, many of whom come from immigrant or migrant families (Gottlieb *et al.*, 1994). Sometimes these placement decisions may be made to avoid accusations of bias due to the greater stigma of the MMR category or out of fear of litigation; other times, as Gottlieb *et al.* suggest, decisions are based on the need to use scarce resources for low-achieving students.

Racial minority overrepresentation: precursors to placement

An alternative strand of overrepresentation research is concerned with the precursors to special education placement. Thus, studies have examined referral, assessment, and decisionmaking processes (Artiles & Pak, 2000; Harry, Klingner, Sturges, & Moore, 2002; Mehan, Hartwick, & Meihls, 1986; Varenne & McDermott, 1999). Some studies have examined bias in referral and placement decisions as associated with teacher gender, race, classroom management ability, and beliefs, whereas other work has assessed the influence of examiner and test (content and development) biases in disability diagnoses (see Donovan & Cross, 2002, for a review of this literature).

Overrepresentation has received closer scrutiny in recent years and a new wave of evidence on the potential antecedents of placement is emerging (e.g., Losen & Orfield, 2002). For instance, funding seems to be associated with minority placement patterns. Parrish (2002) concluded that

> variation in the type of special education funding system suggests that funding systems based on category of disability are particularly prone to troubling patterns of minority overrepresentation and resource distribution. These systems appear much more likely to show over-representation of minority students into the disability category mental retardation, while at the same time providing greater special education funding to districts enrolling the lowest percentages of minority students.
>
> (p. 33)

Studies have also begun to document the complex interactions between school location, disability category, ethnic group, poverty, and proportion of minority school enrollment. For instance, Oswald, Coutinho, Best, and Singh (1999) documented interactions between demographic variables and over-representation patterns and found that Black overrepresentation in MR programs is associated with an increase in poverty, while overrepresentation in the ED category is associated with a decrease in poverty (Oswald *et al.*, 1999). More recently, Oswald, Coutinho, and Best (2002) reported that American Indians were overrepresented in predominantly minority commu-nities, most visibly in ED. Furthermore, "as communities become increasingly Nonwhite, however, white students are substantially less likely to be identified as LD. For Black students, particularly Black male students, living in a community with few Nonwhite students is a substantial risk factor for MR and SED [serious emotional disturbance] identification" (p. 9).

Another factor that could shape placement patterns is the availability of alternative programs (e.g., bilingual education), proportional representation in the district population, and district size. There is evidence, for instance, that Latino overrepresentation as MR was sizable in small districts with high Latino enrollment (i.e., over 70%) (Finn, 1982). Finn reported that overrepresentation was negatively related to the proportion of students placed in bilingual programs. A significant gap in the recent NRC report (Donovan & Cross, 2002) was the discussion of ELL placement in special education; there is indeed an urgent need to conduct more research with this population (Artiles *et al.*, 2002; Ortiz, 1997).

Several important reforms are being implemented in general and special education that may ultimately influence placement in special education. Three such reforms include standards, high-stakes testing, and zero tolerance policies. Minority students are predicted to be most affected by these initiatives, but we are only beginning to study the impact of these reforms (Advancement Project & Civil Rights Project, 2000). For instance, we need more research to understand the impact of high-stakes tests on minority students and on the referral rates to special education. The results of these tests should be examined in conjunction with other indicators such as dropout rates (paying attention to who was included/excluded in this index) and grade retention rates (Heubert, 2002). Impact assessments of these tests should also verify who was included or excluded in the tests, the procedures used to give the tests (particularly with minority students), and the potential impact of inappropriate accommodations (Heubert, 2002). Although increasing numbers of students with disabilities are passing high-stakes tests in recent years, these students continue to lag behind their nondisabled peers.

The specter of bias is always (tacitly or explicitly) present in discussions and analyses of this problem. Unfortunately, little unequivocal evidence is available. In this vein, the latest NRC report concluded that "the evidence available is insufficient to support a claim that *either* discrimination does or does not play a significant role" (Donovan & Cross, 2002, p. 78, emphasis in original). Nevertheless, given the historical legacies of discrimination and racism in our society, we cannot afford to ignore the potential mediating effect of bias on overrepresentation. Two key tasks for future efforts include addressing bias explicitly in research efforts and broadening the conceptualization of bias. As we suggested recently, "bias is not restricted to the actions and decisions of individuals. Bias can also take the form of historical residue and can be found in the social structures of educational settings and institutional regulations and practices that shape institutional discrimination" (Artiles *et al.*, in press).

Overrepresentation is a multidimensional predicament with deep historical and systemic roots, and there are many areas and factors that need to be studied and initiatives that need to be pursued. Perhaps the two most urgent areas of action are the production of more and better data to understand this problem and the need to enforce IDEA's mandates to monitor and prevent it.[9] However, it is beyond the scope of this manuscript to discuss future directions (see Artiles *et al.*, in press; Donovan & Cross, 2002; Losen & Orfield, 2002).

To conclude, it is important to ask, what is at the heart of the overrepresentation problem? Would the problem be solved with quotas so that racial minority students are proportionally represented in general and special education? Is overrepresentation a symptom of massive bias toward racial minorities? Is racial minority overrepresentation justified, given the higher poverty rate in these populations? Why is special education placement deemed negative if it embodies desirable features (e.g., individualized education, higher per-pupil expenditures, smaller teacher-student ratio) (Reschly, 1997)? Answers to these questions are not straightforward. The problem will not be solved with quotas, and it is an oversimplification to blame it on either massive bias or child poverty. Part of the problem is whether we are adequately addressing students' educational potential and needs, from this perspective, false positives and negatives are equally problematic. Let us remember that special education placement is a highly consequential decision, as disability labels carry visible stigma and have other high-cost repercussions. It adds another layer of difference to racial minorities, restricts their access to high-currency educational programs and opportunities, and further limits their long-term educational outcomes, as special education populations have lower graduation, higher dropout, and lower academic achievement rates than their general education counterparts. We should be aware, however, that the overrepresentation debate affords us the opportunity to shift our gaze inward and examine our assumptions about culture. We need to ask tough questions about the role of culture and power in learning and dis/ability and the visions that inform the work we do with students who have historically faced great adversity because of their skin color or the language they speak. My expectation is that such introspection will contribute to the creation of a pluralistic educational system that informs its research knowledge base with a historical and cultural consciousness. The analyses presented in this manuscript represent one step in this direction.

Silence in the inclusion and overrepresentation discourses

A troubling fact evident in the preceding review of the overrepresentation and inclusion scholarship is the silence in and between these literatures. Special education is indeed engaged in an active process of identity transformation as it strives to make services and policies more inclusive. However, such efforts seem to portray educators and students as devoid of sociohistorical identities, even though a sizable segment of the special education population comes from nonmainstream racial, social-class, and linguistic backgrounds. Furthermore, the majority of students entering the special education system in the largest U.S. school districts are ethnic and linguistic minorities. The scholarship on minority placement in special education is silent about the implications of the inclusive education movement. The fact that there is silence in both the overrepresentation and inclusion literatures suggests that it is socially shared. But how can we interpret these silences? And what can we learn from theorizing silence?

The silence on issues of race in the implementation discourse of inclusive education is a major oversight, considering that the history and status of minority groups in our society play major roles in minority students' educational experiences and outcomes. Historically, minority students have been perceived as lacking the skills, experiences, and dispositions to be successful in general education, and, indeed, we know academic achievement is correlated with ethnicity, language background, and social class (Valencia, 1997). Thus, minority students exit general education and move into special education with a deficit identity that foregrounds the aforementioned markers of difference. When diversity is summoned in the inclusion literature (mainly in the rationale scholarship), it is generally associated with diversity of ability levels — indeed an important aspect of diversity — but the plight of minority students is tangentially recognized in the implementation discourse. It is paradoxical that, as the inclusive education movement represents the emergence of empowered voices about disability rights and better educational services for this population, it has been painfully silent about the plight of minority students.

It is also paradoxical that, due to the inclusion movement, minority students might be returning to general education, but with an identity that adds an additional layer of difference — that is, a label adding ability to the composite of racial, linguistic, and social-class markers.[10] This new identity dispensed by the special education system legitimizes the surveillance of these students through legal and technical means (Erickson, 1996). It can also help to perpetuate the poor school outcomes of minorities, since disability status (particularly MR) is correlated with high dropout rates, low school completion rates, low special education exit rates, and poor employment outcomes (Gottlieb *et al.*, 1994; U.S. Department of Education, 1997; Wagner *et al.*, 1993).

Moreover, let us remember that minority students with disabilities are returning to a general education system that is fraught with paradoxical policies and reform pressures, as reflected in the tensions between the push for individual entitlement to the same treatment (same standards and curriculum access) and entitlement to differential treatments (individualized education) (McLaughlin, Fuchs, & Hardman, 1999). It is not clear how this paradoxical situation will be resolved, and it will be interesting to trace whether these reforms are enforced differentially with various segments of the population with disabilities (e.g., minority v. nonminority students) or whether these reforms will benefit certain groups (e.g., nonminority students).

Scholars working on overrepresentation (including myself) are guilty of a silence on the implications of the realization of inclusion for minority students. Although culture (as a way of life) is acknowledged, the dominant overrepresentation discourse seems to favor a deficit view of traditionally silent groups — that is, racial minority groups (Donovan & Cross, 2002). There is a conspicuous silence about the oppressive weight of structural discrimination and about the cultural power, legitimacy, and competence of minority groups; furthermore, this scholarship is painfully devoid of the voices of minority families and students. However, as Sheriff (2000) warns, silence should not be interpreted as oppressed groups' "acceptance of dominant ideology" (p. 118). I argue that we will enhance our understanding of overrepresentation as we scrutinize the contradictory explanations of this predicament and face the silences that emerge from such analyses.

The discourse on the realization of inclusion, on the other hand, assumes White middle-class student experience as the norm, because race and student cultural practices are rarely mentioned. If we consider that the history of a field is built in part through the production of scholarship, we cannot deny that inclusion will be regarded in the future as a critical era in the history of special education. But how will we explain to the future generation of educators and the families they serve that those who benefited from inclusion had no race, class, or culture? We must contest this approach to the production of collective memory.

One potentially fruitful path is to analyze these silences as forms of cultural censorship. Sider explains that "the creation of culture is also, simultaneously and necessarily, the creation of silence. . . . We can have no significant understanding of any culture unless we also know the silences that were *institutionally* created and guaranteed along with it" (cited in Sheriff, 2000, p. 118, emphasis in original). Historically, the research community has created a silence about ethnic, racial, class, gender, and linguistic differences, as evidenced in a major analysis of contemporary special education research. Less than 3 percent of the empirical research published in four peer-reviewed special education journals over a 22-year period (1975–1994) examined data across ethnic and social class lines (Artiles *et al.*, 1997).[11]

An important implication of this finding is that we must strive to understand the goals and functions of the institutionalization of silences about difference in the culture of special education scholarship. Walker (1999) explains that questions about culture are kept on the periphery of educational researchers' socialization. Future researchers are taught that culture should be controlled, that it amounts to variance that ought to be held constant, or worse, it is ignored because the lessons learned from White middle-class samples are assumed to be universal. Similar to the process of historical production (Trouillot, 1995), silences enter research processes at various crucial points: the moment of question formulation or problem statement, the moment of source identification or participant recruitment, the moment of fact creation or assembly (design of data collection tools and actual data collection), or the moment of fact retrieval and retrospective significance (data analysis and final writing).

As I acknowledged at the beginning of this manuscript, special education researchers have made important advances in the development of a scientific knowledge base. However, as this analysis suggests, researchers need to make visible the object of analysis, the language of analysis, and the position of the analyst (Geertz, 1983) to interrogate the identified silences and begin the critique and transformation of the existing knowledge base, the curricula, and the apprenticeship systems of doctoral and teacher education programs. Critiques and analyses of past research efforts should be mindful of the fact that there is always a presence in the past; as Trouillot (1995) reminds us, "It could not just be The Past. It had to be someone's past" (p. 142). Whose past is represented in the special education scholarship? What is the presence that authored the special education scholarship? To conclude, we find ourselves in a situation in which culture or "culturally different" students are "overlooked" (Bhabha, 1994) in the double sense of social surveillance, as in the overrepresentation literature and of invisibility as in the inclusion scholarship. We must end these silences so that we better inform future analysis of inclusion and overrepresentation and deepen our understanding of the processes that lead to and the consequences of overrepresentation patterns in inclusive contexts.

Visions of culture

The inclusion and overrepresentation discourse communities are concerned with issues of culture; the former in terms of issues of professional and organizational cultures, the latter of cultural issues related to student characteristics. Culture, however, is not easily defined, as is reflected in its multiple definitions. In fact, Williams (1983) states that culture is one of the most complicated notions in the English language. In his review of the concept, Brightman (1995) concludes, "Unstable in meaning and reference both synchronically and over time, the culture construct has exhibited exceptional lability" (p. 539). Space constraints prevent me from presenting an exhaustive analysis of this construct (see reviews in Brightman, 1995; Eagleton, 2000; Eisenhart, 2001; Erickson, 2001; Gallego *et al.*, 2001; Rogoff & Angelillo, 2002; Varenne, 1984). Instead, I discuss the most common views of culture that permeate scholarship on inclusion and overrepresentation. I frame this discussion in the context of a description of culture's five primary underlying dimensions: cohesion, stability, location, temporality, and power.[12]

The cohesion and stability of culture

Culture's underlying dimensions of cohesion and stability embody dialectical tensions between culture as homogeneous v. variable, ahistorical v. ever-changing, and reproductive v. improvisational (Brightman, 1995; Rogoff & Angelillo, 2002; Varenne, 1984). The scholarship on overrepresentation and inclusion favors distinct poles in each of these dialectical tensions.

Culture is assumed to be cohesive, to embody characteristics that are distinctive and clearly differentiate cultural groups. Group patterning serves a critical function, for it provides a sense of identity; it allows members of a group to recognize who is and who is not a member of their group (Erickson, 2001). It is also important to recognize that within-group diversity exists in every culture, as individuals are not mere replicas of their cultural histories. Individuals use their agency as they cope with life circumstances to create unique life histories, and such a process contributes to the creation of within-group and within-individual diversity (Anzaldúa, 1999). Culture is also assumed to be stable and can be regarded as fossilized. In such cases, culture is both cohesive and stable, since it is conceptualized as if there is a bounded culture that never changes. Although culture must be transmitted across generations so that newcomers can build on their ancestors' legacies, it is equally critical that cultures evolve and change in order to survive (Erickson, 2001).

An important insight is that cohesion and stability of culture embody dialectical tensions between group traits and within group diversity and between enduring legacies and cultural change. Disparate conceptions of culture emerge, depending on whether scholars privilege certain elements of these dialectical tensions over others. For instance, a common conception of culture in special education scholarship is "culture as a way of life." According to this view, the work of researchers is to document the cohesion and stability of a group's culture. A key assumption is that culture has effects that are independent from other potentially salient variables, which "warrants reification and essentialization" (Handwerker, 2002, p. 108); moreover, culture represents a successful adaptation to relatively constant external conditions. It is further assumed that such a cohesive "way of life" (culture) is transmitted to the next generation through socialization processes (e.g., child rearing). Thus, unless external conditions vary, culture remains stable over time; culture is seen as cohesive and stable.

The overrepresentation scholarship tends to stress two distinct analyses of the problem that ultimately rest on the view of culture as a way of life. One argument is that minorities are disproportionately placed in special education because these groups have distinctive cultures that are incongruent with the school culture.[13] This thesis assumes that misunderstandings and conflict arise when groups that have developed different ways of life come into contact (see Heath, 1983; Vogt, Jordan, & Tharp, 1993, for discussions of this theory in general education contexts). Prescriptions, interventions, and models have been advanced (and often succeeded) to bridge these discontinuities and improve minority students' experiences and outcomes in school (Eisenhart, 2001). The second argument is that racial minority students are disproportionately exposed to the culture of poverty that hinders their development and may put them in a situation that merits special education interventions (Donovan & Cross, 2002).

In turn, the inclusion discourse community uses various perspectives on culture. Let us remember that this literature focuses on the rationale and implementation of inclusion (Dyson, 1999). The work on the rationale tends to focus on the culture of institutions (e.g., schools, classrooms, groups), particularly their histories, assumptions, and traits, and bases its arguments on a view of culture as cohesive and stable over time. Schools organize activities, define roles for teachers and students, and create rules to privilege nondisabled middle-class students. Procedures and other institutional processes are orchestrated to instill in students particular (affective, cognitive) dispositions that reproduce their status in society. A critique of this view is that it is deterministic; the agent is stripped of strategy and improvisation (Brightman, 1995).

Although not always articulated explicitly, this literature relies on a social reproduction thesis. Social reproduction theory is grounded in Marxist precepts of the role of social class in society. Individuals relate to the means of production in routine activities and by assuming particular occupations. Over time, constellations of groups and families develop a shared history of relations to these means of production, which in turn produces a collective cosmovision, "a set of symbolic and conceptual forms by which a group's social class circumstances are made to seem reasonable and 'natural'" (Eisenhart, 2001, p. 212). This view of culture privileges a sociological imagination and foregrounds how cultures are reproduced across generations so that groups maintain their status; school is regarded as a primary site where reproductive processes take place (Anyon, 1997; Bowles & Gintis, 1976; Willis, 1977). This strand of the inclusion literature does not do justice to the perennial tension between cultural reproduction and cultural transformation. Instead, the rationale discourse privileges the reproduction thesis to justify inclusion.

In contrast, the implementation discourse is concerned primarily with cultural change as inclusionists strive to transform the culture of traditional schools. Because there is hardly any acknowledgement of the presence of minorities in special education in the inclusion implementation literature, and considering the history of marginalization of racial minorities in our society, I argue that attention to cultural reproduction processes is imperative. The implementation of inclusion must take into account the reproduction of the historical circumstances that marginalize minority students in the general education system and society at large. This means inclusion scholarship ought to transcend notions of difference based on ability and acknowledge more structural forces that shape minority students' experiences in general and special education alike.

Interestingly, the implementation-of-inclusion literature is grounded in two perspectives of culture, namely, a way-of-life and an interpretivist view. The former is reflected in descriptions of the cohesive and stable cultures of inclusive schools or in comparisons between inclusive and non-inclusive schools. This perspective highlights distinctive structures and processes, with prescriptions for practitioners for the engineering of cogent school cultures that are mindful of inclusion. The interpretivist perspective holds that individuals can actively transform the meanings brought from home as they negotiate their place and roles in the groups they encounter in schools and other contexts (Erickson, 1996); as a result, new meanings, ways to interpret the world, and practices (i.e., idiocultures) can be created. The inclusion work in this tradition either describes inclusive conditions/experiences or assesses the impact of interventions by looking at the meaning-making processes between disabled and nondisabled students in general education instructional (e.g., peer tutoring, cooperative learning groups) or social contexts (e.g., peer networks, communication skills, status, friendships, types of assistance to mediate interactional processes and outcomes). A vision of culture as a meaning-making process privileges the situatedness of social events and implicitly honors the within-group diversity embodied in the individual-in-action (though it does not disregard cohesion). Culture as a meaning-making process opens a space for cultural transformation since it concentrates on the unpredictable construction of local processes.

The location of culture

Depending on its definition, culture can be located internally and externally.[14] The former locates culture in the values, beliefs, worldviews, schemas, and knowledge that people develop locally to navigate the world, solve problems, and attain goals. When located internally, culture is ideational; it is inside the mind of individuals. The work on overrepresentation relies heavily on the internal location of culture. This "subjective knowledge" view assumes that membership in a given ethnic, racial, gender, social-class, ability, or linguistic group will produce distinctive patterns of beliefs, behaviors, customs, values, and so forth. It follows that such groups possess distinctive and homogeneous cognitive, communication, and relational patterns (Cole, 1996); a popular example is the idea of minorities' unique learning styles (see a critical review of the learning styles literature in Irvine & York,

1995). The interactions between markers of difference (e.g., race, ability, gender, language background, social class) are not explored. The scholarship on overrepresentation either argues that educators must be mindful of the distinctive traits of racial groups to avoid misunderstandings that lead to special education placement, or that the distinguishing cognitive and social deficits that characterize poor racial minorities explain their greater need for special education.

Culture can also be located externally, in the historical residues of institutional rules and practices, in the routines and expected ways of using language and nonverbal behavior, and in the social rituals, practices, and predictable means to coordinate actions. Note that these "external" aspects are typically invisible to members of a cultural group, for they have grown accustomed to them (Cole, 1996). The external or "material practices" view is applied to any group that interacts over time; studies of the dominant discourse in U.S. classrooms along with its concomitant social and cognitive consequences illustrate this perspective. The inclusion literature has used an external view of culture as the characteristics, values, and practices of either traditional or inclusive school organizations are identified. The internal/external dichotomy oversimplifies the complex locations of culture.

The temporality of culture

Culture has temporal properties. Researchers study the cohesion, stability, and location of culture across time. To illustrate, we know that changes in a group's culture (cultural history) occur at a faster speed than changes in the history of a species (phylogeny), while cultural historical change proceeds at a slower pace than changes in the life history of an individual (ontogeny) (Cole, 1996). Moving down one level in this hierarchy of temporal scales to the microgenesis of events (moment-to-moment history), one could ask, "How do moments add up to lives? How do our shared moments together add up to social life as such?" (Lemke, 2000, p. 273). Lemke uses the term *temporal heterarchy* to describe the "interdependence of processes at very different timescales . . . of an organizational hierarchy in a complex self-organizing system" (p. 280). These levels of history unfold simultaneously and are interdependent (Scribner, 1985).[15]

The integration of these scales enables us to depict the temporality of culture (see Figure 1). The vertical axis represents the time scales that correspond to phylogenetic (the history of a species), cultural historical (the history of a group, institution, or society), ontogenetic (history of an individual over his or her lifespan), and microgenetic (the history of moment-to-moment lived experience) levels. The vertical axis also suggests that there is a hierarchy of embedded temporal scales that vary according to the level of temporal aggregation at which we examine culture. The horizontal axis depicts the temporality of culture with respect to the past, present, and

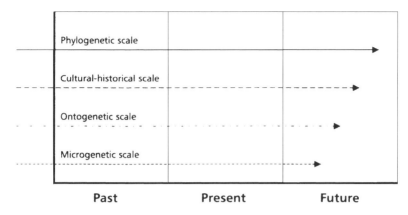

Figure 1 Distribution of Culture across Time Scales (adapted from Cole & Engestrom, 1993).

future, which allows us to conduct synchronic (at a given point in time) and diachronic (across time) analyses; in this vein, Cole and Engestrom (1993) remind us that "only a culture-using human being can 'reach into' the cultural past, project it into the future, and then 'carry' that (purely conceptual) future 'back' into the present in the shape of beliefs that then constrain and organize the present sociocultural environment" (p. 21).[16]

This differentiation of time scales contributes to explanations of cultural reproduction and cultural change. The cultural historical level represents the cultural patterning of a group, community, institution, or society that is reproduced from one generation to the next via apprenticeship processes (e.g., child-rearing practices).[17] When culture is studied at the cultural historical level, we find an emphasis on aspects such as ethnic groups' distinctive traits (e.g., learning or cognitive styles), or the distinctive features of "school cultures," "classroom cultures," or even "the culture of a reading group" (Jacob, 1995). The microgenetic level enables us to understand how an individual both acquires and reproduces such patterns. Individuals also have the potential to contribute to the transformation of cultural history as they exert their agency, though as we know, cultural change is a slower and more complex process. Depending on how one deals with the tensions between reproducing culture and crafting one's own life trajectory, individuals end up composing unique ontogenetic pathways and, ultimately, contribute to within-group diversity. In other words, inherent in ontogenetic development is the tension between normative views of developmental trajectories (i.e., what members of the cultural group are expected to achieve at different life stages) versus the hybridity of individuals (i.e., the within-individual diversity of a person).

The scholarship on overrepresentation tends to emphasize the cultural historical level. For example, recommendations from this discourse community exhort sensitivity toward the cultural historical characteristics of minority groups (e.g., dialect and language preferences, learning styles). It is paradoxical that, in their attempt to affirm cultural diversity, these suggestions end up advocating for essentialist and more static views of culture and cultural history. Furthermore, the risk of stressing a cultural historical view of minorities is that it might implicitly suggest that group traits are immutable features with no previous histories — that is, cultural reproduction is stressed.

Let us contrast the overrepresentation discourse community's traditional views of cultural history with a more dynamic perspective (Cole, 1996). In the case of Latinos/as, for example, we often ignore the fact that Latin America's evolution is fraught with political instability, oppression, ethnic, political, and religious conflict, and fragmented identities (Comas-Díaz, Lykes, & Alarcón, 1998). As a result, generations of Latinos/as, particularly in nations with sizable indigenous or Black populations, have been raised under savage economic, social, and educational inequalities and brutal repression; thus many of them (particularly members of racial minorities) have learned to live with fear, distrust, and/or despair (Galeano, 1989; Seed, 2001). However, these communities have not been merely passive recipients. They have developed and maintained incredible resiliency and persever-ance to survive in such adverse circumstances (Comas-Díaz *et al.*, 1998; Poniatowska, 1985).

When Latinos/as who have lived for generations under these conditions migrate to the United States, they engage in a complex process of coping and adapting to the host society that is inextricably intertwined with the cultural histories crafted in their homelands. Meanwhile, let us not forget that the cultural history of the dominant U.S. society has also influenced the evolving cultural histories of Latinos/as. In this process, recent immigrants begin to compose new cultural histories. As these immigrants weave new hybrid cultural histories in the context of U.S. society, generational differences emerge between themselves and their fellow ethnic peers who have lived in the United States for generations. Generational differences also arise between the recent immigrants and their own children as they are raised in the United States (Delgado-Gaitán, 1994; Suárez-Orozco & Suárez-Orozco, 1995). The result is that we find different combinations of stances (e.g., submission, resistance, assimilation, accommodation) among Latinos/as toward the values, institutions, and demands of the U.S. main-stream society, depending on their previous cultural histories, generation in the country, and the nature of experiences and contacts with dominant and subjugated communities (Suárez-Orozco & Suárez-Orozco, 1995).

This more complex perspective on the cultural histories of Latinos/as differs dramatically from the static view that permeates the overrepresentation discourse. It is indeed imperative that this discourse community take into account the interplay between historical legacies of domination and oppression in the U.S. society and the role of coping strategies, resilience mechanisms, and social and cultural capital in the construction of hybrid cultural histories in Latino and other minority communities. More importantly, researchers need to ask how these insights can inform research on placement patterns and the precursors of overrepresentation.

The inclusion literature, in turn, tends to focus on two time scales, namely, the cultural historical and ontogenetic levels. As explained above, inclusion has concentrated on the culture of traditional or inclusive schools (cultural history of institutions) or on the impact of inclusion on individuals' development or adaptation at certain ages and/or grade levels (ontogenesis); this work has examined one scale at a time (either cultural history or ontogenesis), and most investigators have preferred cross-sectional analyses. This is not surprising, given that special education research relies heavily on developmental psychology, which is inherently organized around chronological age as the primary index of the passage of time (i.e., ontogenetic development). Inclusion scholars face at least two major challenges. The first is to avoid an exclusive focus on single time scales so that the multiple developmental trajectories of students (ontogenetic level) that emerge within the cultural history of a given inclusive school can be documented. The second is to add complexity by acknowledging the racial, ability, language, gender, and class dimensions of students' and teachers' identities. Both challenges call for more complex research designs, as investigators will need to maintain a focus on both time scales throughout data collection and analysis activities while simultaneously considering multiple dimensions of identity.

Power in culture

Even as we complicate the notion of culture around the dimensions identified thus far, we run the risk of grasping only a partial understanding of the construct if we do not include the role of power and its link to historicity. Gallego *et al.* (2001) define culture as "the socially inherited body of past human accomplishments that serves as the resources for the current life of a social group ordinarily thought of as the inhabitants of a country or region" (p. 362). From this perspective, culture is constituted in the sedimentation of historical experience and it is at the intersection of history and social processes that the political nature of culture emerges. As Erickson (2001) explains:

> We live in webs of meaning, caring, and desire that we create and that create us, but those webs also hang in social gravity. Within the webs all our activity is vested in the weight of history; that is, in a social world of inequality all movement is up or down.
>
> (p. 38)

Note that this view of culture embodies visible and invisible elements, and its production and reproduction are achieved in social interactions "from the partial and mutually dependent knowledge of each person caught in the process. It is constituted, in the long run, by the work they do together" (Varenne & McDermott, 1999, p. 137).

Let us remember, though, that the maintenance of domination (i.e., hegemony) by a segment of society is achieved by "supplying the symbols, representations, and practices of social life in such a way that the basis of social authority and the unequal relations of power and privilege remain hidden" (McLaren, 1989, p. 174). Thus, the dominant culture is naturalized and used as a reference point against which all other cultural practices are compared and evaluated. This explains why groups' cultural practices have differential status and prestige in a given society and opportunities to learn valued practices are restricted and controlled. Various groups learn disparate portions or sets of culture and occupy dissimilar power positions. The processes by which culture is unequally distributed across individuals, groups, and generations is the result of profoundly political processes (Erickson, 2001).

Research and scholarship on racial minority placement in special education has overlooked issues of power and history. The bulk of this literature is concerned with placement patterns of discretely defined groups in disability categories or programs. Although some work is mindful of the political dimension of special education placement, we have a long way to go in this area. This oversight is even more intriguing if we consider that work in this area involves cultural groups that have a long history of oppression in U.S. society. Although reviews of the literature and the research base continue to report mixed evidence about bias and discrimination, I argue that overrepresentation scholarship must be mindful of the legacy of deficit thinking about racial minorities in U.S. history that continue to inform policy and scholarly writings (Artiles, 1998). We must acknowledge that unidimensional and deficit-based views of racial minorities permeate societal perceptions and thus mediate educators' and schools' ideologies. The challenge becomes how to develop research approaches that enable us to disentangle and examine the role of power in the construction of minority overrepresentation in special education.

Inclusion, on the other hand, features power to support the rationale for inclusive educational systems. Critiques of the traditional educational system grounded in a disability rights perspective are exemplary in this regard, as they denounce the power differentials and discriminatory assumptions and practices that curtail people with disabilities' access and outcomes in mainstream society. Research on the implementation of inclusion, however, has ignored power issues. Although some work on the social dimension of inclusion (e.g., social status in classrooms, friendships) has the potential to shed light on power issues, most studies neither theorize nor problematize the compelling force of power issues in inclusive classroom and school cultures.

Space: discontinuities in understanding and uses

A limited conception of space plays a critical role in the discourses on overrepresentation and inclusion. One central concern in the inclusion movement is access to general education spaces. Placement data suggest that, despite important variations across states, the nation's students with disabilities are increasingly educated in general education schools and classrooms, particularly students with LD (McLeskey, Henry, & Axelrod, 1999). We also know that discussions and investigations about minority overrepresentation are concerned with placement in various programs and the level of integration of such programs. It is important, therefore, to discuss the theoretical underpinnings of the concept of "space" and examine the inclusion and overrepresentation scholarships from this notion.

Systematic theorizing about space has intensified in recent years, particularly within the study of social life (Daniels & Lee, 1996; Foucault, 1986; Keith & Pile, 1993; Soja, 1996). I use the notion of space from the perspective of social geography to transcend the idea of space as simply physical location or destination. This perspective calls for "the study of physical space and human constructions, perceptions, and representations of spatiality as contexts for and consequences of human interaction" (Hargreaves, 1995, p. 7). Lefebvre (1991) argues for the creation of a "science of space," a unitary theory that aims to bridge the separation between the conception and analysis of space as physical/perceived space and the conception of space as conceived/mental space. Soja (1996) refers to the former as "FirstSpace" and to the latter as "SecondSpace." In this view, space is simultaneously physical, ideal, and the product of social translation and transformation (Lefebvre, 1991; Soja, 1989). The notion of space I am working from, therefore, transcends the traditional view of an a priori fixed entity and is conceived as "an achievement and an ongoing practice" (Shields, 2000, p. 155).

FirstSpace in the inclusion and overrepresentation literatures

FirstSpace refers to physical space that is perceived; it entails the processes and forms of social "spatiality." The social or spatial practice of a society "is thus presented as both medium and outcome of human activity, behavior, and experience" (Soja, 1996, p. 66). Space structures and is structured by people's actions; that is, there is a dialectical tension between the deterministic force of space and people's agency to counter its reproductive weight. As Soja (1989) explains, "We make our own history and geography, but not just as we please; we do not make them under circumstances chosen by ourselves, but under circumstances directly encountered, given and trans-mitted from the historical geographies produced in the past" (p. 129).

FirstSpace represents our commonsense understanding of space in which physical/perceived space (or what is readily visible) plays a significant role. FirstSpace analysis thus "concentrates on the accurate description of surface appearances . . . [or] searches for spatial explanation in primarily exogenous social, psychological, and biophysical processes" (Soja, 1996, p. 75). Inclusion research has assumed that placement of special education students in the physical spaces of general education classrooms has an effect on disabled and nondisabled students' learning and development. Studies that are concerned with the description of practices in inclusive classrooms or that test the impact of instructional approaches on student learning (e.g., Baker & Zigmond, 1995; Mortweet *et al.*, 1999), focusing on human activity, behavior, and/or experience, are examples of research that con-ceptualizes the space of inclusive classrooms simply in terms of FirstSpace. It is not uncommon that researchers assess such practices using data from published research or address process variables (e.g., participation in cooperative groups) indirectly through statistical analysis (Elbaum, Vaughn, Hughes, & Watson-Moody, 1999). Researchers have also examined parents', teachers', administrators', and students' understandings (cognitive/social skills, perceptions) of the physical spaces of inclusive classrooms. These studies have been conducted in an attempt to assess the viability of inclusive models, anticipate potential constraints, and inform inclusion approaches (e.g., Cook *et al.*, 1999; Soodak, Podell, & Lehman, 1998).

Although it is important to address parents' and students' understandings of physical/perceived spaces of inclusion, it is also necessary to obtain detailed or moment-to-moment accounts of the construction processes of academic and social outcomes in those spaces. Evidence of the need for this line of research is apparent in studies reporting mixed results. In such instances the authors allude to contextual aspects. For example, in the case of the outcomes of mixed-ability groups, it was reported that "factors such as partner selection, teacher monitoring, and the establishment of a cooperative ethic appeared to influence the outcomes. Clearly, the structure and support are essential to the success of these arrangements" (U.S. Department of Education, 1999, p. III-29). Another example of studies that conceptualizes classrooms simply in terms of physical space is found in the research on the mixed impact of program models on students with disabilities; the reviewers conclude that such findings underscore "the need to pay greater attention to specific organizational and instructional practices in heterogeneous classrooms" (p. III-22).

The bulk of the overrepresentation literature is equally concerned with FirstSpace analyses as reflected in the almost exclusive attention to placement patterns for various ethnic groups in disability programs. Outcomes (i.e., placement patterns) are foregrounded in these analyses, and static markers of difference (e.g., ethnic labels) are included in studies to discern their association with various physical spaces (e.g., school location, type of special education program). For example, researchers have studied whether placement patterns are differentially shaped by student race, poverty level, academic achievement level, and school location (urban v. suburban) (Artiles *et al.*, 1998; Oswald *et al.*, 1999). With a few exceptions, the social practices that precede placement decisions are ignored. The under-standings of physical/perceived spaces by teachers and other school personnel are also assessed (generally via surveys and questionnaires), typically to test a bias hypothesis (Donovan & Cross, 2002). Given the strong social desirability associated with measures of cultural bias, it is not surprising, that this evidence is mixed.

SecondSpace in the inclusion and overrepresentation scholarship

SecondSpace refers to space as conceptualized by people; it encompasses conceived spaces and includes "representations of power and ideology, of control and surveillance. . . . It is the primary source of utopian thought and vision" (Soja, 1996, p. 67). SecondSpace is "the ideological content of codes, theories, and the conceptual depictions of space linked to production relations" (Shields, 2000, p. 163). Lefebvre (1991) referred to it as "concep-tualized space, the space of scientists" (p. 38). There are far-reaching conceptualizations (conceived space) of inclusive education that situate the meaning and place of special education in larger societal and historical contexts (e.g., Ferguson, 1995; Lipsky & Gartner, 1996). These concep-tualizations emphasize complexity, are comprehensive and ambitious, and generally suggest a revamping of the educational system's premises, values, and practices (Ferguson & Ferguson, 1997). Interestingly, these frameworks contrast with the more outcome-oriented focus of the inclusion research literature. In other words, there seems to be a discontinuity between the rep-resentations of inclusive education (the SecondSpace dimensions of space) and the actual examination of inclusion processes and outcomes (FirstSpace).

Unlike inclusion, the overrepresentation discourse has devoted hardly any effort to developing conceptualizations and visions of the types of spaces needed by students in inclusive classrooms. Given that Secondspace is "entirely ideational, made up of projections into the empirical world from conceived or imagined geographies" (Soja, 1996, p. 79), the lack of utopian thinking or imagination in the overrepresentation discourse has potentially devastating consequences. This scholarship runs the risk of merely accumulat-ing descriptions of spatial practices that are not guided by a theoretical imagination about the role of cultural differences in education or a vision of an ideal state of affairs in a pluralistic society. Unlike the inclusion discourse, the scholarship devoted to address solutions to this problem tends to lack a transformative bent.

There are gaps in the spaces examined by the inclusion and over-representation discourse communities. Although both communities tend to concentrate on the production of spatial practices (on space as FirstSpace), the inclusion community seems to be guided by visions of an inclusive education system (space conceptualized as SecondSpace). In contrast, overrepresentation lacks such conceived space. Without finding a way to bring the two literatures together, special educators risk reconstructing the educational system based on visions that ignore the history and implications of racial, ethnic, class, and linguistic differences in the social organization of learning in culturally and politically charged contexts. Likewise, we cannot afford to reconstruct the system without a vision of what we want to achieve in a heterogeneous educational system to consolidate a socially just society.

Challenges for a new generation of inclusion and overrepresentation research: the productions of culture, lived spaces, and difference

The convergence of inclusion and overrepresentation exposes the fact that the educational system may be educating more students with disabilities in general education contexts, but many of those being included are poor racial and linguistic minorities that have additional ability deficits superimposed onto their identities. It seems that both phenomena have stressed a technical perspective. The inclusion movement has focused on a redistribution of resources so that students with disabilities are educated in a presumed new breed of general education, whereas overrepresentation has been largely reduced to the study of placement proportions. These discourses have also emphasized legalistic issues. Inclusion has focused on new requirements for placement in general education, access to the curriculum, and accountability, while overrepresentation has pushed for the creation of antidiscriminatory regulations generally enforced by the Office for Civil Rights (Losen & Orfield, 2002). However, I argue that the overrepresentation and inclusion literatures have used partial perspectives on culture, have not adequately theorized space, and have been silent about difference. Future research cannot afford to ignore these aspects as we live in an increasingly pluralistic society.

Beyond "ways of life" and places: the productions of culture and lived spaces

Both inclusion and overrepresentation scholarship need to adopt more complex and dynamic conceptions of culture and multiple time scales (cultural, historical, ontogenetic, microgenetic) in order to obtain a deeper understanding of human development as situated in cultural, historical, and social contexts. Traditional views of culture have faced mounting criticism due to the limits of their assumptions and premises. Scholars have criticized traditional views because they project an image of culture that (a) privileges group patterns at the expense of within-group diversity, (b) portrays culture as stagnant in time with clearly demarcated boundaries between groups, (c) ignores individual agency, and (d) overlooks the role of power in cultural processes (Eisenhart, 2001). Researchers face the challenge of incorporating "the fact of constant individual creativity into a theory of culture" (Varenne, 1984, p. 282). At the same time, we must avoid dichotomizing the individual and the society. As Rosaldo (1984) warns us, the "view of the repeated struggle between sacred individualism and sociological wisdom reduces complex historical processes to timeless conflicts" (p. 294).

One of the most ambitious projects that aims to transcend the limits of traditional views of culture is represented in the so-called cultural productions turn (Eisenhart, 2001). This view accounts for individual (e.g., beliefs, values) and societal (e.g., structures) cultural forces, and it argues that the convergence of such forces must be examined as situated in and shaped by the local social conditions of everyday practice. From this perspective, culture not only constrains but also enables individual performance. It constrains in the sense that a person enters a context where a culture is represented in the structural and historical legacies embedded in the artifacts, rules for interaction, and prescribed roles available in the setting. The subject, therefore, is constrained to operate with those elements and pressured to reproduce cultural tradition. At the same time, the individual's agency enables her to use artifacts in novel ways, challenge prescribed roles, and modify established rules. In this sense, culture can also enable the individual to disrupt tradition and promote change (see examples of this research in Engestrom, Miettinen, & Punamaki, 1999; Nespor, 1994).

The cultural productions view uses a unit of analysis that requires researchers to study classroom cultures "as a hybrid of the local and the social historical levels of analysis" (Gallego *et al.*, 2001, p. 957). That is, it uses a unit of analysis that accounts for cultural acquisition, use, reproduction, and change. The recent work on cultural productions enhances our understanding of "how local practices of cultural production become meaningful and consequential to participants; differentiate otherwise similar individuals; make similar otherwise different people; are connected to wider processes of nationalism, stratification, globalization, and professionalism; and sometimes motivate change" (Eisenhart, 2001, p. 218). This perspective on culture, therefore, can help researchers generate knowledge that honors the complexities of the spaces, histories, and cultural practices of both overrepresentation and inclusion.

Similarly, inclusion and overrepresentation scholarship can benefit from a new science of space, building on knowledge of how First- and Second-Spaces interact and influence one another in the lived spaces of inclusive classrooms. Within the interactions between FirstSpace and SecondSpace, a

ThirdSpace is created, capturing lived space, or spaces of representation (Soja, 1996). Lived space both encompasses and is distinct from the other two spaces. ThirdSpace is the "habitus of asocial practices, a constantly shifting and changing milieu of ideas, events, appearances, and meanings" (Kahn, 2000, p. 7). According to Soja (1996), counterspaces or spaces of resistance can be created in ThirdSpace because it is filled with ideology and politics, with relations of dominance and subordination, with the intricate interdependency of the real and the imagined. ThirdSpace is a powerful tool because it enables us to question simplifications of space as "site" or "destination" and to transcend dichotomies of representations such as insiders and outsiders. At the same time, ThirdSpace is a dynamic construct that surfaces as a result of the dialectic of the physical and the mental, the concrete and the abstract; it contains the perceived and conceived spaces simultaneously (Soja, 1996, Tejeda, 2000).

At a time when politically and ideologically charged reforms will likely have devastating consequences for poor and racial minority students, future research ought to focus on the genesis and transformation of ThirdSpaces — the site where attention to ideology and politics is prominent and where resistance is created. Attention to ThirdSpaces will inevitably compel us to be mindful of social justice as issues of power, subordination, and dominance are central. Researchers must conduct participatory research with teachers, families, and students and focus explicitly on the role of institutional forces in their lived experiences in schools, households, and communities.

Beyond diversity: toward an understanding of difference and perspective

Ultimately, inclusion and overrepresentation researchers face dilemmas related to underlying assumptions about difference. Both discourse communities tend to use the notion of cultural "diversity," which is typically defined as "the recognition of pre-given cultural contents and customs" (Bhabha, 1994, p. 34). Two problems exist with this notion. First, the notion of diversity embodies a "transparent norm" (Alsayyad, 2001, p. 7) that essentializes culture and "turns the other into something monolithic, partly out of not only ignorance but also fear" (Viswanathan, 2001, p. 238). Second, racism is very much alive in *all* societies precisely because "the universalism that paradoxically permits diversity masks ethnocentric norms, values, and interests" (Bhabha, cited in Alsayyad, 2001, p. 7).

Cultural difference in turn questions binary distinctions (diverse, nondiverse) and foregrounds "the problem of the ambivalence of cultural authority" (Bhabha, 1994, p. 34). Minow (1990) stated that difference has been equated with deviance or stigma, and thus sameness is a prerequisite of equality. Therefore, it is not surprising that traditional treatments of difference ultimately reaffirm difference and offer options that signal the deficits or disadvantages typically associated with difference — it is paradoxical then that to recognize "difference reinforces hierarchy" (Abu-Lughod, cited in Brightman, 1995, p. 532). Special education has historically faced the dilemma of affirming or ignoring difference. On the one hand, it was argued that equal instructional treatment was unfair, institutionalizing an individualized educational system. On the other hand, the inclusion movement has argued that equal access to general education spaces, curriculum, and accountability standards are just. The former strategy recognizes difference while the latter diffuses it; ultimately, both are organized around it. In the case of minorities we observe a similar ambivalence in the solutions offered to the dilemma of difference — again, the underlying question has been whether we should ignore or affirm it. Indeed, access to the same (integrated) educational contexts was a major achievement for racial minorities in the civil rights era while linguistic minorities have fought for differential treatment in the form of bilingual education programs.

The inclusion and overrepresentation discourses have offered ambivalent and even conflicting responses to the question of how to handle difference due to their underlying assumptions. A first step is to make explicit the underlying assumptions of difference and counter them with alternative assumptions. As we use more complex views of culture in the discourses of inclusion and overrepresentation to address issues ultimately concerned with difference, we must ask, When does a difference count, under what conditions, in what ways, and for what reasons? (Varenne & McDermott, 1999).

Attention to culture and space as a way to understand notions of difference demands that we acknowledge the role of power in the creation of borders. It particularly calls our attention to the perspective of the observer, an issue that has been historically invisible and unquestioned in research practices. Implications of the role of perspective are twofold. First, the perspective of the observer or analyst (e.g., teacher, researcher) must be recognized. Second, we can gain greater insight from examining how people use notions of difference to create borders during social interactions in particular institutional contexts rather than studying the distinctive features of a group's cultural history (Barth, 1969). This is a particularly important theoretical insight, as overrepresentation and inclusion focus on borders, such as race, that possess great historical currency in U.S. society. As Rosaldo (1984) explains, "Race relations in North America involve a blend of assimilationist efforts, raw prejudice, and cultural containment that revolves around a concerted effort to keep each culture pure and in its place" (p. 212).

In turn, systematic attention to culture in research practices will force us to be aware of and disclose our assumptions about difference (e.g., researchers' understandings of development, time, space, and culture). Such heightened awareness will compel us to envision difference as produced in relationships and rooted in comparisons between a person and culturally based norms that can be unveiled, evaluated, and contested (Minow, 1990). Minow also challenges us to enable those who have been dispensed identities of difference, such as disability, to share alternative perspectives that are not always aligned with culturally based norms and expectations. This practice will allow us to reflect on the culturally based assumptions that underlie the design and implementation of school rules, curricula, and assessment practices. The practice of honoring multiple perspectives on inclusion and overrepresentation will also enable us to read these knowledge bases (borrowing from Said) "contrapuntally, to use the metaphor from music. [This practice would enable us to go] over the same history but from a different point of view" (Viswanathan, 2001, p, 245). This way, we could transcend the traditional dilemmas of difference (e.g., to provide equal or preferential treatment). Instead, analysis of culture-based notions of difference should focus on "the ways in which institutions construct and utilize differences to justify and enforce exclusions — and the ways in which such institutional practices can be changed" (Minow, 1990, p. 86). The potential role of institutional histories and contexts must be taken into account in such analyses; this is why it is critical to situate overrepresentation and inclusion analyses in the larger cultural politics of special education reforms.

Overrepresentation and inclusion are ultimately about how educators and educational systems deal with "difference" in politically and culturally charged contexts. I argue that we must examine these phenomena beyond special education placement issues, using more sophisticated views of culture and space. The present emphasis on reporting only the number of students with disabilities being educated in general education classrooms and schools is creating the illusion that the inclusive education movement is consolidating. This emphasis also disregards both the historicity and sociality of who is being identified as disabled and the sociocultural roots of disability constructions. As the complexity of the cultural politics of educational reform surfaces and as its influence on special education transformations intensifies, we must concern ourselves with the study of disability, inclusion, and overrepresentation in an elaborate cultural medium, mediated by multiple scales and planes of space and time. In this manner, disability and special education scholarship will transcend the traditional individualistic perspective and infuse a social justice dimension so that the improvement of educational experiences and life opportunities for historically marginalized students are of central concern.

Notes

I presented various versions of this paper as keynote addresses at the International Special Education Conference (Manchester, England, July 2000), the ninth annual

Inclusive Schools and Communities for Children and Youth Conference (Tarrytown, New York, May 2001), and the IDEA Summit (Washington, DC, June 2001). The analyses presented in this manuscript were refined while I received support from the Spencer Foundation/National Academy of Education (Postdoctoral Fellowship Program), the COMRISE Project under grant #H029J60006 awarded by the U.S. Department of Education (USDOE), Office of Special Education Programs (OSEP), and the National Center for Culturally Responsive Educational Systems (NCCRESt) under grant #H326E020003 awarded by the USDOE, OSEP. Endorsement of the ideas presented in this article by these funding agencies should not be inferred. I am indebted to many colleagues for their feedback on different versions of this paper, particularly to Fernando Diniz, Alan Dyson, Diane Ferguson, Phil Ferguson, Doug Fuchs, Kris Gutierrez, Beth Harry, Elizabeth Kozleski, Huong Tran Nguyen, Denis Poizat, Kim Reed, Mike Rose, Robert Rueda, Carlos Tejeda, and Stan Trent. My thinking and writing were sharpened by their insights, though I remain responsible for the manuscript's shortcomings.

1 "The term inclusion has been used so widely that it has almost lost its meaning" (Skrtic, Sailor, & Gee, 1996, p. 149). Some definitions stress physical placement — for example, "placement (full or partial) of students with mild disabilities in general education classrooms" (Cook, Semmel, & Gerber, 1999, p. 207). Others stress the notion of inclusive schools, which, according to Skrtic, Sailor, and Gee (1996), "are those designed to meet the educational needs of all their members within common, yet fluid, environments and activities" (p. 149). Inclusion is also seen as a process of developing a unified educational system that serves students with disabilities and their nondisabled peers "as active, fully participating members of the school community; that views diversity as the norm; and that ensures a high-quality education for students by providing meaningful curriculum, effective teaching, and necessary supports for each student" (Ferguson, 1995, p. 286).

2 Overrepresentation is defined as "unequal proportions of culturally diverse students in [special education] programs" (Artiles & Trent, 2000, p. 514); typically, this phenomenon is calculated in relation to a group's representation in general education or in reference to the representation of a comparison group (e.g., White students).

3 I use the notion of "discourse community" to describe groups (e.g., researchers, practitioners) that coalesce around a common interest or an object of study or labor. A discourse community devotes efforts and resources to produce knowledge about its object "and establishes conditions for who speaks and what gets heard.... Because it is institutionally sanctioned, their discourse is powerful ... its 'regime' or 'politics of truth' sets standards for the field" (Brantlinger, 1997, p. 432). Although the notion of discourse community emphasizes cohesion, note that there are diverse perspectives within the over-representation and inclusion discourse communities.

4 Special education relies on a categorical model of disabilities. High-incidence disabilities include learning disabilities (LD), emotional disturbance (ED), mild mental retardation (MMR), and speech or language impairments; students with LD comprise about half of the special education population (Smith, 2001). Low-incidence disabilities include autism, deafness/hearing impairments, multiple disabilities, visual impairments, other health impairments, deaf-blindness, orthopedic impairments, and traumatic brain injury.

5 To the dismay of debate participants, general education hardly pays attention to these deliberations. To this day, large-scale efforts to monitor the implementation of major general education reforms "have generally ignored the issue

of disability and . . . the information that is available has been collected in a piecemeal fashion" (Vanderwood, McGrew, & Ysseldyke, 1998, p. 366).

6 For instance, the federal government in recent years has funded the National Longitudinal Transition Study (Wagner *et al.*, 1993), the COMRISE and LASER Projects, the National Institute for Urban School Improvement, and the National Center for Culturally Responsive Educational Systems (among others) to support research and technical assistance activities with an explicit attention to race and minority special education placement and urban education issues.

7 The risk index offers a measure of the proportion of students from a group that is placed in a disability category. It is calculated "by dividing the number of students in a given racial or ethnic category served in a given disability category by the total enrollment for that racial or ethnic group in the school population" (Donovan & Cross, 2002, pp. 42–43). The odds ratio divides the risk index of one racial/ethnic group by the risk index of another racial/ethnic group in order to provide a comparison. If the risk indices are identical for two groups, the odds ratio will equal 1.0. Odds ratios greater than 1.0 indicate that the minority group students are at greater risk for identification, while odds of less than 1.0 indicate that they are less at risk (Donovan & Cross, 2002). To illustrate, let us assume that a comparison of Latino and White student LD identification in a given district results in an odds ratio of 1.36. This means Latino students would be 36 percent more likely than White students to be given the LD label in that school district.

8 Based on OSEP data, the NRC report concluded there is no "evidence that minority children are systematically represented in low-incidence disability categories in numbers that are disproportionate to their representation in the population" (Donovan & Cross, 2002, p. 61).

9 The reauthorization of IDEA in 1997 strengthened the nondiscriminatory requirements of the law, which include using nondiscriminatory assessment, collecting and monitoring placement data by race and class, providing educational services for expelled students or for school-age youngsters in correctional facilities, providing procedural safeguards for parents, and documenting the quality of instruction and opportunity to learn prior to special education referrals (Hehir, 2002; Smith, 2001).

10 As stated above, data are scarce on the types of placement contexts (segregated v. integrated) in which minority students with disabilities are being placed.

11 Artiles *et al.* acknowledged that "although we are not advocating the use of ethnicity or race as the most important proxies of culture in LD research, we chose to examine the research using these proxies to obtain baseline information about this knowledge base" (p. 83).

12 The five dimensions of culture are intricately interrelated, and I discuss them separately for heuristic purposes.

13 Several objections have been made to the cultural discontinuity hypothesis (Gallego *et al.*, 2001; Varenne & McDermott, 1999). One criticism is that cultural discontinuities do not always result in miscommunications and school failure for minorities. Ogbu (1992), for instance, argues that groups create cultural frames of reference based on their unique histories (e.g., immigration, societal power status), which explains why various groups sometimes exhibit distinct responses to similar external conditions. This explains why a minority group that experiences a discontinuity between its own culture and the school's culture still exhibits educational success. Another criticism of the way-of-life view is that it is overly deterministic, as it assumes that home or group culture defines what people do when they enter new contexts.

14 Scholars have taken issue with the internal-external dualism and have advanced more complex views (Erickson 2001; Gallego *et al.*, 2001). I differentiate these locations to explain that many definitions of culture artificially create this dichotomy and tend to privilege one location over the other.

15 Researchers are only beginning to investigate the embededdness of multiple historical domains and their mutual influences to understand the temporal distribution of culture in human development (Cole, 1996; Dien, 2000). For examples of this emergent scholarship, see Cole and Engestrom (1993), Cole (1996), Lemke (2000), and Dien (2000).

16 See Artiles, Gutierrez, and Rueda (2002), Cole (1996), and Stone (1993) for discussions of prolepsis and other processes that can help us understand how culture mediates learning.

17 Note that cultural history also embodies the transformed elements of cultural legacies that result from cultural change processes.

References

Advancement Project & Civil Rights Project. (2000). *Opportunities suspended: The devastating consequences of zero tolerance and school discipline policies.* Cambridge, MA: Civil Rights Project at Harvard University. Retrieved on December 10, 2000, from http://www.law.Harvard.edu/groups/civilrights/conferences/zero/zt_report2.html

Alsayyad, N. (2001). Hybrid culture/hybrid urbanism: Pandora's box of the "third place." In N. Alsayyad (Ed.), *Hybrid urbanism: On the identity discourse and the built environment* (pp. 1–18). Westport, CT: Praeger.

Anyon, J. (1997). *Ghetto schooling: A political economy of urban educational reform.* New York: Teachers College Press.

Anzaldúa, G. (1999). *Borderlands/La frontera: The new mestiza* (2nd ed.). San Francisco: Aunt Lute Books.

Apple, M. W. (1996). *Cultural politics and education.* New York: Teachers College Press.

Artiles, A. J. (1998). The dilemma of difference: Enriching the disproportionality discourse with theory and context. *Journal of Special Education, 32,* 32–36.

Artiles, A. J., Aguirre-Muñoz, Z., & Abedi, J. (1998). Predicting placement in learning disabilities programs: Do predictors vary by ethnic group? *Exceptional Children, 64,* 543–559.

Artiles, A. J., Gutierrez, K., & Rueda, R. (2002, April). *Teacher education in a culturally diverse inclusive era: Implications of a cultural historical vision for teacher learning research.* Paper presented at the annual meeting of the American Educational Research Association, New Orleans.

Artiles, A. J., & Pak, M. (2000, July). *Becoming an inclusive education teacher in an urban multicultural school: Tensions, contradictions, and implications for inclusion research.* Paper presented at the International Special Education Conference, Manchester, England.

Artiles, A. J., Rueda, R., Salazar, J., & Higareda, I. (2002). English-language learner representation in special education in California urban school districts. In D. J. Losen & G. Orfield (Eds.), *Racial inequity in special education* (pp. 117–136). Cambridge, MA: Harvard Education Press.

Artiles, A. J., & Trent, S. C. (2000). Representation of culturally/linguistically diverse students. In C. R. Reynolds & E. Fletcher-Jantzen (Eds.), *Encyclopedia of special education, Vol. 1* (2nd ed., pp. 513–517). New York: John Wiley.

Artiles, A. J., Trent, S. C., & Kuan, L. A. (1997). Learning disabilities research on ethnic minority students: An analysis of 22 years of studies published in selected refereed journals. *Learning Disabilities Research and Practice, 12*, 82–91.

Artiles, A. J., Trent, S. C., & Palmer, J. (in press). Culturally diverse students in special education: Legacies and prospects. In J. A. Banks & C. M. Banks (Eds.), *Handbook of research on multicultural education* (2nd ed.). San Francisco: Jossey-Bass.

Baker, J., & Zigmond, N. (1995). The meaning and practice of inclusion for students with learning disabilities: Themes and implications from the five case studies. *Journal of Special Education, 29*, 163–180.

Barth, F. (1969). *Ethnic groups and boundaries: The social organization of culture difference*. Boston: Little Brown.

Bhabha, H. K. (1994). *The location of culture*. London: Routledge.

Bowles, S., & Gintis, H. (1976). *Schooling in capitalist America: Educational reform and the contradictions of economic life*. New York: Basic Books.

Brantlinger, E. (1997). Using ideology: Cases of nonrecognition of the politics of research and practice in special education. *Review of Educational Research, 67*, 425–459.

Brightman, R. (1995). Forget culture: Replacement, transcendence, relexification. *Cultural Anthropology, 10*, 509–546.

Christensen, C., & Rizvi, F. (Eds.). (1996). *Disability and the dilemmas of education and justice*, Buckingham, Eng.: Open University Press.

Cole, M. (1996). *Cultural psychology: A once and future discipline*. Cambridge, MA: Harvard University Press.

Cole, M., & Engestrom, Y. (1993). A cultural-historical approach to distributed cognition. In G. Salomon (Ed.), *Distributed cognitions: Psychological and educational considerations* (pp. 1–46). New York: Cambridge University Press.

Comas-Díaz, L., Lykes, M. B., & Alarcón, R. D. (1998). Ethnic conflict and the psychology of liberation in Guatemala, Peru, and Puerto Rico. *American Psychologist, 53*, 778–792.

Cook, B. G., Semmel, M. I., & Gerber, M. M. (1999). Attitudes of principals and special education teachers toward the inclusion of students with mild disabilities. *Remedial and Special Education, 20*, 199–207.

Daniels, S., & Lee, R. (Eds.). (1996). *Exploring human geography: A reader*. New York: Halstead Press.

Delgado-Gaitán, C. (1994). Socializing young children in Mexican-American families: An intergenerational perspective. In P. Greenfield & R. Cocking (Eds.), *Cross-cultural roots of minority child development* (pp. 55–86). Hillsdale, NJ: Lawrence Erlbaum.

Dien, D. S. (2000). The evolving nature of self-identity across four levels of history. *Human Development, 43*, 1–18.

Donovan, S., & Cross, C. (Eds.). (2002). *Minority students in special and gifted education*. Washington, DC: National Academy Press.

Dunn, L. M. (1968). Special education for the mildly retarded: Is much of it justifiable? *Exceptional Children, 35*, 5–22.

Dyson, A. (1999). Inclusion and inclusions: Theories and discourses in inclusive education. In H. Daniels & P. Garner (Eds.), *World yearbook of education 1999: Inclusive education* (pp. 36–53). London: Kogan Page.

Eagleton, T. (2000). *The idea of culture*. Oxford, Eng.: Blackwell.

Eisenhart, M. (2001). Changing conceptions of culture and ethnographic methodology: Recent thematic shifts and their implications for research on teaching. In V. Richardson (Ed.), *Handbook of research on teaching* (4th ed., pp. 209–225). Washington, DC: American Educational Research Association.

Elbaum, B., Vaughn, S., Hughes, M., & Watson-Moody, S. (1999). Grouping practices and reading outcomes for students with disabilities. *Exceptional Children, 65*, 399–415.

Engestrom, Y., Miettinen, R., & Punamaki, R. (Eds.). (1999). *Perspectives on activity theory*. New York: Cambridge University Press.

Erickson, F. (1996). Inclusion into what? Thoughts on the construction of learning, identity, and affiliation in the general education classroom. In D. L. Speece & B. K. Keogh (Eds.), *Research on classroom ecologies* (pp. 91–105). Mahwah, NJ: Lawrence Erlbaum.

Erickson, F. (2001). Culture in society and in educational practices. In J. Banks & C. M. Banks (Eds.), *Multicultural education: Issues and perspectives* (pp. 31–58). New York: Wiley.

Ferguson, D. L. (1995). The real challenge of inclusion: Confessions of a rabid inclusionist. *Phi Delta Kappan, 77*, 281–287.

Ferguson, D. L., & Ferguson, P. M. (1997). Debating inclusion in Synecdoche, New York: A response to Gresham and MacMillan. *Review of Educational Research, 67*, 416–420.

Finn, J. D. (1982). Patterns in special education placement as revealed by the OCR surveys. In K. A. Heller, W. H. Holtzman, & S. Messick (Eds.), *Placing children in special education: A strategy for equity* (pp. 322–381). Washington, DC: National Academy Press.

Foucault, M. (1986). Of other spaces. *Diacritics, 16*, 22–27.

Fuchs, D., & Fuchs, L. S. (1994). Inclusive schools movement and the radicalization of special education reform. *Exceptional Children, 60*, 294–309.

Fujiura, G. T., & Yamaki, K. (2000). Trends in demography of childhood poverty and disability. *Exceptional Children, 66*, 187–199.

Galeano, E. (1989). *Las venas abiertas de América Latina*. Mexico DF: Siglo Veintiuno Editores.

Gallego, M. A., Cole, M., & Laboratory of Comparative Human Cognition. (2001). Classroom cultures and cultures in the classroom. In V. Richardson (Ed.), *Handbook of research on teaching* (4th ed., pp. 951–997). Washington, DC: American Educational Research Association.

Gándara, P., Maxwell-Jolly, J., García, E., Asato, J., Gutiérrez, K., Stritikus, T., & Curry, J. (2000, April). *The initial impact of Proposition 227 on the instruction of English learners*. Santa Barbara: University of California Linguistic Minority Research Institute.

García, E. (1996). Preparing instructional professionals for linguistically and culturally diverse students. In J. Sikula (Ed.), *Handbook of research on teacher education* (pp. 802–812). New York: Macmillan.

Gartner, A., & Lipsky, D. K. (1987). Beyond special education: Toward a quality system for all students. *Harvard Educational Review, 57*, 367–395.

Geertz, C. (1983). *Local knowledge: Further essays in interpretive anthropology*. New York: Basic Books.

Gersten, R., Baker, S., Pugach, M., with Scanlon, D., & Chard, D. (2001). Contemporary research on special education teaching. In V. Richardson (Ed.), *Handbook of research on teaching* (4th ed., pp. 695–722). Washington, DC: American Educational Research Association.

Gottlieb, J., Alter, M., Gottlieb, B. W., & Wishner, J. (1994). Special education in urban America: It's not justifiable for many. *Journal of Special Education, 27,* 453–465.

Gutiérrez, K., Asato, J., Santos, M., & Gotanda, N. (2002). Backlash pedagogy: Language and culture and the politics of reform. *Review of Education, Pedagogy, and Cultural Studies, 24,* 335–351.

Handwerker, W. P. (2002). The construct validity of cultures: Cultural diversity, culture theory, and a method for ethnography. *American Anthropologist, 104,* 106–122.

Hargreaves, A. (1995). Toward a social geography of teacher education. In N. K. Shimahara & I. Z. Holowinsky (Eds.), *Teacher education in industrialized nations* (pp. 3–40). New York: Garland.

Harry, B., Klingner, J., Sturges, K. M., & Moore, R. F. (2002). Of rocks and soft places: Using qualitative methods to investigate disproportionality. In D. J. Losen & G. Orfield (Eds.), *Racial inequity in special education* (pp. 71–92). Cambridge, MA: Harvard Education Press.

Heath, S. B. (1983). *Ways with words: Language, life and work in communities and classrooms.* Cambridge, Eng.: Cambridge University Press.

Hehir, T. (2002). IDEA and disproportionality: Federal enforcement, effective advocacy, and strategies for change. In D. J. Losen & G. Orfield (Eds.), *Racial inequity in special education* (pp. 219–238). Cambridge, MA: Harvard Education Press.

Heller, K. A., Holtzman, W. H., & Messick, S. (Eds.). (1982). *Placing children in special education: A strategy for equity.* Washington, DC: National Academy Press.

Heubert, J. P. (2002). Disability, race, and high-stakes testing of students. In D. J. Losen & G. Orfield (Eds.), *Racial inequity in special education* (pp. 137–165). Cambridge, MA: Harvard Education Press.

Individuals with Disabilities Education Act Amendments of 1997 (IDEA), 20 U.S.C. §1400–87 (1997) (1994 & Supp. V 1999) (originally enacted as the Education for All Handicapped Children Act of 1975, Pub. L. No. 94–142, 89 Stat. 773).

Irvine, J. J., & York, D. E. (1995). Learning styles and culturally diverse students: A literature review. In J. A. Banks & C. A. McGee Banks (Eds.), *Handbook of research on multicultural education* (pp. 484–497). New York: Macmillan.

Jacob, E. (1995). Reflective practice and anthropology in culturally diverse classrooms. *Elementary School Journal, 95,* 451–463.

Kahn, M. (2000). Thaiti intertwined: Ancestral land, tourist postcard, and nuclear test site. *American Anthropologist, 102,* 7–26.

Kauffman, J. M., & Hallahan, D. P. (Eds.). (1995). *The illusion of full inclusion.* Austin, TX: Pro-Ed.

Keith, M., & Pile, S. (Eds.). (1993). *Place and the politics of identity.* New York: Routledge.

Lefebvre, H. (1991). *The production of space.* Oxford, Eng.: Blackwell.

Lemke, J. L. (2000). Across the scales of time: Artifacts, activities, and meanings in ecosocial systems. *Mind, Culture, and Activity, 7,* 273–290.

Lipsky, D. K., & Gartner, A. (1996). Inclusion, school restructuring, and the remaking of American society. *Harvard Educational Review, 66*, 762–796.

Lipsky, D. K., & Gartner, A. (1999). Inclusive education: A requirement of a democratic society. In H. Daniels & P. Garner (Eds.), *World yearbook of education 1999: Inclusive education* (pp. 12–23). London: Kogan Page.

Losen, D. J., & Orfield, G. (Eds.). (2002). *Racial inequity in special education.* Cambridge, MA: Harvard Education Press.

Manset, G., & Semmel, M. I. (1997). Are inclusive programs for students with mild disabilities effective? A comparative review of model programs. *Journal of Special Education, 31*, 155–180.

McDonnell, L., McLaughlin, M. J., & Morison, P. (Eds.). (1997). *Educating one and all: Students with disabilities and standards-based reform.* Washington, DC: National Academy Press.

McLaren, P. (1989). *Life in schools.* New York: Longman.

McLaughlin, M. J., & Tilstone, C. (1999). Standards and curriculum: The core of educational reform. In M. J. McLaughlin & M. Rouse (Eds.), *Special education and school reform in the United States and Britain* (pp. 38–65). London: Routledge.

McLaughlin, M. J., Fuchs, L., & Hardman, M. (1999). Individual rights to education and students with disabilities: Some lessons from U.S. policy. In H. Daniels & P. Garner (Eds.), *World yearbook of education 1999: Inclusive education* (pp. 24–35). London: Kogan Page.

McLaughlin, M. J., Henderson, K., & Rhim, L. M. (1998, September). *Snapshots of reform: How five local districts are interpreting standards-based reform for students with disabilities.* Alexandria, VA: Center for Policy Research.

McLeskey, J., Henry, D., & Axelrod, M. I. (1999). Inclusion of students with learning disabilities: An examination of data from reports to Congress. *Exceptional Children, 66*, 55–66.

McLoyd, V. C. (1998). Socioeconomic disadvantage and child development. *American Psychologist, 53*, 185–204.

Mehan, H., Hartwick, A., & Meihls, J. L. (1986). *Handicapping the handicapped: Decision-making in students' educational careers.* Stanford, CA: Stanford University Press.

Minow, M. (1990). *Making all the difference: Inclusion, exclusion, and American law.* Ithaca, NY: Cornell University Press.

Mortweet, S. L., Utley, C. A., Walker, D., Dawson, H. L., Delquadri, J. C., Reddy, S. S., Greenwood, C. R., Hamilton, S., & Ledford, D. (1999). Classwide peer tutoring: Teaching students with mild mental retardation in inclusive classrooms. *Exceptional Children, 65*, 524–536.

Nespor, J. (1994). *Knowledge in motion: Space, time, and curriculum in undergraduate physics and management.* London: Falmer Press.

Ogbu, J. U. (1992). Understanding cultural diversity and learning. *Educational Researcher, 21*(8), 5–14.

Ortiz, A. A. (1997). Learning disabilities occurring concomitantly with linguistic differences. *Journal of Learning Disabilities, 30*, 321–332.

Oswald, D. P., Coutinho, M. J., & Best, A. M. (2002). Community and school predictors of overrepresentation of minority children in special education. In D. J. Losen & G. Orfield (Eds.), *Racial inequity in special education* (pp. 1–13). Cambridge, MA: Harvard Education Press.

Oswald, D. P., Coutinho, M. J., Best, A. M., & Singh, N. N. (1999). Ethnic representation in special education: The influence of school-related economic and demographic variables. *Journal of Special Education, 32*, 194–206.

Parrish, T. (2002). Racial disparities in the identification, funding, and provision of special education. In D. J. Losen & G. Orfield (Eds.), *Racial inequity in special education* (pp. 15–37). Cambridge, MA: Harvard Education Press.

Poniatowska, E. (1985). *Fuerte es el silencio.* Mexico DF: Ediciones ERA.

Pugach, M., & Lilly, S. (1984). Reconceptualizing support services for classroom teachers: Implications for teacher education. *Journal of Teacher Education, 35*, 48–55.

Reschly, D. J. (1997). *Disproportionate minority representation in general and special education: Patterns, issues, and alternatives.* Des Moines: Iowa Department of Education.

Reynolds, M. C., & York, J. L. (1996). Special education and inclusion. In J. Sikula (Ed.), *Handbook of research on teacher education* (pp. 820–836). New York: Macmillan.

Rizvi, F., & Lingard, B. (1996). Disability, education and the discourses of justice. In C. Christensen & F. Rizvi (Eds.), *Disability and the dilemmas of education and justice* (pp. 9–26). Buckingham, Eng.: Open University Press.

Rogoff, B., & Angelillo, C. (2002). Investigating the coordinated functioning of multifaceted cultural practices in human development. *Human Development, 45*, 211–225.

Rosaldo, R. (1984). Comments. *Current Anthropology, 25*, 293–294.

Rueda, R., Artiles, A. J., Salazar, J., & Higareda, I. (2002). An analysis of special education as a response to the diminished academic achievement of Chicano/Latino students: An update. In R. R. Valencia (Ed.), *Chicano school failure and success: Past, present, and future* (2nd ed., pp. 310–332). London: Routledge/Falmer.

Scribner, S. (1985). Vygotsky's uses of history. In J. V. Wertsch (Ed.), *Culture, communication, and cognition* (pp. 119–145). New York: Cambridge University Press.

Seed, P. (2001). *American pentimiento.* Minneapolis: University of Minnesota Press.

Sheriff, R. E. (2000). Exposing silence as cultural censorship: A Brazilian case. *American Anthropologist, 102*, 114–132.

Shields, R. (2000). *Lefebvre, love and struggle: Spatial dialectics.* London: Routledge.

Skrtic, T. M. (1991). The special education paradox: Equity as the way to excellence. *Harvard Educational Review, 61*, 148–206.

Skrtic, T. M., Sailor, W., & Gee, K. (1996). Voice, collaboration, and inclusion: Democratic themes in educational and social reform initiatives. *Remedial and Special Education, 17*, 142–157.

Slee, R. (1996). Disability, social class and poverty: School structures and policing identities. In C. Christensen & F. Rizvi (Eds.), *Disability and the dilemmas of education and justice* (pp. 96–118). Buckingham, Eng.: Open University Press.

Smith, D. D. (2001). *Introduction to special education: Teaching in an age of opportunity* (4th ed.). Boston: Allyn & Bacon.

Soja, E. (1989). *Postmodern geographies: The reassertion of space in critical social theory.* New York: Verso.

Soja. E. W. (1996). *Thirdspace: Journeys to Los Angeles and other real-and-imagined places.* Oxford, Eng.: Blackwell.

Soodak, L. C., Podell, D. M., & Lehman, L. R. (1998). Teacher, student, and school attributes as predictors of teachers' responses to inclusion. *Journal of Special Education, 31,* 480–497.

Stainback, W., & Stainback, S. (1991). Rationale for integration and restructuring: A synopsis. In J. W. Lloyd, A. C. Repp, & N. N. Singh (Eds.), *The Regular Education Initiative: Alternative perspectives on concepts, issues, and models* (pp. 225–239). Sycamore, IL: Sycamore.

Staub, N. (2000). *On inclusion and the other kids: Here's what research shows so far about inclusion's effect on nondisabled students.* Retrieved on March 1, 2001, from http://www.edc.org/urban

Stone, C. A. (1993). What's missing in the metaphor of scaffolding? In E. A. Forman, N. Minick, & C. A. Stone (Eds.), *Contexts for learning: Sociocultural dynamics in children's development* (pp. 169–183). New York: Oxford University Press.

Suárez-Orozco, C., & Suárez-Orozco, M. (1995). *Transformations: Migration, family life, and achievement motivation among Latino adolescents.* Stanford, CA: Stanford University Press.

Tejeda, C. (2000). *Mapping social space: A study of spatial production in an elementary classroom.* (Doctoral dissertation, University of California, Los Angeles, 2000). Ann Arbor: UMI 2001, Microform 9993008.

Trouillot, M. (1995). *Silencing the past: Power and the production of history.* Boston: Beacon Press.

U.S. Department of Education. (1997). *Nineteenth annual report to Congress on the implementation of the IDEA.* Washington, DC: Author.

U.S. Department of Education. (1999). *Twenty-first report to Congress on the implementation of the IDEA.* Washington, DC: Author.

Valencia, R. (Ed.). (1997). *The evolution of deficit thinking.* London: Falmer.

Vanderwood, M., McGrew, K. S., & Ysseldyke, J. E. (1998). Why we can't say much about students with disabilities during education reform. *Exceptional Children, 64,* 359–370.

Varenne, H. (1984). Collective representation in American anthropological conversations: Individual and culture. *Current Anthropology, 25,* 281–291.

Varenne, H., & McDermott, R. (Eds.). (1999). *Successful failure: The school America builds.* Boulder, CO: Westview Press.

Villa, R. A., & Thousand, J. S. (Eds.). (1995). *Creating an inclusive school.* Alexandria, VA: Association for Supervision and Curriculum Development.

Viswanathan, G. (Ed.). (2001). *Power, politics, and culture: Interviews with Edward W. Said.* New York: Pantheon.

Vogt, L., Jordan, C., & Tharp, R. (1993). Explaining school failure, producing school success: Two cases. In E. Jacob & C. Jordan (Eds.), *Minority education: Anthropological perspectives* (pp. 53–65). Norwood, NJ: Ablex.

Wagner, M., Blackorby, J., Cameto, R., Hebbler, K., & Newman, L. (1993). *The transition experiences of young people with disabilities: A summary of findings from the national longitudinal transition study of special education students.* Menlo Park, CA: SRI International.

Walker, V. S. (1999). Culture and commitment: Challenges for the future training of education researchers. In E. C. Lagemann & L. S. Shulman (Eds.), *Issues in education research: Problems and possibilities* (pp. 224–244). San Francisco: Jossey-Bass.

Wang, M. C., & Walberg, H. J. (1988). Four fallacies of segregationism. *Exceptional Children*, *55*, 128–137.

Will, M. (1984). Let us pause and reflect — but not too long. *Exceptional Children*, *51*(1), 11–16.

Williams, R. (1983). *Culture and society*. New York: Columbia University Press.

Willis, P. (1977). *Learning to labor: How working class kids get working class jobs*. New York: Columbia University Press.

Zeichner, K. M., & Hoeft, K. (1996). Teacher socialization for cultural diversity. In J. Sikula, T. J. Buttery, & E. Guyton (Eds.), *The handbook of research on teacher education* (pp. 525–547). New York: Macmillan.

8

OVERREPRESENTATION OF MINORITY STUDENTS

The case for greater specificity or reconsideration of the variables examined

Donald L. MacMillan and Daniel J. Reschly

Source: *The Journal of Special Education* 32(1) (1998): 15–24.

The topic of overrepresentation certainly commands attention in the literature on "judgmental categories" of disability (e.g., learning disabilities, mild mental retardation), yet the evidence reported to date bearing on the issue are less than precise. Clearly, the issue is broader than simple overrepresentation, given that far more egregious examples of overrepresentation in Head Start and Chapter 1 have yet to be criticized, let alone taken to court. In this article the authors distinguish between the *percentage of category or program by group* and *percentage of group in category or program*, which provide quite different perspectives. Futhermore, the authors caution drawing causal inferences from what are descriptive data relating "race/ethnicity" to "placement in disability category." Caution is in order because the data reported by OCR represent aggregated data on race/ethnicity from sources that use different approaches to recording a child's race, fail to account for biracial children, and fail to consider the possibility that social class rather than race/ethnicity may be implicated. The second variable considered is placement in state-sanctioned disability categories. The variability in rates across states reported in *Annual Reports to Congress*, coupled with research data demonstrating the lack of decision reliability, raises serious doubts concerning the validity of these designations. Cross-tabulating two categorical variables so fraught with measurement problems compromises any conclusions that might be drawn.

The issue of overrepresentation was touched on in Dunn's (1968) classic article when he characterized the population of "educable mentally retarded" as follows: "In my best judgment, about 60 to 80 percent of the pupils taught by these teachers are children from low-status backgrounds— including Afro-Americans, American Indians, Mexicans, and Puerto Rican Americans; those from nonstandard English speaking broken, disorganized and inadequate homes; and children from other nonmiddle class environments" (p. 5). The subsequent examination of this problem focused on the ethnic overrepresentation, largely ignoring the main effects of poverty and the interaction of poverty and ethnic group. Nevertheless, overrepresentation data have figured prominently in court cases (e.g., *Larry P. v. Riles*, 1972, 1974, 1979, 1984, 1986) when introduced to support allegations of de facto segregation. Overrepresentation has been examined primarily in cases of children identified as mildly mentally retarded (MMR; see Reschly, 1988), but it has also been an issue concerning other disability categories (e.g., emotional and behavioral disorders [EBD], learning disabilities [LD]). In addition, concerns have been expressed over the "underrepresentation" of certain minority groups in programs for the gifted and talented (Chinn & Hughes, 1987; Harry, 1994).

Evidence of overrepresentation has focused on simple proportions of a given ethnic group (e.g., African American) qualified for special education in a given sanctioned disability category (e.g., LD). The underlying assumption is that the proportion of different ethnic groups in any category or program should be equal to the proportion of that ethnic group in the general school population if there is no discrimination. When the proportion of a given ethnic group enrolled in a given category exceeds the proportion of that ethnic group in the school population (i.e., in a district, state, or nationally), the interpretation suggested is that the disproportion is due to discrimination. It is important to note that ethnic proportions in clearly biologically determined disability categories (e.g., blind, deaf, orthopedic disability) and those cases of mental retardation considered severe and profound do not yield dramatic deviations from proportions one would expect. Efforts by the U.S. Office of Civil Rights (OCR) to monitor overrepresentation are restricted in the disability categories with which it is concerned; data from districts OCR monitors reflect enrollments in only four categories (whereas 13 reporting categories are recognized under the Individuals with Disabilities Education Act of 1990 [IDEA]). OCR secures data on mental retardation, serious emotional disturbance (SED), specific learning disabilities (SLD), and speech and language impairments (SLI). Futhermore, it divides the single IDEA category of mental retardation into MMR and trainable mentally retarded (TMR) counts. This restriction of OCR reflects the absence of compelling, or even suggestive, evidence that a "problem" exists in the remaining IDEA disability categories with regard to overrepresentation. Two further points should be noted: (a) Among certain biologically caused entities there is "overrepresentation" of certain ethnic groups. For example, disproportionately high rates of PKU are found in White children, Tay-Sachs disease in Jewish children, and sickle cell anemia in Black children; (b) some studies do report a significantly higher incidence of biologically based disabilities among Black children and youth (U.S. Department of Education, 1992, p. 16, reporting results from the National Longitudinal Transition Study).

Essentially, then, the "problem" of overrepresentation is evident only in the categories we characterize as "judgmental" disability categories (Gelb & Mizokawa, 1986)—that is, those in which subjective judgments may influence decisions because the disabilities involved do not have a clear biological basis and in which contextual factors (what is tolerated in the specific environment, such as a third-grade classroom in a specific school building) are important and in which cases are filtered through the referral process of general education teachers. The sequence of referral by general education teacher, attempted prereferral intervention, assessment by a multidisciplinary team, and qualification by committee as eligible for special education services characterizes the diagnostic process for children subsequently placed in these judgmental disability categories. If discrimination existed, it could occur at virtually any step in this sequence. However, the work of Mercer (1970, 1973) proved highly influential in the *Larry P.* case. She had reasoned that since there was no disproportion among the population refererred for psychological evaluation and yet there was overrepresentation in the segment actually placed in MMR programs, the discrimination must be occurring in the intervening step—that is, the psychological evaluation. That reasoning was accepted by the court, yet a reanalysis of Mercer's data by Gordon (1980) demonstrated that she had included among the "referred cases" those referred for suspected giftedness. Had she examined only cases referred for "suspected academic and/or behavioral problems," the conclusions drawn might have differed substantially.

Calculation of percentages: the denominator is the key

As noted, simple proportions are employed to examine representativeness. However, there are two different formulas used and they each provide a slightly different perspective on the "problem." Keep in mind that these calculations can be made for a school district, a state, or the nation. One estimate calculates the percent of children *in a disability category* who are members of a given ethnic group. That is, the first estimate asks the question, "What percent of the children classified as MMR are Black?" Reschly (1997) has described this statistic as the "percent of category or program by group." In this calculation, the number of Black children classified as MMR serves as the numerator and the total number of children classified as MMR serves as the denominator. Calculations using this formula are the most frequently employed and were cited in the litigations to demonstrate the magnitude of the overrepresentation of Black children in MMR (as in *Larry P., Marshall et al. v. Georgia*, 1984; *S-1 v. Turlington*, 1979). To illustrate, when the *Larry P.* trial began in 1971, Black students constituted 10% of the California school enrollment, but 25% of the enrollment in MMR programs. The 25% figure was calculated based on the formula shown above (Reschly, 1988, 1997).

A second formula that has been employed provides the "percent of group in category or program," and this estimate asks the question, "What percent of Black students are enrolled in MMR programs?" The same numerator serves (the number of Black children classified as MMR), but the denominator in this calculation uses the total number of Black children in the district, state, or national school population. This second formula provides a perspective on the percent of children in a certain ethnic group that are classified into one of the sanctioned disability categories. Typically, it is a much smaller percentage. For example, at the time of *Larry P.*, as noted, whereas 25% of the total MMR enrollments were Black, only 1.1% of Black students in California were enrolled in MMR programs.

The calculations are simple and straightforward, but the variables involved are not that simple and, in our opinion, warrant much closer examination. We will return to the discussion of these variables with particular attention paid to "ethnicity," "qualifying for certain disability categories" (e.g., MMR, SLD, SED), and the utilization of national databases that aggregate data from the school building to the district to the state level. Before examining these variables, however, we look at why overrepresentation is a problem and some of the estimates of overrepresentation upon which authors and attorneys have relied in discussing the issue.

Why is overrepresentation a problem?

In describing the work of the committee of the National Academy of Sciences, Heller, Holtzman, and Messick (1982) wrote: "Our initial question 'What are the causes of disproportionate representation of minorities and males in special education' became 'Why is disproportionate representation of minorities and males a problem?" (p. x). In fact, the overrepresentation of males in EMR at the time of *Larry P.* was greater than the disproportion of Black students (Lambert, 1981), yet it did not elicit the same degree of attention or debate. The magnitude of the disproportion of Black students in Head Start, Follow Through, and Chapter 1 was at least as great as the overrepresentation of minority students in EMR, and yet these examples of overrepresentation have never been the subject of litigation or come in for criticism. Why is overrepresentation a problem when it appears in special education enrollments? The answer, we believe, resides in the perceptions held regarding the effectiveness of treatment afforded by the various programs and the perceived stigma associated with specific labels. In the *Larry P.* case alleging erroneous classification of Black children as "mentally retarded," the nature–nurture issue lurked in the wings as a result of the writings of Jensen (1969) and Shockley (1971), which received considerable attention in the San Francisco Bay Area. These authors were employed at the University of California and Stanford University, respectively.

Overrepresentation in EMR was viewed as "problematic" in part because the educational treatment provided students was perceived to be ineffective. In his opinion, Judge Robert Peckham described special classes as "deadend," "inferior," and "stigmatizing" no fewer than 27 times despite the fact that little, if any, evidence directly bearing on child outcomes was provided. Moreover, the cases (e.g., *Diana v. Board of Education*, 1970; *Guadalupe v. Tempe Elementary School District No. 3*, 1972) heard prior to 1975 did, in fact, involve districts engaged in poor, and sometimes unethical, practices. These districts were targeted because they represented the worst in special educational practices, not because they were representative of typical programming, but the impression was given that such abuses were widespread. In both of these cases, the defendant districts and state departments of education agreed to several reforms imposed by the courts designed to remedy the poor practices—interested by some as an admission of complicity. It is less clear whether special education treatments for LD and SED are similarly perceived as ineffective or whether they simply suffer from a reputational bias by association and being subsumed under the umbrella of "special education services."

A number of issues, however, are implicitly involved in the perception that overrepresentation is a problem; the interested reader can consult Reschly (1988) for a discussion.

Estimates of disproportionate enrollments in special education

A number of authors have reported on disproportionate enrollments (e.g., Chinn & Hughes, 1987; Harry, 1994; Reschly, 1988) in special education categories, and others have examined the case law pertaining to alleged overrepresentation (e.g., Bersoff, 1979; Elliot, 1987). Here we provide a brief summary of the pattern of the data pertaining to this issue. In the *Larry P.* case, Black students constitued approximately 10% of the California school-age population yet accounted for about 25% of the students served as EMR (this figure represents the percent of category by group). A commonly relied on source of data concerning overrepresentation are surveys reported by OCR. One of the six current OCR priorities is "minorities and special education." It is important to note that the OCR surveys do not involve a nationally representative sample of school districts; rather, OCR includes the 50 largest school districts and a sample of other districts. Moreover, the method for selecting districts has varied over the different surveys, thereby compromising comparisons of results. The use of the largest 50 districts also results in oversampling of Black students—that is, it yields a larger proportion of Black students than are in the general population. Finally, the proportion of Black students in the districts sampled has varied considerably in the different OCR surveys (1978 = 15.7%, 1980 = 20.1%, 1982 = 25.8%, 1984 = 24.5%, 1986 = 16%, and 1990 = 16%). With these limitations in mind, the OCR survey data provide some basis for estimating changes in the enrollment of minority students in various special education programs.

The percent of White, Black, and Hispanic students qualified for special education as MMR, SLD, and SED are shown for 3 years (1978, 1986, 1990) in Table 1. Several trends are evident from these figures. First, there has been an increase in the total percent of children served in the combined three program categories for all three ethnic groups over the 12-year period. Second, the increase in percentages for all three ethnic groups is primarily attributable to the increase in the percent of each ethnic group classified as SLD. Third, the percentage of Hispanic students served in individual and combined categories is substantially lower than the percentages of Black and White students in both the 1986 and 1990 surveys—suggesting that Hispanic students are not overrepresented in these categories at the national level. Fourth, the Black–White difference for the percent in all three categories combined (see row for Total in Table 1) gradually diminished from 2.51% in 1978 to 2.04% in 1986 to 1.47% in 1990. This trend is also evident in Black–White differences in MMR over this same period; however, MMR continues as the category in which Black–White differences are most pronounced and accounts for nearly all of the overrepresentation found for the combined categories. Finally, the dramatic increase across years in the percent of each ethnic group served in SLD appears to be of comparable magnitude for all three ethnic groups.

In order to provide the reader with data reflecting the distinction between *percent of a group in a category* and *the percent of a category by group*,

Table 1 Percentage of White, Black, and Hispanic Students Enrolled in Three Sanctioned Disability Categories for 1978, 1986, and 1990.

Category	1978 OCR[a]			1986 OCR[b]			1990 OCR[c]		
	White	Black	Hispanic	White	Black	Hispanic	White	Black	Hispanic
MMR	1.07	3.46	0.98	0.87	2.30	0.56	0.81	2.10	0.65
SLD	2.32	2.23	2.58	4.29	4.43	4.31	4.97	4.95	4.68
SED	0.29	0.50	0.29	0.57	1.04	0.46	0.69	0.89	0.33
Total	3.68	6.19	3.85	5.73	7.77	5.33	6.47	7.94	5.66

Note: MMR = mild mental retardation; SLD = specific learning disability; SED = serious emotional disturbance.
[a]*Source*: Finn (1982, pp. 324–330). [b]Analyses by Reschly and Wilson (1990), using 1986 OCR survey data compiled by the National Council of Advocates for Students. [c]*Source*: U.S. Department of Education (1994, pp. 198, 201, and 202).

Table 2 contains OCR survey data for 1990 for MMR, SLD, and SED for three ethnic groups. The bottom line in this table reports the percent of each ethnic group receiving Chapter 1 services. The table provides two different "snap shots" of enrollments in high-incidence special education categories. Data such as those provided in Tables 1 and 2 are *descriptive* in nature and lend themselves to a variety of competing interpretations. Do these descriptive data reflect a systematic bias in the process of identifying children for special education? Or, do these data merely mirror the higher incidence of academic learning problems among Black students reflected in dropout rates, Chapter 1, Head Start, and Follow Through enrollments?

Need for greater specificity in variables under study

Data bearing on overrepresentation involve linking information on the ethnicity of the child to the categorical membership of that child in one of the high-incidence disability categories—MMR, SLD, SED, and SLI. Moreover, data on ethnicity and categorical affiliation are typically aggregated across school sites to a district, across districts to the state, and across states to the national level. Although these data may provide a very crude approximation of what is happening nationally, a degree of caution is needed in interpreting the meaning and significance of the findings. In this section we examine the meaning and precision of the two fundamental variables in overrepresentation data sets—ethnicity and disability category. Before one is tempted to infer explanations for these descriptive data, one must consider just how precisely the variables involved are measured.

Ethnicity

A box is checked on a school form determining the ethnic group to which a child belongs. One box, and only one, can be checked and there are no

Table 2 1990 OCR Survey Data Shown by Percentage of Group by Category and by Percentage of Category by Group for Three Sanctioned Disability Categories.

	White		Black		Hispanic	
Category	% group in category	% category by group	% group in category	% category by group	% group in category	% category by group
MMR	0.81	55.82	2.10	34.64	0.65	7.60
SLD	4.97	69.83	4.95	16.61	4.68	11.49
SED	0.69	70.65	0.89	21.47	0.33	5.81
Chapter 1	7.7		22.5		31.3	

Note: MMR = mild mental retardation; SLD = specific learning disability; SED = serious emotional disturbance.

147

uniform guidelines applied from district to district within a state, let alone from state to state. Does a school employee decide the appropriate box based on the child's appearance? Does the parent select the appropriate box? Does a child's surname determine whether he or she is classified as Hispanic? If parents select the appropriate box, is there a box for "mixed"? Although variability exists in the method at the district level, by the time data are aggregated at the national level, it is easy to ignore this variability. The Office of Management and Budget's Statistical Directive 15 urges that racial and ethnic categories should not be interpreted as scientific or anthropological in nature (Hodgkinson, 1995); yet, that is exactly how they are treated in the OCR overrepresentation data set. For any ethnic category, ". . . we have to assume that everyone in the category belongs completely in that box" (Hodgkinson, 1995, p. 175).

In a recent article examining the utility of ethnicity in psychological research, Phinney (1996) concluded that "it is necessary to unpack the packaged variable of ethnicity" (p. 918). She went on to explain that "even within an ethnic group whose members share a relatively precise ethnic label there is tremendous heterogeneity" (p. 919). That is, they differ in terms of social class, income, education, generation of immigration, geographical region, and family structure. In discussing overrepresentation, it might be helpful to specify what aspect of ethnicity is believed implicated in special education placements. Phinney distinguished between three aspects that may account for the psychological importance of ethnicity: "(a) the cultural values, attitudes, and behaviors that distinguish ethnic groups; (b) the subjective sense of ethnic group membership; and (c) the experiences associated with minority status, including powerlessness, discrimination, and prejudice" (p. 919). Illustrations of the heterogeneity among those who share an ethnic label were provided by Hodgkinson (1995) when he noted that in the United States there are a minimum of 3 million Black Hispanics (from the Carribbean, with dark skin, and who speak Spanish), and that Argentine immigrants are labeled Hispanic, yet are primarily of White European ancestry.

The case for "multiracial" children is even more confusing. The "one drop of blood" rule was applied to define a person as Black, but this rule was never applied to the defining of individuals as White, Asian, or Hispanic (Hodgkinson, 1995, p. 174). One school district in which the first author has conducted research reported that in cases of multiracial children the child is classified according to the mother's ethnicity *unless* the father has a Spanish surname, which overrides the mother's ethnicity. In another district, the child is classified as whatever the mother is "because that's the only parent we can be sure of." In yet another, the child is classified as whatever the parents want him or her classified. This was most evident in the case of *Crawford v. Honig* (1988), in which the schools refused the mother's request to administer to Desmond Howard a test of intelligence.

Desmond's mother was Hispanic and his father Black, but on the school ethnicity code the box checked for Desmond was "Black." If his mother agreed to change his ethnicity (i.e., cheek the Hispanic box), he could be tested, but under the prohibition against testing Black children imposed by Judge Peckham in *Larry P.*, he could not be administered a test of intelligence if he was designated as Black. Under current ethnic categories provided in the U.S. Census, one cannot be a "little bit" of anything. Like pregnancy, ethnicity is an all-or-nothing entity. When we read that 25% of the children in EMR programs are Black, we assume that everyone in that ethnic category belongs completely in that box. However, "on direct measurement, the darkest quarter of the white population is darker than the lightest quarter of the black population" (Hodgkinson, 1995, p. 175). Hodgkinson concluded that "If a box labeled 'multiracial'—meaning any racial/ethnic mixing back four more generations—were added to the next Census, estimates are that 80% of blacks and a majority of Americans in general would check the box" (p. 176). Overrepresentation data require that a child be cast into one of the existing "ethnic boxes" and no further breakdown is provided. Interpretability of overrepresentation data is challenged by several of Phinney's (1996) conclusions. First, she wrote that "ethnicity cannot be treated like an independent variable that explains an outcome." She concluded that "the best way to control for ethnicity is to hold it constant, that is, to study processes within groups, rather than make comparisons across groups" (p. 924). Although she focused on psychological processes, it is instructive to note that overrepresentation data do treat ethnicity as an independent variable and essentially consist of comparisons across ethnic groups.

Ethnicity as proxy for SES

As more Americans marry across racial and ethnic boundaries, the utility of ethnicity as a variable will become even weaker than it is today. In the case of MMR, the differing decisions in *Marshall* and *Larry P.* were, in part, due to the appreciation the defense in *Marshall* had for the long-demonstrated relationship between MMR and poverty. The data published in Richardson (1981), shown in Figure 1, compare the prevalence of three forms of mental retardation by social class. The form of mental retardation described by Richardson that is associated with MMR is that with an IQ > 50 and no evidence of central nervous system involvement. The figure demonstrates that there are no occurrences of this form of mental retardation in the highest social class, but in lower social classes this form of mental retardation becomes more prevalent. This study was conducted in Aberdeen, Scotland, involving only White subjects, thereby avoiding the confound of ethnicity and social class.

Hodgkinson (1995) argued that desegregation efforts focused on race. He wrote:

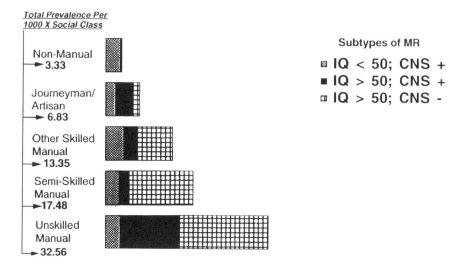

Figure 1 Prevalence per 1,000 of three subtypes of mental retardation × social class for 8- to 10-year-olds born in 1952–1954.

To some extent, race diverted our attention from the most urgent issue: *poverty reduces the quality of the lives of all children, regardless of race or ethnicity.* Had we spent the 40 years since the *Brown* decision systematically seeking to lower the poverty level for *all* American children, we would be in a different, and probably better, condition today. As racial and ethnic characteristics blur over the coming decades, poverty will become an even more obvious problem than it has been.

(pp. 178–179)

In the United States, and particularly in the urban settings included among the 50 largest school disticts in the country sampled by OCR, a disproportionate number of minority children live in poverty. Ethnicity and poverty are inextricably interwoven in our society and the OCR data (and other data sets used to inform us on overrepresentation) fail to break out cases of MMR, SLD, and SED by ethnicity *and* social class. We are willing to wager that in such a matrix, the intercorrelation between ethnicity and social class would be moderately high and that social class, and not ethnicity, would explain more variance in the rates of detection for these high-incidence disabilities, particularly MMR. When ethnicity is the only independent variable, interpretations tend to emphasize "the figment of the pigment."

Classification of students into disability categories

The second fundamental variable considered in the overrepresentation data is the classification into one of the sanctioned disability categories—

150

MMR, SLD, SED, and SLI. We have already noted the error present in "measures" of ethnicity and the possible confound of ethnicity and socio-economic status. In the next few pages we examine the other variable involved in overrepresentation figures—how children are classified by the schools into the various disability categories. It is our position that this variable is fraught with a tremendous amount of error. In order to interpret overrepresentation data meaningfully, one must be certain that there is interrater reliability in the classification decisions, where the "raters" are the school site committees responsible for certifying that a child qualifies under one of the existing categories. Related to the foregoing is the fact that different states employ different criteria for children to qualify under a given disability category. Validity of the classification system refers to the extent to which membership in a given category determines the number of meaningful correlates of class membership. For example, in a review of state department of education IQ cutoff scores for defining mental retardation, Frankenberger and Fronzaglio (1991) reported that 81% of the states specified an IQ cutoff score, but the requisite cut scores ranged from 69 to 84. Clearly, it is reasonable to expect that a state with a more stringent classification criterion would appear to have a lower prevalence of the disability: however, even this expectation may not be true. In Patrick and Reschly's (1982) study of state classification criteria and mental retardation prevalence, the stringency of the IQ cutoff score was unrelated to MR prevalence! States with more stringent criteria, such as IQ < 70, did not have a lower prevalence than states with more lenient criteria, such as IQ < 80 or 84. A further example is provided in California, with one of the most stringent SLD discrepancy criteria (IQ–achievement > 22 standard score points), but a prevalence of SLD that approximates the national SLD average.

Mercer, Jordan, Allsopp, and Mercer (1996) performed a similar survey of criteria for defining LD and also found considerable variability in the magnitude of the IQ–achievement discrepancy required (1 SD, $1^{1}/_{2}$ SDs), as well as in the basis for establishing the discrepancy (e.g., standard score discrepancy, regressed discrepancy), and that some states required an achievement–achievement discrepancy. Our point is that what qualifies a child as mentally retarded or LD in one state differs from the criteria in other states. Overrepresentation data, however, do not make adjustments for such differences—if a child is called LD, the data treat all such cases *as though they represented the same psychological profile*. Clearly, this is not the case.

Let us first examine the extreme variability within given categories (e.g., MR, SED) in terms of the identification rates reported in the annual reports to Congress. The summary data for a recent report (U.S. Department of Education, 1996) are shown in Table 3. The data reflect cases between the ages of 6 and 17 years and show the percent of the overall estimated enrollment served nationally in each of the four categories. The variations across states in the percent of children served under each of these categorical

Table 3 School Population Ages 6–17 Classified as Disabled.

Disability	Number of children served	Percentage of overall pop.	State Variations		
			Lowest	Highest	Factor
SLD	2,231,566	5.34%	2.86 (GA)	9.27 (MA)	3 ×
SLI	1,013,058	2.28%	1.28% (GA)	3.94% (NJ)	3 ×
MR	469,257	1.14%	1.28% (NJ)	3.11 (AL)	10 ×
SED	373,194	0.91%	0.05% (MS)	2.06% (CT)	41 ×
All	4,415,775	10.45%	7.34% (HI)	14.98% (MA)	2 ×

Note: SLD = specific learning disability; SLI = speech and language impaired; MR = mental retardation; SED = serious emotional disturbance; All = all disabilities combined. Data taken from U.S. Department of Education (1996) Tables AA6 and AA13.

designations are noticeable. Three times as many children are served as LD in Massachusetts as in Georgia, and 10 times as many children are served as mentally retarded in Alabama as in New Jersey. The percentage of children served as SED in Mississippi compared to Connecticut differs by a factor of 41! How can this be *if* we are talking about the same "kind" of child? Definitional variations can account for some of the variability and demographic factors may explain additional variance. However, these are "judgmental categories," and we submit that profiles characterizing many children classified as MMR in Alabama are probably being classified as LD in other states with lower overall reported rates of mental retardation. When these data are aggregated nationally, such variations are obscured and the results of overrepresentation data rendered hopelessly uninterpretable when considered by specific categories.

Several studies illustrate the extreme unreliability in the classification decisions reached by schools. These studies may have to be interpreted to reflect practices in the states in which they were conducted, but findings probably generalize to states with comparable criteria for respective disabilities and rates of identification. Gottlieb and his colleagues (Gottlieb, Alter, Gottlieb, & Wishner, 1994) reported on children identified as LD in a large urban district in comparison with suburban districts in a neighboring state. The mean IQ for the urban LD sample was 81.4 ($SD = 13.9$), whereas the mean IQ for the suburban LD sample was 102.8 ($SD = 13.4$)— a difference of approximately $1^1/_2$ standard deviations! For the urban LD sample, 16.6% had IQs less than 70, whereas only 25.7% had IQs above 90. Recall that the Frankenberger and Fronzaglio (1991) analysis revealed that the *lowest* IQ cutoff score for mental retardation is 69. Hence, close to 16%

of the children called LD in this urban district scored lower in IQ than required in *any* state for qualifying a child as mentally retarded. Clearly, an urban LD presents a very different psychometric profile from a child classified as LD in a suburban district—even *within the same state.*

In another series of publications (MacMillan, Gresham, & Bocian, in press; MacMillan, Gresham, Siperstein, & Bocian, 1996), the congruence between characteristics of school-identified students and the criteria specified in the state education codes was investigated. These studies examined students referred by regular class teachers for prereferral intervention. Soon after referral for prereferral services, these students were administered a battery of assessments (IQ, individual achievement) and teachers completed ratings of the children on social skills, problem behaviors, and academic skills. These children were then monitored to determine how the schools dealt with them and how they were qualified as eligible for special education—if indeed the schools did formally evaluate them. Findings from this project have been disseminated in professional journals (Gresham, MacMillan, & Bocian, 1996a, 1996b; Lopez, Forness, MacMillan, Bocian, & Gresham, 1996; MacMillan, Gresham, & Bocian, in press; MacMillan, Gresham, Lopez, & Bocian, 1996; MacMillan, Gresham, Siperstein, & Bocian, 1996; MacMillan, Siperstein, Gresham, & Bocian, 1997). Findings revealed very low levels of adherence by the schools to the state education code criteria in classifying students. Using research diagnostic criteria patterned after education code criteria, the project identified 43 children with Full Scale IQs (FSIQs) on the Wechsler Intelligence Scale for Children–III (WISC-III; Wechsler, 1991) below 75. Of the 43, the schools ultimately reached decisions on 35 cases (4 had moved and 8 were still pending). Only 6 children with FSIQ < 75 were classified as mentally retarded, while 19 of these 35 children were classified as LD, 6 others were found ineligible for special education, and 4 were placed as SLI (MacMillan, Gresham, Siperstein, & Bocian, 1996). A total of 61 children referred for prereferral intervention were ultimately classified as LD by the schools. Fewer than half ($n = 29$) of those 61 children classified as LD by the schools met the research diagnostic criteria (modeled after the state education code criteria; average intelligence and a standard score discrepancy of 22 points between aptitude and achievement), while 7 students who met the research diagnostic criteria (and had been refererred by their regular class teachers) were *not* identified as LD. Comparisons of this "false negative" group with the students the schools did identify as LD revealed several reliable differences on IQ, problem behaviors, teacher ratings of academic competence, and social skills, with the false negative group scoring higher or being perceived by teachers more favorably than the children school identified as LD.

Similar findings were reported by Shaywitz, Shaywitz, Fletcher, and Escobar (1990), although their sample was not referred. Based on an epidemiological sample composed of 84.3% White children, only 45% of school-identified (SI) children with LD met research-identified (RI) criteria (IQ > 79; 22-point discrepancy). The two groups (SI and RI) differed significantly on teachers' ratings of problem behavior; the RI group was perceived to exhibit fewer behavior problems. IQ and achievement differences were not tested; however, descriptive data suggested that the RI group had higher intelligence and math scores but were comparable on reading achievement. Again, fewer than half of the children classified as LD by schools met criteria required for certification.

In an earlier study, Shepard, Smith, and Vojir (1983) found that in a representative sample of 800 children classified as LD by the schools, only 30% met the IQ–achievement discrepancy criterion and only 43% of the cases reflected either clinical or legal signs of LD. Thirty percent of the cases were assigned more properly to low achievement, second language learners, or environmental concerns (e.g., attends many schools, excessive absences). Thus, since 1978, when P.L. 94-142 was to be fully implemented, there has been consistent evidence that between 52% and 70% of children identified by the schools as LD do not meet the standards as conceptualized in federal and state definitions of the disability category. These are startling figures when one considers that the research has been conducted in different states, at different times, and with different strategies for selecting the samples of students with LD. How are we to interpret overrepresentation data when over half the children classified as LD by the schools do not meet the criteria? If we combine the children who are correctly classified as mentally retarded by the schools with those children classified as LD by the schools but meeting criteria for mental retardation, would overrepresentation of Black students in the "corrected" mental retardation category be lessened, increased, or remain the same?

Conclusions and recommendations

Local and state departments of education have been sued in federal courts due to overrepresentation of minority students receiving programs and services that on the surface appear ideal—that is, programs in which (a) the pupil–teacher ratio is considerably lower than that in general education, (b) per-pupil expenditures are two to four times what is spent on general education students, (c) the child's program is individually tailored with written goals and objectives specified and evaluated, and (d) services are delivered by a teacher with specialized training (Reschly, 1988, 1997). Despite these very desirable characteristics of special education programs, *something* weighs so heavily on the minds of critics that it more than offsets these apparently desirable features. This, in part, explains why the National Academy of Sciences panel (Heller *et al.*, 1982) posed the question, "Why is overrepresentation of minorities and males a problem?" We believe that the answer to that question is twofold. First, the treatments are perceived to be ineffective, with the positive features described above believed to be more than offset by the negative consequences derived from being removed from general education to receive services and the necessity of having a pejorative label appended in order to receive these services.

We also hypothesize that the attitudes held by many toward categories such as MMR and SED are both stronger and more negative when over-representation is evident because such evidence might reinforce negative portrayals and stereotypes of minority groups. For example, the fact that *Larry P.* followed on the footsteps of the publication of Jensen's (1969) monograph may suggest that the Black community was resentful of the sug-gestion of racial differences in intelligence, and a disproportionately high percentage of Black children being enrolled in classes for "mentally retarded" students, taken at face value, might provide support for Jensen's assertions, creating an understandable sensitivity among Black citizens. As discussed elsewhere in this issue, the underrepresentation of minority group children in programs for the gifted and talented is also perceived as a problem. On the surface it might appear contradictory to object to *both* overrepresenta-tion and underrepresentation unless one considers (a) the perceived benefits of the services and programs and (b) what these two sets of figures (overrepresentation in MR and underrepresentation in gifted and talented) suggest vis-à-vis the broader issue of racial differences in intelligence.

We have emphasized that overrepresentation data are descriptive and, as such, do not permit causal inferences, however tempting such inferences may be. We would also point out that interpretation of these figures as evidence of discrimination in identification and placement procedures must await additional evidence that the placements of majority students in these programs are "correct" and those involving minority students are "erroneous." Overrepresentation figures are not linked in any way to characteristics of the specific children of any ethnic group placed into one of the judgmental categories. Moreover, it is important to recognize that discrimination is a two-edged sword. Although we must remain vigilant in scrutinizing placement practices in order to prevent the qualification of *any* children for services for which they do not qualify and from which they will not benefit, we must be equally on guard to prevent the *denial* of access to services for which children do qualify and from which they are likely to benefit *because* of their ethnicity. Efforts to "correct" overrepresentation by denying services to children of a particular ethnic group that is "at quota" when one of those children needs the services and supports provided are equally repugnant and constitute educational malpractice.

We have pointed out the oversimplification of the ethnicity variable in the tabulations of overrepresentation in published reports. In addition, we presented evidence documenting the fact that many children categorized into any number of the judgmental categories do not evidence the criteria defining that category of children. When data are aggregated to a national level, the frailties of data at the school site level are lost and we come to believe that the figures reflect reality. Were one to submit a competitive proposal for funding to a federal agency (e.g., Office of Special Education Programs, National Institute of Health and Human Development) to describe the bivariate relationship between two variables in which the scaling of the independent variable was as weak as is "ethnicity" and the dependent variable as unreliable and invalid as the categorical affiliation in the overrepresentation data, that proposal would be rightfully "disapproved."

It has been argued elsewhere (MacMillan, Siperstein, Gresham, & Bocian, 1997) that since passage of P.L. 94-142 the assignment of children to specific categories is no longer the "high stakes" venture that it was previously. That is, differential diagnosis of EMR and LD in the early 1970s was important because the specific classification carried with it consequences for *placement* and *program*. If you were classified as EMR, you got a different functional program and it was delivered in a special day class. Conversely, the diagnosis of LD resulted in academic remediation delivered in a resource room. Since passage of P.L. 94-142, however, regardless of whether a specific child is classified as MR, LD, or SED, the specifics of the treatment or program are negotiated on an individual basis in the formulation of the Individualized Education Program, and the placement is individually determined consistent with the least restrictive environment mandate. Given that the specific diagnostic category into which a given child is placed has no specific programmatic or placement consequences, the tendency on the part of the schools has been to append the "most optimistic label" (LD) and to avoid those labels that are perceived as pessimistic in prognosis (e.g., mental retardation).

We believe strongly that the extant evidence points to socioeconomic status rather than ethnicity as the risk factor for children encountering severe and persistent academic problems in our public schools. As poor as the data are on overrepresentation, the OCR figures continue to point to one primary disability category accounting for the overall excess of Black children in high-incidence disability categories—and that category is MMR. MMR and low socioeconomic status have been empirically linked for decades (Richardson, 1981), and in urban settings the children currently being classified as LD closely resemble those identified as EMR in the past (Gottlieb *et al.*, 1994). How much unique variance in enrollment rates is explained by ethnicity after that explained by social class has been partitioned out? Relatively little, we suspect. In future reports it would be helpful if investigators would examine this issue. Special education services should be provided according to a child's need and not according to a child's ethnicity.

Authors' notes

1 Preparation of this manuscript was supported in part by Grant No. H029J60006 from the U.S. Department of Education, Office of Special Education Programs,

to the University of Virginia for the Center of Minority Research in Special Education.

2 The present work was supported, in part, by Grants No. H023C20002 and H023C30103 from the U.S. Department of Education. Opinions expressed herein are those of the authors alone, and should not be interpreted to have agency endorsement.

References

Bersoff, D. N. (1979). Regarding psychologists testing: Legal regulation of psychological assessment on public schools. *Maryland Law Review*, *39*, 27–120.

Chinn, P. C., & Hughes, S. (1987). Representation of minority students in special education classes. *Remedial and Special Education*, *8*(4), 41–46.

Crawford *et al.* v. Honig. (1988). C-89-0014 RFP, U.S. District Court, Northern District of California.

Department of Education. (ERIC Reproduction Service No. ED 203 575).

Diana v. State Board of Education (1970). CA, No. C-70-37 (N.D. Cal., July 1970) (consent decree).

Dunn, L. M. (1968). Special education for the mildly retarded—Is much of it justifiable? *Exceptional Children*, *35*, 5–22.

Elliot, R. (1987). *Litigating intelligence*. Dover, MA: Auburn House.

Finn, J. D. (1982). Patterns in special education placement as revealed by the OCR survey. In K. A. Heller, W. Holtzman, & S. Messick (Eds.), *Placing children in special education: A strategy for equity* (pp. 322–381). Washington, DC: National Academy Press.

Frankenberger, W., & Fronzaglio, K. (1991). States' definitions and procedures for identifying children with mental retardation: Comparison over nine years. *Mental Retardation*, *29*, 315–321.

Gelb, S. A., & Mizokawa, D. T. (1986). Special education and social structure: The commonality of "exceptionality." *American Educational Research Journal*, *23*, 543–557.

Gordon, R. A. (1980). Examining labeling theory: The case of mental retardation. In W. R. Gove (Ed.). *The labeling of deviance: Evaluating a perspective* (pp. 111–174). Beverly Hills, CA: Sage.

Gottlieb, J., Alter, M., Gottlieb, B. W., & Wishner, J. (1994). Special education in urban America: It's not justifiable for many. *The Journal of Special Education*, *27*, 453–465.

Gresham, F. M., MacMillan, D. L., & Bocian, K. (1996a). "Behavioral earthquake": Low frequency, salient behavioral events differentiating children at-risk for behavior disorder. *Behavioral Disorders*, *21*, 277–292.

Gresham, F. M., MacMillan, D. L., & Bocian, K. (1996b). Learning disabilities, low achievement, and mild mental retardation: More alike than different? *Journal of Learning Disabilities*, *29*, 570–581.

Guadalupe Organization v. Tempe Elementary School District No. 3, No. 71-435 (D. Ariz., January 24, 1972) (consent decree).

Harry, B. (1994). *The disproportionate representation of minority students in special education: Theories and recommendations*. Alexandria, VA: National Association of State Directors of Special Education.

Heller, K. A., Holtzman, W. H. & Messick, S. (Eds.) (1982). *Placing children in special education: A strategy for equity*. Washington, DC: National Academy Press.

Hodgkinson, H. L. (1995). What should we call people? Race, class, and the Census for 2000. *Phi Delta Kappan, 77*, 173–179.

Individuals with Disabilities Eduction Act of 1990, 20 U.S.C. §1400 *et seq*.

Jensen, A. R. (1969). How much can we boost IQ and scholastic achievement? *Harvard Educational Review, 39*, 1–123.

Lambert, N. M. (1981). Psychological evidence in *Larry P. v. Wilson Riles*: An evaluation by a witness for the defense. *American Psychologist, 36*, 937–952.

Larry P. v. Riles, 324 F. Supp. 1306 (N.D. Cal. 1972) (preliminary injunction) affirmed 502 F, 2d 963 (9th cir. 1974); 495 F. Supp. 926 (N.D. Cal. 1979) (decision on merits) affirmed (9th cir. No. 80-427), January 23, 1984. Order modifying judgment, C-71-2270 REP. September 25, 1986.

Lopez, M. F., Forness, S. R., MacMillan, D. L., Bocian, K. M., & Gresham, F. M. (1996). Children with attention deficit hyperactivity disorder and emotional or behavioral disorders in primary grades: Inappropriate placement in the learning disability category. *Education and Treatment of Children, 19*, 272–285.

MacMillan, D. L., Gresham, F. M., & Bocian, K. M. (in press). Discrepancy between definitions of learning disabilities and what schools use: An empirical investigation. *Journal of Learning Disabilities*.

MacMillan, D. L., Gresham, F. M., Lopez, M. F., & Bocian, K. (1996). Comparison of students nominated for pre-referral interventions by ethnicity and gender. *The Journal of Special Education, 30*, 133–151.

MacMillan, D. L., Gresham, F. M., Siperstein, G. N., & Bocian, K. M. (1996). The labyrinth of I.D.E.A.: School decisions on referred students with subaverage general intelligence. *American Journal on Mental Retardation, 101*, 161–174.

MacMillan, D. L., Gresham, F. M., Bocian, K. M., & Siperstein, G. N. (1997). The role of a assessment in qualifying students as eligible for special education. What is and what's supposed to be. *Focus on Exceptional Children, 30*(2), 1–18.

Marshall *et al.* v. Georgia. U.S. District Court for the Southern District of Georgia, CV482-233, June 28, 1984; affirmed (11th Cir. No. 80-8771, October 29, 1985).

Mercer, C. D., Jordan L., Allsopp, D. H., & Mercer, A. R. (1996). Learning disabilities definitions and criteria used by state education departments. *Learning Disability Quarterly, 19*, 217–232.

Mercer, J. R. (1970). Sociological perspectives on mild mental retardation. In H. C. Haywood (Ed.). Social–cultural aspects of mental retardation (pp. 378–391). New York: Appleton-Century-Crofts.

Patrick, J., & Reschly, D. (1982). Relationship of state educational criteria and demographic variables to school-system prevalence of mental retardation. *American Journal of Mental Deficiency, 86*, 351–360.

Phinney, J. S. (1996). When we talk about American ethnic groups, what do we mean? *American Psychologist, 51*, 918–927.

Reschly, D. R. (1988). Minority mild mental retardation overrepresentation: Legal issues, research findings, and reform trends. In M. C. Wang, M. C. Reynolds, & H. J. Walberg (Eds.), *Handbook of special education: Research and practice* (Vol. 2, pp. 23–41). Oxford: Pergamon.

Reschly, D. J. (1997). *Disproportionate minority representation in general and special education programs: Patterns, issues, and alternatives.* Des Moines, IA: Mountain Plains Regional Resource Center.

Reschly, D. J., & Wilson, M. S. (1990). Cognitive processing vs. traditional intelligence: Diagnostic utility, intervention implications, and treatment validity. *School Psychology Review, 19,* 443–458.

Richardson, S. A. (1981). Family characteristics associated with mild mental retardation. In M. J. Begab, H. C. Haywood, H. L. Garber (Eds.). *Psychosocial influences in retarded performance. Vol. II: Strategies for improving competence* (pp. 29–43). Baltimore: University Park Press.

S-1 v. Turlington, Preliminary injunction, U.S. District Court, Southern District of Florida, Case No. 79-8020-Div-CA WPB, June 15, 1979. Affirmed United States Court of Appeals, 5th Circuit, January 26, 1981, 635 F. 2nd 342 (1981). Trial on merits, May 19–June 4, 1986. Order on motion to dismiss, No. 79-9020-Civ-Atkins, U.S. District Court, Southern District of Florida, October 9, 1986.

Shaywitz, S. E., Shaywitz, B., Fletcher, J. M., & Escobar, M. D. (1990). Prevalence of reading disability in boys and girls: Results from the Connecticut Longitudinal Study. *Journal of the American Medical Association, 264,* 998–1002.

Shepard, L. A., Smith, M. L., & Vojir, C. P. (1983). Characteristics of pupils identified as learning disabled. *American Educational Research Journal, 20,* 309–331.

U.S. Department of Education. (1992). *Fourteenth annual report to Congress on the implementation of the Individuals with Disabilities Education Act.* Washington, DC: Author.

U.S. Department of Education. (1994). *Sixteenth annual report to Congress on the implementation of the Individuals with Disabilities Education Act.* Washington. DC: Author.

U.S. Department of Education. (1996). *Eighteenth annual report to Congress on the implementation of the Individuals with Disabilities Education Act.* Washington, DC: Author.

Wechsler, D. (1991). *Wechsler intelligence scale for children–III.* San Antonio, TX: Psychological Corp.

9

EVALUATING SPECIAL EDUCATION SERVICES FOR LEARNERS FROM ETHNICALLY DIVERSE GROUPS

Getting it right

Jill Bevan-Brown

Source: *Journal of the Association for Persons with Severe Handicaps* 26(3) (2001): 138–47.

One of the greatest challenges in evaluating special education services for ethnically diverse groups is obtaining accurate, valid, reliable, and relevant information. This can be achieved by the right person asking the right questions of the right people in the right way at the right place and time. These deceptively simple requirements are discussed in the context of research studies evaluating special education services for indigenous Maori children in New Zealand. Examples of cross-cultural misunderstanding and miscommunication are described and strategies to avoid them are discussed.

Any research requiring input from people, whether it is an evaluation, assessment, or a scientific investigation, seeks to gather accurate, valid, reliable, and relevant data. This task is especially challenging when working with ethnically diverse groups, as evidenced by the widespread concern about cultural bias (Bishop & Glynn, 1992; Ford, 1998; Ishii-Jordan, 1997; McCollum & McBride, 1997; Smith, 1999; Zurcher, 1998). Weinfurt and Moghaddam (2001) contended that "the methods and instruments developed by researchers who share a particular culture may involve assumptions that are not valid in other cultures" (p. 101). The potential danger could be that information gathered from participants whose culture is different from the researchers may be invalid or unreliable. This concern has resulted in the development and use of a range of approaches and strategies to overcome or minimize cultural bias. Weinfurt and Moghaddam (2001) mention several methodological adaptations that researchers can make, such as developing culturally equivalent questions, sampling procedures, and other related strategies. There is also support for the use of multiple and complementary methodologies (Bempechat & Drago-Severson, 1999; Meyer, 1991; Serna, Forness, & Nielsen, 1998), including ethnographic case studies (Canen, 1999), video surveys[1] (Stigler, Gallimore, & Hiebert, 2000), and collaborative research approaches such as participatory action research (Meyer, Park, Grenot-Scheyer, Schwartz, & Harry, 1998a; Turnbull, Friesen, & Ramirez, 1998). In addition, in the assessment area, there is a repeated call to abandon traditional standardized tests that disregard the cultural background and prior knowledge of students from ethnically diverse groups, and to replace them with performance based, authentic assessment approaches (Artiles & Zamora-Duran, 1997; Hiebert, Afflerback, & Valencia, 1994; Ishii-Jordan, 1997; Lee, 1998; Patton, 1997; Rueda, 1997; Zamora-Duran & Reyes, 1997).

Although these strategies to achieve culturally appropriate and sensitive research, evaluation, and assessment are seemingly beneficial for learners from ethnically diverse groups, they are not without their critics. Lee (1998), for example, maintained that there is no evidence that African American, Native American, and Latino students perform any better on performance based assessments than they do on standardized measures. Although performance based assessment is potentially empowering, culturally appropriate, and supportive, it may not draw on students' cultural knowledge and experiences (Lee, 1998). Similarly, Stigler *et al.* (2000) warned of limitations of video survey research in securing "within-culture understandings and perspectives" (p. 99). They argued for the use of additional strategies such as interviews of participants, observations, and input from cultural experts. A message that can be taken from Lee (1998), Stigler *et al.* (2000), and others (McCollum & McBride, 1997; Smith, 1999; Weinfurt & Moghaddam, 2001) is that we must not accept without question seemingly culturally sensitive methodologies, approaches, strategies, and measures. Although they may have the potential to overcome cultural bias and provide accurate, valid, reliable, and relevant data, achieving this requires constant vigilance and effort.

This lesson has been learned in the author's research experiences in New Zealand. In her research involving Maori[2] learners with special needs, despite using culturally sensitive approaches and strategies, the author has not always been successful in collecting accurate, valid, reliable, and relevant data. This article presents some of the challenges that have arisen in two particular research projects that the author has been involved in. It also describes the strategies used to overcome them.

The first project evaluated special educational resources and best practice for Maori children with special needs in the early childhood area (hereafter, "early childhood research project"). A random sample of 30 four year old Maori children was selected from a larger, national sample. Their disability levels ranged from mild to severe in the categories of physical, communication, behavior, sensory, learning, medical fragility, and multiple disabilities. Data were collected utilizing a variety of sources: interviews with individual parents, educators, and service providers; group consultation meetings with parents and family members; documentary analysis of special education case files; service provider questionnaires; and observation of the children in their homes and early childhood centers. The second research project was part of a national, ongoing, 3 year study to monitor and evaluate New Zealand's new special education policy, "Special Education 2000" (hereafter, "SE 2000 research project"). The author investigated how this new policy initiative met the specific needs of Maori children at early childhood centers and at primary, intermediate, and secondary schools. Some of these children attended English medium schools, whereas others attended "kohanga reo" (total immersion early childhood centers) and "kura kaupapa Maori" (total immersion primary schools). The sample included children with mild to severe disabilities in every special education category provided for in New Zealand. From 1999 to 2001, 2,874 schools and early childhood centers participated in the study. Data were gathered from written surveys, interviews with principals, teachers, teachers' aides, and special education service providers, forums, and questionnaires involving 1,500 parents.

The guidelines presented here were derived from a thematic analysis of data in these two research projects. The data include interview transcripts, written and oral feedback from fieldwork interviewers, and all written data including surveys, questionnaires, and transcripts of consultation meetings and forums. It is proposed that in order to obtain accurate research and evaluation data, the right person must ask the right questions of the right people in the right way at the right place and time (the six "Rs"). Although this formula may appear relatively straightforward, putting it into practice is far from easy.

The right person must ask the questions

Ideally, this should be someone of the same ethnic and cultural identity as the person being interviewed, someone the person knows and trusts. The importance of this requirement was illustrated in the early childhood research project. The author interviewed a Maori mother about the speech language services that her son received. Being part of a random sample of research participants, this mother was unknown to the author.

> Before the interview I spent some time establishing rapport as all good interviewers are meant to do. However I didn't do as well at this as I should have because during the interview I got the distinct feeling the woman was "holding back." This came to a head when I asked whether

162

the ethnicity of the speech language therapist was an issue for her. She replied, "No it wasn't, as long as the therapist was good at her job." At this point I mentioned that when my son was at kohanga reo [a total immersion early childhood center] I would have preferred a Maori speech language therapist because he was more comfortable among Maori people. She looked at me in astonishment and asked, "Are you a Maori?" I had just taken it for granted that she knew I was Maori. I forget sometimes that I am a very pale looking Maori. Then it was as if the dam had broken. She said, yes it did matter to her that the speech language therapist was Maori but she didn't say this because she thought I was a Pakeha [a white New Zealander] and that I would think she was racially prejudiced. She then proceeded to change most of the answers to the questions I had asked her previously.

(Bevan-Brown, 2000a)

This mother's change in attitude must be interpreted from a Maori perspective. Kohanga reo are chosen by parents who have a commitment to their children learning to speak their native tongue and maintaining their Maori culture. By disclosing that her son also attended a kohanga reo, the interviewer signaled her support of the mother's educational choice and a similar commitment to their Maori heritage. Therefore, the mother's change in attitude did not relate solely to the interviewer's declared ethnicity but also to her similar cultural identity and commitment.

Having someone of the same ethnic and cultural identity pose the questions may make many people feel more at ease and lessen the chances of misinterpretation and miscommunication caused by differing body language, communication patterns, intonation, vocal cues, cultural vocabulary, culturally determined behavior, and sense of humor. Similar concerns contribute to the demand for the increased involvement of culturally diverse personnel in special education and research in the United States (Artiles, 1998; Ishii-Jordan, 1997; Miramontes, 1990; NAEYC, 1996; Serna et al., 1998; Washington, 1996).

The ideal is to have interviewers who have the same ethnic background and cultural identity as the people being interviewed. If this is not possible, the person involved must have the cross-cultural competence required to interview people from a different ethnic background and culture, as well as to interpret accurately the information given. In New Zealand, the task of developing cross-cultural competence among teachers, special education professionals, and researchers is being addressed by including compulsory multi-cultural content and perspectives in the preservice and in-service education of teachers and special education professionals (Bevan-Brown, 2000b). In the United States, there is a similar demand for preservice and in-service education and multi-cultural teaching practice experiences to educate all professionals who work with culturally diverse students including those with special needs (Artiles & Zamora-Duran, 1997; Artiles, Trent, Hoffman-Kipp, & Lopez-Torres, 2000; Ford, 1992; Ishii-Jordan, 1997; Lynch & Hanson, 1998; Trent & Artiles, 1998; Valles, 1998).

Other considerations for Maori research are having interviewers of similar age and socioeconomic status and preferably of the same tribe and gender. Although these considerations may not be relevant to other ethnic groups, it is likely that these groups will have their own important requirements. For example, the interviewer and interviewee may need to come from similar religious backgrounds or from the same geographic area.

The right questions must be asked

The second requirement is to ask the right questions. This may appear to be a straightforward task, although it is, in fact, fraught with difficulties. These arise from differing cultural concepts, beliefs, worldviews, attitudes, values, norms, customs, experiences, skills, knowledge, practices, language, and cognitive structures.

Cultural concepts, beliefs, and worldviews

The concept of special needs is socially and culturally determined. What is perceived as a special need by one ethnic group may not be considered so by another (Harry, 1992; Joe & Miller, 1993; Lynch & Hanson, 1998; Mallory, Nichols, Charlton, & Marfo, 1993). Researchers must take account of this in framing questions that probe the adequacy of special education services for learners from diverse cultures.

The Maori concept of special needs is much broader than the Pakeha concept on which special education services are based. This was taken into account in the questions posed in both research projects. For example, Maori participants were asked about their concept of special needs and about any special needs that were not being addressed. The data revealed children with special needs who were not receiving services according to Maori, but who did not qualify as having special needs according to Pakeha. These included Maori children who cannot speak Maori. Although Maori is one of New Zealand's two "official" languages, owing to many causes including a past education policy banning Maori from being spoken in all schools, only a minority of Maori speak their native tongue. Total immersion early childhood centers and schools are being established in an effort to revive the language. However, as these were not introduced until the 1980s and cater only to 10% of Maori learners, most Maori children do not speak Maori. This was first identified as a special need by Huirangi Waikerepuru (cited in King, 1995). His rationale is that Maori who cannot speak their own language are disabled because they cannot participate fully in their Maori culture. This is certainly the case for a number of children in total immersion education who struggle to understand and communicate with their teachers and peers because of their limited ability to speak Maori. However, this situation is not recognized as a special need by the Ministry of Education unless the children have been identified as having learning or intellectual disabilities.

The converse may also apply. For example, Maori society is not as dominated by time as Pakeha society. Traditionally, a time frame was not placed over human development. In one study, the author asked a "kaumatua" (respected Maori elder), "Do you think that Maori have an understanding of intellectual disability that is different from the Pakeha meaning?" His reply was:

> I think a lot of Maori kids are classified as intellectually disabled when in fact they are not, so yes, I think there is a difference. They are classified through a misunderstanding or through a different cultural perspective. You know we have some kids who are pretty slow at picking things up but they are not intellectually disabled. . . . Maori people think more in the sense that people need to come to different stages of development through their own time you know, and time is — well you don't measure time. . . . Each kid is different. They have a different time of learning scale and one will learn today and another one might not learn until next year the same sort of skill. But, I mean that is their time, that is their individuality. So you have to accept that and fit around that instead of saying, "Well OK, I'm going to make the time scale. I'm going to say what you are going to learn, what you must learn in this time and what you must learn in that time and it's on your head if you don't!" I mean that is really stupid. So what I am saying is a lot of what we do in schools is wrong. It shouldn't be done. . . . If we just stop categorizing kids like that, we might find that these people who are labeled as slow or handicapped, are not really.
>
> (Bevan-Brown, 1989, pp. 95, 103)

Examples of differing cultural concepts of disability can also be found in the American literature. Harry (1992) found that Puerto Rican American children identified as having mild mental retardation by school authorities were considered to be within a normal range of intelligence by their parents. Likewise, in a study conducted by Mendez Perez (cited in Garcia, Mendez Perez, & Ortiz, 2000), Mexican American children identified as having communication disorders were considered to be within the norma l parameters of language development by their mothers.

Cultural values, attitudes, norms, customs, experiences, skills, knowledge, and practices

Special education services are influenced greatly by cultural values, attitudes, norms, customs, experiences, skills, knowledge, and practices. For example, people from a culture that values collectivism, interdependence, and extended family involvement require different services than people from a culture that values individualism, independence, and nuclear family involvement. This fact needs to be recognized in any evaluation of special education services. In the early childhood research project, one parent commented on the physiotherapy service provided for her daughter who had severe disabilities. Although she was very grateful for being shown correct handling techniques, toileting procedures, and manipulative exercises, she wished her "whanau" (extended family) had been included in these teaching sessions as they shared in her daughter's upbringing. The mother was "too whakama" (shy and embarrassed) to request their involvement. The physiotherapist, however, considered her service to this child as "one of my success stories." Obviously, her evaluation had not included questions that would have elicited the need for whanau involvement.

Language and cognitive structures

Even when English is the first language of both the interviewer and the interviewee, misunderstanding can still arise from differing dialects, language patterns, cognitive structures, body language, and the use of special education jargon. An example is provided in the following research excerpt. The situation involved a speech language therapist who was assessing a child's language skills. Part of the assessment involved the therapist showing the child a series of pictures where something was missing — a car with only three wheels, a person with only one arm, and so forth.

> ... I found that with one of the kids that I was dealing with last year, this specialist would do these games and always ask the same question, "What isn't there?" And I kept saying to her, "He doesn't understand what you're saying, he's come through kohanga [a total immersion early childhood center]. We don't speak about what's not there, we speak about what is there." She just kept doing it and I kept saying to her, "Look lady, he doesn't understand what you mean by 'what isn't there?' But if you asked him, 'What is there?' he will tell you." It's the culture of the language, you see, the structure of the language and how you implement it, the way you say things and all that ... Maori people do not ask what isn't there, what they ask is, "what is in front of you? What do you see? What do you know?" They don't ask you what don't you know. ... I thought well this is a big problem because the specialist isn't listening to what I'm saying and it was culturally inappropriate for her to be asking questions like that.

> (Bevan-Brown, 2000a)

Needless to say, the child in question failed the assessment. This scenario illustrates cultural bias in standardized tests. It is a long-standing concern of parents, teachers, and special educators (*Diana v. California State Board of Education*, 1970; *Larry v. Riles,* 1979; Nitko, 1983; Overton, 1996; Williams, 1975; Zurcher, 1998). In the United States, a range of measures to overcome cultural bias has been suggested, including the use of tests in the child's native language (IDEA, 1990), the use of "culture-free" tests such as the Naglieri Nonverbal Ability Test (NNAT; Naglieri, 1996), and the Comprehensive Test of Nonverbal Intelligence (CTONI; Hammill, Pearson, & Wiederholt, 1996), and the use of performance based, authentic assessment approaches (Artiles & Zamora-Duran, 1997; Garcia & Pearson, 1994; Hiebert *et al.*, 1994). In New Zealand, authentic assessment is also increasing in popularity. However, when standardized tests are used, the preference is to have them administered by a person from the same culture as the child being tested. The shortage of Maori qualified to administer standardized tests is a major problem. One answer has been to partner the person administering the test with a Maori adult the child knows and trusts. However, if a culturally biased test is used and the advice of the Maori helper is ignored, an inaccurate assessment is inevitable. The speech language therapist in the previous scenario easily could have made adaptations to ascertain whether the child's lack of understanding signaled a language problem or cultural difference. A perfect opportunity to ask the right question was missed.

A further consideration relates to the actual purpose of the evaluation. Are the reasons for it being undertaken important, relevant, empowering, and beneficial to the ethnic community involved? Is this reflected in the questions being asked? If the answer to the second question is no, then the evaluation questions should be changed. If the answer to the first question is no, then the evaluation itself is probably not worth doing.

Questions must be directed at the right people

The third requirement is to ask the right people. Although seemingly simple, problems often arise from not consulting widely enough. This may occur because of limited funding, tight research time frames, and not knowing whom to consult. Evaluation involving ethnically diverse groups is particularly susceptible because the protocols and processes involved are often more time-consuming and expensive.

The importance of wide consultation can be illustrated using an example from the early childhood research project. As explained previously, the evaluation of early intervention services involved interviews with service providers, educators, parents, and family members. The variation in information received from these groups was amazing. Differences emerged not just in the perception and evaluation of services, but even at the fundamental level of ethnic identity. A number of educators did not know that the children they were teaching were Maori. This arose in cases where parental contact was with the mother only, who was a Pakeha. Although these mothers were

Pakeha, without exception, they wanted their child's indigenous Maori heritage to be taken into account in the services they received. However, no one had ever given them this option. By considering data collected from a wide range of people, a balanced picture of the early childhood services provided was obtained and their strengths and weaknesses from a cultural perspective were identified. This would not have been possible if questioning had been limited to just one group.

Similarly, superficial consultation within a group can result in an inaccurate evaluation. In the early childhood study, 79% of a general sweep of service providers believed that Maori children with special needs were being cared for appropriately. However, in-depth interviewing of randomly selected service providers revealed that a 40% figure was more accurate.

Questions must be asked in the right way

When evaluating special education services for learners from ethnically diverse groups, culturally appropriate protocols and practices must be followed. Being from the same ethnic group has not given the author automatic entry into the Maori community. Appropriate procedures and protocols have had to be followed both in gaining access and in conducting interviews. For example, in the evaluation of special education services to kura kaupapa Maori, the first step involved attending a meeting of all local kura kaupapa Maori to explain the research and gain their permission and support. Next, the chairperson from the local group presented the research proposal at a national meeting to obtain the approval and support of the national organization. Only at this stage could the evaluation proceed. When conducting interviews in Maori homes, interviewers must leave their shoes at the door, bring food to share, and spend time establishing whakapapa (genealogy) links with the people involved. This can be very time-consuming, but it must be done before getting down to the "business" of interviewing. When interviewers do not adhere to these protocols, they are likely to gather limited or inaccurate data as evidenced in the previously related story of the mother who was concerned about being thought racially prejudiced. In that interview, if the author had spent more time and care establishing whakapapa links with the mother before the interview, her Maori heritage would have been evident and the mother would have felt at ease from the outset.

Another example of appropriate Maori procedures being ignored is related in the following story.

At a special education conference in New Zealand, I attended a presentation given by a Pakeha researcher. During this presentation he made certain claims that caused the heckles of every Maori present to rise. Afterwards I challenged him about these offending claims and he assured me that he had consulted with a number of prominent Maori in preparing his paper. He named the people he had consulted with which, coincidentally, included a friend of mine. I was quite taken aback as I knew her views were diametrically opposed to what he was saying. So I queried him further and discovered he had sent copies of his paper to a number of Maori for them to comment on. When he did not hear back from any of them, he construed their silence as affirmation. In actual fact, silence is often used by Maori to convey the opposite message and this was confirmed by my friend. When I asked her about the paper, she said she had filed it in the rubbish bin where it belonged.

(Bevan-Brown, 2000a)

This researcher made two mistakes. First, he misinterpreted the meaning of silence. Second, he consulted by correspondence. Maori place great store on what is called "kanohi-ki-te-kanohi" (face-to-face) communication. The most appropriate way for this researcher to consult would have been to approach these prominent Maori in person, but at the very least by phone. By asking his questions in the right way, he would not have received the silent treatment. Instead, he would have been given an honest appraisal of his paper.

The Maori preference for face-to-face communication can be problematic when large-scale evaluations are being conducted over a wide geographic area. This problem was encountered with the SE 2000 research project. The response rate for written questionnaires sent to total immersion schools was disappointing. Face-to-face interviews would, no doubt, have provided much greater feedback. Unfortunately, a lack of time and financial resources precluded widespread interviewing. This illustrates the previously mentioned point of the susceptibility of research involving ethnically diverse groups to restraints imposed by limited time and funding.

When conducting interviews with Maori, another cultural consideration is the involvement of the whanau (extended family). Maori are a very group oriented people. Just as the physiotherapist in a previous example should have included the child's whanau in her services, so also should researchers include whanau in their evaluation. When an interview is requested of parents, they should be invited to bring along any family members or friends they would like to include. The resulting interview may be a transcriber's nightmare but the breadth and depth of the information obtained compensates for this. Different ethnic groups will have different protocols and practices that need to be adhered to when conducting evaluations. However, the requirement to take these into account is equally applicable.

Another consideration is the language that should be used during the interviews. The ideal is that all communication should be in the interviewee's first language. If this is not possible, an interpreter should be employed. However, interviewers must be mindful of the additional complications that may be introduced. Privacy, confidentiality, the difficulty of translating special education terminology, and the appropriateness of the interpreter are all important factors that must be considered.

Questions must be asked at the right place and at the right time

The importance of the right place is illustrated in the following story originating from the SE 2000 research project:

> One of our interviews was with a woman who worked for a tribally based welfare Trust. We interviewed this woman in her office. It was in a large old house. Her desk was strewn with papers and the seats on which we sat had seen better days. As we talked the smell of cooking wafted into the room. At the end of the interview, the papers on her desk were brushed aside and it was laid with a veritable feast in which we all partook. The woman explained that she worked for the tribal Trust in the afternoon but in the morning she worked for a government social service agency. She noted that on some occasions she would see people in the morning at her agency office where they would tell her one thing and in the afternoon, they would turn up at the Trust office and tell her a completely different story. She said she didn't believe they lied on purpose, it was just that they felt uncomfortable in the government office and would say anything to expedite the interview. However, in the Trust office, with its Maori carvings and posters on the wall and the ever present smell of kai (food), they felt more at home. In these surroundings they felt comfortable and supported enough to talk at length and honestly about their particular concerns and circumstances. Coincidentally, the next interview we conducted was held in a very flashy, up-town office where I had to punch in a code to gain access to the toilet. In their antiseptic interview room I knew exactly what the Trust worker was talking about. This was not a user-friendly environment that encouraged people to open up and share their thoughts and experiences.
>
> (Bevan-Brown, 2000a)

The requirement to conduct interviews at the right time is principally a matter of common sense. Home interviews with a mother at a time when the children return from school or with a father when the TV in the next room is screening the NBA finals is not conducive to gaining in-depth data, nor will it endear the researcher to all concerned. There may also be cultural and religious considerations that need to be taken into account. For example, for Maori, it would not be appropriate to conduct an interview over the 4 day period of a "tangi" (funeral). Other ethnic and religious groups will have similar times and circumstances when interviews would be inappropriate.

However, some people from these groups may be too shy or consider it impolite to refuse the interviewer's request and so the evaluation is conducted in a situation that is far from ideal.

What can be done to ensure the right person asks the right questions of the right people in the right way at the right place and time?

A number of strategies were used in the early childhood and SE 2000 research projects to ensure that the six Rs were addressed. To ensure the first R, the right people asking the questions, Maori interviewers were employed. They were recruited using culturally appropriate methods including "tono" (this involves the researcher or intermediary "shoulder-tapping" a person deemed appropriate by the Maori community). Different ethnic groups will have their own culturally appropriate methods of involving people and these should be followed. When conducting a study in a setting in which participants come from diverse cultural backgrounds (e.g., a school), a researcher may recruit interviewers from the community who demographically represent the setting under study (Meyer *et al.*, 1998a).

Employing interviewers from the community being researched can provide access to people and situations that would otherwise be unavailable to the researcher. However, there is a danger in this approach of "using" people. To ensure that this does not happen, interviewers are chosen who have a vested interest in the evaluation being undertaken and are empowered to have meaningful input into the research process. The empowerment of "hired hands" was emphasized in studies applying participatory action research. Using this approach, interviewers became collaborative research team members and were also empowered to bring about positive changes at the personal level. For example, they pursued further education and achieved goals for their children (Biklen & Larson, 1998; Meyer *et al.*, 1998a, 1998b; Turnbull *et al.*, 1998). Involving community interviewers can be expensive and time-consuming, but the richness and reliability of the data gathered and the possibility of initiating positive personal changes outweigh any barriers or inconveniences experienced.

To ensure the second R, asking the right questions, in the SE 2000 research project, Maori people were involved in their formulation. For example, in order to ascertain how New Zealand's new national policy was impacting children with special needs in kura kaupapa Maori, a reference group of kura kaupapa Maori teachers and parents was formed. Group members were nominated by kaumatua (respected Maori elders) and kura kaupapa whanau (extended families). The group met in the author's home. Their first task was to formulate a set of questions that arose from their own concerns and perspective. Once these were developed, questions from the Ministry of Education and the researchers were presented. The group considered these carefully, discarding and amending as necessary. Each member then took a copy of all questions to their school community for discussion and amendment. They sought feedback not only on the value and appropriateness of the questions posed but also on the Maori language used. The final questionnaire incorporated all the feedback received. This approach, which seeks the active participation of stakeholders in generating meaningful research questions, is also validated in studies utilizing participatory action research (Park, Meyer, & Goetz, 1998).

To ensure the third R, asking the right people, both the early childhood and SE 2000 research projects consulted national and local committees representing various Maori organizations, tribal councils, schools, and early childhood centers about who should be interviewed in the projects. Whanau networks, Maori, local and national publications, and a radio talk show were used to advertise projects. Also, a free phone line was provided for parents and whanau of children with special needs to contact researchers with their concerns and suggestions. These strategies resulted in the right people being consulted.

To ensure the fourth R, asking questions in the right way, the author consulted with the particular Maori group being researched and with people experienced in working with them. While this method of consulting with appropriate constituent group members is effective, relevant books and articles are also helpful in this respect (e.g., Harry, 1992; Klein & Chen, 2001; Lynch & Hanson, 1998). Whatever the information source used, the following warning should be heeded (Lynch & Hanson, 1998):

> Each individual and each family is different and culture-specific information cannot be assumed to apply in every situation. Its value is that it raises issues that should be considered, poses questions that may need to be answered, and underscores the interventionist's desire to respond sensitively to each family and each family member.
>
> (p. 497)

To ensure the fifth and sixth R's, asking questions at the right place and time, interviewees in the early childhood and SE 2000 research projects were asked to choose a convenient time and place for their interview. The same approach is recommended when consulting with parents or conducting individualized education plan (IEP) meetings. A choice of venues can be suggested — perhaps the parents' home, the neighborhood school, or a local church meeting room. For people who have bad memories of their school days, returning to a school environment can be an uncomfortable experience. Similarly, some people may feel uncomfortable having an interviewer visit their home and would prefer a neutral meeting place. Each person will have his/her own preference. The majority of research interviews conducted by the author have been in people's homes. However, interviews have also

172

been held at schools, early childhood centers, work places, "marae" (tribal community complexes), on the beach, in the author's home, in the home of mutual friends, at cafes, in churches, and even in a tent. The deciding factors have always been the most convenient time and most comfortable environment for the interviewee. On a few occasions in the more public venues that have been chosen, confidentiality has become a concern. The interviewer must be prepared to change locations or even abandon an interview if privacy is threatened.

Finally, when the evaluation is complete, findings should be shared with the interviewees and the ethnic community concerned. Again, this is not a straightforward matter. Dissemination should be done in a manner that is empowering and culturally appropriate. A popular way of sharing research results with the Maori community is to present them at a "hui" (meeting) especially called for that purpose. This should be done before research findings are presented elsewhere. By opening their evaluations to cultural scrutiny in this way, Maori researchers accept the responsibility of addressing any criticisms that arise. When agreement cannot be reached, the disputed issues should be recorded and published as part of the research findings (R. A. Selby, personal communication, May 8, 2001). A range of strategies was used to disseminate the findings from the SE 2000 and early childhood research projects. Interested people were invited to information meetings held throughout the country and draft reports were sent to key individuals, group, and Maori organizations for their feedback. Where possible, recommended changes were included in the final reports, which are available on request and free of charge from the Ministry of Education. The similar approach of validating study findings with the stakeholders is advocated in the literature dealing with participatory action research. Furthermore, it is desirable to include relevant stakeholders/interviewers as co-authors of publications or co-presenters at conference presentations (Park *et al.*, 1998).

Conclusion

Special education services for learners from ethnically diverse groups are generally designed, delivered, and evaluated by people from the majority culture and are usually based on a majority culture concept of special needs. If a learner's ethnic background is not taken into account in the services provided, these services are likely to be less than effective. Included as an Appendix to this article is a checklist that provides some guidelines for achieving ethnically appropriate evaluation and research in special education. However, although the author has focused on evaluation, ethnically appropriate strategies should be incorporated into every phase of service provision from initial planning, through implementation to evaluation. Any evaluation is only as good as the improvement it initiates.

Expending time and effort to collect culturally appropriate, accurate data is a wasted exercise if it is not used to benefit the learners who were the focus of the evaluation.

Finally, it should be noted that Maori are a diverse group. They differ in many areas including education level, lifestyle, beliefs, values, socioeconomic status, religious and tribal affiliations, geographic location, knowledge and practice of Maori culture, and the degree of assimilation into Pakeha society. The examples cited in this article and the recommendations made are appropriate for Maori children and families who identify with and adhere to traditional cultural values and cannot be generalized to all Maori children. However, the author maintains that the requirements of the right person, asking the right questions of the right people in the right way at the right place and time are generally applicable. It is the responsibility of educators, evaluators, and researchers to find out exactly what "right" means for the children and families with whom they work.

Notes

The author thanks Hyun-Sook Park for her valuable input into this article and for her dedication to the editing process.

1 Video survey: A research method that videotapes the topic being investigated in various sites/countries and later analyzes videos according to established criteria. Usually, it is utilized in large cross-cultural studies.
2 Maori: New Zealand's indigenous people. They are of Polynesian extraction and represent approximately 15% of New Zealand's population.

Appendix

A checklist for ethnically appropriate evaluation and research in special education

1　The Right Person
   * Is the interviewer from the same ethnic group as the person being questioned/receiving the special education service?
   * If not, does the interviewer have the cross-cultural competence needed to interview people from a different culture and to accurately interpret the information given?
   * Are the interviewer and interviewee suitably matched (e.g., same gender, similar age, and socio-economic status)?
   * Where interviewers from the ethnic community are employed:
     — has the method of recruitment been culturally appropriate?
     — have the interviewers received adequate training?
     — is involvement an empowering experience for the interviewers?
2　Asking the Right Questions
   * Has the ethnic group's concept of special needs been incorporated into the evaluation/research?

- Have differing cultural concepts, beliefs, values, attitudes, norms, customs, experiences, skills, knowledge, and practices been taken into account?
- Are culturally appropriate and relevant standards and measures used to evaluate special education services?
- Are differing language patterns, cognitive structures, and dialects taken into account?
- Is the evaluation/research important, relevant, empowering, and beneficial to the ethnic community concerned?
- Have both the service providers and the ethnic community been involved in formulating evaluation/research questions?

3 Of the Right People
- Has evaluation/research involved wide, in depth consultation (e.g., have all relevant groups been included)?
- Has the ethnic community involved been consulted in the selection of appropriate interviewees?

4 In the Right Way
- Have culturally appropriate practices and protocols been incorporated into the evaluation/research process?
- Have approval and support of the evaluation/research been gained from the community concerned or their representatives?
- Have culturally appropriate means been used and sufficient time allowed for rapport building prior to commencing interviews?
- Are culturally appropriate evaluation/research designs and methods used?
- Have interviewees been given the option of inviting family members or colleagues to support them in the interview situation?
- Are interviews conducted in the first language of the people being interviewed?
- Where an interpreter is used, is this person appropriate, and have confidentiality and privacy concerns been addressed?
- Has jargon been avoided?
- When evaluation/research is complete, have appropriate means been used to share findings with interviewees and the ethnic community concerned?

5 & 6 At the Right Place and the Right Time
- Is the interview being conducted at a place that is both convenient and comfortable for the interviewee?
- Does the interview venue afford privacy?
- Is the interview being conducted at a time that is convenient to the interviewee?

References

Artiles, A. J. (1998). The dilemma of difference: Enriching the disproportionality discourse with theory and context. *The Journal of Special Education, 32*, 32–36.

Artiles, A. J., & Zamora-Duran, G. (Eds.). (1997). *Reducing disproportionate representation of culturally diverse students in special and gifted education*. Reston, VA: The Council for Exceptional Children.

Artiles, A. J., Trent, S. C., Hoffman-Kipp, P., & Lopez-Torres, L. (2000). From individual acquisition to cultural-historical practices in multicultural teacher education. *Remedial and Special Education, 21*, 79–89.

Bempechat, J., & Drago-Severson, E. (1999). Cross-national differences in academic achievement: Beyond etic conceptions of children's understandings. *Review of Educational Research, 69* (3), 287–314.

Bevan-Brown, J. (1989). *Intellectual disability: A Maori perspective.* Unpublished master's thesis, Massey University, Palmerston North, New Zealand.

Bevan-Brown, J. (2000a, April). *Evaluating special education services for learners from ethnically diverse groups: Getting it right.* Paper presented at the Special Education World Congress, CEC, Vancouver, Canada.

Bevan-Brown, J. (2000b, July). *Why are learners with special needs from ethnically diverse groups missing out on effective, culturally appropriate services and what can be done about it?* Paper presented at the International Special Education Congress, University of Manchester, Great Britain. Available from the World Wide Web: http://www.isec2000.org.uk/abstracts/papersindex.htm

Biklen, S., & Larson, M. (1998). The academy and the street: Using community fieldworkers to study children's social relations in school. In L. Meyer, H. S. Park, M. Grenot-Scheyer, I. Schwartz, & B. Harry (Eds.), *Making friends.* Baltimore: Paul H. Brookes.

Bishop, R., & Glynn, T. (1992). He kanohi kitea: Conducting and evaluating educational research. *New Zealand Journal of Educational Research, 27* (2), 3–13.

Canen, A. (1999). The challenges of conducting an ethnographic case study of a United Kingdom teacher education institution. *Journal of Teacher Education, 50* (1), 50–56.

Department of Education. (1987). *Draft review of special education.* Wellington, New Zealand: Author.

Diana v. California State Board of Education, No. C-70-37 RFP (Dist. Ct. Northern California, February, 1970).

Ford, B. A. (1992). Multicultural education training for special educators working with African-American youth. *Exceptional Children, 59*, 107–114.

Ford, D. (1998). The underrepresentation of minority students in gifted education: Problems and promises in recruitment and retention. *The Journal of Special Education, 32*, 4–14.

Garcia, G. E., & Pearson, P. D. (1994). Assessment and diversity. In L. Darling Hammond (Ed.), *Review of research in education* (Vol. 20, pp. 337–391). Washington, DC: American Education Research Association.

Garcia, S. B., Mendez Perez, A., & Ortiz, A. A. (2000). Mexican American mothers' beliefs about disabilities. Implications for early childhood intervention. *Remedial and Special Education, 21*, 90–100, 120.

Hammill, D. D., Pearson, N. A., & Wiederholt, J. L. (1996). *The comprehensive test of nonverbal intelligence.* Austin, TX: Pro-Ed.

Harry, B. (1992). *Cultural diversity, families and the special education system. Communication and empowerment.* New York: Teachers College Press.

Hiebert, E., Afflerback, P., & Valencia, S. (Eds.). (1994). *Authentic reading assessment: Practices and possibilities.* Newark, DE: International Reading Association.

Individuals with Disabilities Education Act (IDEA) of 1990, 20 U.S.C. s1400 et seq.

176

Ishii-Jordan, S. R. (1997). When behaviour differences are not disorders. In A. Artiles & G. Zamora-Duran (Eds.), *Reducing disproportionate representation of culturally diverse students in special and gifted education* (pp. 28–46). Reston, VA: The Council for Exceptional Children.

Joe, J., & Miller, D. (1993). *American Indian cultural perspectives on disability.* Tucson: The University of Arizona.

King, J. (1995, March 4). Arts award winner sees language value. *Evening Post,* p. 5.

Klein, M. D., & Chen, D. (2001). *Working with children from culturally diverse backgrounds.* Albany, NY: Delmar Thomas Learning.

Larry, P. v. Riles, No. C-71-2270-RFP (N.D. Cal., October 16, 1979).

Lee, C. D. (1998). Culturally responsive pedagogy and performance-based assessment. *The Journal of Negro Education, 67* (3), 268–279.

Lynch, E., & Hanson, M. (1998). *Developing cross-cultural competence: A guide for working with young children and their families* (2nd ed.). Baltimore: Paul H. Brookes.

Mallory, B., Nichols, R., Charlton, J., & Marfo, K. (1993). *Traditional and changing views on disability in developing countries, causes, consequences and cautions.* Durham, NH: IEER University of New Hampshire.

Massey University. (2000). *Special education 2000: Monitoring and evaluation of the policy.* Phase one final report. Report commissioned and funded by the Ministry of Education, New Zealand. February, 2000.

McCollum, J. A., & McBride, S. L. (1997). Ratings of parent-infant interation: Raising questions of cultural validity. *Topics in Early Childhood Special Education, 17* (4), 494–507.

Meyer, L. H. (1991). Advocacy, research and typical practices: A call for a reduction in the discrepancies between what is and what ought to be and how to get there. In L. H. Meyer, C. A. Peck, & L. Brown (Eds.), *Critical issues in the lives of people with severe disabilities* (pp. 629–649). Baltimore: Paul H. Brookes.

Meyer, L. H., Park, H. S., Grenot-Scheyer, M., Schwartz, I., & Harry, B. (1998a). Participatory research: New approaches to the research to practice dilemma. *Journal of The Association for Persons with Severe Handicaps, 23* (3), 165–177.

Meyer, L., Park, H., Grenot-Scheyer, M., Schwartz, I., & Harry, B. (1998b). Participatory research approaches for the study of the social relationships of children and youth. In L. Meyer, H. S. Park, M. Grenot-Scheyer, I. Schwartz, & B. Harry (Eds.), *Making friends.* Baltimore: Paul H. Brookes.

Miramontes, O. B. (1990). Organizing for effective paraprofessional services in special education: A multilingual/multiethnic instructional service team model. *Remedial and Special Education, 12,* 29–36.

NAEYC. (1996). NAEYC position statement: Responding to linguistic and cultural diversity — recommendations for effective early childhood education. *Young Children, 52* (2), 4–12.

Naglieri, J. A. (1996). *The Naglieri nonverbal ability test.* San Antonio, TX: Psychological Corp.

Nitko, A. J. (1983). *Education tests and measurement: An introduction.* New York: Harcourt Brace Jovanovich.

Overton, T. (1996). *Assessment in special education: An applied approach* (2nd ed.). Englewood Cliffs, NJ: Prentice Hall.

Park, H. S., Meyer, L. H., & Goetz, L. (1998). Special series on participatory action research (PAR). *Journal of The Association for Persons with Severe Handicaps, 23* (3), 163–164.

Patton, J. M. (1997). Disproportionate representation in gifted programs: Best practices for meeting this challenge. In A. Artiles & G. Zamora-Duran (Eds.), *Reducing disproportionate representation of culturally diverse students in special and gifted education* (pp. 59–85). Reston, VA: The Council for Exceptional Children.

Rueda, R. (1997). Changing the context of assessment: The move to portfolios and authentic assessment. In A. Artiles & G. Zamora-Duran (Eds.), *Reducing disproportionate representation of culturally diverse students in special and gifted education* (pp. 7–25). Reston, VA: The Council for Exceptional Children.

Serna, L., Forness, S. R., & Nielsen, M. E. (1998). Intervention versus affirmation: Proposed solutions to the problem of disproportionate minority representation in special education. *The Journal of Special Education, 32,* 48–51.

Smith, L. (1999). *Decolonising methodologies: Research and indigenous people.* London/Dunedin: Zed Books/University of Otago Press.

Stigler, J. W., Gallimore, R., & Hiebert, J. (2000). Using video surveys to compare classroom and teaching across cultures: Examples and lessons from the TIMSS video studies. *Educational Psychologist, 35* (2), 87–100.

Trent, S. C., & Artiles, A. J. (1998). Multicultural teacher education in special and bilingual education. *Remedial and Special Education, 19,* 2–6.

Turnbull, A. P., Friesen, B. J., & Ramirez, C. (1998). Participatory action research as a model for conducting family research. *Journal of The Association for Persons with Severe Handicaps, 23* (3), 178–188.

Valles, E. (1998). The disproportionate representation of minority students in special education: Responding to the problem. *The Journal of Special Education, 32,* 52–54.

Washington, V. (1996). Valuing diversity: A key to grassroots success. *Journal of Early Intervention, 20,* 179–182.

Weinfurt, K., & Moghaddam, F. M. (2001). Culture and social distance: A case study of methodological cautions. *The Journal of Social Psychology, 141* (1), 101–110.

Williams, R. L. (1975). The BITCH-100: A culture specific test. *Journal of Afro-American Issues, 3,* 103–116.

Zamora-Duran, G., & Reyes, E. I. (1997). From tests to talking in the classroom: Assessing communicative competence. In A. Artiles & G. Zamora-Duran (Eds.), *Reducing disproportionate representation of culturally diverse students in special and gifted education* (pp. 47–58). Reston, VA: The Council for Exceptional Children.

Zurcher, R. (1998). Issues and trends in culture-fair assessment. *Intervention in School and Clinic, 34,* 103–106.

10

DISPROPORTIONATE REPRESENTATION OF MALES IN SPECIAL EDUCATION SERVICES

Biology, behavior, or bias?

Michael L. Wehmeyer and Michelle Schwartz

Source: *Education and Treatment of Children* 24(1) (2001): 28–45.

Abstract

It is a common circumstance that males receiving special education services outnumber females nearly two to one. The primary explanation for this has been that boys exhibit behavior patterns that are more likely to result in their referral to special education. A second reason for this situation may be biological differences in boys and girls. A third reason, one not widely discussed in the special education literature, relates to the impact of gender bias on referral and admission. To examine the latter, we conducted a comprehensive records review for all students admitted to special education across three school years to examine gender differences in referral, admission, and placement decisions while accounting for known biological and behavioral variables. Our findings support a hypothesis in the literature that males are not necessarily over-represented in the special education population, but instead females who could benefit from special education services are underrepresented. One factor accounting for this underrepresentation is gender bias.

One of the most consistent characteristics of special education services in the past two decades has been the disproportionate number of males served.

Many reports show that boys receiving special education services outnumber girls 2 to 1. For example, the 1992 Report to Congress on the implementation of IDEA reported that more than two-thirds (68.5%) of secondary age students served in special education were males, even though the percentage of school-age males without disabilities was 49.7%. Males were disproportionately represented in every disability category except for deaf-blindness. Learning and emotional disabilities were the most disproportionate categories, with males comprising 73.4% and 76.4% of each, respectively.

As the Report to Congress stated, the reasons for such a high number of males "is not straightforward" (p. 11). Three hypotheses have been forwarded to explain the preponderance of males in special education. First, overrepresentation is attributable to biological factors because boys are more vulnerable to some genetically-determined disorders and predisposed to have some specific learning disabilities. It is established that females have some biological advantages over males like fewer birth defects and more rapid maturation (Harmon, Stockton, & Contrucci, 1992). Second, because boys are more active and more likely to act out or misbehave in classroom settings, it has also been suggested that the overrepresentation of males is a function of behavior problems. Although genetic, biological or neuropsysiological differences may contribute to activity for boys, behavior problems based on early learning may also influence referral and placement decisions. Kedar-Voivodas (1983) noted that child rearing practice, sex role modeling, imitation, socialization, and a student's individual reaction to school can influence the repertoire of behavior that girls and boys perform in the classroom. Boys may learn early that adults are tolerant of their more active behavior while girls are encouraged to behave in more inhibited manners; passive, quiet, obedient, and pleasant (Wagner-b, 1976). Third, researchers in gender equity propose that the disproportionate number of males is also due to influences of gender bias on the referral, classification, and placement process where bias refers to an inclination toward taking a position or reaching conclusions about a person based on their sex or gender. Kratovil and Bailey (1986) suggested that at the root of gender bias in identification for special education services is the gender-stereotyped societal expectations for girls and women, resulting in teachers expecting more from boys and setting high standards, while tolerating lower achievement in girls. Little research has been done to examine gender bias or discrimination as a contributor to the preponderance of males receiving special education services (Anderson, 1997; Kratovil & Bailey, 1986; Karlen, 1985; Phipps, 1982).

The present study reports findings from an exploratory analysis of student admissions to special education to determine the degree to which referral, admission, and placement services are provided in an equitable manner. There is no assumption that gender equity means, *a priori*, that there will or should be an equal number of males and females receiving special education services. Gender equity or fairness, used interchangeably here, refers to conditions in which one's position, conclusion, or behavior is impartial, free from discrimination, prejudice, or judgment based on gender (Reber, 1985). Equitable practices are those in which both males and females who qualify for and can benefit from special education are served (Rousso & Wehmeyer, 2001). Additionally, the term gender bias should not be associated only with regard to its impact on females. Societal based discrimination, bias, and stigma can impact both males and females who are perceived as different and admission to special education is not a panacea for good or desired outcomes. Students can experience negative consequences from being labeled with a disability and boys may disproportionately experience such negative outcomes. On the other hand, girls who are not succeeding and need learning supports may not be able to gain access to those supports and obtain the benefits of special education. If the higher proportion of males reflects inequitable access, then girls certainly experience negative outcomes resulting from that circumstance.

Biological

The utility of the hypothesis that disproportionate gender representation in special education reflects underlying physiological or biological factors depends, primarily, in the etiology of learning disabilities and severe, multiple disabilities. It is well established that, in part due to sex-linked chromosomal abnormalities and risk factors, males are at greater risk, and sometimes exclusively at risk, for significant impairments due to disorders like Klinefelter's syndrome, Fragile X syndrome, or Hurlers syndrome (Type II) (Hagerman, 1997; Menolascino & Egger, 1978). Also, students with significant disabilities are more easily identified as needing special education services, more likely to be identified with a disability at birth or early in life, and often have concomitant physical, health, and sensory impairments; all of which make referral and diagnosis less reliant on subjective indicators, and thus more immune to individual biases. However, students with severe disabilities make up a small percentage of the total population of students receiving special education services and even large gender discrepancies due to biological differences in this population cannot account for the disproportionate representation of males receiving special education services.

Alternatively, because the learning disabilities category constitutes the largest disability category in which students receiving special education are served, often in excess of 50% of the special education population in a district (Lyon, 1996), a biological explanation for the diagnosis of a learning disability could account for the gender gap. Some research, however, has refuted the presumption that reading disorders are more prevalent in males (Shaywitz & Shaywitz, 1994; Lyon 1996). For example, Shaywitz, Shaywitz, Fletcher, and Escobar (1990) used the Connecticut Longitudinal Study data to determine the prevalence of reading disorders in males and females based upon criteria selected by the researchers and thought to be more objective or based upon the school's identification of a reading disorder. They found no significant gender differences in the prevalence of reading disabilities using the ability-achievement criteria, but discovered a significant discrepancy in the prevalence of reading disabilities based on school identification records, where boys were 2 to 4 times more likely to have been referred and identified.

According to Reschly (1996), research has linked "biological factors to mild disabilities such as learning disability, and in particular reading disabilities." However, genetic relationships to severe reading disabilities and biological differences in the brain functioning of students with reading disabilities have not been reliably established (Reschly, 1996). Lyon (1996) noted that federally funded research shows that as many females as males have dyslexia, despite the fact that schools identify 3 to 4 times more boys. Lyon (1996) summarized twin-studies, designed to parse out the relative genetic contributions to reading disorders, and concluded that environment and genetic factors contributed equally to reading difficulties, and gender was a non-significant contributor. Lyon concluded that longitudinal studies of the linguistic, neurobiological, and genetic factors in reading disabilities provide support for the hypothesis that reading disorders are heritable, but not that they are gender specific.

Behavior

Most articles addressing male overrepresentation focus on the role of behavior — both student behavior and teacher perception of behavior — in the referral process (Andrews, Wisniewski & Mulick, 1997). Shaywitz *et al.* (1990) found that students identified as having a reading disability by objective, research-based standards differed from students who were identified by the school in that students referred and identified by the school exhibited higher activity rates and more frequent behavior problems. However, determining the degree to which problematic behaviors contribute to *inappropriate* placements in special education is complex. Even when eligibility for special education services is based on academic performance, as is the case in the diagnosis of a learning disability, there is frequently a co-occurrence of problematic behavior. For example, Epstein, Cullinan, and Lloyd (1986) examined the social-emotional adjustment of students with learning disabilities and concluded that social-emotional problems as well as behavior "represent an important aspect of learning disabilities" (Epstein, *et al.*, 1986, p. 43). The presence of a problematic behavior, in other words, does not constitute a reason to conclude that the special education placement was inappropriate.

Is there any reason to suspect that boys are more likely than girls to be admitted based solely on their behavior? Researchers have consistently noted for some time that boys have a more difficult time conforming to school-based expectations for behavior, independent of disability status or disability category (Maccoby & Jacklin, 1978). The child development literature documents that, for a variety of reasons ranging from biology to sex-typed modeling to differential parent and teacher interactions based on sex-stereotyped roles, boys are more active than girls and engage in higher rates of problem behaviors (Maccoby & Jacklin, 1978). In other words, boys are more likely to have higher activity levels and exhibit behaviors that do not conform with classroom regimens, and as such may be admitted to special education for those reasons.

Given the above, is there evidence that disproportionate representation of males reflects the performance of problematic behaviors and increased activity levels instead of actual learning deficits? Students identified under the learning disabilities category who have an attention deficit hyperactivity disorder (ADHD) with or without hyperactivity, may partially explain the higher number of males receiving special education services. Unlike reading disabilities, ADHD is more prevalent in males, and there is considerable co-occurrence of ADHD with reading disabilities, although the two are separate disorders. Lyon (1996) suggested that "given the frequent co-occurrence of ADHD with reading disabilities, and given the tendency of boys with ADHD to attract considerable attention from teachers, this combination may make boys with disabilities in reading much more likely than girls with disabilities in reading to come to the attention of teachers and to be referred for testing" (p. 67). The higher prevalence of ADHD in males may have a biological basis, as the child development literature has found a biological component to the higher levels of activity and aggressive behavior exhibited by boys (Maccoby & Jacklin, 1978). More recently, according to Lyon (1995), research conducted at Yale University, the University of Colorado, the Bowman Gray School of Medicine, and the University of Miami suggests that the classroom behavior of boys is "naturally more active and some-times rowdy" and leads to identification of their reading disability, while the quieter girls equally reading disabled are often overlooked (p. 5). Consequently, it seems tenuous to attribute a predisposition for ADHD as accounting for the disproportionate representation of males in special education as this confounds the putative biological predisposition for increased activity levels and aggression with problems of learned behavior and referral bias.

Ysseldyke and colleagues (Ysseldyke, Algozzine, & Richey, 1982) concluded that factors unrelated to discrepancies between ability and achievement accounted for placement in special education. Shaywitz *et al.* (1990) concluded that their data "indicate that school-identified samples are almost unavoidably subject to a referral bias" (p. 1002). Referral bias is the degree to which persons, typically teachers in regular education classrooms who are responsible for referring students for evaluation for eligibility in special education make such referrals based upon personal and professional opinions and not objective indicators. There are a number of biases that might impact the referral process, from those due to different levels of tolerance for specific behaviors or actions, to biases based on student characteristics, like gender, race, or ethnicity. Racial or ethnic referral bias is suggested by the fact that more African-American students than white students are referred and placed in special education, and a disproportionate number of African-American students are identified as having mild mental retardation (Reschly, 1996; Russo & Talbert-Johnson, 1997). According to Reschly (1996) several "commonly suggested causes of disproportionate minority representation in special education include poverty, discrimination or cultural bias in referral and assessment, and unique factors directly related to race or ethnicity".

Shaywitz and colleagues (1990) suggested that referral bias indicates that "teachers' perceptions of what constitutes inappropriate behavior enter into the decision and that, in particular, overactivity and behavioral difficulties are likely to be disruptive to a classroom and to influence decisions regarding such children" (p. 1002). Additional research suggests, however, that the problem is more complex than simply teachers referring males due to behavior problems. Shinn, Tindall, and Spira (1987) studied teacher referral, focusing on two types of errors possible in teacher referrals: (1) bias, as described previously, and (2) teacher inaccuracy, or "the extent to which teachers' appraisal of pupil performance is confirmed by objective criteria" (p. 33). These authors identified all students in a school district referred for special education because of a reading problem during one school year. They administered a measure of reading to each referred student, and then determined the local norms for reading level using the same measure with students in the general population. Teacher accuracy was determined by whether referrals were accurate or inaccurate when compared with the objective measure of reading ability. Teacher bias was determined by using student achievement data as a primary dependent measure and documenting the proportion of referred students as a function of sex and ethnicity. Referred males and females were equivalent in performance on measures of their reading skills, but relative to the population base-rates of poor readers, there were significantly more males than females referred.

Interestingly, Shinn and colleagues' examination of teacher accuracy concluded that teachers were, in fact, quite accurate about the reading abilities of students they referred. Across all grades and all analyses, referred students had significant reading problems when compared with local norms. However, the distribution of achievement scores for the referred students fell within the normative distribution for the measure, and Shinn and colleagues noted that "for every referred student, a substantial number of others in the normative population performed similarly" (p. 39). These authors suggested that, given the reality of limited teaching resources, teachers decide that not *all* low readers need to be referred, but instead only those who are poor readers and have some associated school-related problems, like hyperactivity or aggression, or those that "do not meet the biases of the teacher" (p. 39).

MacMillan, Gresham, Lopez, and Bocian (1996) studied the nomination of students to prereferral interventions in California. They administered a battery of assessments to 150 students, grades 2–4 (60% male, 40% female), who had been nominated for prereferral interventions. There were no significant difference by gender on intelligence or achievement tests for this sample, although teachers rated females as having higher academic competence and there were significant main effects for gender on teacher ratings of problem behaviors and social skills. Males were rated to exhibit more problem behaviors and lower scores on social skills than females on one scale, and to score higher on scales measuring conduct problems, hyperactivity, and inattentiveness on the other instrument. These authors suggested that the combination of more, and more severe, behavior problems combined with poor achievement led to their referral, compared with females whose poor achievement was not compounded by behavior problems.

Bias

Biases based on stereotypes about gender and gender roles in our society can take many forms, including the referral biases discussed earlier. Research in educational equity and child development shows that parents, teachers, and the general public treat girls quite differently than boys and have different expectations based on gender (AAUW, 1992; Maccoby & Jacklin, 1974). The AAUW report summarized the literature in this area as showing that "gender bias in the classroom takes many forms, some direct and some indirect, with teachers calling on boys more often than girls, encouraging more assertive behavior in boys than in girls, evaluating boys' papers for creativity and girls' for neatness, and giving boys the time and help to solve problems on their own, but 'helping' girls along by simply telling them the right answers" (p. 9). Teachers hold the same gender biases and expectations based on differential socialization patterns and sex role stereotyping held by the general public, and they bring that with them to the school setting. The fact that most teachers are women, particularly in the elementary years, further compounds the problem of sex role stereotyping and sex-typed modeling. Activists suggest that the preponderance of such role models tend to perpetuate and reinforce sex-stereotyped roles and behaviors for school-age girls (Rousso & Wehmeyer, 2001). Such sex-stereotyped roles and behaviors include quiet, acquiescent behavior. At the elementary ages, girls are reinforced to be more adult-oriented than are boys, tend to seek teacher feedback, and tend to achieve more when adults are present than when they are absent (Grossman & Grossman, 1994). By secondary ages, girls tend to have lower self-confidence and self-esteem than male peers, and perceive themselves as having limited control over out-comes in their lives. While male problem behaviors are often associated with aggression and activity, female-specific problem behaviors are often more internalized, leaving girls at higher risk for depression and learned helplessness (Grossman & Grossman, 1994). This portrait is admittedly broad-brushed in nature, and does not depict every girl, but illustrates why girls who may have achievement problems may not be referred for the services they might need. Many girls are likely to be quiet or withdrawn, and, if they are having difficulties, they may perceive any effort to address this problem as futile.

Study purpose and hypothesis

The purpose of this study was to examine the proportion of males and females *admitted* to special education services and to examine some of the factors contributing to admission. This study differs from previous studies in that the "event" that triggered a student's inclusion to this sample was being admitted to special education services, as opposed to students pre-referred or referred to special education for testing. Our intent, within the constraints introduced by a records review study, was to examine the degree to which admission to special education programs and services would be gender equitable. The study sample was limited to students with mental retardation and specific learning disabilities admitted to special educa-tion for the first time in a specific school year. The literature we reviewed previously suggests that the disproportionate representation of males in special education is not necessarily evidence of male overrepresentation but female underrepresentation. It seems that boys who receive special educa-tional services, by and large, have legitimate, academic-specific learning needs or challenges that should be addressed. However, we suggest that boys outnumber girls 2 to 1 not because fewer girls need special educational assistance, but because a combination of behavioral issues and biases based on gender make them less likely to be referred.

Method

Participants

The population from which the sample was drawn consisted of all students enrolled during one of three school years (1992–93, 1993–94, or 1994–95) in one of three school districts. District A was a rural district in the southern United States, serving students across an entire county. Total enrollment in this district was between 14,473 and 14,659 during the three study years. District B served a medium-sized city in the same state with a total student population between 10,405 and 10,452 across the three study years.

District C was a suburban district situated near a large metropolitan area in the southwestern United States. The student population for this district ranged from 18,852 to 19,235 across the three years.

Procedure and analyses

In each school district, we conducted a records review for one or more of the study years to identify, as nearly as possible, every student who had been admitted to special education for the first time during these years under the categories of learning disability or mental retardation. We limited the data collection to students with mental retardation or significant learning disabilities because issues of gender inequity across the life span have largely been ignored for this population and because it is within this group that referral bias and bias due to gender stereotyping are more likely to have influence. We also limited the sample to students who were six years of age or older. Most admissions to early childhood or early intervention services are initiated by parents or by medical professionals and children served in these programs typically have identifiable disorders that result in early and significant developmental delays. As such, it seems much less likely that biases of educators or service providers come into play. In District A, the review occurred only for the 1992–1993 school year. In District B, the review occurred only for the 1994–1995 school year. In District C, the review occurred across all three school years.

During the records review, the second author collected demographic data and the indicators available in student records of the contribution (if any) of the three factors (biology, behavior, and bias) on admission. To accomplish this, the second author obtained a list of students admitted for special education services by year from each school district. Working with the school district to ensure informed consent, the reviewer obtained data from each district's archival records. Data were collected about students' gender, ethnicity, and date of admission to special education, the person who referred the student for eligibility examination, primary and secondary disability category, placement (regular classroom, resource room, self-contained classroom, separate campus, other), and standardized intelligence and adaptive behavior scores used at time of admission. Data related to sex-linked conditions, early childhood referrals due to parent or medical intervention, severe health conditions, sensory disorders, co-occurrence of reading problems and non-conforming behavior (disorders of conduct, disorders of overactivity and or aggression) were collected to provide some information about the presence of biological or behavioral factors discussed earlier. This information was recorded directly from the records onto a data record sheet developed by project personnel.

Our intent was to examine the degree to which admission to special education was gender equitable. To do so, we first needed to account, as much as possible for disorders with any hypothesized or identified biological or behavioral explanations for admission. For the former, we gathered information on diagnosis (e.g. information on disorders such as Fragile X, Klinefelters syndrome, ADD with Hyperactivity, and so forth). To examine the latter (impact of behavior) we collected data from a referral sheet completed by general education teachers who referred the student for examination for eligibility for special education services. Detailed referral information was made available from District C only for two study years and referral sheets were not available for every student record, resulting in a sample of 115 student referral sheets (74 males, 41 females). From the referral sheet, we gathered data about gender, the reason for referral, and information about the student's grade. In addition, teachers completed a classroom observation form quantifying the student's receptive and expressive language skills, emotional/behavioral/social skills, motor coordination, and academic characteristics.

To further examine gender equitable admission practices we considered bias due to gender stereotyping and examined several of the indicators proposed by Kratovil and Bailey (1986) and Gillespie and Fink (1974) as indicative of gender bias in special education. The first was the age at which students were admitted to special education. Kratovil and Bailey (1986) cited anecdotal evidence that girls are older when admitted to special education, suggesting they wait longer to receive assistance. A second indicator we examined was differences by gender on IQ scores. Again, the suggestion raised by Kratovil and Bailey (1986) was that girls must have more significant deficits in order to be referred and admitted to special education. The third indicator examined was type of placement. Gillespie and Fink (1974) suggested that girls are more likely than boys to be placed in more restrictive classroom settings.

Data analysis consisted of tabular representation of the data to describe trends and outcomes. Differences by gender on age, IQ, and referral counts (from referral sheet) were examined by analysis of variance. Because all analyses were conducted with unequal group sizes (e.g., males outnumbered females), we conducted analyses of unweighted means, where a single harmonic mean was computed for all groups creating homogeneous subsets for all tests (Keppel, 1982). Differences in classroom placement were examined by chi-square analysis. All analyses were conducted using SPSS for Windows.

Results

The examination of school records to identify all students, age 6 years and over, with cognitive disabilities admitted to special education during study years yielded a total of 695 admissions. This included 462 males (66% of the total sample) and 233 females (33%). The majority ($n = 609$) of students had a learning disability, with only 86 students having mental retardation. Of students with learning disabilities, 417 were males (68.5%), 192 were females (31.5%). For students with mental retardation, 45 were males, 41 were females. The percentage of racial groups represented in this sample was generally representative of the nation, with Caucasian students representing 67.5% of the students across all three districts, African-American students representing 19.8%, Hispanic students representing 7.9% of the student body, Asian American students representing 2.8%, and Native American students representing .5%. Data on ethnicity was absent for 1.4% of the sample.

The mean age at time of admission for all males in the sample was 9.41 years ($SD = 2.41$), while the mean age for females was 9.45 years ($SD = 2.40$). The mean intelligence score was 94.38 ($SD = 14.72$) for males and 90.11 ($SD = 15.72$) for females. Analysis of variance for gender by age and IQ score yielded no significant differences for age, but significant differences for IQ score at time of referral and admission to special education services [$F(691,1) = 12.43$, $p = .0001$]. One explanation for this finding is the higher number of females with mental retardation relative to the total sample of girls (18% of total females had mental retardation) versus boys (10% of males had mental retardation). To examine this, we ran a separate analysis of variance examining IQ by gender only for students identified as having a learning disability. This analysis again showed significant differences by gender in IQ [$F(607,1) = 4.92$, $p = .027$], with the mean IQ scores for males at time of admission as 97.55 and the mean IQ scores for females at time of admission as 95.31.

The predominant placement for students in this sample was in the resource room ($n = 488$). Of other placements, 72 students received their education in a regular education classroom, 33 in a separate classroom in the same building, and 103 in off-campus vocational and life skills training program, or in borne-based programs for medical purposes. Since we were interested in the degree to which gender might impact admission to special education services, we opted to compare only students in the same building as same age peers, who were placed in the more typical special education setting; regular classrooms verses separate classrooms, in the same building as same age peers. Chi-square analysis by gender between these two settings (depicted in Table 1) found significant differences (*Chi Square* = 4.39, $p = .032$) and indicated that females were proportionately less likely to be placed in regular classrooms and more likely to be placed in self-contained classrooms than expected, while the opposite trend was true for males.

The next step of our analyses was to account, within the limits of the research design, for factors offered so far as biological or behavioral explanations for the disproportionate representation of males, by eliminating students from the sample (either male or female) who were diagnosed with a disability whose etiology or hypothesized etiology was sex-linked or whose behavior problems might better be explained by a biological

Table 1 Student placement by gender.

Placement		Sample		Sample Without Biology	
		Male	Female	Male	Female
Regular	Frequency	54	18	44	15
Classroom	Expected	49.4	22.6	39.3	19.7
	% of Placement	75%	25%	74.6%	25.4%
	% of Gender	75%	54.5%	75.9%	51.7%
	% of Total	51.4%	17.1%	50.6%	17.2%
Self-Contained	Frequency	18	15	14	14
Classroom	Expected	22.6	10.4	18.7	9.3
	% of Placement	54.5%	45.5%	50%	50%
	% of Gender	25%	45.5%	24.1%	48.3%
	% of Total	17.1%	14.3%	16.1%	16.1%

relationship. To be conservative, we also excluded all students whose record indicated the co-occurrence of a learning disability and non-conforming behavior, a conduct disorder, over-active or aggressive behavior, or whose secondary disabling condition was related to an emotional disorder. At this juncture, there were 598 students remaining, 388 of whom were male (65% of the sample) and 210 who were female (35% of the sample). The mean age of the males was 9.36 (SD = 2.39) while the mean age for females was 9.37 (SD = 2.32). The mean IQ score was 93.76 (SD = 14.83) for males and 89.86 (SD = 15.72) for females. Again, there were no significant differences between genders by age, but significant differences on IQ scores [$F(597,1)$ = 9.03, p = .003]. Findings from the chi-square analysis replicated the initial analysis, with girls significantly (Chi Square = 5.16, p = .02) more likely than expected to be placed in self-contained classrooms and less likely to be placed in general education classrooms, and vice versa for males. Table 1 also reports data from that analysis.

The first section of the referral sheet was titled "reason for referral" and teachers described in narrative form why the student was referred for evaluation. This section was completed on 108 of the 115 forms (68 males, 40 females). Males and females had a similar mean number of academic reasons listed (Male = 1.89, Female = 1.95), but males had more behavioral reasons listed (Males = 2.84, Females = .002). Analysis of variance indicated no significant differences by gender on the number of academic referrals, but a significant difference on behavioral referrals [$F(107,1)$ = 6.03, p = .0161. Of the 40 females, only one student (2.5% of the females) had a behavioral reason listed at all, and she had only a single behavioral reason indicated. Of the 68 males, thirteen (19.1%) had behavioral referrals, and six male students had only behavioral reasons listed.

Referring teachers were then asked to rate the student's grades in relation to his or her past performance and in comparison with other students, both on Likert scales. On the former, teachers responded to the query "this student's grades" with one of four responses (1 = have become steadily higher, 2 = have remained the same, 3 = have become steadily lower, 4 = dropped suddenly). They were then asked to compare whether the student's grades were higher, approximately the same, or lower than other students in the school. In both cases, there were no differences in ratings by gender.

Finally, referring teachers completed a classroom observation form indicating the student's performance in receptive and expressive language skills, emotional/ behavioral/ social skills, motor coordination and academic characteristics. For questions in each area, teachers recorded a score from 1 (poor) to 5 (superior). Table 2 provides the questions in each domain, the point total possible for each domain, and the mean scores in each domain by gender. There were no significant differences by gender on analysis of variance for any domain area.

Discussion

This study provides preliminary support to emerging suggestions that females with disabilities are underrepresented in special education services largely due to biases based on behavior and gender stereotyping. Of all students admitted to special education for the first time, boys outnumbered girls exactly 2 to 1. From that total of 695, we excluded all students whose reason for referral, according to the information available in a records review, might be explained by a heritable or biologically based disabling condition, males and females alike. This resulted in the reduction of the sample by 97 students but the male to female ratio of 2 to 1 did not shift dramatically after these students were taken into account. The gender proportion remained almost 2/3 males (65% males, 35% females). Of the three indicators of gender bias examined for the remainder of the sample, (age and I.Q. at time of admission, type of placement), there were significant differences in two. Females had lower IQ scores at admission and were disproportionately more likely to be placed in self-contained classrooms than males. The latter cannot adequately be explained by the former (e.g., lower IQ scores) because mean IQ scores for females were still quite high relative to other students placed in separate classroom settings. It also seemed that behavioral factors were influencing referral even when we excluded cases where higher levels of overactivity, aggression, or non-conforming behaviors had been documented. Only one female (2.5% of females) had behavioral reasons given for referral, while nearly 20% of males had behavior reasons listed. Six males had only behavior reasons provided. However, there were no differences between males and females on grade estimates (either when

Table 2 Questions on Classroom Observation Form and Mean Scores by Gender.

Skill Area	Mean Scores	
	Male	*Female*
Receptive Language Skills **(scores range from 5–25, 5 = poor, 25 = superior)** Comprehends word meanings Follows oral instructions Comprehends classroom discussion Remembers information just heard	11.46	13.76
Expressive Language Skills **(scores range from 4–20, 4 = poor, 20 = superior)** Displays adequate vocabulary Uses adequate grammar for general understanding Expresses self fluently when called upon to speak Relates a sequence of events in order Organizes and relates ideas and factual information	8.74	8.86
Emotional/Behavioral/Social **(scores range from 10–50, 10 = poor, 50 = superior)** Generally cooperates or is compliant with teachers' requests Adapts to new situations without getting upset Accepts responsibility for own actions Makes and keeps friends at school Works cooperatively with others Has an even, usually happy, disposition Is pleased with good work. Initiates activities independently Responds appropriately to praise and correction Resists becoming discouraged by difficulties or minor setbacks	27.03	29.31
Motor Coordination **(scores range from 2–10, 2 = poor, 10 superior)** Exhibits adequate gross motor coordination Displays adequate fine motor coordination	5.37	5.83
Academic Characteristics **(scores range from 5–25, 5 = poor, 25 superior)** Reads aloud grade level material Comprehends grade level material read Performs math computations at expected grade level proficiency Spells grade level material adequately Writes appropriately for grade level Retains instruction from week to week Exhibits organization in accomplishing tasks Completes tasks on time	14.86	15.07

compared with the student's past performance or with the school as a whole) or on estimations of academic skills provided by referring teachers on an observation form.

The case for the role of biases and expectations about behavior issues was strengthened by the fact that the more objective indicator of behavior problems, a Likert-scale classroom observation form, indicated no significant differences between males and females. In essence, when teachers were asked to provide a narrative of their reason for referral, they emphasized behavior problems for the males. When they completed a less subjective indicator, however, the differences between genders disappeared.

Before discussing these results further, it is important to note the limitations to the study. The primary limitations are those introduced by the conduct of a record review study. Using such a procedure, we can only infer the existence of bias. The indicators for both gender bias and behavioral biases are imperfect, and without actually measuring teacher attitudes, expectations and, more importantly, conducting classroom observations, we cannot say conclusively that these biases exist. Such research has been conducted within regular education settings, and could (as well as should) be conducted with relation to students with disabilities. Until this happens, however, the existence of bias remains hypothetical. We also recognize that there are other influences on the referral process, particularly issues of racial stereotyping. These analyses do not take these considerations into account, other than attempting to configure a sample representative of students across the nation. Nonetheless, other studies have found that gender and ethnicity contribute orthogonally to bias, and the existence of one does not abrogate the impact of the other. Third, the process for excluding students whose disability is biologically based from analyses was dependent upon documentation of such basis in the school record. We recognize that such records may not contain sufficient information on medical causes for disability and, as such, we cannot unequivocally claim to have controlled for biology as a factor. Fourth, because referral data were available only from one school district and involved teacher report indicators, we must emphasize that our findings are quite tentative and should be interpreted with caution. Within these limitations, however, we suggest that these findings complement data reported in previous studies and, at the least, should provide impetus for further research and examination.

The primary message, we believe is that while there is a tendency to refer to the issue of disproportionate representation of males in special education as a problem of male overrepresentation, it may well be a viable alternative explanation for the disproportionate number of males is that females who do need some academic support and special education services but who do not exhibit concomitant behavior problems are not being referred or served in special education. The problem is, potentially, one of female underrepresentation. Findings related to the placement of students by gender lead to another trend that might be called the paradox of placement. Boys are more likely to be referred by regular education teachers, presumably because they are more disruptive and difficult to manage (as well as having academic problems), but are also more likely to be placed back in regular education. On the other hand, girls were disproportionately likely to end up in quite restrictive placements once referred, despite the fact that their behavior was not a concern to teachers.

It appears that the present system may be inequitable, not because more boys are being served than girls, but because girls who have equivalent educational needs are not provided access to supports and services that might address these needs. Follow-up and follow-along studies show consistently that girls with cognitive disabilities graduate to less positive adult outcomes. Research indicates that males with disabilities are more likely than females to be employed, work full-time, and to remain employed. Females with disabilities are more likely than males to be employed in unskilled jobs despite of a lack of differences between sexes in I.Q, achievement, and basic job skills. Hasazi, Gordon, and Roe (1985) found that males with disabilities leaving school were 30% more likely to be employed. Sitlington and Frank (1993) found that females with mental retardation and learning disabilities were less likely than males to find competitive employment after high school and earned significantly less per hour when employed. Scuccimarra and Speece (1991) determined that, among students with mild disabilities two years out of high school, females had a significantly higher rate of unemployment than males (91% employment for males, 52% for females), females were more likely to work in unskilled occupations, and more males (25%) earned $5.00 or more per hour than females (9%).

There are multiple reasons for these outcomes, but bias may play a role. In addition to the impact of gender bias on admission to special education services, gender stereotypes and biases impact the type and content of coursework students receive, the interactions in classrooms, and the expectations others hold for students (AAUW, 1992). Although largely ignored, there is reason to believe that the same forces negatively impact females with cognitive disabilities.

Biases about behavior are a form of gender bias, and attempts to address gender biases will impact both areas. We have gathered guidelines for what special educators should know about gender equitable education (Rousso & Wehmeyer, 2001) to provide direction for practice. In the classroom, teachers can create a learning environment in which students are encouraged to fully participate so that no members dominate and none are silenced, use diverse teaching strategies to take into account differing learning strengths, minimize gender-segregated activities, and encourage cooperation. Teachers should be aware of their communications with students and ensure that praise and recognition is equitably given and that all students are provided answers that lead to independent thinking and problem solving. Curricula needs to be gender equitable, portraying the experiences of and contributions of women and presenting women in nontraditional roles. At the campus and district level, administrators can make sure that policies do not promote gender segregation, and put in place mechanisms to assess the impact of gender biases on processes like special education placement. District wide tests and other evaluative methods need to be free of gender bias and stereotyping. Finally, teachers should be provided opportunities to learn more about equitable education through inservice training.

References

AAUW (1992). *How schools shortchange girls: a study of major findings on girls and education.* Washington, D. C.: American Association of University Women.

Anderson, K. G. (1997). Gender bias and special education referrals. *Annals of Dyslexia, 47,* 151–162.

Andrews, T. J., Wisniewski, J. J. & Mulick, J. A. (1997). Variables influencing teachers' decisions to refer children for school psychological assessment services. *Psychology in the Schools, 34*(3), 239–244.

Epstein, M. H., Cullinan, D., & Lloyd, J. W. (1986). Behavior-problem patterns among the learning disabled: III — Replication across age and sex. *Learning Disabilities Quarterly, 9,* 43–54.

Gillespie, P. H., & Fink, A. H. (1974). The influence of sexism on the education of handicapped children. *Exceptional Children, 41,* 155–162.

Grossman, H., & Grossman, S. H. (1994). *Gender issues in education.* Boston: Allyn & Bacon.

Hagerman, R. J. (1997). Fragile X syndrome: Meeting the challenge of diagnosis and care. *Contemporary Pediatrics, 14*(3), 31–59.

Hasazi, S. B., Gordon, L. R., & Roe, C. A. (1985). Factors associated with the employment status of handicapped youth exiting high school from 1979–1983. *Exceptional Children, 51,* 455–469.

Karlen, A. (1985). Are boys really more vulnerable to learning disabilities than girls? *Academic Psychology Bulletin, 7,* 317–325.

Kedar-Voivodas, G. (1983). The impact of elementary children's school roles and sex roles on teacher attitudes: An interactional analysis. *Review of Educational Research, 53*(3), 415–437.

Keppel, G. (1982). *Design and analysis: A researcher's handbook.* Englewood Cliffs, NJ: Prentice Hall.

Kratovil, J., & Bailey, S. M. (1986). Sex equity and disabled students. *Theory Into Practice, 25,* 250–256.

Lyon, G. R. (1995). Impediments to scientific developments in learning disabilities: An historical perspective. *Research in learning disabilities at the NICHD,* 1–14. Bethesda MD: National Institute of Child Health and Human Development, National Institute of Health.

Lyon, G. R. (1996). Learning disabilities. *The Future of Children, 6,* 54–76.

Maccoby, E. E., & Jacklin, C. N. (1978). *The psychology of sex differences.* Stanford, CA: Stanford University Press.

MacMillan, D. L., Gresham, F. M., Lopez, M. F., & Bocian, K. M. (1996). Comparison of students nominated for prereferral interventions by ethnicity and gender. *The Journal of Special Education, 30,* 133–151.

Menolascino, F. J., & Egger, M. L. (1978). Medical dimensions of mental retardation. Lincoln, NE: University of Nebraska Press.

Phipps, P. (1982). The LD learner is often a boy — why? *Academic Therapy, 17,* 425–430.

Reber, A. S. (1985). *Dictionary of psychology.*: London: Penguin.

Reschly, S. J. (1996). Identification and assessment of students with disabilities. *The Future of Children, 6*(1), 40–53.

Rousso, H., & Wehmeyer, M. L. (2001). *Double jeopardy: addressing gender equity in special education services.* Albany, NY: State University of New York Press.

Russo, C. J., & Talbert-Johnson, C. (1997). The overrepresentation of African American children in special education: the resegregation of educational programming? *Education and Urban Society, 29*(2), 136–148.

Shaywitz, S. E., Shaywitz, B. A., Fletcher, J. M., & Escobar, M. D. (1990). Prevalence of reading disability in boys and girls: Results of the Connecticut Longitudinal Study. *Journal of the American Medical Association, 264,* 998–1002.

Shinn, M. R., Tindal, G. A., & Spira, D. A. (1987). Special education referrals as an index of teacher tolerance: Are teachers imperfect tests? *Exceptional Children, 54,* 32–40.

Sitlington, P. L., & Frank, A. R. (1995). Success as an adult — does gender make a difference for graduates with mental disabilities? *Career Development of Exceptional Individuals, 16,* 171–182.

Succimarra, D. & Speece, D. L. (1991). Employment outcomes and social integration of students with mild handicaps: The quality of life two years after high school. *Journal of Learning Disabilities, 25,* 213–219.

Ysseldyke, J. E., Algozzine, B., & Richey, L. (1982). Judgment under uncertainty: How many children are handicapped? *Exceptional Children, 48,* 53–534.

11

ISSUES OF EQUITY IN SPECIAL NEEDS EDUCATION FROM A GENDER PERSPECTIVE

Harry Daniels, Valerie Hey, Diana Leonard and Marjorie Smith

Source: *British Journal of Special Education* 26(4) (1999): 189–95.

This article is concerned with gender issues in resource allocation for special needs in mainstream schools. The ways in which categories operate in academic life and professional practice in schools raise dilemmas for the development of the concept and practice of equality of opportunity. Data are drawn from a recent ESRC study (R000237346) and used to illustrate some of the ways in which significant problems for the management of special needs services are revealed from the perspective of gender.

Introduction

For many years the analysis of a broad range of social phenomena has been influenced by a general concern for equality of opportunity. This article will explore some of the ways in which categories of analysis in education function, and illustrate the way in which focusing on gender (by race and class) casts light on the processes of the identification of need. The resource allocation in special needs provision in mainstream schools is highlighted.

In the UK there has been a long-term concern for refining concepts of educational difficulty, and one of the key recommendations of the Warnock Report (DES, 1978) was that categories of handicap in education should be abolished and replaced with a concept of special educational need:

We wish to see a more positive approach, and we have adopted the concept of *Special Educational Need*, seen not in terms of a particular disability which a child may be judged to have, but in relation to

197

everything about him, his abilities as well as his disabilities – indeed all the factors which have a bearing on his educational progress.

Para. 3.6, p.37 (stress as in original)

The *Education Act of 1981* was heavily influenced by the Warnock Report, and one of its key aspects was a change in the definition of SEN. Instead of practitioners allocating children to fixed categories of existing special needs provision, they were to formulate children's needs in terms of the provision required to help an individual to make progress, and school governors were required to ensure their pupils' specific needs were identified and met (Section 2 (5)). Much of the subsequent development in SEN provision took the form of LEA-provided resources and support services, including support within mainstream classrooms; together with each school's development of its own special needs policies and practices. Norwich (1990) argued that:

... behind the Warnock rhetoric of abolishing categories lie complex issues which need to be explored ... the central importance of values in education is evident in an educational perspective on disability and in the social movement towards educating children with special educational need in ordinary schools.

(p. 17)

At a general level it would seem reasonable to suggest that many of those who seek to analyse matters of gender, race and special educational need do so on the basis of at least some common values, albeit they have somewhat different perspectives. A series of statements from international bodies has helped to create the climate in which political pressure is ensuring that state run agencies, at least, accede to the notion of special needs as a human rights issue. While the inclusionist, 'schooling for diversity' or 'school for all' movement (eg *The United Nations Standard Rules on the Equalization of Opportunities for People with Disabilities*, 1993; The *UNESCO Salamanca Statement*, 1994) seeks to unite many practitioners and academics in the common purpose of creating an educational system that ensures equality of opportunity, equity and a humanitarian concept of effectiveness.

The public appeal for integration is also witnessed in the *Code of Practice on the Identification and Assessment of Special Educational Needs* (DfE, 1994a) which provides practical guidance for LEAs and school governing bodies on their responsibilities towards pupils with special educational needs. Schools and LEAs have been required 'to have regard to' its recommendations from September 1994. The Department for Education (1994b) also issued Circular 6/94 on *The Organization of Special Educational Provision* which provided suggestions on how schools should manage their provision alongside that of other local schools. These documents embody the twin strategies of individual pupil support and whole school development, although many commentators have noted the somewhat over-individualising impact of the Code. Thus Booth (1996), Lewis, Neill & Campbell (1996) and Ofsted (HMCI, 1996) all report on the implementation of the Code and note that there is still much to be done in ensuring that a system (designed to introduce some sense of regularity into a context in which there were disparities between schools and LEAs) is implemented and developed into a realistic and effective working tool. This problem has also been recognised in the recent *Meeting Special Educational Needs: a Programme of Action* (DfEE, 1998), which seeks to promote the development of more sophisticated and comprehensive forms of regional and local planning.

Despite this torrent of legislation and recommendations, there are still a number of key concerns, such as the extent to which:

- SEN are seen as a matter for analysis at the level of the individual, whether in terms of causation or intervention;
- individual needs are met by *provision* rather than *reformulation* in the light of the provision that is available.

Equality, sameness and difference

The wish to respond to individual need may conflict with principles of equity and equality where the primary concern is with the development of bureaucratic systems. For example, it is possible to apply a principle of equality of opportunity in order that boys and girls are given equal access to SEN support. If provision is looked at from this perspective, stark inequalities are revealed. Data from the USA suggest an over-referral of males, especially African-Americans (Haigh & Malever, 1993–1994; Weinstein, 1993–1994), while the National Longitudinal Transition Study of Special Education Students (NLTS) reported by Wagner (1992) emphasised that, although girls are under-represented, those who are certified are more seriously impaired:

> Females in secondary special education represented a different combination of abilities and disabilities than males. As a group, females were more seriously impaired; even among males and females with the same disability category, females had marginally greater functional deficits than males.
>
> (pp.33–34)

We also know that there has been a marked disparity of provision for boys and girls in access to many special schools in the UK. This has recently been confirmed by large-scale surveys (eg Cooper, Upton & Smith, 1991). But if boys and girls were treated equally, and equal numbers were sent to special schools, would this be equitable?

This tension has led White (1991) to propose the compromise strategy of developing solutions which are 'good enough' for individuals, yet assure equity for all those 'in need'. Although this strategy offers some way forward in a perennial dilemma, it tends to underplay the concept and reality of power relations. The categories used in practice owe their existence to the relations of power and serve to demarcate and maintain the boundaries which form them. Some categories of SEN are more desirable and acceptable than others, which, in the context of SEN practices, is well illustrated by the boundary between the category 'Mental Retardation' (MR) and 'Learning Disability' (LD) in the USA. Entry into the more socially acceptable category (LD) is much more difficult to achieve than into the MR category and therefore it is likely to be the educationally informed middle class who push to ensure the LD label for their children and especially for their sons (Carrier, 1983).

The research reported here attempts to supplement the understandings which are brought to bear on the problem of reconciling concepts of need and equality in the context of power relations, and the categories of gender and SEN. We know that different groupings within the research community have tended to be associated with different categories of social analysis, such as race, class, gender and SEN, and hence these categories remain conceptually and practically distinct (especially SEN) from gender, race and class. This situation is apparent in university departments and local authority services and is made manifest in publications and policy documents. We suggest that these boundaries are also seen in the actual practice of special needs education in schools.

Solstad (1994) suggests that the concept of equity may be embedded in two distinct sets of referents. Equity may be referenced to equality, and the principle may be realised through centralised and centralising actions by agencies such as the state. Alternatively, the principle of equity may be referenced to diversity, and realised in particular settings, regions and localities. Evans (1995) provides an extended discussion in the context of feminist theory:

> We might then want to see 'equality', 'sameness', and 'difference' as forming not a continuum, but three corners of a triangle. Then the notion of 'equality in difference' enters in. (This is the idea that we merit equal though not identical treatment; equal in the sense of 'equally good, and appropriate to us'). Though so does 'equality through difference', as opposed to 'equality through sameness'.
>
> (p.3)

Evans suggests that to treat people equally it is not necessary to treat them in exactly the same way; on the contrary, '. . . to treat people as equals may *require* that they not be treated the same way . . .' (p.4). It is, however, essential that they be treated fairly. The data suggest that girls and boys are not treated in the same way, in that more boys are sent to special schools. The argument is *not* that more girls should be sent to special schools, nor to suggest that girls are being treated fairly as, in fact, their needs are possibly being ignored (Haddock & Malcolm, 1992). If questions concerning equity are important, appropriate tools or categories of analysis (sophisticated enough to encompass the complexity of issues surrounding the term equality) are necessary.

Categories as tools of analysis

Categories, as tools of analysis, may be thought of as relays of social priorities and assumptions in the way they enter the discourses and practices of resource allocation and management. For example, it is clear that monitoring systems, such as LEA SEN audits of need, take account of some groups and not of others. In our own work we did not find an example of an LEA which held central Code of Practice data referenced according to gender.

Many of the terms in popular use have highly situated meanings. This *flakiness* of categories was all too apparent in the research discussed in this article and we found many examples of headteachers having access to information which was not available to Special Needs Co-ordinators (SENCos). We also found that descriptors applied to children and services were used in an inconsistent manner across the LEA; there was also evidence of an idiosyncratic use of services across schools and large differences in levels of Statementing. It was also clear that the use of some categories implied permanency, whilst others were suggestive of potential resolution (eg 'learning difficulty' and 'specific learning difficulty'). Categories formed by provision may also be used to formulate need (eg children who are a cause for concern owing to their behaviour may be referred to a literacy support service simply because there is no other service available). Above all, these categories are, as Norwich (1990) suggests, 'value laden'.

In the two LEAs we considered (in an ESRC funded study R000235059 entitled 'Gender and Special Educational Needs Provision in Mainstream'), difficulties in monitoring were compounded by a general difficulty in collating systems of records within and between schools. (The variation between and within LEAs in the use of specific categories may, in part, be seen to depend on the quality and nature of the provision available within mainstream schools). In addition, resource allocation devices seemed to generate categories into which data were forced. We may only speculate as to whether this actually results in the manipulation of perceptions into administrative categories at LEA level. Certainly, there are complex relations between the language of description, with its categories and criteria, the administrative procedures and practices, and the pedagogic reality. The very complexity and obscurity of these systems may allow for the relative autonomy of local ideologies and our findings suggest that different schools interpret 'SEN' in very different ways. This is particularly in terms of implicit models of causality (eg societal, familial, individual) and in responses (eg whole-class or individual; uniform or differentiated; outside or inside the school). The suggestion was prompted by the finding that there was no association between the level of SEN activity and resource allocation, and the Additional Educational Needs (AEN) budget for the schools we surveyed.

In an earlier small pilot study, we had collected information on the gender ratios in special schools from several LEAs with established Equal Opportunities (EO – gender) policies and asked LEA Advisors to indicate 'good' EO schools which would be 'least likely to show gender inequalities'. We also looked in more detail at two mainstream primary schools (to see how they handled in-school SEN provision) in order to examine the interplay between two major sets of categories: SEN and gender. We found:

a) Significant gender differences exist in the numbers of children receiving extra support, irrespective of the identification procedures.
b) There were gender differences in the effective reasons for referral, although these were rarely made explicit if referral was made to agencies outside the school or, in some cases, the classroom.
c) Boys were often given forms of support which were not designed to meet the needs identified (eg instruction in reading as a response to inappropriate behaviour).

These data supported the suggestion that constructs of SEN remain highly individualised and are tacitly associated with 'within-person' accounts. It is, therefore, often seen as quite distinct from the social processes which bias resource allocation across gender and race boundaries and consequently, in practice, provision is not 'answerable' to EO monitoring procedures (Daniels, Hey, Leonard & Smith, 1995). We then explored a tentative suggestion about the interplay between categories in analysis, and practice was explored in a much larger ESRC funded study. We aimed to test the hypothesis that significant gender differences exist in the allocation of special needs provision and also sought to establish whether significant gender differences exist in the effective criteria used to identify need. That is, we were concerned to establish whether gender differences exist in the processes of matching different forms of provision to need and to understand the consequences for pupils.

The first of the three phases of the ESRC project involved a survey of the allocation of the special provision. This was followed by a series of in-depth studies of processes of identification, referral and allocation. Finally we conducted an evaluation of the consequences for pupils of inappropriate provision and/or over-representation, as well as lack of provision in the case of those underrepresented.

The data we present here are mainly from phase one which involved a broad survey of the allocation of the special provision made available at Key Stage 2 in one LEA. This took place during the first year of the implementation of the *Code of Practice* and the gender ratio data were collected initially for the schools and subsequently by individual pupils within the schools. Thirty-five schools responded to the first survey and information was gathered on:

- the Additional Educational Needs budget
- the proportion of bilingual pupils
- reading test results
- SATs results.

Twenty-one schools provided access to data on each pupil receiving additional support and information was gathered on:

- gender
- date of birth
- ethnic background
- first language
- eligibility for free school meals
- home background (parents living with the child, type of accommodation)
- type of SEN registered by the school
- provision allocated by the school.

The variation between schools suggested that schools as institutions may exert considerable influence over local practice with respect to gender.

Categories in practice

The first gender ratio was aggregated for all the pupils in 35 schools of the 42 schools that we approached. The ratio of boys to girls receiving additional support was adjusted for the ratio of overall numbers of boys to girls in each school; a mean ratio of 1.7, with a standard deviation of1.71.

We then analysed data on each pupil receiving additional support in 21 of the 35 schools, to give 358 pupil profiles. The overall gender ratio here was then 1.84 (232 boys and 126 girls). However, when the ratios are calculated for each school, on the basis of this second survey, the data did not concur with the school-based data of the first survey. The mean adjusted ratio for this data set was 2.5 with a standard deviation of 1.49.

A comparison of adjusted ratios from the first (school-based) survey against the second (pupil-based) survey reveals that the greatest disparities are associated with the highest reported ratios, which suggests that there may be a relationship between the quality and accuracy of school-based records and

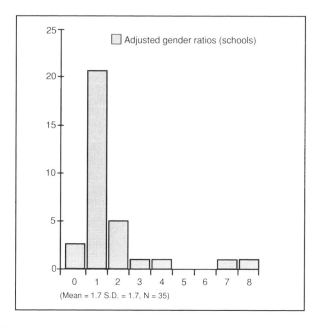

Figure 1 Whole school returns on gender ratios.

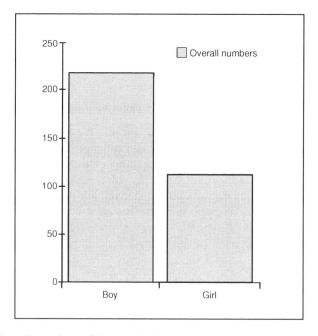

Figure 2 Overall numbers of boys and girls in the sample.

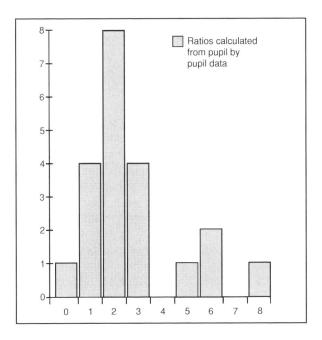

Figure 3 Gender ratios collected from the pupil audit.

gendered inequalities in SEN resource allocation. We therefore decided to use only the pupil-based survey data in further analyses.

Resource allocation

It was with some surprise that we noted no discernible relationship between the level of AEN per head of pupil population and the level of SEN activity in the school. Many SEN co-ordinators and teachers in schools appeared to be unaware that an AEN budget existed, how much had been allocated, or who was responsible for the decisions about its use. Schools studied in the project did, however, seem to make a significant difference in the way that AEN budgets are spent, *and* to the extent to which boys are favoured in the distribution of this resource. To find one school working with a gender ratio of one (when adjusted for the overall numbers of boys and girls in the school) and another school with an adjusted gender ratio of eight, in situations which appear remarkably similar within one LEA, most surely raise the eyebrows of those concerned with equity in resource allocation practices. These are significant school differences which appear to stand outside the gaze of current monitoring procedures and this variation *between* schools suggests that schools as institutions may exert a considerable influence over local practice with respect to gender.

Within schools, gender differences were seen to vary as a function of the category of SEN used by the teachers and SENCos to describe the pupils. As can be seen in Figure 4, the most marked difference was revealed within the category EBD; the least in the mild learning difficulty category.

Gender differences also appeared to vary as a function of ethnicity as categorised by parents. We experienced great difficulty in collecting these data since there was significant variation by school in the extent to which categories of ethnicity were applied and variation in the actual categories used. In Figure 5 (below) the category 'black' comprises African-Caribbean and 'black other'; the category 'white' includes 'white English' and 'white Irish' (there were very few Asian children living in the LEA). Children who are in the process of acquiring English as a second language have been omitted from this analysis. The male/female ratio is close to 1.0 in the African-Caribbean group and above 2.0 in the white English and Irish groups. When examined by ethnicity and gender, patterns of categorizations appear to vary significantly.

Within both 'black' and 'white' groups gender differences are greatest in the emotional and behavioural difficulty category; and gender differences are much greater in the 'white' group than the 'black' group. In addition, 'black' children appear to be more likely to be allocated to the category 'general learning difficulty' than 'reading difficulty' when compared with their 'white' peers. If we are concerned about equity for all, we need to understand much more about SEN practices from the perspectives of both gender *and* race considered simultaneously.

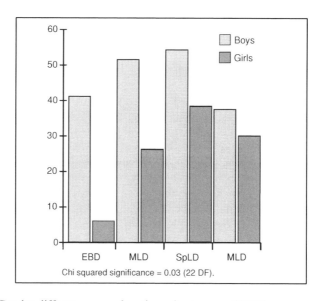

Figure 4 Gender differences as a function of category of SEN.

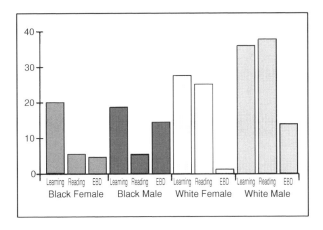

Figure 5 Race by gender by SEN.

Our data also suggest that not only are significantly more boys than girls allocated additional help in mainstream schools, but also that they are given more time. Figure 6 shows how the gender difference tends to increase as the allocation of hours of support increases, while Figure 7 suggests that boys are usually allocated the more prestigious and expensive forms of support.

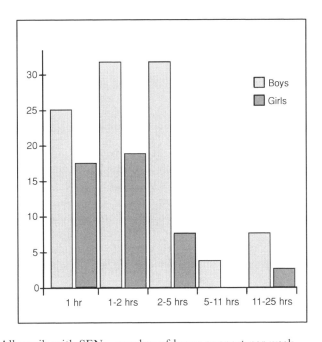

Figure 6 All pupils with SEN – number of hours support per week.

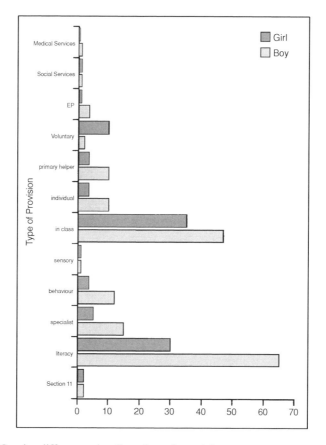

Figure 7 Gender differences in allocation of provision.

We could find no overall relationship between measures of attainment and gender ratios, apart from a slight positive association between poor performance in science SATs and increased gender ratios. In schools where overall performance in science SATs was poor, more boys tended to be allocated special help. When the home background of pupils is considered, a first analysis suggests a strong association between children who live with a single parent (mother) and all forms of SEN. This appears to be particularly marked in the case of pupils (referred to by teachers) as exhibiting emotional and behavioural difficulties (see Figure 4). However, when this same data set is analysed by an index of poverty, namely eligibility for free school meals, as in Figure 6, a very strong association between poverty and SEN is also suggested. Subsequent analysis of the data, suggests that many of the mothers living alone with their children are eligible for free school meals, providing a good example of the dangers of confusing correlation with causation. A confusion which is politically malleable.

Conclusion

The pursuit of equity in education has been guided and enhanced by an analysis-focused equality of opportunity. But this has often involved analyses of educational practice which consider one category of inequality at a time. Similarly groups of analysts and practitioners have developed interests and analyses which have been single-category driven and, moreover, injudicious averaging may be seen to be in play in the context of SEN resource allocation. The data presented here suggest that averaging across schools and that considering categories of SEN, race and gender in isolation are both 'injudicious'. There is most certainly an over-representation of boys in SEN provision, particularly in certain types of learning difficulty and emotional and behavioural difficulty. The undoubted over-referral may in turn give rise to the creation of more provision for boys, which could be seen as a reasonable response to need. The data presented in this paper would suggest that patterns of referral vary from school to school, which should cause us to reflect on those aspects of schooling that give rise to such disparity.

We would argue that social processes bias and distort the allocation of mainstream support for SEN and therefore that the allocation of scarce and precious resources should be monitored and decision making processes evaluated in order to improve the chances of equitable distribution. However, the pursuit of equity through equal opportunities initiatives is constrained by the extent to which the diversity of the client group is captured in the analysis. The power relations that establish and maintain categories in the discourses of analysts and practitioners create inequalities which must be challenged if *equity* is to be achieved.

In this sense we must recognise that the categories are analytical tools with which we understand the social processes we seek to monitor and ultimately change. Categories of analysis need to be selected to serve both general and local purposes. Without such tools we cannot ask whether systems are providing equality let alone equity.

If we wish to treat all children equally fairly, then we must first try and understand how we make decisions, and then monitor the outcomes of those decisions. We know that boys and girls are not treated in the same way. We do not know whether this is fair. It may well be that we should seek to establish new forms of difference rather than impose sameness. In order to match pedagogical needs with provision, we need to be flexible in our response to diversity, rather than offering fixed solutions under the name of equality.

References

Booth, T. (1996) 'A perspective on inclusion from England', *Cambridge Journal of Education.* 26 (1), 87–100.

Carrier, J. G. (1983) 'Explaining educability: an investigation of political support for children with learning disabilities', *British Journal of Sociology of Education.* 4 (2), 121–136.

Cooper, P., Upton, G. & Smith, C. (1991) 'Ethnic minority and gender distribution among staff and pupils in facilities for pupils with emotional and behavioural difficulties in England and Wales', *British Journal of Sociology of Education.* 12 (1), 77–94.

Daniels, H., Hey, V., Leonard, D. & Smith, M. (1995) 'Gendered practice in special educational needs', in L. Dawtrey, J. Holland & M. Hammer (eds.) *Equality and Inequality in Education Policy.* Milton Keynes: Open University Press.

Department for Education (1994a) *Code of Practice on the Identification and Assessment of Special Educational Needs.* London: DfE.

Department for Education (1994b) *The Organization of Special Educational Provision* (Circular 6/94). London: DfE.

Department for Education and Employment (1998) *Meeting Special Educational Needs: a Programme of Action.* London: The Stationery Office.

Department of Education and Science (1978) *Special Educational Needs: Report of the Committee of Enquiry into the Education of Children and Young People* (The Warnock Report). London: HMSO.

Department of Education and Science (1988) *Education Reform Act* (1988) London: HMSO.

Evans, J. (1995) *Feminist Theory Today.* New York: Sage.

Haddock, L. & Malcolm, L. (1992) 'Make trouble: get results: provision for girls in support services', *Educational Psychology in Practice.* 8 (2), 19–32.

Haigh, J. A. & Malever, M. G. (1993–1994) 'Special education referral practices by gender, ethnicity, and comparison to state and district enrolments', *CASE in Point.* 8 (1), 13–24.

HMCI (1996) *The Implementation of the Code of Practice for Pupils with Special Educational Needs.* London: HMSO.

Lewis, A., Neill, S. R. St. J. & Campbell, R. J. (1996) *The Implementation of the Code of Practice in Primary and Secondary Schools.* Coventry: University of Warwick.

Norwich, B. (1990) *Reappraising Special Needs Education.* London: Cassell.

Solstad, K. J. (1994) Equity at risk: schooling and change in Norway. PhD thesis. Norway: National Education Office, Nordland Office.

United Nations (1993) *The Standard Rules on the Equalization of Opportunities for People with Disabilities* (adopted by the United Nations General Assembly at its 48th Session on 20 December 1993 – Resolution 48/96). New York: United Nations.

United Nations Educational, Scientific and Cultural Organization (UNESCO) and The Ministry of Education and Science, Spain (1994) *The Salamanca Statement and Framework for Action on Special Needs Education* (adopted by the World Conference on Special Needs Education 'Access and Quality', Salamanca, Spain, 7–10 June 1994). New York: UNESCO.

Wagner, M. (1992) Being female: a secondary disability? Gender differences in the transition experiences of young people with disabilities. Paper presented at the annual meeting (April, 1992) of the American Educational Research Association, San Francisco.

Weinstein, D. E (1993–1994) 'Special education referral and classification practices by gender, family status and terms used (a case study)', *CASE in Point.* 8 (1), 25–36.

White, J. (1991) 'The goals are the same . . . are they?', *British Journal of Special Education.* 18 (1), 25–27.

12

DISABILITY ON A DIFFERENT MODEL

Glimpses of an Asian heritage

Michael Miles

Source: *Disability & Society* 15(4) (2000): 603–18.

Abstract

The paper reviews common uses of models and terminology, then sketches a few social responses to disablement in historical Zoroastrian, Jaina and Daoist philosophies. Accompanying a discussion of the 'merits of uselessness', Chuang-tzu's holistic social model is reconstructed. A Buddhist tale of 'hunchback Khujjutara' suggests that karma may usefully be seen as an educational, rather than retributive force. Contested histories of blind Japanese and Chinese people, and the dramatic enactment of contradictory behaviour towards them, support the view that Asian meanings of disablement should not be forced into modern European categories, but may challenge and refresh them.

We met some kids who were lame, and some who were blind, and some who were made on a different model. (*Child from Finland visiting disability centre in Pakistan.*)

Why models?

For interpreting human life and activity, all cultures construct and juggle with verbal models and metaphors, whether descriptive—'it is this'—or analogical—'it is like this'. Thus, for example, 'life is one damned thing after another', 'life is a journey to meet oneself', 'life is a bridge: cross it, don't build on it', give pictures or models of varying profundity, which may illuminate a moment, period or activity. None of them can be mistaken for a comprehensive description of life. None is useful to sociology or the biological sciences—though perhaps of more use than a sociological or biological model if it came to motivating a depressed person to resume the role-play of ordinary life. A well-constructed verbal model should provide satisfying insight to a substantial number of users in a particular culture, society or field of knowledge. Users will find it appropriate in its descriptive sense and also in providing some further dimension or extension, so that it can be applied productively or predictively in many situations.

A spectrum from ability, facility, access, inclusion, through opposites such as inability, difficulty, inaccessibility, appears in most aspects of human life and activity. These possibilities and restrictions are felt by individuals, and undergo change from infancy through the subsequent life stages, with higher value and esteem accruing usually at the 'can' end of the spectrum. Not surprisingly, most human cultures provide verbal models for understanding the range of 'can and cannot'. Some apparent extremes of ability/inability become fixed points of reference in these models.

Through much of human history, the darkness of night around most human habitations has been unrelieved by public lighting, while portable lamps have cast very limited illumination. Most people had periodic experience of being able to see practically nothing if they had to move around on a moonless night, and of needing to use touch, hearing and smell for navigation, at some risk of being bitten by snake or scorpion, tripping over an obstruction, being stabbed by an enemy, or other hazard. The vulnerability experienced in such conditions is very unwelcome. The person with total blindness has therefore widely been perceived as being 'in darkness', in a permanent state of vulnerability, and in a condition that everyone understands and would find most undesirable. This 'transferred experience' model of blindness is not one of total helplessness nor is stupidity necessarily attributed. Smallpox, trachoma and other widespread diseases ensured that in most times and places blind people of all ages were familiar. Some were elderly, wise and respected, others might be stupid or clumsy. They were all, nonetheless, considered to be in a state that nobody would wish to be in. Many folk tales around the world involve blind people wishing to regain their sight, and extraordinary means for doing so.

Impotence and infertility and their consequences have also appeared widely as disability conditions in the world's folklore, and again have been experienced as common temporary conditions, so that the permanent condition is thought to be well understood by adults. At any moment in history a significant number of men have been drunk or drugged to the point of unexpected impotence, circumstances often associating mirth and derision with a disability which, when permanent, has usually been a personal and social tragedy. In any year, a vast number of men and women have wished for a son or hoped for another son to replace the one who died. The period of waiting, hoping and fearing has perhaps brought some participatory understanding of the personal and social disability felt by those whose hope has expired and for whom no socially acceptable alternative (e.g. adoption) could be arranged.

In these examples, an ability and opportunity very widely considered normal and desirable may be temporarily unavailable to many people, is permanently unavailable to some, and cannot (yet) be construed as a basic human right or entitlement, for the absence of which a government can be sued.[1] In the case of sight, practically no society and culture considers its absence anything other than a major personal disaster from infancy to the beginning of senescence. The lack of a son has been a still greater tragedy or curse in many cultures; yet in a few modern societies it has become a matter of public indifference and even a personal choice. Thus, even with two of the most widely recognised and clearly defined of disability conditions, there remain some ambiguities and areas of exception where any verbal model may become strained.

The often passionate tone of trans-Atlantic anglophone academic debates on disability models during the 1990s has not always allowed for the ambiguities and imprecisions of any verbal model when faced with the variety of human life and thought within that region and period. Those debates have very seldom drawn on the vastly greater variety of human experience in the Asian heritage, in which many of the current thoughts and arguments seem to have been foreshadowed during two millennia or more. A few illustrations of that heritage will be sketched here to try to broaden the horizons of debate.[2] Anyone seeking definitive answers is recommended to cross this cultural bridge with light baggage and to build nothing weighty on it. The Asian tradition has been to teach by stories, earthy practical examples and repetition, with some elaboration of an inclusive 'both/and' nature. The analytical, male-confrontational obsession with 'either/or' arguments has played a smaller part—certainly it existed, but its inherent limitations have excluded most of it from the heritage sifted by centuries.

Use and abuse of words

The Jaina community in South Asia recognised, probably in the fifth or sixth century BC, that people with visually apparent disabilities or diseases can become annoyed if their condition is publicly announced. The *Akaranga Sutra* counselled against provocative behaviour:

A monk or a nun, seeing any sort (of diseases), should not talk of them in this way: 'He has got boils, or leprosy, &c.' [Note: this '&c.' calls up earlier lists adding 'consumption, falling sickness, blindness and stiffness, lameness and humpbackedness, Dropsy and dumbness, look! apoplexy (?) and eye-disease, trembling and crippledness, ele-phantiasis and diabetes'], 'his hand is cut, or his foot, nose, ear, lip is cut.' For as all such people, spoken to in such language, become angry, hence, considering well, they should not speak to them in such language.

(Jacobi, transl. 1884, pp. 152–153 [and 53–54])

The law-code of Manu and the Arthasastra went further in prescribing fines for abusive language, including the irritation of 'reverse' or euphemistic terms. None of these prescriptions can be shown actually to have made any difference to public or private use of language; nevertheless, the annoyance has been noticed for the past 2500 years.

The removal of negative, pejorative or diminishing terms from the world's languages, or significant restriction in their application in speech or thought to people with disabilities, diseases, differences, deficits or deviations, would entail cutting substantial parts of all known cultures and languages. Such an exercise, by enthusiasts for a 'global ethic' and similar totalising efforts, seems likely to remain marginal in the next few decades in face of the resurgence of indigenous cultures. More interesting is the attempt since the 1950s to develop a controlled international *scientific* vocabulary, starting with the aim

to re-orient professional attitudes and services towards individualized evaluation of the person as a human being, rather than the possessor of some detrimental condition.

(Riviere, 1970, p. 8)

These efforts evolved into the World Health Organisation's *ICIDH. International Classification of Impairments, Disabilities and Handicaps*, first produced in 1980 and now undergoing further revision. The ICIDH originally viewed impairment as what was wrong with the person's body or mind; disability was what he or she could not do as a result; handicap was the problem arising in social functioning as a result of the disability. Terminology based on social models of disability attempts to reduce the IDH triad to a dyad of Impairment and Disability. Disability then arises when people with impairments encounter a so-called 'oppressive social environment', e.g. one designed principally for able-bodied young men. One problem in reducing from three terms to two is that the useful distinction in the triad between impairment and disability disappears. A critique of social model terminology and application has been advanced by Bickenbach *et al.* (1999), who note that the reduction to two terms was useful in advocacy debates, but now causes great problems in formulating propositions that might underpin the model with research results. The 'disappearing body' linked with social model theorisation,[3] and the stretching of 'impairment' to cover for 'disability', are further flaws regretted by Williams (1999), among many others who propose to wheel 'bodies' back into the fray.

The World Health Organisation has been evaluating comments obtained worldwide, with a view to producing *ICIDH-2. International Classification of Impairments, Activities and Participation.* The intended positive spin, replacing 'Disability' with 'Activities', and 'Handicap' with 'Participation', unfortunately has failed to placate those who perhaps see any 'classification' as a step towards such 'scientific solutions' as the Nazi gas chambers. A more credible purpose in trying to improve the classification would be to unite the efforts of participants in the disablement field towards finding solutions to problems of functioning. The very activity of *seeking* global terminologies that are more accurate and more acceptable to a majority of disablement participants is a remarkable human achievement, certainly the first such globally endorsed activity since the Jaina prophet issued his early warning on terminology. Against a time scale of 2500 years, progress in the past 40 years has been substantial and another century of effort using new information technology might achieve a significant consensus. To move toward a carefully controlled and evaluated 'positive' terminology may be the most realistic strategy for diminishing the influence of the world's vast negative terminologies.

Revulsion

A facet of human response now largely omitted from western disability discourse is that of strong revulsion, sometimes accompanied by nausea, at the sight of someone with grossly deformed facia or limbs, perhaps comparable with reactions to corpses where parts have been severely traumatised. The modem omission probably results from the increased availability and efficacy in the past 50 years of cosmetic surgery and devices in western countries. Yet, in much of Asia, people with severe leprosy deformities, bomb blast damage, and artificially contrived scars and limb deformations continue to beg in public, sometimes causing visible revulsion in passers-by. The reaction goes much beyond the curiosity with which people in western countries may stare at prosthetic aids or ask intrusive questions about support apparatus. There is genuine difficulty in maintaining an equable response when accosted by a being in whom all the major facial features are replaced by what seem to be dark holes or indentations in the flesh. The nausea experienced by some people in this encounter does not fit readily into a 'biomedical', 'social' or 'religious' model of disability response—there is no model or classification at all. Against this the advanced Jaina may acquire the 'quality called *nirvicikitsā*, freedom from disgust' and may achieve indifference to the usual dualities of good, bad, attractive, unattractive. The adept will then 'feel no revulsion at the sight of human sickness, insanity, or ugliness' (Jaini, 1979, p. 152). Such a level of detachment, all passion spent and all compassion absent, might seem ideal to modern disability campaigners keen to 'Piss on Charity';[4] yet the same detachment would certainly extend to much of the life expected in a society notionally based on 'human rights' and consumer demands.

Of equal antiquity is a sort of moral revulsion reported by people in various eras and regions, evoked by the perceived disorderliness of people whose visible 'difference' is associated (in the reporter's mind) with disease and moral depravity. Thus, in the Zoroastrian Vendidad, the prophet's vision of an ideal future state provided for eugenic selection so that:

> There shall be no humpbacked, none bulged forward there, no impotent, no lunatic; no one malicious, no liar; no one spiteful, none jealous; no one with decayed tooth, no leprous . . .
>
> (transl. Darmesteter, 1895, p. 17)

The physically and the morally 'undesirable' are here so closely intertwined as to form apparently one category. The viewpoint has certainly been echoed down the centuries in most parts of the world, with varying virulence. Parents reasonably enough exhort small children that 'You don't want to grow up with painful, nasty-looking teeth, so be a Good Girl and brush them!' On a grander scale, the Human Genome project envisions the elimination or improved management of diseases and impairments having genetic origins or predispositions. Justification for what might seem to be hubristic meddling is advanced on grounds varying from socio-economic benefits to the fact that practically nobody wishes themselves or their children to suffer preventable disease or impairment. Reversals in the social expression of physical and moral revulsion can sometimes be engineered with surprising swiftness, as tobacco smokers in Britain have discovered in the past twenty years; but there are much hardier perennials, perhaps universals, such as Ganguly's (1927–28) complaint of being assailed in the streets of Calcutta by

> specimens of degenerate humanity suffering from loathsome and contagious diseases—the lepers, the insane, the idiotic, the feeble-minded—men of abnormal deformities of body and mind . . . The professional beggars in that city form a multifarious body, and they range from those who are no better than stinking bundles of flesh to the well-fed, pestering rogue.

Even that professional angel of mercy the Victorian Missionary Miss-Sahiba, rescuing severely damaged Indian famine orphans, was not immune from revulsion and could describe the utterly wretched state these poor little ones are sometimes found—almost idiotic, often, at first; gradually the mind wakes up as the body gets stronger, but in the early days the care of them was often most trying; some of them were really almost repulsive objects, so diseased and neglected! One felt it was an effort not to shrink from them, though of course such a feeling would never be yielded to.

(Whately, 1878)

The Jaina adept's dispassionate view of human difference, described above, might render models or explanations unnecessary—disability, or the infant's moribund body, is not *like* this or that, it simply *is*, without need for emotion or intellectualisation. Yet this view may also leave the non-viable or borderline infant to die uncared for. Such a result has been apparent from antiquity to modern times, as mothers, grandmothers and midwives have quietly and privately decided that 'this one is not going to make it', 'that one will be unable to cope with life', 'we cannot afford to raise this useless girl', so the necessary care should be reduced until death occurs.[5] Similar decisions, spoken or unspoken, have accompanied the diminution or withdrawal of care from elderly people. How to achieve on the larger public scale a reduction of revulsion, so that 'such a feeling would never be yielded to', yet without encouraging indifference, is a question no government has solved, even if it got as far as thinking that it would be useful to solve it.

The merits of uselessness

The Daoist philosopher Chuang-tzu (now usually Zhuangzhi) in the 4th century BC recorded unusually frank views about disability.[6] His major interpreter, Angus Graham, notes that

beggars, cripples and freaks are seen quite without pity and with as much interest and respect as princes and sages.

(Chuang-tzu, 1981, p. 4)

Chuang-tzu told of Carpenter Shih, who ignored a huge oak tree. When his apprentice expressed amazement Shih remarked that it was wretched timber, which was why the oak had survived long after more useful trees had been cut and planked. The story repeats with various turns, and the paradox recurs that 'All men know the uses of the useful, but no one knows the uses of the useless', the useless thereby outsmarting those who get used up. It appears in company with 'Cripple Shu—his chin is buried down in his navel, his shoulders are higher than his crown' (etc.), who makes a good living by fortune-telling. When the press-gang is out seeking war fodder, Cripple Shu shuffles to the bazar and mocks able-bodied men who risk being pressed into service (Chuang-tzu, 1981, pp. 72–75).

Sinologist Gudula Linck (1995, pp. 190–191) contrasts such views of disability with the ancient Greek idealisation of the body beautiful. The difference was 'especially apparent in early *Daoism*, which considered the outer appearance to be merely a temporary constellation in the process of cosmic transformations'; however, the consequent acceptance and tolerance towards people with disabilities seems to have been confined to the educated classes in Chinese history.[7] Chuang-tzu, celebrated several people with deformities who acquired exceptional influence. Thus,

> Pitcherneck with the big goitre advised Duke Huan of Ch'i; the Duke was so pleased with him that when he looked at normal men their necks were too scrawny . . . Uglyface T'o is trusted before he says a word, is accepted as an intimate without any deed to his credit . . . he is evidently one in whom the stuff is whole but the Power has failed to shape the body.
>
> (Chuang-tzu, 1981, pp. 79–80)

A later Japanese example would be the wily sixteenth century *bonze* Nichijo Shonin, in whom

> the beauty and vivacity of his mind amply indemnified him for the deformity of his body; above all he possessed in sovereign degree that courtierly address and dexterity of which princes are so frequently the dupes.
>
> (Murdoch, 1903, vol. II, p. 158)

This description could equally have applied to his contemporary, the strategist Hideyoshi, notoriously monkey-faced and short-statured, who rose from humble origins to become ruler of Japan (Murdoch, 1903, vol. II, pp. 158–160.)

How did these physiognomically improbable people come to exert such influence? To sketch an ancient East-Asian explanation, Graham collates dislocated fragments of Chuang-tzu, such as a graphic description of water finding its own level, filling a space of whatever shape. The remarkable teaching emerges that the Power/Spirit invests the one with deformed body and attractive personality, but may (as seen above) 'fail to shape the body' as water fails to shape its container (in the short term—though the Daoist paradox of weak water breaking solid rock is well-known). Graham notes that

> For ancient Chinese thought, which does not make a distinction in kind between the mental and the physical, it is the Power, the capacity to respond without reflection according to the Way, which enables the body to grow into its proper shape.
>
> (Chuang-tzu, 1981, p. 81)

Yet this only sharpens the observable paradox that some people who clearly have *not* 'grown into the proper shape' are nonetheless possessed of a power to attract, lead or advise ordinary folk of 'proper' shape. Graham's interpretation is that, in the Daoist Way,

> the sage is sensitive to and adapts to all pressures from outside. The Power in shaping the body is like the water which, irrespective of its source, has a shape imposed on it by the topography of the place. It seems indeed that it is we ourselves, we ordinary folk, who by crowding round T'o from the day of his birth because the charm of pure spontaneity so attracts us, have forced his superbly sensitive and malleable organism into a shape we judge to be ugly.
>
> (Chuang-tzu, 1981, p. 81)

Here is a 'social model' more holistic than merely seeing disability created by environmental and attitudinal obstacles and pressures. It extends to the continuous interface of deforming and enabling aspects of each society upon each individual; yet it also reflects the possibility for the individual's response to have a powerful effect on society.

The insights of Chuang-tzu are of more than philosophical or antiquarian interest. The question of how to sustain an adequate self-image and public standing—or perhaps to dispense altogether with the illusion of 'self'?—in the face of redundancy, and non-worker or non-paid status is a matter of growing concern in post-industrial countries where millions of young, middle-aged and elderly people, whether disabled or able-bodied, are passing substantial periods of their lives with little or no formal work or socially esteemed activity. Observably, in such a situation some people make a life full of meaning for themselves and their circle; some transform their 'uselessness' into a cutting edge; many would like to do so, but are overcome by social and psychological pressures; many more lack any vision of a worthwhile life and self-image. The 'disabled' or 'victim' identity may have its attractive side as a temporary haven or a money-spinner, more so if parleyed into a 'successful survivor' identity. Making good use of one's uselessness has become a desirable modern skill, with perhaps hidden ancient Chinese roots.

Karma as educational force

The major European and Asian philosophies and religions have all contemplated questions of suffering, its origins, possible meanings, reality or unreality, and connections with the progress of the soul (if any). Disablement often entered the picture as a sort of 'permanent state of suffering'. Models of suffering (and therefore of disablement) needed to accommodate beliefs such as that

1   We live one earthly life, followed by
    (A)   nothing; or by
    (B)   a long-lasting spirit existence dependent on the rights and wrongs of the earthly life; or
2   We each live many lives, the conditions in each successive life depending on conduct in the earlier ones.
3   The life or lives are influenced or controlled by
    (A)   social/environmental influences, but no external transcendental power(s); or by
    (B)   an external transcendental power or powers; or by
    (C)   the internal interactions of a transcending Whole within which we are atoms.

Middle Eastern and European civilisations during the past 1500 years mostly favoured explanations involving beliefs l(A), or 1(B) plus 3(B). Such beliefs were also present in Asian civilisations, but beliefs 2 plus 3(B) or 3(C) predominated. Explanations based on the latter beliefs have varied enormously as they balanced ideas of good and evil, fair and just reward or punishment, the possibility of progress toward final liberation from the cycle of lives, etc. Within these variations the observable fact that some people live with a life-long severe impairment of body or mind has often been interpreted as an inevitable outcome of personal misdeeds in earlier lives; and this understanding has shaped the immensely variable doctrines of *karma*.[8] In both 'western' and 'eastern' beliefs, the element of ascribed personal responsibility did not necessarily preclude the idea that society as a whole was rotten, e.g. the ruler misbehaved, the people failed in religious duties, so 'monstrous' babies were born to de-monstr-ate divine displeasure, or perhaps as rebounding ill-effects within the interconnected Whole.

For the western audience, the notion of *karma* may more usefully be packaged not as inescapable doom or retributive fate, but as a neutral, chastening, educational force. This is well illustrated in the character of Khujjutara, one of the legion of hunchbacked maids who traditionally attended the royal women of Indian antiquity. Khujjutara was Queen Samavati's servant, charged with obtaining flowers every day. Her habit was to spend half the daily allowance correctly and the other half on herself. One day the flowers she would normally have bought were already in use, for the Buddha was preaching in the neighbourhood. The florist suggested that if Khujjutara cared to attend the Buddha's sermon, she could collect the flowers afterwards. Hearing the Law preached, Khujjutara was converted to the Buddha's Way and realised that she must reform her conduct. She therefore returned to the palace with twice the usual number of flowers. Being questioned by the queen about the floral abundance, she promptly admitted her previous theft of the petty cash. Queen Samavati, instead of tearing lumps out of the penitent maid, wanted to know why she had changed her practice. As a result, Khujjutara was invited to preach the Law to five hundred ladies at court. She soon attained a pre-eminent position as a religious teacher (Burlingame, 1921, vol. I, pp. 281–282).

Thus far, a simple tale of religious morality; yet the unprecedented transformation from deformed maidservant to honoured teacher of the Law was endorsed by the Buddha, who also sketched Khujjutara's history for his disciples' instruction. In an earlier birth she had mocked a deformed holy man at the royal court of Benares, imitating his stoop. She thus earned herself a 'corrective' or educational rebirth as a hunchback, so that the progress of her soul should not be impeded by a continuation of Wrong Thinking and Wrong Conduct (Burlingame, vol. I, p. 292). Other 'genetic links' existed between the early Buddhist disability stories. A 'dullard' mentioned in one tale was revealed to have been previously a learned person who mocked a slow-learning monk and thus earned what looked like the penalty of being reborn himself as a dullard (Burlingame, vol. I, p. 302). Rather than being a 'penalty', the experience of a lifetime of intellectual incompetence with its attendant social humiliations was needed for this soul to make progress towards perfection—or so the teaching claimed. The tendency among the learned to treat unlettered people as irredeemable clods has been documented from antiquity to the present, and continues in many countries. As long as this attitude thrives, the idea of awarding arrogant intellectuals a few years' experience of cleaning the latrines may continue to appeal to the Red Guards, of China or elsewhere. Where such an educational sabbatical cannot be arranged, rebirth as a slow-learning child may be considered a suitable alternative.

Blind people handling their own fate

Models and stories embodying them arise in social situations and any different conceptualisations in Asia cannot be understood without dipping into social history. Accounts of earlier social responses to blind people particularly in Japan, and to some extent in China, indicate a measure of both group and individual autonomy within reserved and valued occupations, ostensibly reflecting a status model more 'normal' than blind people enjoyed in much of European history. Improved status in Japan traditionally dates from the blind son of a ninth century emperor, for whom 'many blind men of good families' were recruited as companions (Dixon, 1891; Yoshimoto, 1908). A national revenue was supposedly devoted to the welfare of blind people from this time (Golay, 1973). Contrary interpretations have also appeared. Susan Matisoff (1978, pp. 19–22, 28–31, 39–46) assembles detailed evidence suggesting that blind, lute-playing, mendicant friars (*biwa hoshi*) originated in China and reached Japan in the sixth century. Their successors slowly constructed a semi-legendary past, conflating stories of more than one blind prince in an effort to raise their very modest social status—an interesting reminder that disabled people have not always been helpless targets for model-making by a dominant environment.

Whatever may underlie these legendary beginnings the traditional professions of musical performance, song and recitative became a recognised speciality of blind people, with the less elevated alternative vocations of massage, acupuncture, fortune-telling and later money-lending. Various schools emerged, teaching the standard professional curricula with local innovations or flavours. The training and certification process was controlled by powerful blind guilds. Over several centuries, the Proper Path Guild of blind *Heike* reciters eventually

> extended its control to include all blind lute performers in Japan. They became, in effect, a country of the blind, controlled by their own system of regulations outside direct government management.
>
> (Matisoff, 1978, p. 43)

The original apprentice-style training also became a broader education. 'Music' on the curriculum extended beyond learning to play the lute—blind musicians were expected to have a repertoire of stirring songs, so parts of the literary heritage were memorised by students.[9] The therapy skills of acupuncture and massage extended to coverage of body parts and functions together with a grasp of client psychology.

Thus, it was that in 1760 young Hokiichi Hanawa, who would become one of Japan's founding academic bibliographers, went to a private school for blind youths at Edo, now Tokyo (Yoshimoto, 1908). There he should have learnt skills of music and acupuncture under Ametomi Kengyo. Failing to gain proficiency in those skills, he succeeded 'only' in learning classical literature, and was taught later by the famous Kamo no Mabuchi. This sort of well established and differentiated educational provision in urban Japan (and systems with some similarities in China) compares favourably with the situation in eighteenth century Europe. Hokiichi Hanawa was already launched on his bibliographical career by the time Valentin Haüy, at Paris in 1771, was shocked to see a mock orchestra of blind people pretending to read and play music, a jape meant to attract passers-by to a café. Eventually in 1784 Haüy founded a school to provide more dignified work for blind people, and the chance genuinely to learn to read and play music (Farrell, 1956, pp. 18–29). He was a pioneer in Europe—it is only a pity that Haüy could not first have visited Japan and China to learn how some blind men had for centuries managed their own education and professions.

The extent of education and employment for blind people in Japan is hard to quantify, even more so in China where earlier developments of the same professions and 'blind guilds' had taken place, at least in cities. Perhaps a majority of blind young people learnt some local craft or skill within their families, while people losing their sight in old age were cared for by relatives. Occasionally such familial concern brought a wider practical application. The northern Chinese provincial governor Lü K'un (1536–1618) was an enthusiast for welfare measures. Reportedly,

> Lü ordered the officials of each city to train the blind in a profession such as music, singing, storytelling, and fortune telling. Although he did not believe in the last himself he compiled a simple textbook from which the younger people among the blind might be orally taught.
> (Goodrich & Chaoying Fang, 1976, vol. I, p. 1007)

Lü's particular concern for blind people arose from the experience of his mother losing her eyesight suddenly in 1547, the family's unavailing search for treatment and their hiring of a succession of blind women musicians to restore her spirits. Joanna Handlin (1983, pp. 161–163) suggests the pattern of Lü K'un's thoughts in which crisis, the power of music, and the means for self-reliance recurred to take him beyond a 'charitable' model of response, to one in which independence and self-support were central, and the government's duty was to provide skill training and work tools.

Some rather positive glimpses appear above, for which evidence is available; yet for large numbers of blind people there was certainly no ideal Asian world. Beggars were plentiful, particularly on urban streets, and during the periodic famines those with disabilities were swept away by disease, neglect and starvation along with millions of other people. An archetypal image of early nineteenth century dispensary clients showed 'old, blind, decrepit men, "with staff in hand", led thither by their little grand-children' (Canton Dispensary, 1833). The condition of blind Chinese women was often pitiful. In the sixteenth century, Juan Gonzalez de Mendoza (1588, p. 68) reported of such that

> when she commeth vnto age, she doth vse the office of women of loue [i.e. works as a prostitute], of which sorte there are a great number in publike places.

The evidence is strong that some children were deliberately blinded for urban begging and prostitution, an activity not unknown also in Europe (Lockhart, 1861, p. 250; Hanks, 1872, p. 13). Twentieth century writers such as Susanna Hoe (1991, pp. 173–176) and Lucy Ching (1982, pp. 19–21, 47, 50, 274–275) remark on the ongoing sexual exploitation of blind women, the latter because it was still commonly assumed to be her own destiny in the 1940s. Blindness was turned to advantage in prostitution presumably because the client's own identity and defects were thereby spared the scrutiny of a knowing 'professional gaze'—there was only a defenceless, sightless body for temporary hire. On the other hand, the absence of physical sight benefitted blind women working as spirit mediums (*itako*) in some north-eastern Japanese prefectures, because of the widespread belief that blind people 'see' things that sighted people cannot see. Carmen Blacker (1975, pp. 140–163, 337–339), who studied these mediums and their personal experiences, realised that what she witnessed was far from the original shamanistic practice:

> A girl is impelled to become an *itako* purely and simply because she is blind . . . By becoming a medium she will become a viable member of her community rather than a burden.
>
> (p. 141)

What these mediums performed for their clients seemed to Blacker all too clearly a stilted act rather than a genuine trance. Yet the aura of 'otherness' attached to their blindness seemed sufficient for rural participants to suspend any disbelief and to be greatly moved by what they took to be evidence of communication with the dead. Blacker made no comparisons with the performance of blind prostitutes, nor delved into questions of who was exploiting whom.

Ambivalence of relations between the blind and the sighted worlds was exploited in several Kyogen dramas. These poignant farces originating in thirteenth century Japan depict humankind in the raw. The peculiarities of blind people are fair game, as 'not only were blind people very much a part of everyday life in Japan, but they were also intimately involved with the performing arts' (Golay, 1973). One of the best known, *Tsuki-mi Zato*, opens with a blind man in a field at full moon, soliloquizing about the delightful voices of the insects. A sighted man from a posh locality enters, also to view the moon, and they strike up an amicable conversation, even sharing a jug of wine. Eventually, the two men part with warm thanks for each other's company. The blind man moves away, cheered by this chance encounter. The sighted man is cheered by his own kindly condescension; but suddenly it occurs to him that he could have a little more fun by sneaking back and 'accidentally' bumping into the blind man, then roughing him up. He promptly does so, shouting abuse in a disguised voice, before running off. This dramatic *bouleversement* shocks the audience into nervous laughter. Picking himself up, the blind man bitterly confides to the stunned audience that he is 'amazed at how different from the man before this pitiless rascal was' (Kenny, 1989, p. 211); the double-edged irony forces the audience to laugh again in spite of itself. The blind man's conduct throughout is a model of decent if naive human behaviour—no 'disability model' is required; but the sighted audience is confronted by its own recognition that other people's trust and vulnerability may evoke sharply contradictory responses in oneself. The advanced model of human intercourse slips readily into the barbaric.

225

Cross-cultural mis-identification

The Asian traditions, models and experiences, of which the merest glimpse and taste is indicated above, lend themselves readily to mis-identification—especially after being (mis-)described in English by a foreign devil! If the West European and North American disability models of the past 30 years are believed (on no very obvious grounds) to be universal, then historical reports from distant lands can be categorised as 'essentially' religious model, charity model, deficit, personal tragedy, individual, biomedical, administrative, social, social construction, etc. Yet it is apparent that, for example, Chuang-tzu contemplated a sort of socio-religious or socio-philosophical model having dimensions significantly different from those discussed nowadays (by a small minority of academics) in London or Los Angeles; he did so some 2300 years before the current advocates were born; his ideas have been the subject of debate and puzzlement through two millennia among the small minority of East Asian intellectuals who have ever heard of them; and the social functioning of at least some disabled Chinese and Japanese during that period has been substantially different from that of their counterparts and contemporaries in Europe. These points may serve to correct any Eurocentric tendency to assume that the rest of the world's ideas are more or less primitive and can be stowed definitively in pigeonholes devised during recent decades of anglophone disability debate.

Nor do these glimpses provide sufficient basis for any new Grand Theory. Angus Graham, after spending many years of linguistic study and philosophical pondering to build a cultural bridge towards Chuang-tzu, cautions that

> When in an ancient text we stumble on what looks like a modern idea, we are always faced with the question whether thinkers within different conceptual schemes can be saying the same thing. It is pointless to exclaim in wonder 'So they knew that thousands of years ago!', but stimulating to explore these unexpected points of contact as critical places where ancient thinkers reveal both their nearness and their remoteness from ourselves.
>
> (Chuang-tzu, 1981, p. 183)

Among the illustrations given by Graham is Chuang-tzu's story (1981, p. 188) about a criminal, entitled 'It isn't his fault, it's society . . .'

In conclusion

Of what use then are glimpses of the Asian heritage, to European debate? First, they do not have to be immediately 'of use'—the ones seemingly 'useless', i.e. that hang around because they are not easily pigeonholed, might eventually prove the most stimulating. As Europeans have been keen to offer their ideas to Asians during the colonial and subsequent periods, and hoped for the offers to be welcomed, it would be merely reciprocal politeness to contemplate some of the Asian heritage, without a utilitarian yardstick in hand. Secondly, in common experience some facets of disability and disablement are absorbed within everyday life without demanding either a change of thinking or an explanatory model. Some facets seem to fit well under a biomedical explanation while others are catered for under social or social construction models. Religious and philosophical models continue to serve some purpose in explaining disability in much of the world. There remain some aspects of disablement which, by their marginal, liminal or interstitial nature, are not easily absorbed when they surface in everyday life, nor do they fit easily into available models. They are not this, they are not like that, there is something that is sensed but is not easily explained or cannot be pinned down at all. Might they be the grit that provokes pearls among forthcoming models?

Finally, all terms that are in uncontrolled public use tend to veer and decay, becoming useless for precise communication. As terms decay, models lose their explanatory bite and power. Thus, Vic Finkelstein (1999) laments that the once revolutionary 'social model' argument has been blunted, domesticated and 'rectified' to fit snugly in an unmoved world. The philosopher Henri-Jacques Stiker (1999, p. 371) sees the same model declining because, in addition to denying some painful realities perceived by the rest of the world, it belongs to a mode of thought that has had its day. There is a need for regular reformulation or refreshment with new symbols. For these tasks, there is merit in broadening the horizons of debate by approaching the models, metaphors and historical contexts of the vast Asian disablement heritage. It should be noted, however, that broader horizons, while refreshing, are unlikely to make life any easier. The way forward is from certainty to uncertainty. (Cross it; don't build a model of it . . .)

Notes

1 The introduction of 'rights' terminology to disability models has made very modest progress in most Asian countries, where 'rights' are more often conceived in terms of moral conduct in society than as legally enforceable entitlements of individuals. Some discussion of disability and rights in Islamic Asian contexts appears in Miles & Hossain (1999).

2 The potential of Asian materials to illuminate European social history relevant to disablement is exemplified in fascinating studies by Frank Dikötter (1998), tracing Chinese theories and polemics concerning birth defects through five centuries, with European echoes.

3 Over-focus on *physical* impairment has obscured the fact that a 'social theory of mental deficiency' began to be formulated in the 1940s by Lewis Dexter, an able-minded person, highlighting the mismatch between social demands and learnt ability to meet those demands, while noting ways in which 'failure' was generated

by socially sanctioned obstacles imposed on those with lesser abilities. This led the latter 'to acquire a negative or hostile self-image' and thus 'to live according to a self-definition of themselves as worthless or contemptible' (Dexter, 1958).

4 A century before this inelegant slogan appeared, the philosopher Friedrich Nietzsche (1883–92, transl. 1961, pp. 275–278, see also pp. 35, 271), who was himself about to experience severe disablement, captured the abhorrence felt by 'The Ugliest Man', one who was 'shaped like a man yet hardly like a man, something unutterable', for the pity and alms usually cast at him. Especially loathsome was the pity of the 'over-compassionate god', the divine peeping Tom and intrusive forgiver who 'crept into my dirtiest corners', and whose elimination Nietzsche considered imperative for humankind's maturation.

5 The abandonment of an infant because of its severe impairment is enshrined in Japan's Creation Myth, which continues to puzzle commentators. The first-born of the primal progenitors, Izanagi and Izanami, was 'Hiruko' the leech-child, 'which even at the age of three years could not stand upright. They therefore placed it in the rock-camphor-wood boat of Heaven, and abandoned it to the winds' (*Nihongi*, 1896, vol. I, p. 19). The legend and the impaired offspring are linked by Fuminobu Murakami (1988) with other early brother-sister incest materials; yet it remains extraordinary as a tale of 'national origins'. Recently, its various strands and historical developments have been strikingly repackaged by a well-known disabled Japanese poet: Syuncho Hanada (1998) depicts the rejected Hiruko, 'rehabilitated' in popular imagination as the god Ebisu, still piloting his little craft through cosmic space.

6 Similar frankness appeared in response to a visitor boasting of having 'got-rich-quick'. Chuang-tzu noted that when the Ruler called for his doctors, 'the one who bursts a carbuncle or drains a boil gets a single chariot, the one who licks his piles gets five. The viler the treatment the more chariots one gets. You wouldn't have been treating his piles of course? What a lot of chariots you have!' (Chuang-tzu, 1981, pp. 119–120). If Chuang-tzu's Daoist writings sometimes seem to travel from a remote world, his political repartee needs no sharpening for 21st century Europe.

7 Blyth (1959) gives examples of traditional Chinese humour at the expense of disabled people, and also notes among the twelfth century Japanese *Yamaizoshi* 'Pictures of Illness', a dwarf who 'walks here and there asking for food. Children follow him, laughing at him. He looks back angrily, but they are unabashed, and laugh at him the more' (Plate XXIII).

8 The simplicity and complexities of *karma* are discussed in detail in O'Flaherty (1980), and a useful modern paper by Goldman (1985).

9 Hrdličková (1965) cites a field study where blind or illiterate Chinese story-tellers, 'could sing and recite three months on end without repeating themselves' (p. 229), suggesting the formidable immersion expected of learners.

References

BICKENBACH, J. E., CHATTERJI, S., BADLEY, E. M. & ÜSTÜN, T. B. (1999) Models of disablement, universalism and the international classification of impairments, disabilities and handicaps, *Social Science & Medicine*, 48, pp. 1173–1187.

BLACKER, C. (1975) *The Catalpa Bow* (London, Allen & Unwin).

BLYTH, R. H. (1959) *Oriental Humour* (Tokyo, Hokuseido Press).

BURLINGAME, E. W. (transl.) (1921, reprint 1969) *Buddhist Legends* (London, Luzac).

CANTON DISPENSARY (1833) *Chinese Repository*, II, pp. 276–277.

CHING, L. (1980, reprint 1982) *One of the Lucky Ones* (London, Souvenir).

CHUANG-TZU (1981) *The Seven Inner Chapters and Other Writings* transl. A. C. GRAHAM (London, Allen & Unwin).

DARMESTETER, J. (transl.) (1895) *The Zend-Avesta, Part 1, The Vendidad* (Oxford, Clarendon).

DEXTER, L. A. (1958) A social theory of mental deficiency, *American Journal of Mental Deficiency*, 62, pp. 920–928.

DIKÖTTER, F. (1998) *Imperfect Conceptions* (London, Hurst).

DIXON, J. M. (1891) The habits of the blind in Japan, *Transactions of the Asiatic Society of Japan*, 19(iii), pp. 578–582.

FARRELL, G. (1956) *The Story of Blindness* (Cambridge, MA, Harvard University Press).

FINKELSTEIN, V. (1999) Extended review, *Doing Disability Research*, COLIN BARNES & GEOF MERCER (Eds), 1997, Leeds, Disability Press, *Disability & Society*, 14, pp. 859–878.

FUMINOBU MURAKAMI (1988) Incest and rebirth in *Kojiki, Monumenta Nipponica*, 43, pp. 455–463.

GANGULY, B. N. (1927–28) The street-beggars of Calcutta: a study of the problem and its solution, *Indian Journal of Economics*, 8, pp. 373–386.

GOLAY, J. (1973) Pathos and farce: Zatō plays of the Kyōgen repertoire, *Monumenta Nipponica*, 28, pp. 139–149.

GOLDMAN, R. P. (1985) Karma, guilt, and buried memories: public fantasy and private reality in traditional India, *Journal of the American Oriental Society*, 105, pp. 413–425.

GOODRICH, L. C. & CHAOYING FANG (Eds) (1976) *Dictionary of Ming Biography 1368–1644* (New York, Columbia University Press).

HANADA, S. (1998) *Ebisu Mandara* (Japanese & English). Japan Council on Disability website: [www.vcom.or.jp/project/jd/Ebisu]

HANDLIN, J. F. (1983) *Action in Late Ming Thought* (Berkeley, CA, University of California Press).

HANKS, L. W. (1872) *Blindness and the Blind* (London, Chapman & Hall).

HOE, S. (1991) *The Private Life of Old Hong Kong* (Hong Kong, Oxford University Press).

HRDLIČKOVÁ, V. (1965) The professional training of Chinese storytellers and the storytellers' guilds, *Archiv Orientální*, 33, pp. 225–248.

JACOBI, H. (transl.) (1884) *Gaina Sûtras* (Oxford, Clarendon).

JAINI, P. S. (1979) *The Jaina Path of Purification* (Delhi, Motilal Banarsidass).

KENNY, D. (transl.) (1989) *The Kyogen Book* (Tokyo, The Japan Times).

LINCK, G. (1995) *Befähigung anderer Art? Zur Lebenswelt köperlich Behinderten in China* (Pfaffenweiler, Centaurus-Verlagsgesellschaft).

LOCKHART, W. (1861) *The Medical Missionary in China* (London, Hurst & Blackett).

MATISOFF, S. (1978) *The Legend of Semimaru, blind musician of Japan* (New York, Columbia University Press).

DE MENDOZA, J. G. (1588, reprint 1853) *The Historie of the Great and Mightie Kingdome of China*, transl. R. PARKE (London, Hakluyt Society).

MILES, M. & HOSSAIN, F. (1999) Rights and disabilities in educational provision in Pakistan and Bangladesh: roots, rhetoric, reality, in: F. ARMSTRONG & L. BARTON

(Eds) *Disability, Human Rights and Education: cross-cultural perspectives* (Buckingham, Open University Press).

MURDOCH, J. (1903) *A History of Japan* (Kobe, Office of the 'Chronicle').

NIETZSCHE, F. (1883–1892) *Thus Spoke Zarathustra* transl. R. J. HOLLINGDALE (1961) (Harmondsworth, Penguin).

NIHONGI. Chronicles of Japan (1896) transl. W. G. ASTON (London, Kegan Paul).

O'FLAHERTY, W. D. (Ed.) (1980) *Karma and Rebirth in Classical Indian Traditions* (Berkeley, CA, University of California Press).

RIVIERE, M. (1970) *Rehabilitation Codes* (US National Institute of Neurological Diseases and Blindness).

STIKER, H.-J. (1999) Using historical anthropology to *think* disability, in: B. HOLZER, A. VREEDE & G. WEIGT (Eds) *Disability in Different Cultures* (Bielefeld, Transcript).

WHATELY, E. J. (1878) Leaves from the history of a missionary auxiliary, *Church Missionary Gleaner*, 5, pp. 28–29.

WILLIAMS, S. J. (1999) Is anybody there? Critical realism, chronic illness and the disability debate, *Sociology of Health & Illness*, 21, pp. 797–819.

YOSHIMOTO, T. (1908) Past, present, and future of the blind in Japan, in: *Report of the Second Triennial International Conference on the Blind and Exhibition*, Manchester, July 24th–August lst, 1908, pp. 174–181.

WORLD HEALTH ORGANISATION (1980) *ICIDH. International Classification of Impairments, Disabilities and Handicaps* (Geneva, WHO).

230

13

COMMUNITY BASED REHABILITATION IN DEVELOPING COUNTRIES

Alice Bradley

Source: P. Lacey and C. Ouvrey (eds), *People with Profound and Multiple Learning Disabilities: A Collaborative Approach to Meeting Complex Needs*, London: David Fulton, 1998, pp. 215–25.

Introduction

Community based rehabilitation is a concept which has been analysed, debated and refashioned countless times over recent years. Like *Care in the Community* in the UK, it has given rise to greater controversy than almost any other issue about disability in developing countries. So, what are the contentions, and how is community based rehabilitation relevant to the central theme of this book, collaborative multidisciplinary work with people with profound and multiple learning disabilities?

The origins of community based rehabilitation

Caring for disabled people in the community is nothing new in developing countries, as several writers point out (Kisanji 1995; Miles 1993); it has been going on for generations. But it was not until the 1970s that community based rehabilitation (CBR) became a recognised term. The World Health Organisation (WHO), drawing on the community based model of Primary Health Care (PHC), sought to extend provision for people with disabilities to meet increasing demand. Most services at that time were based on the institutional model prevalent in industrialised nations and had several short-comings. Fewer than 2 per cent of people with disabilities benefited, and most provision was in cities, inaccessible to the vast majority who lived in rural areas. Families struggling with poverty were unable to pay the fees required by many services. It was clear that other solutions had to be found.

As O'Toole (1993) explains, 'There was a need for new patterns of service with fewer experts, less advanced forms of training and simplified methods of rehabilitation' (p.201).

Institutionalised models of rehabilitation were increasingly becoming discredited globally. To continue to separate people with disabilities from their own communities was clearly unacceptable and a flagrant infringement of basic human rights. Disabled people themselves, and their families, were beginning to question the paternalistic, authoritarian approach which prevailed in traditional services.

In instigating community based rehabilitation, WHO sought to disseminate basic rehabilitation knowledge and techniques to families and communities with no access to conventional rehabilitation services. Communities would be involved in the design, implementation and evaluation of rehabilitation strategies. To encourage the spread of community based rehabilitation, WHO produced a manual, *Training the Disabled in the Community*, which presented simple rehabilitation techniques and covered all disabilities. The emphasis was predominantly medical and on functional skills such as might normally be taught by occupational therapists or physiotherapists.

The large scale transfer of rehabilitation techniques envisaged by WHO was to be accomplished through the use of local supervisors selected by the community. They would train families, or disabled people, using the appropriate parts of the manual. Specialist rehabilitation professionals would train the local supervisors for their role, and would monitor their work. Governments were expected to be active partners, and commit themselves to the promotion of CBR, using available resources to support programmes initiated at community level. Community resources would complement government resources and communities would, as a result, become partners in the rehabilitation process. Partnership was an essential component of CBR from the outset. People from different backgrounds and different sectors would have to work together if the approach was to be effective.

The WHO manual was piloted in several countries, outcomes reviewed and the CBR concept officially accepted by WHO in 1982. CBR was well and truly launched and attracted a great deal of international interest. It was subsequently endorsed by all of the major international organisations. By 1984, 40,000 copies of the WHO manual had been produced and translated into twenty languages (O'Toole 1993).

CBR in action

CBR in some form now operates in most developing countries. One of its greatest strengths lies in its flexibility, and this is evident in the myriad approaches adopted. Some projects draw heavily upon the WHO model, and others have followed their own path. Whatever the approach, collaborative multidisciplinary teamwork is essential. A few examples illustrate the diversity which exists.

The CBR project in Negros Occidental in the Philippines, which began in 1981, is based upon the WHO model. Local supervisors are residents of their respective communities and the project is supported externally by a non-government organisation (NGO). Community awareness is a fundamental aspect of the programme, and is demonstrated by the way in which disabled people are regarded as integral members of local life. The project has a strong multidisciplinary element both at community level and through its referral network, with links at district, provincial and national level. This is essential for sustainability (Valdez 1991).

By contrast, the CBR project in Janakpuri, an outlying area of Delhi, owes its origins to a woman who had never heard of community based rehabilitation, let alone the WHO model. Started in 1990 in response to the needs of one child with polio, the project now serves over 200 people, children and adults of all ages and with all types of disability. Families of children with PMLD are given loans to start businesses in their homes, which means that they can keep their children with them rather than put them into institutional care or leave them with relatives. CBR workers are drawn from various sectors of the community, include the mothers and some disabled people, and work together closely. The project has minimal financial and administrative help from a local non-government organisation and a strong network of medical, rehabilitation, vocational and educational support (Saxena 1993).

Some CBR projects are government initiated, such as those started by the Ministry of Health in Kenya and integrated into primary health care (PHC), as was first envisaged by WHO. District CBR teams are multidisciplinary, drawn from various ministries and NGOs (Lagerwall 1992). Others begin as outreach programmes from centre based rehabilitation services, such as one in Tamil Nadu, in India, which started as a disability awareness programme in the community and evolved into CBR. The CBR team uses volunteers from the community and includes parents and disabled people (Spastics Society of Tamil Nadu, 1995–96).

Sometimes projects owe their origin to disabled people's organisations, to families or to parents' groups, with or without help from outside agencies. The Zanzibar Association of the Disabled (an organisation *of* rather than *for* disabled people) runs a CBR project, with support from an international NGO. The intention in starting the project was to convince both the community and the government that CBR is the best way of rehabilitating disabled people, especially those from rural areas. The project has grown considerably since it began in 1988 and includes education, employment, housing and transportation, as well as parents' workshops and playgroups for disabled children. Establishing partnership with parents was difficult in the early stages. Several families had hoped for curative facilities or material help and saw little benefit in CBR. The government had low expectations of the programme and it took time to convince them of its value. Now, however, there is strong family involvement and the project leaders are instrumental in influencing government policy and raising community awareness (Khalfan 1992).

The Nairobi Family Support Service (NFSS) was started by families in 1981, and is today used as a model by the Kenyan government. The project is managed by a local committee of parents, community leaders, disabled people and professionals. Over 200 children are catered for in various parts of Nairobi, several with profound and multiple learning disabilities. Activities include playgroups, home visits, vocational training, workshops for families and the production of equipment (Asindua 1995).

It will be clear from these examples, a few selected from many, that there are differences in the way in which the CBR concept is interpreted and implemented in different situations. It will also be obvious that CBR without teamwork is impossible. If programmes are to meet individual needs and improve life for all disabled people, collaboration and flexibility are crucial. WHO had always intended their CBR model to be flexible, but just how flexible is not clear, and this is one of the issues which has caused greatest conflict. What can and cannot justifiably be called 'community based rehabilitation'? As often happens, the arguments became polarised. Purists declared that only programmes which were home based could rightly be called CBR, while those at the other end of the spectrum simply re-named practically everything CBR, even programmes which were quite clearly institutional. In many ways, this debate resembles that associated with *Care in the Community*.

One thing that emerged from experience was that CBR is much more than just a rehabilitation programme. You cannot 'do' CBR as you can 'do' therapy, assessments or exercises. The CBR concept embodies philosophy, ideology and strategies for effecting change, The goal is to work towards social justice and equity for disabled people and their families. If CBR is effective, it should change communities, bring people together, increase understanding about disability and result in improved quality of life for people with disabilities. Like *Care in the Community* in the UK, community based rehabilitation should be a process of empowerment for disabled people and their families.

Werner (1993) reminds us that both primary health care and CBR have emphasised empowerment and community participation, but that, in practice, planning and implementation has been top-down. He asserts,

> Participation was too often reduced to compliance, which in terms of self determination was counter-productive. Obedient compliance to the designs of those in positions of authority and control only perpetuates the low social status and powerlessness of underprivileged groups.
>
> (p.vii)

He contests the idea of 'involvement' for disabled people and families, saying that this is not enough. 'Only when programs for disabled people are led and controlled by disabled people (and/or their families) are they likely to help disabled persons gain self determination and a respected, equal position in society (p.viii).

In the 20 years that have elapsed since WHO first mooted the idea of community based rehabilitation, the concept has developed considerably, shaped by the experiences of individuals, communities and governments across the world, and by the criticisms levelled at the WHO model. There has been increasing resistance to top-down prepackaged solutions in which communities are expected merely to cooperate with what has been planned for them, rather than initiate and control what happens. In many parts of the developing world, disabled people themselves, and to a lesser extent, the families of disabled children, have reacted strongly to having their lives managed for them. Like their counterparts in industrialised nations, they are demanding more control over what is happening. Disabled people's organisations in several countries are beginning to influence the design and implementation of CBR programmes (Miles 1996).

But what of people with PMLD? While many of them may be able to advocate for themselves in some situations, it is unlikely that they will be able to do so on a large scale. So how does CBR serve their interests?

CBR and people with PMLD

It is difficult to obtain an overall picture of CBR coverage for people with PMLD. One reason for this is the generic nature of CBR. Since it is a strategy for people with all types of disability, it tends to be non-categorical in approach. Some projects are designed to provide for people with a specific disability, but many more are for everyone, regardless of the type of disability. While people may keep records for their own information, few generic projects formally record the different disabilities of their participants. This is commendable ethically and philosophically, but it does make it more difficult to find out just how many projects cater for children and adults with PMLD, and to ascertain whether people with PMLD are sharing in the benefits of community based initiatives. Another reason for the shortage of information is that the term 'profound and multiple learning disabilities' is relatively unknown in developing countries. Children and adults with PMLD are often referred to as 'mentally retarded' or 'spastic'. Thus, when questioned about whether a project provides for people with multiple disabilities, many project workers will be unclear about what is meant.

There are several ways in which CBR projects provide for people with PMLD and their families. These include:

- direct work with the disabled child or adult, either in the home or in a community based centre;
- work with the family, such as livelihood loans, grants or home based employment, usually for mothers;
- parent-to-parent programmes, where a more experienced parent will support other families with disabled children;
- providing low cost aids and adaptations, such as seating, buggies or wheelchairs;
- referring the child or adult on to more specialised services and meeting financial costs;
- parent support groups;
- integrated play or activity schemes where able bodied siblings participate;
- family based activities, such as outings or social events.

The Janakpuri project in Delhi, referred to earlier, does not work directly with the children, but the loans and the employment given to mothers benefit the whole family. This means that it is less likely that parents will seek institutional placements for their children. The Nairobi Family Support Service, also mentioned earlier, caters for all children, including those with PMLD, through playgroups, home visits, the provision of equipment and parent support groups.

Parents themselves are often instrumental in developing services. Florence Chitiyo, a mother of a disabled child, writes about a neighbourhood centre run by parents. The centre, she tells us 'offers a range of activities – stimulation for children, relief care for exhausted mothers and a mothers' group for income generating activities' (p.3). Profits are divided between mothers and the centre. She says, 'Both the support offered by the centre and the income we make helps us. Many of us have children who are too handicapped ever to find a school place' (Chitiyo 1996, p.3).

In the KASAMAKA community based projects in the Philippines, all of which cater for children and adults with PMLD, the CBR workers are mothers of disabled children. The Portage style programme organisers decided to use mothers as home visitors because volunteer workers kept dropping out. These same mothers now manage the programme. As well as home teaching, they organise community workshops and have an advocacy role. They have established strong links with schools, hospitals and re-habilitation centres. Disabled people and families have become empowered through active participation in planning, implementation and decision making. Opportunities to come together in groups provide support and solidarity, and help parents and disabled people work together with professionals to effect change (McGlade and Aquino 1995). How many projects in industrialised countries have achieved the same degree of collaboration?

236

In Mexico the families of children with physical, intellectual and multiple disabilities have established mutual support groups, rehabilitation facilities and a school for children unable to gain admission to state schools. They are pressurising the government for better services. The programme was started by a social worker, but elected family members are gradually assuming control. Some of the teachers are severely disabled and are good role models for disabled children (Werner 1993).

There are similar stories from other countries. Empowerment is vital for the families of people with PMLD if things are to change. 'Parent empowerment is a tool in the fight against stigmatisation and low social status felt among parents of disabled' (NAMH 1996). Empowerment happens in a variety of ways and professionals have an important role as facilitators, as they have in every country across the world.

A CBR programme, run by the Christian Foundation for the Deaf and Blind in the Philippines, originally catered only for people with sensory impairments, but now works with multiply disabled children and their families. As well as direct work with the children, they also supply custom-made mobility aids such as buggies and wheelchairs, which means that many children are able for the first time to be taken out. Poor families are given grants to help them care for their children, or livelihood loans which will enable them to start small businesses at home. Professionals train and support community workers. Parents and children now have much more of a visible presence in the community, an essential prerequisite for community inclusion (Campos 1992).

Most project participants find great strength and solidarity in group activities, and parent-professional boundaries often disappear when people share common goals. But different expectations can mean that relationships between families and CBR workers, whether professionals or non-professionals, do not always go smoothly. Some parents are hoping only for a residential placement for the disabled person. Convincing them that community based intervention is a better option is a difficult task. Lagerwall (1992) tells of a return visit to a family with a twelve year old daughter with severe cerebral palsy, whose family had intended to leave her to the CBR team or an institution, and remarks, 'Although it was disturbing to find the girl lying on the sack on the ground with a severe scoliosis, she was now clean and well dressed which had not been the case at previous visits' (p.3). Most parents, however, struggle to keep their children at home, whatever their circumstances.

Shared vision is essential in CBR, and vision develops as a result of exposure to other people's ideas and aspirations. This is another reason why partnerships are vital: partnerships which include families, disabled people, professionals and front line workers, all working towards a common goal.

237

Partnership through collaborative multidisciplinary practice

Multidisciplinary collaboration is one of the goals of CBR. Projects which are urban based are much more likely to have easy access to professionals than those in more remote rural areas. But even in urban projects professionals are few in number compared to the need. CBR was designed specifically to deal with the shortage of services and of specialists. But it was also intended as a means of de-mystifying professionalism; sharing rehabilitation techniques and practice with 'non-professionals'. It is a move towards power sharing, so that disabled people and their families will no longer be at the bottom of the hierarchy.

Professionals may not be the best people to implement CBR. They may have the technical expertise, but do not necessarily have the community skills, the organisational skills or the management experience required. They are unlikely to understand community needs and community development as well as the people who actually belong to the community. At the same time, CBR workers who are not professionals need access to the technical skills if they are to be able to understand the effects of different disabilities. Collaborative multidisciplinary practice in CBR is much broader than that normally experienced in more traditional services. It includes disabled people, families, CBR workers who are likely to be drawn from various sectors, professionals from various disciplines, community leaders and government officials, amongst others.

Projects employ professionals in a variety of ways, according to need and the nature of the project. Most professionals have to assume a number of different roles:

- that of front line workers; visiting homes and running sessions in centres;
- advisers, helping to steer the programme in the right direction; giving advice on problems in their own field of expertise;
- consultants, visiting from time to time, receiving referrals, dealing with children or adults with particular types of disbilities or problems;
- members of management bodies, helping to run or monitor the project;
- supervisors, supporting and advising front line workers;
- trainers;
- counsellors, working with families;
- a link between community groups and national organisations, particularly government bodies;
- disseminators of ideas and information.

CBR is primarily about power sharing, and not everyone finds this easy. Community members are accustomed to deferring to professionals, while professionals have their status to consider. As Miles (1996) says, 'The transition from omniscient professional to facilitator in the community requires an enormous shift in thinking and, too often, institutional attitudes are carried over' (p.501). Different disciplines have their own professional boundaries and few professionals are trained in collaboration. But once the initial hurdles are overcome and everyone adjusts to the new roles, CBR is fertile ground for collaborative multidisciplinary practice.

There are many advantages. Collaborative multidisciplinary work makes available a larger pool of ideas and expertise. Professionals have access to resources the community might not have. They are also part of larger networks and of the infrastructures which exist in a country. Projects which use a team approach are much more likely to be sustained than those which rely on one leader, however strong or charismatic that person might be. Professionals are surprised how much there is to learn when they begin to listen to disabled people and families. A group of Malaysian teachers, doctors and social workers found that the most successful feature of a three week course on CBR was an ad hoc session where a group of parents from a CBR project came to talk about their own experiences. Participants and visitors worked in small groups and the session continued long after the official closing time. The professionals, all experienced in the field of disability, said that they had learned more from that session than from any other training they had done (Bradley 1993).

Collaborative multidisciplinary training facilitates working partnerships, especially when it also involves disabled people and families. Training through video courses, designed and produced locally, has proved particularly useful. Trainers collaborate in the production of the materials, are trained in their use and then take the training back to the people in their project. The package acts as a catalyst, giving guidelines and ideas, and providing a basis for discussion and planning (McConkey 1993). One example from India, designed for those working with children with PMLD, is based on a play project. Components include drama, painting, locally made toys and equipment, movement activities, basic positioning and handling, simple aids and adaptations. The children filmed were in a residential situation, but the programmes were also designed for families in home settings as well as CBR workers. The purpose was to show how many different things children with PMLD can achieve if given the right kind of support and encouragement, rather than being left lying all day doing nothing (Bradley 1994).

Interactive training is particularly suitable for people who have to work as part of a multidisciplinary team in a CBR project. It provides opportunities for discussion, exchange of ideas, learning from others and problem solving. If a programme is to reflect the needs and wishes of a community there is little point in training people in prepackaged, standardised approaches. In fact, CBR needs not just to be multidisciplinary, but multisectoral. Unless CBR is integrated as part of community development, and has links with all relevant government and non-government organisations, the chances of sustainability are low. Collaboration at all levels means that there is more chance of capitalising on lessons learned both locally and nationally.

Evaluation, interdisciplinary practice and CBR

In some places CBR seems to have been ground breaking: empowering parents, raising public awareness, bringing people closer together and steering government policy. In others, projects started with great hope and enthusiasm have died away leaving no tangible sign of change. The most successful projects are built on collaboration. McGlade and Aquino (1995) write: 'The value of CBR may be rooted as much in the relationship between CBR workers and family members, as in the actual practical interventions carried out' (p.187). So what constitutes success in CBR, particularly with regard to collaborative multidisciplinary practice and people with PMLD? To date we have little evidence to draw upon, but we can at least begin to ask the right questions.

- To what extent are people with PMLD being served by CBR projects in different countries?
- What kinds of interventions are most effective as perceived by the different people involved? Is there agreement?
- What kinds of support do non-professional practitioners need from professionals (Brar 1992)?
- Which factors are instrumental in making multidisciplinary teams effective?
- Which combination of services suit families and people with PMLD?
- What part do families and communities play in the project?
- How are parent-to-parent supports utilised?
- How does the project build on pre-existing community support systems?
- How can technical expertise about PMLD best be disseminated?

Evaluations are influenced by the role and perspective of the person or persons in control. There is little sense in promoting a collaborative multidisciplinary strategy such as CBR and then adopting a traditional, one-dimensional approach to evaluation. And yet this is what often happens. Projects are evaluated by outsiders who understand little about the community in which the project is located. Rural projects are evaluated by professionals from the urban elite, whose lifestyles are at the other end of the spectrum. Programme workers have vested interests. Consumers feel constrained and give the answers they think workers want to hear. Projects are evaluated separately by outsiders and insiders with contradictory results. There are also problems finding evaluation measures which will allow comparison across projects and across countries. By definition each project should reflect the needs, aspirations and demands of individual communities. What is appropriate in one situation may be entirely unworkable in another. CBR projects are not easily replicated or compared. And most evaluations deal with methodology and outcomes, rather than process, which is a fundamental element of CBR (Thomas and Thomas 1995).

Participatory evaluation is the approach that seems most suited to CBR, based as it is on partnership, collaboration and equality. However, many of those who are central to the CBR process are too busy getting on with the job, and are reluctant to spend time on monitoring and evaluation, especially if they feel it has little value. So, how do you convince front line workers that evaluation is important and within their capabilities? Thomas and Thomas (1995) tell of a phased strategy designed to change CBR workers' attitudes to evaluation. They used a proactive, phased approach to convince workers that evaluation was in their own interests, and not just that of the NGO supporting the programme. By means of newsletters, discussions, workshops and joint action, they showed that monitoring and evaluation could lead to better and more cost effective services and that evaluation was not as difficult as workers thought.

Evaluation, if done properly, will enable us to capitalise on the knowledge and expertise accumulated by CBR projects across the world. It will help us compare strategies and uncover some of the factors which facilitate effective teamwork, while still maintaining the diversity necessary in CBR. Most fundamentally, it will deepen our understanding of how families and professionals can complement one another's expertise. CBR is a two way learning process: families learn more about disability and rehabilitation techniques; practitioners learn about the real lives of disabled people (Brar 1992). Participatory evaluation will facilitate ownership, a prerequisite for sustainability.

Dissemination of information is equally vital. Brar (1992) highlights the weaknesses in dissemination, asserting that we must find a range of methods of making information accessible to those who need it. In Indonesia, she tells us, this was done by means of traditional research reports, slide shows, question and answer formats, case histories and network mapping. Thomas (1997) pinpoints a reluctance of CBR projects to share information with one another. Because of this, valuable lessons have been lost and people have had to reinvent the wheel. 'There is a need for donor organisations to recognise the importance of pooling resources, developing strategies for collaboration and coordination, avoiding duplication of efforts and aiming for optimal resource utilisation.' (p.31). Miles (1989) reminds us that there is a fund of rehabilitation knowledge and skills dispersed in the community, acquired from people's own experiences.

Concluding comments

There are parallels to be drawn between CBR in the developing world and community based initiatives in industrialised countries, notably *Care in the Community* in the UK. At the root of all such initiatives is the empowerment of disabled people and their families, and a shift from top-down development to true collaboration between families and professionals. For children and young people with PMLD, the role of the family is crucial. Parents must be at the forefront of development and not just followers. Even in the best informed communities, in both industrialised and developing countries, there is little spontaneous effort to improve the lives of disabled people. Where communities have changed, this has seldom been due to altruism. The origins of education and integrated services for disabled children in industrialised nations are usually to be found in parental effort. In developing countries, it is unrealistic to expect that all parents will play a leading role, since the sheer act of daily survival is challenge enough for many. But there are those who can, and who are already doing so. There are similarities, albeit different in degree, with their counterparts in more affluent societies.

The Parent Mobilisation Resource Group (PMRG), working under the umbrella of Inclusion International (formerly the International League of Societies for People with Mental Handicap), has parent representatives from several African countries, Jamaica and Norway, and is a good example of partnership across nations. Through high profile activities and parent empowerment seminars, the group aims to share experiences, exert political pressure and work towards full inclusion for all persons with intellectual disability (NAMH 1996).

The most effective community based initiatives recognise that the person with PMLD is part of a larger network, comprising both the immediate and extended family. Improving the circumstances of the family can often be the best way of improving the quality of life for the person with PMLD. The livelihood loans to parents, discussed earlier in the chapter, make a difference to the life situation of the disabled child or young person. Similarly, in an industrialised country, providing child care which allows a mother to work alters the circumstances of both child and family. In both, there is respite and support for the mother, a recognition of her individuality and needs and an improvement in economic status.

There are similarities too, in the way in which the best community based services worldwide have evolved to match local circumstances. There is no such thing as a typical community, nor a blueprint for service provision. One of the strengths of community based provision lies in its flexibility; an ability to take on the nature and shape required to suit the needs of those it serves and to capitalise on available resources.

Partnership has an increasingly important part to play, although it is not always easy, especially where professional boundaries and lines of demarcation between professionals and non-professionals are clearly marked. Specialist expertise within institutional settings can be made available to community groups through joint ventures. Communities can influence professionals, drawing upon their own experiences of real life situations. Governments can play a coordinating role, as some already do, facilitating and supporting partnerships between government and non-government organisations, communities, families and disabled people.

Disabled people's organisations have been a powerful voice for change within and across nations. But so far most have neglected the rights and needs of those who are more severely disabled. If empowerment and equality for all is the goal, it makes no sense to be selective about which types of disability will and will not be represented.

In both CBR and *Care in the Community*, the relationship between education and other sectors providing services is still much too tenuous. Stronger links are essential if multidisciplinary collaboration is to become a reality. In CBR, emphasis is largely on health, with little on education. Children are referred to school from CBR projects, but these are generally children with less severe disabilities. In developing countries it is unlikely that many children with PMLD will be in mainstream schools in the short, or even medium term, but this must be the ultimate goal. In the meantime, there are imaginative ways of integrating children with PMLD and able bodied children, such as play schemes and family activities. Integrated activities should be a planned component of all CBR projects.

Even those professionals who are committed to multidisciplinary collaboration struggle with both the concept and its practice. Many professionals remain role bound. Shared training at qualifying level is rare. Experience suggests that it may be more common at post qualifying level in developing countries than in industrialised, possibly because professional organisations are stronger in the latter, and numbers greater. Yet, if community based services are to succeed, we need to move far away from the style of professionalism we have grown up with. Professionalism may be the biggest obstacle to multidisciplinary collaboration at community level.

Like *Care in the Community*, CBR has not yet proved its true worth, and is not without its critics. Momm and Konig (1990), from their experiences of reviewing projects in several countries, cast doubts on its sustainability without outside support. But, at least for the present, it is the best hope for many people with PMLD and their families. The challenge is to strive for sustainability, to increase the number of people with PMLD who benefit, and to strengthen the impact. It is not an antidote to the inequalities experienced by large numbers of people with PMLD and their families, but it is a genuine attempt to even out some of them. It is a learning experience with potential for change, and there is still a long way to go.

Fundamentally, provision in the community for people with profound and multiple disabilities depends on a vision of a more equitable society, locally, nationally and internationally. Vision is shaped and altered by exposure to other people's ideas and aspirations. Monitoring and evaluating our services enables us to draw upon experience, deepen our understanding and share achievements. Together, internationally, we have much to learn from one another.

References

Asindua, S. (1995) 'Comparing urban and rural CBR', *CBR News*, **19**, Jan.–April, 6–7.

Bradley, A. (1993) 'Evaluation of Community Based Education Course', Unpublished Report to Ministry of Education, Malaysia.

Bradley, A. (1994) Better Chances – Better Lives. Video course for Children with Multiple Disability, Leonard Cheshire Foundation International, London.

Brar, B. (1992) 'Research and evaluation in community based rehabilitation – some views derived from UNICEF experience', *ActionAid Disability News* **3** (2) 35–41.

Campos, M. (1992) Personal Interview.

Chitiyo, F. (1996) Letter to *CBR News*, **22**, Jan.–April, 3.

Khalfan, K. H. (1992) 'CBR in Zanzibar', *CBR News* 12 Sept.

Kisanji, J. (1995) 'Attitudes and Beliefs about Disability in Tanzania', in O'Toole, B. and McConkey, R. (eds) *Innovations in Developing Countries for People with Disabilities*. Chorley, Lancashire: Lisieux Hall Publications.

Lagerwall, T. (1992) *Review of Community Based Rehabilitation Services run by the Ministry of Health in Kenya*. Vallingby, Sweden: The Swedish Handicap Institute.

McConkey, R. (1993) *Training for All: Developing Video-based Training Packages for Parent and Community Education*. Paris: UNESCO.

McGlade, B. and Aquino, R. (1995) 'Mothers of Disabled Children as CBR Workers', in O'Toole, B. and McConkey, R. (eds) *Innovations in Developing Countries for People with Disabilities*. Chorley, Lancashire: Lisieux Hall Publications.

Miles, M. (1989) 'Information-Based Rehabilitation for Third World Disability', *Social Science and Medicine* **28** (3), 207–10.

Miles, M. (1993) 'Service development by information, not ideology', in Finkenflugel, H. (ed.) *The Handicapped Community*, Amsterdam: VU University Press.

Miles, S. (1996) 'Engaging with the Disability Rights Movement: the experience of community based rehabilitation in southern Africa', *Disability and Society*, **11**, (4), 501–17.

Momm, W. and Konig, A. (1990) *From Community Based Rehabilitation to Community Integration Programmes*. Geneva: International Labour Organisation.

NAMH (1996) *A Society for All*. Norwegian Association for Mentally Handicapped.

O'Toole, B. (1993) 'Community Based Rehabilitation', in Mittler, P., Brouillette, R. and Harris, D. (eds) *World Yearbook of Education 1993*. London: Kogan Page.

Saxena, M. (1993) Personal Interview.

Spastics Society of Tamil Nadu, India (1996) *Annual Report*.

Thomas, M. (1997) 'CBR in Developing Countries – The Shifts and Changes in the Last Decade', *Asia Pacific Disability Rehabilitation Journal* **8**, (1), 2.

Thomas, M. and Thomas, M, (1995) 'Evaluation based Planning for Rehabilitation Programmed in India', in O'Toole, B. and McConkey, R. (eds) *Innovations in Developing Countries for People with Disabilities*. Chorley, Lancashire: Lisieux Hall Publications.

Valdez, J. (1991) Personal Interview.

Werner, D. (1993) 'Preface: What should be the goal of Community Based Rehabilitation: to normalize or to liberate?', in Finkenflugel, H. (ed.) *The Handicapped Community*. Amsterdam: VU University Press.

World Health Organisation (WHO) (1992b) *Training the Disabled in the Community*. Geneva: WHO.

14

EXECUTIVE SUMMARY

Department of Education

Source: *Education White Paper 6. Special Needs Education: Building an Inclusive Education and Training System*, Pretoria: Republic of South Africa, Department of Education, 2001, pp. 5–8.

1   In this White Paper we outline what an inclusive education and training system is, and how we intend to build it. It provides the framework for establishing such an education and training system, details a funding strategy, and lists the key steps to be taken in establishing an inclusive education and training system for South Africa.

2   In October 1996, the Ministry of Education appointed the National Commission on Special Needs in Education and Training and the National Committee on Education Support Services to investigate and make recommendations on all aspects of 'special needs and support services' in education and training in South Africa.

3   A joint report on the findings of these two bodies was presented to the Minister of Education in November 1997, and the final report was published by the Department of Education in February 1998 for public comment and advice (Report of National Commission on Special Needs in Education and Training and National Committee on Education Support, Department of Education, 1997).

4   The central findings of the investigations included: (i) specialised education and support have predominantly been provided for a small percentage of learners with disabilities within 'special' schools and classes; (ii) where provided, specialised education and support were provided on a racial basis, with the best human, physical and material resources reserved for whites; (iii) most learners with disability have either fallen outside of the system or been 'mainstreamed by default'; (iv) the curriculum and education system as a whole have generally failed to respond to the diverse needs of the learner population, resulting in massive numbers of drop-outs, push-outs, and failures; and, (v) while some attention has been given to the schooling phase with regard to 'special needs and support', the other levels or bands of education have been seriously neglected.

5 In the light of these findings, the joint report of the two bodies recommended that the education and training system should promote education for all and foster the development of inclusive and supportive centres of learning that would enable all learners to participate actively in the education process so that they could develop and extend their potential and participate as equal members of society.

6 The principles guiding the broad strategies to achieve this vision included: acceptance of principles and values contained in the Constitution and White Papers on Education and Training; human rights and social justice for all learners; participation and social integration; equal access to a single, inclusive education system; access to the curriculum, equity and redress; community responsiveness; and cost-effectiveness.

7 The report also suggested that the key strategies required to achieve this vision included: (i) transforming all aspects of the education system, (ii) developing an integrated system of education, (iii) infusing 'special needs and support services' throughout the system, (iv) pursuing the holistic development of centres of learning to ensure a barrier-free physical environment and a supportive and inclusive psycho-social learning environment, developing a flexible curriculum to ensure access to all learners, (v) promoting the rights and responsibilities of parents, educators and learners, (vi) providing effective development programmes for educators, support personnel, and other relevant human resources, (vii) fostering holistic and integrated support provision through intersectoral collaboration, (viii) developing a community-based support system which includes a preventative and developmental approach to support, and (ix) developing funding strategies that ensure redress for historically disadvantaged communities and institutions, sustainability, and – ultimately – access to education for all learners.

8 Based on the recommendations in the joint report, the Ministry released a Consultative Paper (Department of Education. Consultative Paper No. 1 on Special Education: Building an Inclusive Education and Training System. August 30, 1999). The submissions and feedback of social partners and the wider public were collated and have informed the writing of this White Paper.

9 In this White Paper, we outline the Ministry of Education's commitment to the provision of educational opportunities in particular for those learners who experience or have experienced barriers to learning and development or who have dropped out of learning because of the inability of the education and training system to accommodate their learning needs. We recognise that our vision of an inclusive education and training system can only be developed over the long term and that the actions we will take in the short to medium term must provide us with models for later system-wide application. Our short-term to medium-term actions will also provide further clarity on the capital,

material and human resource development, and consequently the funding requirements, of building an inclusive education and training system.

10   We also define inclusive education and training as:
   •   Acknowledging that all children and youth can learn and that all children and youth need support.
   •   Enabling education structures, systems and learning methodologies to meet the needs of all learners.
   •   Acknowledging and respecting differences in learners, whether due to age, gender, ethnicity, language, class, disability, HIV or other infectious diseases.
   •   Broader than formal schooling and acknowledging that learning also occurs in the home and community, and within formal and informal settings and structures.
   •   Changing attitudes, behaviour, teaching methods, curricula and environment to meet the needs of all learners.
   •   Maximising the participation of all learners in the culture and the curriculum of educational institutions and uncovering and minimising barriers to learning.

11   The Ministry appreciates that a broad range of learning needs exists among the learner population at any point in time, and that where these are not met, learners may fail to learn effectively or be excluded from the learning system. In this regard, different learning needs arise from a range of factors including physical, mental, sensory, neurological and developmental impairments, psycho-social disturbances, differences in intellectual ability, particular life experiences or socio-economic deprivation.

12   Different learning needs may also arise because of:
   •   Negative attitudes to and stereotyping of difference.
   •   An inflexible curriculum.
   •   Inappropriate languages or language of learning and teaching.
   •   Inappropriate communication.
   •   Inaccessible and unsafe built environments.
   •   Inappropriate and inadequate support services.
   •   Inadequate policies and legislation.
   •   The non-recognition and non-involvement of parents.
   •   Inadequately and inappropriately trained education managers and educators.

13   In accepting this inclusive approach we acknowledge that the learners who are most vulnerable to barriers to learning and exclusion in South Africa are those who have historically been termed 'learners with special education needs,' i.e. learners with disabilities and impairments. Their increased vulnerability has arisen largely because of the historical nature and extent of the educational support provided.

14 Accordingly, the White Paper outlines the following as key strategies and levers for establishing our inclusive education and training system:

- The qualitative improvement of special schools for the learners that they serve and their phased conversion to resource centres that provide professional support to neighbourhood schools and are integrated into district-based support teams.
- The overhauling of the process of identifying, assessing and enrolling learners in special schools, and its replacement by one that acknowledges the central role played by educators, lecturers and parents.
- The mobilisation of out-of-school disabled children and youth of school-going age.
- Within mainstream schooling, the designation and phased conversion of approximately 500 out of 20,000 primary schools to full-service schools, beginning with the 30 school districts that are part of the national district development programme. Similarly, within adult basic, further and higher education, the designation and establishment of full-service educational institutions. These full-service education institutions will enable us to develop models for later system-wide application.
- Within mainstream education, the general orientation and introduction of management, governing bodies and professional staff to the inclusion model, and the targeting of early identification of the range of diverse learning needs and intervention in the Foundation Phase.
- The establishment of district-based support teams to provide a co-ordinated professional support service that draws on expertise in further and higher education and local communities, targeting special schools and specialised settings, designated full-service and other primary schools and educational institutions, beginning with the 30 districts that are part of the national district development programme.
- The launch of a national advocacy and information programme in support of the inclusion model focusing on the roles, responsibilities and rights of all learning institutions, parents and local communities; highlighting the focal programmes; and reporting on their progress.

15 The development of an inclusive education and training system will take into account the incidence and the impact of the spread of the HIV/ AIDS pandemic and other infectious diseases. For planning purposes the Ministry of Education will ascertain, in particular, the consequences for the curriculum, the expected enrolment and drop-out rates and the funding implications for both the short and long term. The Ministry will gather this information from an internally commissioned study as well as from other research being conducted in this area.

15

EQUALITY FIFTEEN YEARS ON

Mary Warnock

Source: *Oxford Review of Education* 17(2) (1991): 145–53.

An enormous amount has happened in the last 15 years, both politically and ideologically, and nowhere has this change been more marked than in the world of education. In the early 1970s, as well as in the 1960s, school education had come to be widely regarded as primarily an instrument of social engineering. There was an accurate perception that our education system, totally unlike that of all other countries, was somehow to blame for the social ills we suffered, and especially the class divisions which seemed to stifle growth. It is true that such a concept of education was subject to a great deal of criticism and indeed aroused deep hostility among many. There were those who demanded, unrealistically, that politics should be kept out of education. There were others who, though they realised that education was inevitably a political issue, wanted to be allowed to stand back and consider what went on at school in a purely educational way, putting the class war low on the agenda. Nevertheless because as a country we recognised our obsession with class it seemed to many that the only logical step we could take towards the classless society was through the education system.

The Welfare State after the war had promised education, free, to everyone. But real equality, though it was the inspiration of the welfare state, had not materialised, and the only step forward seemed to be to educate all, or nearly all, children in the same kind of school, teaching them as far as possible together when they got there. The expansion of the comprehensive system, originally introduced as an experiment, and mixed ability teaching within the system seemed necessary for equality. Those who opposed such measures believed that equality must be abandoned as an ideal, and something more properly educational substituted for it.

Three things have changed this emphasis on social engineering, and have made the old objections to equality as an ideal seem somehow misdirected and off-target. The first was the so-called Great Debate, which began in

1977. This event has been fairly widely discussed, and I do not want to go into the story again in detail. What happened was not a debate at all but a series of rather tedious meetings where local education officers and a handful of politicians spoke at various venues all over the country, airing their often very strong views. What is now of interest is the motivation for setting it all up. Increasingly it had become clear that education was failing. Children were leaving school as soon as they could legitimately do so (or rather before), and in many cases they were illiterate and innumerate when they left, 11 years of school appearing to have helped them in no way at all. They were virtually unemployable, except as unskilled labourers. Employers complained ceaselessly about educational standards. Parents, fearful of unemployment for their children began to be vociferous in their demands that their children should be better served. The emphasis shifted with dramatic speed from the structure of the system (what sorts of schools there should be) to its content (what should be taught).

James Callaghan, the then Prime Minister, set the Great Debate in motion in a speech at Ruskin College, the workers' college just outside Oxford. This was October 1976. Already before this concern had been mounting, James Hamilton, a Permanent Secretary at the DES had said, in June of that year, 'I believe that the so-called secret garden of the curriculum cannot be allowed to remain so secret after all, and that the key to the door must be found and turned' (Annual Conference of the Association of Education Committees, 25 June 1976). His was by no means a lone voice. Increasing numbers of parents, joined by industrialists, began to demand that the curriculum itself must be changed so as better to serve both children themselves and the economy.

It was in 1975 that the notorious case of the William Tyndale primary school in Islington hit the headlines. This was a school where relations between teachers and management appeared to have broken down completely. Teachers were accused by the governors and some parents of having become so 'progressive' in their methods that children were learning nothing at all. The headmaster was said to have asserted that learning to write was outdated; and at least one teacher was supposed to have refused to teach reading, and sent children off to play or watch television instead. There was an enormously long drawn-out formal enquiry into the case, and a report on it was published in 1976.

The recommendations of the report were soon forgotten, but the effect on the public attitudes to education were permanent. There was an overwhelming demand for a central curriculum which could be delivered to all children at school. They must not be short-changed. Their own futures and that of society demanded that they should, all of them, be taught what it would be useful for them to know. A new concept of equality was beginning to emerge in embryo: there should be a common curriculum, mandatory for all state schools, and this would ensure that all children equally were provided, educationally, with what they would need in their future lives. Sadly the teachers emerged from the Great Debate as the villains. It was thought to be they who had been so much carried away by their waging of the class war that they had, it seemed, become totally political, and forgotten about the educational needs of their pupils. Their reputation has hardly recovered.

The second event of the later 1970s was in some ways closely connected with the Great Debate, though at first sight quite different in its motivation. In the early 1970s responsibility for those children hitherto designated 'ineducable', the severely mentally handicapped, was transferred from the Department of Health to the Department of Education and Science. This was an event not much noticed at the time, and probably too little noticed by social historians. It was nevertheless a profound change. One man can take a large measure of responsibility for the outcome, and that is the energetic and ebullient Stan Segal, who ceaselessly lobbied every MP, including Mrs Thatcher when she was Secretary of State for Education, and who wrote an influential book called *No Child is Ineducable*. The immediate response from government was to set up a committee of enquiry into the education of the handicapped; and, after a change of government, this committee finally started work in 1974, publishing its report in 1978, while the Great Debate was still in progress. Committees of enquiry are on the whole strange creatures, partly innovative, partly following sheep-like where civil servants lead. This committee, of which I was chairman, was no exception. We did not know at the time quite what we were doing, because, as soon as we started to look into it, so many problems arose in the matter of educating children with handicaps in vast variety, temporary or permanent, that our task seemed overwhelmingly hard. But in the end what arose out of this committee, by genuine consensus, was a belief that education was a track along which *every* child and adult had a right to walk, a *right of way*. For some it was a relatively smooth and easy track, for others it was set about with obstacles. These might arise from a variety of causes, and might in some cases be terribly daunting. It was the duty of the education service, we thought, to enable children as far as possible to progress along this track, by helping them to overcome the obstacles. To provide such help was to provide for those children's *special needs*. And thus the concept of educational need, always latent in educational thinking, and certainly by no means new, came to have prominence in the late 1970s and early 1980s, and was incorporated in the 1981 Education Act.

The notion of need is one that is essentially relative to some end. Thus if you are to live you need food and water and air. If you are to become a top-class ballet dancer you need not only the right physique, but time to practise, and the development of a sophisticated ear for rhythm. If we as a committee were prepared to talk about educational need we had to be able to specify what end constituted and created that need. We had thus to state in our report, however briefly, what we thought the proper goals of education were, such that in order to move towards them children needed to have certain services provided, needed to be allowed access to a curriculum which would advance them towards these goals. We set out the goals, perhaps dogmatically, as independence, the ability to do useful work and the ability to enjoy life, by imaginatively understanding it and participating in it. Now these were, in our view, common goals. The very severely handicapped might advance only a very short way to their achievement. But, for them, each step was of immense importance. Thus, for example, a child who had been for years doing nothing but sitting in a corner waiting to be fed, and who could exercise no choice of any kind, could, as we discovered, by patient teaching learn how to point to things, to choose whether to accept chocolate or raspberry flavoured instant whip, to indicate that she wanted to have the radio to play with rather than the teddy bear. Such advances in the ability to choose seem incredibly small to those of us who have been choosing since infancy. But to the individual who can make and communicate such preferences for the first time the advance is enormous. The quality of her life has vastly improved. Such communication is a step towards independence, even though for some children independence will never get much further than this; and choice, however limited, is a step towards enjoyment.

The committee had considerable difficulty in persuading people, especially, at first, members of the medical profession, that severely handicapped people could be educated. Surely what they needed was what they had hitherto had, namely care or, perhaps, therapy, treatment, or at best training. We were fortunate in this matter to be able to rely on the law. All children were now entitled by law to education, not just care. However, if the concept of education was to be made to apply in reality as well as in theory and in law to all, we had to try to show that the purpose of education was the same for everyone. With regard to education all were equal in the eyes of the law, a law that had been made specifically with equality of provision in mind.

To say that education is, as to its purpose, common to all is entirely different from saying that education must be the same for all. For once you embrace the project of educating everyone, the most severely disabled as well as the potentially brilliant, within the context of *meeting their educational needs* then this becomes obvious, for the idea of an educational need is, and must be, extremely flexible.

Up till 1981 it had been assumed that about 2% of those who were at school were so disabled one way or another that they must have special education in special schools. A different sort of education altogether with different goals could then be given to the remaining 98% of children who were normal. Once it was recognised, however, that the goals of education were the same for all, that there was only one kind of education, that which was designed to meet a child's needs, and that everyone had educational needs which had to be met, the picture changed. It began to be seen that there were far more children than the 2% in special schools who had educational needs for which a school ought to lay on something special if their needs were to be met. At any one time there might be as many as 20% of children (and in some schools far more) who would need special help if they were to be able to overcome the obstacles in their way and progress down the educational road. Many of these special needs were temporary and could be met by a bit of extra help to catch up with lessons missed through illness or for other reasons; or, say, a place in the front of the class for a child deaf after an infection. Some were permanent and could be met only by long-term provision. It was the duty of teachers to be alert to such needs and spot them early. Schools increasingly became aware that they must make provision for this kind of flexibility. For it was the duty of a school to ensure that as far as possible everyone could make educational progress whatever their abilities. In the light of the concept of need, then, equality was seen as equality of entitlement, not identity of provision.

The 1981 Education Act incorporated these ideals. They were not realised in practice (though the Act had considerable influence). It would doubtless have been impossible at any time to realise them completely, because of the costs involved, as well as the need for changes in attitude. Nevertheless attitudes *did* change, not only to the disabled but to equality itself. It began to seem possible to marry the idea of equality with that of variety, within a common framework of provision. To some extent then the ideal embodied in the Act was accepted.

What really made it inevitable that the 1981 Act should be more or less still-born was the financial crisis. This gave birth to a new ideal in education, that of cost-effectiveness. This has been the third great change since 1975. At first what we saw seemed entirely negative. We saw nothing but 'the cuts', savage measures inhibiting the realisation of any ideals whatsover. Gradually, however a new philosophy began to be received behind the cuts, the positive philosophy of the market. We were beginning to see the rise of Thatcherism, the ideology that will be forever associated with the 1980s.

For Thatcherism, inefficiency is the major sin. Whatever is must be cost-effective and what is not cost-effective must either be cut away, or allowed to wither away for lack of support. All the metaphors of education which in the 1960s were notoriously drawn from the garden and the greenhouse were suddenly changed, deriving now from industry and the management schools. Indeed the language of industry became more than metaphorical. Schools and universities were not simply to be run like businesses; they were businesses.

Thus in education one could no longer afford to be soft. Whatever could not be shown to be efficient must go. The thought that the education service was meant to satisfy educational needs was held to be paternalistic and was therefore condemned. The admired 1980s person was in no need of a father, nor even a father-figure. He had an independence, born of having risen from the bottom, pulled up by the strength of his own boot laces, not by any help given him by the State. There were to be no more hand-outs, no free lunches, no assumption that free education was a right. Nothing except the spirit of self-reliant independence, nothing but a determination to get on, better yourself and make money (in order to own your own house, buy your own car, send your children to fee-paying schools) would qualify you for admiration. In the market economy, people would be free, it was held, to decide what they wanted and pursue it. The 'Nanny State' would not dictate to them what it was they ought to want. Intellectual educational theorists could shut up shop. They had always been in the business of trying to influence policy, and even to deliver, through the maintained system, what they thought children should have in the way of education. Now, instead, people untainted by theory, parents, were to be able to decide. They would put up with no nonsense. Had they not already, in the William Tyndale case, shown that they could stand only so much, and in the end could call the tune? And it was assumed that parents would always choose for their children schools where they would be prepared for gainful employment, and where they would learn only what was useful.

The market philosophy thus assumed that schools would become more efficient in response to parental demands and that this would be true both of independent and of maintained schools. In both categories, those schools which failed to deliver would ultimately simply disappear.

That this philosophy was widely accepted was shown by the enormous increase in the number of parents prepared to pay for private education in the last decade: and the trend continues. Very large numbers of parents who did not themselves go to independent schools are anxious to pay for their children to do so, on the grounds that in this way they will get on. They will get an education that fits them either for employment immediately after school, or for higher education and a degree, and thence the glittering prizes. Parents cannot and should not be blamed for this determination to do what they see as best for their children, often at considerable cost to themselves. But of course there are numbers of parents who cannot take action or who are too ignorant or apathetic to do so. Many of them are simply too poor. For them there is a new idea: that of the safety net. The safety net is meant to pick up the real no-hopers whether by giving them a social services hand-out, or by ensuring that their children get educated somehow, even if they do not go to the successful and competitive schools. It was for some of these children that the new City Technology Colleges were invented, schools intended to be set up by industry and then funded by direct grant from the DES. They were supposed to be for those children who would benefit by a high-powered technological education and whose parents were prepared to guarantee that they would stay at school till their course was concluded and would work extra hard for extra long hours as long as they were at school. In the event those CTCs that have come into existence have not turned out quite like that. They seem to be selective; few are in inner cities, and they are mainly established by government funds. They certainly do not seem much of a safety net for the disadvantaged.

I shall return to the safety net in a moment. First it is worth commenting in more detail on the concept of utility on which the Thatcherist educational philosophy is founded. That education must be useful to those who are being educated would hardly ever have been denied. Only extreme fanatics for a concept of purity in education would ever have refused to allow that we educate people 'for' something—if only for a more satisfactory life after education is over. Certainly the concept of educational needs implied as much. For an educational need, as I have argued, is determined by the non-educational goals a child is aiming for, goals which are described in terms of what the child wants to do, or how he wants to live. And it has been generally supposed that usefulness to the individual will add up in the end to usefulness to society. The educated person would serve society the better for his education.

However, in the late 1970s the idea of utility took on a narrower aspect. The country was failing commercially and economically. We were quite manifestly being overtaken by our European neighbours and by Japan. It was generally held that our failure was caused by our lack of skilled technologists. And so usefulness in education came to be identified with what was confusingly lumped together as 'science and technology'. It was an assumption of Thatcherism that parents and employers would agree that education should be technology-orientated. It was necessary only to set market forces loose, and the desired vocational education would overtake all other forms. Producer and consumer would work together in harmony. The invisible hand would ensure it.

This new concentration on applied science and technology was far from all bad. The scientific and mathematical incompetence of the average British school child had become notorious. They were often genuinely unemployable without a further course in basic arithmetic, because without it, they could not even begin to master the technological skills they were supposed to be able to use in industry or commerce. Such incompetence is by no means yet a thing of the past.

The trouble was that the concentration on applied science and technology went too far. It began to mean that every element of education not obviously usable or not technological would be thrown away. Even the universities, traditionally thought to be centres of scholarship and learning, of theoretical science, fundamental research and philosophy were told that they must sell their services to industry, or close their departments. There are still threats in the air. It has become a matter of urgency and ingenuity to defend the humanities and theoretical science in such a way as to make it seem that these disciplines too are worth funding, even though industry cannot be expected to fund them. We have to make them seem in some way as useful as the rest. A liberal education cannot any longer be defended on the grounds that it leads to a civilised or enjoyable life, nor on the grounds that people continue to want it. It must also be shown to produce value for money, in a market economy.

Fortunately, the narrow notion of utility is gradually being abandoned by many industrialists in favour of something wider and more realistic. It is recognised that employers want people who can communicate and co-operate with one another as well as solve problems on their own. They need people who can explain things as well as do them. Above all they need people who can communicate in more than one language. Moreover it is perhaps slowly being recognised that intelligent decisions about the future cannot be made, whether in politics or in industry, without some understanding of how we got to the position we are in, how the past is related to the present and future. The more truly we are parts of Europe the broader this understanding will have to be. Thus history, literature and the history of ideas will gradually have to be let into the concept of the useful. The National Curriculum, mandatory for all maintained schools and in some form voluntarily adopted by almost all independent schools will in the end contain the elements of a liberal or humane as well as a technological education. Reading, writing and thinking historically are there, to be taught to all children, and so are modern languages.

There is, however, a bleak consequence of the new market-led concept of education and that is the inescapable fact that in the market-place some are losers. Some schools, we are told, will simply turn out to be too bad, and will either have to improve or close. But what if such a 'bad' school fails to come up with the proper examination results because it has a lot of 'bad' pupils who cannot pass examinations? What will happen to such pupils in the future? We are already told that schools may 'exempt' certain pupils from the National Curriculum tests. There is a real danger that such pupils may also be 'exempted' from the national curriculum itself. Moreover if a school, or its teachers, are to be judged efficient by the percentage of children entered for tests who pass, there will be a strong temptation to 'exempt' as many potential failures as possible, in order to make the results look good. This is a moral issue which brings us back at last to the idea of equality.

Since 1944 and until the 1980s it had been a matter of genuine consensus that everyone is entitled to the best, or, if they cannot get the best they are entitled to a *chance* of it. Thus in the case of education, a child had a right to be educated, and there was a real commitment to making that education as good as possible. In the health service, though what one got depended inevitably on where one lived, in areas with good hospitals it was a matter of pride that everyone could get the best possible service. The welfare state, though it did not always work, was thus founded as I have already suggested on the concept of equality. The revolution of the 1980s cannot be presented too starkly. Consensus has become in general despised; and consensus with regard to welfare is despised more than any other. The word 'wet' was hijacked to describe those who clung to the ideal of equality, and who found it hard to stomach the 'safety net' for the helpless as a true alternative.

In the market the underdog does not have his day. There is no place for him. So, educationally, there is no place for the dim, the disadvantaged, the disabled, or the slow. We may be sorry for them and perhaps at Christmas give a little to a charity that helps them. But they are no longer entitled to the best. In the 1981 Education Act, as I have argued, there was an implicit assumption of equal entitlement to education within a global concept of meeting educational needs. Now, though education is to be vocational in order to meet the needs of society, the notion of a pupil's needs has disappeared. For that would entail that in some cases more had to be spent on those whose needs were greatest; and this could never in any circumstances be cost-effective. The handicapped as a group cannot, or not in any obvious sense, as a group be educated efficiently if this is measured in terms of a result valuable to industry for the least possible cost. (There is a different argument, to the effect that educating the disabled for independent living and, where possible, employment, is more cost-effective than not educating them and having to maintain them all their lives. But this argument has never as far as I know found much favour, for it involves spending money first, and saving later.)

If choices are left to parents, only those parents with handicapped children of their own will choose a school which makes good provision for children with special needs. Most parents will continue to choose schools with good test scores and then good A level results. In principle these schools might be the same schools; but when funds are low, and so, within a school, something has to be sacrificed, it will inevitably be the special needs provision that will suffer, especially now that schools manage their own budgets. Thus the position of children with special needs will revert to what it was in the 1960s: they will hardly be thought worth educating. No one will be prepared to spend money on them; little research will be initiated into new innovatory ways of teaching them. The great step forward of placing them under the auspices of the DES will have been wasted. The safety net, whatever form it takes is no substitute for entitlement to education. Neither is the concept of 'caring'. The disabled and disadvantaged do not need 'care'; they need education on a basis of *equal rights*.

Thus I would argue that the idea of equality as an educational ideal must be reinstated in a different form. But my argument does not rest solely on the case of the disabled. We have, very properly, been told by Government that we must increase the numbers of those who stay on at school and proceed to further or higher education. This is an essential aim whether we think of education as primarily vocational or as useful in the wider sense for which I have argued. But it cannot be achieved as long as we set up a series of obstacles in the path of people at school, such as to deter or defeat them. Children tend to think of school as a kind of puissance competition, with the last, vast wall represented by A levels, examinations regarded with awe or simply refused by a vast majority of school children. If we are to increase the number of people going on to higher education, we need as a matter of urgency to abolish A levels. In their place we need a whole series of graded tests, up to the highest standard we can devise, both practical and written in every subject. These tests could serve, in the early stages of school, to test the National Curriculum. But unlike the tests currently envisaged, they would not be taken by groups of children of the same age. They would be taken by anyone, child or adult, when he was ready. In this way both the high and the low flyers would be involved in the same system of examinations. Everyone would leave school with some test success (even if it were only grade 1 practical reading or grade 2 practical car maintenance), and institutions of higher and further education would have a profile of the candidate, showing what he could do. I have no doubt that devising these graded tests would be difficult. But it has already been done in modern languages and some of the sciences as well as music. I believe that with goodwill the system could be extended. And if it were, it seems to me that, beyond doubt, everyone would be better served, as the goal of having pupils aged between 16 and 21 in education would be achieved.

Moreover it would be a *practical* triumph for the idea of equality. I am not arguing that equality should be the only educational ideal; nor that, as our ideal, it is compatible with *all* the other things we want and need from education. But we are becoming, I believe, more accustomed to the notion that we may quite sincerely embrace more than one ideal, and in order to get our policies right, in education and other fields, we have a struggle not to forget any of the things we think worth pursuing, however hard a compromise may be.

Let me quote Noel Annan's book *Our Age* (1990, p. 361). Writing of the twentieth century he says

Like Faust, Our Age discovered that *Zwei Seelen wohnen ach! in meiner Brust*. The first soul, the soul of justice, wanted more children to stay on and work in the sixth form, far more to enter higher education, wanted the disparities between the public school pupils and the children who before the war left school at fourteen to be diminished, wanted them to be taught about things that make life worth living . . . music, literature and art. This was the soul that, analysing statistics, was shocked to see how the scales were weighted against the poor and later the blacks. The other soul, the soul of excellence, wanted the standards of entry to universities raised, and sixth-form studies to multiply but remain as rigorous as ever. This soul dreamed of a society

where merit replaced privilege, longed for boys and girls to study whatever subject stirred their imagination, and admired the high standards
achieved by early specialisation. In all the reports on education ...
in all the sapient articles ... you can see the two souls wrestling for
mastery. The very documents that called for the expansion of education
upheld principles that curtailed it.

It is, in my opinion, our duty as educationalists, to find a way to marry the
ideal of equality of entitlement with that of cost-effectiveness. This is partly
a political task; but, more, it is a task for which the teaching profession
itself, along with the universities and polytechnics, must now give their
formidable and foreseeing minds.

16

SPECIAL EDUCATION FOR THE MILDLY RETARDED—IS MUCH OF IT JUSTIFIABLE?

Lloyd M. Dunn

Source: *Exceptional Children* 35 (1968): 5–22.

A preface

In lieu of an abstract to this article, I would like to preface it by saying this is my swan song for now—as I leave special education and this country for probably the next two years. I have been honored to be a past president of The Council for Exceptional Children. I have loyally supported and promoted special classes for the educable mentally retarded for most of the last 20 years, but with growing disaffection. In my view, much of our past and present practices are morally and educationally wrong. We have been living at the mercy of general educators who have referred their problem children to us. And we have been generally ill prepared and ineffective in educating these children. Let us stop being pressured into continuing and expanding a special education program that we know now to be undesirable for many of the children we are dedicated to serve.

A better education than special class placement is needed for socioculturally deprived children with mild learning problems who have been labeled educable mentally retarded. Over the years, the status of these pupils who come from poverty, broken and inadequate homes, and low status ethnic groups has been a checkered one. In the early days, these children were simply excluded from school. Then, as Hollingworth (1923) pointed out, with the advent of compulsory attendance laws, the schools and these children "were forced into a reluctant mutual recognition of each other." This resulted in the establishment of self contained special schools and classes as a method of transferring these "misfits" out of the regular grades. This practice continues to this day and, unless counterforces are set in motion now, it will probably become even more prevalent in the immediate future due in large measure to increased racial integration and militant teacher organizations. For example, a local affiliate of the National Education Association demanded of a local school board recently that more special classes be provided for disruptive and slow learning children (Nashville *Tennessean*, December 18, 1967).

The number of special day classes for the retarded has been increasing by leaps and bounds. The most recent 1967–1968 statistics compiled by the US Office of Education now indicate that there are approximately 32,000 teachers of the retarded employed by local school systems—over one-third of all special educators in the nation. In my best judgment, about 60 to 80 percent of the pupils taught by these teachers are children from low status backgrounds—including Afro-Americans, American Indians, Mexicans, and Puerto Rican Americans; those from nonstandard English speaking, broken, disorganized, and inadequate homes; and children from other nonmiddle class environments. This expensive proliferation of self contained special schools and classes raises serious educational and civil rights issues which must be squarely faced. It is my thesis that we must stop labeling these deprived children as mentally retarded. Furthermore we must stop segregating them by placing them into our allegedly special programs.

The purpose of this article is twofold: first, to provide reasons for taking the position that a large proportion of this so called special education in its present form is obsolete and unjustifiable from the point of view of the pupils so placed; and second, to outline a blueprint for changing this major segment of education for exceptional children to make it more acceptable. We are not arguing that we do away with our special education programs for the moderately and severely retarded, for other types of more handicapped children, or for the multiply handicapped. The emphasis is on doing something better for slow learning children who live in slum conditions, although much of what is said should also have relevance for those children we are labeling emotionally disturbed, perceptually impaired, brain injured, and learning disordered. Furthermore, the emphasis of the article is on children, in that no attempt is made to suggest an adequate high school environment for adolescents still functioning as slow learners.

Reasons for change

Regular teachers and administrators have sincerely felt they were doing these pupils a favor by removing them from the pressures of an unrealistic and inappropriate program of studies. Special educators have also fully believed that the children involved would make greater progress in special schools and classes. However, the overwhelming evidence is that our present and past practices have their major justification in removing pressures on regular teachers and pupils, at the expense of the socioculturally deprived slow learning pupils themselves. Some major arguments for this position are outlined below.

Homogeneous grouping

Homogeneous groupings tend to work to the disadvantage of the slow learners and underprivileged. Apparently such pupils learn much from being in the same class with children from white middle class homes. Also, teachers seem to concentrate on the slower children, to bring them up to standard. This principle was dramatically applied in the Judge J. Skelly Wright decision in the District of Columbia concerning the track system. Judge Wright ordered that tracks be abolished, contending they discriminated against the racially and/or economically disadvantaged and therefore were in violation of the Fifth Amendment of the Constitution of the United States. One may object to the Judge's making educational decisions based on legal considerations. However, Passow (1967), upon the completion of a study of the same school system, reached the same conclusion concerning tracking. The recent national study by Coleman *et al.* (1966), provides supporting evidence in finding that academically disadvantaged Negro children in racially segregated schools made less progress than those of comparable ability in integrated schools. Furthermore, racial integration appeared to deter school progress very little for Caucasian and more academically able students.

What are the implications of Judge Wright's rulings for special education? Clearly special schools and classes are a form of homogeneous grouping and tracking. This fact was demonstrated in September, 1967, when the District of Columbia (as a result of the Wright decision) abolished Track 5, into which had been routed the slowest learning pupils in the District of Columbia schools. These pupils and their teachers were returned to the regular classrooms. Complaints followed from the regular teachers that these children were taking an inordinate amount of their time. A few parents observed that their slow learning children were frustrated by the more academic program and were rejected by the other students. Thus, there are efforts afoot to develop a special education program in D.C. which cannot be labeled a track. Self contained special classes will probably not be tolerated under the present court ruling but perhaps itinerant and resource room programs would be. What if the Supreme Court ruled against tracks, and all self contained special classes across the nation which serve primarily ethnically and/or economically disadvantaged children were forced to close down? Make no mistake—this could happen! If I were a Negro from the slums or a disadvantaged parent who had heard of the Judge Wright decision and knew what I know now about special classes for the educable mentally retarded, other things being equal, I would then go to court before allowing the schools to label my child as "mentally retarded" and place him in a "self contained special school or class." Thus there is the real possibility that additional court actions will be forthcoming.[1]

Efficacy studies

The findings of studies on the efficacy of special classes for the educable mentally retarded constitute another argument for change. These results are well known (Kirk, 1964) and suggest consistently that retarded pupils make as much or more progress in the regular grades as they do in special education. Recent studies such as those by Hoelke (1966) and Smith and Kennedy (1967) continue to provide similar evidence. Johnson (1962) has summarized the situation well:

> It is indeed paradoxical that mentally handicapped children having teachers especially trained, having more money (per capita) spent on their education, and being designed to provide for their unique needs, should be accomplishing the objectives of their education at the same or at a lower level than similar mentally handicapped children who have not had these advantages and have been forced to remain in the regular grades.
>
> [p. 66]

Efficacy studies on special day classes for other mildly handicapped children, including the emotionally handicapped, reveal the same results. For example, Rubin, Senison, and Betwee (1966) found that disturbed children did as well in the regular grades as in special classes, concluding that there is little or no evidence that special class programing is generally beneficial to emotionally disturbed children as a specific method of intervention and correction. Evidence such as this is another reason to find better ways of serving children with mild learning disorders than placing them in self contained special schools and classes.

Labeling processes

Our past and present diagnostic procedures comprise another reason for change. These procedures have probably been doing more harm than good in that they have resulted in disability labels and in that they have grouped children homogeneously in school on the basis of these labels. Generally, these diagnostic practices have been conducted by one of two procedures. In rare cases, the workup has been provided by a multidisciplinary team, usually consisting of physicians, social workers, psychologists, speech and hearing specialists, and occasionally educators. The avowed goal of this approach has been to look at the complete child, but the outcome has been merely to label him mentally retarded, perceptually impaired, emotionally disturbed, minimally brain injured, or some other such term depending on the predispositions, idiosyncracies, and backgrounds of the team members. Too, the team usually has looked for causation, and diagnosis tends to stop when something has been found wrong with the child, when the why has either been found or conjectured, and when some justification has been found for recommending placement in a special education class.

In the second and more common case, the assessment of educational potential has been left to the school psychologist who generally administers— in an hour or so—a psychometric battery, at best consisting of individual tests of intelligence, achievement, and social and personal adjustment. Again the purpose has been to find out what is wrong with the child in order to label him and thus make him eligible for special education services. In large measure this has resulted in digging the educational graves of many racially and/or economically disadvantaged children by using a WISC or Binet IQ score to justify the label "mentally retarded." This term then becomes a destructive, self fulfilling prophecy.

What is the evidence against the continued use of these diagnostic practices and disability labels?

First, we must examine the effects of these disability labels on the attitudes and expectancies of teachers. Here we can extrapolate from studies by Rosenthal and Jacobson (1966) who set out to determine whether or not the expectancies of teachers influenced pupil progress. Working with elementary school teachers across the first six grades, they obtained pretest measures on pupils by using intelligence and achievement tests. A sample of pupils was randomly drawn and labeled "rapid learners" with hidden potential. Teachers were told that these children would show unusual intellectual gains and school progress during the year. All pupils were retested late in the school year. Not all differences were statistically significant, but the gains of the children who had been arbitrarily labeled rapid learners were generally significantly greater than those of the other pupils, with especially dramatic changes in the first and second grades. To extrapolate from this study, we must expect that labeling a child "handicapped" reduces the teacher's expectancy for him to succeed.

Second, we must examine the effects of these disability labels on the pupils themselves. Certainly none of these labels are badges of distinction. Separating a child from other children in his neighborhood—or removing him from the regular classroom for therapy or special class placement— probably has a serious debilitating effect upon his self image. Here again our research is limited but supportive of this contention. Goffman (1961) has described the stripping and mortification process that takes place when an individual is placed in a residential facility. Meyerowitz (1965) demonstrated that a group of educable mentally retarded pupils increased in feelings of self derogation after one year in special classes. More recent results indicate that special class placement, instead of helping such a pupil adjust to his neighborhood peers, actually hinders him (Meyerowitz, 1967). While much more research is needed, we cannot ignore the evidence that removing a handicapped child from the regular grades for special education probably contributes significantly to his feelings of inferiority and problems of acceptance.

Improvements in general education

Another reason self contained special classes are less justifiable today than in the past is that regular school programs are now better able to deal with individual differences in pupils. No longer is the choice just between a self contained special class and a self contained regular elementary classroom. Although the impact of the American Revolution in Education is just beginning to be felt and is still more an ideal than a reality, special education should begin moving now to fit into a changing general education program and to assist in achieving the program's goals. Because of increased support at the local, state, and federal levels, four powerful forces are at work.

Changes in school organization

In place of self contained regular classrooms, there is increasingly more team teaching, ungraded primary departments, and flexible groupings. Radical departures in school organization are projected—educational parks in place of neighborhood schools, metropolitan school districts cutting across our inner cities and wealthy suburbs, and, perhaps most revolutionary of all, competing public school systems. Furthermore, and of great significance to those of us who have focused our careers on slow learning children, public kindergartens and nurseries are becoming more available for children of the poor.

Curricular changes

Instead of the standard diet of Look and Say readers, many new and exciting options for teaching reading are evolving. Contemporary mathematics programs teach in the primary grades concepts formerly reserved for high school. More programed textbooks and other materials are finding their way into the classroom. Ingenious procedures, such as those by Bereiter and Engelmann (1966), are being developed to teach oral language and reasoning to preschool disadvantaged children.

Changes in professional public school personnel

More ancillary personnel are now employed by the schools—i.e., psychologists, guidance workers, physical educators, remedial educators, teacher

266

aides, and technicians. Furthermore, some teachers are functioning in different ways, serving as teacher coordinators, or cluster teachers who provide released time for other teachers to prepare lessons, etc. Too, regular classroom teachers are increasingly better trained to deal with individual differences—although much still remains to be done.

Hardware changes

Computerized teaching, teaching machines, feedback typewriters, ETV, videotapes, and other materials are making autoinstruction possible, as never before.

We must ask what the implications of this American Revolution in Education are for special educators. Mackie (1967), formerly of the US Office of Education, addressed herself to the question: "Is the modern school changing sufficiently to provide [adequate services in general education] for large numbers of pupils who have functional mental retardation due to environmental factors [p. 5]?" In her view, hundreds—perhaps even thousands—of so called retarded pupils may make satisfactory progress in schools with diversified programs of instruction and thus will never need placement in self contained special classes. With earlier, better, and more flexible regular school programs many of the children should not need to be relegated to the type of special education we have so often provided.

In my view, the above four reasons for change are cogent ones. Much of special education for the mildly retarded is becoming obsolete. Never in our history has there been a greater urgency to take stock and to search out new roles for a large number of today's special educators.

A blueprint for change

Two major suggestions which constitute my attempt at a blueprint for change are developed below. First, a fairly radical departure from conventional methods will be proposed in procedures for diagnosing, placing, and teaching children with mild learning difficulties. Second, a proposal for curriculum revision will be sketched out. These are intended as proposals which should be examined, studied, and tested. What is needed are programs based on scientific evidence of worth and not more of those founded on philosophy, tradition, and expediency.

A thought

There is an important difference between regular educators talking us into trying to remediate or live with the learning difficulties of pupils with which they haven't been able to deal; versus striving to evolve a special education program that is either developmental in nature, wherein we assume responsibility for the total education of more severely handicapped children from an early age, or is supportive in nature, wherein general education would continue to have central responsibility for the vast majority of the children with mild learning disabilities—with us serving as resource teachers in devising effective prescriptions and in tutoring such pupils.

A clinical approach

Existing diagnostic procedures should be replaced by expecting special educators, in large measure, to be responsible for their own diagnostic teaching and their clinical teaching. In this regard, it is suggested that we do away with many existing disability labels and the present practice of grouping children homogeneously by these labels into special classes. Instead, we should try keeping slow learning children more in the mainstream of education, with special educators serving as diagnostic, clinical, remedial, resource room, itinerant and/or team teachers, consultants, and developers of instructional materials and prescriptions for effective teaching.

The accomplishment of the above *modus operandi* will require a revolution in much of special education. A moratorium needs to be placed on the proliferation (if not continuance) of self contained special classes which enroll primarily the ethnically and/or economically disadvantaged children we have been labeling educable mentally retarded. Such pupils should be left in (or returned to) the regular elementary grades until we are "tooled up" to do something better for them.

Prescriptive teaching

In diagnosis one needs to know how much a child can learn, under what circumstances, and with what materials. To accomplish this, there are three administrative procedures possible. One would be for each large school system—or two or more small districts—to establish a "Special Education Diagnostic and Prescription Generating Center." Pupils with school learning problems would be enrolled in this center on a day and/or boarding school basis for a period of time—probably up to a month and hopefully until a successful prescription for effective teaching had been evolved. The core of the staff would be a variety of master teachers with different specialties— such as in motor development, perceptual training, language development, social and personality development, remedial education, and so forth. Noneducators such as physicians, psychologists, and social workers would be retained in a consultative role, or pupils would be referred out to such paraeducational professionals, as needed. A second procedure, in lieu of such centers with their cadres of educational specialists, would be for one generalist in diagnostic teaching to perform the diagnostic and prescription devising functions on her own. A third and even less desirable procedure would be for one person to combine the roles of prescriptive and clinical teacher which will be presented next. It is suggested that 15 to 20 percent of the most insightful special educators be prepared for and/or assigned to prescriptive teaching. One clear virtue of the center is that a skilled director could coordinate an inservice training program and the staff could learn through, and be stimulated by, one another. In fact, many special educators could rotate through this program.

Under any of these procedures, educators would be responsible for the administration and interpretation of individual and group psychoeducational tests on cognitive development (such as the WISC and Binet), on language development (such as the ITPA), and on social maturity (such as the Vineland Social Maturity Scale). However, these instruments—with the exception of the ITPA which yields a profile of abilities and disabilities—will be of little use except in providing baseline data on the level at which a child is functioning. In place of these psychometric tests which usually yield only global scores, diagnostic educators would need to rely heavily on a combination of the various tools of behavior shapers and clinical teachers. The first step would be to make a study of the child to find what behaviors he has acquired along the dimension being considered. Next, samples of a sequential program would be designed to move him forward from that point. In presenting the program, the utility of different reinforcers, administered under various conditions, would be investigated. Also, the method by which he can best be taught the material should be determined. Different modalities for reaching the child would also be tried. Thus, since the instructional program itself becomes the diagnostic device, this procedure can be called diagnostic teaching. Failures are program and instructor failures, not pupil failures. In large measure, we would be guided by Bruner's dictum (1967) that almost any child can be taught almost anything if it is programed correctly.[2]

This diagnostic procedure is viewed as the best available since it enables us to assess continuously the problem points of the instructional program against the assets of the child. After a successful and appropriate prescription has been devised, it would be communicated to the teachers in the pupil's home school and they would continue the procedure as long as it is necessary and brings results. From time to time, the child may need to return to the center for reappraisal and redirection.

Clearly the above approach to special education diagnosis and treatment is highly clinical and intuitive. In fact, it is analogous to the rural doctor of the past who depended on his insights and a few diagnostic and treatment devices carried in his small, black bag. It may remain with us for some time to come. However, it will be improved upon by more standardized procedures. Perhaps the two most outstanding, pioneering efforts in this regard are now being made by Feuerstein (1968) in Israel, and by Kirk (1966) in the United States. Feuerstein has devised a *Learning Potential Assessment*

Device for determining the degree of modifiability of the behavior of an individual pupil, the level at which he is functioning, the strategies by which he can best learn, and the areas in which he needs to be taught. Also, he is developing a variety of exercises for teaching children with specific learning difficulties. Kirk and his associates have not only given us the ITPA which yields a profile of abilities and disabilities in the psycholinguistic area, but they have also devised exercises for remediating specific psycholinguistic disabilities reflected by particular types of profiles (Kirk, 1966). Both of these scientists are structuring the assessment and remediation procedures to reduce clinical judgment, although it would be undesirable to formalize to too great a degree. Like the country doctor versus modern medicine, special education in the next fifty years will move from clinical intuition to a more precise science of clinical instruction based on diagnostic instruments which yield a profile of abilities and disabilities about a specific facet of behavior and which have incorporated within them measures of a child's ability to learn samples or units of materials at each of the points on the profile. If psychoeducational tests had these two characteristics, they would accomplish essentially the same thing as does the diagnostic approach described above—only under more standardized conditions.

Itinerant and resource room teaching

It is proposed that a second echelon of special educators be itinerant or resource teachers. One or more resource teachers might be available to each sizable school, while an itinerant teacher would serve two or more smaller schools. General educators would refer their children with learning difficulties to these teachers. If possible, the clinical teacher would evolve an effective prescription for remediating the problem. If this is not possible, she would refer the child to the Special Education Diagnostic and Prescription Generating Center or to the more specialized prescriptive teacher who would study the child and work out an appropriate regimen of instruction for him. In either event, the key role of the resource room and itinerant clinical educators would be to develop instructional materials and lessons for implementing the prescription found effective for the child, and to consult and work with the other educators who serve the child. Thus, the job of special educators would be to work as members of the schools' instructional teams and to focus on children with mild to moderate school learning problems. Special educators would be available to all children in trouble (except the severely handicapped) regardless of whether they had, in the past, been labeled educable mentally retarded, minimally brain injured, educationally handicapped, or emotionally disturbed. Children would be regrouped continually throughout the school day. For specific help these children who had a learning problem might need to work with the itinerant or resource room special educator. But, for the remainder of the day, the special educator would probably be more effective in developing specific exercises which could be taught by others in consultation with her. Thus, the special educator would begin to function as a part of, and not apart from, general education. Clearly this proposed approach recognizes that all children have assets and deficits, not all of which are permanent. When a child was having trouble in one or more areas of learning, special educators would be available to devise a successful teaching approach for him and to tutor him when necessary. Perhaps as many as 20 to 35 percent of our present special educators are or could be prepared for this vital role.

Two other observations

First, it is recognized that some of today's special educators—especially of the educable mentally retarded—are not, prepared to serve the functions discussed. These teachers would need to either withdraw from special education or develop the needed competencies. Assuming an open door policy and playing the role of the expert educational diagnostician and the prescriptive and clinical educator would place us in the limelight. Only the best will succeed. But surely this is a responsibility we will not shirk. Our avowed *raison d'être* has been to provide special education for children unable to make adequate progress in the regular grades. More would be lost than gained by assigning less than master teachers from self contained classes to the diagnostic and clinical educator roles. Ainsworth (1959) has already compared the relative effectiveness of the special class versus itinerant special educators of the retarded and found that neither group accomplished much in pupil progress. A virtue of these new roles for special education is that they are high status positions which should appeal to the best and therefore enhance the recruitment of master regular teachers who should be outstanding in these positions after having obtained specialized graduate training in behavior shaping, psychoeducational diagnostics, remedial education, and so forth.

Second, if one accepts these procedures for special education, the need for disability labels is reduced. In their stead we may need to substitute labels which describe the educational intervention needed. We would thus talk of pupils who need special instruction in language or cognitive development, in sensory training, in personality development, in vocational training, and other areas. However, some labels may be needed for administrative reasons. If so, we need to find broad generic terms such as "school learning disorders."

New curricular approaches

Master teachers are at the heart of an effective school program for children with mild to moderate learning difficulties—master teachers skilled at

271

educational diagnosis and creative in designing and carrying out interventions to remediate the problems that exist. But what should they teach? In my view, there has been too great an emphasis in special classes on practical arts and practical academics, to the exclusion of other ingredients. Let us be honest with ourselves. Our courses of study have tended to be watered down regular curriculum. If we are to move from the clinical stage to a science of instruction, we will need a rich array of validated prescriptive programs of instruction at our disposal. To assemble these programs will take time, talent, and money; teams of specialists including creative teachers, curriculum specialists, programers, and theoreticians will be needed to do the job.

What is proposed is a chain of Special Education Curriculum Development Centers across the nation. Perhaps these could best be affiliated with colleges and universities, but could also be attached to state and local school systems. For these centers to be successful, creative educators must be found. Only a few teachers are remarkably able to develop new materials. An analogy is that some people can play music adequately, if not brilliantly, but only a few people can compose it. Therefore, to move special education forward, some 15 to 20 percent of our most creative special educators need to be identified, freed from routine classroom instruction, and placed in a stimulating setting where they can be maximally productive in curriculum development. These creative teachers and their associates would concentrate on developing, field testing, and modifying programs of systematic sequences of exercises for developing specific facets of human endeavor. As never before, funds are now available from the US Office of Education under Titles III and VI of PL 89-10 to embark upon at least one such venture in each state. In fact, Title III was designed to support innovations in education and 15 percent of the funds were earmarked for special education. Furthermore, most of the money is now to be administered through state departments of education which could build these curriculum centers into their state plans.

The first step in establishing specialized programs of study would be to evolve conceptual models upon which to build our treatments. In this regard the creative teachers would need to join with the theoreticians, curriculum specialists, and other behavioral scientists. Even the identification of the broad areas will take time, effort, and thought. Each would require many subdivisions and extensive internal model building. A beginning taxonomy might include the following eight broad areas: (a) environmental modifications, (b) motor development, (c) sensory and perceptual training, (d) cognitive and language development including academic instruction, (e) speech and communication training, (f) connative (or personality) development, (g) social interaction training, and (h) vocational training. (Of course, under cognitive development alone we might evolve a model of intellect with some ninety plus facets such as that of Guilford [1967], and as many training programs.)

In the area of motor development we might, for example, involve creative special and physical educators, occupational and physical therapists, and experts in recreation and physical medicine, while in the area of language development a team of speech and hearing specialists, special educators, psychologists, linguists, and others would need to come together to evolve a conceptual model, to identify the parameters, and to develop the specialized programs of exercises. No attempt is made in this article to do more than provide an overview of the problem and the approach. Conceptualizing the specific working models would be the responsibility of cadres of experts in the various specialties.

Environmental modifications

It would seem futile and rather unrealistic to believe we will be able to remediate the learning difficulties of children from ethnically and/or economically disadvantaged backgrounds when the schools are operating in a vacuum even though top flight special education instructional programs are used. Perhaps, if intensive around the clock and full calendar year instruction were provided beginning at the nursery school level, we might be able to counter appreciably the physiological weaknesses and inadequate home and community conditions of the child. However, the field of education would be enhanced in its chances of success if it became a part of a total ecological approach to improve the environments of these children. Thus special educators need to collaborate with others—social workers, public health officials, and other community specialists. Interventions in this category might include (a) foster home placement, (b) improved community conditions and out of school activities, (c) parent education, (d) public education, and (e) improved cultural exposures. For optimal pupil development, we should see that children are placed in a setting that is both supportive and stimulating. Therefore, we must participate in environmental manipulations and test their efficacy. We have made a slight beginning in measuring the effects of foster home placement and there is evidence that working with parents of the disadvantaged has paid off. The model cities programs would also seem to have promise. But much more human and financial effort must be invested in this area.

Motor development

Initial work has been done with psychomotor training programs by a number of persons including Delacato (1966), Oliver (1958), Cratty (1967), Lillie (1967), and others. But we still need sets of sequential daily activities built around an inclusive model. Under this category, we need to move from the early stages of psychomotor development to the development of fine and large movements required as vocational skills. Programs to develop improved motor skills are important for a variety of children with learning problems. In fact, one could argue that adequate psychomotor skills constitute the first link in the chain of learning.

Sensory and perceptual training

Much of our early efforts in special education consisted of sensory and perceptual training applied to severe handicapping conditions such as blindness, deafness, and mental deficiency. Consequently, we have made a good beginning in outlining programs of instruction in the areas of auditory, visual, and tactual training. Now we must apply our emerging technology to work out the step by step sequence of activities needed for children with mild to moderate learning difficulties. In this regard, visual perceptual training has received growing emphasis, pioneered by Frostig (1964), but auditory perceptual training has been neglected. The latter is more important for school instruction than the visual channel. Much attention needs to be given to this second link in the chain of learning. Children with learning problems need to be systematically taught the perceptual processes: they need to be able to organize and convert bits of input from the various sense modalities into units of awareness which have meaning.

Cognitive and language development including academic instruction

This is the heart of special education for slow learning children. Our business is to facilitate their thinking processes. We should help them not only to acquire and store knowledge, but also to generate and evaluate it. Language development could largely be included under this caption—especially the integrative components—since there is much overlap between the development of oral language and verbal intelligence. However, much of receptive language training might be considered under sensory and perceptual training, while expressive language will be considered in the next topic.

A major fault of our present courses of study is failure to focus on the third link in the chain of learning—that of teaching our children systematically in the areas of cognitive development and concept formation. A major goal of our school program should be to increase the intellectual functioning of children we are now classifying as socioculturally retarded. For such children, perhaps as much as 25 percent of the school day in the early years should be devoted to this topic. Yet the author has not seen one curriculum guide for these children with a major emphasis on cognitive development— which is a sad state of affairs indeed!

Basic psychological research by Guilford (1959) has provided us with a useful model of intellect. However, little is yet known about the trainability of the various cognitive processes. Actually, Thurstone (1948) has contributed the one established set of materials for training primary mental abilities.

274

Thus, much work lies ahead in developing programs of instruction for the training of intellect.

We are seeing more and more sets of programed materials in the academic areas, most of which have been designed for average children. The most exciting examples today are in the computer assisted instruction studies. Our major problem is to determine how these programed exercises need to be modified to be maximally effective for children with specific learning problems. Work will be especially needed in the classical areas of instruction including written language and mathematics. Hopefully, however, regular teachers will handle much of the instruction in science and social studies, while specialists would instruct in such areas as music and the fine arts. This will free special educators to focus on better ways of teaching the basic 3 R's, especially written language.

Speech and communication training

This area has received much attention, particularly from speech correctionists and teachers of the deaf. Corrective techniques for specific speech problems are probably more advanced than for any other area, yet essentially no carefully controlled research has been done on the efficacy of these programs. Speech correctionists have tended to be clinicians, not applied behavioral scientists. They often create the details of their corrective exercises while working with their clients in a one to one relationship. Thus, the programs have often been intuitive. Furthermore, public school speech therapists have been spread very thin, usually working with 75 to 100 children. Many have been convinced that only *they* could be effective in this work. But remarkable changes have recently occurred in the thinking of speech therapists; they are recognizing that total programs of oral language development go far beyond correcting articulation defects. Furthermore, some speech therapists believe they could be more productive in working with only the more severe speech handicaps and devoting much attention to the development and field testing of systematic exercises to stimulate over-all language and to improve articulation, pitch, loudness, quality, duration, and other speech disorders of a mild to moderate nature. These exercises need to be programed to the point at which teachers, technicians, and perhaps teacher aides can use them. Goldman (1968) is now developing such a program of exercises to correct articulation defects. This seems to be a pioneering and heartening first step.

Connative (or personality) development

This emerging area requires careful attention. We must accept the position that much of a person's behavior is shaped by his environment. This applies to all aspects of human thought, including attitudes, beliefs, and mores.

Research oriented clinical psychologists are providing useful information on motivation and personality development and before long we will see reports of research in shaping insights into self, the effects of others on self, and one's effects on others. It is not too early for teams of clinical psychologists, psychiatric social workers, creative special educators (especially for the so called emotionally disturbed), and others to begin developing programs of instruction in this complex field.

Social interaction training

Again we have an emerging area which overlaps considerably with some of those already presented, particularly connative development. Special educators have long recognized that the ability of a handicapped individual to succeed in society depends, in large measure, on his skill to get along with his fellow man. Yet we have done little to develop his social living skills, a complex area of paramount importance. Training programs should be developed to facilitate development in this area of human behavior.

Vocational training

Closely tied to social interaction training is vocational training. Success on the job for persons that we have labeled educable mentally retarded has depended on good independent work habits, reliability, and social skills, rather than on academic skills. Consequently, early and continuing emphasis on developing these traits is necessary. In fact, it is likely to be even more important in the years ahead with fewer job opportunities and increasing family disintegration providing less shelter and support for the so called retarded. Therefore sophisticated programs of instruction are especially needed in this area. Even with our best efforts in this regard, it is likely that our pupils, upon reaching adolescence, will continue to need a variety of vocational services, including trade and technical schools, work study programs, and vocational training.

Another observation

It seems to me to be a red herring to predict that special educators will use these hundreds of specialized instructional programs indiscriminately as cookbooks. Perhaps a few of the poor teachers will. But, the clinical teachers proposed in this article would be too sophisticated and competent to do this. They would use them as points of departure, modifying the lessons so that each child would make optimal progress. Therefore, it seems to me that this library of curriculum materials is necessary to move us from a clinical and intuitive approach to a more scientific basis for special education.

276

An epilogue

The conscience of special educators needs to rub up against morality. In large measure we have been at the mercy of the general education establishment in that we accept problem pupils who have been referred out of the regular grades. In this way, we contribute to the delinquency of the general educations since we remove the pupils that are problems for them and thus reduce their need to deal with individual differences. The *entente* of mutual delusion between general and special education that special class placement will be advantageous to slow learning children of poor parents can no longer be tolerated. We must face the reality—we are asked to take children others cannot teach, and a large percentage of these are from ethnically and/or economically disadvantaged backgrounds. Thus much of special education will continue to be a sham of dreams unless we immerse ourselves into the total environment of our children from inadequate homes and backgrounds and insist on a comprehensive ecological push—with a quality educational program as part of it. This is hardly compatible with our prevalent practice of expediency in which we employ many untrained and less than master teachers to increase the number of special day classes in response to the pressures of waiting lists. Because of these pressures from the school system, we have been guilty of fostering quantity with little regard for quality of special education instruction. Our first responsibility is to have an abiding commitment to the less fortunate children we aim to serve. Our honor, integrity, and honesty should no longer be subverted and rationalized by what we hope and may believe we are doing for these children—hopes and beliefs which have little basis in reality.

Embarking on an American Revolution in Special Education will require strength of purpose. It is recognized that the structure of most, if not all, school programs becomes self perpetuating. Teachers and state and local directors and supervisors of special education have much at stake in terms of their jobs, their security, and their programs which they have built up over the years. But can we keep our self respect and continue to increase the numbers of these self contained special classes for the educable mentally retarded which are of questionable value for many of the children they are intended to serve? As Ray Graham said in his last article in 1960: [p. 4.]

We can look at our accomplishments and be proud of the progress we have made; but satisfaction with the past does not assure progress in the future. New developments, ideas, and facts may show us that our past practices have become out-moded. A growing child cannot remain static—he either grows or dies. We cannot become satisfied with a job one-third done. We have a long way to go before we can rest assured that the desires of the parents and the educational needs of handicapped children are being fulfilled.

[p. 4]

Notes

1 Litigation has now occurred. According to an item in a June 8, 1968, issue of the *Los Angeles Times* received after this article was sent to the printer, the attorneys in the national office for the rights of the indigent filed a suit in behalf of the Mexican-American parents of the Santa Ana Unified School District asking for an injunction against the District's classes for the educable mentally retarded because the psychological examinations required prior to placement are unconstitutional since they have failed to use adequate evaluation techniques for children from different language and cultural backgrounds, and because parents have been denied the right of hearing to refute evidence for placement. Furthermore, the suit seeks to force the district to grant hearings on all children currently in such special classes to allow for the chance to remove the stigma of the label "mentally retarded" from school records of such pupils.
2 By ignoring genetic influences on the behavioral characteristics of children with learning difficulties, we place responsibility on an inadequate society, inadequate parents, unmotivated pupils, and/or in this case inadequate teachers. Taking this extreme environmental approach could result in placing too much blame for failure on the teacher and too much pressure on the child. While we could set our level of aspiration too high, this has hardly been the direction of our error to date in special education of the handicapped. Perhaps the sustained push proposed in this paper may not succeed, but we will not know until we try it. Insightful teachers should be able to determine when the pressures on the pupil and system are too great.

References

Ainsworth, S. H. *An exploratory study of educational, social and emotional factors in the education of mentally retarded children in Georgia public schools.* US Office of Education Cooperative Research Project Report No. 171(6470). Athens, Ga.: University of Georgia, 1959.

Bereiter, C., & Engelmann, S. *Teaching disadvantaged children in the preschool.* Englewood Cliffs, N.J.: Prentice-Hall, 1966.

Bruner, J. S., Olver, R. R., & Greenfield, P. M. *Studies in cognitive growth.* New York: Wiley, 1967.

Coleman, J. S., *et al. Equality of educational opportunity.* Washington, D.C.: USGPO, 1966.

Cratty, P. J. *Developmental sequences of perceptual motor tasks.* Freeport, Long Island, N.Y.: Educational Activities, 1967.

Delacato, C. H. (Ed.) *Neurological organization and reading problems.* Springfield, Ill.: Charles C Thomas, 1966.

Feuerstein, R. *The Learning Potential Assessment Device* Jerusalem, Israel: Haddassa Wizo Canada Child Guidance Clinic and Research Unit, 1968.

Frostig, M., & Horne, D. *The Frostig program for the development of visual perception.* Chicago: Follett, 1964.

Graham, R. Special education for the sixties. *Illinois Educational Association Study Unit*, 1960, **23**, 1–4.

Goffman, E. *Asylums: Essays on the social situation of mental patients and other inmates.* Garden City, N.Y.: Anchor, 1961.

Goldman, R. *The phonemic-visual-oral association technique for modifying articulation disorders in young children.* Nashville, Tenn.: Bill Wilkerson Hearing and Speech Center, 1968.

Guilford, J. P. *The nature of human intelligence.* New York: McGraw-Hill, 1967.

Hoelke, G. M. *Effectiveness of special class placement for educable mentally retarded children.* Lincoln, Neb.: University of Nebraska, 1966.

Hollingworth, L. S. *The psychology of subnormal children.* New York: Macmillan, 1923.

Johnson, G. O. Special education for mentally handicapped—a paradox. *Exceptional Children*, 1962, **19**, 62–69.

Kirk, S. A. Research in education. In H. A. Stevens & R. Heber (Eds.), *Mental retardation.* Chicago, Ill.: University of Chicago Press, 1964.

Kirk, S. A. *The diagnosis and remediation of psycholinguistic disabilities.* Urbana, Ill.: University of Illinois Press, 1966.

Lillie, D. L. The development of motor proficiency of educable mentally retarded children. *Education and Training of the Mentally Retarded*, 1967, **2**, 29–32.

Mackie, R. P. *Functional handicaps among school children due to cultural or economic deprivation.* Paper presented at the First Congress of the International Association for the Scientific Study of Mental Deficiency, Montpellier, France, September, 1967.

Meyerowitz, J. H. Family background of educable mentally retarded children. In H. Goldstein, J. W. Moss & L. J. Jordan. *The efficacy of special education training on the development of mentally retarded children.* Urbana, Ill.: University of Illinois Institute for Research on Exceptional Children, 1965. Pp. 152–182.

Meyerowitz, J. H. Peer groups and special classes. *Mental Retardation*, 1967, **5**, 23–26.

Oliver, J. N. The effects of physical conditioning exercises and activities on the mental characteristics of educationally sub-normal boys. *British Journal of Educational Psychology*, 1958, **28**, 155–165.

Passow, A. H. *A summary of findings and recommendations of a study* of *the Washington, D.C. schools.* New York: Teachers College, Columbia University, 1967.

Rosenthal, R., & Jacobson, L. Teachers' expectancies: Determinants of pupils' IQ gains. *Psychological Reports*, 1966, **19**, 115–118.

Rubin, E. Z., Senison, C. B., & Betwee, M. C. *Emotionally handicapped children in the elementary school.* Detroit: Wayne State University Press, 1966.

Smith, H. W., & Kennedy, W. A. Effects of three educational programs on mentally retarded children. *Perceptual and Motor Skills*, 1967, **24**, 174.

Thurstone, T. G. *Learning to think series.* Chicago, Ill.: Science Research Associates, 1948.

Wright, Judge J. S. *Hobson vs Hansen: U. S. Court of Appeals decision on the District of Columbia's track system. Civil Action No. 82–66.* Washington, D. C.: US Court of Appeals, 1967.

17

SPECIAL EDUCATION – THEORY AND THEORY TALK

Garry Thomas and Andrew Loxley

Source: G. Thomas and A. Loxley, *Deconstructing Special Education and Constructing Inclusion*, Buckingham: Open University Press, 2001, pp. 1–20.

> ... since we can never know for certain, there can be no authority here for any claim to authority, for conceit over our knowledge, or for smugness.
>
> Karl Popper (*Conjectures and Refutations*)

In this book we seek to look behind special education[1] to its intellectual foundations. We look at the growth of special education, at its many faces, at its reconstruction of itself in different forms, and at its response to a changing political mood. Most important, though, and running through each part of this inquiry, is an examination of the *knowledge* of special education. Faith in certain kinds of knowledge provides the credence, the believability behind special education's status. Trust in this knowledge secures special education's reputation as a rational, sensible way of educating a portion of the population. But if one takes a questioning disposition to this knowledge, serious challenges to the legitimacy of special education begin to emerge.

Many excellent critiques have located the existence, growth and status of special education not so much in these knowledge-related matters, but in professional, structural and institutional interests at play in society. We do not deny the significance of these analyses, indeed we draw upon them extensively in this book. We believe, however, that to assume that they can proffer anything like a full analysis of the growth of special education is to ignore, or at least to downplay, the impact of ways in which knowledge is arrived at, disseminated and used. At the risk of sounding pompous, it is these *epistemic* features in the growth of special education to which we give special attention in this book. There has often existed over twentieth-century discourse about special education a presupposition almost of rock-solid knowledge. On this solid knowledge the edifices of special education could be confidently built. The very words which have been used to discuss not just special education but more importantly its key concepts – words like 'intelligence' – have been taken to have reasonably straightforward meanings, the *logoi* of Derrida (1978). But, as Derrida points out, there is no ordinary, uncontaminated language. If this is so – and there is a clear case for it to be especially so in the words surrounding the tenuous human 'sciences' from which educators have borrowed liberally – the argument must be strong for a close scrutiny of language as a source of knowledge.

Our focus, then, is the knowledge held and promulgated by special educators and the means by which this knowledge is secured. There have been assumptions in the empirical and rational arguments behind special education almost of a kind of special, privileged knowledge. In this book, this kind of knowledge – or at least assumptions that it can exist – will be critically examined.

Critiques

But before examining these epistemic features, it is important first to set such attention within the context of other critical examinations of special education, for there have been many of these. We need to outline these in order to make clear our points of agreement, and more importantly, disagreement, with them. For much critique which gives rise to an inclusionary mindset emerges from committed theoretical positions which, it seems to us, share a need for scrutiny: the topic of inclusion is hardly uncontroversial (see for example, Dorn *et al.* 1996; Croll and Moses 1998; Hornby 1999) and if fairness is being aimed for, the epistemological premises underpinning these committed inclusionary positions need as much deconstructing as those which preceded them.

What then are these viewpoints and critiques? Slee (1998) provides an excellent summary of the different perspectives from which disability and special education have been viewed and, in certain cases, critiqued. Turning his analysis around notions of disability and basing it on earlier work by Riddell (1996) and Fulcher (1989), he suggests that these perspectives comprise the following:

1   Essentialist perspectives – which locate children's differences and disabilities unproblematically in their individual pathology. This has sometimes been called a *deficit* or *medical* approach.
2   Social constructionist perspectives – which interpret and present disability as a socially contrived construct 'deployed against minorities enforcing social marginalisation' (Slee 1998: 128).
3   Materialist perspectives – which see disability as a form of exclusion created and maintained by the economic system. It is worth noting here

that Abberley (1987), an exponent of this view, has said that '. . . the main and consistent beneficiary [of exclusion] must be identified as the present social order, or more accurately, capitalism'. These are, then, Marxist analyses (though are not offered explicitly by Slee as such).

4   Postmodern perspectives – which reject the theoretical explanations offered by materialist accounts, seeing the experiences of excluded children and adults as discontinuous and ungroupable. Though Slee does not give examples, it is worth noting that Young (1990) suggests that the mere existence of excluded groups forces us to categorize – and the categories encourage a particular mindset about a group, while in reality the 'groups' in question are 'cross-cutting, fluid and shifting' (Young 1990: 45). Meekosha and Jacubowicz (1996) make a similar point: there is no discrete class of people who are disabled.

5   Disability movement perspectives – which, Slee says, 'devote less attention to the production of a coherent theoretical explication of disability in their eclectic quest for social change . . .' (Slee 1998: 129).

Others have taken different angles on the conceptualization surrounding disability and special education. Söder's (1989) stance is interesting since it is critical of some of the received wisdom of critics themselves. He outlines four distinct approaches:

1   The medical/clinical perspective (similar to Slee's first perspective).
2   The epidemiological approach – which sees disability as an abnormality but seeks to account for this abnormality with a range of social and other explanations.
3   The adaptability approach – wherein disability arises out of some maladaptation of the individual to the environment, due perhaps to the expectations imposed by people in that environment.
4   The social constructionist approach – in which disabilities are constructed on the basis of interpretations made because of social values and beliefs.

Söder sees much of the critical analysis surrounding this field as being off the mark. He suggests that there is an 'epistemological error' in the assumptions behind the fourth of the categories of analysis he identifies, namely the social constructionist approach, which has been at the root of much of the progressive thinking behind moves to inclusion. He suggests that this analysis rests in a hope that 'structure' can be changed – that the meanings ascribed to structures can be altered by goodwill. He calls this kind of thinking 'voluntarism' and puts it down to researchers trying to be reformers, change agents and politicians.

Many disagree with Söder's position. They would challenge his view that there is an epistemological error at the base of this, and – in direct contradiction to his point that researchers are trying to be politicians – take the position that researchers' engagement with the political and social in this area is an imperative. Their view is, in other words, that critique and analysis cannot disengage itself from social and political issues (see, for example, Gitlin *et al.* 1989; Armstrong *et al.* 1998). It is from this perspective that analysis has taken into account what Tomlinson (1987) has called the 'social, economic and political structures of a society'. She locates her own critique of special education specifically in *critical theory*, which she finds useful 'in interpreting events and explanations in the expanding area of special educational needs' (Tomlinson 1987: 33). It is worth quoting her at some length since she summarizes her position and the position of many critics of special education with great clarity:

> Critical theorists have suggested that the answers to questions about 'why children fail' might lie as much in the social, economic and political structures of a society as in anything intrinsic to children or 'lacking' in a child. From a critical theorist's viewpoint, it becomes easier to question the deficit model of children, which assumes that negative properties intrinsic to children – low IQ, disability, inability – are wholly responsible for his or her educational failure. It becomes easier to examine the social processes by which 'achievement' is defined. Who, for example, decides what achievement is in a society where the highest achievers are almost always white, upper- or middle-class males? Why does being a poor reader *and* working class seem to have much more serious and long-term social consequences than being a poor reader and upper or middle class?
>
> (Tomlinson 1987: 34)

Not the first, Tomlinson is one of the most articulate advocates of this theoretical position and she has done as much as anyone to drive debate and analysis about special education forward. As she notes, her work has paid particular attention to the institutional and professional[2] interests at play in the growth of special education: 'I have been concerned in my work in special education to use critical theories to question the part professionals and practitioners play in the social and cultural reproduction of a particular class in our society' (Tomlinson 1987: 39).

The resilience of special education

Such critical commentary is well developed and has since the mid-1970s helped to lay the platform for many notionally progressive changes in legislation across the world. The United States was among the pioneers in this legislative sea-change with its Public Law 94–142, which mandated public education for students with disabilities in 'the least restrictive environment' – or, in other words, the most natural, mainstream or integrated environment.

Despite the legislation, though, and despite the critical commentaries, there has, as the analysis of Skrtic (1991) has pointed out, continued to be a re-emergence of the kind of thinking which leads to ever-newer forms of segregative and exclusionary practice. As Skrtic (1991: 150) puts it, 'the new practices associated with . . . mainstreaming simply reproduced the special education problems of the 1960s in the 1980s'. The exclusionary practices are still there: there is still labelling; exclusion shows no sign of declining (see Parsons 1999).

The critical theorists might see the resilience of special education as a clear demonstration of education's inevitable *reproduction* of the existing social system. As Tomlinson (1987: 34) puts it: 'critical theorists have noted the way that education often helps to *reproduce* the children of blacks, minorities, working-class – and the handicapped – into inferior, powerless, social positions'. The process being referred to by Tomlinson is exactly the same as that referred to (only half-flippantly) by the French social philosopher Simone Weil in *The Need for Roots* (1949): 'Culture is an instrument wielded by professors to manufacture professors, who when their turn comes will manufacture professors.' Educational culture, at whatever level, is predisposed to remake itself and the society from which it draws. Pierre Bourdieu, the French sociologist, has done most to explicate this process of reproduction (see for example Bourdieu and Passeron 1977; Bourdieu 1984), pointing to the role of 'cultural capital' in this.[3]

Some observers of the social and political scene subscribe to a distinction in the management of human affairs between what is popularly known as 'conspiracy theory' versus 'cock-up' (McLynn 1999). Those who do subscribe to such distinctions will notice something of the conspiracy theory in analysis of special education which rests in critical theory. For the existence of special education is seen through this particular theoretical template in terms of maintenance and reproduction of the existing social order for the benefit of those who already possess power and 'cultural capital'. There is an assumption of intentionality in the system.[4] The system is assumed to be *about* the reproduction of the social order. There could be said to be strong and weak versions of intentionality here, and one doesn't have to subscribe to a strong version of intentionality in order to assent to Archer's (1979) analysis of the development of educational systems as related to the interests of those who manage the system.

Clearly, the interests at play in the education system have contributed to the manufacture and maintenance of segregation. But there are other more prosaic ways of interpreting the perpetually re-emerging exclusionary practices of education – ways which avoid any kind of intentionality. A good example of an approach which might be considered less conspiracy-orientated is the analysis of Skrtic (1991), which locates the phenomenon more in *functionalism*. If functionalism, which 'presupposes that social reality is objective, inherently orderly, and rational and thus that social problems are pathological' (Skrtic 1991: 152), is consciously or unconsciously adhered to by planners and practitioners, it will lead to a particular mindset about the way to deal with education's problems, namely the children who don't fit or won't learn. He continues:

> . . . when industrialization and compulsory school attendance converged to produce large numbers of students who were difficult to teach in traditional classrooms, the problem of school failure was reframed as two interrelated problems – inefficient organizations and defective students.
>
> (Skrtic 1991: 152)

He is surely right about the framing of school failure in notions of bad schools or bad children and his analysis is borne out by the contemporary discourse of education and special education, with its discussion of effective (and, by implication, ineffective) schools. He goes further to suggest that it is what he calls the 'machine bureaucracy' of schools, itself a product of functionalism, which is responsible for the re-emergence of old thinking and old practice in new clothes – even when schools are notionally moving to inclusion. Instead of achieving the 'adhocracy' which he looks forward to, schools retain (presumably because they are tacitly cleaving to the tenets of functionalism) the organizational structure which perpetuates exclusionary responses to children who are difficult to teach. We do not demur from this analysis in any way; indeed, we find it helpful and draw on it, especially in Chapter 2 of this book.

Theories of special education – and theoretical critique: reasons to be different

However, we try to cast the net even wider and to avoid theoretical analysis.[5] If 'atheoretical analysis' in education is a contradiction in terms to some, it is anathema to others, who see any such analysis typifying a philistine and anti-intellectual stance. Some commentators – such as Suppes (1974) and Garrison (1988) – have even claimed that atheoretical research in education is impossible. Non-theoretical research seems taboo for a large part of the research community in education.

But one of the problems, as we see it, of analysis in education is that it is discipline-orientated: it tends to follow the theoretical and methodological furrows of disciplinary preference – of sociology, psychology, history, or whatever. The trouble is that in education, and in special education in particular, foci for analysis do not usually lend themselves to the analytical instruments borrowed from the major disciplines. We take up this theme in the next chapter, borrowing from the neurologist-turned-anthropologist Oliver Sacks who argues that research and diagnostic instruments fashioned for one set of questions are inappropriate for another set. Back in the 1960s Barker (1968), in arguing for a more 'ecological psychology', made the same point. He highlighted the need for recognition of different forms of enquiry and analysis by giving an example of alternative, but equally valid, explanations for the same event. He asks us to imagine the movement of a train of wheat across the Kansas plains. How is this movement to be explained? An economist will explain it in one way, while an engineer will explain it in another. 'Both the laws of economics and the laws of engineering are true; both operate in predictable ways on the train' (Barker 1968: 12).

The train analogy is a nice one, for it points to the diverse number of analytical frames which can be lain over any phenomenon. The crude questions asked about an event (such as 'how is the train's movement to be explained?') disguise the multiplicity of levels at which analytical purchase can be made. It may be easy to ask certain questions, yet those questions may be wholly inappropriate for the task in hand.

Theory-shaped critique

Life is monstrous, infinite, illogical, abrupt and poignant; a work of art, in comparison, is neat, finite, self-contained, rational, flowing and emasculate.

Robert Louis Stevenson (Stevenson 1999: 85)

For the words 'a work of art' in Stevenson's presciently postmodern statement, one could easily substitute the words 'theory' or 'research'. Art, theory and research are all examples of artifice: the attempt to draw a narrative, a theme out of the 'monstrousness' and 'abruptness' of life. The theory of our educational scholarship, and this applies especially to special education, seeks order. It is measured for its effectiveness by the extent to which it is logical, clear, tidy, parsimonious, rational, consistent. The disciplines in which theory is framed encourage attempts at explanation in a social world which is singularly lacking in order or intentionality. As Oakeshott (1967) puts it, the rational mind behind the attempt to forge theory has

> ... none of that *negative capability* [his emphasis] ... the power of accepting the mysteries and uncertainties of experience without any irritable search for order and distinctness, only the capability of subjugating experience ... [The rationalist has] no aptitude for that close and detailed appreciation of what actually presents itself.
>
> (Oakeshott 1967: 2)

It is a freedom to make a 'close and detailed appreciation of what actually presents itself' which a loosening of grasp on theory offers. If we are seeking to understand why one child isn't reading, or why another refuses to go to school, we should perhaps trust in our own knowledge as people – trust in our experience and understanding of fear, interest, friendship, worry, loneliness, boredom. We know what it is to be confident, over-confident, or to feel self-doubt. We understand lying, openness, hypocrisy. We understand guile and the possibility of being deceived. We have self-knowledge, and this is our principal tool in helping us to understand others. As Joynson (1974: 2) puts it, 'Human nature is not an unknown country, a *terra incognita* on the map of knowledge. It is our home ground. Human beings are not, like the objects of natural science, things which do not understand themselves.'

We can use our understanding of these facets of being human, though, only if we feel confident in the knowledge that using them does not restrict our understanding – only if we feel that we are not missing out on some important empirical knowledge or missing some key theoretical insight. One of the points which we wish to make in this book is that the models, theories and intellectual castles created in the field of special pedagogy have helped little in improving learning – helped little in understanding why children fail at school,[6] (and this is discussed further in the next chapter). This is unfortunate enough in itself, but the even more unfortunate corollary is that the existence of this kind of supposedly privileged knowledge has persuaded teachers in ordinary schools across the globe that they may not be sufficiently knowledgeable or sufficiently expert to help children who are experiencing difficulty: that they do not have sufficient technical expertise or theoretical knowledge to teach all children.

To say merely this, though, is to make the case too weakly: this privileged knowledge, these theories and models have, by satisfying Oakeshott's 'irritable search for order and distinctness' distracted attention from the ways in which we may use our common humanity to understand others, and use our common sense to make schools more humane, inclusive places. For the knowledge is compartmentalized and disbursed according to the frames provided by academic disciplines most obviously adjacent to special education. Free thinking is difficult in such an intellectual atmosphere. When Foucault (1970: 49) said that 'knowledge [has] closed in on itself' he was referring to the codification of knowledge into disciplinary compartments. It would be a brave set of practitioners who would dare to move outside the professional edifices and procedural imperatives generated by those codifications. Procedural and professional responses and reflexes thus emerge from schools when problems with pupils arise, but these are often no more than what Skrtic (1991) calls 'symbols and ceremonies', distracting attention from more obvious and straightforward (but probably less prestigious, and certainly less immediately credible) action based on humanity and common sense. As Kohler (1947) put it in his masterpiece *Gestalt Psychology* (in the gendered language of the time – for which, apologies):

I feel that I must take sides with the layman; that, for once, he rather than our science is aware of a fundamental truth. For the layman's conviction is likely to become a major issue in the psychology, neurology and philosophy of the future.

(Kohler 1947: 323)

Kohler's prediction, made halfway through the twentieth century, looks to have been a little too optimistic at the beginning of the twenty-first. Even though there has been a turn away from the mechanistic behaviourism of his time, there is still strongly detectable a sense that those who urge the need for a more humanistic turn are slightly soft in the head. And this applies particularly at the 'applied' level of implementation: even in the 1970s and 1980s there was a feeling among applied psychologists that behavioural psychology had been drawn from the white heat of contemporary psychological discourse. This was despite the warnings of those like psychology's elder statesman Sigmund Koch (1964), who warned of the necessity to remember that

In every period of our history we psychologists have looked to external sources in the scholarly culture – especially natural science and the philosophy of science – for our sense of direction. And typically we have embraced policies long out of date in those very sources ... Psychology is thus in the unenviable position of standing on philosophical foundations which began to be vacated by philosophy almost as soon as the former had borrowed them.

(Koch 1964: 4–5)

The warning is about the transposition of one kind of thinking to a different arena and it applies today as much as when Koch wrote. Theoretical, model-making, grand-explanatory effort is in a human field bound to be not only short of the mark, but possibly misleading. It is especially so if it leads to the belief that practice – practice in schools and with children – involving know-how knowledge can be extracted from such endeavour.

The tack taken in this book is that the theories and models of special education are no exception in this respect. Indeed, they provide an exemplary case of how grand explanatory frameworks can be misleading, and we give examples of this in Chapters 3 and 4 where we look especially at children's behaviour at school and at their difficulty with reading. Especially worrying in this is how these frameworks can seem to make us lose confidence in ourselves as teachers and, indeed, as people.

The problem as we see it, though, lies not just in these theories and models of special education and special pedagogy, but also in the theories employed in its critique. One of the difficulties of taking an explicitly theoretical stance – like that of critical theory – in trying to understand a phenomenon like special education is that things become shaped according to the theoretical lens through which one is viewing them. Barrett (1978) poses the danger thus:

> The greater and more spectacular the theory, the more likely it is to foster our indolent disposition to oversimplify: to twist all the ordinary matters of experience to fit them into the new framework, and if they do not, to lop them off.
>
> (Barrett 1978: 149)

The warning here is about the simplifying tendency of theory in the social and symbolic sciences in general – the problems are not restricted by any means to special education or even education. Theoretical moulds, from wherever they derive, the argument goes, are the Procrustean bed of the educationist; there is the danger that in compacting, trimming and generally forcing the worlds with which we work into these theoretical moulds we may distort and misperceive those worlds. And education is by no means peculiar in this respect: Wright Mills (1970) described and attacked this theoretical tendency in socio-historical analysis, where he suggested that theory (in particular in the philosophies of Comte, Marx, Spencer and Weber) creates a 'transhistorical strait-jacket' into which the evidence of history is coerced.

Thus, while many have seen theory as the *sine qua non* of educational analysis, we view it here with profound scepticism. This is not to dismiss it: where it can provide what Bourdieu calls a 'thinking tool', it can be valuable, enabling the perception of something in a different light or from a different perspective. However, where it dominates thought, permanently dictating the direction of analysis, it can become hypnotic and even dangerous. This is how Bourdieu puts it himself:

> Let me say outright and very forcefully that I never 'theorise', if by that we mean engage in the kind of conceptual gobbledygook . . . that is good for textbooks and which, through an extraordinary misconstrual of the logic of science, passes for Theory in much of Anglo-American social science . . . There is no doubt a theory in my work, or, better, a set of thinking tools visible through the results they yield, but it is not built as such . . . It is a temporary construct which takes shape for and by empirical work.
>
> (Bourdieu, in Wacquant 1989, cited in Jenkins 1992: 67)

Theory is, then, for Bourdieu, a thinking tool – a *temporary construct*. It is something that comes and goes: a brief model, a metaphor, an idea or set of ideas which come out of one's thinking, one's reading and one's experience of the world. It is evanescent and fragile, to be captured and cradled when useful but discarded when it begins to dominate and steer the analysis.[7] Foucault says something similar. For Foucault, while Piagetian or psychoanalytic theory may form useful stepping-off points, they are useful only in the sense that they are caricatured or theatricalized. The conclusions which one draws thus emerge from a disrespectful tossing around of the notions of the grand theory builders. They cannot emerge, according to Foucault, from the very architecture of the theorists' palaces. To use theorists' ideas in this way, as totalities which provide a useful explanatory framework, can lead us on interminable wild goose chases and down infinitely long culs de sac. Foucault suggests that when social theories have been used as explanatory frameworks they have proved a 'hindrance to research' (Foucault 1980: 81). Likewise with Bourdieu: theory should never be a dogma – an unvarying liturgy of principles for the operation of some analytical process.

This is important for three distinct reasons. First, it is important because of the direct effects which the grand theory of the Great Thinkers has had in special education. In Chapter 3 we examine how special education has suffered from the influence of psychoanalytic theory on the understanding of behaviour difficulty at school. That which is, notionally at least, 'theory' has a particularly powerful influence since it confers academic legitimacy on the subject of the supposedly 'theoretical' analysis.

So, in a field like special education, which has always suffered something of an inferiority complex about its academic status, there is the danger that 'theory' may be used to add cachet to simple ideas or propositions – and to claim some epistemological legitimacy and explanatory currency for these ideas and propositions. But those ideas and propositions lent credibility by theory are as likely to be incorrect as correct. Indeed, the imprimatur of correctness, while proffered by supposedly theoretical analysis, is probably entirely inappropriate for a field like education, given the plasticity of the stuff with which we work and which we study. There is no means in educational research of enabling what the philosopher of science Canguilhem (1994: 41) calls the 'elimination of the false by the true'. Educational theory is (and we are thinking here of its 'grand theory' which has been particularly influential in special education: Freudian, Piagetian, behavioural), unlike science's theory, non-progressive – in science there *is* an eventual elimination of false by true or at least (for those who balk at the starkness of false versus true) an elimination of less reliable knowledge by more reliable knowledge (Ziman 1991).

But in education that process of elimination of less reliable by more reliable is far more problematic – because of the kind of *knowledge* we trade in, as educators. The knowledge that we have and which we seek as educators of whatever kind – teachers, planners, researchers – is not progressive knowledge. Today's school student *knows* more about electricity than Faraday, *knows* more about chemistry than Mendeleyev and more about genetics than Mendel, because of the cumulative, transferable nature of the knowledge involved. It is unlikely, however, that today's student of education knows more about education than great educators such as Froebel, Pestalozzi or Rousseau – although today's experienced teacher in any and every school in the land may well 'know' more than these luminaries. The reasons for the contrast between the education student and the practising teacher lie in the difference between what the philosopher Gilbert Ryle (1990) called *know-how* knowledge and *know-that* knowledge. The know-how knowledge is practical knowledge – and the practising teacher's know-how knowledge may (or may not) be more sophisticated than that of Froebel. The 'know-that' knowledge is the accreted knowledge of facts, collectable and progressive and clearly demonstrable in the sciences; but this latter has offered little progress that one can discern in education: there has been little conspicuous elimination of the false by the true – and nor should we expect there to be. The problem with the cachet imputed by theory, though, is that it suggests that the truth, the right path *has* been found, or at least is in some way findable.

All those who work in education, and particularly special education, should be concerned about this: concerned about the consequences of theory, since those consequences are in the real world of classrooms and the real lives of teachers and children. Theories are not simply the playthings of bored academics: they have often been used to 'explain' how children learn, and why they fail. Piaget's thinking, for example, has been responsible for many ideas and initiatives in education. Reliance on Piagetian theory and what Bruner (1966: 214) calls 'the cloying concept of "readiness"' led to wholly mistaken notions about readiness for reading. Bryant (1984: 257), indeed, contends that 'there can be no question that the implications of Piaget's theories about children's logical skills are, as far as teachers are concerned, restrictive and negative'. It is surely not too early to say that certain elements of that theory proffer a serious misrepresentation of the way children think. This has happened for two main reasons: from unrealistic expectations about the place and limits of theory in education, and from the understandable fascination of professional and academic communities by a particularly powerful nexus of theoretical knowledge.

It is worth saying a word or two about Vygotsky here, since his genius in thinking about learning has often been presented as the anti-venom to Piaget's genetic determinacy. One wonders whether his reputation is entirely justified, or whether the fascination with him is due to his romantically short life, his clever flirting with the aparatchiks of the USSR (in contrast to the leaden political correctness of Lysenko),[8] and his bright acceptance of the importance of the social element in learning. His, after all, was an optimistic way of seeing learning – and the message with which Vygotsky leaves the teacher contrasts with that left by Piaget, which Bryant (1984: 257) says is 'a pretty bleak one'. But while Vygotsky's ideas are refreshing, most educators (outside the scholarly world of Vygotsky-interpreters) would probably flounder if asked to expound, without waffling, in more than three or four sentences exactly what Vygotsky said. Their answers would probably be of the variety: (i) 'Learning is social: children learn from those – usually adults – who know more than they do about something' and (ii) 'Learning happens best when children are being stretched a little bit – but not too much; what they are learning shouldn't be too easy and it shouldn't be too hard.'

The extraordinary fact is that neither of the latter ideas is particularly startling and neither is particularly new. Their consistency rings through the work of all the great educators: Pestalozzi, Froebel, Montessori, Rousseau. The reason that they have been so interesting recently is that they have presented an alternative to the crystal-hard theorizations with which they were contemporary. Theorists like Freud and Piaget seemed to be constructing channels within which our ideas about children's thinking were to be constrained. Vygotsky, along with these other educators, returns to unadorned knowledge of learning which comes from our knowledge, as people, of what it is to learn. That knowledge is, then, by no means new to us: it has not been revealed by some remarkable theoretical disclosure. It comes from Ryle's 'know-how' which we gain of others (as learners, friends, deceivers, trusted colleagues, or whatever) and that knowledge arrives from our experience as teachers and as people. While Rousseau shocked the world with *Émile* ([1762] 1993), he said only what *good* teachers know (and probably have always known) about learning:

Instead of keeping [Émile] mewed up in a stuffy room, take him out into a meadow every day; let him run about, let him struggle and fall again and again, the oftener the better; he will learn all the sooner to pick himself up. The delights of liberty will make up for many bruises. My pupil will hurt himself oftener than yours, but he will always be merry; your pupils may receive fewer injuries, but they are always thwarted, constrained, and sad. I doubt whether they are any better off.

(Rousseau 1993: 49)

The contrast drawn by Rousseau seems remarkably prescient, and rather like a contrast between good nursery education and that which might be offered by Direct Instruction, Doman Delacato or one of the other miracle methods of special pedagogy. No miracle pedagogy has been discovered since his day, or is ever likely to be revealed by the theoretical endeavours of educators or psychologists.

We reject the view, then, that special educators (or, indeed, any educators) have to adopt some formulaic schema for collecting data, some analytical sieve for sifting it or some theoretical frame for synthesis. As the historian of ideas Isaiah Berlin (1979: 86) says, 'What do the greatest classical scholars of our time know about ancient Rome that was not known to Cicero's servant girl? What have they added to her store?' If, in other words, practitioners are immersed in the practice and observation of education, its traditions, literatures and the literatures of cognate areas, there is no need for some external validation of their action.

The second reason for mistrusting theory, as we have indicated already, is that theory may dominate analysis when one is seeking to understand a phenomenon like special education. This is so even with a theoretical system as open-ended, personal and 'emancipatory' as critical theory.[9] The argument of critical and emancipatory theorists is that theorizing which excludes or ignores meaning, significance and social and historical contexts denies the possibility of social critique. Theory, these advocates would say, has to emerge out of political stance. In addressing the critique of Clark *et al.* (1998) of certain kinds of sociological theory applied to special education, Slee (1998) says the following:

> There is a failure to recognise that imported sociological theorising of disability and education is not a quest to force theoretical closure to eliminate doubt. It is essentially a political project demanding ever-clearer explanations of complex realities in order that we know 'what's going on, why and how we change it' (Troyna 1994). In this respect it is what Troyna (1995) referred to as partisan research . . .
>
> (Slee 1998: 129)

Stanley Fish (1989) is one of the most forthright critics of the kind of theoretical enterprise of which Slee speaks here. The disavowal of forced 'theoretical closure' is not enough, Fish would argue, not only because it is contradicted by the subsequent commitment to 'partisan research' (which surely loads one's reasoning toward some expected end-point), but because the analysis which is sought and proffered with the honorary title 'theoretical' assumes some kind of privileged status. But in reality this discourse, this 'theory talk', possesses no epistemological advantage over any other. There is no way of showing that it is right or wrong. Neither is there any way of showing that the undoubted commitment to social and personal improvement – the partisan-ness of which Troyna writes, and which lies behind it – can in any way be validated. Many sincere people at the turn of the century, for example, believed – no doubt after due dialectic and reflection – that it was right and proper to ship children from England to Australia for a 'new life' (Newman and Roberts 1996). It is now recognized, of course, from the personal accounts which have come from the 'beneficiaries' of such well-meaning policy, that it often caused unquantifiable misery. The problem is that critique and theory which comes out of one political stance is as likely to be right or wrong as another. That which determines to provide critique is liable to be undermined by it. Fish (1989) notes that the critical theorist

... is unable to show that critical self-reflection is something it is possible to do ... [this] means that critical theory is faced with two unsatisfactory alternatives: either it admits an inability to distinguish between its own agenda and the agenda it repeatedly exposes, admits, in short, that it is, like everything else, merely 'interested' and not possessed of a special interest called the emancipatory or it preserves its specialness by leaving its agenda without content, operating forever at the level of millenarian prophecy, issuing appeals in the name of a generalised human potential, calling for actions that have no particular content, celebrating goals that remain unachievable because they remain unthinkable.

(Fish 1989: 455–6)

The problem stems not from taking a political stance, for part of our argument is that to pursue a value-orientated education system is a more valid project than to seek an evidence-led one (and this is explored in Chapter 7). Rather, the problem stems from the assumption that a particular stance is validated and given credibility by its association with a certain theory. Again, the problems emerge from the privileges which theory confers.

The third reason for mistrusting theory, aside from its Procrustean and legitimizing tendencies, is that it may distract us from action, and from concern with the kind of social justice which is necessary for a movement to inclusion. This may seem a strange proposition, and is certainly one which would be disputed by those who promote their theoretical analysis as 'emancipatory'. The argument for the proposition is articulated powerfully by Richard Rorty (1998). Academics since the mid-sixties, he says, have become so preoccupied with the weighty matters of theory and theorizing that they no longer bother to concern themselves with the mundanity of reform – of the kind of efforts at social justice which are behind inclusion. It is the 'mundanity' which is important: effecting social justice is, for Rorty, about a difficult, dirty agenda of change in statute, regulation and ways of operating public organizations like schools. Recently, though, concern with this kind of agenda has become submerged under a welter of theorizing. Academics nowadays, he asserts, in their fascination with theory, have turned away from secularism and pragmatism. Academics seem to want always to see things 'within a fixed frame of reference, a frame supplied by theory' (Rorty 1998: 36).

The 'fixed frame of reference' argument is the one articulated by Barrett and others and which was addressed earlier. But Rorty is going further: he contrasts the contemporary academy with pre-sixties reformers whose uncomplicated agenda was to protect the weak from the strong. Rorty's message, if it is right, surely has particular resonance for special educators. The message is that for those in fields like education, the priority should be change. Change is effected only through an unremitting focus on the particular – by concentrating energy on a detailed, unglamorous agenda of administrative, legal and financial matters. But a focus on these mundane but necessary matters is subverted by the contemporary intellectual's obsession with theory. The product of the theorizing academy has been '... many thousands of books which represent scholastic philosophizing at its worst' (1998: 93). Rorty asserts that this kind of academic theorizing '... produces dreams not of political reforms but of inexplicable, magical transformations' (1998: 102).

This theorizing (and these dreams) of academic special educators would be harmless enough if they didn't have consequences. But the trouble is that our theories in special education do have consequences – consequences of both omission and commission. On the omission side, if we are too busy theorizing, we may neglect to act, as Rorty asserts; we become too obsessed with our own theory-projects. On the commission side, theory – of whatever kind – legitimizes some potty ideas and practices. 'Theory' carries with it such academic cachet that it is taken to be a sound basis from which to proceed. That which is 'theoretically grounded' is taken to be more worthy of respect and support than that which, more simply and prosaically, seems right and sensible.

Rorty says that this theorizing often offers 'the most abstract and barren explanations imaginable' (1998: 93) and that it distracts from the proper job of the academic in the social sciences, which is to reform. Special education is surely one of the clearest cases in point, where reform should supersede theorization. This is one of the clearest messages from this book: that the kind of theory employed by all branches of social scientific endeavour over the twentieth century often channelled thinking about special education inappropriately. Further, it provided misleading metaphors for understanding some of the social and psychological processes in which we are most interested.

Think small: the need for local enquiry

Because of this, we would want to reassert, theory should be seen better as the 'temporary construct' of Bourdieu: the thinking tool. Dewey said much the same: take Meiklejohn's (1966) summary of Dewey's position:

> It is unwise, Dewey tells us, to philosophize, to have and to use 'general theories' ... 'What is needed,' Dewey says, 'is specific inquiries into a multitude of specific structures and interactions. Not only does the solemn reiteration of categories of individual and organic or social whole not further these definite and detailed inquiries but it checks them ...'
>
> (Meiklejohn 1996: 83)

Dewey's emphasis on 'specific enquiries' is very similar to Rorty's emphasis on a particular, detailed agenda and Skrtic's *adhocery*. The corollary of such a way of thinking is that we should invest less dependence in the grand theoretical edifices and rigid castles of metaphor constructed by education's intellectual heroes. And we should place less faith in theory's methodological handmaidens. As the iconoclastic critic of social science, Stanislav Andreski (1972: 108–9) puts it, 'The overemphasis on methodology and techniques [in social science], as well as adulation of formulae and scientific-sounding terms, exemplify the common tendency . . . to displace value from the end to the means.' In education in general, and special education in particular, there has been this tendency to displace value from the end to the means as the legitimacy and value of research is determined less by common-sense evaluations of its status and likely impact and more by notions such as 'reliability', imported from the natural sciences.

Not only does a focus on means rather than ends deliver a particular kind of knowledge, one that may well distort the sort of practice we feel that it is right to implement, it also may, again in Andreski's (1972: 116) words, provide 'an alibi for timorous quietism'. It may, that is to say, distract attention from important yet challenging matters for the educator – away, in other words, from critical thought, inquiry and innovation about the curriculum; away from children as people.[10] It may lead the gaze instead towards the less challenging paraphernalia of measurement and research procedure. Postman (1996) puts it well. He notes that Confucius

> insisted on students studying what we would call 'good manners'. Can you imagine a school today requiring as a major subject the study and practice of good manners? Surely, no one can say it is not an important subject. Perhaps it is not in the curriculum because the Educational Testing Service would be hard-pressed to figure out how to assess it.
>
> (Postman 1996: 104)

Thus, for example, with the kudos which learning theory invested in behavioural methods, more attention was devoted to the proper application of task analysis procedures, or the correctness of behavioural objective specification[11] than was given to the question of what was actually wanted from an education of children for whom the procedures were devised. It was only when critical voices reached sufficient volume – from a number of directions (see for example, Stenhouse 1975; Wood and Shears 1986), and from the protestations of teachers – that serious questions began to be asked about what was going on.

If one doesn't think small, one is in danger of being guided by the safety of prestigious theory, by the putatively secure knowledge emerging from the findings of supposedly empirical enquiry. The problem with a theory, as distinct from Bourdieu's 'thinking tool', is that it always returns to a guiding path. The underlying assumption is that there is a proper way of examining things. As Foucault put it (in discussion with Gérard Raulet) in interpreting the behaviour of revolutionary Marxists in the 1960s, there came to be an 'antidogmatic violence':

Gérard Raulet: An antidogmatic violence in search of references . . .

Foucault: And looking for them, on occasion, in an exasperated dogmatism.

Gérard Raulet: Via Freud or via structuralism.

Foucault: Correct. So, once again, I would like to reassess the history of formalism . . . within the larger phenomenon of formalism in the twentieth century, as important in its way as Romanticism or even positivism during the nineteenth century.

(Foucault 1994: 111)

None of this is to deny the particular and specific insights which may come from particular kinds of theory and which may be used as thinking tools in considering particular problems which arise out of children's reluctance to learn. It is the seeking of form, in Marx, Freud, the Frankfurt School or wherever, which is of concern – and this is important when we are looking to explain the history of special education, since the grand theory postulated by the grand theorists has been highly influential. Even to the present day, as we discuss in Chapter 3, notions of emotional disturbance dominate explanations of behaviour difficulty and these rely for their legitimacy on a Freudian ontology, even if that ontology is, as Crews (1997: 298) has put it, an 'ontological maze peopled by absurd homunculi'. Even with, as Rorty (1998: 76) puts it, a 'partial substitution of Freud for Marx as a source of social theory', there remains the seemingly willing dependence on the structure of a theory or what Dewey (1982: 187) called the 'logic of general notions under which specific situations are to be brought'. Dewey asserted that instead of these general notions, 'What we want is light upon this or that group of individuals, this or that concrete human being, this or that special institution or social arrangement' (1982: 187).

When Foucault says that his 'genealogy' entertains '. . . the claims to attention of local, discontinuous, disqualified, illegitimate knowledges against the claims of a unitary body of theory which would filter, hierarchise and order them in the name of some true knowledge', he sounds distinctly like the Dewey of nearly a century ago who warned of theory – of 'true knowledge'. Indeed, Rorty (1991: 193) suggests that 'Foucault can be read . . . as an up-to-date version of John Dewey.'

Concluding comment

The picture drawn in this chapter is of special education as something of an epistemic jumble. Its 'jumbleness' has not evidently been a source of concern to many, or even a source of note. Indeed, the very legitimacy of special education is proudly constructed out of its 'theory', even though the theory is an agglomeration of bits and pieces from Piagetian, psychoanalytic, psychometric and behavioural theoretical models.

We make an argument here for a loosening of hold on the erstwhile theoretical knowledge behind special education, contending that less of our inquiry into children's difficulties at school – and, more importantly, less of our response to those difficulties – should be defined and tackled in the way that it has hitherto. An argument is made, if we are looking to the shape of an education system for the future, for more reliance by all in education – practitioners, planners, academics, researchers – on ideals about equity, social justice and opportunity for all. In pursuing these ideals, in improving the education system, we should accept rather than deny the insights which emerge by virtue of being human – insights which emerge from our own knowledge of learning; our own knowledge of failure, success, acceptance or rejection. There is nothing to be lost in so doing, for the evidence is that there are no magic fixes or startling insights to emerge from the traditional knowledge-base of special education. Indeed, there is a great deal to be regained through a recourse to our common humanity. Joynson (1974) begins his book *Psychology and Common Sense* by précising a G. K. Chesterton story that makes the point well:

> . . . a man dreams of emulating the great explorers. One day he sets sail from the West Country and heads out into the Atlantic, confident that he is destined to discover an unknown land. For many weeks he wanders across the ocean, buffeted by storms and uncertain of his position. At last, a coastline comes in view and, as he approaches, he sees the towers and domes and minarets of a strange civilisation. Greatly excited, he makes his way ashore. To his astonishment, the natives speak English. He has landed at Brighton.
>
> (Joynson 1974: 1)

Maybe the research indicating the ineffectiveness of special education (reviewed briefly in Chapter 2) has landed us at Brighton. Maybe the realization that we haven't found a new civilization, nor are ever likely to, leads us to a separate set of questions about failure at school. Maybe it leads us to re-evaluate our research and its methods and to place more value in what we – as people – already know and want.

Analysis framed by the research methodology of special education and the discourse which surrounds it tends always to push discussion about alternatives to special education into boxes. Discussion tends to lead to this method versus that method, or segregation versus integration, or exclusion versus inclusion. In Vygotsky's metaphor, words are the tools we use for thinking and the words we use in our discourse here tend always to channel discussion along predictable furrows. The tools for thinking – the vocabulary, the theory, the research methodology – encourage particular ways of thinking. Worked with these tools, failure – whether it is perceived to be failure of children at school, or failure of schools to educate children – becomes yet another special education discourse.

In the next few chapters we proceed to examine the consequences of this discourse, such as the influence which it has had on professional and popular thinking about learning difficulty. Suggesting that much of the 'knowledge' of special education is misconceived, we proceed to make the case that arguments for inclusion have to emerge out of ideas about social justice and human rights.

Summary

Much critique has focused on the place of special education in the wider social system. Special education has been taken by critics to act as a kind of service industry to the mainstream; acting in that role, the argument goes, it is discriminatory and oppressive. While such critiques are not invalid, they leave much unsaid. The point made in this chapter is that notions of learning difficulty which underpin special education and special pedagogy rely for their status on some questionable kinds of knowledge and reasoning. They rely on notions which have been elevated by 'scientific' methodology and theory to something more than they really are. The great thinkers of the 'ologies' (usually psychology) have built impressive theory which gives credibility and kudos to particular (and often mistaken) ways of viewing learning, viewing children and viewing the difficulties that they experience at school. Often, these theories distract attention from simpler explanations for children's failure to thrive. An argument is made for a renewal of confidence in practitioners' knowledge as teachers in understanding the failure of children at school. Only outside the confines of the disciplinary and professional knowledge which enjoys such status in special education will there be a restoration of faith in the kind of principles which must guide inclusive practice.

Notes

1 Special education is taken throughout to mean not just segregation in special schools, but also the special procedures and systems – sometimes in the mainstream – which exclude certain children.
2 It is worth noting that Fish (1989) makes a critique of 'anti-professionalism' which highlights what he takes to be an epistemological arrogance among anti-professionals. He notes that the anti-professional position assumes: '. . . let us free ourselves from the confining perspective of particular beliefs (even when they are our own) and with the help of *acontextual* and transcultural

algorithm . . . come to see things as they really are' (Fish 1989: 277). He argues that what anti-professionals '. . . seem never to realise . . . is that power not only constrains and excludes, but also enables, and that without some institutionally articulated spaces in which actions become possible and judgments become inevitable (because they are obligatory), there would be nothing to do and no values to support' (Fish 1989: 239).

3 By cultural capital, Bourdieu means the accumulated resources and insignia which can be 'cashed in' for society's goods and services.

4 Intentionality in the philosophical sense is different from intention in the familiar sense. Deliberate intention to oppress others may or may not be assumed (in the people who populate a society) by theorists to exist. The existence of *intentionality*, however, on the part of the model maker or theory constructor is different. It is described by Dennett (1996: 46–8) as 'aboutness': 'Something exhibits intentionality if its competence is in some way *about* something else . . . Intentional phenomena are equipped with metaphorical arrows, you might say, aimed at something or other . . . But of course many phenomena that exhibit this minimal sort of intentionality do not do anything *intentionally*, in the everyday sense of the term.'

5 Many would seek to disabuse us of the notion that we are not theorizing (see Rajagopalan 1998). However, we stick to our guns on this and draw in for support the American academic Stanley Fish, who has had a lot to say about the overuse of the notion of 'theory'. He (1994: 378) highlights the highly varied activities shoved under the billowing cloak of 'theory,' concluding that '. . . to include such activities under the rubric of theory is finally to make everything theory, and if one does that there is nothing of a *general* kind to be said about theory'. He distinguishes between theory and what he calls *theory talk*; the latter being 'any form of talk that has acquired cachet and prestige' (Fish 1989: 14–15). When informed analysis occurs, we are in Fish's terms 'not following a theory, but extending a practice, employing a set of heuristic questions' or, as E. D. Hirsch (1976) puts it, 'making calculations of probability based on an insider's knowledge'. This is *not* using theory. We can, says Fish, always call such kinds of thinking 'theory' but nothing whatsoever will have been gained and we will have lost any sense that theory is special. We discuss this further elsewhere (Thomas 1997; 1999).

6 As Baker, Wang and Walberg (1995: 14) put it, 'There is no separate knowledge base for teaching children classified as mildly retarded or learning disabled.'

7 Bourdieu's drawing of this distinction is not unique. Mouzelis (1995) makes the point that there is a classic distinction (drawn by S. F. Nadel) between (i) theory as a set of substantive statements, provable by empirical investigation, which try to tell us something new about the world, and (ii) theory as a set of tools. Mouzelis further points out that Althusser makes a similar distinction between theory as tool/means (which the calls Gen. II) and theory as provisional end product (which he calls Gen. III). In education (as distinct from sociology) Chambers (1992) identifies no fewer than nine meanings for 'theory' as it is used in this field. Only one of those meanings concerns theory as 'thinking tool'.

8 Trofim Denisovich Lysenko was the Soviet agronomist and geneticist who progressed in the Soviet scientific establishment by developing a genetic theory that was consistent with Marxist–Leninist thought. Darwinian evolution and Mendelian genetics, he asserted, could not be correct because it conflicted with Marxist–Leninist ideology. His ideas received official support, being taught in biology courses in the USSR, and they were incorporated, with disastrous consequences, into agricultural programmes.

9 Commentators such as Armstrong *et al.* (1998) make a persuasive case for the social value of theory, arguing for a Habermasian extension of personal theory to critical and emancipatory theory.

10 James and Prout (1990) make the case persuasively with respect to the damage which has been done to our view of children as people. In particular they point to ways in which models such as those of Piaget have inappropriately 'constructed' notions of childhood. Readers of Piaget will have noticed that he calls himself not an educator, nor even a psychologist or a biologist but rather a 'genetic epistemologist'. The phrase gives some clues about Piaget's mission and his core beliefs. As Toulmin (1972) points out, there are two ways in which this *épistemology génétique* can be understood: as 'intellectual phylogeny' of human cultures, on a collective level, or to 'intellectual ontogeny' (p. 424) of individual human beings. The former, he says, is the correct interpretation of Piaget's meaning. The rational adult is in other words seen as the butterfly at the end of some ugly but necessary pre-rational stages. Seen through such a theoretical lens, all kinds of implications follow for teaching and for an understanding of failure to learn in the child.

11 It is worth noting that those who promulgated behavioural objectives insisted on the observability of the behaviour which was being promoted and that this insistence owes a lineage directly to logical positivism via Skinner's behaviourism. The insistence that a child be seen to *do* something, rather than merely be noted vaguely to *enjoy* it is traceable with no difficulty at all to the logical positivists' insistence on the verification of meaningfulness through observation. Carnap (leader of the logical positivists' Vienna Circle) would no doubt have turned in his grave at the knowledge that the philosophical school which he helped to form had, fifty years later, provided the intellectual lead for a system of teaching which involved breaking down learning into dozens of 'behavioural objectives'.

References

Abberley, P. (1987) The concept of oppression and the development of a social theory of disability, *Disability, Handicap and Society*, 2(1): 5–19.

Andreski, S. (1972) *Social Sciences as Sorcery*. London: André Deutsch.

Archer, M. S. (1979) *The Social Origins of Educational Systems*. London: Sage.

Armstrong, D., Armstrong, F. and Barton, L. (1998) From theory to practice: special education and the social relations of academic production, in C. Clark, A. Dyson and A. Millward (eds) *Theorising Special Education*. London: Routledge.

Baker, E. T., Wang, M. C. and Walberg, H. J. (1995) The effects of inclusion on learning, *Educational Leadership*, 52(4): 33–5.

Barker, R. G. (1968) *Ecological Psychology*. Stanford, CA: Stanford University Press.

Barrett, W. (1978) *The Illusion of Technique*. New York, NY: Anchor-Doubleday.

Berlin, I. (1979) The divorce between the sciences and the humanities, in I. Berlin, *Against the Current*. London: The Hogarth Press.

Bourdieu, P. (1984) *Distinction*. London: Routledge and Kegan Paul.

Bourdieu, P. and Passeron, J.-C. (1977) *Reproduction in Society, Education and Culture*. London: Sage.

Bruner, J. (1966) After John Dewey, What? in R. D. Archambault (ed.) *Dewey on Education*. New York, NY: Random House.

Bryant, P. E. (1984) Piaget, teachers and psychologists, *Oxford Review of Education*, 10(3): 251–9.

Canguilhem, G. (1994) The various models, in F. Delaporte (ed.) *A Vital Rationalist: Selected Writings from Georges Canguilhem*. New York, NY: Zone Books.

Chambers, J. H. (1992) *Empiricist Research on Teaching: A Philosophical and Practical Critique of its Scientific Pretensions*. Dordrecht: Kluwer Academic Publishers.

Clark, C., Dyson, A. and Millward, A. (1998) Theorising special education: time to move on? in C. Clark, A. Dyson and A. Millward (eds) *Theorising Special Education*. London, Routledge.

Crews, F. (1997) *The Memory Wars: Freud's Legacy in Dispute*. London: Granta.

Croll, P. and Moses, D. (1998) Pragmatism, ideology and educational change: the case of special educational needs, *British Journal of Educational Studies*, 46(1): 11–25.

Dennett, D. C. (1996) *Kinds of Minds: Towards an Understanding of Consciousness*. London: Phoenix.

Derrida, J. (1978) *Writing and Difference*. London: Routledge and Kegan Paul.

Dewey, J. (1982) Reconstruction in philosophy, in *The Middle Works of John Dewey*, Vol. 12. Carbondale, IL: Southern Illinois University Press.

Dorn, S., Fuchs, D. and Fuchs, L. S. (1996) A historical perspective on special education reform, *Theory into Practice*, 35(1): 12–19.

Fish, S. (1989) *Doing What Comes Naturally*. Oxford: Clarendon Press.

Fish, S. (1994) *There's No Such Thing as Free Speech*. Oxford: Oxford University Press.

Foucault, M. (1970) *The Order of Things: An Archaeology of the Human Sciences*. London: Tavistock.

Foucault, M. (1980) Two lectures, in C. Gordon (ed.) *Power/Knowledge: Selected Interviews and Other Writings 1972–1977 – Michel Foucault*. London: Harvester Wheatsheaf.

Foucault, M. (1994) Critical theory/intellectual history, in M. Kelly (ed.) *Critique and Power: Recasting the Foucault/Habermas Debate*. Cambridge, MA: MIT Press.

Fulcher, G. (1989) *Disabling Policies?* London: Falmer.

Garrison, J. W. (1988) The impossibility of atheoretical educational science, *Journal of Educational Thought*, 22(1): 21–6.

Gitlin, A., Siegel, M. and Boru, K. (1989) The politics of method: from leftist ethnography to educative research, *Qualitative Studies in Education*, 2(3): 237–53.

Hirsch, E. D. (1976) *The Aims of Interpretation*. Chicago IL: University of Chicago Press.

Hornby, G. (1999) Inclusion or delusion: can one size fit all? *Support for Learning*, 14(4): 152–7.

James, A. and Prout, A. (1990) A new paradigm for the sociology of childhood? Provenance, promise and problems, in A. James and A. Prout (eds) *Constructing and Reconstructing Childhood: Contemporary Issues in the Sociological Study of Childhood*. London: Falmer.

Jenkins, R. (1992) *Pierre Bourdieu*. London: Routledge.

Joynson, R. B. (1974) *Psychology and Common Sense*. London: Routledge and Kegan Paul.

Koch, S. (1964) Psychology and emerging conceptions of knowledge as unitary, in T. W. Wann (ed.) *Behaviourism and Phenomenology*. Chicago, IL: University of Chicago Press.

Kohler, W. (1947) *Gestalt Psychology*. New York, NY: Liveright.

McLynn, F. (1999) History isn't always a cock-up, *New Statesman*, 20 September: 25–7.

Meekosha, H. and Jacubowicz, A. (1996) Disability, participation, representation and social justice, in C. Christensen and F. Rizvi (eds) *Disability and the Dilemmas of Education and Justice*. Buckingham: Open University Press.

Meiklejohn, A. (1966) Knowledge and intelligence, in R. D. Archambault (ed.) *Dewey on Education*. New York, NY: Random House.

Mouzelis, N. (1995) *Socioloical Theory: What Went Wrong?* London: Routledge.

Newman, T. and Roberts, H. (1996) Meaning well and doing good: interventions in children's lives, in P. Alderson *et al. What Works? Effective Social Interventions in Child Welfare*. London: Barnardos.

Oakeshott, M. (1967) *Rationalism in Politics and Other Essays*. London: Methuen.

Parsons, C. (1999) *Education, Exclusion and Citizenship*. London: Routledge.

Popper, K. R. (1989) *Conjectures and Refutations*, 5th edn. London: Routledge.

Postman, N. (1996) *The End of Education*. New York, NY: Alfred A. Knopf.

Rajagopalan, K. (1998) On the theoretical trappings of the thesis of anti-theory; or why the idea of theory may not, after all, be all that bad: a response to Gary Thomas, *Harvard Educational Review*, 68(3): 335–52.

Riddell, S. (1996) Theorising special educational needs in a changing political climate, in L. Barton (ed.) *The Sociology of Disability: Emerging Issues and Insights*. London: Longman.

Rorty, R. (1991) *Essays on Heidegger and Others: Philosophical Papers, Vol. II*. Cambridge: Cambridge University Press.

Rorty, R. (1998) *Advancing our Country: Leftist Thought in 20th-century America*. Cambridge, MA: Harvard University Press.

Rousseau, J.-J. ([1762] 1993) *Émile* (trans. B. Foxley). London: J. M. Dent.

Ryle, G. (1990) *The Concept of Mind*. London: Penguin.

Skrtic, T. M. (1991) The special education paradox: equity as the way to excellence, *Harvard Educational Review*, 61(2): 148–206.

Slee, R. (1998) The politics of theorising special education, in C. Clark, A. Dyson and A. Millward (eds) *Theorising Special Education*. London: Routledge.

Söder, M. (1989) Disability as a social construct: the labelling approach revisited, *European Journal of Special Needs Education*, 4(2): 117–29.

Stenhouse, L. (1975) *An Introduction to Curriculum Research and Development*. London: Heinemann.

Stevenson, R. L. (1999) *A Humble Remonstrance*, in G. Norquay (ed.) *R. L. Stevenson on Fiction: an Anthology of Literary and Critical Essays*. Edinburgh: Edinburgh University Press.

Suppes, P. (1974) The place of theory in educational research, *Educational Researcher*, 3(6): 3–10.

Thomas, G. (1997) What's the use of theory? *Harvard Educational Review*, 67(1): 75–105.

Thomas, G. (1999) Hollow theory: a reply to Rajagopalan, *Harvard Educational Review*, 69(1): 51–66.

Tomlinson, S. (1987) Critical theory and special education, CASTME Journal, 7(2): 33–41.

Toulmin, S. (1972) *Human Understanding, Volume I*. Oxford: Clarendon Press.

Troyna, B. (1994) Blind faith? Empowerment and educational research. Paper presented at the International Sociology of Education Conference, University of Sheffield.

Troyna, B. (1995) Beyond reasonable doubt? Researching 'race' in educational settings, *Oxford Review of Education*, 21(4): 395–408.

Wacquant, L. D. (1989) Towards a reflexive sociology: a workshop with Pierre Bourdieu, *Sociological Theory*, 7: 50.

Wood, S. and Shears, B. (1986) *Teaching Children with Severe Learning Difficulties: A Radical Re-appraisal*. London: Croom Helm.

Wright Mills, C. (1970) *The Sociological Imagination*. London: Pelican.

Young, I. M. (1990) *Justice and the Politics of Difference*. Princeton, NJ: Princeton University Press.

Ziman, J. (1991) *Reliable Knowledge*. Cambridge: Canto.

18

COMMENTARY

Today's special education and its messages for tomorrow

James M. Kauffman

Source: *The Journal of Special Education* 32(4) (1999): 244–54.

Ten characterizations of contemporary special education and five major implications for the future of the field are offered. Special education today is characterized as (a) ignorant of history, (b) apologetic for existing, (c) preoccupied with image, (d) lost in space, (e) unrealistic in expectations, (f) unprepared to focus on teaching and learning, (g) unaware of sociopolitical drift, (h) mesmerized by postmodernist/deconstructionist inanities, (i) an easy target for scam artists, and (j) immobilized by anticipation of systemic transformation. The implications are (a) changes in the boundaries of special education, (b) shifts in service delivery patterns and staffing patterns for special educators and in special education's relationship to general education, (c) changes in state standards and patterns of funding for special education and in personnel preparation, (d) additional changes in state and federal legislation and regulation, and (e) possible loss of special education's focus on the scientific understanding of instruction. A final note of optimism is offered, as special education is a relatively young profession with a history that includes reliable research and considerable capacity for self-correction. We could turn our attention unambiguously and forcefully to empirical research—generating reliable common knowledge of effective instruction of students with disabilities.

Characterizing today's special education is in many ways a dangerous undertaking. It is risky because no particular view is likely to be entirely accurate, and there is much diversity of opinion among special educators on nearly every issue. Furthermore, prognostication may make the forecaster look foolish. Had I been asked 20 years ago, or even 10, to guess what the future held, I would not have forecast the developments that have occurred in our field. I am thus acutely aware that my commentary about the meaning of today's special education for the future may be inaccurate and that in 10 or 20 years, or in even fewer, I will be embarrassed by my lack of understanding and foresight. However, in all candor, I am not very happy with most of what I see in our field today. I think we are in a period of considerable upset and danger, and our future could look rather bleak depending on how we respond to current pressures. Consequently, I offer a series of cautions about our present course.

The one sentence or metaphor that I believe best characterizes special education today is this: We are a middle-aged profession going through a profound identity crisis that includes self-destructive behavior. I refer here to the middle age of our profession's evolution, of course, not to the middle age of its members. Some might think that my characterization of special education merely reflects my own middle age or struggle with personal identity. Be that as it may, I offer more specific observations of our present-day characteristics and what they portend. Although there are exceptions, including individuals and pockets of our professional culture, I think the majority in our field could be said to have the following attributes: They are (a) ignorant of our history, (b) apologetic for existing, (c) preoccupied with image, (d) lost in space, (e) unrealistic in expectations, (f) unprepared to focus on teaching and learning, (g) unaware of sociopolitical drift, (h) mesmerized by postmodern/deconstructivist inanities, (i) an easy target for scam artists, and (j) immobilized by anticipation of systemic transformation.

Each of these 10 attributes has implications for our future, and I discuss each briefly. Because I am not single-mindedly negative and pessimistic about our field today, I conclude with a brief commentary on some positive characteristics that merit attention.

Ten attributes of today's special education

Ignorant of history

As a group of professionals, we are woefully ignorant of our past. I have two bases for stating this. First, I have observed among many of the students I teach (I refer here mostly to undergraduate and master's students) great apathy, ignorance, or even outright hostility toward history. Their ignorance and disinterest are revealed in their impression that special education really began in the 1960s or 1970s. Some of these students had not been born in 1970, of course, and it is difficult to understand a world that existed before your memory or that you can see only through the eyes of your early childhood. Occasionally, I have encountered students who explicitly state that they see no value in the history of our field and wish to be spared the useless effort of thinking and talking about it. I've been told, for example, "I want to know what's current, not what's outdated; don't tell me about the past, tell me about the future." Second, some reformers' commentaries on the history of special education are extremely superficial and seriously distorted. In some cases, our colleagues are advocating radical restructuring and the abandonment of special education as a distinctive, separable part of public schooling with little serious attention to how exceptional children fared in our schools when general and special education were indistinguishable. They do not seem to grasp what our history tells us—that without a separate, distinctive, visible structure, the interests of exceptional children are going to be lost. Moreover, they confuse the history of civil rights of racial minorities and women with the history of civil rights of persons with disabilities (cf. Dupre, 1997; Kauffman & Lloyd, 1995).

We appear to be highly likely to repeat our mistakes. Perhaps it is unreasonable to expect that we will learn very much from history. One clear lesson we *could* learn from our history, however, is that unrestrained advocacy is self-defeating. More specifically, we could observe that over-enthusiasm for inclusion is likely to suffer the same fate as overenthusiasm for exclusion. In fact, we might expect that unrestrained advocacy for full inclusion is even now laying the foundation for some future reformers' radical, unrestrained advocacy of full separation of exceptional children from the educational mainstream. Now, you may believe that the only thing we learn from history is that we don't really learn much from it (see Blatt, 1987). But I am just persistently optimistic enough to believe that we do not have to be caught in a cycle of constant forgetting, rediscovery, and disappointment. I think that we can do better—that is, I think we can avoid repeating our mistakes—but only if we have a firm grasp of our past. A firm grip on our history would, in my opinion, make us less apologetic about our existence. Historically, as Gerber (1996) has pointed out, we have been the *added* structure requiring and enabling public education to accommodate students with disabilities, to become truly universal public education.

Apologetic for existing

Notwithstanding our history, my impression is that some of our colleagues today see our very existence in public education as both unfortunate and avoidable (e.g., Brantlinger, 1997; Danforth & Rhodes, 1997; Lipsky & Gartner, 1996). Their line of argument seems to be roughly as follows: If we had done our job as we should have, then we would quickly have worked ourselves out of business. Perhaps we should just quit special education now. The only reason we exist is that general education is flawed and we are evil co-conspirators, maintaining harmful domination over those we label as needing so-called special education. If we reform education in the right way, there will be no more need for labels or so-called special services because education will be a seamless and flexible web of indistinguishable supports for all students. We do not really belong in public education; we were grafted on as an ugly appendage when general education was weak and needed us to help maintain a stratified society by giving privilege to high performers and keeping the so-called disabled powerless.

The loathing of special education is evident in scurrilous reviews of special education and calls for radical transformation (e.g., Brantlinger, 1997; Lipsky & Gartner, 1996) rather than the incremental improvement suggested by others (e.g., Carnine, 1997; Kauffman, 1993; Zigmond, 1997). We are at a curious juncture in our profession's development, a point at which the value of science in special education policy and practice is being attacked by those—including some special educators—who believe that special education has become an evil empire (see Walker *et al.*, in press, for a discussion of such issues in behavioral disorders). Brantlinger, for example, uses concepts of postmodern, deconstructivist philosophy to condemn the presumed power of special education "traditionalists," which she sees as coercive of the powerless—those who, like herself, seek to transform education so that special education is unnecessary. If Brantlinger and others who condemn special education acquire the power or "voice" they feel they are now denied, it will be interesting to see not only whether they then loathe their own dominance but also whether students with disabilities benefit and what language, if any, is used to describe the students we now say have disabilities. Perhaps some prefer the role of victim and the pretense that difference and disability can be acknowledged without labels.

People who are apologetic about their very existence often self-destruct. They may accomplish their own demise in a variety of ways, including their imagined transformation to a new level of existence. If we are going to survive as a viable professional field, then I think we are going to need to change the way we view our legitimacy in public education and develop a sense of self-worth and pride in what we do. I would like to see us become unapologetic about our function, our identity, our distinctiveness, our visibility. I hope we can become unafraid to suggest that students *can* be better off for their contact with us, actually helped more than harmed by our services, including services delivered outside general education when that is appropriate. But many in our field today are preoccupied with an image as antisegregationist to the near exclusion of concern for our substance.

Preoccupied with image

As I suggested in an article on radical reform (Kauffman, 1993), we live in a society that shows a strong preference for image over idea. The popularity of the word *inclusion* reflects, I think, more a desire to polish the image of antisegregationism than any substantive idea. In fact, the term *inclusion* has become virtually meaningless, a catch-word used to give a patina of legitimacy to whatever program people are trying to sell or defend. It appears to be part of what writer Salman Rushdie has humorously called "the new incomprehensibility" (Rushdie, 1996). Perhaps the most startling example of the term's incomprehensibility to date is a news report in which Vermont school officials describe a special, separate school as part of their full inclusion plan (Sack, 1997). Certainly, we have had inclusion of this type for many decades in special education. In fact, special education began with just such inclusion, which is indeed legitimate but contrary to the contemporary meaning of the term. *Inclusion*, as the term is used by most of its proponents, means students with disabilities being taught alongside or in the presence of, or at least in the same school if not in the same classroom space as, their nondisabled neighbors. But image makers typically use words in self-contradictory ways so that the words are drained of meaning. This allows image makers to claim that whatever they do is "inclusion."

Some have complained that special education has a Statue of Liberty image—that our image is that of a haven for general education's castoffs. Ironically, full inclusion represents the ultimate Statue of Liberty image appeal. It says not just "Give me your tired, your poor, your huddled masses," but "Give me everyone; that's right, all of the students, and 'all means all, no exceptions.'" Only now it is general education that beckons as the land of opportunity and special education is seen as the cruel land from which students are said to be seeking shelter.

I hope that our future will be one of greater concern for ideas and comprehensible language and less concern for image. I would like to see us say openly and without shame that the word "segregation" has varied meanings and that segregation per se—setting apart—is not inherently evil. We can and do repudiate the evils of forced racial segregation. Nevertheless, we do not need to taint every deliberate grouping of people, including the deliberate grouping of students in school for specialized instruction, by invoking the image of racial segregation. We need to get beyond concern for our image and concentrate on substantive issues, as preoccupation with image leaves us lost in space.

Lost in space

By "lost in space" I mean that we have lost a clear point of reference in the debate about least restrictive environment (LRE). That point of reference is students' progress in learning, their academic achievement and social competence. LRE has become the focal issue of special education reformers, as if the space occupied by students was the supremely important variable in their learning and self-worth and in judging our success. Crockett (1997) has noted how the meanings of LRE have proliferated over the years, with concern for appropriate education often taking second place. I have written and spoken about this trouble in our field ad nauseam, and I will not belabor the point. Suffice it to say that in the pursuit of what people call "inclusion" we've lost our heads about place, about the spaces occupied by people with disabilities. I believe that moving students into a particular space called general education will prove to be a largely empty victory in most cases.

We are likely to find that inclusion in general education provides physical access but not instructional access for most students to the supposedly rich and varied general education curriculum offered in general education classrooms. But physical access to a place can restrict access to the instructional procedures that are most effective for students with learning problems. Many advocates of including all students in general education seem to believe that if we move the children, then the effective instruction will follow. Or, at the very least, they are convinced that it is possible to teach students with extremely diverse instructional needs effectively in a common space. It does not seem to occur to them that common space may in some cases present insurmountable obstacles to needed instruction. I see this refusal to recognize the implications of placement for instruction as part of a larger difficulty of our profession, namely expectations that are disconnected from realities.

Unrealistic in expectations

Today there is great unhappiness with special education and its outcomes, and unhappiness with general education, too. Rightfully so. Certainly, I agree that we need to improve outcomes. But what will happen if special education really works and general education does, too? That is, what would we expect to happen to the distribution of outcomes and our students' relative position in that curve if both special education and general education worked the way we think they should? What some reformers seem to be suggesting is that we should expect all children to be successful by a common standard—that is, that we should have the same high standards and expectations for all students and include all students in the same curriculum and assessment procedures, as if by some magic participation therein defines success. In the February 23, 1998, issue of *The New Yorker*, cartoonist Jack Ziegler depicted a California business executive exhorting a subordinate, "Damn it, Henderson, New York is *still* three hours ahead of us. Get on that!" (p. 168). Just as ludicrous would have been an educator saying, "Damn it, Kauffman, some students are *still* two standard deviations below average. Get on that!"

Special education can never be successful in terms of all or even most students with disabilities catching up with their nondisabled peers unless general education is really awful. In fact, if general education begins to provide truly effective instruction for all students, then we might expect that the population variance will increase and that the performance of students with disabilities will become more discrepant than ever from the mean. Perhaps our understanding of these problems at some level predisposes us to shy away from focusing on teaching and learning. After all, we tend to do things at which we are successful. If we are unable to achieve the goal of helping students with disabilities learn academic skills within a standard deviation or so of the normal population mean, then why not turn our efforts to things more easily accomplished: placing children in neighborhood schools and general education classes and telling their teachers to collaborate?

Unprepared to focus on teaching and learning

Special education can be no better than the instruction offered by teachers. Today, much of the instruction received by students with disabilities is provided by general educators, many of whom are very poorly trained, if trained at all, to teach atypical students. The training and support these teachers are given are, in most cases, wholly inadequate. Unfortunately, many of today's special education teachers also are ill prepared to teach particularly difficult students and poorly supported by infrastructure (which includes instructional materials, trained paraprofessionals, and access to consultants). The number and proportion of special education teachers employed on emergency or provisional certificates is scandalous (e.g., in Virginia in 1996–1997, the number was over 1,000, approximately 13% of the special education teaching force). Many teacher education programs emphasize consultation and collaboration even though they are training prospective teachers who have had little or no teaching experience in general education, much less experience in teaching very difficult students. The approaches to teaching and learning that are most popular among general educators today are those we know are extremely likely to fail with most students with disabilities. They emphasize indirect, discovery-oriented, radical constructivist teaching. Furthermore, much of the research in special education today is not about teaching and learning, and many special educators do little or no direct, intensive instruction using the best teaching procedures we have to offer.

What this means for the future of special education is that if we are to survive to help students with disabilities, we are going to have to change course. We cannot continue to avoid focusing on instruction suited to the special needs of students with disabilities. We cannot ignore the difference between such special instruction and instruction that is appropriate for typical students. We cannot continue to imagine that general educators can be prepared to do our job. We cannot continue to suppose that consultation and collaboration will somehow make up the deficit in instruction. We cannot continue to rely on substitutes for the specialized, individualized, intensive, relentless, instruction that special education is supposed to be in all cases but actually is today in too few cases (see Zigmond & Baker, 1995).

This kind of special education is very expensive and highly visible. As such, it is out of step with today's sociopolitical currents.

Unaware of sociopolitical drift

I think many of us tend to forget that education, including special education, is a social welfare program of government. All such programs are under attack today, especially if they are conceptualized as entitlement programs. In fact, special education is being attacked in the popular media and by some special educators as a wasteful and ineffective government entitlement program that should be drastically downsized or eliminated. Government assistance of all kinds—except, perhaps, that offered to business and industry—is increasingly difficult to obtain. The prevailing opinion of our citizens, as reflected by the people elected to public office, is that government benefits for children at risk and their families should be smaller and harder to get. Today, more of our children are being reared in poverty and under conditions that we would expect to produce elevated risk of disability. Yet today sentiment is building against the increasing number of students served by special education and the increasing cost of such services. We are being told—and some of us are buying the big lie—that government programs serving those with special needs, including special education, do not work and should be largely abandoned.

We are virtually certain, in my opinion, to be "downsized," possibly dramatically so in both the size of the population we now serve and the size of our budget. Perhaps a case can be made for turning back responsibility for some of the children we serve to general education. However, if we are to serve even the remaining students adequately, then surely we will need an increase, not a decrease, in the fiscal resources devoted to the task. Our expectations of our programs to normalize children have been unrealistically high, and our estimates of the cost of delivering high-quality services have been unrealistically low. Today, Americans want to ignore social welfare problems as much as possible, to abandon government commitments to all but the spectacularly needy, and to deal with what cannot be ignored by purchasing services from private vendors on the cheap. As a profession, we seem unaware that we are in grave danger of being torched by public sentiment and that some members of our profession are fueling the fire. Our vulnerability is being worsened by postmodern rejection of scientific evidence. Maybe we are attracted to any kind of claptrap if it seems to be capturing the popular imagination, as postmodernism and deconstructionism are now doing.

Mesmerized by postmodern/deconstructivist inanities

I recognize that mine may be an unpopular and risky position that in a few years will look silly or worse, but I now believe that some in our field today have taken a bad cognitive tumble into postmodernism and radical deconstructivist philosophy. I refer here specifically to essays on postmodern and deconstructivist descriptions of education, and more particularly of special education (e.g., Brantlinger, 1997; Danforth, 1997; Danforth & Rhodes, 1997; Elkind, 1997, in press; Sailor & Skrtic, 1996; Skrtic, Sailor, & Gee, 1996). In my view, their teachings undermine progress in serving the needs of students with disabilities. I am not able to identify any practical applications of these writers' work to special education or comprehend how applying their ideas might make a positive contribution to teaching students with disabilities or researching special education problems. This may reflect my own cognitive limitations, but if my assessment is widely shared among special education researchers, it may say something about the observation of an eminent scientist. "Consider this rule of thumb: to the extent that philosophical positions both confuse us and close doors to further inquiry, they are likely to be wrong" (Wilson, 1998, p. 59). I do comprehend the value of context and understand the conditional nature of truth, but the recognition that scientific "truth" is tentative is not a uniquely post-modern insight, nor is the observation that science is affected by its social context a revelation of postmodernists (see Walker *et al.*, in press).

The terms *postmodernism* and *deconstructivism*, though difficult to define precisely, are often linked (see Wilson, 1998). I refer to them together as "PD" to indicate the general notions that logical positivism (i.e., what we have come to know as science) is untrustworthy and that alternative ways of knowing or constructing truth have equal merit. The worldview presented by PD is singularly egocentric, as one's own experience (text or narrative) is the only one knowable. Much of the PD thinking put forward by educators is, in my view, based on nonsequiturs and serious misunderstandings of science. According to PD, disability is a social construction that we could eliminate (deconstruct, subvert, redefine; see Danforth, 1997; Danforth & Rhodes, 1997), a view seriously at odds with the science of exceptionality (see Kauffman, in press). Elkind (1997, in press) has suggested that post-modernism challenges the ideas of progress, universality, and regularity that are part of modern science. For example, Elkind (1997) noted:

> We acknowledge today that some phenomena, such as the weather, are inherently irregular. So too are phenomena such as the dispersion of cream in a coffee cup. Each time we place cream in a coffee cup, the dispersion pattern is different from what it was before. Some phenomena are, by nature, chaotic and have no underlying regularity.
>
> (p. 243)

First, it is important to understand that modern scientists do not claim to be able to predict all phenomena or all cases. In fact, it is precisely the irregularities in phenomena that give rise to shifts to new paradigms that can predict additional phenomena for which older ones could not account, bringing a new level of regularity and predictability to phenomena that previously were assumed to be chaotic. Second, the fact that some phenomena are or appear to be chaotic means neither that all are chaotic nor that the apparent unpredictability of a particular phenomenon will never be understood as a predictable sequence of events. Third, some chaotic phenomena are trivial for achieving a particular purpose in which they play a part. The fact that the dispersion of cream in coffee is chaotic in no way impairs our ability to predict with a high degree of accuracy, and with good effect, the color, taste, and caloric value of a given amount of coffee to which a given amount of cream is added. Likewise, the fact that an individual child's immediate response to a praise statement may be unpredictable in no way invalidates the use of social approval as a strategy for reinforcing desired behavior. Finally, the grand metanarrative of progress attributed to modern science by some proponents of PD (e.g., Danforth, 1997) is caricature, a clever and amusing set of exaggerations. But, if my understanding is correct, in the PD worldview, caricature cannot be discriminated from reality.

The demise of the modern era and of logical positivism as the prevailing scientific paradigm are ballyhooed by those who speak—out of their academic element and inappropriately, I think—of a "paradigm shift." Many of those writers who urge a radical change in view invoke a book by Thomas Kuhn (1996), who described the process by which science progresses from less defensible to more accurate and complete explanations of phenomena. But we are not experiencing a shift in scientific paradigm to postmodern or deconstructivist views in any sense compatible with the observations of Kuhn (1996), who popularized the term *paradigm shift*. His treatise dealt only with how paradigms shift within science itself, in which replicable evidence in the positivist tradition is essential. "Any conception of nature compatible with the growth of science by proof is compatible with the evolutionary view of science developed here" (Kuhn, 1996, p. 173).

Those who say education paradigms are shifting have no reliable data—no proof—with which to create or legitimize a shift (see Brigham & Polsgrove, in press). In fact, PD rejects such proof as unnecessary. The changes of view proposed by PD are based on mere assertion. That is, the proponents of PD seem to suppose that a new paradigm can be created merely by saying or believing that science (that is, positivism) no longer provides valid explanations for our work. However, *scientific* paradigms are not shifted by chutzpah. A scientific paradigm shifts only if reliable, publicly verifiable data are obtainable in support of it; without the data, a new paradigm dies an ignominious death. Moreover, a new scientific paradigm does not necessarily discredit the old, as Kuhn (1996) has shown in the case of Newton's and Einstein's physics. Scientific paradigms offer solutions to problems: they are not merely interesting, novel ideas. Kuhn observed that "novelty

314

for its own sake is not a desideratum in the sciences as it is in so many other creative fields" (p. 169). Nevertheless, in higher education, at least in the social sciences and humanities, data are often ignored for the glitter of novelty. Glazer (1997) wrote of novelty in academia:

One gets ahead in academia by developing a new point of view, perhaps indeed an outrageous one. When one promotes this new point of view in literature or some other field of the humanities, or in some parts of the social sciences . . . there is little constraint from an external world of experiments and facts and numbers to limit the unleashed mind.

(p. 6)

So far, I see no evidence that PD approaches to education offer superior solutions to puzzles (in fact, as I suggested earlier, I am unable to discern what the solutions suggested by PD might be). The absence of better solutions to educational problems offered by PD suggests to me an alternative view of shifting paradigms in education. Researchers during the past several decades have provided clear problem-solving theory (e.g., Engelmann & Carnine, 1982). Education may be considered preparadigmatic in that no consensus has existed that teaching and learning can be studied scientifically or that educational policy decisions should be based on reliable data (see Carnine, 1993; Watkins, 1996). The rise of applied behavior analysis and the formulation of an explicit and testable theory of instruction (e.g., Engelmann & Carnine, 1982) may represent the shift to a scientific paradigm of education against which PD assertions are now being directed. An initial scientific paradigm may emerge over a period of decades, and there are always countercurrents that seek to discredit science or, once established, the scientific paradigm that ultimately becomes dominant. To me, a plausible explanation of shifting paradigms in education is that PD represents a struggle to discredit the paradigm that ultimately will be adopted because it solves problems better than the nonpositivist alternatives.

In the end—in science, anyway—the paradigm that wins the wars is the one that offers the most practical and reliable tools for problem solving. As the history of science shows, though, paradigms can be squelched, at least in the short term, by political philosophy or religious beliefs or superstitions. Positivism has won the day in the natural sciences for several hundred years only because political and religious authorities have allowed it to emerge from the dark ages. But persons who do not believe the scientific data or do not like them can still squelch scientific evidence in favor of political correctness, religious faith, or greed, as has been demonstrated by despots, religious zealots, some industrial giants, and occasionally by scientists themselves (see Wilson, 1998).

We should not underestimate the popularity of nonscientific and aggressively *anti*scientific beliefs today. Nor should we dismiss the danger of such

315

sentiments and frames of mind for education. *The New Yorker* magazine of April 14, 1997 devoted its entire "Talk of the Town" feature to commentary on the mass suicide of Marshall Applewhite and his Heaven's Gate cult. Applewhite and his followers rejected evidence in favor of belief in the supernatural. *The New Yorker* commentary concluded: "Though science is stronger today than when Galileo knelt before the Inquisition, it remains a minority habit of mind, and its future is very much in doubt. Blind belief rules the millennial universe, dark and rangy as space itself" (p. 31). As if to provide supporting evidence, *Life* magazine subsequently featured an article on the recent resurgence of belief in astrology, hyped on its cover under the banner "ASTROLOGY RISING: Why So Many of Us Now Believe the Stars Reflect the Soul" (Miller, 1997). Belief in astrology has burgeoned in the past 20 years, in the absence of any scientific evidence whatever to support its claims and in the face of reliable scientific evidence that its perceived "success" is a function of people's suggestibility and desire for personal validation (see Miller, 1997).

Postmodern/deconstructivist philosophy would have us embrace the subversion of the concepts of disability and special education, particularly their positivist research bases. It suggests that the scientific way of looking at things is a cognitive house of cards created solely by White males, mostly ones now dead. In fact, it would have us believe that all apparent realities are merely convenient constructions and power relations that need deconstructing. It is difficult, if not impossible, to construct a defensible philosophy of special education, or anything else, on the assumption that reality is always constructed to fit convenient power relations and fictions. Moreover, there is comic irony in the proposition that all realities are convenient fictions derived from power relations that enslave the powerless—except this one. It recalls the paradox embedded in any proposition made by someone who says, "I always lie." If we accept such notions we will be left with little or nothing but cognitive demolition debris. Guess who will be buried deepest in the rubble? Children with disabilities will be, of course.

The detonation of PD in our profession leaves us with profoundly weak defenses against the glossy assertions of charlatans that they have discovered something miraculous. We become easy marks for those peddling junk science and other frauds. Why wouldn't we believe a spaceship from comet Hale-Bopp might rescue us, if not our students, and transform our earthly vessels? Who is to say that it will not? I am reminded of the cartoon by Robert Mankoff in *The New Yorker* for April 14, 1997 (p. 6), with the caption, "What lemmings believe." Mankoff's drawing shows a stream of lemmings ascending into heaven rather than plunging off a cliff. As I have suggested elsewhere (Kauffman, 1997b), our profession has a considerable history of enchantment by scam artists, and today's special education seems to me ripe for pied pipers.

316

An easy target for scam artists

In my view, PD philosophy helps make us sitting ducks for the quack—pun intended. The list of instructional and therapeutic procedures that have very little or no reliable data to support them is long. It would include such curious items as applied kinesiology and neurological organization technique (NOT), ocular training said to address learning disabilities, facilitated communication (FC), and a wide range of other new age nostrums. In some cases, these quack methods are popularized and sold shamelessly by special educators. Jacobson, Mulick, and Schwartz (1995) and Danforth (1997) drew clear linkages among PD, antiscientific sentiment, and FC. As Sailor (cited in Jacobson *et al.*, 1995) explained, "Facilitated communication can be looked at as a post-modern idea ... It is social constructivism in communication" (p. 759). In defense of FC, Danforth (1997) noted that "postmodern philosophers propose that the sources of hope in the field of mental retardation services erupt from precisely those mouths and writing (or typing) that do not speak the language of science" (p. 104).

We have always had quacks, and we will have them in perpetuity. But PD notions of the invalidity of science and the arbitrary construction of truth have great potential for diverting us from progress and into perfidy. For example, in the 1990s, we have seen remarkable scientific progress in the positivist tradition in harnessing electronic technology to help individuals with highly specialized communicative needs to express themselves clearly, reliably, and independently. However, at the same time, we have seen the communication of some children with disabilities perverted by the inventive fantasies of "facilitators" (see Jacobson *et al.*, 1995). What a cruel hoax—that some in our profession are now communicating *for* individuals with disabilities while pretending that these individuals are communicating for themselves. A predictable defense of such sham is that the phenomena of facilitated communication are beyond the reach of traditional scientific verification (see Danforth, 1997). This is the familiar dodge of accountability that is used by the magician, the charlatan, the cultist, or the astrologer (see Miller, 1997).

My guess is that in 20 years or so many of those now believing in FC and other frauds will look back on today's quackery with considerable chagrin and wonder why they were so eager to play the fool. I think many of us will wonder why we thought we were about to be transformed, along with the rest of social science if not the world, by ideas that were disconnected from scientific method and not open to public verification. But even if we do not accept PD inanities and scams, we seem spellbound by the idea of systemic transformation, a notion that can distract us from the humbler task of ensuring the integrity and adequacy of *our* component of the array of services exceptional children need—special education.

Immobilized by anticipation of systemic transformation

Like the gambler who awaits the big jackpot, many in our profession await the wholesale change of all of public education, if not of all social services. They do not want incremental change; they want total system transformation. They have fallen into a pattern of "thinking up ever more abstract and abusive names for 'the system'" (Rorty, 1998, p. 136). Some advocates for children with disabilities have complained that change in schools has been piecemeal and limited "because they focus on the individual child and not on the educational system that perpetuates and sometimes produces disadvantage" (Rizvi & Christensen, 1996, p. 3). This statement and many others in today's literature reveal weariness with focusing on individuals and component services such as special education. Some anxiously await and strive to precipitate total systems change that will not just improve special education a little but radically transform our capacities to serve children. As I have noted in a critique of the National Agenda for Achieving Better Results for Children and Youth with Serious Emotional Disturbance,

> "Systemic" is among the most popular modifiers used in contemporary complaints and advertisements for objects and actions. Virtually everything, even the simplest tools, is at risk of being described as a system. We should not be surprised to see nails described as fastening systems or claw hammers as fastening system driving and pulling systems. When anything or anyone fails, we are tempted to see system failure, not the failure of a part or individual. Likewise success; we tend to see it as dependent upon the integral functioning of a wholeness, not as the product of particulars. We forget the parable about the loss of a nail causing the loss of a kingdom.
>
> (Kauffman, 1997a, p. 79)

The notions of system and wholeness, for all their merits, can be used to dodge the angst that goes with responsibility for the particular. Social welfare programs, including general and special education, have a distinguished record of failing to meet our expectations. Many special educators and related service providers are weary of examining the component parts of these systems and of not being able to find and correct the flaws that prevent them from working as they should. Integrated, comprehensive meta- or mega-systems are now much more interesting to talk about, topics on which papers are likely to be published and about which people are often asked to speak or consult. However, I fear that in looking primarily at larger and more complex systems rather than the smaller, more discrete components of them we are merely avoiding the truth that each part must work properly or the system is in shambles. Our attention to the whole system cannot make up for the weakness of its components any more than a singular focus on components will always improve a system.

In the heat of our passion for total system transformation we could find, in a decade or two, that although the structure of the system has changed, its outcomes have not. The outcomes are likely to be no better for this reason, even if the system is transformed: We have failed to take the less glamorous but essential action of ensuring the integrity and fidelity of our own component of the service system.

Five implications of today's special education

Taken together, I believe these 10 characteristics of today's special education have at least five primary implications for our future, each of which I comment on only briefly.

First, I think there are likely to be major changes in the boundaries of special education, in part as a consequence of the very low self-esteem we seem to have developed and the incessant hammering special education has taken in the popular press and the academic literature. We will likely be serving a smaller and more obviously disabled population of students. One factor contributing to this change is the shifting demographics of our school population. Concern about the over-representation of children of color, who disproportionately experience poverty and its disadvantages, may help fuel resistance to early intervention and prevention and may accelerate the decertification of children for special education. The downsizing of special education and the decertification of students as having disabilities may occur in an era in which poverty, neglect, abuse, and other demographic factors are putting higher percentages of children of all colors at risk of disability. We may thus be setting the stage for a substantial reduction in reliance on special education for addressing students' needs. However, we may simultaneously be laying the foundation for a drastic decline in access to special education for those who need it and for the seriously diminished capacity of special education for early intervention and prevention. We need to be at least as careful not to hamper early intervention and prevention and to ensure access to special education for those who need it as we are careful to keep special education from touching those whose nondisabling differences are mistaken for disabilities.

Second, I think we are likely to see a major shift in service delivery patterns and staffing patterns for special educators and in our relationship to general education. We appear to be at a crossroads in our search for the proper role of special educators. The direction we take may well depend on what we see as the most desired outcomes of special education. If we are focused on students' presence in general education, regardless of their acquisition of particular skills in academics, self-care, or employment, then we may see a dramatic and nearly total shift in special educators' roles toward collaboration. However, if we are intent on ensuring that students have instructional access to the general education curriculum—or access to alternative curricula better suited to their needs—then we may see renewed interest in special education teachers with special instructional skills who teach individuals and small groups, often in pull-out settings. Data to date may support the claim that some students with disabilities can be taught appropriately in general education if support services are provided. However, the data to date do not support the claim that *all* students with disabilities can be taught appropriately in neighborhood schools or in general education. We need to take at least as much care to prepare special educators who will offer truly specialized instruction in special settings as we do to prepare special educators who will collaborate and work in general education settings.

Third, I think we may see a major change in state standards and patterns of funding for special education and in personnel preparation programs. The devolution of central authority and the movement toward site-based management are virtually certain to affect special education. State and local authorities will be given more freedom to do what they want, and they will also be required to set aside fewer dollars for students with disabilities. Those who claim to be erasing the lines between general and special education teacher preparation and service delivery may be leading us into a new era of neglect of the educational needs of students with disabilities. We need to monitor carefully the effects of devolution and deregulation on special education funding and services and urge corrective legislation and regulation if exceptional children's access to appropriate education is eroded.

Fourth, it seems possible that we will have additional major changes in state and federal legislation and regulation. I think we might expect changes similar to those that have occurred in other social welfare programs—the rollback of funding and services. Our society has become increasingly punitive and retentive during the past two decades, and I do not think we are about to turn the corner toward a kinder and gentler and more supportive social structure. It is extremely unfortunate that some members of our own profession are contributing to pressures for legislative and regulatory changes that put students with disabilities at a more serious disadvantage, but in language that is at once incomprehensible and appealing in today's socio-political climate. For example, Lipsky and Gartner (1996) inveigh against special education as it is now structured and recommend the following:

- unfettered access to publicly and adequately funded education;
- educational services provided in an inclusive setting, that is in the same school available to their non-disabled peers in age-appropriate classes;
- educational programs that offer effective opportunities for success, in schooling and life; and

- holding those who govern and manage schools accountable for the achievement of that success.

(p. 153)

"Unfettered," "inclusive," "opportunity," "success," and "accountability" are particularly appealing words, but their meanings in this list must be examined thoughtfully. Questions about the logical consistency and comprehensibility of these four recommendations of Lipsky and Gartner for restructuring are many. Consider the following for starters: What fetters access? Is it conceivable that being educated in the same school and classroom as one's age-mates can fetter the access of some students? What is an effective opportunity for success, and how does it differ from an ineffective opportunity? Can an effective opportunity fail? How should we define success in schooling—or in life? How do we hold those who govern and manage schools accountable for a student's success in schooling? Why should school personnel be held accountable for students' success in *life*? Recommendations such as these can easily be seized upon by those who are interested primarily in the nondisabled student population and be used to argue that what is good for one is good for all. Our recommendations should be subjected to a higher level of critical thinking than we urge our elementary and high school students to use in examining advertising, political rhetoric, and other propositions.

Fifth, the lure of postmodernism and radical deconstructivism is strong and growing. Anti-positivist sentiment is strong, and most citizens, including many teachers and teacher educators, have a very poor understanding of the methods and advantages of positivist science. We may well see even more virulent vilification and rejection of the scientific method by those who misunderstand the meanings and uses of evidence. Special education may lose much more of its focus on the scientific understanding of instruction and find itself lost in a cognitive dead end (see Kauffman, in press). We need to weigh very carefully the statements of those who would reform the foundational concepts of our field. We must think our way through the implications of propositions made with "little constraint from an external world of experiments and facts and numbers to limit the unleashed mind" (Glazer, 1997, p. 6), especially propositions to subvert the idea of disability. We must remember that "disengagement from practice produces theoretical hallucinations" (Rorty, 1998, p. 136). Minds unleashed from the constraints of external realities typically dodge responsibilities, leaving people with disabilities stuck in a social niche made more cruel by the avoidance of real-world issues.

A note of optimism

Our future looks bleak for many reasons, some of which I have addressed. We are a middle-aged profession that I believe is showing some signs of being "middle-age crazy," as the condition is called in the vernacular. As a professional group we seem to have lost our buoyancy, sense of purpose, and self-esteem. We appear to have forgotten much of our history, with two particular consequences. First, we tend to romanticize our profession's youth, when we were relatively free of regulation, definition, and respons-ibility, able to lead our professional lives ad hoc—without concern for the broader consequences of our actions. Second, we appear not to have learned much from our prior decades, as we seem ready to dismiss early mistakes as social aberrations and buy "new" ideas (or, if you prefer hype, "paradigms") with virtually no pragmatic analysis of their merits. This is not a pretty picture. If we are to get a grip on our situation and avoid decades of disastrous floundering, then we must do some serious stock-taking.

Our problem of conceptual foundations is not unique. Writers in many fields appear to be forcing a choice between common knowledge (universals) and idiosyncratic understandings of individuals or groups (constructivist knowledge) (Wilson, 1998). The differences in representation of truth are stark, and the consequences of rejecting common knowledge may be profound. But in the face of PD challenges, we can look with considerable confidence to the writing of numerous scholars in other fields who have studied the relationship of knowledge to culture and illuminated the value of common knowledge and truths that are independent of our idio-syncracies. The commentaries of several are particularly instructive and serve to give us hope that our profession will not abandon the science of human behavior for the alternatives:

> Some things in nature just are—even though we can parse and interpret such real items in wildly various ways. A lion is a lion is a lion—and lions are more closely tied by genealogy to tigers than to earthworms. (Of course, I recognize that some system of human thought might base its central principle upon a spiritual or metaphorical tie between lion and earthworm—but nature's genealogies would not be changed thereby, even though the evolutionary tree of life might be utterly ignored or actively denied.)
>
> (Gould, 1997, p. 17)

> No one can deny that science has often misunderstood the limits of its explanatory power, succumbing to a hubristic claim to the Truth. But hubris can be corrected without destroying the underlying confidence in the possibility of a common knowledge—or at least so one hopes. For without a common understanding, a common knowl-edge, prospects for coexistence among the world's many contending truths grow precariously faint.
>
> (Tolson, 1998, p. 12)

How did they [liberal politicians since the 18th century] accomplish that [realize the goals of greater social justice]? Why, by identifying true (or nearly true) universals, such as the common origins, physiologies, aspirations, and feelings of all humankind, *and refuting the false ones*, such as the divine right of kings, natural slavery, and the general inferiority of women. Yes, by some scientists, and at various times, science has offered false universals, but those have been overthrown *only by better science*. And without reaching for true, or better-approaching-true commonalities, we would have only the idiosyncrasies of tribes, including those of whatever tribe you or I happen to belong to.

(Gross, 1998, p. 48)

What these quotes have in common is the recognition that although individuals and groups may indeed see different truths from their idiosyncratic perspectives, there is also a body of information that is not only common or universal but able to free us from egocentrism and tribalism. Such universal knowledge—indeed, the admission of its existence and the recognition of its unique power to free people from separation into warring factions—is under serious attack as a modern failure. Nothing compels us to join the attack. The "modern" universal knowledge that has prevailed for several hundred years frees us as individuals and as a professional cadre to continue the pursuit of universally shared knowledge that brings the greatest liberation and habilitation to all people. The fact that contrary perspectives emerge should neither discourage us nor lead us to conclude that conceptual chaos is inevitable. E. O. Wilson has stated:

I suggest that there have always been two kinds of original thinkers—those who upon viewing disorder try to create order, and those who upon encountering order try to protest it by creating disorder. The tension between the two is what drives learning forward. It lifts us upward on a zigzagging trajectory of progress. And in the Darwinian contest of ideas order always wins, because—simply—that is the way the real world works.

(1998, p. 59)

Looking only on the dark side is a serious mistake. Special education is a relatively young profession with a history that includes reliable empirical research on what works for students at the margins of the distribution of abilities and performance. We have considerable capacity for self-correction and finding order where others see disorder. We could turn our efforts unambiguously and forcefully to our historic mission of seeking reliable, common knowledge about how best to teach students with disabilities—researching and applying instruction that is intensive, urgent, relentless, goal directed according to individual need, and delivered in the setting where it is most effective (see Zigmond & Baker, 1995).

Author's notes

1 This paper is based on a panel presentation at the annual convention of the Council for Exceptional Children, Salt Lake City, April 11, 1997.
2 I am grateful to Fredrick J. Brigham, Jean B. Crockett, and Mark P. Mostert for their helpful feedback on an earlier draft of this paper, but in no way does my gratitude for these reviewers' comments imply their agreement with the opinions I express.

References

Blatt, B. (1987). *The conquest of mental retardation.* Austin, TX: PRO-ED.

Brantlinger, E. (1997). Using ideology: Cases of nonrecognition of the politics of research and practice in special education. *Review of Educational Research, 67,* 425–459.

Brigham, F. J., & Polsgrove, L. (in press). A rumor of paradigm shift in the field of children's emotional and behavioral disorders. *Behavioral Disorders.*

Carnine, D. (1993, December 8). Facts over fads: Testing out "innovations" might save money, time, and good will. *Education Week,* p. 40.

Carnine, D. (1997). Bridging the research-to-practice gap. In J. Lloyd, E. Kameenui, & D. Chard (Eds.), *Issues in educating students with disabilities* (pp. 363–373). Mahwah, NJ: Erlbaum.

Crockett, J. B. (1997). *Instructional settings for exceptional learners: A conceptual, historical, and empirical examination of the least restrictive environment.* Unpublished doctoral dissertation, University of Virginia.

Danforth, S. (1997). On what basis hope? Modern progress and postmodern possibilities. *Mental Retardation, 35,* 93–106.

Danforth, S., & Rhodes, W. C. (1997). Deconstructing disability: A philosophy for inclusion. *Remedial and Special Education, 18,* 357–366.

Dupre, A. P. (1997). Disability and the public schools: The case against "inclusion." *Washington Law Review, 72,* 775–858.

Elkind, D. (1997). The death of child nature: Education in the postmodern world. *Phi Delta Kappan, 79,* 241–245.

Elkind, D. (in press). Behavior disorders: A postmodern perspective. *Behavioral Disorders.*

Engelmann, S., & Carnine, D. (1982). *Theory of instruction: Principles and applications.* New York: Irvington.

Gerber, M. M. (1996). Reforming special education: Beyond "inclusion." In C. Christensen & F. Rizvi (Eds.), *Disability and the dilemmas of education and justice* (pp. 156–174). Philadelphia: Open University Press.

Glazer, N. (1997). *We are all multiculturalists now.* Cambridge, MA: Harvard University Press.

Gould, S. J. (1997). *Questioning the millennium. A rationalist's guide to a precisely arbitrary countdown.* New York: Harmony Books.

Gross, P. R. (1998). The Icarian impulse. *The Wilson Quarterly, 22,* 39–49.

Jacobson, J. W., Mulick, J. A., & Schwartz, A. A. (1995). A history of facilitated communication. Science, pseudoscience, and antiscience silence working group on facilitated communication. *American Psychologist, 50,* 750–765.

Kauffman, J. M. (1993). How we might achieve the radical reform of special education. *Exceptional Children, 60*, 6–16.

Kauffman, J. M. (1997a). Conclusion: A little of everything, a lot of nothing is an agenda for failure. *Journal of Emotional and Behavioral Disorders, 5*, 76–81.

Kauffman, J. M. (1997b). Guest editorial: Caricature, science, and exceptionality. *Remedial and Special Education, 18*, 130–132.

Kauffman, J. M. (in press). Foreword: What we make of difference and the difference we make. In D. H. Saklofske & V. L. Schwean (Eds.), *Handbook of psychosocial characteristics of exceptional children.* New York: Plenum.

Kauffman, J. M., & Lloyd, J. W. (1995). A sense of place: The importance of placement issues in contemporary special education. In J. M. Kauffman, J. W., Lloyd, D. P. Hallahan, & T. A. Astuto (Eds.), *Issues in educational placement: Emotional and behavioral disorders* (pp. 3–19). Hillsdale, NJ: Erlbaum.

Kuhn, T. S. (1996). *The structure of scientific revolutions* (3rd ed.). Chicago: University of Chicago Press.

Lipsky, D. K., & Gartner, A. (1996). Equity requires inclusion: The future for all students with disabilities. In C. Christensen & F. Rizvi (Eds.), *Disability and the dilemmas of education and justice* (pp. 144–155). Philadelphia: Open University Press.

Miller, K. (1997, July). Star struck: A journey to the new frontiers of the zodiac. *Life*, pp. 39–53.

Rizvi, F., & Christensen, C. (1996). Introduction. In C. Christensen & F. Rizvi (Eds.), *Disability and the dilemmas of education and justice* (pp. 1–8). Philadelphia: Open University Press.

Rorty, R. (1998, April 3). The dark side of the academic left. *The Chronicle of Higher Education*, 134–136.

Rushdie, S. (1996, September 23). Reservoir frogs (or places called mama's). *The New Yorker*, p. 104.

Sack, J. L. (1997, April 16). Disruptive spec. ed. students get own school. *Education Week 16*(29), 1, 24–25.

Sailor, W., & Skrtic, T. M. (1996). School-linked services integration: Crisis and opportunity in the transition to a postmodern society. *Remedial and Special Education, 17*, 271–283.

Skrtic, T. M., Sailor, W., & Gee, K. (1996). Voice, collaboration, and inclusion: Democratic themes in educational and social reform initiatives. *Remedial and Special Education, 17*, 143–157.

Tolson, J. (1998). At issue: The many and the one. *The Wilson Quarterly, 22*, 12.

Walker, H. M., Forness, S. R., Kauffman, J. M., Epstein, M. H., Gresham, F. M., & Nelson, C. M. (in press). Macro-social validation: Referencing outcomes in behavioral disorders to issues and problems society wants solved. *Behavioral Disorders.*

Watkins, C. L. (1996). Follow through: Why didn't we? *Effective School Practices, 15*, 57–66.

Wilson, E. O. (1998, March). Back from chaos. *The Atlantic Monthly*, pp. 41–62.

Zigmond, N. (1997). Educating students with disabilities: The future of special education. In J. Lloyd, E. Kameenui, & D. Chard (Eds.), *Issues in educating students with disabilities* (pp. 377–390). Mahwah, NJ: Erlbaum.

Zigmond, N., & Baker, J. M. (1995). Concluding comments: Current and future practice in inclusive schooling. *The Journal of Special Education, 29*, 245–250.

325

19

INCLUSIVE EDUCATION IN THE MARKET-PLACE

Martyn Rouse and Lani Florian

Source: *International Journal of Inclusive Education* 1(4) (1997): 323–36.

Abstract

For many, the concept of inclusive schools is seen as the logical development of a more tolerant and accepting society. Recent debates about inclusion have centred on the rights of children with disabilities to attend mainstream schools and the ways in which schools must change to make this a reality. At the same time, a competitive climate, brought about by a 'new orthodoxy' of educational reform in the developed world, is affecting the context in which schools are working. There has been a shift from policies based on equity, social progress and altruism to new laws underpinned by the philosophy of the market-place. In such a climate, students with special educational needs are particularly vulnerable. This paper explores some of the issues that are emerging in England and Wales as policies designed to extend the concept of inclusive education are affected by the market-place philosophies that have driven recent reforms.

Introduction

Much has been written recently about the concept of inclusion. For many, it is seen as the logical development of a more tolerant and accepting society, an extension of the basic human right for all people to participate in that society regardless of any difference or disability. Inclusion is a notion that extends to many areas of social policy, including anti-discrimination laws, care in the community, employment and education.

Within education, the debate about inclusion has focused primarily on the rights of children with disabilities to attend mainstream schools (e.g. Ainscow 1991, Forest 1988, Slee 1993, Stainback and Stainback 1992, 1996). It is an international debate (Sebba and Ainscow 1996) that has been the subject of deliberation at the highest level (e.g. Unesco 1994).

Many advocates of inclusive education have argued that segregation, particularly by placement in special schools, is morally wrong and educationally inefficient. They are convinced that the opportunities for socialization and development offered by mainstream schools represent the best chance for eventual social acceptance of people with disabilities within mainstream society. The benefits of such thinking are potentially significant because, by definition, inclusive schools value diversity and strive to offer the maximum learning opportunities for all students.

Even within a supportive legislative framework, the implications of inclusion for schools are enormous, affecting such issues as: organization, teaching styles, curriculum, assessment, staff development and community links. In this paper, we argue that the task has been made greater because schools are operating in a hostile legislative context. During the past decade, there has been a shift from legislation and policies based upon principles of equity, social progress and altruism, to new legislation underpinned by a market-place philosophy based on principles of academic excellence, choice and competition. In a climate in which educational reforms are based upon the principles of the market, students with disabilities and/or special educational needs are particularly vulnerable. For schools, the task of becoming inclusive is to swim against the tide of educational reform.

This paper explores some of the issues that are emerging as attempts to extend inclusive education are affected by the market-place philosophies that have driven recent reforms. It is written in the context of developments in England and Wales, but as we have suggested elsewhere (Rouse and Florian 1996), there are many parallels with the situation in other countries. Our arguments draw upon an ongoing research project that considers the implications of recent educational reform on students with special educational needs (Rouse 1996). To help set the scene for the discussion, some background to the reforms is provided and consideration is given to the ways in which the special needs task has been reconceptualized in recent years.

Developments in special education:
from integration to inclusion

Throughout the world, recent years have seen considerable questioning about the purpose, practice and location of special education (e.g. Skrtic 1991, Slee 1993). In writing about England and Wales, Wedell (1990) pointed out that few areas of education have seen such major developments during the past 20 years as special needs education. The thinking that informed these developments was articulated in the Warnock Report (DES 1978) and led to a reconceptualization of the special needs task based upon the following principles:

- *Interactive nature of difficulty*: special educational needs result from a complex interaction of factors, only some of which exist within the child. Other factors are found in the learning environment in which the child is educated.
- *Non-categorical nature of disability*: special needs are relative and context specific. It is therefore impossible to draw a clear line between different disability groups or the so-called handicapped and non-handicapped.
- *Common aims*: the aims of education are the same for all children, although the means may be different, as might the extent to which the aims are achieved.
- *Integration*: children have the right to be educated alongside their peers as long as their needs can be met. Additional support may be required if this is to be achieved.
- *Positive discrimination*: some children's rights should be protected by a 'statement of special educational need', a legal document detailing the form of provision and additional support required.

There were those who argued that the principles underlying this reconceptualization of the special needs task led to a simplistic rejection of medical explanations of disability and also to a denial of individual differences. For example, Norwich (1990) was unconvinced that the use of categorical labels inevitably led to negative outcomes for children. He argued for the adoption of a general systems approach which would merge biological, psychological and social explanations of disability in order to avoid sterile debates about causation.

Despite these concerns, evidence from many parts of the UK suggested that progress was made in implementing new policies and practice based upon these principles (Wedell *et al.* 1987). In 1981 a new special education law was passed, spending on special education increased, LEAs appointed new advisory teams and there was a series of new teacher and school development initiatives designed to help develop whole-school policies for meeting special needs (Rouse and Balshaw 1991). Although many of these developments could be seen as positive, some critics (e.g. Ainscow 1991, Barton 1986) were unconvinced that the growth of special education worked to the benefit of students. To add to the confusion, the government started to ask questions about the quality and efficiency of special education provision (Audit Commission 1992a, 1992b). There were concerns that the system was not delivering value for time and money.

Many advocates and professionals began to question the necessity and appropriateness of segregated provision. The most radical suggested that special schools were a form of educational apartheid (Jordan and Goodey 1996). In addition, a number of parental pressure groups were established to further the cause of integration. This pressure, together with increasing professional and political interest, led to a series of *ad hoc* local integration schemes in many parts of the UK. Some local authorities, most famously the London Borough of Newham, made a commitment to close segregated special schools and to develop integrated mainstream schools by relocating expertise and facilities.

More recently, the concept of inclusion has largely replaced integration, which has come to be seen by some as unsatisfactory. According to Lewis (1995), there are two reasons for this. The first is that integration has been too narrowly interpreted as placement, without any regard to the quality of that placement. Furthermore, much integration practice not only involved the relocation of students from special to mainstream, but also the transfer of many special education practices. Ainscow (1997: 3) questions the use of individualized methods of teaching to support integration; he argues that individualized approaches to learning are not desirable, nor are they feasible in mainstream schools: 'when integration efforts are dependent upon the importing of practices from special education they seem almost certain to lead to difficulties. Indeed they are likely to lead to new forms of segregation, albeit within mainstream settings.'

The second and more complex reason has to do with a critique of the concept of *normalization*, a key influence on integration policies throughout the world. Nirje (1985) defined normalization as 'making available to all persons with disabilities, patterns of life and conditions of everyday living which are as close as possible to or indeed the same as the regular circumstances and ways of life of society'. Critics (e.g. Peters 1995) claim that to do so involves a denial of difference and ask whether the concept itself has contributed to a devaluing of people who are different.

In response, the term *inclusion* has come to refer to the opportunity for people with a disability to participate fully in all of the educational, employment, consumer, recreational, community and domestic activities that typify everyday society (Inclusion International 1996). The 'opportunity to participate' is quite different from 'making available patterns of life and conditions of everyday living'. Opportunity to participate implies active involvement and choice, as opposed to the passive receipt of a pattern or condition that has been made available. Such thinking requires a radical reappraisal of the purpose and nature of special education, together with the reconfiguration of mainstream schools, rather than the mere relocation of techniques developed in segregated settings.

The permissive and enabling education policies throughout the 1970s and much of the 1980s stimulated much thinking about children and young people with special educational needs. Throughout this period, many people assumed that special education provision would continue to grow because of the permissive policy framework. Few people anticipated that the political climate would change so radically that it would threaten the assumptions upon which both existing and emerging practice and provision were based.

Educational reform

Over the past decade, many countries around the world have taken up initiatives designed to improve and restructure education. According to O'Neill (1995: 9), government interventions in many countries appear to have been driven by a range of motives, including:

- improving national economies by tightening a connection between schooling, employment, productivity and trade;
- enhancing student outcomes in employment related skills and competencies;
- attaining more direct control over curriculum content assessment;
- reducing the costs to government of education;
- increasing community input to education by more direct involvement in school decision making and pressure of market choice.

Whilst the pace and detail of the reforms between countries has been varied, a 'new orthodoxy' has emerged in many complex post-industrialized societies. Mitchell (1996) suggests it may be characterized by the following:

- *choice*: providing parents with greater choice of schools for their children;
- *competition*: between schools for students and resources;
- *privatization*: reducing public monopolies by contracting out services to private sector suppliers;
- *separation*: of organizational, advisory, regulatory, and delivery functions, to prevent too much power being in the hands of the providers;
- *decentralization*: of decision-making through local management;
- *prescription*: of curriculum content and assessment systems;
- *surveillance*: through more rigorous quality-control procedures utilizing quantifiable outcome indicators.

In England and Wales laws based upon this 'new orthodoxy' introduced a series of radical reforms embodied in the 1988 Education Reform Act (ERA) which were to have a profound impact upon the education landscape. The ERA was designed to raise standards by introducing a National Curriculum closely linked to national assessment and testing. In addition, control of the education service would pass from the providers (local education authorities and teachers) to the consumers (parents) through a series of measures designed to impose the rigours of the market-place on schools. It has been considered the most important and far-reaching piece of educational legislation in England and Wales since the Education Act of 1944 (which ensured universal access to secondary education), because it altered the basic power structure of the education system (Maclure 1988).

Table 1 summarizes the major reforms introduced by the Education Reform Act 1988. It may appear paradoxical that legislation designed to empower parents as consumers of education should have at its heart a centralized National Curriculum and a set of national standards. Whilst politicians may have trusted parents and school governors with the day-to-day running of schools, they were not prepared to let them decide what schools should teach or how it should be assessed. In the following section, we explore the impact of the market-place reforms in more detail. Market-place reforms are defined as those pertaining to local management of schools, choice and competition. Although other reforms such as the introduction of a National Curriculum and national assessment and testing procedures have also had a significant impact on the education of pupils with special educational needs, space limitations have led us to focus in this paper on market-place reforms. The events leading up to the introduction of the Education Reform Act 1988 in England and Wales have been powerfully described and insightfully analysed by others, including Ball (1990) and Lawton (1989).

The impact of marketplace reforms on the education of children with special educational needs

In many countries, children with special educational needs have been given no more than a passing reference in recent educational reform legislation. In a climate which stresses the need for high achievement, it could be argued that such children are at best irrelevant, or at worst an encumbrance. Many commentators from the special education community in the UK (e.g. Copeland 1991, Heward and Lloyd-Smith 1990, Wedell 1988) predicted that the reforms would undermine and dissipate much of the progress made for students with special needs following the Warnock Report (DES 1978). Indeed, Mary Warnock in a lecture at the Cambridge Institute of Education, in 1992, predicted that just as housing policies of the 1980s had led to an increase in homelessness, the educational reforms would lead to 'school-less children'. Children with learning difficulties or emotional and

Table 1 Major reforms of ERA (1988).

National Curriculum
National testing and assessment
Publication of test results
Local management of schools (LMS)
Competition between schools for students
Open enrolment and parental choice
Grant-maintained schools
City technology colleges (CTCs)

behavioural problems were seen as being particularly vulnerable. It was argued that such students would be unattractive to schools because they would depress the schools' test results or cost more to educate than they brought into school in resources. A new climate had been created. There was a spirit of 'educational Darwinism' in the air in which it was expected that only the fittest schools, teachers and students would survive.

By the 1990s, it was becoming clear that many of the 1988 reforms were incompatible with the earlier 1981 special education legislation which linked additional resources to a 'statement of special educational need'. Mainstream schools were under pressure from some of the reforms and many sought to secure additional funding by identifying (statementing) increasing numbers of students with special needs (Lunt and Evans 1994). New legislation introduced a *Code of Practice on the Identification and Assessment of Special Educational Needs* (DFE 1994) in an attempt to deal with these problems. However, it may not have had the desired effect as some schools have continued to pursue additional resources by identifying increased numbers of children as having special educational needs. Paradoxically, the Code of Practice may be undermining school-wide developments which could be beneficial to all students by focusing teachers' attention on the difficulties faced by individuals (Sebba 1996). As a result, the special needs debate, which should be focused on the development of quality provision, has been dominated by an undignified scramble for extra resources.

Nevertheless, there were those who saw potential benefits from some of the reform proposals. Bowers (1993) saw greater opportunities for schools resulting from the introduction of local financial management because many decisions about spending are better taken at the local level. Thomas and Bullock (1994: 49) argued that increased local management of schools (LMS), including 'delegation, transparent formula-based funding and more information for parents [were] in principle, welcome innovations'. They noted that the national framework for local management was sufficiently flexible for some LEAs to direct extra resources to schools with the highest proportion of 'additional needs'.

Yet historically, equal opportunity and inclusion policies in schools were often the result of local authority (LEA) initiatives. Although the law states that LEAs still have responsibility for students with special educational needs, in many cases reduced resources and facilities make it more difficult for them to meet these requirements. The demise of LEAs, as a consequence of LMS and the delegation of decision-making to schools, has threatened the future development of equal opportunity and inclusion policies, particularly where schools feel driven by the need to achieve excellence at the expense of equity. There is considerable evidence to suggest that LEAs now have only limited ability to monitor and/or guide school policy and provision for students with special educational needs in comparison to the period prior to the 1988 reforms (Vincent *et al.* 1995).

Due to the demise of the LEA, open enrolment and greater parental choice, there is now no overall management of school admissions. There is evidence to suggest that some schools, given the greater autonomy they now enjoy, are overtly or covertly discriminating against students with disabilities while trying to attract greater numbers of high-achieving students (Copeland 1994). It is possible that in the market-place, students with special needs are unattractive to those schools trying to improve their position in the league tables in which test results are published and compared. Selection by ability is once again a major factor in the English educational system.

The research of Ball *et al.* (1994) confirms negative outcomes for students with special needs. They suggest that the publication of performance indicators has meant that schools are keen to attract 'motivated' parents and 'able' children, who are more likely to enhance their competitive edge, rather than children who might find learning difficult. They also report that there has been a shift in resources away from students with special needs in favour of students who are more likely to enhance the school's performance in the league tables. Popular schools can increasingly select the students they admit. In such cases, it is likely that they will reject students who are not perceived as contributing to the academic status of the school.

It is apparent that the consequences of the reforms are seen by some people as being predominantly negative, whilst others see them more positively. For example, the extension of parental choice has been warmly welcomed by some parents and by the headteachers of those schools that have benefited from increased student numbers and funding (Le Grand and Bartlett 1993). However, research by Knill and Humphreys (1996) has questioned the ability of parents to make informed choices about schools when they lack the relevant knowledge. This has particular significance in special education because until recently professionals were more likely to make the decisions about school placement. Parents may have been consulted, but they did not have choice. We would argue that in spite of the growth of support groups intended to empower parents (Wolfendale 1997), many parents still do not have choice because of the knowledge and status differences between parents and professionals. A 1989 Harris poll conducted in the United States found poorer and less educated parents to be less informed about their rights and choices than more highly educated, affluent parents, despite a federal law requiring LEAs to disseminate the relevant information to parents of children with disabilities in their native language (Harris and Associates 1989).

Thus middle-class parents are able to exploit the market in education by bringing their social and cultural advantages to bear. They are more likely to have the knowledge, skills and contacts to understand and take advantage of a deregulated system. Some teachers point out that their schools are now finding it more difficult to manage the demands from their articulate middle-class parents for special treatment for their children (Riddell and

Brown 1994), particularly when these demands are backed by politically astute pressure groups (cf. Chasty and Friel 1993). Teachers claim that there is a growing group of vulnerable children who do not have parents able to advocate on their behalf with the school. This is problematic because decisions about resource allocation are now increasingly taken at the school level, rather than by the LEA. School managers and govenors may find it more difficult to apply the principle of equity in the face of an articulate parental campaign based upon the principle of self-interest, particularly now that market forces are operating. When parents exercise their right to send their children to schools outside their neighbourhood, there is likely to be a negative effect on the funding and viability of other schools which are often situated in less prosperous areas (Adler *et al.* 1989). A consequence is that students who have learning difficulties or are from poor working-class backgrounds are more likely to find themselves being educated in the same (low-status) school. As Whitty (1997) points out, markets have exacerbated the inequalities between schools.

No school can afford to ignore the market-place, but some schools are more vulnerable in the new competitive world. Even some 'good' schools may suffer from the new funding arrangements because of geography (the school may be hard to get to), or demography (the area might have a reduced number of children). Declining rolls result from a number of complex factors. Schools serving disadvantaged communities could be doing a successful job but this may not be reflected in their league-table position. In schools where the student numbers are in decline, the low morale of the teachers may be seriously affecting the quality of education that is available (*Times Educational Supplement* 17.1.97).

In some schools the reforms have led to a shift in the value framework upon which previous policies were based. Some headteachers report that financial, rather than educational, principles now underpin many of the decisions (Rouse 1996). Schools increasingly see themselves in competition with other schools and therefore act as individual units (Vincent *et al.* 1995). The increase in demand for statutory assessment of children is symptomatic of this self-interest as schools scramble for a greater share of the resource cake. In some LEAs there has been a two fold increase in the number of statemented children during the last five years. Such behaviour is motivated by self-interest, rather than being informed by wider considerations of service development.

There has been a reported increase in marketing activity by special schools. Bowers (1996) claims that salary incentives are available to special school headteachers if they can demonstrate to their governors that they have recruited more students and therefore received more income for the school. Bowers asks whether the aggressive marketing of segregated special provision can be reconciled with an expressed desire to increase inclusive education.

There is increasing evidence that schools are under considerable pressure. One indicator of this is the alarming growth in the number of children who are excluded from school (Stirling 1992; OFSTED 1996). It is not claimed that the reforms are the only, or even the main cause of these problems, but there is evidence from the Association of Metropolitan Authorities (1995) that the pressure on schools has increased as a result of the reforms. Official statistics indicate that in 1991/92 some 3,833 children and young people were permanently excluded from schools in England and Wales (DFE 1993b), an increase of 25 per cent since 1991/92. Parsons (1994) claims that this figure would be doubled if children who were indefinitely excluded were to be counted in the official figures. Even then, according to Stirling (1992), this would show only the tip of the iceberg. In addition to the formal exclusions recorded in the official statistics, it is estimated that there are tens of thousands of children who are 'school-less'. For example, in one LEA, Stirling claims to have found that for every two pupils who were formally excluded, a further 30 pupils were excluded by various 'unofficial' means such as bogus medical circumstances, collusion with parents or 'imaginative' use of authorized absence procedures. She estimates that there are 60,000 children and young people currently without a school place, and that students with special educational needs are disproportionately over-represented in this group.

The overall impact of local management, competition and parental choice has been uneven. There may have been improvements in decision-making at the school level, leading to greater efficiency and cost savings; but there has also been an increase in the number of pupils excluded from school. Some schools have clearly been winners as resources have been redistributed. However, as in any competition, there have also been losers. The impact on the development of inclusive schools has been substantial. Rouse (1996) found that many teachers who claimed to be committed to the development of inclusive education feel pulled in a different direction by the overwhelming power of the reforms.

In spite of the evidence that leads to these negative conclusions, it is interesting to note that some schools that are committed to the development of inclusive practice have been able to make significant progress in educating a more diverse group of students whilst, at the same time, improving academic results and their position in the league tables. In the conclusion of this paper, we consider how it might be possible for schools to be academically effective and inclusive in the current climate.

Conclusion

The past ten years has been a period of uncertainty and turbulence as the effects of various reforms become apparent. Many of the earlier predictions about the impact of the reforms have been realized, others have produced unexpected and positive outcomes. For example, although we have not addressed it here, the implementation of a National Curriculum has led to greater progression and continuity of learning experiences for many pupils with disabilities (Sebba and Byers 1992); and Lewis (1996) claims that the modified assessment arrangements may provide the basis for developments in inclusive practice.

However, it is apparent that the reforms have led to a series of tensions within the educational system as different ideologies and priorities compete with one another. We suggest that an identifiable set of tensions (see table 2) has emerged as a result of the clash between the principles that underpin market-based reforms and the principles that underpin the development of inclusive education. These tensions may be used to provide a framework for analysing the impact of the reforms on the development of inclusive schools.

One way forward for those advocating more inclusive schools is to understand these tensions and try to find ways of reducing the negative impact and confusion that has been produced. As noted above, some schools are working successfully and creatively within the current climate. Such schools manage to be both excellent (as defined by the reforms) and to be inclusive. We would suggest that such schools do not see the tensions as bipolar or either–or opposites. They have clear policies that have been developed by all the staff and have a commitment to educating all children. Our impression is that they are using what Handy (1994) calls a 'third angle' or 'trinitarian' approach for resolving these tensions. For example, a bipolar approach makes it difficult to resolve the equity–excellence dilemma. If a third element is introduced into the debate—in this case, effectiveness—then resolution is possible because an effective school does not have to choose between being either equitable or excellent. It can be both, by aiming at excellence for all. Of course, the third angle in our example (effectiveness) is not without its own complexity, as the school effectiveness and school improvement literature makes clear. What research on effectiveness does clarify, however, is that school variables have a significant impact upon pupils' learning. Our research on inclusive schools suggests a specific refinement of the factors associated with effective schools. Effectiveness in an inclusive school is more than efficiency or excellence for some. If an effective school is characterized in part by a common mission, an inclusive school's common

Table 2 The tensions.

Inclusion : Exclusion
Equity : Excellence
Producers : Consumers
Choice : Planning
Entitlement : Differentiation
Altruism : Self-interest
Individuals : Groups

mission includes a philosophy of zero-reject (Rouse and Florian 1996). In this way, effectiveness can mediate the equity–excellence dilemma.

The Improving the Quality of Education for All (IQEA) project (Hopkins *et al.* 1996) is a 'school improvement' approach that contains realistic and workable solutions to resolving some of the tensions we have identified. By focusing on whole-school development, the project aims to strengthen a school's capacity for managing change (i.e. as required by external reforms) and pupil diversity (as implied by the principles of inclusive education policies, i.e. 'all means all'). The 'third angle', in this case, is a condition of participation in the project, that schools select their own individual development projects, but must do so in a way that accepts the five principles of IQEA. The principles include a vision of the school that embraces *all* members of the school community as both learners and contributors, and that the school will view external pressures for change as an opportunity to secure its internal priorities.

The enhancement of 'consumer' rights has exacerbated the tensions between parents and education professionals. In turn, this has been associated with the growth in the numbers of parents directly challenging decisions made on their behalf through the legal system. However, these tensions are less apparent where collaborative systems of governance have been established (Brighouse 1997). In some areas, the development of parental partnership schemes is well advanced which have the effect of reducing the tensions between parents and professionals (Wolfendale 1997). Though complex and difficult to establish, such partnership arrangements reduce the potential for conflict which is apparent in 'us and them' situations. Because partnership requires cooperation and negotiation, it mediates between producers and consumers, enabling perspectives to be shared and common goals to be established.

Although there are examples of promising practice, further work is required to identify the conditions that allow some schools to be successful for all students in the current climate. Such knowledge would provide a starting-point for other schools as they attempt to resolve the tensions that have been produced by the reforms. The need for such a starting-point is underscored by a recent National Foundation for Educational Research study which found that 'the effects of league tables as deterrents to taking in [more] pupils with statements, was seen as a minor issue in LEAs where all schools had the expectation and acceptance that they would provide for all the pupils in the area' (Lee and Henkhuzens 1996: 12–13). Certain tensions (i.e. between inclusion and exclusion) were found to be less acute in LEAs with clear policies on inclusion and higher levels of integration.

Of course, schools would find it easier to develop inclusive policies and practice if they were publicly acknowledged for such developments. This could be helped by redefining the criteria of a successful school and broadening the concept of achievement beyond the uni-dimensional emphasis on test scores in a limited range of the curriculum, to include acknowledgement of all students' learning across a broader range of outcomes. As Stainback and Stainback (1996) point out, it is not only students with disabilities who benefit from inclusion. They claim benefits for all students, as well as for their teachers and society at large. For this claim to be accepted by policy-makers, it is necessary to develop a series of outcome indicators that could be used to demonstrate the benefits of inclusive education for all.

There are likely to be long-term costs resulting from some of the reforms. The increase in the numbers of school-less children and the growing inequalities between schools are leading to social exclusion and the creation of an educational underclass. We would suggest that these costs will be greater than any benefits that may have resulted from the application of market-place philosophies to education. However, we would not argue for a return to the old order, for as Whitty (1997) points out, this is not feasible or sensible. Instead, new policies designed to encourage community empowerment and involvement are required. Such policies could help redress the worst excesses that have been caused by the individual's right to choose at the expense of disadvantaged groups.

Inclusive education has been bruised by the harsher elements of the reforms, but even in this unsupportive climate, there are schools that are currently demonstrating that inclusion is not incompatible with excellence. Politicians as well as educators could learn from such schools if they are interested in providing the highest standard of education to all students and the creation of a more inclusive society.

Acknowledgment

We would like to thank Judy Sebba, of the University of Cambridge School of Education, for her helpful critique of an earlier version of this paper.

References

Alder, M., Petch, A. and Tweedie, J. (1989) *Parental Choice and Education Policy* (Edinburgh: Edinburgh University Press).

Ainscow, M. (1991) *Effective Schools for All* (London: David Fulton).

Ainscow, M. (1997) Towards inclusive schooling. *British Journal of Special Education*, **24** (1), 3–6.

Association of Metropolitan Authorities (1995) *Reviewing Special Educational Needs* (London: AMA).

Audit Commission (1992a) *Getting in on the Act* (London: HMSO).

Audit Commission (1992b) *Getting the Act Together* (London: HMSO).

Ball, S. J. (1990) *Politics and Policy Making in Education* (London: Routledge).

Ball, S. J., Bowe, R. and Gerwitz, S. (1994) Market forces and parental choice: self interest and competitive advantage in education. In S. Tomlinson (ed.), *Educational Reform and its Consequences* (London: IPPR/Rivers Oram Press).

Barton, L. (1986) The politics of special educational needs. *Disability, Handicap and Society*, **1** (3), 273–290.

Bowers, T. (1993) Funding special education. In J. Visser and G. Upton (eds), *Special Education in Britain after Warnock* (London: David Fulton).

Bowers, T. (1996) Some dilemmas in imposing marketplace philosophies on special needs provision. In L. Florian and M. Rouse (eds), *School Reform and Special Educational Needs: Anglo-American Perspectives* (Cambridge: University of Cambridge Institute of Education).

Brighouse, T. (1997) Urban education: taking differentiation beyond the classroom. Inagural Lecture, University of Birmingham, 28 January.

Chasty, H. and Friel, J. (1993) *Children with Special Needs: Assessment, Law and Practice* (London: Jessica Kingsley).

Copeland, I. (1991) Special educational needs and the Education Reform Act 1988. *British Journal of Educational Studies*, **39** (2), 190–206.

Copeland, I. (1994) The secondary school prospectus and the challenge of SEN. *Educational Studies*, **20** (2), 237–250.

Department for Education and Science (DES) (1978) *Special Educational Needs* (The Warnock Report) (London: HMSO).

DFE (Department for Education) (1993) Press Release on national exclusions reporting system. (DFE, London).

DFE (1994) *The Code of Practice on the Identification and Assessment of Special Educational Needs* (London: DFE).

Forest, M. (1988) Full inclusion is possible. *IMPACT*, **1**, 3–4.

Handy, C. (1994) *The Empty Raincoat: Making Sense of the Future* (London: Hutchinson).

Harris and Associates (1989) *International Center for Disabled Survey III: A Report Card on Special Education* (New York: Harris and Associates).

Heward, C. and Loyd-Smith, M. (1990) Assessing the impact of legislation on special education policy—an historical analysis. *Journal of Education Policy*, **5** (1), 21–36.

Hopkins, D., West, M. and Ainscow, M. (1996) *Improving the Quality of Education for All: Progress and Challenge* (London: David Fulton).

Inclusion International (1996) Policy directions. *Inclusion: News from Inclusion International*, **18** (34), 4.

Jordan, L. and Goodey, C. (1996) *Human Rights and School Change: The Newham Story* (Bristol: Centre for Studies in Inclusive Education).

Knill, B. and Humphreys, K. (1996) Parental preference and its impact upon a market force approach to special education. *British Journal of Special Education*, **23** (1), 30–34.

Lawton, D. (1989) *Education Culture and the National Curriculum* (London: Hodder and Stoughton).

Lee, B., and Henkhuzens, Z. (1996) *Integration in Progress: Pupils with Special Needs in Mainstream Schools* (Slough: National Foundation for Educational Research).

Le Grand, J. and Bartlett, W. (eds) (1993) *Quasi-Markets and Social Policy* (London: Macmillan).

Lewis, A. (1995) *Children's Understanding of Disability* (London: Routledge).

Lewis, A. (1996) Summative National Curriculum assessments of primary aged children with special needs. *British Journal of Special Education*, **23** (1), 9–14.

Lunt, I. and Evans, J. (1994) Dilemmas in special educational needs: some effects of local management of schools. In S. Riddell and S. Brown (eds) *Special Educational Needs Policy in the 1990s* (London: Routledge).

Maclure, S. (1988) *Education Re-formed: A Guide to the Education Reform Act* (London: Hodder and Stoughton).

Mitchell, D. (1996) The rules keep changing: special education in a reforming education system. *International Journal of Disability and Education*, **43** (1), 55–74.

Nirje, B. (1985) The basis and logic of the normalisation principle. *Australia and New Zealand Journal of Developmental Disabilities*, **11**, 65–68.

Norwich, B. (1990) *Special Needs in Ordinary Schools: Re-appraising Special Education* (London: Cassel).

OFSTED (1996) *Exclusions from Secondary Schools* (London: HMSO).

O'Neill, M. (1995) Introduction. In D. Carter and M. O'Neill (eds), *International Perspectives on Educational Reform and Policy Implementation* (London: The Falmer Press).

Parsons, C. (1994) *Excluding Primary School Children* (London: Family Policy Studies Centre).

Peters, S. (1995) Disability baggage: changing the educational research terrain. In P. Clough and L. Barton (eds), *Making Difficulties: Research and the Construction of SEN* (London: Paul Chapman).

Riddell, S. and Brown, S. (1994) *Special Educational Needs Policy in the 1990s* (London: Routledge).

Rouse, M. (1996) An analysis of the educational reforms in England and Wales: Implications for students with disabilities. Report submitted to the Center for Policy Research, University of Maryland, College Park, MD.

Rouse, M. and Balshaw, M. (1991) Collaborative INSET and special educational needs. In G. Upton (ed.), *Staff Training and Special Educational Needs* (London: David Fulton).

Rouse, M. and Florian, L. (1996) Effective inclusive schools: a study in two countries. *Cambridge Journal of Education*, **26** (1), 71–85.

Sebba, J. (1996) Assessing standards and quality for students with special needs. In L. Florian and M. Rouse (eds), *School Reform and Special Educational Needs: Anglo-American Perspectives* (Cambridge: University of Cambridge Institute of Education).

Sebba, J. and Ainscow, M. (1996) International developments in inclusive schooling: mapping the issues. *Cambridge Journal of Education*, **26** (1), 5–18.

Sebba, J. and Byers, R. (1992) The National Curriculum: control or liberation for pupils with learning difficulties? *The Curriculum Journal*, **3** (2), 143–160.

Skrtic, T. (1986) *Behind Special Education* (Denver, CO: Love).

Slee, R. (ed.) (1993) *Is There a Desk with My Name on It? The Politics of Integration* (London: The Falmer Press).

Stainback, S. and Stainback, W. (1992) *Curriculum Considerations for Inclusive Classrooms: Facilitating Learning for All Students* (Baltimore, MD: Paul H. Brookes).

Stainback, S. and Stainback, W. (eds) (1996) *Inclusion: A Guide for Educators* (Baltimore, MD: Paul H. Brookes).

Stirling, M. (1992) How many pupils are being excluded? *British Journal of Special Education*, **19** (4), 128–130.

Thomas, H. and Bullock, A. (1994) The political economy of school management. In S. Tomlinson (ed.), *Educational Reform and its Consequences* (London: IPPR/ Rivers Oram Press).

Times Educational Supplement (1997) Staff dissatisfaction peaks. *Times Educational Supplement*, **4203**, 17 January.

Unesco (1994) *The Salamanca Statement and Framework on Special Needs Education* (Paris: Unesco).

Vincent, C., Evans, J., Lunt, I. and Young, P. (1995) Policy and practice: the changing nature of special needs provision in schools. *British Journal of Special Education*, **22** (1), 4–11.

Wedell, K. (1988) The new Act: a special need for vigilance. *British Journal of Special Education*, **15** (3), 98–101.

Wedell, K. (1990) Overview: the 1988 Act and current principles of special educational needs. In H. Daniels and J. Ware (eds), *Special Educational Needs and the National Curriculum* (London: Kogan Page).

Wedell, K., Evans, J., Goacher, B. and Welton, J. (1987) Policy and provision under the 1981 Act. *British Journal of Special Education*, **14** (2), 50–53.

Whitty, G. (1997) Creating quasi-markets in education: a review of recent research on parental choice and school autonomy in three countries. In M. Apple (ed.), *Review of Research in Education, 22* (Washington, DC: American Educational Research Association).

Wolfendale, S. (ed.) (1997) *Working with Parents of SEN Children after the Code of Practice* (London: David Fulton).

20

MARKET IDEOLOGIES, EDUCATION AND THE CHALLENGE FOR INCLUSION

Len Barton

Source: H. Daniels and P. Garner (eds), *World Yearbook of Education 1999: Inclusive Education*, London: Kogan Page, 1999, pp 54–62.

Introduction

The topic of this paper is a very serious one and I am conscious of the dangers of approaching it in a sterile, obtuse and dispassionate manner. My stance is, thus, one of anger and moral indignation, and expresses 'an attitude' (Ladwig, 1996). It partly derives from a recognition that the impact of market-ideology on the governance, process and outcomes of education has been to establish a more hierarchical, status-ridden, selective system, in which exclusionary policies and practices have become more prominent. And this question of social exclusion is not solely applicable to the area of education. It is a feature of the welfare and social system generally (Walker and Walker, 1997).

Another factor influencing my stance concerns my critical attitude towards those individualistic within-the-person explanations that have been a powerful force in the field of 'special education'. They have significantly informed policies and practices which legitimate deficit models and dependency-sustaining relations between professional bodies and disabled people. This form of atomized thinking has failed to engage with the deep structural socio-economic conditions and relations of society, which maintain divisive inequalities, discriminations and exclusionary practices. It is important, therefore, to recognize that education cannot be viewed in a vacuum and, as Sultana (1997) contends,

> schooling cannot be divorced from the wider social order, and schools and educators are not and cannot be 'neutral' and 'apolitical' channels

for equally 'neutral' and 'apolitical' knowledge. Whatever we make happen in schools – constantly and inevitably – gives messages defining what it means to be 'human', 'good' and 'normal' in particular social contexts.

(pp 26–7)

This perspective reminds us that educational issues cannot be adequately understood in merely technical and resource terms. They are fundamentally social questions, involving struggles over, for example, social justice, equity and citizenship (Brown and Lauder, 1992).

New Right ideologies

Under consecutive Conservative governments a cultural and economic revolution has taken place in Britain. A new vision of the 'good society' has been articulated, involving the celebration of individualism, competition and the decentralization of planning and decision-making.

A political language has been developed influenced by free-market ideas and, as Taylor (1990) notes, has been 'constructed around notions of "choice" and the "freedom" of the market and "the rights of the individual" over and above the notions of social justice, the "community" and, indeed, of "welfare" as such' (p 5).

Through, for example, economic advisers and right-wing intellectuals writing and being interviewed on radio and television, and the tabloid press, in particular, this discourse has been tirelessly presented (Taylor, 1990). Central to this powerful discourse have been concerns over issues of policy, provision and practice in relation to questions of cost and efficiency. Coupled with this has been a strong moral component, which has sought to discredit existing social democratic values, presenting alternative ones, as part of a more general intention of introducing a new political and moral leadership in the country (Gamble, 1994).

The influence and comprehensive range of the critiques involved in this market-driven discourse are enormous. For example, the family is presented as being under threat, and its authority is assumed to be breaking down. A commitment to greater equality is viewed as both economically inefficient and morally reprehensible. Schools are depicted in terms of their failure to maintain standards and discipline, thereby reducing the nation's international competitiveness in the market place (Gamble, 1994; David, 1990; Ball, 1994).

Underpinning the drive for change is a belief that market forces are more efficient at allocating resources, more responsive to the needs of individuals, and will inevitably lead to the improvement of standards, and to more public accountability on the part of providers of services. In this new world, markets are viewed as more democratic than democracy itself (Henig, 1994).

343

Many of these values and intentions had a particular poignancy during the Thatcher administrations; what Hall (1980) has called 'authoritarian populism' led to the means becoming available by which the extensive restructuring of the educational system took place. It was, as Gamble (1994) so shrewdly notes,

> populist because it drew upon popular discontent with many aspects of the social democratic state to win support for a radical right programme. It was authoritarian because in the implication of its programmes it further increased the power of the state and weakened opposition to it.
>
> (p 182)

The political strategy entailed confrontational politics, and reflected the determination of a strong government to be victorious over groups, such as trade unions, that sought to question its authority, and develop alternative ideas and practices (Atkinson and Savage, 1994).

It is important to recognize that the contributory factors influencing the powerfulness of the New Right discourse included its accessibility, its self-confirming, self-evident rhetorical style and its capacity to play down questions of the social effects and costs of a market-driven system of provision and practice (Taylor, 1990).

Fundamental to the New Right approach is a belief in a free economy and a strong state. This involves both a paradox, and a reminder that the New Right does not entail a coherent, homogeneous set of ideas. The paradox is, as Gamble (1994) illustrates,

> The state is to be simultaneously rolled back and rolled forward. Non-interventionist and decentralized in some areas the state is to be highly interventionist and centralized in others. The New Right can appear by turns libertarian and authoritarian, populist and elitist. This ambiguity is not an accident. It derives in part from the fact that the New Right has two major stands: a liberal tendency, which argues the case for a freer, more open and more competitive economy, and a conservative tendency, which is more interested in restoring social and political authority throughout society.
>
> (p 36)

Both the neo-liberal and neo-conservative elements within the Conservative tradition do share some common interests. They are both critical of egalitarianism and collectivism, which they maintain have encouraged an anti-enterprise and permissive culture. They are also united in their emphasis on such themes as 'authority, tradition, stability, order, the family and morality' (Atkinson and Savage, 1994, p 7). This has provided the basis for warnings about the 'enemies within society', and the demands for returning to 'back to basics' in all aspects of civil life.

Through the activities of the New Right we have seen the mobilization of a new legitimating discourse – that of the market. The emphasis has been on the desirability of creating an enterprise culture based on free-market economic policies. Responsibilities previously equated with the welfare state must now be properly discharged privately by individuals and/or the family. In redefining what is politically acceptable, an emphasis has been given to notions of 'choice', 'efficiency', 'diversity of provision' and 'rights of the individual'. Policy programmes formulated around such concerns have been based on a fundamental assumption that 'success has to be earned through improved competitiveness' (HMSO, 1994, p 8).

It is this commitment that provides the driving force for establishing new ways of thinking about the individual and the state, and about the relationship between the two.

The State

In a paper concerned with research agendas for philosophy of education and, in particular, the contribution that the discipline can make to meta-theoretical debates, Jonathan (1998) argues that education is a peculiar and complex good. It can be understood as both a private and a public issue. In so far as education at an individual level is an exchange value for achievement and, thus, social status in a competitive ethos, it can be viewed as a *private* good. In so far as education is an institutional arrangement that brings 'collective benefit to a society as a whole in enhancing social climate and national economy, it is a *public* good' (p 81). One of the impacts of a system of policy and practice increasingly informed by economic rationality is that education is viewed as a *private* good. In terms of both the public and private dimensions, there are important disputes over the purpose and degree of the role of the state in this process.

One analyst, Neave (1988), examines the development of what he calls the 'evaluative state' through a comparative analysis of the rise of mass higher education in Western Europe. He makes a distinction between evaluation concerned with system maintenance and evaluation for strategic change. The 'evaluative state' represents a fundamental shift in the timing, purpose and location of evaluation. He contrasts *a priori* evaluation with *a posteriori* evaluation. The latter is a new and innovatory form of state activity, which 'works through the control of *product*, not through the control of process' (p 10).

Whilst this approach specifically engages with higher educational issues, it has very important implications for all aspects of the educational system, including schools. They include, first, a much more radical way of *steering* institutions in terms of key goals. Second, by signifying the centrality of *outcome*, the purpose of education in terms of the economy is given a much more privileged position. Finally, this perspective introduces a different way of *conceiving* 'quality' and 'social justice'.

The education context

The system of educational provision and the values underpinning it have been the subject of a most radical transformation. This powerful programme of change has been directed at the governance, content and outcome of all aspects of the educational system. The role of undemocratically elected quangos and extensive legislation have been influential in this process of policy creation and implementation.

The impact of marketization on schools can be seen, for example, in the following changes:

* increased diversity of school provision;
* the introduction of the local management of schools;
* opting-out opportunities;
* the changing nature of governing bodies;
* the published league tables of examination results and low truancy rates;
* the reduction of the role of LEAs in planning and decision-making;
* an emphasis on parental choice;
* changes to the financing of education;
* vouchers for pre-school nursery children;
* the intensification of competitiveness within and across institutions; and
* new forms of assessment and examination.

In research conducted in 1991–94 at the Centre for Educational Studies, at King's College, London, the focus has been on a set of specific educational networks – three clusters of secondary schools (15 in all). The research included monitoring the market behaviour of schools, conducting interviews with parents in such clusters, and collecting from LEAs the overall patterns of parental choice. The findings support the view that the principle of self-interest is increasingly driving the market system, and that existing patterns of inequalities expressed in the cultural capital of parents are influencing patterns of participation and opportunity. These include opportunities for transport, flexibility for moving house, child-care support, and extra coaching for school placement (Ball, 1994). The notion of 'parental choice' from the insights derived from this research becomes highly problematic and obfuscates major inequalities between families.

Inclusive education

Inclusive education is not integration and is not concerned with the assimilation or accommodation of discriminated groups or individuals within existing

346

socio-economic conditions and relations. It is not about making people as 'normal' as possible. Nor is it about the well-being of a particular oppressed or excluded group. Thus, the concerns go well beyond those of disablement. Inclusive education is not an end in itself, but a means to an end – the creation and maintenance of an inclusive society. As such, the interest is with all citizens, their well-being and security. This is a radical conception, not satisfied with piecemeal, short-term reforms. It is ultimately about the transformation of a society and its formal institutional arrangements, such as education. This means change in the values, priorities and policies that support and perpetuate practices of exclusion and discrimination (Barnes, 1991; Oliver, 1995).

The desire for an inclusive society and educational system is motivated by a deeply held, informed conviction that discrimination is a stubborn and long-standing feature of a society based on inequalities and disadvantage. In an analysis of the past two decades in British society, Walker (1997) provides an important definition of social exclusion:

> [it is] . . . the dynamic process of being shut out, fully or partially, from any of the social, economic, political and cultural systems which determine the social integration of a person in society. Social exclusion may, therefore, be seen as the denial (or non-realization) of the civil, political and social rights of citizenship.
>
> (p 8)

The collection of papers in Walker's book support the proposition that, during the past two decades, inequalities, discrimination and poverty have been exacerbated, and that 'a narrow focus on economic efficiency and economic growth will not solve problems such as poverty and social exclusion but, rather, will make them worse'. (p 11)

This harrowing perspective is a reminder that there is no single, 'quick-fix' solution to these stubborn, long-standing inequalities. Within education, as Mortimer and Whitty (1997) maintain, those who come from families that are disadvantaged, and have most to gain, are those who most experience the stigma and exclusion of failure. Education has a part to play in combating injustice and discrimination both within and outside the educational system. However, it cannot carry out this task alone; new alliances and creative relationships with parents, the community and wider organizations will be necessary if these problems are to be overcome.

The struggle for inclusive education involves an identification, challenge and removal of all forms of barriers to participation, including social, cultural, ideological and physical factors. Armstrong (1998) maintains that schools are crucially involved in the generation and regeneration of social differences and stereotypes. This, she argues, is powerfully exemplified in the ways in which *space* within schools is designed and divided up, and thus contributes to the practice of exclusion based on negative conceptualizations of difference. The curriculum, she contends, is given a particular cultural space, a privileged position.

The processes by which this position is maintained and legitimated are complex and contradictory and open to resistance and challenge by teachers and pupils. Part of that challenge needs to take place over particular categories within the official discourse that are routinely used to define pupils. The individual is enveloped by a label such as 'special needs pupil' or 'disruptive pupil'. Thus, pupils take up specific social spaces informed by the labels attached to them.

From this perspective, the historical significance of segregated special schooling set within distinct physical spaces can be viewed as representing the disabling barriers within a society. Such provisions and practices have legitimated reciprocal ignorance between disabled and non-disabled peers, leading to various forms of stereotypes, suspicion and fear (Morris, 1990).

Empowerment and the social context

An inclusive society is concerned with the issue of empowering individuals, and engaging in constructive ways with the question of power. Critical theorists such as Giroux and McLaren in the United States have provided a range of ideas relating to the question of the nature of empowerment and the pedagogical task. To 'empower' can be understood in terms of something being given, conferred and even taken away. In a discussion of the empowering impact of critical pedagogy, McLaren (1995) contends that

> it is a praxis that seeks to engage history with the intent of helping the powerless locate themselves in it . . . In other words, we need to resituate the challenge of teaching as a task of empowering the powerless from states of dependency and passivity as both an informed movement for revolutionary social and economic transformation and as areas of achieving what Brian Fay (1987) calls a 'state of reflective clarity'.
>
> (p 23)

Such a perspective has been criticized, for attributing extraordinary abilities to the teacher, for its failure adequately to address the work context of teachers, and for its over-reliance on the assumed power of critical discourse. In a critique of such ideas, and through an exploration of the position of Foucault with regard to the notion of power, Gore (1992) raises some further important issues. Refuting the idea that power can be *given*, she maintains that, 'When the agent of empowerment assumes to be already empowered, and so apart from those who are to be empowered, arrogance can underlie claims of "what we can do for you"'. (p 61)

Gore argues that power needs to be conceived as being *exercised* in an attempt to help others exercise power. This requires attention being given to the micro aspects of interactions and the importance of context. This, she contends, should involve a greater reflexivity and degree of humility with regard to 'what we can do for others'.

The discourse of empowerment tends to be presented in a romantic and context-free manner. For those concerned with the desire for an inclusive society, and with the position of excluded people and our relationship to them, Core's analysis is a timely reminder of the need for greater self-criticism and humility.

Conclusion

Essential to a democratic participatory process of social interaction is the encouragement and opportunity to debate issues relating to the well-being both of the individual and the society as a whole. This form of engagement requires the development of sensitive listening skills, openness, humility and a willingness of all involved to acknowledge mistakes and/or the limitation of their own position. Part of overcoming dogmatism and exclusiveness will involve a recognition that all of us are *learners* and thus 'do not possess all the answers, are aware of the complexities of social reality and are confused or uncertain about many significant issues' (Lawn and Barton, 1981, p 248).

The task involved in the struggle for an inclusive society is a difficult and urgent one. We cannot afford to be complacent and part of the process of change will involve risk-taking. Several important questions arising from this brief overview are examples of the issues that need to be debated. They include (in no particular order of priority) the following.

- Is there a difference between 'integration' and 'inclusion'?
- To what extent is inclusive education a human rights issue?
- How should we educate teachers and what rights and entitlements should they enjoy?
- What do we mean by 'teaching to diversity' and is this a requirement of all teachers?
- How useful is it to conceive of education in terms of a 'market'?
- Does a market-led policy of provision and practice encourage exclusionary values and demands?
- In what ways and why is the issue of difference central to an inclusive perspective?

Many voices have been excluded from participating in discussions and decisions over issues affecting the quality of their lives. Historically, disabled people have been part of an oppressed group who have experienced the indignity, frustration and dehumanization of being treated as an inferior, less-than-human species. The pursuit of an inclusive society is concerned with issues of equity and non-discrimination, in which the good of *all* citizens is a central commitment. By setting the issue of disability and all forms of oppression within a human rights perspective, the possibilities for the realization of a society based on community, solidarity and in which difference can be viewed in dignified ways, becomes much stronger.

Acknowledgement

I am grateful to Felicity Armstrong for her comments on an earlier draft of this paper.

References

Armstrong, F. (1998) 'Inclusion, Curriculum and the Struggle for Cultural Space', *International Journal of Inclusive Education*, 3 (3)

Atkinson, R. and Savage, S. (1994) 'The Conservatives and public policy', in S. Savage, R. Atkinson and L. Robins, (eds) *Public Policy in Britain*, Macmillan, Basingstoke

Ball, S. J. (1994) *Education Reform: A Critical and Post-Structural Approach*, Open University Press, Buckingham

Barnes, C. (1991) *Disabled People in Britain and Discrimination: A Case for Anti-Discrimination Legislations*, Hurst and Company, London

Brown, P. and Lauder, H. (1992) 'Education, economy and security: an introduction to a new agenda', in P. Brown and H. Lauder (eds) *Education for Economic Survival: From Fordism to Post-Fordism?*, Routledge, London

David, M. (1990) 'Looking after the cubs: Women and "work" in the decade of Thatcherism', in I. Taylor (ed.) *The Social Effects of Free Market Policies: An International Text*, Harvester Wheatsheaf, London

Fay, B. (1987) *Critical Social Science: Liberation and its Limits*, Polity Press, Cambridge

Gamble, A. (1994) *The Free Economy and the Strong State* (2nd edn), Macmillan, Basingstoke

Gore, J. (1992) 'What we can do for you! What can "we" do for "you"? Struggling over empowerment in critical and feminist pedagogy', in C. Luke and J. Gore (eds) *Feminisms and Critical Pedagogy*, Routledge, New York

Hall, S. (1980) 'Popular democratic versus authoritarian populism', in A. Hunt (ed.) *Marxism and Democracy*, Lawrence and Wishart, London

Henig, J. R. (1994) *Rethinking School Choice: Limits of the Market Metaphor*, Princeton University Press, Princeton

HMSO (1994) *Competitiveness Helping Business to Win* (CM 2563), HMSO, London

Jonathan, R. (1998) 'When there are urgent concerns about education, why worry about metaphysics', in W. Bauer, W. Lippitz, W. Marotzki, J. Ruhoff, A. Schäfer and C. Wulf (eds) *Fragen nach dem Menschen in der umstrittenen Moderne*, Schneider Verlag Hohengehren GmbH

Ladwig, J. (1996) *Academic Distinctions: Theory and Methodology in the Sociology of School Knowledge*, Falmer Press, London

Lawn, M. and Barton, L. (1981) 'Curriculum politics and emancipation', in M. Lawn, and L. Barton (eds) *Rethinking Curriculum Studies*, Croom Helm, London

McLaren, P. (1995) *Critical Pedagogy and Predatory Culture: Oppositional Politics in a Post-Modern Era*, Routledge, London

Morris, J. (1990) 'Progress with humanity: The experience of a disabled lecturer', in R. Rieser, and M. Mason (eds) *Disability Equality in the Classroom: A Human Rights Issue*, ILEA, London

Mortimore, P. and Whitty, G. (1997) *Can School Improvement Overcome the Effects of Disadvantage?*, Institute of Education, University of London, London

Neave, G. (1998) 'On the cultivation of quality, efficiency and enterprise: an overview of recent trends in Higher Education in Western Europe', *European Journal of Education*, 23 (1/2), pp 7–23

Oliver, M. (1995) *Understanding Disability: From Theory To Practice*, Kingsley Press, London

Sultana, R. (1997) 'Towards a Critical Sociology of Education', in R. Sultana (ed.) *Inside/Outside Schools: Towards a Critical Sociology of Education in Malta*, Publishers Enterprises Group (PEG) Ltd, Malta

Taylor, I. (1990) 'Introduction: The concept of "social cost" in free market theory and the social effects of free market policies', in I. Taylor (ed.) *The Social Effects of Free Market Policies: An International Text*, Harvester Wheatsheaf, London

Walker, A. (1997) 'Introduction: The Strategy of Inequality', in A. Walker and C. Walker (eds) *Britain Divided: The Growth of Social Exclusion in the 1980s and 1990s*, CPAG Ltd, London

Walker, A. and Walker, C. (eds) (1997) *Britain Divided: The Growth of Social Exclusion in the 1980s and 1990s*, CPAG Ltd London

21

STANDARDS-BASED REFORM AND STUDENTS WITH DISABILITIES

Reflections on a decade of change

Martha L. Thurlow

Source: *Focus on Exceptional Children* 33(3) (2000): 1–16.

Calls for higher and more rigorous standards for all students turned out to be the educational battle cry of the 1990s. State after state defined its content and performance standards, and a major push for change in education became known as "standards-based reform." Near the beginning of standards-based reform, special educators asked whether all students, in particular students with disabilities or the individuals who worked with them, were included in various aspects of the reform—setting standards, developing assessments, taking tests, getting data on test results, and so on.

Nearly a decade has now passed. What has happened? What has standards-based reform meant for students with disabilities? These questions are important to answer because the push for standards-based education continues to make the headlines and to be pushed forward by federal and state initiatives. I hope to answer the questions about where we are now in standards and standards-based reforms for students with disabilities.

First, I provide a brief history of standards and what standards-based reform has entailed. Then I describe what has occurred in including students with disabilities in all aspects of standards-based reform—setting standards, participating in assessments, making assessment accommodations, reporting results, developing accountability systems, and teaching/learning. Much of the information that I cite is based on investigations and analyses conducted by the National Center on Educational Outcomes (NCEO), a federally funded center that has followed these issues for 10 years. I conclude by highlighting what I believe to be some of the lessons we have learned about including students with disabilities in standards-based reform.

A brief history of standards and standards-based reform

Content standards define what students should know and be able to do (i.e., knowledge and skills) as a result of their schooling and other educational experiences. Performance standards define how well students must perform to demonstrate adequate knowledge and skills—"how good is good enough?" Together, content and performance standards have formed the kernal of standards-based reform in the United States in the past decade.

States started defining content standards in the early 1990s, often spurred by work on national standards (e.g., National Council of Teachers of Mathematics, 1989; National Research Council, 1993) or by the 1989 educational summit at which the national educational goals were first identified (see National Council on Education Standards and Testing, 1992). Various groups and news media began to rate standards (e.g., American Federation of Teachers, 1999; Fordham Foundation, 2000; State Policy Updates, 2000), further elevating their importance in the eyes of the public.

Federal laws also were written to promote the development and implementation of standards and educational reforms based on them. Table 1 summarizes three of the most important of these laws: Goals 2000, Title I of the Improving America's Schools Act, and the Individuals with Disabilities Education Act. These federal laws have helped to solidify the importance assigned to standards and the standards-based reform movement, as well as to highlight the notion that standards and reforms are meant for all students, including students with disabilities.

Standards-based reforms, however, have involved more than just setting standards. Hand-in-hand with them have come state and district assessments, reporting systems, and accountability mechanisms. Today, all except two states have state-level assessments. District-level assessments exist in the majority of districts spread throughout the states. High-stakes assessments that have significant consequences for districts, schools, administrators, educators, or the students themselves have mushroomed in an attempt to improve the performance of students (Education Commission of the States, 1999).

By the end of the century, 40 of the states had implemented (or were in the process of implementing) assessments that resulted in significant consequences (rewards or sanctions) for schools or the educators within them. More than 20 states had implemented (or were in the process of implementing) assessments that resulted in significant consequences for students (high school diplomas, promotion from one grade to the next). Assessment has become big business, a business that now is addressing how to include students with disabilities (and other formerly excluded students, such as students with limited English proficiency).

Table 1 Key Standards Provisions in Goals 2000, IASA (Title I), and IDEA.

Federal Law	Year Enacted	Standards-related Provisions
Goals 2000: Educate America Act	1994	"It is the purpose of this part to establish a bipartisan mechanism for— . . . reviewing the voluntary national content standards, voluntary national student performance standards, and voluntary national opportunity to learn standards certified by the National Education Standards and Improvement Council . . ." [Sec. 201 (3)]
		"It is the purpose of this part to establish a mechanism to—(1) certify and periodically review voluntary national content standards and voluntary national student performance standards that define what all students should know and be able to do; (2) certify state content standards and State student performance standards submitted by States on a voluntary basis, if such standards are comparable or higher in rigor and quality to the voluntary national content standards and voluntary national student performance standards certified by the National Education Standards and Improvement Council." [Sec. 211 (1) (2)]
Improving America's Schools Act (Title I)	1994	"[Title I] programs need to become even more effective in improving schools in order to enable all children to achieve high standards; and in order for all students to master challenging standards in core academic subjects." [Sec. 1001 (b) (4) (5)]
		"If a state has not adopted State content standards and State student performance standards for all students, the State plan shall include a strategy and schedule for developing State content standards and State student performance standards for elementary and secondary school children served under this part in subjects as determined by the State, but including at least mathematics and reading or language arts by the end of the one-year period. . . ." [Sec. 1111 (b) (1) (C)]
		"State rules, regulations, and policies under this title shall support and facilitate local educational agency and school-level systemic reform designed to enable all children to meet the challenging State content standards and challenging State student performance standards." [Sec. 1603 (a) (2)]

354

Table 1 (cont'd)

Federal Law	Year Enacted	Standards-related Provisions
Individuals with Disabilities Education Act (IDEA)	1997	"All educational programs for children with disabilities in the State, including all such programs administered by any other State or local agency— . . . meet the educational standards of the State education agency. . . ." [Sec. 612 (a) (11) (A) (ii) II]
		"PERFORMANCE GOALS AND INDICATORS— . . . are consistent, to the maximum extent appropriate, with other goals and standards for children established by the State. . . ." [Sec. 612 (a) (16) (A) (ii)]
		"The Federal Government has an ongoing obligation to support programs, projects, and activities that contribute to positive results for children with disabilities, enabling them to meet their early intervention, educational, and transitional goals and, to the maximum extent possible, educational standards that have been established for all children." [Sec. 671 (a) (1) (A)]

Including students with disabilities in standards-based reform

The finding that students with disabilities were being excluded from national and state assessments (Ingels, 1993, 1996; Ingels & Scott, 1993; McGrew, Thurlow, Shriner, & Spiegel, 1992) was one of the first indicators that students with disabilities might not receive the benefits associated with standards-based reforms. Evidence of this exclusion came from parents and students themselves, who indicated that students were purposely being excluded (e.g., Why Johnny stayed home, 1997), as well as from surveys of states and attempts to collect data from national and state assessment data bases (McGrew, Algozzine, Ysseldyke, Thurlow, & Spiegel, 1995; McGrew, Vanderwood, Thurlow, & Ysseldyke, 1995), as well as from school districts (Zlatos, 1992). Inquiry into the exclusion of students with disabilities revealed that the problem existed at several points, each of which was a point of possible change.

Setting standards

Probably the first point of exclusion occurred when standards were being developed. Initially, evidence of exclusion was found in the national standards under development by various national associations (Hofmeister, 1993;

355

Shriner, Kim, Thurlow, & Ysseldyke, 1992; Ysseldyke, Thurlow, & Shriner, 1992). As states began to develop their own standards, analyses of them suggested that students with disabilities had not been considered (Thurlow, Ysseldyke, Gutman, & Geenen, 1998). This conclusion was supported by the findings that (a) only 17% of the states with standards (47 at the time of the analysis) had included individuals with disabilities (or those who were familiar with them) in developing their standards, and (b) 23.4% did not mention students with disabilities in any of their core subject area documents.

As part of the Improving America's School Act (IASA), Title I provisions, states must have standards in math and English/Language Arts, at minimum. And, when measuring adequate yearly progress, the performance of all students against these standards must be measured (U.S. Department of Education, 1999). Thus, standards (content and performance) must apply to all students (Thurlow & Ysseldyke, 2000) and, more important, these standards should be tied to effective assessments (Business Roundtable, 1996).

Participating in assessments

Assessment is the mechanism by which states are measuring whether students are meeting standards. Yet, for nearly half of the past decade, students with disabilities were excluded from assessments not just during the time when assessments were administered but also when the items were developed and when results were tabulated and reported. In the early 1990s (Shriner & Thurlow, 1992), the rate of participation of students with disabilities in assessments ranged from 0% to 100%. Within a few years of this finding, it became evident that many states and districts did not really know how many students with disabilities had participated in assessments because their data management systems were not designed to address the participation of students with disabilities or they had not figured out how to keep track of whether these students had actually taken the test (Erickson, Thurlow, & Ysseldyke, 1996; Erickson, Ysseldyke, & Thurlow, 1997).

Excluding students with disabilities during administration of the test generally decreased over time, even as states began to have better estimates of participation rates. In the early 1990s, most states had 10% or fewer of their students with disabilities in assessments (Shriner & Thurlow, 1992). By the mid-1990s, this had changed somewhat. More states indicated that they knew how many students participated in assessments, and the number of states indicating that fewer than 10% of their students with disabilities were included in assessments decreased (Elliott, Erickson, Thurlow, & Shriner, 2000).

The reauthorization of IDEA in 1997 escalated these changes because it required that states include students with disabilities in their state and districtwide assessments and report on their findings by July 1, 1998 (see Table 2 for large-scale assessment requirements of Title I and IDEA).

356

Table 2 Key Assessment Provisions in IASA (Title I), and IDEA.

Federal Law	Year Enacted	Assessment-Related Provisions
Improving America's Schools Act (Title I)	1994	"... high-quality, yearly student assessments ... that will be used as the primary means of determining the yearly performance of each local educational agency and school served under this part in enabling all children served under this part to meet the State's student performance standards. (A) Such assessments shall be the same assessments used to measure the performance of all children, if the State measures the performance of all children (F) ... provide for the participation in such assessments of all students (i)." [Sec. 1111 (b) (3) (A) (F) (i)] "A State educational agency shall— ... publicize and disseminate to local educational agencies, teachers and other staff, parents, students, and the community the results of the State review, including statistically sound results, as required by section 1111 (b) (3) (1)." [Sec. 116 (d) (1) (B)] "... enable results to be disaggregated with each State, local educational agency, and school by ... students with disabilities as compared to nondisabled students. ..." [Sec. 1111 (b) (3) (I)]
Individuals with Disabilities Education Act (IDEA)	1997	"Children with disabilities are included in general State and district-wide assessment programs, with appropriate accommodations, where necessary." [Sec. 612 (a) (17) (A)] "As appropriate, the State or local educational agency develops guidelines for the participation of children with disabilities in alternate assessments for those children who cannot participate in State and district-wide assessment programs." [Sec. 612 (a) (18) (A) (i)] "The national assessments shall examine how well schools, local educational agencies, States and other recipients of assistance under this Act ... including improving the performance of all children with disabilities in general scholastic activities and assessments as compared to nondisabled children; providing for the participation of children with disabilities in the general curriculum." [Sec. 673 (b) (3) (A) (B)]

Table 2 (cont'd)

Federal Law	Year Enacted	Assessment-Related Provisions
		"The State educational agency makes available to the public, and reports to the public with the same frequency and in the same detail as it reports on the assessment of nondisabled children, the following: the number of children with disabilities participating in regular assessments. The number of those children participating in alternate assessments. The performance of those children on regular assessments (beginning not later than July 1, 1998) and on alternate assessments (not later than July 1, 2000), if doing so would be statistically sound and would not result in the disclosure of performance results identifiable to individual children." [Sec. 612 (a) (17) (B) (i) (ii) (iii) (I) (II)]

In 1999, estimates of participation rates by states were still variable, ranging from 15% to 100% (Thompson & Thurlow, 1999), but most states now had estimates of about 60%–65% of their students with disabilities participating in the statewide assessment.

Another indicator of participation that has changed over time is the written policies that states have about the participation of students with disabilities in the general state assessment. In the early 1990s, written-participation policies existed in fewer than half of the states (Thurlow, Ysseldyke, & Silverstein, 1993) and often indicated that students with disabilities need not take the general assessment. By the mid-1990s, 43 states had written participation policies, more of them indicating an intent to include students with disabilities in assessments (Thurlow, Scott, & Ysseldyke, 1995b). And, by the end of the century, all states with active assessment systems have written policies about participation in assessments (Thurlow, House, Boys, Scott, & Ysseldyke, 2000).

IDEA also required that states begin the development and implementation of alternate assessments, to be used with students unable to participate in the general state assessment. This would mean that every student with a disability would be included in some type of state or districtwide assessment. The first known alternate assessment was developed in Kentucky, in response to the Kentucky Educational Reform Act (KERA) (Ysseldyke, Thurlow, Erickson, Gabrys, *et al.*, 1996). In Kentucky, the alternate assessment is a portfolio system, designed to be consistent with portfolio assessments used with other students.

As states neared the time when they were to have alternate assessments in place, most states had developed something (Thompson & Thurlow, 2000). As might be expected, however, states were at a variety of stages in their development process. Similarly, they had taken many different approaches in their alternate assessments. This might be expected, since their general assessments were also quite varied in purpose and characteristics (Olson, Bond, & Andrews, 1999).

With the development of alternate assessments, it would be expected that all students with disabilities now will be included in each state's assessment system. The same should be true for district-wide assessments, although the extent to which this has happened is still unclear. The expectation that all students would be included in state and district assessments was made clear in an answer about alternate assessments given in a question-and-answer memo prepared for states by the Office of Special Education Programs (Heumann & Warlick, 2000):

12. Do the requirements to establish participation guidelines for alternate assessments and to develop alternate assessments apply to both SEAs and LEAs?

Yes. 34 CFR §300.138 specifically requires inclusion of children with disabilities in both State and district-wide assessment programs and requires both the SEA and the LEA, as appropriate, to develop guidelines for the participation of children with disabilities in alternate assessments for those children who cannot participate in State and district-wide assessments, and develop alternate assessments.

Of course, if an LEA does not conduct district-wide assessments other than those that are part of the State assessment program, then the LEA would follow SEA guidelines and use the SEA alternate assessment(s). The requirements apply to district-wide assessments regardless of whether or not there is a State assessment. (Heumann & Warlick, 2000, p. 10)

Assessment accommodations

Participation of students with disabilities in general state and district-wide assessments is intimately linked to the availability of accommodations for students with disabilities. Accommodations are "changes in testing materials or procedures that enable students with disabilities to participate in an assessment in a way that allows abilities to be assessed rather than disabilities" (Thurlow, Elliott, & Ysseldyke, 1998, pp. 28–29). More specifically, accommodations generally are considered to include changes in presentation, response, timing, scheduling, setting, and other aspects of the testing situation. A few examples of each of these are shown in Table 3.

Table 3 Examples of Accommodations.

Setting	Presentation
Study carrel	Repeat directions
Special lighting	Larger bubbles on multiple-choice questions
Separate room	Sign language presentation
Individualized or small group administration	Magnification device
Timing	**Response**
Extended time	Mark answers in test booklet
Frequent breaks	Use reference materials (e.g., dictionary)
Unlimited time	Word process writing sample
Scheduling	**Other**
Specific time of day	Special test preparation techniques
Subtests in different order	Out-of-level test

For some time, researchers and others suspected that by allowing accommodations (or more accommodations than before), the participation rates of students with disabilities in assessments probably would increase (Thurlow, Elliott, & Ysseldyke, 1998; Ysseldyke, Thurlow, McGrew, & Shriner, 1994; Ysseldyke, Thurlow, McGrew, & Vanderwood, 1994). A study commissioned by the National Center for Education Statistics (Anderson, Jenkins, & Miller, 1996) showed empirically that this was true. A special study using the National Assessment of Educational Progress (NAEP), which is used as a report card for the country, evaluated whether participation rates would increase with the availability of accommodations. Reporting on the findings of that study, Mazzeo, Carlson, Voekl, and Lutkus (2000) noted that the participation rates did not increase as a result of changing inclusion criteria, but did increase when some accommodations were available during testing.

Although convincing evidence now exists that providing accommodations increases the participation of students with disabilities, accommodations remain controversial. This is a result, in part, of concerns that accommodations provide students who use them with an advantage that other students do not have. It also is related to some specific accommodations linked to the constructs being assessed (e.g., reading to the student a test of decoding skills), and therefore may produce invalid or noncomparable scores (e.g., Koretz, 1997).

Despite these concerns, state policies on accommodations have changed dramatically. In 1991, when NCEO first requested information from states about accommodations, fewer than half the states had written policies or guidelines (Shriner & Thurlow, 1992). In 1993, 21 states had written guidelines (Thurlow, Ysseldyke, & Silverstein, 1993), and by 1995, 38 states had them (Thurlow, Scott, & Ysseldyke, 1995a). By 1999, all states with state-level assessments had written policies or guidelines about the use of accommodations during state assessments (Thurlow, House, Boys, Scott, & Ysseldyke, 2000).

Although information about allowed accommodations existed (see also Olson *et al.*, 1999), this information did not reflect the extent to which students with disabilities were using accommodations. NCEO had encouraged states to collect data on the use of accommodations, and by the end of the decade, several states had these data (Elliott, Bielinski, Thurlow, DeVito, & Hedlund, 1999; Thompson & Thurlow, 1999; Trimble, 1998). The data were very revealing (see Table 4) because variability in the use of accommodations was so great from state to state. In one state the use of accommodations at a particular grade level was less than 8% of the students; in another state the use of accommodations at a particular grade level was more than 80% of the students (Thompson & Thurlow, 1999). These data hint at the confusion surrounding the term "accommodation," the way in which accommodations are counted, and differences in beliefs about the appropriateness of using accommodations.

Confusion about what an "accommodation" is

Terminology has plagued our understanding of accommodations. *First*, different terms are sometimes used to mean the same thing. Thus, in some states acceptable testing changes are called accommodations, in others they are called modifications, and in others they are called adaptations. *Second*, the same term may be used to mean different things. For example, in some states and districts the term "modification" refers to an acceptable change in the test itself, such as a braille or large-print version. In other states and districts the term "modification" is used to mean a change that is not acceptable—a change that may compromise the construct being assessed (such as reading a test to a student that is designed to assess reading decoding skills).

Confusion about which accommodations to count

Given the variability in terminology, it should be apparent that states and districts think about different accommodations in different ways. For example, if State A counts using a pencil holder or a slantboard on the desk as an accommodation, but State B does not, there will certainly be a difference in the number of students counted as using accommodations, and in the number of accommodations used during a test. This scenario reflects the current status of states that are tracking the use of accommodations. Some states are counting only those changes in testing about which they have concerns. Other states are counting all changes in the testing, regardless of whether they were considered to be perfectly acceptable or ones that challenged the meaningfulness of scores obtained when they were used.

Table 4 State-reported Levels of Use of Accommodations.

State	Assessment/Subject Area	Elementary Grades (K–5)	Middle School Grades (6–8)	High School Grades (9–12)
Florida	FL Writing Assessment	51% (Gr 4)	39% (Gr 8)	34% (Gr 10)
	FCAT (Reading)	47% (Gr 4)	38% (Gr 8)	40% (Gr 10)
	FCAT (Math)	50% (Gr 5)	38% (Gr 8)	39% (Gr 10)
Indiana	Statewide Assessment—Math	28% (Gr 3)	34% (Gr 6)	80% (Gr 10)
			38% (Gr 8)	
	English/Language Arts	29% (Gr 3)	34% (Gr 6)	82% (Gr 10)
			38% (Gr 8)	
Kansas	KS Assessment Program—Math	21% (Gr 4)	14% (Gr 7)	08% (Gr 10)
	Reading	19% (Gr 3)	13% (Gr 7)	08% (Gr 10)
	Writing	23% (Gr 5)	17% (Gr 7)	09% (Gr 10)
Kentucky	Kentucky Core Content Test	82% (Gr 4)	72% (Gr 7)	50% (Gr 10)
		82% (Gr 5)	70% (Gr 8)	57% (Gr 11)
				55% (Gr 12)
Massachusetts	Comprehensive Assessment System	61% (Gr 4)	38% (Gr 8)	25% (Gr 10)

State	Test			
Maryland	MSPAP—Reading	53% (Gr 3)	25% (Gr 8)	
	Language Usage	51% (Gr 5)	16% (Gr 8)	
		44% (Gr 3)		
		41% (Gr 5)		
	Math	20% (Gr 3)		44% (Gr 10)
Nevada	Terra Nova Complete Battery	51% (Gr 4)	42% (Gr 8)	
New York	PEP Test—Reading	50% (Gr 3)	50% (Gr 6)	
	Math	31% (Gr 3)	32% (Gr 6)	
	Writing	33% (Gr 5)		
Pennsylvania	Reading and Math Assessment	67% (Gr 5)	52% (Gr 8)	45% (Gr 11)
Rhode Island	Writing Performance Assessment	49% (Gr 3)	55% (Gr 7)	60% (Gr 10)
	Health Performance Assessment	39% (Gr 5)	61% (Gr 9)	
South Dakota	Stanford Achievement Test (Language, Math, Reading, Science, Social Science)	63% (Gr 2)	59% (Gr 8)	46% (Gr 11)
		67% (Gr 4)		
West Virginia	SAT 9—Language, Math, Reading, Science, Social Studies	64% (Gr 3–11)		

Source: From *1999 State Special Education Outcomes*, by S. J. Thompson & M. L. Thurlow (Minneapolis: University of Minnesota, 1999), Table 7: Percent of Students Receiving Special Education Services Who Used Testing Accommodations, reprinted by permission of the National Center on Educational Outcomes.

Differences in beliefs about the appropriateness of accommodations

Remaining at the core of confusion about how accommodations interact with the participation of students who have disabilities in assessments is an array of beliefs about the acceptability of either specific accommodations or accommodations in general. Clear evidence of these differences exists in the written policies and guidelines that states have developed. Although all states with assessments now have written information about which accommodations are allowed, the specific accommodations allowed and not allowed vary tremendously.

The variation extends beyond that expected from the different tests that states use. Even in states using the same test, accommodations on the allowed and not-allowed lists are different (Thurlow, House, Boys, Scott, & Ysseldyke, 2000). This indicates, in part, that the policies are not based on research findings about the appropriateness of specific accommodations.

In fact, test developers are just beginning to address accommodations issues (e.g., CTB/McGraw-Hill, 2000). For many years, information on the accommodations that students could use when taking the major achievement tests used by districts and states (e.g., California Achievement Test, Iowa Test of Basic Skills, Metropolitan Achievement Test, Stanford Achievement Test) was either nonexistent or very limited (see summary in Thurlow, Elliott, & Ysseldyke, 1998). Today, a host of research efforts is underway to address the effects of specific accommodations on score comparability, as well as the decision-making process to identify specific accommodations needed by individual students. Many of these efforts are funded either by the Office of Special Education Programs (OSEP) or the Office of Educational Research and Improvement (OERI). In addition, several additional research efforts are emerging, often supported by states as they struggle with their own policies on accommodations.

Reporting of assessment results

Simply having students with disabilities take tests, with the accommodatons they need, is not enough to provide students with the benefits to be derived from standards-based reform. The importance of reporting the performance results of students with disabilities emerged as another critical aspect of including students with disabilities in standards-based reforms (Erickson, Ysseldyke, Thurlow, & Elliott, 1997). Although changes in individual programs may result from providing large-scale assessment information to teachers and parents, public reporting is what prompts programmatic improvements (Elmore & Rothman, 1999).

The first effort to determine the extent to which states reported on the performance of students with disabilities occurred just before the amendments to IDEA were enacted (Thurlow, Langenfeld, Nelson, Shin, &

Coleman, 1998). The amendments required states to publicly report on the performance of students with disabilities in the same way and with the same frequency as they reported on the performance on other students.

This analysis, based on 1996 state reports, indicated that only 11 states provided test-based data on students with disabilities. Five of these states reported on the performance of students with disabilities in documents separate from those in which data on other students were presented.

Follow-up analyses, using state reports from 1998 (Ysseldyke *et al.*, 1998) and 1999 (Thurlow, Nelson, Teelucksingh, & Ysseldyke, 2000) showed meager increases—12 states in 1998 reports and 17 states in 1999 reports. The number of states publicly reporting will certainly increase in the next couple years, as data management, policy, and other issues are slowly resolved.

These data are important for a number of reasons, other than the importance of knowing how students with disabilities across the nation are performing. Besides confirming that, in general, students with disabilities are performing below their peers, the data open up avenues to exploring changes over time. Two such analyses have revealed important increases in the performance of students with disabilities over time in standards-based educational systems (Keller, 2000; Trimble, 1998). Other analyses have helped to identify how states can get better information when looking at trends in performance (Bielinski & Ysseldyke, 2000).

Accountability systems

Accountability is one facet of standards-based reform that generates considerable emotion and controversy. Accountability systems can be focused either on the student (such as a graduation exams and tests used to decide on promotion from one grade to another) or on the system (such as when schools are taken over, when staff members receive rewards, or when accreditation in based on student performance). State accountability systems vary in their approaches and in the consequences tied to them (Education Commission of the States, 1999).

Student accountability

Holding the student responsible for his or her performance on state and district tests is increasing in popularity among governors and legislators. At the same time, concern about including students with disabilities in assessments is heightened because of these kinds of assessments (Thurlow, in press; Thurlow & Johnson, 2000). There is concern about large numbers of students with disabilities not passing these tests, and thereby being relegated to a pathway that is sure to lead to dropping out of school or eventually having poor prospects for employment and post-secondary training (Thurlow & Johnson, 2000). Despite numerous warnings that systems should be held accountable for student learning and have their systems in place for ensuring equal opportunity to learn to all students (Heubert & Hauser, 1999), this has not stopped the proliferation of these tests (see American Federation of Teachers, 1999; Guy, Shin, Lee, & Thurlow, 1999).

Guy *et al.* (1999) explored states' graduation requirements and found a confusing array of requirements designed specifically for students with disabilities, even in states using graduation exams. This confusion is exemplified not only in variations in course requirements and testing requirements for students with disabilities—in some states but not in others—but also in an array of diploma options, from IEP diplomas, special education diplomas, and modified diplomas to the same diploma but different documentation on transcripts.

In an NCEO report (Thurlow & Thompson, 2000), we highlighted these variations and related some thoughts about how all students can have access to the same array of diploma options (see Table 4). Unfortunately, this does not represent what is happening in most states.

High stakes exams that punish or reward students are going to continue to be a controversial topic until it is clear that all students have equal opportunity to learn. Court cases are addressing these issues now with increasing frequency (e.g., Olson, 2000), and the number of cases of this nature probably will continue to increase until some of the issues surrounding appropriate opportunity to learn for all students are adequately addressed.

Systems accountability

When consequences are significant, complex formulas often are used to determine how accountability scores are calculated for schools and districts. Yet, these formula are not accessible to the public (Krentz, Thurlow, & Callender, 2000). Further, finding out how students with disabilities are included (or not) in these formula was nearly impossible. Some states do have clear information, often because their state legislatures have required it. The goal of the Improving America's School Act, of course, is that all students are to be included in the accountability system.

Because students with disabilities now are included in the assessments that form the basis of most accountability systems, we should expect to begin to see clear evidence of their inclusion in this component of standards-based reform. Through their inclusion in the accountability system, states and districts will begin to see the importance of ensuring that their instructional programs and placements are the best they can be.

Teaching and learning

When the discussion turns to assessments and accountability systems, perhaps the most important elements of standards-based reform—teaching and learning—are often forgotten. It is important to remember that the impetus for standards-based reform was the desire to improve teaching and learning so all students could demonstrate the knowledge and skills needed in the global economy of today and the future.

With the emphasis given to assessments as the measures of whether students were achieving standards, several unintended consequences of standards-based reforms began to emerge. One was the tendency for the curriculum to narrow—to focus only on the knowledge and skills included in assessments (Heubert & Hauser, 1999; Linn, 2000; Linn & Herman, 1997; Shepard, 1991). Although some states argued that narrowing of the curriculum was appropriate if the test was measuring the appropriate standards, there continues to be concern about teaching to the test, and teaching students only how to take tests better—not to gain a broad knowledge base and set of skills that will be reflected in higher test performance (Heubert & Hauser, 1999; Kohn, 2000; Shepard, 1991).

Beyond this, when looking at state standards, it soon became apparent that not all standards were the same. Some states had relatively broad standards such as, "Students compare patterns of change and constancy in systems," whereas others had quite narrow standards such as, "Students describe the basic processes of photosynthesis and respiration and their importance to life" (examples from states cited in American Federation of Teachers, 1996). The extent to which standards are broad or narrow affects the nature of the curriculum for students with disabilities, particularly those who may be determined to be eligible to participate in the assessment system through the alternate assessment.

Discussions about how broad or narrow standards are is particularly relevant when considering the curriculum for students with disabilities. In the early 1990s the National Center on Education Outcomes devoted considerable time, and involved hundreds of stakeholders, in efforts to identify the important outcomes of education for students with disabilities (Ysseldyke, Thurlow, & Gilman, 1993a, 1993b, 1993c, 1993d; Ysseldyke, Thurlow, & Erickson, 1994a, 1994b). The outcome models that were developed were for all students, since the broad group of stakeholders kept all students in mind as the outcomes were developed. They reflected broad domains, including Presence & Participation, Accommodation and Adaptation, Physical Health, Social/Emotional Adjustment, Independence & Responsibility. Contribution & Citizenship, and Satisfaction, as well as Academic & Functional Literacy (see also Ysseldyke, Krentz, Elliott, Thurlow, Erickson, & Moore, 1998).

Regardless of what kinds of standards the states developed, however, state assessments tended to focus on material that was easy to test. The tendency not to use performance assessments, but instead to consider extended response items to be a proxy for performance assessments, turned around the discussion once again to concerns about the nature of the curriculum that might be directed only to doing well on a test.

Although this concern about narrowing of the curriculum permeated education, its effects might be most devastating for students with disabilities, particularly those who might not be headed for college. Would students who were not eligible for the alternate assessment be short-changed because their curriculum focused only on academics, with little concern about ensuring that they were learning broader skills or being prepared for transition into the world of work? These were legitimate concerns as the focus on standards-based education continued into the new century.

Elliott and Thurlow (2000) identified several characteristics of a standards-based classroom:

"Students know the standards and level of proficiency required," (b) Students are provided multiple opportunities to learn," (c) Student assignments reflect an integration of facts, concepts, and strategies," and (d) "Each assignment is an assessment in itself."

(pp. 42–43)

They suggest that IEPs must be linked to standards—a concept that aligns with access to the general education curriculum—and that standards must be backmapped to instruction. Nowhere is there the implication that the purpose is to narrow the curriculum or teach to the test. In fact, time and again, researchers have verified the importance of teaching broadly, using the best instructional procedures available.

The themes about the importance of the instructional process and an appropriate, standards-based curriculum were echoed by the National Research Council's report (Elmore & Rothman, 1999), *Testing, Teaching and Learning: A Guide for States and School Districts*. The importance of "authentic pedagogy" (see Newmann & Associates, 1996) for all students was highlighted. The instruction involves higher-order thinking, deep knowledge, substantive conversation, and connections to the world beyond the classroom. Classroom studies find that these qualities are rarely present (David, 1997; Spillane, 1997).

The National Research Council report presented five recommendations for ways to ensure that instruction is appropriate for standards-based learning (Elmore & Rothman, 1999):

• Schools and districts should monitor the conditions of instruction—the curriculum and instructional practices of teachers—to determine if students are exposed to teaching that would enable them to achieve the standards they are expected to meet.

• Districts and schools should use information on the conditions of instruction to require and support improvement of instruction and learning in every classroom.

- Teachers should use the information on conditions of instruction in their classroom, along with data on student performance, to improve the quality of instruction. Districts have a responsibility to assist schools in collecting and using such information.
- Schools should use the information on the conditions of instruction to organize the time and resources provided to teachers and demand support from the district.
- Districts should use the information on the conditions of instruction to improve the quality and effectiveness of the resources and support they provide to schools for instructional improvement. (p. 77)

With evidence that students who are lower-performing are least likely to get equal access to a standards-based curriculum, and are more likely to receive poorer instruction (Bradley, 2000; National Association of State Boards of Education, 1998; U.S. Department of Education, 1995), curriculum and instructional issues are likely to remain among the most important for students with disabilities as the move into standards-based education continues.

Lessons learned about including students with disabilities in standards-based reforms

Just prior to passage of the reauthorization of the Individuals with Disabilities Education Act in 1997, the National Research Council conducted a study of students with disabilities and standards-based reform (McDonnell, McLaughlin, & Morison, 1997). One product of this effort was the development of a set of recommendations as follows:

Recommendation 1. States and localities that decide to implement standards-based reforms should design their common content standards, performance standards, and assessments to maximize participation of students with disabilities.

Recommendation 2. The presumption should be that each student with a disability will participate in the state or local standards; however, participation for any given student may require alterations to the common standards and assessments. Decisions to make such alterations must have a compelling educational justification and must be made on an individual basis.

Recommendation 3. The committee recommends strengthening the IEP process as the formal mechanism for deciding how individual students with disabilities will participate in standards-based reform.

Although these recommendations address critical topics, they do not highlight some of the key lessons that have been learned about including students with disabilities in standards-based reform. I share some of the key lessons here.

Participation in assessments is only the first step—it is an important step, but not the most important goal of standards-based reform.

Low expectations and the belief that students with disabilities should be protected from harm continue to characterize too many special educators, creating a great disservice to students who will have to function in employment and postsecondary settings when they leave school. Standards-based reform, of course, focuses on much more than just assessments. Key elements include the following:

- Goals (content standards)
- Indicators of success (performance standards)
- Measures of progress
- Reporting
- Consequences

The measures of progress are the assessments, clearly just one piece of the picture. The most critical piece is the notion that we provide all students with the opportunity to learn. For students with disabilities, this often means access to the general education curriculum first, then the provision of accommodations during instruction to ensure equal access to the general curriculum.

One of the notions behind participation in assessments is that we cannot know how students are progressing unless we have data to show us that performance. A common argument is that state and district assessments are not the best way to measure student performance, and that for students with disabilities, it is better to continuously measure student progress toward achieving the goals noted on their IEPs. This argument has created difficulties for special education because it has resulted in the field having little meaningful data on the performance of students (McGrew, Vanderwood, Thurlow, & Ysseldyke, 1995). And it has created a situation in which it is easy to think that everything is okay and that any amount of progress is all right. This is not the case. Most students with disabilities should be meeting the same high standards as other students. We are unlikely to realize this goal unless instruction is significantly ratcheted up and directed toward the learning needs of students who are receiving special education services.

Accountability is the key to standards-based reform for all students. Anecdotal evidence has been accumulating for some time about the expectations held for students receiving special education services. This evidence suggests that special educators have low expectations for students with disabilities. Some special educators also hold the attitude that they are more devoted to their students and know better than anyone else how to protect them and care for them. This attitude is a disservice to students with disabilities.

One of the advantages of standards-based reform is that it points out the inappropriateness of too much protection. It also begins to challenge the low expectations that have been held for many students with disabilities by showing what they know and can do.

Views on accommodations reflect attitudes—accommodations
are a key part of access to assessments, yet they are
shrouded in conflicting attitudes.

Views about accommodations perhaps are one of the most telling indicators of individual views about including all students in standards-based reforms. For years we have respected assessments that have sterilized the information we collect on students: Everyone must perform under exactly the same conditions so we then can compare them to each other. A standards-based system looks at progress toward standards; it is not about comparing students to each other. Yet, we are unwilling to give up the old model of assessment, which, of course, then makes it more difficult to be accepting of accommodations.

To some extent, views on accommodations seem to reflect tolerance for differences. They also reflect, to some extent, views on how people work as adults. Today increasing numbers of accommodations are provided as natural supports for individuals to be successful in employment settings. These accommodations, furthermore, often are provided to all employees, not just those who have disabilities. Should our assessment system not reflect the conditions under which we expect individuals to work after they have left the educational system—that is, with the availability of lifelong accommodations?

The extent to which students are using accommodations during assessments also highlights some instructional problems. When NCEO began to talk about needed assessment accommodations, the link to instructional accommodations was apparent. If students are surprised by being provided an assessment accommodation to which they have never been exposed before, it likely will be of little help, and may actually be a hinderance to performance. Most state policies on accommodations now refer back to what happens during instruction (Thurlow, House *et al.*, 2000). Yet, we find that teachers' knowledge about how to identify and use instructional accommodations is limited (DeStefano & Shriner, in press; Fuchs, Fuchs, Eaton, Hamlett, & Karns, 2000; Scott, Vitale, & Master, 1998).

Consequences create complications—incentives to exclude
students continue to exist and often are bolstered by
high stakes accountability.

Accountability or, rather, counting all students equally is going to be the force that drives forward the benefits of standards-based reform for students with disabilities. Until students with disabilities count in the same way as other students do, it is too easy to discount their performance, and in discounting, to ignore it and the instructional need it identifies.

IDEA 97 required that students with disabilities be included in assessments, and that their performance be reported publicly in the same way and with the same frequency as performance is reported for other students. Even though states are having difficulty meeting the reporting requirement (Thurlow, Nelson *et al.*, 2000), that requirement is not really enough. Today's schools are driven by accountability systems that produce significant rewards or sanctions for the schools (Education Commission of the States, 1999)—teachers receive cash awards, schools lose their accreditation, and so on—all on the basis of student performance. These systems existed in 40 states in 1999, and the number is likely increasing.

Children who count in these high-stakes systems are the ones who most likely will be attended to first. For this reason, students with disabilities must not only participate in assessments and have their scores reported, but their scores must count just like those of other students. Is this happening? Analyses (Krentz, Thurlow, & Callender, 2000) suggest that finding out who exactly counts in state accountability formula is difficult—if you can even find the formulas being used for accountability. This is a huge gap in ensuring that all students have exposure to high standards and that they benefit from educational reforms. Unfortunately, as in the past, the students most likely to be left out are those with disabilities (along with those students of limited English proficiency).

Policy has outpaced the technology of standards-based education and assessment.

Policies surrounding the participation of students with disabilities in assessments, their access to the general education curriculum, and their inclusion in Title I services and evaluation systems have moved forward rapidly during the past decade. The policies have moved forward so rapidly that educators are still catching up. But not only educators are having to catch up. The test development industry is having to catch up as well. Test developers and publishers have not retooled their assessment instruments either to be accessible to all students or to be standardized appropriately with all students (along with their accommodation needs) included.

Technology is beginning to catch up to policy. For example, CTB/McGraw Hill's (2000) guidelines on accommodations are way ahead of the current thinking of most test publishers, at least in comparison to the information provided on accommodations in their test manuals.

There still is a need to go farther, however. At the time that items are developed, all students should be considered. I suspect that if items were developed to be more accessible to all students, the need for accommodations would be less. In addition, at the time of item reviews, a trained disability representative should participate on the bias review team to identify any nonaccessible items the item developers produced. This person has to be trained so inaccessibility can be identified for the entire range of disabilities. NCEO currently is in the process of putting together a manual that could be used to train individuals for participation on bias review teams and that item developers also could use.

The bottom line—instruction!

This lesson regarding the importance of instruction probably has come through already in the other lessons I have identified. It is an important lesson, however, and deserves repetition. As we have come to realize that students must be included in standards-based reform and as we have pushed students into assessments from which they were previously excluded, we have taken many side trails (including cheating), in an attempt to avoid the most important path of all: Students must receive appropriate instruction, characterized both by access to the general education curriculum and by appropriate accommodations. The instruction must reflect high expectations and data-based instructional corrections. Students with disabilities must have access to all the remedial and honors programs to which other students have access.

We have come a long way in the past decade. Although there are indications of changes in instruction as a result of the emphasis on standards and participation in state and district assessments, we still have a way to go. As we proceed through the next decade, the challenge remains to move beyond simply participation to full-blown success through comprehensive, inclusive, standards-based education for all students.

References

American Federation of Teachers. (1996). *Making standards matter 1996: An annual fifty-state report on efforts to raise academic standards*. Washington, DC: Author.

American Federation of Teachers. (1999). *Making standards matter 1999*. Washington, DC: Author.

Anderson, N. E., Jenkins, F. F., & Miller, K. E. (1996). *NAEP inclusion criteria and testing accommodations: Findings from the NAEP 1995 field test in mathematics*. Princeton, NJ: Educational Testing Service.

Bielinski, J., & Ysseldyke, J. (2000). Interpreting trends in the performance of special education students. Minneapolis: National Center on Educational Outcomes.

Bradley, A. (2000, Jan. 13). The gatekeeping challenge. *Quality counts 2000: Who should teach? (Education Week)*, *19*(18), pp. 20, 22–24, 26.

Business Roundtable. (1996). *A business leader's guide to setting academic standards*. Washington, DC: Author.

CTB/McGraw-Hill. (2000). *Guidelines for using the results of standardized tests administered under nonstandard conditions.* Monterey, CA: Author.

David, J. M. (1997). *The role of standards-based assessment in schoolwide instructional improvement: Necessary, perhaps, but not sufficient.* Paper presented for New Standards Evaluation Steering Committee (cited in Elmore & Rothman, 1999 *Testing, Teaching and Learning,* p. 76.

DeStefano, L., & Shriner, J. G. (in press). The role of teacher decision-making in participation and accommodation of students with disabilities in large-scale assessments. *Exceptional Children.*

Education Commission of the States. (1999). *Education accountability in 50 states.* Denver: Author.

Elliott, J. L., Bielinski, J., Thurlow, M. L., DeVito, P., & Hedlund, E. (1999). *Accommodations and the performance of all students on Rhode Island's performance* (Rhode Island Report 1). Minneapolis: University of Minnesota, National Center on Educational Outcomes.

Elliott, J. L., Erickson, R. N., Thurlow, M. L., & Shriner, J. (2000). State-level accountability for the performance of students with disabilities: Five years of change? *Journal of Special Education, 34*(1), 39–47.

Elliott, J. L., & Thurlow, M. L. (2000). *Improving test performance of students with disabilities on district and state assessments.* Thousand Oaks, CA: Corwin Press.

Elmore, R. F., & Rothman, R. (1999). *Testing, teaching, and learning: A guide for stares and school districts.* Washington, DC: National Academy of Sciences.

Erickson, R. N., Thurlow, M. L., & Ysseldyke, J. E. (1996). *Neglected numerators, drifting denominators, and fractured fractions* (Synthesis Report 23). Minneapolis: University of Minnesota, National Center on Educational Outcomes.

Erickson, R., Ysseldyke, J., & Thurlow, M. (1997). Neglected numerators, drifting denominators, and fractured fractions: Determining participation rates for students with disabilities. *Diagnostique, 23*(2), 105–115.

Erickson, R., Ysseldyke, J., Thurlow, M., & Elliott, J. (1997). *Reporting educational results for students with disabilities* (NCEO Policy Directions 8). Minneapolis: University of Minnesota, National Center on Educational Outcomes.

Fordham Foundation. (2000). *The state of state standards 2000.* Washington, DC: Thomas H. Fordham Foundation.

Fuchs, L. S., Funchs, D., Eaton, S. B., Hamlett, C. L., & Karns, K. M. (2000). Supplementing teacher judgments of mathematics test accommodations with objective data sources. *School Psychology Review, 29*(1), 65–85.

Guy, B., Shin, H., Lee, S. Y., & Thurlow, M. L. (1999). *State graduation requirements for students with and without disabilities* (Technical Report 24). Minneapolis: University of Minnesota, National Center on Educational Outcomes.

Heubert, J., & Hauser, R. (1999). *High stakes: Testing for tracking, promotion, and graduation.* Washington, DC: National Academy Press.

Heumann, J. E., & Warlick, K. R. (2000, Aug. 24). *Questions and answers about provisions in the Individuals with Disabilities Education Act Amendments of 1997 related to students with disabilities and state and district-wide assessments* (Memorandum to State Directors of Special Education, OSEP 00-24). Washington, DC: Office of Special Education Programs.

Hofmeister, A. M. (1993). Elitism and reform in school mathematics. *Remedial & Special Education, 14*(6), 8–13.

Ingels, S. J. (1993). *Strategies for including all students in national and state assessments: Lessons from a national longitudinal study*. Paper presented at National Conference on Large-Scale Assessment, Albuquerque, NM. (ERIC Reproduction Service No. ED 363-645).

Ingels, S. J. (1996). *Sample exclusion in NELS:88: Characteristics of base year ineligible students; changes in eligibility status after four years* (NCES Technical Report 96-723). Washington, DC: U.S. Department of Education, Office of Educational Research and Improvement.

Ingels, S. J., & Scott, L. A. (1993). *Exclusion of students with barriers to participation in NELS:88—Baseline excluded students two and four years later*. Paper presented at annual meeting of American Educational Research Association, Atlanta. (ERIC Document Reproduction Service No. ED 360-371)

Keller, B. (2000. April 12). More N. Y. special education students passing state tests. *Education Week on the Web* (http://www.edweek.org/ewstory.cfm?slug=31ny.h19&keywords=new%20york).

Kohn, A. (2000). Burnt at the high stakes. *Journal of Teacher Education, 51*(4), 315–327.

Koretz, D. (1997). *The assessment of students with disabilities in Kentucky* (CSE Technical Report 431). Los Angeles: National Center for Research on Evaluation, Standards, and Student Testing.

Krentz, J., Thurlow, M., & Callender, S. (2000). *Accountability systems and counting students with disabilities* (Technical Report). Minneapolis: University of Minnesota, National Center on Educational Outcomes.

Linn, R. L. (2000). Assessments and accountability. *Educational Researcher, 29*(2), 4–16.

Linn, R. L., & Herman, J. L. (1997). *Standards-led assessment: Technical and policy issues for meaningful school and student progress* (CSE Technical Report 426). Los Angeles: University of California. CRESST.

Mazzeo, J., Carlson, J. E., Voekl, K. E., & Lutkus, A. D. (2000). *Increasing the participation of special needs students in NAEP: A report on 1996 NAEP research activities* (NCES Statistical Analysis Report 2000-473). Washington, DC: U.S. Department of Education, Office of Educational Research and Improvement.

McDonnell, L., McLaughlin, M., & Morison, P. (1997). *Educating one & all: Students with disabilities and standards-based reform*. Washington, DC: National Academy Press.

McGrew, K. S., Algozzine, B., Ysseldyke, J. E., Thurlow, M. L., & Spiegel, A. N. (1995). The identification of individuals with disabilities in national databases: Creating a failure to communicate. *Journal of Special Education, 28*(4), 472–487.

McGrew, K. S., Thurlow, M. L., Shriner, J. G., & Spiegel, A. N. (1992). *Inclusion of students with disabilities in national and state data collection systems* (Technical Report 2). Minneapolis: University of Minnesota, National Center on Educational Outcomes.

McGrew, K. S., & Vanderwood, M. (1993). *The identification of people with disabilities in national data bases: A failure to communicate* (Technical Report 6). Minneapolis: University of Minnesota, National Center on Educational Outcomes.

McGrew, K. S., Vanderwood, M., Thurlow, M. L., & Ysseldyke, J. E. (1995). *Why we can't say much about the statutes of status of students with disabilities during educational reform* (Synthesis Report 21). Minneapolis: University of Minnesota, National Center on Educational Outcomes.

National Association of State Boards of Education. (1998). *The numbers game: Ensuring quantity and quality in the teaching workforce.* Alexandria, VA: Author.

National Council on Education Standards and Testing. (1992). *Raising standards for American education.* Washington, DC: U.S. Government Printing Office.

National Council of Teachers of Mathematics. (1989). *Curriculum and education standards for school mathematics.* Reston, VA: Author.

National Research Council. (1993). *National science education standards.* Washington, DC: National Committee on Science Education Standards and Assessment.

Newmann, F. M., & Associates. (1996). *Authentic achievement: Restructuring schools for intellectual quality.* San Francisco: Jossey-Bass.

Olson, J. F., Bond, L., & Andrews, C. (1999). *Data from the annual survey: State student assessment programs.* Washington, DC: Council of Chief State School Officers.

Olson, L. (2000, May 31). Indiana case focused on special ed. *Education Week on the Web* (http://www.edweek.org/ewstory.cfm?slug=38stateshl98keywords=Indiana%20special %20education).

Scott, B. J., Vitale, M. R., & Master, W. G. (1998). Implementing instructional adaptations for students with disabilities in inclusive classrooms: A literature review. *Remedial & Special Education, 19*(2), 106–119.

Shepard, L. A. (1991). *Will national tests improve student learning?* Los Angeles: University of California, CRESST.

Shriner, J. G., Kim, D., Thurlow, M. L., & Ysseldyke, J. E. (1992). *IEPs and standards: What they say for students with disabilities* (Technical Report No. 5). Minneapolis: University of Minnesota, National Center on Educational Outcomes.

Shriner, J. G., & Thurlow, M. L. (1992). Special education outcomes 1991. Minneapolis: University of Minnesota, National Center on Educational Outcomes.

Spillane, J. P. (1997). *External reform initiatives and teachers' efforts to reconstruct their practice: The mediating role of teachers' zones of enactment.* Paper presented at annual meeting of Association for Public Policy Analysis and Management (cited in National Research Council, 1999, pp. 75–76).

State policy updates (2000, Jan. 13). Quality counts 2000: Who should teach? (*Education Week*), *19*(18).

Thompson, S. J., & Thurlow, M. L. (1999). *1999 State special education outcomes.* Minneapolis: University of Minnesota, National Center on Educational Outcomes.

Thurlow, M. L. (in press). Focusing on state and local assessments. *ALERTS.*

Thurlow, M. L., Elliott, J. L., & Ysseldyke, J. E. (1998). *Testing students with disabilities: Practical strategies for complying with district and state requirements.* Thousand Oaks, CA: Corwin Press.

Thurlow, M. L., House, A., Boys, C., Scott, D., & Ysseldyke, J. (2000). *State assessment policies on participation and accommodations for students with disabilities: 1999 update* (Synthesis Report 33). Minneapolis: University of Minnesota, National Center on Educational Outcomes.

Thurlow, M. L., & Johnson, D. R. (2000). High stakes testing of students with disabilities. *Journal of Teacher Education, 51*(4), 305–314.

Thurlow, M., Langenfeld, K., Nelson, J. R., Shin, H., & Coleman, J. (1998). *State accountability reports: What are states saying about students with disabilities?*

(Technical Report 20). Minneapolis: University of Minnesota, National Center on Educational Outcomes.

Thurlow, M. L., Nelson, J. R., Teelucksingh, E., & Ysseldyke, J. E. (2000). *Where's Waldo? A third search for students with disabilities in state accountability reports* (Technical Report 25). Minneapolis: University of Minnesota, National Center on Educational Outcomes.

Thurlow, M. L., Scott, D. L., & Ysseldyke, J. E. (1995a). *A compilation of states' guidelines for accommodations in assessments for students with disabilities* (Synthesis Report 18). Minneapolis: University of Minnesota, National Center on Educational Outcomes.

Thurlow, M. L., Scott, D. L., & Ysseldyke, J. E. (1995b). *A compilation of states' guidelines for including students with disabilities in assessments* (Synthesis Report 17). Minneapolis: University of Minnesota, National Center on Educational Outcomes.

Thurlow, M., & Thompson, S. (2000). *Diploma options and graduation policies for students with disabilities* (NCEO Policy Directions 10). Minneapolis, MN: University of Minnesota, National Center on Educational Outcomes.

Thurlow, M. L., & Ysseldyke, J. E. (2000). Standard-setting challenges for special populations. In G. Cizek (Ed.), *Standard setting on peformance assessments* (Ch. 12). Mahwah, NJ: Lawrence Erlbaum Associates.

Thurlow, M., Ysseldyke, J., Gutman, S., & Geenen, K. (1998). *An analysis of inclusion of students with disabilities in state standards documents* (Technical Report 19). Minneapolis: University of Minnesota, National Center on Educational Outcomes.

Thurlow, M. L., Ysseldyke, J. E., & Silverstein, B. (1993). *Testing accommodations for students with disabilities: A review of the literature* (Synthesis Report 4). Minneapolis: University of Minnesota, National Center on Educational Outcomes.

Trimble, S. (1998). *Performance trends and use of accommodations on a statewide assessment* (NCEO Assessment Series, Maryland/Kentucky Report 3). Minneapolis: University of Minnesota, National Center on Educational Outcomes.

U.S. Department of Education. (1995). *Teacher supply, teacher qualifications, and teacher turnover, 1990–91*. Washington, DC: National Center for Education Statistics.

U.S. Department of Education. (1999). *Peer reviewer guidance for evaluating evidence of final assessments under Title I of the Elementary and Secondary Education Act*. Washington, DC: Author.

Why Johnny stayed home. (1997, Oct. 6). *Newsweek, 130*(34), 60.

Ysseldyke, J., Krentz, J., Elliott, J., Thurlow, M., Erickson, R., & Moore, M. (1998). *NCEO framework for educational accountability*. Minneapolis, MN: University of Minnesota, National Center on Educational Outcomes.

Ysseldyke, J., Thurlow, M., & Erickson, R. (1994a). *Educational outcomes and indicators for grade 4*. Minneapolis: University of Minnesota, National Center on Educational Outcomes.

Ysseldyke, J., Thurlow, M., & Erickson, R. (1994b). *Educational outcomes and indicators for grade 8*. Minneapolis: University of Minnesota, National Center on Educational Outcomes.

Ysseldyke, J., Thurlow, M., Erickson, R., Gabrys, R., Haigh, J., Trimble, S., & Gong, B. (1996). A *comparison of state assessment systems in Maryland and Kentucky with a focus on the participation of students with disabilities* (Maryland/

Kentucky Report 1). Minneapolis: University of Minnesota, National Center on Educational Outcomes.

Ysseldyke, J., Thurlow, M., & Gilman, C. (1993a). *Educational outcomes and indicators for early childhood (age 3)*. Minneapolis: University of Minnesota, National Center on Educational Outcomes.

Ysseldyke, J., Thurlow, M., & Gilman, C. (1993b). *Educational outcomes and indicators for early childhood (age 6)*. Minneapolis: University of Minnesota, National Center on Educational Outcomes.

Ysseldyke, J., Thurlow, M., & Gilman, C. (1993c). *Educational outcomes and indicators for individuals at the post-school level*. Minneapolis: University of Minnesota, National Center on Educational Outcomes.

Ysseldyke, J., Thurlow, M., & Gilman, C. (1993d). *Educational outcomes and indicators for students completing school*. Minneapolis: University of Minnesota, National Center on Educational Outcomes.

Ysseldyke, J. E., Thurlow, M. L., Langenfeld, K. L., Nelson, J. R., Teelucksingh, E., & Seyfarth, A. (1998). *Educational results for students with disabilities: What do the data tell us?* (Technical Report 23).

Ysseldyke, J., Thurlow, M., McGrew, K. S., & Shriner, J. G. (1994). *Recommendations for making decisions about the participation of students with disabilities in statewide assessment programs* (Synthesis Report 15). Minneapolis: University of Minnesota, National Center on Educational Outcomes.

Ysseldyke, J., Thurlow, M., McGrew, K., & Vanderwood, M. (1994). *Making decisions about the inclusion of students with disabilities in large-scale assessments* (Synthesis Report 13). Minneapolis: University of Minnesota, National Center on Educational Outcomes.

Ysseldyke, J. E., Thurlow, M. L., & Shriner, J. G. (1992). Outcomes are for special educators too. *Teaching Exceptional Children, 25*, 36–50.

Zlatos, B. (1992). Don't test, don't tell: Is "academic red-shirting" skewing the way we rank our schools? *The American School Board, 191*(11), 24–28.

22

DECLARATION ON THE RIGHTS OF DISABLED PERSONS

United Nations

Source: New York: United Nations, 1975.

UN Document Series Symbol: ST/HR/
UN Issuing Body: Secretariat Centre for Human Rights
© *United Nations*

Proclaimed by General Assembly resolution 3447 (XXX) of 9 December 1975

The General Assembly,

Mindful of the pledge made by Member States, under the Charter of the United Nations to take joint and separate action in co-operation with the Organization to promote higher standards of living, full employment and conditions of economic and social progress and development,

Reaffirming its faith in human rights and fundamental freedoms and in the principles of peace, of the dignity and worth of the human person and of social justice proclaimed in the Charter,

Recalling the principles of the Universal Declaration of Human Rights, the International Covenants on Human Rights, the Declaration of the Rights of the Child and the Declaration on the Rights of Mentally Retarded Persons, as well as the standards already set for social progress in the constitutions, conventions, recommendations and resolutions of the International Labour Organisation, the United Nations Educational, Scientific and Cultural Organization, the World Health Organization, the United Nations Children's Fund and other organizations concerned,

Recalling also Economic and Social Council resolution 1921 (LVIII) of 6 May 1975 on the prevention of disability and the rehabilitation of disabled persons,

Emphasizing that the Declaration on Social Progress and Development has proclaimed the necessity of protecting the rights and assuring the welfare and rehabilitation of the physically and mentally disadvantaged,

Bearing in mind the necessity of preventing physical and mental disabilities and of assisting disabled persons to develop their abilities in the most varied fields of activities and of promoting their integration as far as possible in normal life,

Aware that certain countries, at their present stage of development, can devote only limited efforts to this end,

Proclaims this Declaration on the Rights of Disabled Persons and calls for national and international action to ensure that it will be used as a common basis and frame of reference for the protection of these rights:

1 The term "disabled person" means any person unable to ensure by himself or herself, wholly or partly, the necessities of a normal individual and/or social life, as a result of deficiency, either congenital or not, in his or her physical or mental capabilities.
2 Disabled persons shall enjoy all the rights set forth in this Declaration. These rights shall be granted to all disabled persons without any exception whatsoever and without distinction or discrimination on the basis of race, colour, sex, language, religion, political or other opinions, national or social origin, state of wealth, birth or any other situation applying either to the disabled person himself or herself or to his or her family.
3 Disabled persons have the inherent right to respect for their human dignity. Disabled persons, whatever the origin, nature and seriousness of their handicaps and disabilities, have the same fundamental rights as their fellow-citizens of the same age, which implies first and foremost the right to enjoy a decent life, as normal and full as possible.
4 Disabled persons have the same civil and political rights as other human beings; paragraph 7 of the Declaration on the Rights of Mentally Retarded Persons applies to any possible limitation or suppression of those rights for mentally disabled persons.
5 Disabled persons are entitled to the measures designed to enable them to become as self-reliant as possible.
6 Disabled persons have the right to medical, psychological and functional treatment, including prosthetic and orthetic appliances, to medical and social rehabilitation, education, vocational training and rehabilitation, aid, counselling, placement services and other services which will enable them to develop their capabilities and skills to the maximum and will hasten the processes of their social integration or reintegration.
7 Disabled persons have the right to economic and social security and to a decent level of living. They have the right, according to their capabilities, to secure and retain employment or to engage in a useful, productive and remunerative occupation and to join trade unions.
8 Disabled persons are entitled to have their special needs taken into consideration at all stages of economic and social planning.

9   Disabled persons have the right to live with their families or with foster parents and to participate in all social, creative or recreational activities. No disabled person shall be subjected, as far as his or her residence is concerned, to differential treatment other than that required by his or her condition or by the improvement which he or she may derive therefrom. If the stay of a disabled person in a specialized establishment is indispensable the environment and living conditions therein shall be as close as possible to those of the normal life of a person of his or her age.

10 Disabled persons shall be protected against all exploitation, all regulations and all treatment of a discriminatory, abusive or degrading nature.

11 Disabled persons shall be able to avail themselves of qualified legal aid when such aid proves indispensable for the protection of their persons and property. If judicial proceedings are instituted against them, the legal procedure applied shall take their physical and mental condition fully into account.

12 Organizations of disabled persons may be usefully consulted in all matters regarding the rights of disabled persons.

13 Disabled persons, their families and communities shall be fully informed, by all appropriate means, of the rights contained in this Declaration.

23

THE SALAMANCA STATEMENT AND FRAMEWORK FOR ACTION ON SPECIAL NEEDS EDUCATION

Adopted by the World Conference on Special Needs Education: Access and Quality. Salamanca, Spain, 7–10 June 1994

UNESCO

Source: Paris: UNESCO, 1994, pp. vii–xii.

Reaffirming the right to education of every individual, as enshrined in the 1948 Universal Declaration of Human Rights, and renewing the pledge made by the world community at the 1990 World Conference on Education for All to ensure that right for all regardless of individual differences,

Recalling the several United Nations declarations culminating in the 1993 United Nations Standard Rules on the Equalization of Opportunities for Persons with Disabilities, which urges States to ensure that the education of persons with disabilities is an integral part of the education system,

Noting with satisfaction the increased involvement of governments, advocacy groups, community and parent groups, and in particular organizations of persons with disabilities, in seeking to improve access to education for the majority of those with special needs still unreached; and recognizing as evidence of this involvement the active participation of highlevel representatives of numerous governments, specialized agencies and intergovernmental organizations in this World Conference,

1.

We, the delegates of the World Conference on Special Needs Education representing ninety-two governments and twenty-five international organizations, assembled here in Salamanca, Spain, from 7–10 June 1994, hereby reaffirm our commitment to Education for All, recognizing the necessity and urgency of providing education for children, youth and adults with special educational needs within the regular education system, and further hereby endorse the Framework for Action on Special Needs Education, that governments and organizations may be guided by the spirit of its provisions and recommendations.

2.

We believe and proclaim that:

- every child has a fundamental right to education, and must be given the opportunity to achieve and maintain an acceptable level of learning,
- every child has unique characteristics, interests, abilities and learning needs,
- education systems should be designed and educational programmes implemented to take into account the wide diversity of these characteristics and needs,
- those with special educational needs must have access to regular schools which should accommodate them within a child-centred pedagogy capable of meeting these needs,
- regular schools with this inclusive orientation are the most effective means of combating discriminatory attitudes, creating welcoming communities, building an inclusive society and achieving education for all; moreover, they provide an effective education to the majority of children and improve the efficiency and ultimately the cost-effectiveness of the entire education system.

3.

We call upon all governments and urge them to:

- give the highest policy and budgetary priority to improve their education systems to enable them to include all children regardless of individual differences or difficulties,
- adopt as a matter of law or policy the principle of inclusive education, enrolling all children in regular schools, unless there are compelling reasons for doing otherwise,
- develop demonstration projects and encourage exchanges with countries having experience with inclusive schools,
- establish decentralized and participatory mechanisms for planning, monitoring and evaluating educational provision for children and adults with special education needs,

- encourage and facilitate the participation of parents, communities and organization of persons with disabilities in the planning and decision-making processes concerning provision for special educational needs,
- invest greater effort in early identification and intervention strategies, as well as in vocational aspects of inclusive education,
- ensure that, in the context of a systemic change, teacher education programmes, both pre-service and in-service, address the provision of special needs education in inclusive schools.

4.

We also call upon the international community; in particular we call upon:

- governments with international cooperation programmes and international funding agencies, especially the sponsors of the World Conference on Education for All, the United Nations Educational, Scientific and Cultural Organization (UNESCO), the United Nations Children's Fund (UNICEF), United Nations Development Programme (UNDP), and the World Bank:
    - to endorse the approach of inclusive schooling and to support the development of special needs education as an integral part of all education programmes;
    - the United Nations and its specialized agencies, in particular the International Labour Office (ILO), the World Health Organization (WHO), UNESCO and UNICEF:
    - to strengthen their inputs for technical cooperation, as well as to reinforce their cooperation and networking for more efficient support to the expanded and integrated provision of special needs education;
- non-governmental organizations involved in country programming and service delivery:
    - to strengthen their collaboration with the official national bodies and to intensify their growing involvement in planning, implementation and evaluation of inclusive provision for special educational needs;
- UNESCO, as the United Nations agency for education:
    - to ensure that special needs education forms part of every discussion dealing with education for all in various forums,
    - to mobilize the support of organizations of the teaching profession in matters related to enhancing teacher education as regards provision for special education needs,
    - to stimulate the academic community to strengthen research and networking and to establish regional centres of information and documentation; also, to serve as a clearinghouse for such activities

and for disseminating the specific results and progress achieved at country level in pursuance of this Statement,

– to mobilize funds through the creation within its next Medium-Term Plan (1996–2002) of an expanded programme for inclusive schools and community support programmes, which would enable the launching of pilot projects that showcase new approaches for dissemination, and to develop indicators concerning the need for and provision of special needs education.

5.

Finally, we express our warm appreciation to the Government of Spain and to UNESCO for the organization of the Conference, and we urge them to make every effort to bring this Statement and the accompanying Framework for Action to the attention of the world community, especially at such important forums as the World Summit for Social Development (Copenhagen, 1995) and the World Conference on Women (Beijing, 1995).

Adopted by acclamation, in the city of Salamanca, Spain, on this 10th of June, 1994.

24

TRANSFER OF BELIEFS, KNOWLEDGE, AND EXPERIENCES BETWEEN COUNTRIES

David Mitchell

Source: P. Retish and S. Reiter (eds), *Adults with Disabilities: International Perspectives in the Community*, Mahwah, NJ: Lawrence Erlbaum, 1999, pp. 259–85.

In recent years, beliefs, principles, knowledge, and practices relating to special education and rehabilitation increasingly have been transferred between countries, with the result that there is a remarkable degree of convergence, both in ideology and in practices, across all types of nations. This chapter will examine the following questions:

- Who transfers beliefs, knowledge, and experiences?
- What beliefs, knowledge, and experiences are transferred?
- What are the issues involved in transferring beliefs, knowledge, and experiences?

Who transfers beliefs, knowledge and experiences?

Knowledge and experiences relating to people with disabilities are transferred between countries in varied ways by a range of organizations and individuals. These sources fall into seven categories:

1 International governmental and intergovernmental organizations.
2 Regional governmental and intergovernmental organizations.
3 International and regional nongovernmental organizations.
4 Bilateral arrangements between countries.
5 Influential legislation and policies from specific countries.
6 Associations and individuals involved in rehabilitation.
7 The Internet.

International governmental and intergovernmental organizations

International agencies have been actively promoting a consistent set of philosophies regarding persons with disabilities. These have been expressed in several key documents that have been promulgated by the United Nations and associated agencies (e.g., UNESCO, UNICEF, UNDP, WHO, ILO) over the past half century. The most important of these are as follows:

- The Universal Declaration of Human Rights, adopted by the UN General Assembly (1948).
- The Declaration on the Rights of Mentally Retarded Persons, adopted by the UN General Assembly (1971).
- Declaration of the Rights of Disabled Persons, adopted by the UN General Assembly (1975).
- The International Covenant on Economic, Social and Cultural Rights adopted by the UN General Assembly in 1966, and entered into force in 1975.
- The International Year of Disabled Persons (1981).
- The UN Decade of Disabled Persons (1983–1992), and the associated UN World Programme of Action Concerning Disabled Persons (1983).
- The International Labour Organization Convention concerning Vocational Rehabilitation and Employment of Disabled Persons (1983).
- The Convention on the Rights of the Child adopted by the UN General Assembly in 1989, and entered into force in 1990.
- The World Declaration on Education for All (1990).
- The Standard Rules for the Equalization of Opportunities for Persons with Disabilities, adopted by the UN General Assembly (1993).
- The Salamanca Statement and Framework of Action on Special Needs Education, adopted by UNESCO (1994).

Several of the aforementioned documents warrant special mention. The International Year of Disabled Persons, and the follow-up Decade of Disabled Persons with its 201-paragraph World Programme of Action Concerning Disabled Persons, both had major impacts on the development of policies around the world. Several countries—Senegal, Pakistan, India, Japan, and the Republic of Korea, to name a few, created legislation that can be directly attributed to the policies promoted during this period (Kim, 1993; Lynch, 1994; Mazurek & Winzer, 1994). For example, in India, it led to a National Plan of Action that included the following objectives: (a) to evolve a national policy for full social integration and legal protection for disabled persons, (b) to initiate a few practical programs that would carry immediate benefit for the integration of disabled persons, and (c) to initiate public campaigns to create greater awareness among the people regarding the causes, prevention, and effects of disability and the potentials of disabled persons

(Agrawal, 1994). According to O'Hanlon (1995), the International Year of Disabled Persons also formed a basis for the European Union's response to the social and economic needs of people with disabilities, and led directly to the establishment of the first action program, the Social Integration of Disabled People—a Framework for Community Action. This document contained the recommendation that member states should promote measures to prepare handicapped people for an active life, in particular by integrating them in normal education and training whenever possible. This first action program led directly to the second action program, Handicapped People in the European Community Living Independently in an Open Society (HELIOS), which ran from 1988 to 1991. A third program, known as HELIOS II (1993–1996), focused on the exchange of information, experiences, and good practices in the fields of functional rehabilitation, education, employment, and independent living. For the first time, older disabled people have been identified as a separate priority group within the European Union program (Merceron, 1996).

The 1983 World Programme of Action was further clarified by the UN Secretary-General in 1984, when he emphasized nine priorities for member states: continuing and extending national disability committees established during the International Year, reviewing national legislation, collecting basic data, preventing disability, establishing regulations to ensure accessibility, providing technical aids, equalising opportunities in education, informing the public, and—at the international level—establishing effective services for the exchange of information.

In turn, the World Programme of Action led to the development of *The Standard Rules for the Equalization of Opportunities for Disabled Persons*, which were adopted by the UN General Assembly in 1993 (United Nations, 1994). This document is of special significance because it represents a contemporary and authoritative distillation of all preceding UN documents on disability. It was drafted by representatives of 74 governments who took part in three different conferences from 1991 to 1992. The *Standard Rules* comprises 22 general rules, with a total of 132 more detailed guidelines. As Rowland (1996) points out, one of the attractive features of the *Standard Rules* is that while they are specific, they are not overly detailed and are thus adaptable to different legal systems and cultures. In countries that are in transition, they provide a basis for formulating disability policy and legislation as witnessed, for example, in South Africa and Namibia (Rowland, 1996). The UN was not satisfied with merely promulgating the *Standard Rules*, but instead set up a mechanism for monitoring and furthering their implementation, with three responsible agents, the Permanent Commission of the UN, the Commission for Social Development, and a Special Rapporteur assisted by a 10-member panel of experts. Initially, the Rapporteur and panel of experts have focused on surveying and promoting six of the rules: education, employment, legislation, accessibility, the position of organizations of disabled people, and the distribution of government responsibilities.

Almost contemporaneous with the development of the *Standard Rules* was the development of the *Salamanca Statement and Framework of Action on Special Needs Education*. The latter document had its specific origins in the World Declaration on Education for All (1990), which resulted from the World Conference on Education for All held in Jomtien, Thailand in 1990 and convened by UNESCO, UNICEF, UNDP, and the World Bank (Inter-Agency Commission, 1990). This conference brought together government representatives from 155 countries and over 150 organizations. One of the major outcomes of this conference was the convening by UNESCO of a series of high-level regional seminars on policy, planning, and organization of education for children and young people with special needs, with an emphasis on inclusive education. These seminars culminated in a meeting in 1994 of representatives of 92 governments and 25 international organizations who drew up the document known as the *Salamanca Statement* (UNESCO, 1994). Included in this document were statements of beliefs and an appeal to governments to give priority to developing and implementing policies on special education, with particular attention to inclusive education. It provides a "Framework for Action" that contains 85 specific recommendations to do with policy and organization, school factors, recruitment and training of educational personnel, external support services, priority areas, community perspectives, resource requirements, and guidelines for action at the regional and international levels.

Many examples can be found of the direct role played by the UN and its agencies in transferring policies and practices to countries around the world. A few will suffice here. Firstly, Diaconescu, Ionescu, Chis, and Daunt (1995) outline how, in 1991, with the sponsorship of UNESCO and UNICEF, the Romanian authorities organized a conference to review the system of special education. While there were some reservations, considerable interest was shown in the concepts of integration and normalization. The three foreign consultants attending the conference under UNESCO's auspices prepared a draft proposal for the setting up of pilot projects to promote the educational and social integration of children and young people with disabilities of whatever kind or severity. In 1993, the government accepted the proposal and two projects were launched, with UNESCO continuing to provide technical support and UNICEF some funding.

One of the major determinants of international convergence of policies and practices in social areas is undoubtedly the World Bank. While it has not been particularly active in defining policies related to people with disabilities, the World Bank, as noted by Torres (1995–96), is already a major player in the transnationalization of knowledge, influencing the discourse of education and educational reforms, not only in developing countries, but worldwide. The underlying ideology thus projected, according to Torres, is that of neoliberalism. The World Bank made its first loan for education in 1963 and is now the largest single source of external financing for education in developing countries, accounting for about a quarter of all such aid (World Bank, 1995). In developing countries, it has the ultimate influence to bring about change: money. In its own words, "Bank financing will generally be designed to leverage spending and policy change by national authorities" (World Bank, 1995, pp. 14–15). Its priorities for reform therefore bear close study in the broader context of forces underlying the transfer of ideology and knowledge. In a recent publication, these were summarized as being in six key areas: (a) giving higher priority to education, (b) setting priorities with reference to outcomes, (c) emphasizing basic education, (d) attending to equity, (e) involving households in the governance of schools, and (f) granting schools the autonomy to use instructional inputs according to local school and community conditions, with accountability to parents and communities. The bank's principal policy instrument for reducing the high incidence of physical and learning disabilities in developing countries is through the improvement of child nutrition and health. It notes, too, that the "unit costs" for special education can be reduced by using community-based approaches, referring in this context to the existence of community-based rehabilitation programs (see next section) in many countries, including India, Indonesia, Jamaica, Kenya, Malaysia, Nepal, the Philippines, and Zimbabwe.

In the light of its relevance to the theme of this book, it is appropriate to look more closely at the World Bark's view on equity, which it defines as having two principal aspects:

> (a) everyone's right to a basic education—the basic knowledge and skills necessary to function effectively in society—and (b) the government's obligation to ensure that qualified potential students are not denied education because they are poor or female, are from disadvantaged ethnic minorities or geographically remote regions, or have special educational needs.
>
> (World Bank, 1995, pp. 10–11)

It will be noted that the reference to "qualified potential students" raises doubts as to whether this statement's coverage extends to all learners with special needs.

Regional governmental and intergovernmental organizations

Regional-level governmental and intergovernmental organizations have adopted and promoted policies on persons with disabilities. Examples drawn from Europe, Asia, and Latin America will suffice to illustrate this point.

Europe

In Europe, as O'Hanlon (1993, 1995) points out, the movement towards integration has been heavily influenced by the Community's (and now the Union's) belief in human rights. Observance of human rights was originally embedded in the Convention for the Protection of Human Rights and Fundamental Freedoms within the Council for Europe, which was signed by member states in 1950. Since that time, the preservation of basic human rights has formed the foundation of all measures adopted by the Council for Europe. However, while the European Union (EU) has wide powers to formulate and implement policy, it does not have harmonization of educational systems as an overt aim and individual countries can opt out of certain policy instruments such as the Social Charter (which the UK has done). O'Hanlon notes that although there is no specific EU legislation for inclusive education, there is evidence of the development of similar policies within member states in relation to this matter. The Council of Ministers, for example, has been considering the possibility of developing more prescriptive general guidelines for the inclusion of pupils with special educational needs in education, with the intent that member states will bear these in mind when passing their own legislation. Such a development would be consistent with the *Resolution of the Council and the Ministers of Education of 31 May 1990* concerning the integration of children and young persons with disabilities into ordinary systems of education (O'Hanlon, 1995). Also, as noted by Merceron (1996), the treaties are currently being revised and discussions on Social Europe are high on the agenda.

As well as legislative moves, there are other mechanisms in place in Europe that play an important role in transferring knowledge and practices among countries, both within the EU and between it and countries in the former Communist bloc. At the governmental and intergovernmental level, the most important of these would be the ERASMUS and TEMPUS programs of the EU (Mittler & Daunt, 1995). The European Community Action Scheme for the Mobility of University Students (ERASMUS) aims at increasing the number of EU students undertaking a period of study in another member state, promoting cooperation among higher education institutions, and promoting the mobility of teaching staff. One such program was concerned with the integration of children with disabilities and involved universities in Bologna (Italy), Cologne (Germany), Malaga (Spain), and Manchester, Birmingham, and London (UK). TEMPUS is the acronym for Trans European Mobility Programme for University Staff, a program in which several universities collaborate on joint projects involving, especially, countries in Central and Eastern Europe. One such project is that between Manchester Metropolitan University, the Institut Universitaire de la Formation des Maîtres, Grenoble, and the Siauliai Pedagogical Institute in Lithuania, which is concerned with good practice in inclusive education and the teacher training structures that underlie it. As described by Johnson, this project aims "to empower the teachers by encouraging them to have confidence in their personal expertise and not to look constantly for the advice of 'experts' " (1995, p. 83). A second TEMPUS project deals with special educational needs in the mainstream and involves a partnership between the Bárczi Gusztáv College for Special Education in Hungary, which acts as both coordinator and contractor, along with the Budapest Teacher Training College, Manchester and Cambridge Universities in England, the Heidelberg Pädagogische Hochschule in Germany and the Instituut voor Doven (a school for the deaf) in the Netherlands (Csanyi, 1995).

Asia

During the last decade or so, several conferences and seminars relevant to special education have been held in the Asia Pacific Region and have yielded a wide range of policy recommendations in the field of special education (Mitchell & Chen, 1996). Preeminent among these is the series of regional seminars on special education, which have been held annually since 1981 under the auspices of UNESCO's Asia Pacific Programme of Educational Innovation for Development. These seminars have been hosted by Japan's National Institute of Special Education and largely funded by the Japanese National Commission for UNESCO. Participants have usually included representatives from Australia, Bangladesh, China, India, Indonesia, Japan, Malaysia, Nepal, New Zealand, Pakistan, the Philippines, the Republic of Korea, and Sri Lanka. As an example of these seminars, the one held in 1996 focused on the transition from schooling to post-compulsory education.

Another important regional initiative in Asia is the Asia Pacific Decade of the Disabled (1993–2002), with an agenda that includes national coordination, legislation, information dissemination, public awareness, training and employment, education, rehabilitation services, and regional cooperation.

Latin America

In 1993, the *Declaration of Managua* was signed by representatives of 36 Latin American countries who had come together to develop policies concerning the human rights of people with intellectual disabilities. The impact of this declaration is shown, for example, in the Dominican Republic where in 1995 the Catholic Church issued a public statement at every mass supporting its principles. As well, the church is gradually moving towards inclusive education in its schools and is recognizing the needs of children with disabilities in its policy on strengthening the Dominican family (Inclusion International, 1996).

Other regional or multinational organizations that are having or have the potential to impact on policies and practices of their member states include OECD, APEC, the Organization of American States, the Organization of African Unity, and the Arab League.

International and regional nongovernmental organizations

Nongovernmental organizations (NGOs) play a very important role in developing and promoting policies on people with disabilities. As pointed out by Mitchell & Chen (1996), although NGOs are not in a position to take on nationwide responsibility, they can join forces with the national authorities, assisting in areas like community-based programs and working on small-scale innovative projects to demonstrate new approaches. In this respect, they act as catalysts for change. Thus, it is very important that NGOs be involved in planning and coordinating their work with the public sector provision.

Of particular relevance here is the impact of worldwide organizations such as Rehabilitation International and Inclusion International (formerly known as the International League of Societies for Persons with Mental Handicap), Disabled People's International, the World Blind Union, the World Federation for the Deaf, the Islamic World Council on Disability and Rehabilitation, and the World Federation of Psychiatric Users (Helander, 1993).

A second group of NGOs comprises those that have their origins in a single country, but are involved in one or more other countries. For example, the German NGO Blindenmissen operates in several countries, Diakonia from Sweden operates in areas such as the West Bank and the Gaza Strip (Mazurek & Winzer, 1994, p. 62), and the Swedish voluntary organization, Radda Barnen, is introducing community rehabilitation centers in the Republic of Yemen (Qirbi, 1993). As well, the Japanese Society for the Rehabilitation of Disabled Persons is developing cooperation with Thailand, Vietnam, and the Philippines, is assisting in the establishment of a printing and computer training workshop in Thailand and is marketing products made in Vietnamese workshops in Japan (Niwa, 1996). A useful case study of the role of NGOs is afforded by Romania, where, since 1990, many new developments have been initiated by NGOs. As noted by Diaconescu *et al.* (1995), the Romanian NGOs that promoted these activities began to be important elements in the implementation of reform, "able to transmit messages to and from the citizens and the authorities, and even more importantly, able to establish international contacts and cooperation" (p. 68). Of particular interest is the contact generated by the Danish Red Barnet (Save the Children) between three Romanian NGOs in County Dolj and a number of different Danish counties.

Lynch (1994) also draws attention to the role played by NGOs in developing services with national counterparts. For example, Helen Keller International has established an Asia Pacific regional office in Bangkok where it conducts regional training workshops; it has also set up field offices in nearly all developing Asian nations. A similar range of programs has been established by the UK Save the Children Fund. Yet another example is the work of the Cheshire Foundation, which has established projects for disabled children and adults in over 50 countries throughout the world (McConkey, 1996).

At times, the range of NGOs operating can create problems in coordination —a point developed in more detail in the next section. Lynch (1994) cites the case of Nepal in 1988, when there were no fewer than 32 international agencies assisting in the development of services:

> Helen Keller International, the German Blindenmission, Norwegian, British and American Save the Children, Action Aid, SEVA, United Missions to Nepal, Norwegian Association for the Mentally Retarded, Mary Knoll Fathers, the World Union of the Blind, Perkins School for the Blind, Special Olympics, Sight Savers, and Jaycees, among others.
>
> (p. 12)

The role of NGOs is also apparent in Indonesia, where private voluntary agencies provide 55% of the resources for special education (World Bank, 1995). Private organizations and NGOs also play a significant role in the provision of special education in the Philippines. Of the 4,470 special education facilities, one-third are operated by NGOs or private corporations/ foundations; this is especially the case with special and residential schools. (Mitchell & Chen, 1996). While not all of the NGOs in Indonesia and the Philippines are from outside the country, these figures serve to illustrate the critical role that NGOs play in some countries' provisions for individuals with disabilities.

While, strictly speaking, they are not classifiable as NGOs, it is worth mentioning here the important role that church groups and missionaries have played in the evolution of special education in several developing countries. Some such influences are noted in the above description. Another example is afforded by the Republic of Korea, where Kim (1993) acknowledges the work of an American missionary, Rosetta S. Hall, who set up education programs for the blind and the deaf in the late 19th and early 20th centuries, and another American missionary, Edward Adams, who initiated education for physically disabled children in 1959. In Jordan, the first school for children with disabilities was set up in 1964 by Father Andeweg, a Dutch Anglican priest (Moulton, Andrews, & Smith, 1996).

Bilateral arrangements between countries

Several countries are active in providing bilateral aid to developing countries in the field of disability and rehabilitation. As noted by Lynch (1994), the Scandinavian countries in particular have made significant contributions to Asian national efforts to train personnel and provide initial services in provisions for people with disabilities. For example, the Swedish International Development Agency supported the Sri Lankan Ministry of Education in the area of staff training, development of sign language, the establishment of a resource and teacher training center for special education, and the maintenance of a Braille press; the Norwegian Agency for Developmental Cooperation helped to provide teacher training facilities in Bangladesh and services development in Nepal; the Australian International Development Assistance Bureau funded a Childhood Disabilities Project in some of the island states of the South Pacific; the Canadian International Development Agency funded the development of a disability diploma in the Gaza Strip (Brown, Abu Ghazaleh, and Neufeldt, 1996); and the United States Agency for International Development provided funding for programs for disabled people in the Gaza Strip. The Japanese Government-funded National Institute for Special Education is another example of bilateral aid that has had a pronounced influence on regional development.

Influential legislation and policies from specific countries

In the field of disability, there are perhaps three landmark reports or sets of legislation, with associated research, which have had effects well beyond the countries that generated them. The first of these is undoubtedly the Scandinavian legislation and practices that gave rise to the notion of "normalization" (e.g., Nirje, 1969, 1985) These have been acknowledged by several writers as having had a major impact on their countries' approaches to special education and rehabilitation: for example, Australia (Swan, 1994), New Zealand (Mitchell and Mitchell, 1987), and Japan (Misawa, 1994).

The second influential event is the U.S. Public Law 94–142 and its successor, the Individuals with Disabilities Education Act (IDEA) 1990. Their significance has been acknowledged in countries as diverse as Australia (Brown, 1997; Swan, 1994), Brazil (Kerns & Cavalcante, 1997), Canada (Winzer, 1994), Japan (Misawa, 1994), New Zealand (Mitchell & O'Brien, 1994), Nigeria (Abang, 1994), and Taiwan (Chen & Lu, 1994).

The Warnock Report in the UK (Warnock, 1978) is the third landmark event to have had an impact, with countries such as Japan (Misawa, 1994), Hong Kong (Crawford & Bray, 1994), Australia (Brown, 1997; Swan, 1994), and New Zealand (Mitchell and O'Brien, 1994) all being influenced by its principles.

Associations and individuals involved in rehabilitation

The final major way in which knowledge and experiences are transferred between countries is via various associations and individuals with interests in disabilities. In the field of mental retardation, the pre-eminent bodies in this regard are probably the International Association for Scientific Studies on Intellectual Disability and the American Association for Mental Deficiency, with the Asia Federation for the Mentally Retarded playing a very important regional role. Networks of organizations in the field of disability and rehabilitation also facilitate the dissemination and implementation of knowledge. An example of such a network is given by Hekking (1996), who describes the European Platform of Vocational Rehabilitation, a transnational network of European rehabilitation institutions, established in 1993. This was set up in part because of the growing political integration of the EU and the likelihood of a growing integration of the European labor market. It has four main strategies: (1) the development of a common European understanding of vocational rehabilitation, (2) the promotion of research and innovation in vocational rehabilitation, (3) developing the skills of professionals, and (4) improving service quality by such means as establishing common guidelines for European quality standards.

The Internet

Including all of the above, but extending beyond them, is the Internet, with its enormous and growing array of information on disability, special education, and rehabilitation. As noted by Mitchell (1996), the Internet, with its access to E-mail and the World Wide Web, is the prime current exemplar of how technology facilitates one's capacity to independently reach out and find information. The introduction of E-mail has dramatically changed the character and speed of communication, with participants able to simultaneously exchange information with a large number of people in a way that uniquely combines ease, speed, immediacy, and (increasingly) cheapness.

In recent years there has been a burgeoning network of sites on disability, special education, and rehabilitation. For example, GLADNET (Global Applied Disability Research and Information Network on Employment and Training) has been developed by the ILO to promote policies, programs, and projects to further equal opportunities for people with disabilities. This network is based in Geneva with a mirror home page in Ottawa and hyperlinks with over 50 disability sites. As of mid-1996, it comprised 160 members. Similarly, in 1995 ILO published a network of 53 organizations on the Web with information to do with disability. A third network of relevance is the one on inclusive education (inclusive-education@mailbase.ac.uk). One of its originators, David Skidmore of the University of Reading, UK, has also compiled a list of World Wide Web sites about inclusive education, disabilities, and other related subjects. The list (updated frequently) comprises a mix of U.S., Canadian, and U.K. sites. It may be accessed at http://www.mailbase.ac.uk/lists/inclusive-education/files/inclusion_sites.txt.

What beliefs, knowledge, and experiences are transferred?

Taking the foregoing organizations together, the philosophies expressed by them cohere around principles such as the following:

- disability should be seen in a societal, rather than an individualized context;
- persons with disabilities should be treated as being self-responsible, rather than dependent;
- persons with disabilities have the right to access physical environments, information, education, health care services, rehabilitation services, communication, employment, and recreation; and to make choices, develop individuality, and participate fully in citizenship;
- multisectorial approaches to dealing with disability should be implemented at national levels, with coordinated, complementary, and collaborative approaches among different agencies and ministries;
- the public should be educated and informed about the rights of disabled persons to participate in and contribute to various aspects of economic, social, and political life;
- persons with disabilities should be helped in their physical and psychological adjustment to society;
- every child has a fundamental right to education and must be given the opportunity to achieve and maintain an acceptable level of learning;
- those with special educational needs must have access to regular schools that should accommodate them within a child-centered pedagogy capable of meeting these needs;
- regular schools with an inclusive orientation are the most effective means of combating discriminatory attitudes, creating welcoming communities, building an inclusive society, and achieving an education for all; moreover, they provide an effective education to the majority of children and improve the efficiency and ultimately the cost-effectiveness of the entire education system;
- greater effort should be invested in early identification and intervention strategies;
- transition programs should be seen as an integral part of a continuous process of development ranging from early childhood and school to postschool programs; these programs need to include greater employment opportunities and other appropriate activities;
- emphasis should be placed on the provision of programs that include the development of vocational skills.

In terms of vocational inclusion, the *Standard Rules for the Equaliza-tion Of Opportunities for Persons with Disabilities* (United Nations, 1994) contains a clear indication of what is being asserted as internationally acceptable principles pertaining to persons with disabilities. Rule 7, which deals with employment, asserts that states should recognize the principle that persons with disabilities must be empowered to exercise their human rights, particularly in the field of employment. It goes on to note that in both rural and urban areas, they must have equal opportunities for productive and gainful employment in the labor market and that laws and regulations in the employment field must not discriminate against them and must not raise obstacles to their employment. Further, states should actively support the integration of persons with disabilities into open employ-ment, through such measures as vocational training, incentive-oriented quota schemes, reserved or designated employment, loans or grants for small business, exclusive contracts or priority production rights, tax concessions, and contract compliance or other technical or financial assistance to enterprises employing workers with disabilities. States' action programs should include measures (a) to design and adapt workplaces and work premises in such a way that they become accessible to persons with different disabilities; (b) to support the use of new technologies and the develop-ment and production of assistive devices, tools, and equipment for persons with disabilities to enable them to gain and maintain employment; (c) to provide appropriate training, placement, and ongoing support for workers with disabilities; (d) to initiate and support public awareness-raising campaigns designed to overcome negative attitudes and prejudices concerning workers with disabilities; and (e) to create training and employ-ment opportunities through such means as flexible hours, part-time work, job-sharing, self-employment, and attendant care for persons with dis-abilities. Over all, the aim should always be for persons with disabilities to obtain employment in the open labor market. For persons with disabilities whose needs cannot be met in open employment, small units of sheltered or supported employment may be an alternative, with the caveat that the quality of such programs should be assessed in terms of the extent to which they provide opportunities for persons with disabilities to gain employment in the open labor market.

In recent years, one of the major philosophies to have taken root in developing countries is Community-Based Rehabilitation (CBR), defined by ILO, UNESCO, and WHO (1994) in a joint position paper, as

a strategy within community development for the rehabilitation, equalization of opportunities and social integration of all people with disabilities. CBR is implemented through the combined efforts of disabled people themselves, their families and communities, and the appropriate health, education vocational and social services.

The aim of CBR is to allow people with disabilities to live in their communities and to fully participate in all types of activities, including employment (Murray, 1996). It is a comprehensive approach that should involve the community in the planning, implementation, and evaluation of the program and, as such, is part of the process of community development whereby the community seeks to improve itself (O'Toole, 1991). As noted by Tjandrakusuma (1996), an underlying assumption of CBR is that problems faced by people with disabilities result not only from their individual impairments, but from the attitudes and beliefs of their communities. It therefore aims at enabling community members to increase their understanding about disability issues, to become involved in the disability prevention activities and to "provide a positive environment . . . to improve the quality of life of persons with disabilities" (p. 2).

As well as promulgating broad principles, international and regional bodies have been increasingly involved in attempting to ensure the implementation of policies at a very practical level. Two examples will suffice. Firstly, as alluded to above, major steps have been taken in several developing countries to implement CBR (Narayan, 1996; O'Toole, 1991; Thorburn, 1996; Tjandrakusuma, 1996). Secondly, in the field of education the impact of UNESCO's *Teacher Education Resource Pack* (Ainscow, 1994) must be noted. This is aimed at encouraging member states to develop strategies for responding to children's special needs in ordinary schools and was developed through regional and national workshops sponsored largely by UNESCO. It contains four modules: (1) introduction to special needs in the classroom, (2) special needs: definitions and responses, (3) towards effective schools for all, and (4) help and support. Each module contains several units with instruction sheets discussion materials and videos. Developments such as those reflected in the *Resource Pack* are very timely as countries strive to upgrade the quality of teaching. Referring to special education in the Asian region, Lynch (1994) noted that "much of the useless theory, often deriving from models current in western teacher education in the 1960s and 1970s" (p. 14), is being replaced by curriculum-led developments, with an increasing emphasis on group work, multigrade teaching, continuous pupil assessment, and ways to motivate a diversity of children to learn.

What issues are involved in transferring beliefs, knowledge, and experiences?

The transfer of beliefs, knowledge, and experiences between countries is a complex matter that raises both technical and moral issues. In this section, five such issues will be discussed: coordination of international assistance, the universal design of technology, differential access to the Internet, convergence or diversity among cultures, and guidelines for introducing innovations.

Coordination

In most countries where rehabilitation provisions exist, they come under the auspices of a diverse range of governmental, NGO, and private service providers, a diversity that is often compounded by the involvement of several governmental ministries or departments—social welfare, health, employment, and education. Even in the most developed countries, the issue of service coordination is one that has constantly to be addressed, notwithstanding the arguments of advocates of the market economy that there are merits in having some duplication of services, as this introduces an element of contestability and competition that will lead to improved service efficiency and quality, provided consumers have genuine choice.

In developing countries, where there are often negligible resources available for the rehabilitation sector, the notion of contestability may seem to be an esoteric, if not luxurious, Western economic model, even if it is promoted by the World Bank. Perhaps a higher priority in such countries is the need to attend to international coordination. This has received attention from the UNDP, where Helander (1993) talks about his personal frustrations in bringing this about. He cites difficulties arising from (a) the choice of representatives attending meetings (too many administrators without technical knowledge of disability, too many professionals from industrialized countries with limited experience in developing countries, and too few national rehabilitation managers); (b) the choice of subject matter (too much on industrialized countries, too much focus on information exchange, and too little on cooperative planning); (c) the expected outcomes (mainly confined to annual repetitions of rituals of producing documents that do not bring forth much in terms of services to persons with disabilities); and (d) the policymaking mechanisms of international organizations (insufficient concern for innovation, inward-looking structures). Helander concludes his critical review by stating that "the present forum for international co-ordination is not effective as an instrument of change" and that "a thorough review is needed of the entire effort of international co-ordination" (p. 196). He suggests the following steps: (a) creating a new coordination mechanism in particular countries (or in a region), involving all potential partners—UN agencies, governmental international development organizations, and NGOs; (b) commissioning a group of experienced national program managers and field experts to propose a new set of policies for the coordinating agency; (c) formulating detailed guidelines within each developing country regarding the approaches to be applied; (d) reaching an agreement between donor/development agencies on how work can be divided up so as to avoid the present concentration on a few countries; (e) joint planning by all those who work in a specific country under the leadership of the government; and (f) creating a joint mechanism for follow-up and evaluation.

Universal design

As rehabilitation services expand, particularly in the area of assistive technology, there will be an increasing need for some degree of international standardization. In a recent international conference on rehabilitation, the importance of developing universal and adaptable designs—a "design for all"—was emphasized by Seelman (1996). This principle draws attention to the importance of developing standardized approaches to the design of various assistive devices, ranging from the wheelchairs to computer software. Seelman noted that international cooperation between people and nations in assistive technology is at a formative stage, with dialogue about assistive technology and cooperation among nations currently taking place, for example, between the United States and Europe and between the United States and Japan. As well, the European Union has established a program called TIDE (Technology for the Integration of the Disabled and Elderly People) aimed at increasing the availability in technology in Europe. Currently, the European Commission is arguing for the adoption of technical rules and standards before assistive technology devices can be put on the European market.

Differential access to the Internet

Several features of the Web make up its special character. Firstly, like no other form of information sharing, the Web is fundamentally egalitarian in that it gives all people with access to it a forum for expressing their views and for seeking and sharing information (Burbules, 1995; UNESCO, 1996). Interactive media will soon make it possible not only to send and receive information, but to engage in dialogue and to transmit information and knowledge unconstrained by distance or operating time. Secondly, because every node in the Web is linkable to any other node, the structure is decentered and nonhierarchical; or, as described by Burbules (1995) it is "hypertextual and rhizomatic." Thirdly, the Web has multimedia capability (i.e., it is able to integrate multiple sources and forms of information). Networked multimedia systems will provide general, efficient, enduring, and multimodal (as distinct from a hitherto predominantly verbal) access to cultural works of nearly every form conceivable (McClintock, 1995, p. 262).

The Internet is often described as being "anarchic," in the sense that it is not under the control of any authority, nor is it susceptible to such control. This view is somewhat glib, however, for there are various levels of control that can be and currently are being exercised over the medium. While it is true that anyone can put on or pull down information from the Internet, it is not equally accessible. Firstly—and most obviously—not everyone has physical access to it, either because they cannot afford it, or their country lacks the infrastructure of telephones or electricity to support it, or they lack the individual skills to enter into it. Secondly, the Internet has created a new class of what Burbules and Callister call "knowledge producers and knowledge organizers" (1996, p. 44)—those who act as interpreters and makers of knowledge, deciding on the inclusion and exclusion of materials in hypertexts and the links between them and who create the filters that help users sort through the enormous volume of information available. Burbules and Callister feel that these people will control access to information in ways that are potentially much less democratic and more restrictive than is now possible with simpler informational systems. In a similar vein, the International Commission on Education for the Twenty-first Century (UNESCO, 1996) notes with concern the differences that will arise between societies that will be capable of producing the content and those that will merely receive the information without taking a real part in the exchanges.

Finally, we must be aware that the opportunities afforded by information technology and its increasing role in all aspects of life will not be equally accessible to all members of a society, let alone to all societies. This means that there could well be growing disparities in knowledge and basic skills "between those who have access to the wonderworld of opportunities afforded by computers and those who have not, between those who can pay for the service and those who cannot" (Roll, 1995, p. xii).

Convergence or diversity

Perhaps the key issue underlying the transfer between countries of beliefs, principles, knowledge, and practices relating to special education and rehabilitation is the one to do with cultural propriety. Is it appropriate for the ideas generated in one society with a particular culture and world view to be transferred to another? Who should decide? What safeguards should be put in place if cultural imperialism is to be avoided? Is this a real issue, or are the forces of globalization inexorably leading to cultural convergence?

As noted by Mitchell (1996), globalization is a trend that is well under way and will gather pace as we move into the what Kennedy (1993) refers to as the "transnational world" of the 21st century. In this world, we will experience "the intensification of worldwide social relations which link distant localities in such a way that local happenings are shaped by events occurring many miles away and vice versa" (Giddens, 1990, p. 9). In a transnational world, the sovereignty of nation-states will increasingly be challenged by forces that lie well outside their borders (Kennedy, 1993), a process which Torres (1995–96, p. 312) refers to as "denationalization." As nations become more interdependent, there will be more frequent and broadranging exchanges of goods and services across national boundaries (Wilson, 1989). This trend towards globalization is the product of such factors as the emergence of a global economy, the development of intergovernmental and quasi-supranational institutions, the establishment of regional political federations and alliances, and the expansion of transnational economic and cultural links (Held, 1991). To these economic and geopolitical factors, we must add the impact of increasing communications interconnectivity (Negroponte, 1995), which will lead to many of the values of the nation-state giving way to those of both larger and smaller electronic communities, with their own cultures (Rheingold, 1993). Increasingly, we will socialize in digital neighborhoods and engage in electronic commerce on a global scale (Butler, 1996). Societies will increasingly depend on telecommunications to move information to where it is needed, physical space will be irrelevant and time will play a different role (Negroponte, 1995; Tiffin & Rajasingham, 1995). In his controversial book, *The End of History and the Last Man*, Fukuyama (1992), goes so far as to suggest that as countries modernize they must increasingly resemble one another, "regardless of their historical origins or cultural inheritances" (p. xiv). This homogenization reflects the "universal economic nexus of modern consumerism, . . . centering around technologically-driven economic growth and the capitalist social relations necessary to produce and sustain it" (p. 126). It must be noted, however, that contrasting positions are taken on this issue. There are those who, like Fukuyama, perceive a convergence of cultures, but there are others who see the post-Cold War world leading to cultural identities shaping the patterns of cohesion, disintegration, and conflict. Such a view is espoused by Huntington (1996) in his recent book, *The Clash of Civilizations and the Remaking of World Order*. A third position is that there is truth in both views, in that there is both convergence and divergence, depending on the activity. Whatever the mix of values that emerges in different countries, these will have profound implications for education and rehabilitation.

In terms of education, recent years have seen what McNeely and Cha (1994) refer to as "a remarkable degree of convergence in both educational ideology and educational structure across all types of nation states," a situation that reflects the trend towards nation-states becoming increasingly subject to world-level ideological prescriptions and practices, as mediated by such agencies as the UN and the OECD. Such agencies exercise considerable authority, according to McNeely and Cha, influencing national systems through a number of normative and rule-creating activities, four in particular. Firstly, international organizations act as a major forum for the transnational exchange of ideas and information via their publications, through the provision of consultants, and by sponsoring various types of conferences, meetings, and workshops. Secondly, in order to become members of these international organizations, countries have to sign up to their charters and constitutions, which typically contain professions of adherence to global principles, norms, and procedures. A third and related means of bringing about international convergence can be found in standard-setting instruments such as declarations and recommendations. Although these may not be legally binding, "they may be both inspirational and educational."

As noted in a previous section of this chapter, international bodies have already had a major impact on special education and rehabilitation. This is likely to continue, if not accelerate, in the future as the *Salamanca Statement and Framework for Action on Special Needs Education* (UNESCO, 1994) and *The Standard Rules on the Equalization of Opportunities for Persons with Disabilities* (United Nations, 1994) exert their influences. Finally, and in some circumstance perhaps most importantly, international organizations exert their influence through direct financial assistance or through the provision of development experts, both of which are usually linked to the adoption of certain ideas and policies.

Despite the evidence of convergence, the emergence of a transnational world with shared social values will not be achieved easily. Disputes are bound to occur. For example, in a recent publication, UNESCO's International Commission on Education for the Twenty-first Century identify six main tensions that will be central to the problems of the next century (UNESCO, 1996):

- *global and local:* people will need to become world citizens without losing their roots and continuing to participate in their nation and community;
- *universal and individual:* people will need to adapt to a globalized culture without submerging their unique individual character;
- *tradition and modernity:* people will need to adapt to the new information age without turning their backs on the past;
- *long-term and short-term:* this tension is sustained by the prevalence of the ephemeral and instantaneous in a world when an over-abundance of information and fleeting emotion keeps the spotlight on immediate problems;
- *competition and equality of opportunity:* the pressure of competition has driven many authorities to lose sight of their mission to give every human being the means to take advantage of every opportunity; three forces must be reconciled: competition (which provides incentives), cooperation (which gives strength), and solidarity (which unites);
- *spiritual and material:* education should stimulate everyone to reach out to the universal and to a measure of self transcendence. (pp. 16–18)

Some writers have expressed their disquiet regarding the way in which Western principles and practices are often imported into countries in ways that undermine the indigenous culture. In an analysis of the impact of Western practices on Indonesia, Kugelmass (1995) studied a group of parents of 14 mentally handicapped children. She found that all had consulted *dukuns* (spirit doctors) regarding the care and treatment of their child and believed in magic that held out the promise that some day their child would be cured. Notwithstanding this, Indonesian parents have begun to question the value

404

of traditional approaches to caring for one another as they look towards technological and institutional solutions to provide a "cure" for their children: "The physician is replacing the dukun and medical knowledge is becoming his or her magic" (p. 45). Kugelmass notes that while some professionals recognized *dukuns* as an important component of Indonesian health care who, at the very least, provide emotional support for families, most had not incorporated them into their treatments, and were not recognizing the value of the community-based systems that have sustained Indonesian families for centuries. Instead, they were relying solely on Western approaches and were imitating Western practices and styles (e.g., the use of IQ tests). Kugelmass expresses concern at this importation of technologies into a culture based on very different assumptions, values, and patterns of thinking than the culture from which they originated. She cites Fitch and Webb's (1989) summary of the set of values underlying Indonesian belief systems, inviting a comparison with Western values. The former comprise the notions that wisdom always comes from experience; change is always possible, but one cannot change one's destiny; duties of office are predetermined and one must accept them and act accordingly; everything has its place in the universe according to one's status and morality and one must do what is appropriate and avoid what is not; and people should know their place and task. She concludes that in order for the artifacts of one culture to be adopted appropriately by another, the subjective and objective aspects of both must be fully understood and respected.

In a similar vein, Kerns and Cavalcante (1997) note that the model of inclusion developed in the United States cannot be applied directly to Brazilian schools. They argue that Brazilian educators and parents need to create their own model of inclusion, taking into consideration their social, economic, political, and cultural singularities. They cite DaMatta (1987) as describing the spectrum of social life in Brazil and in the United States of America following "radically different logics":

The historical-cultural process of Brazil (and Latin America) is one of having to open a social and political space for local and individual manifestations since everything is rigidly overseen and dominated by an enormous political, religious and legal centralism. The historical North American experience is one of generating laws which can invent or save totalities greater than local systems. In Brazil, individualism is created with effort, as something negative and *against* the laws which emanate from the state and define totality In the United States, individualism is positive, and the thrust has been to create a *union*, a totality.

(p. 314)

The explicit or implicit cultural imperialism that has accompanied much of the transfer of beliefs, knowledge, and experiences in the past is particularly pernicious in the case of countries that have gone though extended periods of colonialism. Ajuwon (1996), for example, is very critical of the ways in which "the forces of urbanisation and the dependency pattern of development, coupled with missionary activities" (p. 192) in Africa have led to the collapse of kinship systems and community-based learning experiences for children.

A further example of the need for senstivity on transferring beliefs and practices across cultures is provided by New Zealand, where the indigenous people, the Maori, embrace a model of well-being referred to as *Whare Tapa Wha*. This model translates literally as "the four walls of the house," with each being necessary to ensure strength and balance (Durie, 1994). These walls comprise *taha wairua* (the spiritual side), *taha hinengaro* (thoughts and feelings), *taha tinana* (the physical side), and *taha whanau* (the extended family). Many cultures have a similar holistic perception of well-being and it behooves those engaged in the cross-cultural transfer of knowledge to work within such models if they wish to have their ideas accepted.

In his review of disability in the context of Eastern religions, Miles (1995) provides a salutory reminder for Westerners of the fact that "at least 70% of global disability is experienced in countries and contexts upon which western ethics and philosophy impinge only peripherally" (p. 50). Furthermore, he asserts, current formulations of the rights of the disabled "rest upon a largely western liberal consensus of views" (p. 61) and as such constitute "unintended cultural colonialism" that largely ignores "the history and anthropology of disability outside the dominant culture of the western educated classes" (p. 62). Miles concludes that as global efforts are made to improve the lot of disabled people, beliefs and attitudes present in the world's major non-Christian religions (Islam, Hinduism, and Buddhism) must be taken more fully into account.

Various projects have taken steps to guard against imposing outside solutions in the process of transferring beliefs, knowledge, and practices. For example, Johnson (1995) outlines how, in the Lithuania project described earlier in this chapter, the philosophy of the project was based on the principle that all those potentially affected by changes should have a voice and, if possible, an involvement in the events leading to such changes: "Application of this principle enhances the likelihood that any resulting structures and processes will be Lithuanian in character because they have been derived by Lithuanians" (p. 79). A second example of an attempt to redress potential power imbalances that are inherent between aid donors and recipients is afforded by UNESCO's Parent Education Project implemented in Malawi, Sri Lanka and Uganda (McConkey, 1993). This project utilizes indigenously produced video programs as a medium for educating families and local communities about childhood disabilities. In a similar vein, a Training for Work video course has been developed by the Chesire Foundation International using video programs recorded on location throughout the Asia Pacific Region (McConkey, 1996).

Introducing innovations

A useful analysis of how educational innovations should be introduced is provided by Baine (1996). He identifies three phases: initiation, implementation, and institutionalization. The initiation phase involves a needs assessment; deciding whether to undertake innovation; mobilizing resources; and developing initial commitment. Planning plays a most important role during this phase. Strategic planning involves selecting and prioritizing objectives and selecting broad implementation strategies. Here a balance has to be struck between narrowing the focus to those objectives that can reasonably be achieved with existing or easily obtainable resources and bringing about sufficient change to improve quality (Rondinelli, Middleton, & Verspoor, 1990). Operational planning involves translating broad program objectives into specific policy actions, implementation schedules, and procedures that will allow the achievement of the strategy objectives. The implementation phase involves putting an innovation into practice, with attention to ongoing personnel training, consultation, project coordination, commitment, maintenance, materials dissemination, conducting pilot studies, program evaluation, innovation revision, and diffusion. Institutionalization involves removing the novelty of the innovation and making it part of the normal, continuing administrative and professional practice. Derham (1988) describes this phase in terms of sustainable systems development, with local responsibility playing the critical role.

A complementary perspective to the foregoing is provided by the Norwegian Agency for Development Cooperation, which has put forward a set of principles it requires NGOs to meet to be eligible for financial support. These coalesce around three basic values: justice (e.g., development assistance should benefit poor and marginalized population groups), participation (e.g., development assistance should promote democratization), and sustainability and self-reliance (e.g., development assistance should promote self-reliance at individual, community and national levels).

Prospects for the future

As we approach the 21st century, it is timely to consider ways in which the transfer of beliefs, knowledge, and experiences relating to special education and rehabilitation should take place in the future. Such projections need to take account of a range of contextual factors—many of which have negative connotations for people with disabilities—which have been identified by writers such as Merceron (1996), Mitchell (1996), Murray (1996), and Rehabilitation International (1996). These include: (a) the acceleration of globalization processes, which are facilitating both integration and fragmentation; (b) the increasing disparities of living standards, both within and between countries; (c) a rethinking of the concept of social protection, arising from concerns at the growing costs of the welfare state and an increased emphasis on economic efficiency at the expense of social justice; (d) longer average life expectancies, resulting in the trend for young people with disabilities to survive to adulthood and to outlive their parents' ability to care for them; (e) the expansion of automation, resulting in the elimination of less sophisticated tasks, especially in industries with a low-skilled, labor-intensive content—the sector frequently occupied by disabled people; (f) the increasing sophistication of assistive devices, but a corresponding diminution of access by many people with disabilities, especially in developing countries; and (g) the wide variation among countries with respect to issues such as human rights, quality of life, and personal choice.

If the negative effects of these social and economic trends for people with disabilities are to be ameliorated, and if greater equality is to be achieved both within and between countries, it is clear that there will have to be improvements in the ways in which beliefs, knowledge, and experiences— and, of course, capital—are transferred. As explained in this chapter, international instruments such as *The Standard Rules for the Equalization of Opportunities for Persons with Disabilities* and the *Salamanca Statement* provide a sound basis for future developments and are already exerting considerable influence on many countries' policies. The challenge remains, however, of finding ways to convert these good intentions into actual practices across the world in all its diversity: the rural areas of Malawi, the isolated mountain villages of Nepal, the subarctic communities of Siberia, the nomadic tribes of Jordan, the slums of Calcutta, the former communist countries of Eastern Europe, the strife-torn societies of Rwanda and Albania, the island states of the South Pacific. As pointed out in this chapter, there already exist complex networks of international, national, and regional agencies working in the field of rehabilitation. In developing countries, some of these networks are coordinated, but more often they are uncoordinated; some work within sustainable parameters, while others create over-dependence on external assistance; some are sensitive to indigenous cultures, whereas others import inappropriate technologies; some can independently access the most recent developments in the field through such means as the Internet, whereas others are dependent on external consultants or "knowledge brokers."

The challenge to both exporters and importers of philosophies and practices is to determine how far should indigenous philosophies, ideologies, and practices be encouraged, respected, challenged, overthrown, or blended with those from "outside." There are ultimately three approaches to this dilemma (Mazurek & Winzer, 1994). One is to adopt a position of social relativism, which asserts that because social enterprises reflect their cultural milieu, it would be inappropriate and culturally imperialistic to seek to radically change their policies or practices, even if authorities in the importing country would seem to encourage such new ideas. A second approach is to have recourse to "human and cultural universals that provide the touchstones against which ideas and practices may be measured and evaluated" (Mazurek & Winzer, 1994, p. xxiii), as expressed, for example, in the recent UN-sponsored *Standard Rules*. The third perspective represents a midpoint of the foregoing and would see change arising from a process of reflection upon existing policies and practices (Ainscow & Hart, 1992), with countries taking ownership of the process (Brown, Baine, & Neufeldt, 1996) and being supported in the development of their own models. An essential element of this approach is that of capacity building, in which institutional and human resources are developed to enhance the countries' abilities to solve their problems in a sustainable manner. In this context, the role of the external consultant is one of facilitating rather than directing change (Brown, Abu Ghazaleh, & Neufeldt, 1996; Davies & Johnson, 1996; Silverman, 1996).

A final word needs to be added. As outlined in this chapter, much of what has taken place in the transfer of beliefs, knowledge, and experiences between countries has been characterized by one-way traffic—from richer to poorer countries, from high-technology to low-technology countries, from Western to non-Western countries. It is to be hoped—and expected—that the future will see sincere steps taken to redress this assymetrical transfer (King, 1991) and that there will not only be an increase in collaborative projects (Barcham & Upton, 1993), but also greater appreciation among developed countries of what can be learned from the experiences and perceptions of those from developing nations (Brown, Baine, & Neufeldt, 1996). Ultimately, wherever one lives, it will be the judicious blending of outside ideas and existing cultural practices that will bring about sustainable changes that are likely to improve the quality of life of people with disabilities.

References

Abang, T. B. (1994). Nigeria. In K. Mazurek & M. A. Winzer (Eds.), *Comparative studies in special education* (pp. 71–87). Washington, DC: Gallaudet Press.

Agrawal, R. (1994). India. In K. Mazurek & M. A. Winzer (Eds.), *Comparative studies in special education* (pp. 179–203). Washington, DC: Gallaudet Press.

Ainscow, M. (1994). *Special needs in the classroom: A teacher education guide*. Paris: UNESCO; London: Jessica Kingsley Publishers.

Ainscow, M., & Hart, S. (1992). Moving practice forward. *Support for Learning*. 7(3), 115–120.

Ajuwon, P. M. (1996). Educational and rehabilitation aspects of visual impairments in developing countries. In R. Brown, A. Neufeldt & D. Baine (Eds.), *Beyond basic care: Special education and community rehabilitation in low income countries* (pp. 183–199). North York, ON: Captus Press.

Baine, D. (1996). Introducing changes to educational and rehabilitation programmes in developing countries. In R. Brown, A. Neufeldt, & D. Baine (Eds.), *Beyond basic care: Special education and community rehabilitation in low income countries* (pp. 307–319). North York, ON: Captus Press.

Barcham, L., & Upton, G. (1993). Towards the comparative study of special education. In R. J. Michael & G. Upton (Eds.), *The Viewfinder, Volume 2: Expanding
boundaries and perspectives in special education* (pp. 50–52). Reston, VA: Division
of International Special Education and Services, The Council for Exceptional
Children.

Brown, R., Baine, D., & Neufeldt, A. H. (1996). Introduction. In R. Brown,
A. Neufeldt, & D. Baine (Eds.), *Beyond basic care: Special education and community
rehabilitation in low income countries* (pp. 1–7). North York, ON: Captus Press.

Brown, R. I. (1997). Legislation in Australian special education intent and effect:
The impact on child, family and teacher. In D. Mitchell & J. Kugelmass
(Eds.), *The Viewfinder: Volume 4, New Models for Re-forming Special Education.*
Reston, VA: Division of International Special Education and Services, The
Council for Exceptional Children.

Brown, R. I., Abu Ghazaleh, H., & Neufeldt, A. (1996). Challenges to rehabilitation—
A case example. In R. Brown, A. Neufeldt, & D. Baine (Eds.), *Beyond basic care:
Special education and community rehabilitation in low income countries* (pp. 280–
306). North York, ON: Captus Press.

Burbules, N. C. (1995). Technology and changing educational communities. Paper
presented to AESA, Fall 1995. Available online at: http://www.ed.uiuc.edu/coe/
eps/NickB.html.

Burbules, N. C., & Callister, T. A. (1996). Knowledge at the crossroads: Some
alternative features of hypertext learning environments. *Educational Theory, 46*(1),
23–50.

Butler, G. (1996). *Impact 2000: How information technology will change New
Zealand.* Wellington: Information Technology Advisory Group and Information
Technology Association of New Zealand.

Chen, Y-H., & Lu, T-H. (1994). Taiwan. In K. Mazurek & M. A. Winzer (Eds.),
Comparative studies in special education (pp. 238–259). Washington, DC: Gallaudet
Press.

Crawford, N., & Bray, M. (1994). Hong Kong. In K. Mazurek & M. A. Winzer
(Eds.), *Comparative studies in special education* (pp. 286–304). Washington, DC:
Gallaudet Press.

Csanyi, Y. (1995). Special education and teacher training in Hungary. In P. Mittler
& P. Daunt (Eds.), *Teacher education for special needs in Europe* (pp. 138–144).
London: Cassell.

DaMatta, R. (1987). The quest for citizenship in a relational universe. In J. Wirth,
E. Nunes, & T. Bogenschild (Eds.), *State and society in Brazil: Continuity and
change* (pp. 307–335). Boulder, CO: Westview Press.

Davies, R., & Johnson, P. R. (1996). Consulting in the Middle East—A personal
perspective. In R. Brown, A. Neufeldt, & D. Baine (Eds.), *Beyond basic care:
Special education and community rehabilitation in low income countries* (pp. 261–
279). North York, ON: Captus Press.

Derham, M. (1988). The right kind of development. *TEAR Times*, 39, 4–6. [Cited by
Ager, A. (1990). Planning sustainable services: Principles for the effective targeting
of resources in developed and developing nations. In W. I. Fraser (Ed.), *Key issues
in mental retardation research* (pp. 385–394). London: Routledge.]

Diaconescu, R., Ionescu, M., Chis, V., & Daunt, P. (1995). Teacher training and
the integration of children with special needs: Romanian initiatives. In P. Mittler

& P. Daunt (Eds.), *Teacher education for special needs in Europe* (pp. 64–74). London: Cassell.

Durie, M. H. (1994). *Whaiora: Maori health development*. Wellington, New Zealand: Oxford University Press.

Fitch, R. M., & Webb, S. A. (1989). Cultural immersion in Indonesia through Pancasila: State ideology. *Journal of Educational Thought*, *23*(1), 44–51.

Fukuyama, F. (1992). *The end of history and the last man*. London: Hamish Hamilton.

Giddens, A. (1991). *Modernity and self-identity: Self and society in the late modern age*. Cambridge: Polity Press.

Hekking, K. (1996). Participant in Joint Seminar of Vocational Commission on Organisation and Administration—Organisation and Administration of Employment Initiatives Through Systems Change. In *Proceedings of 18th World Congress of Rehabilitation International* (pp. 194–200). Auckland, New Zealand, 15–20 September 1996.

Helander, E. (1993). *Prejudice and dignity: An introduction to community-based rehabilitation*. New York: UNDP.

Held, D. (1991). Democracy, the nation-state and the global system. In D. Held (Ed.), *Political theory today*. Cambridge: Polity Press.

Huntington, S. P. (1996). *The clash of civilizations and the remaking of world order*. New York: Simon & Schuster.

ILO, UNESCO, & WHO (1994). *Community-based rehabilitation for and with people with disabilities: A joint position paper*. Unpublished manuscript.

Inclusion International (1996, October). Inclusive education in the Dominican Republic. *Inclusion International*, No. 4.

Inter-Agency Commission (UNDP, UNESCO, UNICEF, World Bank) (1990). *World Declaration on Education for All*. New York: UNICEF House.

Johnson, M. (1995). East-West cooperation for pupils with SEN: A report on a TEMPUS project. In P. Mittler & P. Daunt (Eds.), *Teacher education for special needs in Europe* (pp. 75–86). London: Cassell.

Kennedy, P. (1993). *Preparing for the twenty-first century*. New York: Random House.

Kerns, G. M., & Cavalcante, F. S. (1997). Brazilian special needs education: Conceptual framework and policy for the 1990s. In D. Mitchell & J. Kugelmass (Eds.), *The viewfinder, Volume 4: New models for re-forming special education*. Reston, VA: Division of International Special Education and Services, The Council for Exceptional Children.

Kim, S-K. (1993). Development of special education in the Republic of Korea. In R. J. Michael & G. Upton (Eds.), *The viewfinder, Volume 2: Expanding boundaries & perspectives in special education* (pp. 26–28). Reston, VA: Division of International Special Education and Services, The Council for Exceptional Children.

King, K. (1991). *Aid and education in the developing world: The role of donor agencies in educational analysis*. Harlow, England: Longman.

Kugelmass, J. (1995). The Indonesian system of caring: Beyond technology solutions to human problems. In D. L. Edyburn, R. A. Henderson, & L. Sandals (Eds.), *The viewfinder, Volume 3: International perspectives on special education technology* (pp. 37–48). Reston, VA: Division of International Special Education and Services, The Council for Exceptional Children.

Lynch, J. (1994). *Provision for children with special educational needs in the Asia region*. Washington, DC: World Bank.

411

Mazurek, K., & Winzer, M. A. (1994). Introduction. In K. Mazurek & M. A. Winzer (Eds.), *Comparative studies in special education* (pp. xvii–xxxix). Washington, DC: Gallaudet Press.

McClintock, R. (1995). *Power and pedagogy: transforming education through information technology.* Available online at: http://www.ilt.columbia.edu/academic/texts/mcclintock/pp/title.html.

McConkey, R. (1993). Video training packages for parent education. In R. J. Michael & G. Upton (Eds.), *The Viewfinder, Volume 2: Expanding boundaries and perspectives in special education* (pp. 34–37). Reston, VA: Division of International Special Education and Services, The Council for Exceptional Children.

McConkey, R. (1996). A valued life in the community. In R. Brown, A. Neufeldt, & D. Baine (Eds.), *Beyond basic care: Special education and community rehabilitation in low income countries* (pp. 151–167). North York, ON: Captus Press.

McNeely, C. L., & Cha, Y.-K. (1994). Worldwide educational convergence through international organizations: Avenues for research. *Educational Polity Analysis Archives, 2*(14).

Merceron, A. (1996). Does technology enhance the quality of life for elderly people? In *Proceedings of 18th World Congress of Rehabilitation International* (pp. 374–385). Auckland, New Zealand, 15–20 September 1996.

Miles, M. (1995). Disability in an Eastern religious context: Historical perspectives. *Disability & Society, 10*(1), 49–69.

Misawa, G. (1994). Japan. In K. Mazurek & M. A. Winzer (Eds.), *Comparative studies in special education* (pp. 221–237). Washington, DC: Gallaudet Press.

Mitchell, D., & Chen, Y-Y. (1996). Special education in East and South East Asia. In R. Brown, A. Neufeldt, & D. Baine (Eds.), *Beyond basic care: Special education and community rehabilitation in low income countries* (pp. 8–42). North York, ON: Captus Press.

Mitchell, D., & O'Brien, P. (1994). New Zealand. In K. Mazurek & M. A. Winzer (Eds.), *Comparative studies in special education* (pp. 420–451). Washington, DC: Gallaudet Press.

Mitchell, D. (1996). What will special education look like in 2021? Paper presented at 18th World Congress of Rehabilitation International, Auckland, New Zealand, 15–20 September 1996.

Mitchell, J., & Mitchell, D. (1987). Integration/mainstreaming. In D. R. Mitchell & N. N. Singh (Eds.), *Exceptional children in New Zealand* (pp. 107–117). Palmerston North, New Zealand: Dunmore Press.

Mittler, P., & Daunt, P. (Eds.) (1995). *Teacher education for special needs in Europe.* London: Cassell.

Moulton, R., Andrews, J. F., & Smith, M. (1996). The deaf world. In R. Brown, A. Neufeldt, & D. Baine (Eds.), *Beyond basic care: Special education and community rehabilitation in low income countries* (pp. 168–182). North York, ON: Captus Press.

Murray, B. (1996). Participant in Joint Seminar of Vocational Commission on Organisation and Administration—Organisation and Administration of Employment Initiatives Through Systems Change. In *Proceedings of 18th World Congress of Rehabilitation International* (pp. 178–189). Auckland, New Zealand, 15–20 September 1996.

412

Narayan, J. (1996). Special education in India. In R. Brown, A. Neufeldt, & D. Baine (Eds.), *Beyond basic care: Special education and community rehabilitation in low income countries* (pp. 43–62). North York, ON: Captus Press.

Negroponte, N. (1995). *Being digital.* London: Coronet Books, Hodder and Stoughton.

Nirje, B. (1969). The normalization principle and its human management implications. In R. Krugel & W. Wolfensberger (Eds.), *Changing patterns in residential services for the mentally retarded.* Washington, DC: President's Committee on Mental Retardation.

Nirje, B. (1985). The basis and logic of the normalisation principle. *Australia and New Zealand Journal of Developmental Disabilities, 11*(2), 65–68.

Niwa, S. (1996). Developments in creating an Asia/Pacific Network of Centers for Disabled Persons. Paper presented at 18th World Congress of Rehabilitation International, Auckland, New Zealand, 15–20 September 1996.

Norwegian Agency for Development Cooperation, *Guide to planning and evaluating NGO projects* [five parts]. Oslo: Norwegian Agency for Development Cooperation, Division for Non-Governmental Organizations.

O'Hanlon, C. (1993). Inclusion and integration in Europe: A human rights issue. In R. J. Michael & G. Upton (Eds.), *The viewfinder, Volume 2: Expanding boundaries & perspectives in special education* (pp. 47–49). Reston, VA: Division of International Special Education and Services, The Council for Exceptional Children.

O'Hanlon, C. (1995). A comparison of educational provision for pupils with special educational needs in Europe. In P. Mittler & P. Daunt (Eds.), *Teacher education for special needs in Europe* (pp. 1–16). London: Cassell.

O'Toole, B. J. (1991). *Guide to community-based rehabilitation services.* Paris: UNESCO.

Qirbi, A. (1993). Poverty and handicap in the Republic of Yemen. In R. J. Michael & G. Upton (Eds.), *The viewfinder, Volume 2: Expanding boundaries & perspectives in special education* (pp. 12–17). Reston, VA: Division of International Special Education and Services, The Council for Exceptional Children.

Rehabilitation International. (1996). Summary of Congress outcomes. In *Proceedings of 18th World Congress of Rehabilitation International* (pp. 3–9). Auckland, New Zealand, 15–20 September 1996.

Rheingold, H. (1993). *The virtual community.* Reading, MA: Addison-Wesley.

Roll, R. (1995). Foreword. In J. Tiffin & L. Rajasingham, *In search of the virtual class: Education in the information society* (pp. xxi–xvi). London: Routledge.

Rondinelli, D. A., Middleton, J., & Verspoor, A. M. (1990). *Planning educational reforms in developing countries.* Durham, NC: Duke University Press.

Rowland, W. (1996). Participant in the Roundtable Forum on the UN Standard Rules for the Equalisation of Opportunities for Persons with Disabilities. In *Proceedings of 18th World Congress of Rehabilitation International* (pp. 478–479). Auckland, New Zealand, 15–20 September 1996.

Seelman, K. (1996). Equality through participation. In *Proceedings of 18th World Congress of Rehabilitation International*, Auckland, New Zealand, 15–20 September 1996, pp. 89–99.

Silverman, F. H. (1996). Personal involvement in the development of programmes for persons with disabilities. In R. Brown, A. Neufeldt, & D. Baine (Eds.), *Beyond basic care: Special education and community rehabilitation in low income countries* (pp. 254–260). North York, ON: Captus Press.

Swan, G. (1994). Australia. In K. Mazurek & M. A. Winzer (Eds.), *Comparative studies in special education.* Washington, DC: Gallaudet Press.

Thorburn, M. (1996). Roles and relationships of community-based rehabilitation in Jamaica. In R. Brown, A. Neufeldt, & D. Baine (Eds.), *Beyond basic care: Special education and community rehabilitation in low income countries* (pp. 126–150). North York, ON: Captus Press.

Tiffin, J., & Rajasingham, L. (1995). *In search of the virtual class: Education in the information society.* London: Routledge.

Tjandrakusuma, H. (1996, September). Towards the 21st century: Challenges for community based rehabilitation in the Asian and Pacific Region. Paper presented at 18th World Congress of Rehabilitation International, Auckland, New Zealand.

Torres, C. A. (1995/96). State and education revisited: Why educational researchers should think politically about education. *Review of Research in Education, 21,* 255–331.

UNESCO. (1994). *The Salamanca Statement And Framework For Action On Special Needs Education.* Paris: UNESCO.

UNESCO. (1996). *Report of the International Commission on Education for the Twenty-first Century.* Paris: UNESCO.

United Nations. (1994). *The Standard Rules on the Equalization of Opportunities for Persons with Disabilities.* Paris: United Nations.

Warnock, H. M. (1978). *Report of the Committee into the Education of Handicapped Children and Young People.* London: HMSO.

Wilson, J. (1988). *Politics and leisure.* Boston: Unwin Hyman.

Winzer, M. A. (1994). Canada. In K. Mazurek & M. A. Winzer (Eds.), *Comparative studies in special education* (pp. 370–386). Washington, DC: Gallaudet Press.

World Bank (1995). *Priorities and strategies for education: A World Bank review.* Washington, DC: The World Bank.

414

25

EDUCATING PUPILS WITH INTELLECTUAL DISABILITIES IN ENGLAND

Thirty years on

Peter Mittler

Source: *International Journal of Disability, Development and Education* 49(2) (2002): 145–60.

Abstract

In April 1971, responsibility for the education of all children with intellectual disabilities in England and Wales passed from health to education authorities at national and local level. From that date, no child could be declared to be "ineducable," regardless of the nature or severity of their disability or whether they were living with their families or in residential institutions. The former Junior Training Centres were redesignated as special schools and were administered by the same Local Education Authorities who were responsible for all other publicly funded schools in the community. This paper highlights major developments in the education of children with intellectual disabilities in the light of an early review of progress and problems and subsequent reforms to the education system as a whole. Key issues include access to the National Curriculum, prospects for the education of children with intellectual disabilities in mainstream schools, and the implications of these developments for the professional development of all teachers.

Setting the scene

Although the focus of this paper must by definition be on children with intellectual disabilities, the issues raised are by no means unique or specific to that population. There are obvious areas of overlap with children who have been labelled as having mild, moderate, or specific learning difficulties, as well as those with physical and sensory impairments, emotional and behavioural difficulties, and autistic spectrum disorders. In fact, children

415

labelled as having an intellectual disability illustrate the futility of using such labels since most of them have additional disabilities which also require skilled assessment and intervention. [Please note that "intellectual disability" is used in this article because this term is in increasing use internationally and has been standard in Australia and a number of other countries for some time. It replaces mental handicap, mental subnormality, and mental retardation, although "learning disabilities" (for adults) and "severe learning difficulties" (for children) are still in official use in the UK.]

One of the major lessons of the last 30 years is that we must learn to think less categorically and to put more emphasis on devising methods of working with individual children rather than basing our teaching on generalisations about the learning characteristics or teaching needs of children with specific disorders and syndromes. Knowing that a child has a named condition or a measured level of intellectual functioning may be useful as background information but rarely provides the basis for a program of teaching. The essence of an inclusive approach lies in its emphasis on changing the environment rather than the child. This means looking at the way we organise our schools and classrooms, how we design, deliver and adapt the curriculum, the kind of supports we provide for children experiencing difficulties, and the ways in which schools relate to parents and their local community (Mittler, 2000).

Exclusion to inclusion?

Looking back, England and Wales deserve some credit for being amongst the first to ensure that children with intellectual disabilities became the responsibility of education authorities. The transfer of responsibility from health to education marked the culmination of a campaign by parents and professional organisations during the 1960s. A key influence at that time was the advocacy of the late Stanley Segal and the publication of his book *No Child is Ineducable* (Segal, 1966). Thirty years later, in a *Festschrift* in his honour, some of the early advocates for better services for people with intellectual disabilities revisited their campaigns, while others provided a critical analysis of what had and had not been achieved (Mittler, 1996).

In 1971 *Better Services for the Mentally Handicapped* was published by the Department of Health and Social Security. This proposed a major reorientation of services for adults as well as children, with priority for the running down of long-stay hospitals and time-tabled targets for the development of community-based services. This has now been replaced by a new White Paper *Valuing People: A New Strategy for Learning Disability in the 21st Century* (Department of Health, 2001). The guiding principles underlying this review are based on human rights, independence, choice, and inclusion. People with intellectual disabilities were involved in the process of policy review from the outset and will continue to be involved in monitoring its implementation. This suggests an obvious question—are our schools preparing the present generation of pupils to fight for their rights as citizens and to live in an inclusive society?

An article written shortly after education authorities assumed responsibility for children with intellectual disabilities posed some basic issues which needed to be confronted (Mittler, 1974).

- What should be the aims of education for these children?
- How relevant are existing educational methods?
- What kind of curriculum and what kind of teaching methods are suitable?
- What kind of teachers are needed and how should they be trained?
- How early should education begin and at what point should it end?
- What kind of educational provision should be made for further education after school?

Prospects for integration

Notably absent from this list is the question "Where should the children be educated?" Although the article discussed some early examples of integration, it was generally assumed that the newly designated special schools would be the main providers for some time to come. This assumption is now being challenged—by many teachers in all sectors of education, by parents, by some of the children themselves, by organisations of disabled persons, and to some extent by government policy initiatives.

This is not the place to review the arguments for and against educating children with intellectual disabilities in mainstream schools or to weigh the complex research evidence on educational and social outcomes (but see Farrell, 1997; Hegarty, 1993; Jenkinson, 1997). In any case, the debates around integration have been largely overtaken by the inclusion movement which is based on notions of social justice and human rights, but which is also related to concerns about school effectiveness and school improvement.

As far as children with intellectual disabilities are concerned, in England and Wales the majority still remain in some form of segregated provision. Very few children have been transferred from special to mainstream schools. A survey by the Audit Commission (1992) estimated that the average rate of transfer was one child per year from all types of special school. Nevertheless, it is safe to assume that *some* children who would automatically have been sent to special schools in the 1970s would now attend mainstream schools with varying amounts of support and that others would be attending other special schools or special classes attached to mainstream schools.

Apart from a wealth of anecdotal evidence about individual children and numerous publications describing integration programs, very little national data is available. However, we do have some information about children with Down syndrome—some 30% of all children in the new special schools in the late 1970s (Mittler & Preddy, 1981). Today, according to recent UK surveys, between 70 and 80% of children with Down syndrome can expect to begin their schooling in integrated settings, 35 to 40% to complete four years of primary education, and 20 to 25% to complete secondary education (Cunningham, Glenn, Lorenz, Cuckle, & Shepperson, 1998). There are individual reports of students who successfully pass the ordinary end of school public examinations at the age of 16 and go on to further education and vocational qualifications. Here again, these national trends mask enormous variations between and even within Local Education Authorities (LEAs). In some parts of the country, the proportion of pupils with Down syndrome attending mainstream schools full time can be much higher or much lower than these figures suggest.

Although the present government is strongly committed to inclusive education (Department for Education and Employment, 1997, 1998), current policy is to retain special schools as part of the wide spectrum of provision which is needed to match the even wider spectrum of need. Parents are understandably divided on this issue. Although many are strongly in favour of inclusion, this does not mean that they would be ready to see their child's special school closed, unless they could be convinced that he or she could be fully supported in a mainstream setting (Farrell, 1997). Teachers in mainstream schools also feel strongly that special schools are essential for a minority of children, though their main concerns are about pupils with emotional and behavioural difficulties (Croll & Moses, 2000).

As long ago as 1978, the Warnock Report (Department of Education and Science) envisaged that special schools would become "resource centres" but the concept has not been clearly defined nor effectively implemented. Only one LEA (London Borough of Newham) has closed its special schools and relocated all their pupils to various types of supported mainstream provision (Burke, 1999) and a few others are moving in that direction. All LEAs have to publish their inclusion policies as part of their development plans and are inspected by the Office for Standards in Education but there is no requirement that they should produce a plan for the rundown and closure of any or all of their special schools.

Special schools

We have little national information about the work of special schools because governments no longer publish data by type of special school or categories of disability, only aggregate data about children in all types of special school. Such data tell us that although the total number of special schools decreased by 15% from 1,405 in 1986 to 1,191 in 1996, the number of pupils in all types of special schools has remained constant at just under

100,000. This corresponds to 1.3% of the total school population nationally but there are immense variations between LEAs—ranging from 0.32 to 2.67% of the local school population (Department for Education and Employment, 1999). Around a quarter of children in special schools are attending schools for children with severe learning difficulties.

The most recent data about children with intellectual disabilities come from national surveys conducted by Male (1996a) who compared her findings with a number of earlier surveys of provision for children with severe learning difficulties (Evans & Ware, 1987; Hogg, Lambe, Cowie, & Coxon, 1987; Mittler & Preddy, 1981) as well as with a parallel survey of children in schools for children with moderate learning difficulties (Male, 1996b). According to this survey, a typical special school for pupils with severe learning difficulties (SLD) now contains 60 pupils, 10 teachers, and 14 learning support assistants (LSAs). An increasing number are now catering only for primary or secondary age pupils, sometimes supplemented by pupils of pre-school or post-school age. Although many more LSAs are now being recruited, the ratio of teachers to pupils has remained constant over many years, largely for financial reasons. For some years, schools have had to manage their own budgets from funds delegated through the LEA under the Local Management of Schools initiative.

The pupils

Male's survey (1996a, 1996b) involved 57 special schools for children with severe learning difficulties—one in six of all such schools in England providing for some 4,000 children. Some of the key findings are as follows:

- There has been a marked increase in the number of children with profound and multiple disabilities over the last 20 years, estimates of 40% being the most common, compared with 20% in the 1980s. Whereas such pupils were previously taught together in segregated classes ("special care classes"), the majority are now "integrated" in age-appropriate classes in their special schools.
- In an "average" school of 60 pupils, at least a quarter displayed challenging behaviour—to a severe degree in five children. One in four schools had felt compelled to exclude children for this reason during the previous year.
- Four out of five schools reported that up to a quarter of their pupils had autistic spectrum disorders or physical or sensory impairments—a major increase compared with earlier surveys.
- About 10% of pupils had degenerative disorders, some of them life-threatening and requiring frequent nursing intervention by school staff.
- In addition, Male's survey of 75 schools for children with moderate learning difficulties indicated that head teachers of these schools

considered that at least 10% of their pupils had severe rather than moderate learning difficulties (Male, 1996a, 1996b).

Links between special and mainstream schools

Although the majority of pupils with severe learning difficulties remain in segregated provision, almost all special schools have for many years developed regular, time-tabled links with neighbouring mainstream schools. These were first described in a report from the National Foundation for Educational Research (Jowett, Hegarty, & Moses, 1988). Despite early fears that these links would be reduced as a result of pressures brought about by the National Curriculum and delegated funding, the results of a follow-up study suggested that most of the links were being maintained, indeed strengthened, because all schools were now following the same National Curriculum (Jowett, 1994).

These links were usually developed on the initiative of the head teachers involved, and were only rarely initiated or even suggested by the LEAs. Consequently, they take many forms, depending on local needs and priorities. Sometimes all the children in a class, together with their teachers and support assistants, travel to their neighbourhood school and join in the whole range of activities there, not just music, drama, or physical education. In addition, individual children may regularly go to a mainstream school, usually but not necessarily accompanied by an LSA. Activities in mainstream schools are carefully planned and coordinated between staff of special and mainstream schools.

Information from school inspections

Since 1992, all special schools have been subject to regular inspection by the Office for Standards in Education (OFSTED), using publicly drawn up criteria (OFSTED, 2000). Reports on individual schools are publicly available and are posted on the OFSTED website (www.ofsted.gov.uk).

A national summary report on the work of special schools is broadly positive. For example, in nine out of 10 schools, the quality of teaching was rated as satisfactory or better and the pupils were making at least satisfactory progress. Pupils' behaviour and attitudes to work were satisfactory or good in almost all schools (OFSTED, 1999). On the negative side, there are references to teachers' lack of knowledge of teaching the National Curriculum programs of study, especially in information and communication technology, and poor practice in assessment and recording of pupils' progress and in using such information to support their learning.

An earlier study by Sebba, Clarke, and Emery (1996) provided an independent analysis of the process of inspections, based on reports on 47 special schools, which included 12 schools for pupils with severe learning difficulties. The study highlights the tensions for schools in finding a balance between the demands of a 10 subject National Curriculum and meeting the pupils' individual needs. This is further explored below.

Aims of education

There has been general agreement in principle with the recommendations of the Warnock Report (Department of Education and Science, 1978) that the aims of education should be the same for all children:

> The purpose of education for all children is the same; the goals are the same but the help that individual children need in progressing towards them will be different . . . the aims are first to enlarge a child's knowledge, experience and imaginative understanding, and thus his awareness of moral values and capacity for enjoyment; and secondly to enable him to enter the world of work after formal education is over as an active participant in society and a responsible contributor to it, capable of achieving as much independence as possible.
>
> (para. 1.4)

Although these principles have been reiterated in a variety of contexts both by governments, professional bodies, and parent organisations, translation into practice has proved to be quite challenging. If the aims of education are to be the same for all, how can children who experience severe difficulties in learning be included in a major reform of the education system which is based on a drive to raise academic standards and which forces schools into competing for pupils and resources?

Curriculum entitlement and access

The 1988 Education Reform Act and the various amending Acts which followed represented both a crisis and an opportunity for schools working with pupils with severe learning difficulties. It was a crisis in the sense that the Act originally ignored all children with special educational needs (SEN) and seemed irrelevant for pupils with severe learning difficulties. Although a few head teachers did take that view, the majority saw the new curriculum as a challenge. At least, all schools were now working within the same curricular framework and shared a common language where programs of study were concerned.

The Act introduced a 10 subject National Curriculum, each subject having programs of study and 10 levels of attainment, with nationally designed tests at age 7, 11, 14, and 16 years. As the programs of study were published, it seemed that "Level 1 attainments" in most areas would be beyond the abilities of most of the children attending schools for pupils with severe learning difficulties, even at age 16. Because the Act made it possible to "disapply" some or all of the National Curriculum for individuals or groups of children, there were fears that children who were unable to reach Level 1 would once again be declared ineducable and excluded from the education system.

In the early 1990s, it became clear that the National Curriculum was far too demanding for all children, as well as too prescriptive for teachers. The government commissioned a major review by Sir Ron Dearing which resulted in a slimmer and more flexible curriculum for all pupils, further-more, one which took greater account of pupils with special educational needs (Schools Curriculum and Assessment Authority, 1993).

From an early stage, the National Curriculum Council had introduced a number of cross-curricular themes and dimensions, including personal, social and health education, economic and industrial understanding, careers education, environmental education, and the European dimension. These were found to be particularly helpful in special schools who often used them as a basis for introducing the more traditional subjects (Rose, Ferguson, Coles, Byers, & Banes 1996; Sebba, Byers, & Rose, 1995; see also Tilstone, Florian, & Rose, 1998 for excellent discussions of curriculum access which are informed by an intellectual disability perspective).

From the beginning, teachers insisted on their pupils' entitlement to a National Curriculum by demonstrating ways in which the new curricu-lum could be adapted and differentiated to meet the needs of all children, including those with profound and multiple learning difficulties. Teacher working parties were set up in many parts of the country, some at the level of the school, others working in clusters of schools or at the level of the LEA.

In Manchester, the LEA seconded six teachers from different schools to spend a full year at the University of Manchester with the aim of developing series of nationally published curriculum guides with detailed "worked examples" of good practice not only in accessing the official curriculum, but also in integrating this both with the wider curriculum and pupils' individual educational programs. (See Fagg, Aherne, Skelton, and Thornber (1990) for the original overview volume which was followed by detailed guidance in each subject area.) Indeed, the sector concerned with pupils with severe learning difficulties was by the far the most pro-ductive in developing guidelines for curriculum access for the pupils in its schools. A number of other publications also offered guidance and examples of good practice in accessing and modifying the curriculum (Ashdown, Carpenter, & Bovair, 1991; Carpenter, Ashdown, & Bovair, 1996, 2001; Tilstone, 1991).

Belatedly, the government also took some steps to try to ensure that children with special educational needs (SENs) were included in the National Curriculum. For example, they issued a strong statement on entitlement:

The principle that each pupil should have a broad and balanced curriculum *which is also relevant to his or her particular needs* is now established in law.

(Department of Education and Science, 1989) (italics added)

The government funded a series of national studies which were specifically designed to support teachers working with children with severe and profound and multiple learning difficulties in adapting and differentiating the curriculum (National Curriculum Council, 1992; Qualifications and Curriculum Authority, 2001; Schools Curriculum and Assessment Authority, 1996). In fact, more guidance has been provided for this than for any other sector of special needs provision.

The most recent revision of the National Curriculum which became operational in September 2000 is notable for a well received seven page statement on inclusion which is then adapted to each subject area. In addition, the new curriculum includes health, personal and social education, and citizenship in terms which can be adapted to meet the needs of all pupils with special educational needs, including those with profound and multiple learning difficulties (Department for Education and Employment and Qualifications and Curriculum Authority, 1999; Mittler, 2000).

Testing and assessment

Right from the outset, teachers in all sectors of education resisted the imposition of national tests (originally called Standard Assessment Tasks) at 7, 11, and 14 years, even going to the length of industrial action at one stage and ending the career of an exceptionally unpopular Secretary of State. Teachers of pupils with intellectual disabilities were particularly concerned because the original tests were often pitched too high for many of their pupils, with the result that those unable to reach Level 1 were designated as "W" (working towards) and might be doomed to remain at W for the whole of their schooling in each subject area. Because steps between levels were too large, the progress that others made could not be officially recognised.

These assessment inequalities have been addressed in a number of ways. In the first place, the government accepted that a teacher's assessment of a child's level of attainment in a National Curriculum area could be substituted for national tests. Secondly, the national tests could be administered with much more flexibility—extra time could be given, test papers opened earlier, word processors, information technology, and enlarged print could be used, and amanuenses could be brought in to support pupils. These were all helpful measures for some pupils with sensory and physical impairments but they did not address the fundamental question of the irrelevance of the standard tests to the wider curriculum and personal needs of the pupils in

"SLD provision." Consequently, teachers tend to "disapply" the formal assessment requirements in favour of enriched teacher assessment.

The overall strategy of assessing and recording access to the curriculum has been through a "small steps approach." This was first outlined in a review of good practice in assessment published by the National Foundation for Educational Research (Fletcher-Campbell & Lee, 1995). These were developed by the Qualifications and Curriculum Authority as guidance on formative assessment of pupils who have not reached Level 1 (Department for Education and Employment and Qualifications and Curriculum Authority, 1998) and have most recently been incorporated in new guidelines for teaching and assessing the most recent revisions of the National Curriculum (Qualifications and Curriculum Authority and Department for Education and Employment, 2001).

P (performance) scales provide a framework for charting progress in learning up to Level 1 through eight progress steps: P1 to P3 illustrate general attainment and P4 to P8 are related to specific subjects. For example, the first three levels provide working definitions and examples of seven levels of recognising attainment, ranging from "encounter" to "gaining skills and understanding;" intermediate levels include "awareness, attention and response, engagement, participation and involvement." Detailed work has been done in the core subjects of English and Mathematics but this approach can be used right across the curriculum as a way of recording, reporting, and building on progress, however small.

Despite these positive developments, the government remains committed to using age-related norms in the national program of target-setting for all schools. These are clearly irrelevant in a school for pupils with severe learning difficulties.

Teaching and learning

During the 1970s and early 1980s, the emphasis in schools for pupils with severe learning difficulties had been on the "how" rather than the "what" of teaching. An influential example of this approach was the Education of Developmentally Young (EDY) course in behavioural methods of teaching (Farrell, 1985). The EDY team based at Manchester University developed intensive five day workshops in a day special school (Melland School, Manchester); these were designed to equip educational psychologists, advisers, or head teachers from all over the country to run school-based workshops in their own areas. The workshops provided hands-on training in task analysis, reward assessment, chaining, prompting and imitation, and in planning individual teaching sessions, using role play and role reversal to provide experience of the approach. A cascade model was highly successful in disseminating the approach: 20 five day workshops produced 100 trainers who in turn trained a new generation of staff, eventually totalling well over

6,000 people at local level. Training materials were published and later revised (McBrien, Farrell, & Foxen, 1992) following extensive evaluation (Robson, Sebba, Mittler, & Davies, 1988). The course has been translated and adapted for use in other countries (e.g., India) and has resulted in a substantial number of publications.

Behavioural methods went "out of fashion" in the late 1980s when many schools described themselves as "beyond behaviourism." In some cases, this meant that teachers were competent in the use of behavioural methods but only used them when they considered them to be appropriate or as part of a wider and richer program of teaching. For example, skills such as task analysis, prompting, or reinforcement became a natural part of the teacher's repertoire. But there was also a reaction against behaviourist methods in favour of approaches which emphasised intensive social interactions and following leads given by the child (Nind & Hewett, 1994), thus generating controversy about the role of "age-appropriate" activities in working with this population (see Coupe-O'Kane and Goldbart, 1996 for examples of this and other contentious issues in this field).

Although courses such as EDY helped teachers to develop techniques to help children to learn new skills, their very success postponed serious consideration of curriculum priorities. Each special school followed its own curriculum, but there was a common emphasis on the teaching of skills in the area of self-care, domestic skills, use of money, language, and communication and on helping children to overcome or compensate for their disabilities with the support of speech and physiotherapists. Although some central guidance was provided by the government (Department of Education and Science, 1975) and in a Schools Council Curriculum Development project concerned with the teaching of communication skills (Leeming, Coupe, Swann, & Mittler, 1979), it was the sudden advent of the National Curriculum at the end of the 1980s which confronted schools with the challenge of identifying their curriculum priorities and of finding a balance between the needs of individual pupils, the new National Curriculum and existing best practice in, for example, teaching pupils to become as independent as possible in areas such as self-care, communication, use of money, or public transport. In addition, there was a need for greater emphasis on preparing young people to become self-advocates by supporting students in making choices and in voicing their own opinions (Coupe-O'Kane & Smith, 1994; Mittler, 2001).

These tensions have become even more acute as education in mainstream schools became a possibility. For this to succeed, children in special schools needed to be supported in gaining access to the National Curriculum. By the same token, teachers in special schools would be needed to provide support for pupils in mainstream schools. In practice, as we have seen, very few children transfer from special to mainstream schools, though many travel in the other direction. Children with severe learning difficulties who did attend mainstream schools tended to be supported by learning support assistants, supervised by an experienced peripatetic teacher based on the LEA or by an outreach teacher based on the special school.

Teacher training

Governments introducing change and innovation rarely ensure that teachers receive appropriate training and support and are properly funded to do so. The cataclysm of innovation which has engulfed the English education system since the end of the 1980s has also seen the collapse of structures for training and professional development for all teachers but without a serious attempt to design new systems to match new needs. Although there are now signs that government is giving higher priority to professional development, it will take a long time to provide the training opportunities which all teachers will need to update their knowledge and skills in a more inclusive system.

Throughout the 1970s and early 1980s, specialist initial training courses were available for students who wanted to work with children with intellectual disabilities. When these courses were phased out, schools could no longer rely on newly qualified teachers who wanted to make a career in this field. The government and its advisers took the view that it was better for teachers to gain experience in mainstream schools before working in special schools and seeking advanced specialist training at a later stage. Unfortunately, the whole system of secondment for advanced study collapsed as a result of funding decisions, leaving an enormous gap in professional development opportunities throughout the education system as a whole (Special Educational Needs Training Consortium, 1996; Mittler, 1995, 2000).

Since the mid 1980s, training has been largely funded by schools. Much of the training is therefore school-based or school-focused and generally of very short duration. All schools have five days in the school year which can be devoted to staff development. Most teachers have to pay for additional training themselves and most courses take place in the evenings.

Longer courses leading to awards have all but disappeared. In the past, teachers could take one year full-time or two year part-time courses which led to an additional qualification in the teaching of children with SLD or in which a specialisation in severe learning difficulties was available within a generic special needs qualification. Modular versions could also be taken over a longer period. Less than half the teachers in this sector have such a qualification and few opportunities remain for them to obtain additional qualifications by this route. This is in contrast to teachers of pupils with sensory impairments for whom there is a mandatory requirement for a specialist qualification within three years.

The training needs of teachers working in the SLD field are now inseparable from those of all other teachers. Clearly, all newly qualified teachers need to have some preparation for working with the whole range of pupils with SEN. Furthermore, in an education system moving towards inclusion, training in any area provided for those already in post must be concerned with a much wider range of pupil need than in the past. Such training cannot be provided by the traditional SEN specialists. It must come from trainers who plan their training along inclusive lines, just as training now has to include gender and race dimensions from the beginning and no longer as an afterthought.

Responsibility for training is now divided between the government-appointed Teacher Training Agency (TTA) and the Department for Education and Employment. The TTA has developed "national standards" which take the form of lists of competencies for newly qualified teachers (which include some concerned with SEN), as well as standards for head teachers, subject leaders, and "advanced skills teachers." National standards for SEN coordinators in mainstream schools (TTA, 1998) have been generally welcomed.

National SEN specialist standards (TTA, 1999) have proved more problematic and controversial, largely because of inherent conflicts of interest between those who want to retain training along categorical lines for different groups of specialists and those who were aiming for a non-categorical approach which would be relevant to all teachers working in mainstream schools or in any sector of special needs education. The final version of the specialist standards reflects a less categorical approach than some of the earlier drafts. Although the mandatory training requirements for teachers of children with sensory impairments are retained, the standards are relevant to teachers working in a variety of settings and do not necessarily lead to specialist qualifications in specific disability areas, such as autism or severe learning difficulties. It remains to be seen how these standards will be reflected in training opportunities; clearly, those who provide training will have to take them into account.

The core standards for all specialists include: (a) knowledge, understanding, and skills in identification, assessment, and planning; (b) effective teaching in securing access to the curriculum; (c) development of communication, literacy, numeracy, and information and communication technology (ICT) capability; and (d) promotion of social and emotional development, positive behaviour, and preparation for adulthood.

Extension standards are grouped under four headings: (a) communication and interaction, (b) cognition and learning, (c) behavioural, emotional, and social development, and (d) sensory and physical development.

Each of these is further broken down into knowledge and understanding and skills. with a total of 63 standards under the four headings. The intention is to encourage teachers to develop pathways through these headings rather than encourage too much specialisation. For example, all four headings will be of interest to teachers working with pupils with SLDs. Although cognition and learning will be particularly relevant for teachers working in the SLD field, it is also relevant to those working with pupils with specific learning difficulties or dyslexia.

The TTA has done some valuable groundwork in defining the knowledge, understanding, and skills which teachers will require to work in a system working towards inclusion, but it is not at all clear at this stage how a coherent system of professional development can be created without firmer leadership both from the profession and from government.

The most positive development in the field of teacher education arises from the government's most recent proposals to set up a strong and properly funded framework for continuing professional development for all teachers, up to Masters degree level (Department for Education and Employment, 2000).

Conclusions

Looking back over 30 years and forward to the next 30, there is cause for both confidence and concern. On the one hand, the quality of education for children with intellectual disabilities has changed out of all recognition in this period. Teachers have responded brilliantly to the fundamental challenge posed by the imposition of a national curriculum and its associated regime of testing and inspection and have worked hard at national, local, and individual levels to make the whole curriculum not only accessible but rich and relevant to the needs of children. Despite the collapse of training structures, teachers in this sector have taken advantage of whatever training opportunities have been available and have joined forces with colleagues in mainstream schools, with mutual benefit. Special schools are no longer isolated havens of care but lively centres of teaching and learning.

But how many of the children now in special schools could be satisfactorily educated in mainstream schools, if appropriate supports were available and if the schools were restructured to become more inclusive? Some will argue that all children without exception could be in mainstream provision if these conditions were met and that anything less than this would result in an even more segregated environment for those that remain behind. An alternative strategy is to begin with the youngest children and to guarantee them a fully supported and funded place in integrated provision. At the same time, more could be done to review inclusion possibilities for each child in special schools.

The government is deeply ambivalent on the future of special schools. On the one hand, they talk the language of inclusion and have greatly increased funding for inclusive projects. On the other hand, they consistently fail to grasp the legislative nettle which would make education in the mainstream school the first assumption in the process of assessment and decision making. The 1981 Act included some deeply discriminatory clauses which allowed LEAs and schools to refuse to accept children if this would result in unreasonable expenditure or if it interfered with the education of other children. The new Special Educational Needs and Disability Act (2001) greatly strengthens children's rights to mainstream education and requires schools to make "reasonable adjustments" to enable them to do so but still retains some discriminatory clauses.

Despite lack of clear policies from the centre, many parts of the country are not only moving towards inclusion but working to ensure that it is of high quality. Innumerable reports have been published describing local projects and the experiences of schools and individual children. These reports illustrate beyond a shadow of doubt that education in a mainstream school for children with intellectual disabilities is not only possible, but can be a positive experience both for the children involved and for their teachers.

Finally, new opportunities are opening up for young people after they leave school. Larger numbers of young people are studying part-time or full-time in Colleges of Further Education available to all young people leaving school, some of them while still attending school. Under new legislation, and stimulated by the influential Tomlinson Report *Inclusive Learning* (Further Education Funding Council, 1996; Johnstone 1995), better funded learning opportunities are being made available to pupils with learning difficulties and disabilities.

Despite a great deal of progress, many adults with intellectual disabilities are still living and learning in isolation from their peers and from the local community. A large proportion have no paid work or meaningful occupation during the day and little access to leisure or recreation. Large residential institutions have been replaced by smaller units, but some of these are still run along institutional lines.

The future looks more promising. There has been a major review of services for people with intellectual disabilities (Department of Health, 2001). This outlines a new approach to community services, clearer funding mechanisms, a greater degree of participation by people with intellectual disabilities themselves, and strong support for the development of self-advocacy and independence.

Author note

I am grateful to Judy O'Kane, Head Teacher of Melland High School, Manchester, for 30 years of collaboration and professional support and also for her comments on an earlier draft of this paper.

References

ASHDOWN, R., CARPENTER, B. & BOVAIR, K. (Eds.) (1991). *The curriculum challenge: Access to the national curriculum for pupils with learning difficulties.* London: Falmer Press.

AUDIT COMMISSION AND HER MAJESTY'S INSPECTORATE (1992). *Getting in on the act. Provision for pupils with special educational needs: The national picture.* London: HMSO.

BURKE, B. (1999). LEA Support Services: A Newham perspective. In B. NORWICH (Ed.), *Rethinking support for more inclusive schooling: Policy Option Paper 1* (3rd series, pp. 18–24). Tamworth, UK: National Association for Special Educational Needs.

CARPENTER, B., ASHDOWN, R. & BOVAIR, K. (Eds.) (1996). *Enabling access: Effective teaching and learning for pupils with learning difficulties.* London: Fulton.

CARPENTER, B., ASHDOWN, R. & BOVAIR, K. (Eds.) (2001). *Enabling access: Effective teaching and learning for pupils with learning difficulties* (2nd ed.). London: Fulton.

COUPE-O'KANE, J. & GOLDBART, J. (Eds.) (1996). *Whose choice? Contentious issues for those working with people with learning difficulties.* London: Fulton.

COUPE-O'KANE, J. & SMITH, B. (Eds.) (1994). *Taking control. Enabling people with learning difficulties.* London: Fulton.

CROLL, P. & MOSES, D. (2000). *Special needs in the primary school: One in five?* London: Continuum.

CUNNINGHAM, C., GLENN, S., LORENZ, S., CUCKLE, P., & SHEPPERSON, B. (1998). Trends and outcomes in educational placements for children with Down's syndrome. *European Journal of Special Needs Education, 13,* 225–237.

DEPARTMENT FOR EDUCATION AND EMPLOYMENT (1997). *Excellence for all children.* London: HMSO.

DEPARTMENT FOR EDUCATION & EMPLOYMENT (1998). *Meeting special educational needs: A programme of action.* London: Author. (www.dfee.gov.uk.sen)

DEPARTMENT FOR EDUCATION AND EMPLOYMENT (1999). *Statistics of education: Special educational needs in England 12/99.* London: Author.

DEPARTMENT FOR EDUCATION AND EMPLOYMENT (2000). *Professional development: Support for teaching and learning. Consultation document.* London: Author.

DEPARTMENT FOR EDUCATION AND EMPLOYMENT & QUALIFICATIONS AND CURRICULUM AUTHORITY (1998). *Supporting the target setting process.* London: Department for Education and Employment.

DEPARTMENT FOR EDUCATION AND EMPLOYMENT & QUALIFICATIONS AND CURRICULUM AUTHORITY (1999). *The national curriculum: Handbooks for primary and secondary teachers.* London: Department for Education and Employment. (www.nc.uk.net)

DEPARTMENT OF EDUCATION AND SCIENCE (1975). *Educating mentally handicapped children. Education Pamphlet 60.* London: Author.

DEPARTMENT OF EDUCATION AND SCIENCE (1978). *Special education needs: The Report of the Committee of Enquiry into the Education of Handicapped Children and Young People.* The Warnock Report. Cmnd 7212. London: HMSO.

DEPARTMENT OF EDUCATION AND SCIENCE (1989). *The national curriculum: From policy to practice.* London: Author.

DEPARTMENT OF HEALTH (2001). *Valuing people: A new strategy for learning disability in the 21st century.* Cm. 5086. London: HMSO.

DEPARTMENT FOR HEALTH AND SOCIAL SECURITY (1971). *Better services for the mentally handicapped.* London: HMSO.

EDUCATION REFORM ACT (1988). London: HMSO. Retrieved 15 February, 2002 from http://www.inforoute.hmso.gov.uk/acts/acts1988/Ukpga_19880040_en_1.htm

EVANS, P. & WARE, J. (1987). *Special care provision.* Slough, UK: National Foundation for Educational Research.

FAGG, S., AHERNE, P., SKELTON, S. & THORNBER, A. (1990). *Entitlement for all: A broad, balanced and relevant curriculum for pupils with severe and complex learning difficulties.* London: Fulton.

430

FARRELL, P. (Ed.) (1985). *EDY: Its impact on staff training and mental handicap.* Manchester, UK: Manchester University Press.

FARRELL, P. (1997). *Teaching pupils with learning difficulties: Strategies and solutions.* London: Cassell.

FLETCHER-CAMPBELL, F. & LEE, B. (1995). *Small steps of progress in the national curriculum.* Slough, UK: National Foundation for Educational Research.

FURTHER EDUCATION FUNDING COUNCIL (1996). *Inclusive learning.* The Tomlinson Report. London: FEFC & Department for Education and Employment.

HEGARTY, S. (1993). Reviewing the literature on integration. *European Journal of Special Needs Education, 8,* 194–200.

HOGG, J. LAMBE, L., COWIE, J. & COXON, J. (1987). *People with profound retardation and multiple handicaps attending schools or social education centres.* London: MENCAP.

JENKINSON, J. (1997). *Mainstream or special? Educating students with disabilities.* London: Routledge.

JOHNSTONE, D. (1995). *Further opportunities: Learning difficulties and disabilities in further education.* London: Cassell.

JOWETT, S. (1994). *Still joining forces? A follow-up study of the links between ordinary and special schools.* Slough, UK: National Foundation for Educational Research.

JOWETT, D., HEGARTY, S. & MOSES, D. (1988). *Joining forces: A study of links between ordinary and special schools.* Slough, UK: National Foundation for Educational Research.

LEEMING, J., COUPE, J., SWANN, W. & MITTLER, P. (1979). *Teaching language and communication to the mentally handicapped.* London: Evans Methuen.

McBRIEN, J., FARRELL, P. & FOXEN, T. (1992) *EDY: Teaching people with severe learning difficulties. Trainee workbook* (2nd ed.). Manchester, UK: Manchester University Press.

MALE, D. (1996a). Who goes to SLD schools? *Journal of Applied Research in Intellectual Disabilities, 9,* 307–323.

MALE, D. (1996b). Who goes to MLD schools? *British Journal of Special Education, 23,* 35–41.

MITTLER, P. (1974). Progress and problems in the education of mentally handicapped children in the UK. *The Slow Learning Child, 21,* 140–154.

MITTLER, P. (1995). Professional development for special needs education. In I. LUNT & B. NORWICH (WITH V. VARMA) (Eds.), *Psychology and education for special needs: Recent developments and future directions* (pp. 211–228). Aldershot, Hants, UK: Ashgate.

MITTLER, P. (2000). *Working towards inclusive education: Social contexts.* London: Fulton.

MITTLER, P. (2001). Preparing for self advocacy. In B. CARPENTER, R. ASHDOWN & K. BOVAIR (Eds.), *Enabling access: Effective teaching and learning for pupils with learning difficulties* (2nd ed., pp. 328–345). London: Fulton.

MITTLER, P. & PREDDY, D. (1981). Mentally handicapped pupils and school leavers: A survey in North West England. In B. COOPER (Ed.), *Assessing the handicaps and needs of mentally retarded children* (pp. 33–51). London: Academic Press.

MITTLER, P. (WITH SINASON, V.) (Eds.) (1996). *Changing policy and practice for people with learning disabilities.* London: Cassell.

NATIONAL CURRICULUM COUNCIL (1992). *The national curriculum and pupils with severe learning difficulties.* York, UK: Author.

NIND, M. & HEWETT, D. (1994). *Access to communication: Developing the basics of communication with people with severe learning difficulties.* London: Fulton.

OFFICE FOR STANDARDS IN EDUCATION (1999). *Special education 1994–1998: A review of special schools, secure units and pupil referral units in England.* London: HMSO.

OFFICE FOR STANDARDS IN EDUCATION (2000). *Inspecting schools: The framework.* London: Author.

QUALIFICATIONS AND CURRICULUM AUTHORITY & DEPARTMENT FOR EDUCATION AND EMPLOYMENT (2001). *Planning, teaching and assessing the curriculum for pupils with learning difficulties: General guidelines.* London: Author. (www.qca.org.uk)

ROBSON, C., SEBBA, J., MITTLER, P. & DAVIES, G. (1988). *In-service training and special educational needs: Running short, school-focused courses.* Manchester, UK: Manchester University Press.

ROSE, R., FERGUSON, A., COLES, C., BYERS, R. & BANES, D. (1996). *Implementing the whole curriculum for pupils with learning difficulties* (rev. ed.). London: Fulton.

SCHOOLS CURRICULUM AND ASSESSMENT AUTHORITY (1993). *The national curriculum and its assessment. The Dearing Report.* London: Author.

SCHOOLS CURRICULUM AND ASSESSMENT AUTHORITY (1996). *Planning the curriculum for pupils with profound and multiple learning difficulties.* London: Author.

SEBBA, J., BYERS, R. & ROSE, R. (1995). *Redefining the whole curriculum for pupils with learning difficulties.* London: Fulton.

SEBBA, J., CLARKE, J. & EMERY, B. (1996). How can the inspection process enhance improvement in special schools? *European journal of Special Needs Education, 11,* 82–94.

SEGAL, S. (1966). *No child is ineducable.* Oxford: Pergamon Press.

SPECIAL EDUCATIONAL NEEDS AND DISABILITY ACT (2001). London: HMSO. Retrieved 15 February, 2002 from http://www.legislation.hmso.gov.uk/acts/acts2001/20010010.htm

SPECIAL EDUCATIONAL NEEDS TRAINING CONSORTIUM (1996). *Professional development to meet special educational needs. Report to Secretary of State for Education and Employment.* Stafford, UK: Flash Ley Resource Centre, Stafford ST17 9DR.

TEACHER TRAINING AGENCY (1998). *National standards for special educational needs coordinators.* London: Author.

TEACHER TRAINING AGENCY (1999). *National special educational needs specialist standards.* London: Author.

TILSTONE, C. (Ed.) (1991). *Teaching children with severe learning difficulties: Practical approaches.* London: Fulton.

TILSTONE, C., FLORIAN, L. & ROSE, R. (1998). *Promoting inclusive practice.* London: Routledge.

26

THE EXPANSION OF
SPECIAL EDUCATION

Sally Tomlinson

Source: *Oxford Review of Education* 11(2) (1985): 157–65.

Abstract

This article advances the argument that special education is expanding as part of a restructuring of the education-training system to deal with large numbers of young people who are now defined as unable or unwilling to participate in normal education. The expansion is occurring as attempts are made to change education to fit the perceived needs of a technologically-based society in which a large social group will be partially or permanently unemployed. Evidence for expansion is examined, professional interests in an expanding clientele are noted, and the dilemmas inherent in comprehensive schooling and a disappearing youth labour market are discussed. The concept of special needs is thought to have become an ideological rationalisation which obfuscates the educational, political and economic needs actually served by the expansion.

Special education in Britain, as in other advanced technological societies, is expanding. In changed forms and rationalised by changed ideologies, notably the ideology of special needs, it is becoming a more important mechanism for differentiating between young people and allocating some to a future which, if not as stigmatised as in the past, will be characterised by relative powerlessness and economic dependency. It is expanding primarily as part of a political response to a crucial dilemma facing education systems in late twentieth-century technological societies. This dilemma is centred round restructuring the education-training system to deal with the increasing number of young people who are defined as being unable or unwilling to participate satisfactorily in a system primarily directed towards producing academic and technical elites. Adequate achievements in normal school education or educational training are becoming more important in gaining any sort of employment or income above subsistence level, or exerting any influence on the wider society. The expansion of special education is linked to the question of what sort of education—or preparation for future life-style—can or should be offered to a larger social group who are likely to be partially or permanently non-employed, and thus in traditional industrial-society understandings are not economically profitable or 'useful'. As special education expands it is likely to provide both a rationale and a justification for the economic and social position of at least a part of this social group. Although presented in ideological terms as catering for the 'needs' of pupils, the expansion of special education is the result of rational action on the part of those who control and direct education and training, to restructure the education system to fit the perceived needs of a post-industrial, technologically based society.

This article examines evidence for the claim that special education is expanding and discusses three reasons for the expansion—professional vested interest, comprehensive school dilemmas and the declining youth labour market—and asserts that the ideology of 'special needs' directs attention away from the social, economic and political concerns which have led to the expansion.

Evidence for expansion

Legally, special education is defined as the curriculum and pedagogy offered to pupils who pre-1981 had a 'disability of body or mind' calling for special educational treatment, and post-1981 have a learning difficulty which calls for special educational provision. The number of such children rose from nil in the early 1870s—at the beginning of compulsory state education—to some $1^1/_2$ million in 1981.[1] This argues that a sub-system of special education has been successfully established and has become an important structural component of the educational system. The expansion can be largely accounted for by the number of children who have no physical or sensory handicap, but who are educationally defined as being incapable of participating or unwilling to participate in what is currently defined as the 'normal' curriculum, and being incapable of 'adequate achievements' via this curriculum. Such children have, over the past 100 years, been variously described as feeble-minded, educable defective, educationally sub-normal, those having moderate learning difficulties, dull and backward, remedial, and maladjusted and disruptive.

The expansion is linked to enhanced definitions of 'achievement'. There is increasing pressure on schools to raise standards and to credential more and more pupils. This has led to pressures on schools to devise more and more courses leading to lower-level credentials and to seek ways of separating out

those who are unable or unwilling to achieve even these lower-level qualifications. In this way the sub-system of special education appears capable of
seemingly indefinite expansion. For example, the number of pupils considered
to have a disability of body or mind in 1946 was 2% with a further 8% to 9%
likely to be unable to achieve adequately in schools.[2] In 1978, the number in
need of special provision was considered by the Warnock Committee to be
20% of the school population. By 1982 the Secretary of State was expressing
his concern about the less able 40%, and a DES-sponsored programme for
lower-attaining pupils was instigated. The ideological differences between
the 20% of pupils needing special provision owing to learning difficulties
and the learning difficulties of the bottom 40% are problematic, and in
practice the programme appears to fill a gap between school definitions of
'special needs' and 'CSE material' (NFER, 1984). In Scotland the system
may be expanding faster. A Scottish Inspectorate comment on learning
difficulties in 1984 noted that since 'there is a whole range of difficulties
faced by very many pupils in the lower half of the ability range . . . the
progress report was thinking in terms of up to 50%'.[3] Accurate numbers of
those in special education provision, or 'in need' of this kind of provision
have always been difficult to quantify. One reason for this have been the
changing definitions of special education. Another reason is that LEAs have
always differed in the kinds and amount of special provision they offered.
Perhaps of more interest are the proportional and percentage increases.

Post-war, Booth has worked out that in 1950 2,402 pupils per million
were categorised as ESN-M; by 1977 the proportion had risen to 5,763 per
million. Similarly, in 1950, 93 pupils per million were officially maladjusted,
by 1977 this had risen to 1,416 per million (Booth, 1981, p. 295). In another
entertaining comparison Squibb (1981, p. 47) estimated that in 15 years
(1961–76) there was an increase of 150% in pupils classed as ESN, a 237%
increase for those classed as maladjusted, a 1,332% increase for those
classed as speech defective and an infinite increase (from no pupils in 1961
to 951 in 1976) in those classed as autistic. As Squibb has noted 'we may all
be autistic soon' (1981, p. 48). Further evidence of percentage increases of
pupils segregated into special schools and classes under the pre-1981 system
of classification by handicap has been provided by Swann who worked out
that despite assumptions that integration was occurring and fewer pupils
were being physically removed from mainstream schooling, the proportion
of pupils segregated in special schools actually increased by 4.8% between
1977 and 82 and he particularly noted the increased segregation into
ESN-M and maladjusted provision (Swann, 1984).

From its beginnings special education was concerned to take in those with
obvious and definable physical and sensory handicaps and behaviourally
troublesome pupils, but from 1889 the most likely candidates for inclusion
in an expanding system were those originally classed as feeble-minded or
educable defectives—their heirs being the dull and backward, educationally

sub-normal, remedial, moderate learning and behavioural difficulties, the less-able, etc. I have argued (Tomlinson, 1982) that the persistent connection of this expanding group—and of learning and behavioural problems—with the children of the manual working-class is perenially resilient. The 'social problem' class that worried Cyril Burt continues to worry educationalists from the Secretary of State downwards. Connections between lack of intelligence, inability to learn, bad behaviour, low socio-economic status and a variety of undesirable social attributes continue to ensure that it is largely the children of the lower working class and the unemployed who are candidates for the expanding special education sector. The story of Bill and Daisy included by A. F. Tredgold (1914) in his *Textbook of Mental Deficiency* may still be pertinent:

> Bill, we will suppose, had been a pupil in a special (educationally subnormal) school up to the age of 16 . . . and has since been employed in a number of jobs, starting as an errand boy and graduating to simple machine-minding in a factory. Daisy went to an ordinary school but was very backward and like Bill, is scarcely able to read and write. Daisy, before her marriage to Bill, has held a variety of jobs mainly assembling or varnishing small electrical parts.
>
> After joining a gang for acceptance and a sense of importance Bill was . . . impelled to seek a girl friend, but was so unprepossessing that his only chance would be with a girl equally unattractive who might be available. Daisy was unattractive but simple and compliant and an easy date. Between the pair a bond of sympathy grew up. They each provided for the other what had been lacking all the years—comfort and appreciation.
>
> (Daisy became pregnant and they married and went to live in an attic room in an overcrowded house—going down four flights of stairs for water and six for the WC. Daisy had to give up her job, the couple lacked foresight and planning.)
>
> After the baby's birth, Daisy went out cleaning, Bill lost his job—they had another baby but fear of further pregnancies led Daisy to fail to give Bill comfort and solace. Bill took to staying away from home and he became ripe for any criminal exploitation that might come his way. The children will have a natural backwardness at school, will play truant and delinquent practices will follow. Thus history will have repeated itself.
>
> (p. 394)

Tredgold's documentation of two ESN school-leavers who found semi-skilled work, married and had a family could be read as a eugenist's warning, or as a libel on a couple who lacked an adequate wage, decent housing and contraceptive advice.

Expansion and professional interests

Much of the expansion of special education has been ascribed to accident, spontaneous adjustment, progress and benevolence. These explanations have always proved a stumbling block to the analysis of the emergence and expansion of a special sub-system of education. Archer's (1979) contention that educational structures are the result of the *interests* of those social groups who manage, as a result of conflicts, to achieve educational control, is a more useful starting point. The development and expansion of special education is the result of a variety of conflicting interest groups, both inside and outside education. Indeed, an understanding of the competition and alliances among interest groups in special education is crucial to understanding its expansion.

Pre-1945 (as I have documented in Tomlinson, 1982) educationalists, psychologists and medical practitioners all had vested interests in expanding the numbers of pupils in special education, and government had an interest in the control and direction of numbers of pupils who might prove 'troublesome' in their post-school careers in a variety of ways (principally by unemployment, crime or by requiring resources). Ordinary teachers' interests in the removal of special pupils—who originally interfered with payment-by-results and filled the standard 'O' classes—has proved an enduring and crucial force behind expansion. Then, as now, the public status of ordinary teachers was dependent on their ability to 'raise standards', which called for the removal of defective and troublesome children. This removal coincided with the interests of the new sub-profession of special school teachers who had a vested interest in obtaining clients for their schools. It also coincided with the interests of the eugenists who were concerned to identify and isolate defectives who threatened the 'racial stock'. Psychologists had a crucial interest in developing the tools of assessment for special education, which have proved to be so important in their professional development and claims to specialist expertise. The enduring medical influence in special education has also been well documented (Pritchard, 1963) and the recorded conflicts of educational and medical personnel over the control of access to special education post-1908 provides a good example of the strategic power-play that ultimately determines control of the education system.[4]

Post-1945, medical and psychological interests took precedence over education in vying for control of assessment processes for special education, psychologists partially reaching parity of esteem by 1975 and certainly by 1981. However, by this time all professional interests were becoming united by a suspicion that central and local administrators had annexed control of special education via distribution of resources, control of assessment procedures, parental appeals and decisions on provisions. The 1981 Act did, however, place more control of the expanding sector of special education in the educationalists' area, as its major location became the ordinary school.

In particular the expanding sub-profession of 'special needs' Heads of Departments, teachers and support staff in ordinary schools now has power to shape and control large sectors of special education and in particular to decide who the special clients in the ordinary school will be and what sort of 'special' curriculum and pedagogy they will be offered. The ideology of 'special needs' is currently penetrating the secondary school curriculum and conflicts of interest are developing between 'special needs' specialists and their colleagues. In addition it was not to be expected that teachers in special schools would willingly give up their special expertise or clients as the location changed, and there are currently conflicts of interest between special and ordinary schools over the retention or movement of pupils, particularly in areas where segregated provision was well established.[5] But by the late 1970s 'special' teachers in both segregated and integrated provision had, to some extent, realised that their common interest lay in enhanced professional claims to special expertise. These claims are currently being strengthened and the expansion of special education has created the opportunity for more expert special teachers, support staff, advisers and inspectors to be employed.

Comprehensive school dilemmas

The expansion of special education cannot be understood without reference to developments and changes in the whole education system, particularly changes since the establishment of state comprehensive education during the 1970s. A common school, underpinned by egalitarian ideologies and attended by middle and working class children, was envisaged by comprehensive supporters, but comprehensive education is now dogged by a series of dilemmas. One dilemma which was slowly realised during the 1970s was that if selection by ability was inadmissible, so was selection by disability or inability. The 100-year-old principle of segregation gave way to notions of integration and comprehensive schools were expected to incorporate many non-conformist and troublesome children who would previously have been candidates for exclusion. Other dilemmas included the promise to offer equality of opportunity, while explaining away unequal outcomes in what Shaw has termed 'our incorrigibly competitive and hierarchical society' (Shaw, 1983, p. 37); the pressure to raise standards and credential more pupils by expanding the examination system while offering a suitable curriculum to the 'less able'; and the pressure to incorporate a subject-orientated traditional grammar school-type curriculum while incorporating secondary modern-type pupils.

Reynolds & Sullivan (1979) have argued that initially comprehensives were left relatively free to develop their own curriculum, pedagogies and forms of control with little outside interference, and one response to dilemmas posed by the 'less able' and the 'unwilling' (pupils with learning and behavioural problems) whose numbers increased after 1973 and the raising of the school-leaving age, was to segregate them internally within the schools. The rapid development of behavioural units for disruptive pupils from 1974 and the development of large remedial departments created an unofficial expansion of special education in secondary schools. This expansion was noted by the Warnock Committee which recommended that 'children previously regarded as disruptive' and 'children who have hitherto been seen as requiring remedial rather than special education' should be deemed candidates for special education (Warnock Report, 1978, p. 47). Thus the unofficial expansion was given official recognition. Up to the beginning of the 1980s there was little evidence that comprehensive schools had solved the dilemma of providing a curriculum for the 'less able' or the 'remedial-special'. Evidence (HMI, 1979; Reid *et al.*, 1981) indicated that most comprehensives preferred streaming, setting and banding to mixed-ability teaching, and their curriculum for the less able was narrow and inappropriate. Given the pressures to concentrate on the able and the examinable, this is perhaps not surprising.

The incursion of the new vocationalism and MSC activities into secondary schooling and the blurring of the education-training divide has created more dilemmas for comprehensive schools—one of which is how far 'special needs' pupils will be incorporated into technical and vocational courses, or how far they will be offered watered-down palliatives of 'work experience' and 'social and life skills'.

The disappearing youth labour market

While the comprehensive school curriculum has increasingly become a matter for pressures from political and economic interest groups outside school, a major focus has been on the curriculum for the 'less able'. The DES 14–16 'lower attaining pupils programme', for example, is a direct but little publicised political incursion into this curriculum. DES criticism of the inappropriate curriculum offered to the less able up to the early 1980s was largely a criticism of the apparent slowness of schools to realise the social and political consequences of the disappearance of the youth labour market for less able and special leavers. The pupils to whom the DES and other vocational and educational programmes for the less able are aimed are those who, up the mid-1970s, could be minimally motivated to learn and behave at school by means of the carrot of possible employment. Programmes designed for the less able and special adolescents are part of a political response to the problem of dealing with larger numbers of young people who, despite new vocational initiatives, will probably never acquire employment. The expansion of special education to embrace larger numbers of young people, particularly at post-16 level, may provide both a rationale and a justification for the subsequent economic position of this group.

I suggested in 1982 that 'to have received a special education—with its historical stigmatic connotations, even a non-recorded special education in an integrated setting, may be regarded unfavourably by potential employers' (Tomlinson, 1982, p. 177). However, this kind of assertion now needs much more careful elaboration. The role of special education in preparing large numbers of young people for a workless future or at least one of sporadic, low-skilled employment needs research and analysis.

Any discussion of the relationship between the expansion of special education and the economic situation must start from the premise that to have 'special needs' is not an individual characteristic; it is the product of interaction between individuals and their social environment. It has been an underlying theme of this article that special education expands, not because of intrinsic qualities or lack of qualities in pupils, but because of the social or educational criteria currently being applied. *Similarly, whether or not the handicapped or the special find employment depends on the current economic conditions rather than on the possession of suitable abilities or skills.* Thus, while the economy was in need of low-skilled labour, the majority of special school leavers found employment, even though their mental or physical capacities were judged to be low. It has been an enduring characteristic of the 'handicapped' (as Barnett (1984) has recently elaborated in an interesting discussion of the economics of mental retardation) that they have often been considered retarded or problematic at school, but not outside school, particularly in employment. In Britain one careers officer wrote in 1974 that in his experience 'the majority of special school leavers found jobs with comparative ease ... these included polishing, assembling, building, painting, canteen work and even office work' (City of Birmingham, 1977). A major task of special education has always been to prepare pupils for routine manual work, and some employers came to prefer special school leavers who were often more docile, obedient and punctual than others (see Collman, 1956; Atkinson *et al.*, 1981). By 1975, however, the same careers officer was noting that 'many special school leavers are affected by the recession and those requiring routine or semi-skilled work found most difficulty". In this, of course, special school leavers were joined by the less able and also leavers with school-leaving certificates. In 1974 80,000 under-20-year-olds were unemployed; by 1981 this number was 532,000 (although 360,000 were in government schemes or work experience programmes). The kind of work those who had received a special education formerly undertook has now virtually disappeared, although some low-skilled manufacturing or service jobs may continue to be available for them. Although the question of 'specially educated for what?' can only be answered by empirical investigation of the post-school careers of those leaving special education, an examination of some post-16 college courses for special needs students suggests that for those pupils with severe sensory, physical or mental handicaps traditional supervised provision, usually at Adult Training Centres, is envisaged after they have undertaken college courses to the age of 19 or 21. For those with moderate learning difficulties (as the description now runs) further special courses, including special YTS schemes, transfer to a normal YTS place, or even low-skilled employment is the aim, while for more able but handicapped students transfer to mainstream college courses, YTS or particular kinds of employment is the aim. The courses usually include a large component of 'social and life skills', 'coping and independent living' and 'adult responsibility' as well as college or employer-based introductions to basic manual skills. The expansion of special education may have brought more young people in its orbit but the aims of special education may not have changed too drastically over 100 years. Training for self-sufficiency and controlled social behaviour, and training for low-skilled productive work are traditional aims in special education. The major future difference may be that disappearance of low-skilled work will lead to more and more extensive special courses and more carefully planned supervision for those who will never achieve work. The next expansion of special education will undoubtedly be into 'adult special needs' courses.

The ideology of special needs

To study ideology, as Thompson (1984) has recently pointed out, is to study the ways in which the meaning of particular words or ideas serves to sustain relations of domination. The concept of 'special needs' has become an ideological rationalisation for those who have the power to shape and define the expanding special education system and have vested interests in this expansion. Those who can define the 'needs' of others and give or withold provision have great power, yet the benevolent image with which the notion of 'catering for special needs' has become imbued precludes discussion of the supposed needs, or criticism of provision and practice. This, however, is the purpose of ideology—'ideology is, as it were, the linguistic legislature which defines what is available for public discussion and what is not' (Thompson, 1984, p. 85).

The concept of special needs began to be applied to particular groups of pupils in the 1960s—most notably to ethnic minority pupils whose language and cultural needs were 'special', and to 'disadvantaged pupils'. The liberal child-centred pedagogies of the 1960s focused on children's supposed needs, as did egalitarian programmes to compensate for social disadvantages. The concept was applied to special education in 1965 when a DES report described such education as 'education that is specially well adapted to meet a child's needs'. The Warnock Committee in 1978 adopted the concept both as a rationale for an expanded system of special education ('broader provision', p. 36) and as a more positive description of the clients of special education than description by handicap or disability. While the concept appears to have done the former, all sorts of expansion is now taking place

441

with no further justification than 'the pupil has special needs', the descriptive problem has not been overcome. The child with special educational needs has become the SEN or the SNARC pupil who needs a SNAP!.[6] The extension of the concept to cover 'gifted' pupils, or indeed *all* pupils, has led Mary Warnock to repudiate the use of the concept for those pupils her report had dealt with (*TES*, 12.11.82, 11.11.83).

The whole concept of special needs is ambiguous and tautological. It has become part of a rhetoric that serves little educational purpose. While it does mainly focus on negative psychogenic properties of individual pupils— their difficulty, disability, incapacity or lack of intelligence, it does not provide any mechanism for deciding who has these properties. The current desperate search for improved assessment procedures is an indication that the concept of special needs is no actual help in deciding who the clients of special education should be. At the same time the concept, with its humanitarian overtones, precludes discussion of the needs and interests actually being served by the expansion of special education. Those who find difficulty in moving beyond humanitarian rhetoric, and insist that 'all children have special needs' still have to explain why a whole sub-system of special education has developed and expanded, which is backed by legal enforcement and caters largely for the children of the manual working class. To do this, attention must turn from the psychogenic focus on individual 'needs' to the social interest groupings, the educational, political and economic 'needs' which an expansion of special education is serving. At the present time the ideological obfuscation provided by the focus on the 'child's special needs' prevents an adequate analysis of this expansion.

Notes

1 In 1981 approximately 200,000 pupils were excluded from mainstream education in special schools and classes plus those unofficially counted and excluded in disruptive units. The Warnock Report's suggestion that remedial and disruptive pupils be officially counted as needing special provision—implicitly accepted by the 1981 Act, and that 1 in 5 children may need special provision, brought the number to $1^{1}/_{2}$ million in 1981—a fifth of the (then) 8 million pupils in education.
2 *Special Educational Treatment*, Ministry of Education pamphlet no. 5, 1946, pp. 22–23.
3 In *The Concept of Special Educational Needs* by J. H. Thompson HMCI, paper given to the Conference on Special Educational Needs, Dundee, February 1984.
4 See *Report of the Royal Commission on the Care and Control of the Feeble-minded*, Vol. 1, 1980, HMSO.
5 See, for example, the conflicting evidence offered to the Fish Committee, set up in 1984 to examine segregated special provision in the Inner London Education Authority.
6 Some schools now have Special Educational Needs (SEN) departments, at least one school has a Special Needs and Remedial Children (SNARC) Department and many schools are adopting the Special Needs Action Programme (SNAP) produced in Coventry.

References

ATKINSON, P. *et al.* (1981) Labouring to learn: industrial training for slow learners, in: L. BARTON & S. TOMLINSON (Eds) *Special Education Policies, Practices and Social Issues* (London, Harper & Row).

ARCHER, M. S. (1979) *The Social Origins of Educational Systems* (London, Sage).

BARNETT, W. S. (1984) *The economics of mental retardation, unpublished PhD thesis,* (State University of Utah).

BOOTH, A. (1981) Demystifying integration, in: W. SWANN (Ed.) *The Practice of Special Education* (Milton Keynes, Open University).

COLLMAN, R. P. (1956) *The employment success of ESN pupils, American Journal of Mental Deficiency,* Vol. 60, pp. 247–51.

FISH, J. (1985) *Committee of inquiry into ILEA Special Schools* (London, ILEA).

HMI (1979) *Aspects of Secondary Education: an HMI survey* (London, HMSO).

NATIONAL FOUNDATION FOR EDUCATIONAL RESEARCH (1984) *Lower attaining pupil programme newsletter,* November (Slough, NFER).

PRITCHARD, D. E. (1963) *Education of the Handicapped 1760–1960* (London, RKP).

REID, M. I. *et al.* (1981) *Mixed Ability Teaching: problems and possibilities* (Slough, NFER).

REYNOLDS, D. & SULLIVAN, M. (1979) Bringing school back, in: L. BARTON & R. MEIGHAM *Schools: pupils and deviance* (Driffield, Nafferton).

SHAW, B. (1983) *Comprehensive Schooling; the impossible dream* (Oxford, Blackwell).

SQUIBB, P. (1981) A theoretical, structuralist approach to special education, in: L. BARTON & S. TOMLINSON, *op. cit.*

SWANN, W. (1984) *Statistics of Segregation,* Childright No. 8 (pp. 18–19).

THOMPSON, J. (1984) *Studies in the Theory of Ideology* (London, Polity Press).

TREDGOLD, A. F. (1914) *Text-book of Mental Deficiency,* 2nd edn (Tindall, Balliere & Cox).

TOMLINSON, S. (1982) *A Sociology of Special Education* (Henley, Routledge & Kegan Paul).

WARNOCK REPORT (1978) *Special Educational Needs* (London, HMSO).

WARNOCK, M. (1982) Personal column, *The Times Educational Supplement,* 12.11.82, p. 72.

WARNOCK, M. (1983) Personal column, *The Times Educational Supplement,* 11.11.83, p. 64.

27

EXECUTIVE SUMMARY

President's Commission on
Special Education 2002

Source: *A New Era: Revitalizing Special Education for Children and their Families*, Jessup, MD: Education Publications Center, US Department of Education, 2002, pp. 6–9.

The education of all children, regardless of background or disability . . . must always be a national priority. One of the most important goals of my Administration is to support states and local communities in creating and maintaining a system of public education where no child is left behind. Unfortunately, among those at greatest risk of being left behind are children with disabilities.

— President George W. Bush, Executive Order 13227

On October 2, 2001, President Bush ordered the creation of the President's Commission on Excellence in Special Education. As part of the President's charge to find ways to strengthen America's four decades of commitment to educating children with disabilities, the Commission held 13 hearings and meetings throughout the nation and listened to the concerns and comments from parents, teachers, principals, education officials, and the public.

In this executive summary, we provide the overarching findings illustrated throughout the following pages of the report.

Summary of Findings

Finding 1

IDEA is generally providing basic legal safeguards and access for children with disabilities. However, the current system often places process above results, and bureaucratic compliance above student achievement, excellence, and outcomes. The system is driven by complex regulations,

444

excessive paperwork, and ever-increasing administrative demands at all levels—for the child, the parent, the local education agency, and the state education agency. Too often, imply qualifying for special education becomes an end-point—not a gateway to more effective instruction and strong intervention.

Finding 2

The current system uses an antiquated model that waits for a child to fail, instead of a model based on prevention and intervention. Too little emphasis is put on prevention, early and accurate identification of learning and behavior problems, and aggressive intervention using research-based approaches. This means students with disabilities don't get help early when that help can be most effective. Special education should be for those who do not respond to strong and appropriate instruction and methods provided in general education.

Finding 3

Children placed in special education are general education children first. Despite this basic fact, educators and policy-makers think about the two systems as separate and tally *the cost* of special education as a separate program, not as additional services with resultant add-on expense. In such a system, children with disabilities are often treated, not as children who are members of general education and whose special instructional needs can be met with scientifically based approaches, they are considered separately with unique costs—creating incentives for misidentification and academic isolation—preventing the pooling of all available resources to aid learning. General education and special education share responsibilities for children with disabilities. They are not separable at any level—cost, instruction, or even identification.

Finding 4

When a child fails to make progress in special education, parents don't have adequate options and little recourse. Parents have their child's best interests in mind, but they often do not feel they are empowered when the system fails them.

Finding 5

The culture of compliance has often developed from the pressures of litigation, diverting much energy of the public schools' first mission: educating every child.

445

Finding 6

Many of the current methods of identifying children with disabilities lack validity. As a result, thousands of children are misidentified every year, while many others are not identified early enough or at all.

Finding 7

Children with disabilities require highly qualified teachers. Teachers, parents, and education officials desire better preparation, support, and professional development related to the needs of serving these children. Many educators wish they had better preparation before entering the classroom as well as better tools for identifying needs early and accurately.

Finding 8

Research on special education needs enhanced rigor and the long-term coordination necessary to support the needs of children, educators and parents. In addition, the current system does not always embrace or implement evidence-based practices once established.

Finding 9

The focus on compliance and bureaucratic imperatives in the current system, instead of academic achievement and social outcomes, fails too many children with disabilities. Too few successfully graduate from high school or transition to full employment and post-secondary opportunities, despite provisions in IDEA providing for transition services. Parents want an education system that is results oriented and focused on the child's needs—in school and beyond.

Summary of major recommendations

In response to these findings, the Commission has produced *A New Era: Revitalizing Special Education for Children and Their Families*. This report contains dozens of recommendations addressing each of the Commission's nine major findings and their ramifications.

Overall, federal, state, and local education reform efforts *must* extend to special education classrooms. What we discovered was that the central themes of the *No Child Left Behind Act of 2001* must become the driving force behind IDEA reauthorization. In short, we must insist on high academic standards and excellence, press for accountability for results at all levels, ensure yearly progress, empower and trust parents, support and enhance teacher quality, and encourage educational reforms based on scientifically rigorous research. In addition, we must emphasize identification and assessment methods that prevent disabilities and identify needs early and accurately, as well as implement scientifically based instructional practices.

Three broad recommendations form the foundation of the report.

Major recommendation 1: Focus on results—not on process

IDEA must return to its educational mission: serving the needs of every child. While the law must retain the legal and procedural safeguards necessary to guarantee a "free appropriate public education" to children with disabilities, IDEA will only fulfill its intended purpose if it raises its expectations for students and becomes results-oriented—not driven by process, litigation, regulation, and confrontation. In short, the system must be judged by the opportunities it gives and the outcomes achieved by each child.

Major recommendation 2: Embrace a model of prevention not a model of failure

The current model guiding special education focuses on waiting for a child to fail, not on early intervention to prevent failure. Reforms must move the system toward early identification and swift intervention, using scientifically based instruction and teaching methods. This will require changes in the nation's elementary and secondary schools as well as reforms in teacher preparation, recruitment, and support.

Major recommendation 3: Consider children with disabilities as general education children first

Special education and general education are treated as separate systems, but in fact *share* responsibility for the child with disabilities. In instruction, the systems must work together to provide effective teaching and ensure that those with additional needs benefit from strong teaching and instructional methods that should be offered to a child through general education. Special education should not be treated as a separate cost system, and evaluations of spending must be based on all of the expenditures for the child, including the funds from general education. Funding arrangements should not create an incentive for special education identification or become an option for isolating children with learning and behavior problems. Each special education need must be met using a school's comprehensive resources, not by relegating students to a separately funded program. Flexibility in the use of all educational funds, including those provided through IDEA, is essential.

447

A final challenge

Before signing the *Education for All Handicapped Children Act* of 1975 (since reauthorized as the *Individuals with Disabilities Education Act*), President Ford expressed some concerns about the effect of the law. He worried that it would create new complexities and administrative challenges for public education. But ultimately it was hope and compassion that inspired him to sign the bill into law.

More than a quarter century later, we know that many of President Ford's concerns were realized. But we also know that IDEA has exceeded President Ford's greatest hopes. Children with disabilities are now being served in public schools. And new opportunities abound. This Commission is optimistic that our nation can build on the successes of the past and do even better in meeting the needs of special education children and their families. But we will do so only through a focus on educational achievement and excellence, teacher quality and support, and rigorous research. We will succeed if we work to create a culture of high expectations, accountability, and results that meets the unique needs of every child. Only then can the promise of no child left behind truly be fulfilled.

28

EQUITY INDICATORS BASED ON THE PROVISION OF SUPPLEMENTAL RESOURCES FOR DISABLED AND DISADVANTAGED STUDENTS

Peter Evans

Source: W. Hutmacher, D. Cochrane and N. Bottani (eds), *In Pursuit of Equity in Education: Using International Indicators to Compare Equity Policies*, Dordrecht: Kluwer Academic, 2000, pp. 253–66.

Following the "difference principle" outlined by John Rawls in his *Theory of Justice* (Rawls, 1971), which argues that institutions should be structured with a built-in bias in favor of the disadvantaged, there seems to be little doubt that equity in education should not be based on an equal distribution of resources to all students. Disabled students, for example, need additional resources if they are to access the curriculum on anything like an equal basis with non-disabled students and thus be able to profit, as other students, from "the benefits that education provides opportunities for" (Brighouse, 2000). For instance, deaf students frequently need signing interpretation, which requires an additional assistant in the classroom.

On the other hand, students with severe learning difficulties are unlikely to attain the same outcome levels as non-disabled students no matter how many additional resources are supplied. For this reason, Harry Brighouse (2000) goes on to argue that equity, conceived of as the attainment of equal outcomes for all students, is also undermined by considering the inevitably low educational achievements of severely mentally disabled students. Thus, a simple reduction in inequality in performance cannot be considered an adequate indicator of equity. The focus should more properly be on the degree of inequality that is acceptable.

Such considerations have led to the possibility of considering minimum thresholds of achievement (e.g., Benadusi, Chapter 1) for employability and inclusion into the normal elements of democratic life (Guttman, 1987; Curren, 1995; Demeuse & De Zanet, 1999). Although these threshold conceptions are less demanding than the equality of outcome approach, they still present substantial challenges to most educational systems. Relevant also are Bloom's contentions that an efficient education system should raise mean achievement levels, reduce achievement variance, and decrease the correlation between the student's performance and social background (Bloom, 1976). A full discussion of these issues is beyond the scope of this chapter, but the implications are important for the interpretation of quantitative indicators.

Providing additional resources for disabled students also raises the question of "bottomless pit" funding. It would not be equitable to supply endless resources to students who are most unlikely to ever attain even average levels of achievement at the expense of most other students in the system. Again, this proposition follows Rawls "difference principle:" If the distribution of goods were to be so extreme that this would lead to a general disadvantage, it would be neither fair nor just.

It should be clear that there is philosophical disagreement about how much extra to provide to disabled and disadvantaged students. But there is agreement, among advocates of the two kinds of theory (threshold theory and equality theory), that considerably more resources should be provided to disabled and disadvantaged students than to other students, and for the present this must suffice to inform existing policy. This may be seen at a pragmatic level, where for instance providing additional resources is a central focus of policy-making, in formula funding approaches (Hill & Ross, 1999). Clarity in the philosophical debate would help further to inform decision-making on the resources distribution front, and this would clearly be a goal for the future, but it is a problem that will not be resolved in this chapter, which approaches the issue from a quantitative perspective.

The value of appropriate resourcing levels for improving educational outcomes is also becoming better appreciated. For instance, research in Sweden (Borhagen, 1999) shows that 40 percent of the variance between mean grades can be explained by a resources variable. Cochrane (Chapter 4) also argues that a decrease in class size associated with improved outcomes for students in minority groups is correlated with increased resources. In addition, in the Francophone community of Belgium, government policy has been working towards developing models of resource distribution that will positively discriminate in favor of disadvantaged groups (Demeuse, Crahay & Monseur, Chapter 2). Thus, what is at stake is not the principle but, as suggested above, the extent of the additional resources to be supplied and their distribution among the groups concerned.

As Brighouse (2000) argues:

A full and principled account of educational equality would say something about how much more must be devoted to children with disabilities than to ordinarily-abled children. Even among students without disabilities there is a range of ability levels, such that, assuming that the same level of resources is devoted to each, those in the top ability levels simply have more prospects for the rewards of the labor market than those in the bottom ability levels. So the account must also be able to guide the distribution of resources among more and less able children within the ordinarily-abled group. If the same resources should be devoted, the account needs to explain why, and why such differences do not merit the same response as the differences, between the ordinarily-abled and disabled. If on the other hand, differential resources should be devoted, this needs to be explained.

Two additional points are worth raising. First, the inclusion of disabled students in mainstream schools identifies a further facet of equity. If equity policies should promote educational opportunity for all, and this is seen in terms of access to employment and to involvement in life in general, then education in segregated provision could be inequitable if it prejudiced access to these opportunities. And this is almost certainly the case because of different curricula covered by students in segregated settings, different networks developed, employer prejudice towards the disabled, different experiences of the human condition had by disabled and non-disabled students, etc. Thus, in some countries, such as the United States, the aspiration of full inclusion is driven by a human-rights agenda.

Second, Orfield (Chapter 6) has pointed to the importance of gathering statistical data for informed policy-making. Given the additional costs of educating disabled and disadvantaged students, it is important to ensure that funds are efficiently and effectively spent. Informed policy development is greatly strengthened if appropriate data are readily available. For many countries, in the field discussed in this chapter, this is simply not the case, as OECD (2000) reveals.

In this chapter, data will be presented in a number of key areas relating to the education of these students, in terms of overall resources provided, place of education—i.e., special schools, special classes in regular schools, or regular classes in regular schools—and gender. In the conclusion, some key issues will be identified for further discussion. International comparisons of this type should serve to inform the debate on the balance that should be struck in the appropriate allocation of resources.

A resource-based approach to international comparisons for identifying disabled and disadvantaged students

Earlier work (OECD, 1995) brought together data on students with special educational needs from 21 OECD member countries. It showed clearly that international comparability based on national descriptions of those with special educational needs was severely hampered by different definitions in use among countries of the concept "special education," and in the varying categories through which students with special needs were described and data gathered. For instance, the term "special education" is used in some countries to refer only to those students with disabilities, while in others it covers a much broader range of students including the disadvantaged, ethnic minorities and even gifted students (OECD, 2000). The number of categories used to describe special-needs students also show no pattern. At one extreme, some countries have a non-categorical approach with only one category (e.g., the United Kingdom), while other countries have several categories, such as Switzerland with 19. Furthermore, definitions of categories vary substantially from one country to the next. A summary table is provided in OECD (2000) that reveals clearly the range of definitions and terminology in use. Given the complexity of the picture, a means was needed to provide a coordinating framework, which is described in the next section.

1. Disability, disadvantage and special educational needs

Before introducing the approach taken in this chapter, it is necessary to be absolutely clear about how the issue relating to disabled and disadvantaged students is being approached. Descriptions of *disability* are frequently if not invariably made in terms of factors relating to individuals' impairment; for instance, in terms of sensory, physical or cognitive dysfunction, or all three. These impairments normally imply that a specialized learning environment must be supplied. But whether or not a student has *special educational needs* depends on the extent to which the current educational arrangements can meet those needs as part of the normal provision made for non-disabled students. It follows from this that a student may have a *disability* but not a *special educational need*.

A similar argument can be advanced with regard to the disadvantaged. Definitions of disadvantage are usually couched in terms of essentially non-educational variables such as ethnic status or poverty—factors that cannot be manipulated directly by the education system. Such experiences may indeed lead to students with these backgrounds being in need of a specialized learning environment of some sort, or they may not. Thus, as with disabled students, students from disadvantaged backgrounds may or may not have special educational needs.

What both of these groups have in common is that a special educational need is associated with the requirement to supply additional educational resources in some form or other. They would be intended to help these students access the curriculum; for example, through modifications to teaching materials, extra teachers or different forms of computer hardware and software. In this chapter, the issue is approached in exactly this way. The assay is made on the basis of the additional resources supplied by countries.

Thus, students with special educational needs are those who are in receipt of additional resources so that they can be helped to access the curriculum and benefit as fully as possible from it.

Additional resources are defined as follows:

"Additional resources are those made available over and above the resources generally available for students who have no difficulties in accessing the regular curriculum" (OECD, 1998). Resources may be of many different kinds. They may be *personnel* (e.g., extra teachers), *material* (e.g., specialized teaching materials), or *financial* (e.g., funding formulae that are more favorable to those with disabilities or disadvantages). Financial resources will, of course, include the costs of personnel and materials (OECD, 2000).

Such a definition provides a supply-side approach based on countries' own identification of those perceived to need additional provision to offset or compensate for disadvantage of one sort or another. It allows for the broadest possible numbers of students to be included and is not dependent on idiosyncratic categorical descriptions. Furthermore, such an approach is commensurate with the revised International Standard Certification of Education (ISCED) 97 classification definition of special education (UNESCO, 1997).

2. Cross-national categories A, B and C

While the additional resources supplied provide a practical means of identifying the wider envelope of special-needs students who are receiving additional support, it is at the same time clear that students are included in this definition for different reasons. Students with disabilities and those with disadvantages can have very different types of problems in terms of accessing the curriculum, and the causes of these problems have different roots. Different policies may determine the resources provided for the different groups.

In order not to lose sight of these differences, and their significant policy implications, it then becomes necessary to subdivide those covered under the additional resources definition in a relevant way. It was agreed by member countries of OECD that this could be done in terms of three cross-national categories, named A, B and C.

Category A: Refers to educational needs of students where there is substantial normative agreement—such as in the case of the blind and partially sighted, deaf and partially hearing, severely and profoundly mentally handicapped, and those with multiple handicaps. These are conditions that affect students from all social classes and occupations. Typically, adequate measuring instruments and agreed criteria are available. These are considered in medical terms to be organic disorders attributable to organic pathologies (e.g., related to sensory, motor or neurological defects).

Category B: Refers to educational needs of students who have difficulties in learning that do not appear to be directly or primarily attributable to factors that would lead to categorization as "A" or "C". For instance, students with learning disabilities, as defined in the United States, are classified here.

Category C: Refers to educational needs of students that are considered to arise primarily from socioeconomic, cultural and/or linguistic factors. There is some background factor, generally considered to be a disadvantage, for which education seeks to compensate.

3. Some comparative data

During the work conducted at OECD/CERI, a great deal of data has been gathered in different areas. In consideration of a discussion on equity as described at the outset of this chapter, comparative data will be presented that inform this debate. Thus, information is supplied on the numbers of students identified as receiving additional resources, on gender and on inclusion as indicated by the place in which they are educated, i.e., special schools, special classes in regular schools or regular classes in regular schools.

3.1. *Additional resources made available*

Countries were asked to provide data in terms of the resources definition of special-education needs as described above. The numbers of students they reported as falling within this definition expressed as a percentage of the overall school population in each country are presented in Figure 1 (page 455).

As may be seen from the table, countries vary substantially in the extent to which additional resources are made available. In the United States, 35.5 percent of students receive additional resources in contrast to 0.41 percent in Turkey. The table also shows these data broken down by cross-national categories A, B and C. It reveals substantial differences among countries in the numbers of students in these categories who are receiving additional resources.

It is important to note that these data *per se* do not allow us to conclude that one country's provision is more or less equitable than another's. A great deal more information would be needed to determine this. However, the data do provide a comparative basis for further inquiry.

3.2. *The location of education*

Countries were also asked to report on where special-needs students were educated, whether in special schools, special classes or regular classes. Figures 2, 3, 4 and 5 (pages 456–457) show the data for each of the three cross-national categories separately and for all students added together.

The figures clearly reveal major differences among countries in the place of education for students with special educational needs. It is clear that in

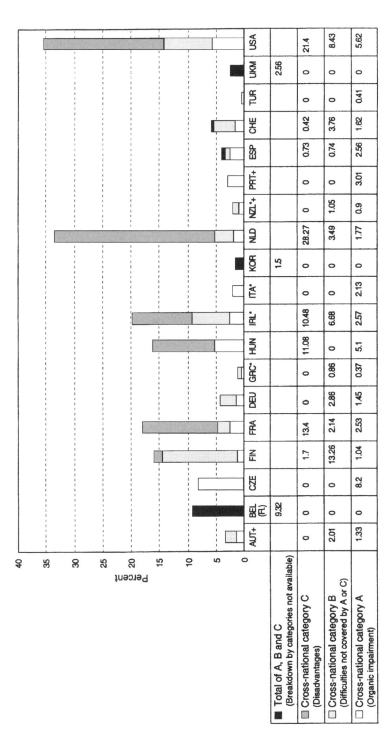

	AUT+	BEL (FL)	CZE	FIN	FRA	DEU	GRC*	HUN	IRL*	ITA*	KOR	NLD	NZL*+	PRT+	ESP	CHE	TUR	UKM	USA
Total of A, B and C (Breakdown by categories not available)		9.32									1.5							2.56	
Cross-national category C (Disadvantages)	0	0	0	1.7	13.4	0	0	11.08	10.48	0	0	28.27	0	0	0.73	0.42	0	0	21.4
Cross-national category B (Difficulties not covered by A or C)	2.01	0	0	13.26	2.14	2.86	0.86	0	6.68	0	0	3.49	1.05	0	0.74	3.76	0	0	8.43
Cross-national category A (Organic impairment)	1.33	0	8.2	1.04	2.53	1.45	0.37	5.1	2.57	2.13	0	1.77	0.9	3.01	2.56	1.62	0.41	0	5.62

Figure 1 Students receiving additional resources to access the curriculum as a percentage of all students in primary and lower secondary education, by cross-national categories (based on head counts, 1996).

Source: Education at a Glance, OECD, 2000.

+Cross national category C not available. Cross category B not available for Portugal.

*Public Institutions only.

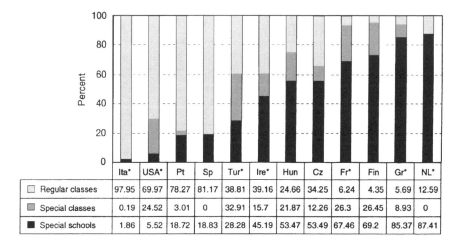

	Ita*	USA*	Pt	Sp	Tur*	Ire*	Hun	Cz	Fr*	Fin	Gr*	NL*
☐ Regular classes	97.95	69.97	78.27	81.17	38.81	39.16	24.66	34.25	6.24	4.35	5.69	12.59
▨ Special classes	0.19	24.52	3.01	0	32.91	15.7	21.87	12.26	26.3	26.45	8.93	0
■ Special schools	1.86	5.52	18.72	18.83	28.28	45.19	53.47	53.49	67.46	69.2	85.37	87.41

Figure 2 Proportions of students in cross-national category A by location.
Source: Education at a Glance, OECD, 2000.
*Greece, Ireland: Public institutions only; Italy: Special classes and regular classes are public institutions only; France, USA: Estimated figures; Turkey: Turkish data refer only to compulsory school period (ISCED1); Netherlands: The data for regular classes are estimated.

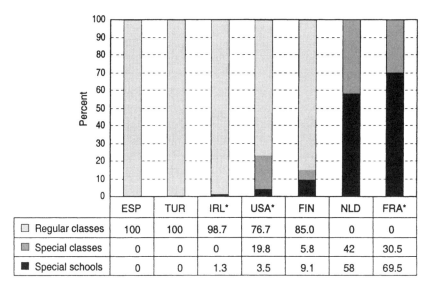

	ESP	TUR	IRL*	USA*	FIN	NLD	FRA*
☐ Regular classes	100	100	98.7	76.7	85.0	0	0
▨ Special classes	0	0	0	19.8	5.8	42	30.5
■ Special schools	0	0	1.3	3.5	9.1	58	69.5

Figure 3 Proportion of students in cross-national category B by location.
Source: Education at a Glance, OECD, 2000.
*Ireland: Schools only; France, USA: Estimated figures.

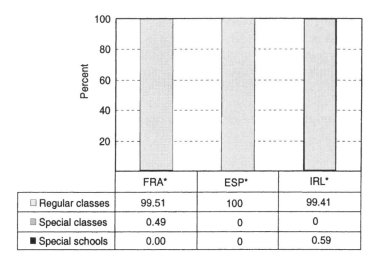

	FRA*	ESP*	IRL*
☐ Regular classes	99.51	100	99.41
▨ Special classes	0.49	0	0
■ Special schools	0.00	0	0.59

Figure 4 Proportion of students in cross-national category C by location.
Source: Education at a Glance, OECD, 2000.
*Ireland: Public institutions only and data on children of refugees in regular classes are missing; France, Ireland, Spain: Data are estimated.

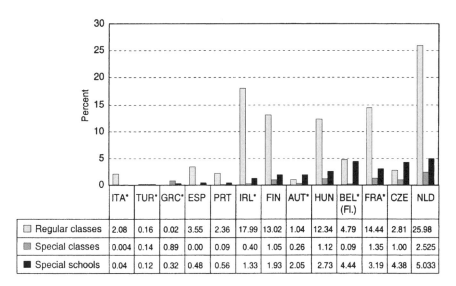

	ITA*	TUR*	GRC*	ESP	PRT	IRL*	FIN	AUT*	HUN	BEL* (Fl.)	FRA*	CZE	NLD
☐ Regular classes	2.08	0.16	0.02	3.55	2.36	17.99	13.02	1.04	12.34	4.79	14.44	2.81	25.98
▨ Special classes	0.004	0.14	0.89	0.00	0.09	0.40	1.05	0.26	1.12	0.09	1.35	1.00	2.525
■ Special schools	0.04	0.12	0.32	0.48	0.56	1.33	1.93	2.05	2.73	4.44	3.19	4.38	5.033

Figure 5 Number of students with special educational needs within resources definition as a percentage of all students in primary and lower secondary education, by location and by country.
Source: Education at a Glance, OECD, 2000.
*Austria: The data in regular classes are estimates; Belgium (Flemish Community): Includes upper secondary students (ISCED3); France: Estimated figures; Greece, Ireland: Public institutions only; Italy: Special classes and regular classes are public institutions only; Turkey: Turkish data refers only to compulsory school period (ISCED1).

cross-national categories A and B, students perceived to need additional resources to access the curriculum might be in special schools in some countries but in regular schools in others. The limited data available for category C students show that the majority of these students are in regular schools.

Again, on their own, these data do not allow the conclusion that segregated education is more or less equitable than inclusive approaches. Further data, for instance on differential availability of opportunities for students in the different settings, would be needed.

3.3. Gender

Countries were also asked to provide breakdowns of data by gender. Figures 6, 7, and 8 (below and page 459) show how gender is distributed in special schools, special classes and regular classes for countries that were able to supply data.

The figures show clearly that in all countries providing data, boys are in the clear majority by a ratio of around 3:2, and by implication as a group are receiving more resources than girls to help them gain access to the curriculum. Such large differences seem unlikely to be wholly due to "natural," randomly distributed biological factors.

Whether these differences are inequitable or not depends on knowledge of other factors. This issue is discussed and interpreted further in the next section.

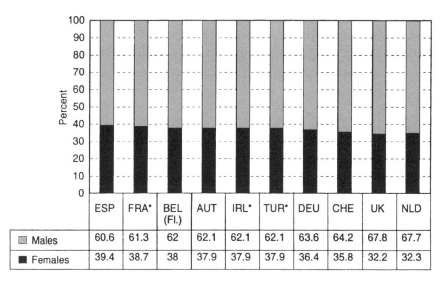

	ESP	FRA*	BEL (Fl.)	AUT	IRL*	TUR*	DEU	CHE	UK	NLD
▨ Males	60.6	61.3	62	62.1	62.1	62.1	63.6	64.2	67.8	67.7
■ Females	39.4	38.7	38	37.9	37.9	37.9	36.4	35.8	32.2	32.3

Figure 6 Gender ratios in special schools.
Source: Education at a Glance, OECD, 2000.
*Ireland: Public institutions only; France: Estimated figures; Turkey: Turkish data refers only to compulsory school period (ISCED1).

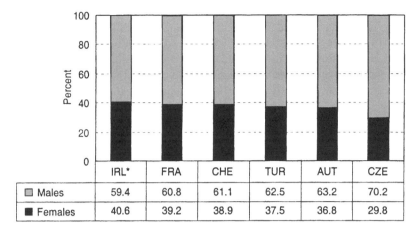

Figure 7 Gender ratios in special classes.
Source: Education at a Glance, OECD, 2000.
*Ireland: Public schools only.

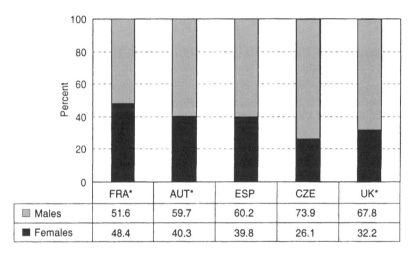

Figure 8 Gender ratios of students with special educational needs in regular classes.
Source: Education at a Glance, OECD, 2000.
*Austria, France, UK: Estimated figures.

4. Discussion

What do these data tell us about issues of equity for disabled and disadvantaged students and provision for their special educational needs? The three indicators will be commented on individually followed by a brief general discussion.

Resources supplied

First, it is clear that in all the countries that provided data, the idea that resources should be distributed equally does not hold. Thus, in general terms, a positive discrimination is practiced in recognition of educational needs. However, there is wide variation among countries (and although the data do not show this, there is regional variation as well) in the extent to which students are given this additional support. This variation raises the question of the adequacy of this additional support. This point touches on the issue of the bottomless-pit question raised by Brighouse (2000) and others on the degree to which substantial additional resources should be given to supplement disabled and disadvantaged students' learning needs. It emphasizes also the importance of quantifying the extent of additional resources being supplied—and ultimately their link with outcomes. The empirical approach adopted in this chapter offers a start in providing such a quantification from which more effective policies, for instance pertaining to the most cost-effective use of resources, could be developed.

Location of education

The location of a student's education raises rather different issues. Here, the provision of additional resources is a given. Thus, the equity argument rests more on whether such provision provides equitable access to the opportunities provided by education. These might be, for instance, to the world of work; to the ability to participate in a democracy; to the possibility of developing friendships; or, more generally, to the avoidance of social exclusion (e.g., Sen, 1999).

As noted above, the data gathered so far cannot address this issue in any direct way, but they do point to the significantly different experiences that students with the same disabilities would receive in different countries. These are quite substantial and likely to lead to different post-school outcomes. Comparative data, collected within the present framework, have not been gathered, so little more may be said conclusively. However, data from individual countries (OECD, 1999) would suggest that segregated settings provide few advantages in many areas of normal life. For instance, students are often educated outside their own communities, thus inhibiting the development of friendship opportunities. Segregation separates the general public from disability; this alone does nothing to reduce prejudice and improve employment opportunities or other social involvement. Access to post-compulsory education may also be hindered, partly because of frequent differences in curricula in special schools. Certainly from this perspective of equity, segregated provision would be viewed as inequitable, additional resources notwithstanding.

Gender

Educational equity for males and females has been a central policy issue in many countries for many years and, at least in terms of access, has been achieved in OECD countries. However, the finding here of a ratio of around 3:2 males to females, for both disabled and disadvantaged groups of students, raises questions of interpretation because it appears that an inequitable situation has arisen where males are provided with more resources than females. Such a situation may arise because of different social and educational expectations of males in contrast to females, or because males or their parents express their dissatisfaction with education in a different and more aggressive way than females.

Following other arguments for positive discrimination for disabled and disadvantaged groups, this unequal distribution would not be inequitable if males were genuinely more in need than females of additional support to access the curriculum and benefit equally from education. There is a hint from Swedish data to support this view (Hard, 1999). This study showed that schools were better at preparing females than males for life in a democracy, covering areas such as willingness to take responsibility, tolerance of minority groups, solidarity with those outside the group and attitude to immigration policy. Thus, if curriculum goals are becoming more accessible to females (at least in part due to changes in content driven by globalization, societal changes and current labor market demands), then additional resources to help males would not be inequitable.

Conclusion

Equity in education can be usefully seen in terms of the way resources are distributed to disadvantaged groups, an approach firmly situated within the theory of justice outlined by Rawls (1971). This supply-side model of equitable provision has the major advantage of being quantifiable, and for this reason can provide a data-based approach to policy development in this field (the significance of which has been discussed by Orfield (Chapter 6), for issues on race and poverty). For instance, it should help to determine whether additional resources are being used efficiently or effectively in segregated school settings in achieving equality of opportunity in access to the labor market. Or, as has been shown, it can provide an additional perspective on the differential resources supplied for males and females. These examples point to the multi-dimensional nature of equity issues and the need for data in making rational decisions for resource distribution that will lead to an equitable education for all.

Comparative approaches have much to offer in this regard. The large range of differences that exist among countries in the way resources are allocated to different disability and disadvantaged groups should help to identify key aspects for policy development for improving equity. However, the paucity of good data in this area is also a considerable barrier, and a major effort to improve data quality is required.

References

Benadusi L. B., "Equity and Education," Chapter 1, this volume, 2000.

Bloom B. S., *Human Characteristics and School Learning*, McGraw-Hill, New York, 1976.

Borhagen K., "Overview of studies from the equity perspective in Swedish child-care, preschool and school," presentation to the OECD/INES ad hoc project on equity, Geneva, 1999.

Brighouse M. H., *School choice and social justice*, Oxford University Press, Oxford, 2000.

Cochrane D. R., "Why Education Matters," Chapter 4, this volume, 2000.

Curren R. R., "Justice and the threshold of educational equality," *Philosophy of education*, 50, pp. 239–248, 1995.

Demeuse M., "La politique de discrimination positive de Commaunauté française de Belgique: une méthode dáttribution des moyens supplémentaires basée sur des indicateurs objectifs," presentation to the OECD/INES ad hoc group on equity in education, Geneva, 1999.

Demeuse M., Crahay M., Monseur C., "Efficiency and Equity," Chapter 2, this volume, 2000.

Demeuse, M., De Zanet, F., *Equity and Efficiency*, Unpublished paper presented at the OECD Ad Hoc Group on Education Equity Indicators, Geneva, 1999.

Guttman A., *Democratic education*, Princeton University Press, Princeton, 1987.

Hard S., *Equity and democracy*, presentation to the OECD/INES ad hoc group on equity in education, Geneva, 1999.

Hill P. W., Ross K. N., "Component 3: Student supplementary educational needs," in Ross K. N., Levacic R. (eds.), *Needs-based resource allocation in education—via formula funding of schools*, IIEP, UNESCO, Paris, 1999.

OECD, *Integrating students with special needs into mainstream schools*, OECD, Paris, 1995.

OECD, *Education at a glance*, OECD, Paris, 2000.

OECD, *Education at a glance*, OECD, Paris, 1998.

OECD, *Inclusive education at work—students with disabilities in mainstream schools*, OECD, Paris, 1999.

OECD, *Special needs education: statistics and indicators*, OECD, Paris, 2000.

Orfield G., "Why Data Collection Matters: The role of race and poverty indicators in American education," Chapter 6, this volume, 2000.

Rawls J., *A Theory of Justice*, Harvard University Press, Cambridge, 1971.

Sen A., *Development as freedom*, Knopf, New York, 1999.

UNESCO, *International standard classification of education*, UNESCO, Paris, 1997.

29

RESTRUCTURING SPECIAL EDUCATION FUNDING IN NEW YORK TO PROMOTE THE OBJECTIVE OF HIGH LEARNING STANDARDS FOR ALL STUDENTS*

Thomas B. Parrish

Source: *Economics of Education Review* 19 (2000): 431–45.

Abstract

New York has given long and careful consideration to the reform of special education funding in the state. The proposal under consideration, as endorsed by the State Department of Education, is based on a count of all students, as opposed to just special education students, and includes a poverty adjustment. This plan appears to support many of New York's special education reform goals, and it aligns with national trends. However, the decision to maintain separate funding systems for special education students with certain disabilities may conflict with the state's goal of educating students with disabilities alongside their nondisabled peers. Also, it is important to realize that achieving high learning standards for students with disabilities will not simply flow from the planned fiscal reforms; it will require careful consideration to ensure that these students are fully included in the state's system of accountability for all students.

1. Introduction

This paper includes two major sections. The first provides a national perspective on special education finance and related reform issues and proposals, with emphasis on those of particular relevance for the state of New York. The second section looks specifically at the current New York funding system as it pertains to students with disabilities and to promoting high learning standards for all students. New York has been considering special education finance reform for some time.

The paper concludes with several observations. First, the proposed state reforms relating to a funding system based on a count of all students—rather than just special education students—and using the proposed poverty adjustment, appears to support many of New York's reform goals. These proposals are also in alignment with national special education reform trends at the federal level and in an increasing number of the states. Second, the decision to maintain separate funding systems for special education students "with excessively high costs in public schools, with disabilities requiring summer programs, and with disabilities educated in approved private special education schools" seems likely to conflict with the state's reform goal of ensuring that students with disabilities are educated with their nondisabled peers to the greatest extent possible. Last, realization of the goal of high learning standards for students with disabilities cannot be expected to simply flow from these fiscal reforms. This objective is likely to be much more difficult to obtain. While the proposed fiscal reforms may foster a more supportive environment for high learning standards, strategies for ensuring that students with disabilities are fully included in the state's system of accountability for all students, thereby benefitting from these high standards, will need to be carefully devised and rigorously implemented if significant gains are to be realized.

2. National context

With the passage of the *Education for All Handicapped Children Act* (P.L. 94-142) in 1975—now called the *Individuals with Disabilities Education Act* or IDEA—programs and related services for students with disabilities have become a major component of public education in the United States. What was previously a patchwork of programs for students with disabilities transformed into a truly national system of services. However, although the federal government has provided, and continues to provide, important leadership in the formulation and interpretation of a national system of special education law, in terms of financial support it remains a junior partner to state and local levels of government.

Lately, there has been a lot of interest in issues related to special education finance. Feature articles have appeared in national publications including *US News and World Report, The New York Times*, and *The Wall Street Journal*. A segment on this topic was featured in a recent edition of television's *60 Minutes*.

There are several reasons for these high levels of interest. First is the estimated national annual expenditure of $32 billion on special education programs and services. Second, and perhaps more important than the absolute magnitude of this expenditure, is the growing number of questions about whether these costs are rising too rapidly and are encroaching upon the resources of the entire public education enterprise.

At the same time, according to the 1996 *Phi Delta Kappa/Gallup Poll of the Public's Attitudes Toward the Public Schools*, 47 percent of adults said that the United States is spending too little of its total education budget on students with special needs (such as physical and mental disabilities), while 41 percent said that about the right amount is being spent. Only 5 percent said that too much is being spent (Elam, Rose & Gallup, 1996).

2.1. How much do we spend and where does the money come from?

While expenditures for special education services in the United States are known to be considerable—one estimate is \$31.8 billion[1]—exact current expenditures are unknown. This is because the states were last required to report these amounts for the 1987–88 school year and the last independent national special education cost study, completed in 1988, was based on data from the 1985–86 school year.

Data from this study showed that, on average, expenditures for students receiving special education services were 2.3 times greater than general education students.

2.1.1. The federal funding system

Federal funding under IDEA has been based on each state's count of children with disabilities who are receiving special education services. No distinction is made for variations in the types of disabilities or patterns of placement of special education children across the states.

However, through the last reauthorization of IDEA, federal special education funding will begin a slow transition to the type of census-based funding system being proposed for New York. The number of school-age children who may be counted for federal funding purposes is limited to 12 percent of the general school-age population. However, a state must provide special education programs and services to all eligible children with disabilities.

2.1.2. State funding systems

The major responsibility for education in the United States lies with the states. All 50 states have special provisions in their funding formulas that acknowledge the excess costs of special education. State special education funding formulas vary from reimbursing a fixed percentage of actual special education expenditures (11 states), to pupil weighting systems (19 states) in which special education students generate a fixed multiple of the general education pupil allocation (e.g., twice as much as is allocated to general education students), to systems that directly fund specified numbers of special education teachers (10 states), to fixed dollar grants per student (10 states). Each is briefly described below.

2.1.2.1. SPECIAL EDUCATION FUNDING BASED ON PERCENT REIMBURSEMENT

Under a percent reimbursement system, the amount of state special education aid a district receives is directly based on its expenditure for this program. Districts may be reimbursed for 100 percent of their program expenditures or for some lesser percentage. Usually there is some basis for determining what costs are allowable, and which are not, under such a system. As with all special education funding systems, there may be overall caps on the number of students any individual district can claim for funding purposes. For example, the district cannot exceed some specified percentage of the statewide average claim per student.

2.1.2.2. SPECIAL EDUCATION FUNDING BASED ON A PUPIL WEIGHTING SYSTEM

Under a weighted special education funding system, of which the current system in New York is an example, state special education aid is allocated on a per student basis. The amount of aid is based on the funding weight associated with each student. For example, in Oregon a single funding weight of 2.0 is applied to all eligible special education students in the state. This means that the amount of state aid for every special education student in a district is twice that received for a general education student in that district. However, most weighting systems differentiate among special education students, with those expected to be at a higher cost to serve receiving a larger weight—and therefore more state aid—than those expected to be served at a lower cost. These weight differentials are based on expected costs because they may not hold true for any one student. However, categories of students with higher funding weights are those who are expected to be, on average, higher cost to serve. Funding weights are differentiated on the basis of placement (as in New York's current system, which will be described in more detail in an upcoming section), disability category (as in Georgia), or some combination of the two (as in New Jersey).

2.1.2.3. SPECIAL EDUCATION FUNDING BASED ON NUMBER OF TEACHERS

Special education funding systems that are based on specific resources generally allocate units of funding based on some determination of the number of staff needed to serve the district's population of special education students. For example, in the case of Missouri, allocations are awarded based on an approved number of teachers, professional staff members other than classroom teachers, and aides.

2.1.2.4. SPECIAL EDUCATION FUNDING BASED ON A FIXED DOLLAR GRANT PER STUDENT

Federal IDEA funding is based on a fixed grant, or fixed amount, per special education student up to a limit of 12 percent of a state's school-age population. Some states also have such a flat grant funding system. For example, in North Carolina the total state funding available for special education is divided by the special education count for the state to determine the amount of state aid to be received by districts per special education student. A newer variation to this approach to special education funding is based on the total number of students in a district, rather than the number of special education students. This is known as a census-based approach, which, as an important basis for the reform proposals in New York, will be discussed at greater length later in this paper.

All of these systems primarily provide funds for the provision of special education services and for the most part are more alike than different. Beyond the state and federal shares of support, the remaining funding for special education programs comes from local district funds (Moore *et al.*, 1988).

2.2. What issues are driving reform of special education funding across the nation?

A recent survey[2] of the states regarding special education finance revealed that 17 states have implemented some type of finance reform in the past 5 years (4 of these states are again considering reform). Twenty-six states are currently considering major changes in their special education funding policies. Table 1 summarizes the finance reform movement by state. Major issues driving these reforms and responses from selected states follow.

2.2.1. Flexibility in placement and use

The degree of flexibility can be affected by the type of funding formula used (column 2) and the basis utilized for allocating funds (column 3). For example, allocations based on type of student placement (e.g., special day class) limit the placement of special education students.

Another important provision relating to flexibility in the use of state special education funds is whether these funds must be spent only on special education students (column 4). These policies can provide more fiscal accountability, but they also reduce local control over program design. Interestingly, while this type of restriction is often presumed to exist, 27 states report that their policies do not require that all special education funds be spent exclusively on special education services.

Table 1 State special education funding systems and reform, 1994–95[a].

State	Current funding formula	Basis of allocation	State special ed. $ for target population only	Implemented reform within last 5 years	Considering major reform
Alabama	Flat grant	Special ed. enrollment	–	–	–
Alaska	Pupil weights	Type of placement			–
Arizona	Pupil weights	Disabling condition			–
Arkansas[b]	Pupil weights	Type of placement	–		–
California	Flat grant	Total district enrollment	–	–	
Colorado	Flat grant	Special ed. enrollment	–	–	–
Connecticut	% reimbursement	Actual expenditures	–		–
Delaware	Resource-based	Classroom unit			
Florida	Pupil weights	Disabling condition			–
Georgia	Pupil weights	Disabling condition	For 90% of funds		–
Hawaii	Pupil weights	Placement and condition			
Idaho	% reimbursement	Actual expenditures	–	–	–
Illinois	Resource-based	Allowable costs		–	–
Indiana	Pupil weights	Disabling condition			
Iowa	Pupil weights	Type of placement			
Kansas	Resource-based	No. of special ed. staff	–	–	–
Kentucky	Pupil weights	Disabling condition		–	
Louisiana	% reimbursement	Actual expenditures	–	–	
Maine	% reimbursement	Allowable costs	–		
Maryland	Flat grant	Special ed. enrollment		–	
Massachusetts	Flat grant	Total district enrollment			
Michigan	% reimbursement	Allowable costs	–		
Minnesota	% reimbursement	Actual expenditures	–		
Mississippi	Resource-based	No. of special ed. staff	–		
Missouri	Resource-based	No. of special ed. staff	–	–	–

State	Funding type	Allocation basis	Notes
Montana	Flat grant	Total district enrollment	—
Nebraska	% reimbursement	Allowable costs	—
Nevada	Resource-based	Classroom unit	—
New Hampshire	Pupil weights	Type of placement	
New Jersey	Pupil weights	Placement and condition	
New Mexico	Pupil weights	Services received	
New York	Pupil weights	Type of placement	—
North Carolina	Flat grant	Special ed. enrollment	—
North Dakota	Flat grant	Total district enrollment	
Ohio	Resource-based	Classroom unit	—
Oklahoma	Pupil weights	Disabling condition	
Oregon	Pupil weights	Special ed. enrollment	—
Pennsylvania	Flat grant	Total district enrollment	—
Rhode Island	% reimbursement	Actual expenditures	—
South Carolina	Pupil weights	Disabling condition	For 85% of funds
South Dakota	% reimbursement	Allowable costs	—
Tennessee	Resource-based	Classroom unit	
Texas	Pupil weights	Type of placement	—
Utah[c]	Pupil weights	Type of placement	—
Vermont[d]	Flat grant	Total district enrollment	—
Virginia	Resource-based	Classroom unit	
Washington	Pupil weights	Special ed. enrollment	—
West Virginia	Flat grant	Special ed. enrollment	—
Wisconsin	% reimbursement	Allowable costs	—
Wyoming	% reimbursement	Actual expenditures	—

[a] Table key. *Pupil weights*: Funding allocated on a per student basis, with the amount(s) based on a multiple of regular education aid. *Resource-based*: Funding based on allocation of specific education resources (e.g., teachers or classroom units). Classroom units are derived from prescribed staff/student ratios by disabling condition or type of placement. *% reimbursement*: Funding based on a percentage of allowable or actual expenditures. *Flat grant*: A fixed funding amount per student or per unit.

[b] Formula also contains a substantial flat grant allocation for selected disabling conditions.

[c] Formula amounts are now frozen and are based on allocations in prior years.

[d] Formula also contains a substantial percent reimbursement component.

2.2.2. Rising special education costs and enrollments

Many, but not all, states are concerned about rising costs and enrollments. Pennsylvania, for example, specifically designed its reform to meet these, as well as other, policy objectives. The two primary objectives of reform were stabilizing special education costs and enrollment, and affecting practice.

2.2.3. Concerns over the efficiency of special education services

Studies have shown that only about 62 percent of the special education dollar is being used to provide direct services to students. As a result, questions are being raised about whether too much is being spent on such support activities as program administration. The Oregon reform represents one state's attempt to cut through some of the program's paperwork requirements, thereby raising program efficiency.

2.2.4. High cost of special education assessment and program administration

The average special education assessment costs $1,206 per student (an estimated $1,648 in 1995–96 dollars), as reported by Moore *et al.* It is used primarily to determine whether a student does or does not qualify for special education services. After a student is placed in special education, teachers often report that their first activity is to reassess the student to determine their instructional needs because expensive eligibility assessments are not useful for this purpose. This raises questions about the usefulness of such assessments for students who are determined to be not eligible for special education services as well as for many students who are deemed eligible.

2.2.5. Strict categorical nature of special education services

Categorical funding refers to dollars allocated for a specific purpose that generally have strict limitations on how they can be used. An important issue in special education finance is how strictly categorical these dollars should remain. For example, as noted by a former Director of Special Education in Florida, "When over one-half of our students qualify for at least one type of special, categorical program, it is no longer clear that it makes sense to refer to them as special".[3]

2.2.6. Fiscal policies that work at cross purposes with special education inclusion policies

Many states are now determining whether their special education funding systems contain disincentives to inclusionary practices. While funding policy should be designed to foster the state's programmatic priorities, the reality is often the opposite. The National Association of State Boards of Education released a strong policy statement, *Winners All: A Call for Inclusive Schools*. It advocates a shift in education policy to foster the development of well integrated services for all students. It argues that the linkages between funding, placement, and disability labels, which have traditionally provided the foundation for special education funding, must be broken.

2.2.7. Summary of national reform issues

Common themes that appear to be driving special education finance reforms nationally are concerns over rising costs, the efficient use of resources, and the relationship between fiscal and program policy. All of these factors, as well as the other issues described above, have led some states and the federal government to consider new approaches to allocating special education funds.

2.3. State and federal reform initiatives

In response to the concerns outlined above, state and federal policymakers have been forging new reform initiatives. Some of these provisions are described below.

2.3.1. Census-based funding

One of the predominant themes in special education finance reform found at the federal level and throughout the states over the past 5 to 10 years is census-based funding. It is the new basis for federal IDEA funding, and it has been adopted in various forms by the states of Vermont, Pennsylvania, Massachusetts, California, Montana, and North Dakota. An understanding of census-based funding is critical to this paper because it constitutes a fundamental component of proposed reforms for New York.

Census-based finance systems are based on total enrollment rather than on special education counts. For example, under a state-level census-based funding system, districts with identical student enrollments receive the same special education aid regardless of the number of students placed in the program, the disabilities of these students, where they are placed, or how they are served.

The rationale for adopting such a system is that the prior, more traditional funding mechanisms may provide fiscal incentives for identifying more students and for designating them in higher reimbursement categories of disability or in higher cost placements. Census-based approaches are often thought to be free of such incentives. However, in reality, incentive-free systems do not exist. For example, while a census-based system may remove incentives for identifying more students for special education and for assigning them to high cost placements, it can be argued that they create new incentives to not identify students for special education and to use lower cost placements. Accordingly, census-based systems have not escaped the controversy that lately appears to be associated with nearly all special education financing alternatives. Some of the pros and cons associated with census-based systems follow.

2.3.1.1. ARGUMENTS SUPPORTING CENSUS-BASED FUNDING

- Working outside special education is less costly. The special education assessment and referral process is costly, and studies show that in many cases the tests and methods for classifying students provide little information useful in planning instructional programs for these students (Ysseldyke, Algozzine, Richey & Graden, 1982).
- Some students may be better served outside special education. Special education programs, as traditionally designed, tend to isolate students in more segregated placements (e.g., pull-out programs or special classes). Labeling students tends to stigmatize them for the remainder of their schooling experiences, and perhaps throughout their lives. Once students are placed in special education, they tend to stay in the program (Shields, Jay, Parrish & Padilla, 1989).
- Overidentification is now the major issue. Before the passage of P.L. 94-142, large segments of the special education population were being underidentified and/or underserved. Now, however, many states are reporting that over- rather than underidentification is their major concern.[4]
- Procedural safeguards would remain in place. Movement to a census-based funding system would not jeopardize any of the procedural safeguards under current law. In addition, all students with disabilities would be protected under Section 504 of the *Americans with Disabilities Act* whether they are labeled as special education or not.

2.3.1.2. ARGUMENTS AGAINST CENSUS-BASED FUNDING

- The system would not be equitable to states and districts with higher identification rates. A census-based funding system assumes comparable prevalence rates of special education students. States and districts might exhibit higher percentages of special education students because of real differences in the characteristics of students (Verstegen, 1991). Even where student populations are comparable, states and districts may have been especially proactive in setting up programs for special needs students, and census-based funding systems penalize those very districts that have been most responsive to the state and federal call to identify and serve all special education students.

472

- Procedural safeguards cannot be maintained if students are not identified as having special needs. Census-based funding would create fiscal incentives to underidentify students with disabilities, abridging their right to a free and appropriate education.
- Fiscal accountability would he jeopardized. Because funds would not be earmarked for the exclusive use of disabled students, a census-based funding system reduces assurances of fiscal accountability at a time when such controls are seen as increasingly important by taxpayers.
- Current levels of special education funding would be threatened. Traditional levels of support for special education services would likely diminish when they can no longer be attributed to specific special education students with legal entitlement.

2.3.1.3. SUMMARY OF CENSUS-BASED ANALYSIS

In reviewing these arguments, it is important to note that they are meant to reflect sentiments often expressed in discussions of the potential merits and demerits of such a system. As such, they do not necessarily reflect the opinion of this author, nor are they necessarily based on fact. Where research is available to support these assertions, citations have been provided.

A full understanding of some of the arguments in favor of, and in opposition to, a census-based funding approach for special education is necessary because it is an issue nationally, and forms an important basis for reform proposals in New York. From a national perspective, in addition to the states that have adopted this approach, the federal Amendments to IDEA, signed into law in June 1997, contained provisions for a gradual conversion to census-based funding.

2.3.2. Adjusting special education funding based on student poverty

In addition to the adoption of a census-based approach, the reauthorized IDEA contains a second important new provision in relation to federal special education funding. Under the new system, federal funding will be adjusted upward in accordance with the percentage of students in poverty in a state. In this way, poverty is used as an alternative to the percentage of students identified for service as an indicator of variation in the need for special education services across the states.

Based on data from CSEF, only three states—Connecticut, Louisiana, and Oregon—currently have some form of poverty adjustment in place within their special education funding formula. However, interest in such an adjustment is receiving added attention across the states with the increased focus on census type funding systems and with the federal inclusion of this type of adjustment. With a poverty adjustment in place, a funding amount is generally determined based on whatever general formula is being used, and then these allocations are further adjusted based on a poverty factor.

Such a factor could take varying forms, but the basic idea is that districts or states with higher percentages of students in poverty receive more special education funds.

As described above, poverty is the adjustment selected for federal Part B funding and that is currently used in one form or another by three states. Poverty variations are also an accepted basis for adjusting special education aid allocations in Great Britain. What are some of the pros and cons most commonly cited for this approach?

2.3.2.1. ARGUMENTS IN FAVOR OF SPECIAL EDUCATION POVERTY ADJUSTMENTS

- Substantial evidence suggests that sustained and intensive poverty results in conditions (e.g., poor health and nutritional care, as well as high levels of drug and alcohol abuse for expectant mothers) that lead to larger proportions of the school-age population needing special education services.
- Although differences in poverty may be an imperfect measure of variations in a district's true need in relation to special education services, it may be the best measure beyond a district's control that is available.
- Although the relationship between student poverty and the need for special education services may be somewhat tenuous, districts with high numbers of students in poverty do need more educational services, and increasing their special education funding is one way to provide it.
- Based on parental reports of disability, prevalence rates climb as personal income declines.
- Other education poverty programs such as federal Title I and state compensatory education would be brought into better alignment with IDEA, appealing to policymakers who call for more integrated approaches across all categorical programs.

2.3.2.2. ARGUMENTS OPPOSED TO SPECIAL EDUCATION POVERTY ADJUSTMENTS

- A special education poverty adjustment brings into question the most appropriate relationship between special education and poverty driven programs such as state compensatory education and the federal Title I program, potentially confusing the unique roles of these programs.
- Data show that minority students, who are more likely to be in poverty, are disproportionately placed in special education. It has been argued that this disproportion is due to the placement of some of these students on the basis of cultural differences rather than disability. Increasing special education funding to high poverty districts may expand these inappropriate placement practices for minority students.
- The inclusion of a poverty factor for special education may accelerate calls for merging this program with Title I or state compensatory

education programs into single block grants to the states or to school districts. Many special educators and parents perceive such a move as a threat to special education.

- The relationship between special education and poverty is unclear. For example, no statistical relationship between the percentage of students in poverty and those in special education is found.

- Current and accurate measures of student poverty at the district level are generally not available across the states. The best national measures are based on census data which are collected every 10 years. Free and reduced lunch counts constitute an alternative, but it is sometimes argued that these data are insufficiently accurate for such purposes.

2.3.2.3. SUMMARY OF POVERTY ADJUSTMENT ANALYSIS

Arguments for and against a poverty adjustment to special education funding present opposite sides of similar themes. For example, while parental reports of disability diminish as family income rises, no relationship between the percentage of students in poverty and those in special education is observed. Some will argue that the first measure showing a positive relationship between disability prevalence and poverty is weak because it is based on parental reports, while others argue that the latter relationship showing no relationship between special education and poverty is not strong because it is based on special education identification rather than prevalence rates. Similarly, while some perceive closer ties between education disability and poverty programs as leading to more coherent education policy, others argue that any attempt to remove the distinctions between these two programs places future special education funding in jeopardy.

2.3.3. Removing fiscal incentives for restrictive placements

A third important issue at the federal and state levels relates to state funding mechanisms that contain incentives for serving special education students in more restrictive settings, which is counter to the least restrictive environment (LRE) provisions of IDEA. For example, some state formulas allow for generous reimbursement to school districts when students are placed in private or regional public settings. However, these formulas do not offer comparable assistance for the establishment of programs in neighborhood schools. In other words, these dollars are not always able to follow students into the less restrictive settings that may be better suited to their education needs. Other states may offer alternative funding levels for placement in specialized settings, but do not include the general education classroom as a placement option. These types of provisions create a disincentive for placing special education students in the least restrictive environment.

The Office of Special Education Programs has initiated challenges to states with such restrictive funding provisions through its monitoring system.

New York was the recipient of one of these challenges. In addition, the reauthorized IDEA requires states to demonstrate that if the state special education funding formula distributes assistance to localities based on the type of setting in which a child is served, the state has policies and procedures to assure that these funding provisions do not result in placements that violate the requirement that children with disabilities be served in the LRE. If such policies are not in place, the state must provide the Secretary with an assurance that it will revise the funding mechanism to ensure that it does not result in restrictive placements.

2.3.4. Change in the federal incidental benefit rule

This change in the reauthorized federal law, relating to the concept of fiscal accountability, also has implications for the placement of special education students in general education classrooms. The prior incidental benefit rule required schools to keep track of how much time special educators spent in regular classes to ensure that IDEA-funded teachers did not provide services to nondisabled students. Through the reauthorized law, special educators are permitted to provide incidental benefits to nondisabled students when serving disabled students according to their Individualized Education Programs (IEPs). The previous rule tended to provide a disincentive for serving students with and without disabilities together in general classroom settings, as would be expected in a truly integrated setting.

2.3.5. Blended funding and service provision

A critical question that confronts the development of future fiscal policy in special education is whether funding should retain its purely categorical nature. There is a natural tension between separate, highly categorical funding streams and overall education reform objectives favoring more unified schooling systems (McLaughlin & Warren, 1992). In such systems, the strict barriers between categorical programs begin to disappear and are replaced by a more seamless set of educational programs and services designed to meet the special needs of all students.

2.4. Looking to the future from a national perspective

The special education population has consistently grown at a faster rate than the general education population. Combine this with the prediction that the general education population will grow by over 10 percent during the next 10 years, and the estimate that special education expenditures per student have been growing at a faster rate than general education expenditures, and it is not hard to imagine considerable strain on special education budgets over the next decade.

At the same time that the need for future programs and services is predicted to escalate appreciably, the demand for services already may be outstripping availability in some states. In addition, with the new emphasis on fiscal constraint at the state and federal levels of government, it is difficult to imagine considerable new growth in special education support. (Despite reasonably substantial new growth in special education funding at the federal level through IDEA, this still constitutes only about 8 to 9 percent of total special education spending.) This suggests a continued restructuring of current programs in an effort to achieve greater efficiency (National Governors' Association and National Association of State Budget Officers, 1994).

These trends suggest a crossroad in special education policy. Current state interest in restructuring education is likely to continue to build, and will focus on efforts to increase the effectiveness of, as well as to contain expenditures on, programs for children with disabilities (themes which are featured in reform proposals for New York). If services are restructured, choices must be made about what changes should occur and which programs and services will be affected.

However, the current period of fiscal stress also presents opportunities. Several states are using this opportunity to look more closely at the effectiveness of programs and services with an eye towards pruning the least efficient while restructuring existing services for greater effectiveness. For example, some states, including New York, are examining the high cost of uniformly providing special education assessments to students with learning problems prior to the provision of support services. The challenge will be to balance the diverse education needs and rights of all students against limited financial resources.

3. Special education funding in New York

Many of the national trends discussed in the previous section are mirrored in New York and in the state's proposed policy interventions. This section of the paper deals specifically with current and proposed special education policy in New York. How does the state's current special education funding system fit into the larger picture of how we fund special education as a nation? In addition, the state has been pursuing special education finance reform over the past several years. How do these reform efforts correspond to the broader range of special education finance reform issues that have been described for the nation? The purpose of this section is to discuss the proposed restructuring of special education funding in New York to promote the objective of high learning standards for all students. Primarily, it will describe and discuss current special education funding provisions in the state, as well as the proposed alternatives. To fully address the topic of restructuring special education funding in New York to promote the objective of high learning standards for all students, however, requires a secondary emphasis on what these learning standards are, how they are to be measured, who is to be included or excluded, how they are reported, and how districts are to be held accountable.

3.1. The current system

3.1.1. Special education funding

As shown in Table 1, New York's base special education funding system falls into the category of a weighted pupil system based on student placement. As described in a recent state publication on aids and entitlements for schools, this system features two basic weights. These differential weights are for students in the following categories of funding:

- funding weight of 1.7 for students who have been determined to require placement for 60 percent or more of the school day in a special class;
- funding weight of 0.9 for students who have been determined to require placement for at least 20 but less than 60 percent of the school day, or who require direct or indirect consultant teacher services at least 2 hours per week.

The funding associated with this formula is wealth adjusted such that the state's share of funding is 49 percent for the district of average wealth, with poorer districts receiving a greater share and richer districts a lesser share.

As described above, a general concern associated with funding systems in which allocations vary according to student placement is that they may provide fiscal incentives for more restrictive placements. For example, the state's current system allocates nearly twice as much in supplemental funding (weight of 1.7) for students who spend the majority of their day in separate special education classes in relation to special education students spending less time in special settings (weight of 0.9). Such formulas are increasingly being considered as too prescriptive in regard to how services will be provided and to create a fiscal disincentive for full compliance with the LRE provisions of IDEA.

In New York, it has been pointed out that these placement weights are not necessarily restrictive. For example, a spokesperson for the New York State United Teachers (NYSUT) reports that in addition to spending up to 60 percent of the day in a special education class, a student may also generate this higher funding weight through the provision of special education services in a general education class for up to 60 percent of the school day (e.g., through the provision of a one-on-one aide). However, this respondent also concedes that this is unusual, and that the NYSUT is working with the Department of Education regarding the appropriate method of writing IEPs to ensure that students receiving special education services in general education classrooms generate appropriate funding weights. While the current New York system may not necessitate more restrictive placements to obtain higher levels of funding, given the wording currently associated with these weights, it may bolster old habits at the local level favoring more restrictive placement models.

While there is debate about the incentives in the current system and the extent to which they actually govern placement decisions, statistics regarding student placement comparing New York to the nation show placements to be comparatively restrictive in the state. According to a recent internal State Education Department document on special education reform, during the 1995–96 school year 34.5 percent of school-age students with disabilities spent more than 60 percent of their day in separate classrooms as compared to the 1993–94 national average of 22.7 percent. This same publication further contends that the current system "provides a fiscal incentive to place students in restrictive environments".

This type of funding system and the resulting patterns of student placement, which appear to be substantially more restrictive than the national average, also raise questions as to whether the current state funding system will be likely to be found in violation of new federal provisions under the reauthorized IDEA. As described above, states are required to demonstrate that if the state special education funding formula distributes assistance to localities based on the type of setting in which a child is served (as is true for New York's current system), the state has policies and procedures to assure that these funding provisions do not result in placements that violate the requirement that children with disabilities be served in the LRE. If such policies are not in place, the state must provide the Secretary with an assurance that it will revise the funding mechanism to ensure that it does not result in restrictive placements. Given the state's placement data in relation to the nation, it may be difficult for the state to establish that these funding provisions do not result in more restrictive placements, thus seemingly necessitating revision to the current mechanism if the state is to continue to participate in this federal program and to retain eligibility for federal special education aid.

3.1.2. Special education funding for students with severe disabilities

Beyond the basic formula, however, a second special education funding mechanism is in place for students with severe disabilities. Under separate formulas, these students may qualify for public excess cost aid or for private excess cost aid. A special education student generates aid under the public excess cost formula when special education costs exceed the lesser of $10,000 or four times the approved operating expense per pupil. Private excess cost aid is available to districts with special education students enrolled in approved private schools and state schools (e.g., the New York State School for the Blind). The private excess cost contribution is based on the cost remaining after a required local district contribution is deducted from the approved tuition.

Separate funding formulas of this type for low incidence, more severe students often are equally, if not more, problematic than the base funding formulas in their propensity to create fiscal incentives for the placement of students with disabilities in more restrictive placements. Rather than a single funding system for students with disabilities, which generates funding for students based on their relative need for supplemental services or on some other basis, funding systems based on student placement, and particularly multiple funding systems based on varying categories of placement, tend to be especially problematic in relation to the LRE requirement of IDEA. That this appears to be true of the New York formula is evidenced by data showing that 10.7 percent of the special education students in the state are served in separate settings (e.g., approved schools for students with disabilities) as compared to the national average of 4.4 percent of special education students in such placements.

3.1.3. Other features of the current state funding system

A unique feature of the current system is the category of available funding known as Declassification Support Services Aid. This aid is intended to help defray the cost of providing additional pupil support for the first year in which a pupil moves from a special education program to a full-time general education program. This category of aid may be designed to somewhat mitigate the fiscal disincentives of moving children out of special education. A state and national problem is that once students are categorized as special education they most commonly are never declassified throughout their public school years. For example, in New York, only 5.8 percent of students with disabilities were declassified during the 1995–96 school year. However, as the amount of aid received under this category is based on the total number of children in the program rather than on the number of students declassified, it is not clear how effective these provisions to remove the disincentives for declassification are likely to be.

Another characteristic of the current state special education funding system is that funding is based on the number of students identified as special education. Although this does not set it apart from the vast majority of other state special education funding systems, it is a major point of distinction in contrast with the Regent's and Governor's reform proposals, which are largely based on total, rather than special education, enrollments. While it is perfectly reasonable on the one hand to have total special education aid based on the number of special education students served, as pointed out by the Regent's reform document and others, such systems provide a disincentive for attempting to build a supportive general education environment

480

which reduces the need for referrals to special education. Under special education head count funding systems, such school districts are likely to have their state aid reduced. Thus, one important argument often cited in favor of census- or total enrollment-based funding systems is that they create fiscal incentives for serving students with mild special learning needs within the general education system. Evidence of the need for incentives to retain students within the state's general education system is found in a rapidly increasing statewide special education identification rate that has risen from 9.9 percent in 1992–93 to 11.1 percent in 1995–96.

3.1.4. High learning standards for students with disabilities

Statistics cited in the Department's publication on strategies for implementing special education reform suggest that high learning standards for students with disabilities are not currently uniformly in place. Students with disabilities were more likely to drop out of school than their nondisabled peers, and of those who completed school, only 4.4 percent received a Regent's diploma compared to 40 percent of all public high school graduates. This publication further describes a phenomenon whereby students with special needs show substantial declines in math as they progress through school.

Furthermore, state policies for excluding students with disabilities from statewide tests seem somewhat unclear. Although a Department spokesperson reported relatively few testing exemptions across the state, with an average participation rate of 91 to 92 percent of students with disabilities, it seems that the policies for allowing for such exclusions are largely determined by local authorities. The 8 to 9 percent of the special education students currently being excluded from the state's assessment system is likely to include many students with disabilities, raising questions about the extent to which these students are fully included in the current system for measuring progress toward the state's learning standards.

3.2. The proposed system

The state has been seriously considering special education finance reform over at least the past half dozen years. A number of alternative approaches to reform have been considered and current separate proposals for reform are being circulated for public consideration by the Regents and by the governor.

3.2.1. Special education reform goals

The basic reform goals associated with these changes in fiscal policy have remained fairly constant and are well specified. As listed in the Department publication on Special Education Reform, they are:

1   Eliminate unnecessary referrals to special education.
2   Assure that students unnecessarily placed, or who no longer need special education services, are returned to a supportive general education environment.
3   Hold special education services to high standards of accountability to improve results for all students with disabilities.
4   Assure that students with disabilities are educated in settings with their nondisabled peers to the greatest extent possible.
5   Provide mechanisms for school districts to develop support and prevention services.
6   Assure that school personnel and families have the knowledge and skills which will enable them to effectively assist students with disabilities in attaining high standards.

The importance of a comprehensive and clearly articulated set of reform goals, as listed above, must be noted. A CSEF publication, *The Politics of Special Education Finance Reform in Three States* (Parrish & Montgomery, 1995), reports on three states—Oregon, Pennsylvania, and Vermont—that had been successful in their reform efforts. It concludes from these states' experiences the importance of tying fiscal reform to a larger set of program reforms and the need for clearly stated reform objectives.

Clearly stated reform objectives are critical to forming linkages between fiscal and program policy objectives. Careful examination of all of the fiscal policy and funding mechanism alternatives presented in the first section of this paper will reveal that they all contain incentives for one type of program practice over another. For example, pure census-based funding systems are said to be incentive-free because overall special education funding is unaffected by the number of students identified for special education or where they are placed for service. However, it can be argued that such policies create fiscal incentives to not identify students for special education and to place them in lower cost settings. Given the fact that there is no such thing as an incentive-free formula, if fiscal and program policy are to be aligned, it is essential to clearly identify program goals prior to attempting to design the state's fiscal policy mechanisms.

New York has clearly stated its goals for reform, as listed above. What funding mechanisms have they designed to complement these reform goals and to what extent do they do so?

3.2.2. Special education finance reform strategies

The state's special education finance reform proposals are closely aligned with the recently enacted revisions to federal law under IDEA. This was true in many respects prior to the federal reauthorization, and the

482

revisions contained in the latest proposals from the Regents make this even more true. Both are predicated on a full census count of students, rather than counts of special education students, both contain adjustment factors favoring higher poverty jurisdictions, and both feature a gradual phase-in period.

The Regents 1998–99 Special Education Finance Reform Proposal features the following strategies:

1   A 100 percent increase in funding for support services and other alternatives for students experiencing learning difficulties.
2   A phased-in approach to basing special education aid on the bases of district enrollment and district poverty.
3   Dramatic investment in general education support and prevention services in 1998–99 and continued increases in subsequent years.
4   Continuance of current laws for students with disabilities with excessively high costs in public schools, students with disabilities requiring summer programs, and students with disabilities educated in approved private special education schools.
5   Current year funding to provide additional state aid to school districts with newly enrolled high cost students with disabilities.
6   An evaluation to determine the effects of the new public excess cost formula and to ensure that the private excess cost requirements are consistent with federal least restrictive environment requirements.
7   A statewide training effort to provide special educators with the skills to educate students with disabilities in the least restrictive environment.

3.2.3. Alignment of proposed funding provisions and reform goals

For the most part, these provisions align well with the specified reform goals. Strengthened prevention and support services (strategy 1), accompanied with proper training (strategy 7), should assist in eliminating unnecessary referrals to special education (goal 1). Although strategies 1 and 3, which call for increased investments in support and prevention services outside of education, appear to be largely the same, these additional funds should assist in assuring that special education students are returned to a supportive general education environment (goal 2) and should provide the desired mechanisms for support and prevention services (goal 6). Breaking the current link between placement and funding, as represented in the current student weighting formula (strategy 2) and the implementation of a statewide training effort to provide the skills needed to educate students with disabilities in the least restrictive environment (strategy 7), should support the objective of having students with disabilities educated in settings with their nondisabled peers to the greatest extent possible (goal 4).

3.2.4. Gaps in alignment

Where are the possible gaps between the specified goals and the proposed fiscal provisions? Primarily they appear to exist in two areas. First, and perhaps most important from the perspective of high learning standards for all students, is the lack of any clear connection between these funding proposals and the reform goal of high standards of accountability for results for all students with disabilities (goal 3). Second, the proposal to continue current laws as they pertain to private excess costs (strategy 4), may in many instances directly contradict the reform objective of educating students in settings with their nondisabled peers to the greatest extent possible (goal 4). The proposal to implement an evaluation of the effects of retaining these provisions in compliance with federal least restrictive environment provisions (strategy 6) may be the state's way of attempting to balance the tension between finance reform proposal strategy 4 and reform goal 4.

3.2.5. The need to remove fiscal incentives for restrictive placements

As described above, separate funding systems for "students with disabilities with excessively high costs in approved private special education schools" appears to pose a threat to the goal of "assuring that students with disabilities are educated in settings with their nondisabled peers to the greatest extent possible". The proposed evaluation of this issue (strategy 6 above) is very likely to find that this is the case. Furthermore the retention of this dual system seems a likely target for future federal monitoring.

The problem is not the existence of a continuum of placements for students with disabilities, including separate public and private schools. However, incentives that favor placement in such systems, from a fiscal perspective, is a problem that may be found to conflict with federal law under IDEA, especially in its reauthorized form. The fundamental question that the state needs to address is that if a local school district finds that the most appropriate future placement of a student currently being served in a separate public or private facility is to return to local placement, will the local share of costs for this student rise? That is, would the state's current level of support for the child remain unchanged in the current year, and over time, if this level of funding is needed to appropriately serve the child in a local setting? Thus, while a continuum of placements is required by federal law, the state's funding mechanism should not favor more restrictive placements. Placement decisions along the continuum of services must be based on the needs of the child, and available state funding for these services should be unaffected by these placement decisions. In the case of the state's excess cost formulas, the state will need to justify separate formulas for public versus private placements. State Department officials argue that the public excess cost formula is not restrictive because students can be served in any public

484

placement—for example, in a fully supported inclusionary setting. However, as private settings are more restrictive, if the private excess cost formula provides more generous support than the public excess cost formula, it would appear to be out of compliance with federal law.

3.2.6. *Accountability for results for all students with disabilities*

The first indication of a possible problem with this goal is in the way it is stated by the Department, "Hold special education to high standards of accountability for results for all students with disabilities". This type of statement may suggest a problem of perspective. Many reform advocates will argue that it is important to move away from the suggestion that special education is uniquely, or solely, responsible for the accountability of special education students. They emphasize the importance of, and need for, educating students with disabilities with their nondisabled peers (goat 4, stated above). To encourage the inclusion of students with disabilities into mainstream education programs means instruction geared to the same high learning standards that are being applied to all children. First of all, children with disabilities are students, and as such are the primary responsibility of general education, which must be held fully accountable for their learning performance.

Although it is believed, and a spokesperson for the Department describes, that it is a goal of the state to fully include special education students in the implementation of general education learning standards and accountability provisions, some of the particulars for achieving this important set of objectives may still be lacking.

For example, in emphasizing that the New York learning standards will indeed be intended for all, a Department spokesperson said that the goal will be for all students, including those with disabilities, to participate in challenging course work in support of these standards. It was reported that the Competency Examination that is currently taken by many students with disabilities will gradually be phased out and replaced by the Regents Examination. However, these objectives for fully including students with disabilities in the state assessment system may result in more questions than answers; for example, "Once we raise the bar, what will be the full impact on students with disabilities?" An NYSUT spokesperson comments that "the proposed change in high school graduation standards contains a phase-in over several years (unspecified) for reporting the scores of most, if not all, disabled students. (School districts do not know this yet, so they are still excluding students from testing or providing unnecessary testing accommodations.)"

These are difficult issues, and other states are undergoing similar struggles to arrive at answers. As described by Erickson (1997), "educational accountability asks the multifaceted question, 'Who must answer to whom, for what, and with what consequences?'" It is essential that the state deal with the concept of educational accountability at the level of detail that will be needed to truly make a difference for students with disabilities.

In addition, without concerted efforts to avoid it, raising of the bar may further swell special education rolls, disenfranchising even more students from the high education standards that the state hopes to achieve for all. As noted by Allington & McGill-Franzen (1992) in reference to New York, it is often found that the greater the emphasis on high stakes accountability systems, the more likely that students with disabilities will be excluded from participation.

The NYSUT spokesperson concurs that "New York State's policies for excluding students from statewide tests seem unclear". School districts are required to publicly report the scores of all students except those excluded from the assessment system. Excluding a student can artificially raise the overall performance of a school, and in the age of public reporting, exclusion represents a needed, but unethical way to accomplish this goal. Without uniform rules for clearly defining and limiting exclusion, comparisons among districts become increasingly suspect (Zlatos, 1994). As noted by Erickson:

> . . . the implications for students with disabilities appear even more serious: they face the prospect of lessened expectations and fewer opportunities to reach higher levels of performance. For results-based accountability systems, the maxim "out of sight, out of mind" has the ring of truth.
>
> (Erickson, 1997)

New York is not alone in its need to deal with this problem. McGrew, Thurlow, Shriner and Spiegel (1992) found between 40 and 50 percent of students with disabilities being excluded from nationwide assessment efforts. Furthermore, in a followup study, Stancavage, McLaughlin, Vergun, Godlewski and Allen (1996) found that 70 percent of the students excluded from the Trial State Assessment of fourth grade reading could have been tested. At the state level, Erickson, Thurlow and McGrew (1995) found that state special education directors could estimate participation rates for special education students in less than 37 percent of the 133 statewide assessments in use across the states. In an attempt to rectify this situation, the states of Kentucky and Maryland now disallow the outright exclusion of students from assessments without clear justification, and require districts to publicly report their assessment exemption rates.

At the federal level, new legislation is increasingly holding schools accountable for the results of all children. For example, *Goals 2000* and the *Improving America's Schools* both require the inclusion of students with disabilities in related assessments. Similarly, the reauthorized IDEA requires states and districts to include students with disabilities in all large-scale assessment programs.

However, in New York, there are indications that students with disabilities have not been fully considered in the overall push to implement high standards for all students. For example, at least in the executive summary, the final report of the New York State Equity Study Group for Elementary, Middle, and Secondary Education makes relatively little mention of students with disabilities despite their charge to consider alternative forms of outcome equity for all students (The Equity Study Group, 1993). Rather than students with disabilities, the focus is almost exclusively on the special challenges facing students in poverty. However, issues relating to concerns about children being left behind and forgotten are likely to pertain in similar ways to the two populations.

It is also telling that a State Department publication, *Update on New York State's Overall Strategy for Raising Standards* (New York State Education Department, 1997b, April) contains little mention of students with disabilities. In at least one mailing of this publication, it is preceded by an attachment titled, *Special Education*, also dated April (New York State Education Department, 1997a). This attachment also says very little about the degree to which, or in what ways, students with disabilities will be included under the state's new system for raising standards other than to raise the question if there might be ways to make accommodations.

Further cause for concern is found in the Department's draft publication, *New York State School Report Card for Example School in Example School District* (February, 1998). Although the proposed report cards are to be commended in that they contain a new section that reports the performance of students with disabilities, it appears that the scores of such students still will be kept separate from their regular education counterparts, and most of the examples show more students being exempted than being given the test.

The State Department clearly expresses resolve around this issue. The Deputy Commissioner for Special Education describes the improvement of student results as the "cornerstone of New York State educational reform efforts". A number of ambitious goals have been set for students with disabilities, for example, considerable expansion of participation in the Regents examinations for graduation. This is laudable, but if these goals are to be realized, students with disabilities will need to be fully exposed to the state curriculum and included in the state assessment system from the beginning of their school years. All students with disabilities must participate in the state assessment system with modifications and adaptations when appropriate, or for a small number of children (e.g., 2 percent) through some form of alternative system. Results for students with disabilities should be reported separately by school, to allow comparative assessment of students as a group, and also be included in the overall scores reported for schools and the district, to ensure that they are fully incorporated into the overall accountability system.

487

4. Conclusion

While fiscal policies that conflict with reform goals can hinder program reform, it is important to recognize that changes in fiscal policy alone are insufficient to result in substantial program change. In New York, fiscal reform can support more inclusive placements and heightened learning standards for students with disabilities, but are likely to be insufficient alone to lead to the realization of these goals, States reporting the most success in coordinating program and fiscal reform emphasize the need for financial incentives, or at least the removal of disincentives, within the context of larger systemic reform.

Within the context of systemic reform, there has been clear recognition of the limitations of traditional accountability mechanisms. Especially in the categorical program areas, accountability checks have been more concerned with the legal use of funds than whether they are being used well. Monitoring based on procedure, rather than student performance, is only likely to be de-emphasized when accountability systems are devised and implemented that can clearly measure the extent to which the children for whom these dollars are intended are making clear and sufficient educational progress. The development of such results-based accountability systems may be among the most critical components in the design of future special education finance policy.

The special education finance reforms proposed for New York will provide more resources, and more flexibility in their use, for most of the state's school districts. In one respect this should assist students with disabilities to be more fully included in the state program for achieving high learning standards for all students. However, the proposal to maintain separate funding systems for certain students with more severe disabilities may work against this inclusion, especially in the case of fiscal incentives for private placements. In addition, until specific and clear provisions for the inclusion of all students with disabilities in the state assessment system are fully in place, these funding reforms alone are not likely to be sufficient to realize the goal of high learning standards for *all* students.

Acknowledgements

This research has received support from the New York State Department of Education. However, the data presented, statements made and views expressed do not necessarily represent the New York State Board of Regents.

Notes

* New York State has recently enacted a new special education funding formula, somewhat different from the census-based approach outlined in this article. Instead, New York has made major modifications to its long-standing formula—a student

weighting system based on placement. However, the new formula includes several innovations including a fiscal incentive for providing intensive services to students with disabilities within the general education classroom. The new formula also provides for preferral interventions and supports to students, provisions to ensure that students with disabilities are involved in the general education curriculum, and requirements for districts with disproportionate placements in special education based on race and ethnicity to take correction action. The new provisions will stay in place through the 2001–02 school year, at which time their impact will be evaluated and used to determine further modifications to the formula beyond 2001–02.

1 This estimate is based on a projection of $265 billion in current expenditures for K-12 public education for the 1995–96 school year (Gerald & Hussar, 1995) and a 12 percent allocation to special education programs (Moore, Strang, Schwartz & Braddock, 1988).
2 Survey done by the Center for Special Education Finance (CSEF), at the American Institutes for Research, Palo Alto, CA.
3 Address given to Florida Futures Conference held in Tampa, FL, September 16–17, 1994. Note that this reference to special, categorical programs extends beyond special education to include such programs as compensatory (poverty), limited-English proficient, and gifted education.
4 This contention is supported by an overall 29.9 percent increase in the number of children served in IDEA, Part B, and Chapter 1 Handicapped programs since the inception of Part B in 1976 through the 1990–91 school year. The 1990–91 school year showed an increase of 2.8 percent, which is the largest increase in a decade. However, the larger increase in this year is primarily due to the additional availability of early childhood programs.

References

Allington, R. L., & McGill-Franzen, A. (1992). Unintended effects of educational reform in New York. *Educational Policy*, 6, 397–414.

Elam, S. M., Rose, L. C., & Gallup, A. M. (1996). The 28th Annual Phi Delta Kappa/Gallup Poll of the Public's Attitudes Toward the Public Schools. *Kappan*, 78 (1), 41–59.

The Equity Study Group (1993). *Summary Report of the Equity Study Group: The Road to Outcome Equity*.

Erickson, R. (1997). *Special Education in an Era of School Reform: Accountability, Standards and Assessment*. Washington, DC: Academy for Educational Development.

Erickson, R., Thurlow, M. L., & MeGrew, K. (1995). *1994 State Special Education Outcomes*. Minneapolis, MN: University of Minnesota, National Center on Educational Outcomes.

Gerald, D. E., & Hussar, W. J. (1995). *Projections of Education Statistics to 2005 (NCES 95-169)*. Washington, DC: US Department of Education, National Center for Education Statistics.

McGrew, K. S., Thurlow, M. L., Shriner, J. G., & Spiegel, A. (1992). *Inclusion of Students with Disabilities in National and State Data Collection Systems*. Minneapolis, MN: University of Minnesota, National Center on Educational Outcomes.

McLaughlin, M. J., & Warren, S. H. (1992). *Issues and Options in Restructuring Schools and Special Education Programs*. College Park, MD: University of Maryland.

Moore, M. T., Strang, E. W., Schwartz, M., & Braddock. M. (1988). *Patterns in Special Education Service Delivery and Cost*. Washington, DC: Decision Resources Corporation.

National Governors' Association and National Association of State Budget Officers (1994). *Fiscal Survey of the States*. Washington, DC: National Governors' Association and National Association of State Budget Officers.

New York State Education Department (1997a). *Special Education*. Albany, NY: New York State Education Department.

New York State Education Department (1997b). *Update on New York States's Overall Strategy for Raising Standards*. Albany, NY: New York State Education Department.

Parrish, T. B., & Montgomery, D. L. (1995). *Politics of Special Education Finance Reform in Three States—State Analysis Series*. Palo Alto, CA: American Institutes for Research, Center for Special Education Finance.

Shields, P. M., Jay, D. E., Parrish, T., & Padilla, C. (1989). *Alternative Programs and Strategies for Serving Students with Leaning Disabilities and Other Learning Problems—Final Report*. Menlo Park, CA: SRI International.

Stancavage, F., McLaughlin, D., Vergun, R., Godlewski, C., & Allen, J. (1996). *Study of Exclusion and Assessability of Students with Disabilities in the 1994 Trial State Assessment (TSA) of the National Assessment of Education Progress (NAEP)*. Paper presented at the meeting of the American Educational Research Association, New York, NY.

Verstegen, D. A. (1991). The economic and demographic dimensions of national education policy. In J. G. Ward, & P. Anthony, *Demographic Trends and Cultural Diversity: Challenges for School Finance Policy*. Newbury Park, CA: Sage Publications.

Ysseldyke, J., Algozzine, B., Richey, L., & Graden, J. (1982). Declaring students eligible for learning disability services: Why bother with the data? *Learning Quarterly*, *5*, 37–44.

Zlatos, B. (1994). Don't ask, don't tell. *The American School Board Journal*, *11*, 24–28.